OLD VENUS

Old Venus
Print edition ISBN: 9781785653360
E-book edition ISBN: 9781783297887

Published by Titan Books
A division of Titan Publishing Group Ltd.
144 Southwark Street, London, SE1 0UP

First paperback edition: September 2016
2 4 6 8 10 9 7 5 3 1

Title page illustration by Stephen Youll

Old Venus is a work of fiction. Names, places, and incidents are either a product
of the author's imagination or are used fictitiously.

This edition published by arrangement with Bantam Books, an imprint of
Random House, a division of Random House LLC, a Penguin Random House
Company, New York.

Book design by Donna Sinisgalli

Printed and bound in Great Britain by CPI Group UK Ltd.

Did you enjoy this book? We love to hear from our readers.
Please email us at readerfeedback@titanemail.com or write to us at
Reader Feedback at the above address.

To receive advance information, news, competitions, and exclusive offers online,
please sign up for the Titan newsletter on our website: www.titanbooks.com

OLD VENUS

Edited by
GEORGE R. R. MARTIN
& GARDNER DOZOIS

TITAN BOOKS

For Bob Walters and Tess Kissinger,
who would love to paint the wallowing
dinosaurs of swampy Venus

Contents

Introduction: Return to Venusport

BY GARDNER DOZOIS

DAWN ON VENUS:

The sleek, furry heads of the web-footed amphibious Venusians break water near one of the rare archipelagos in the world-girdling ocean. Nearby, the toothy head and long, snaky neck of a Plesiosaur-like sea creature momentarily rears above the waves. Elsewhere, vast swamps are pocked and shimmered by the ceaseless, unending rain, while immense dinosaurian shapes grunt and wallow in the mud. Elsewhere, tall, spindly people in elaborate headdresses and jewel-encrusted robes walk across rope bridges strung between huge trees, bigger by far than any Terrestrial Redwood or Sequoia, and the spreading ashen light reveals that there's an entire city up there, up in the trees. Elsewhere, shining silver rockets are landing at the spaceport at Venusport. Still elsewhere, the thick, fetid, steamy jungle is ripped asunder by a dinosaur-like beast, reminiscent of a Tyrannosaurus Rex, who emerges from the dripping vegetation and opens his massive, dagger-studded mouth to roar defiance at the morning.

Then, one day in 1962, all these dreams abruptly vanish, like someone blowing out a candle.

People have always noticed Venus (and sometimes worshipped it), perhaps because it's the brightest natural object in the night sky, other than the Moon. In ancient times, they thought Venus was two separate objects, the Morning Star and the Evening Star—the Greeks called them Phosphoros and Hesperos, the Romans Lucifer and Vesper. By Pythagoras's day in the sixth century B.C., it was recognized as a single celestial object, which the Greeks called Aphrodite, and the Romans called Venus, after the goddesses of love in their respective religions. Somehow, Venus has always been associated with goddesses, perhaps in contrast with the second-brightest object in the night sky, Mars, which because of its ruddy color was associated with war, usually the province of men and of male gods. The Babylonians, who realized it was a single celestial object hundreds of years before the Greeks, called it "the Bright Queen of the Sky," and named it Ishtar, after *their* goddess of love, the Persians would call it Anahita after a goddess of their own, and Pliny the Elder associated Venus with Isis, a similar Egyptian deity. This earned it a nickname, still occasionally used, the Planet of Love.

When telescopes were invented, Venus could be seen to present a bright but featureless face to observation, and the idea slowly developed that Venus was shrouded in a permanent layer of clouds, unlike Mars or Mercury or the Moon, and speculation as to what might be *beneath* the swaddling clouds began, earning Venus its other nickname, the Planet of Mystery.

Clouds meant rain, and a planet permanently shrouded in clouds must certainly be a planet where it *rained*. A lot.

Just as future speculation about Mars was shaped by American astronomer Percival Lowell, who trained telescopes on Mars and believed that he saw canals there, most future speculation about what lay beneath the clouds of Venus was shaped and given direction by Swedish chemist Svante Arrhenius, who speculated, in his 1918 book, *The Destinies of the Stars*, that the Venusian clouds must be composed of water vapor, and went on to say that "everything on Venus is dripping wet ... A very great part of the surface of Venus is no doubt covered with swamps, corresponding to those of the Earth in which the coal deposits were formed ... The temperature on Venus is not so high as to prevent a luxuriant vegetation. The constantly uniform climatic conditions which exist everywhere result in an entire absence of adaptation to changing exterior conditions. Only low forms of life are therefore represented, mostly no doubt, belonging to the vegetable kingdom; and the organisms are nearly of the same kind all over the planet."

This idea, that the surface of Venus was covered with swamps, making it resemble Earth in the Carboniferous Period, would be the ruling paradigm for almost the next fifty years, along with the related idea that Venus was an ocean world, perhaps consisting only of one world-encircling sea. So pervasive was this vision that as late as 1964, Soviet scientists were still designing the *Venera* Venus probes for the possibility of landing in liquid water.

As the subgenre of the Planetary Romance slowly precipitated out of the older body of pulp adventure, the swamps grew jungles and dinosaurs, and the seas grew monsters.

In the heyday of the Planetary Romance, also called Sword and Planet stories, roughly between the 1930s and the 1950s, the solar system swarmed with alien races and alien civilizations, as crowded and chummy as an Elks picnic, with almost every world boasting an alien race that it would be possible for a Terran adventurer to have swordfights or romances with, even Jupiter and Saturn and Mercury. Mars always claimed pride of place, and was the preferred setting for most Planetary Romances—but Venus wasn't far behind.

Venus had appeared as a setting in religious allegories and Fabulous Journey stories throughout the nineteenth century, but the first Planetary Romance to take us there, something recognizable as what we'd today consider to be science fiction, was probably Otis Adelbert Kline's 1929 novel *Planet of Peril* (and its sequels *The Prince of Peril* and *Port of Peril*), in which Earthman Robert Grandon is telepathically transported into the mind of a Venusian, gets involved with warring native races, and has many sword-swinging adventures on a Venus that features forests of giant trees (due to the lower gravity) and dinosaur-like monsters. Kline's novels were almost certainly inspired by Edgar Rice Burroughs's *A Princess of Mars,* which took a similarly swashbuckling Earthman to the Red Planet, called Barsoom by Burroughs, and which had been a sensation upon its publication in 1915. Burroughs would retaliate by sending his own Terran adventurer, Carson Napier, to Venus in 1932 in his *Pirates of Venus* (and its four sequels), and the era of the Planetary Romance was launched.

The purest expression of the Planetary Romance story was probably to be found between 1939 and 1955 in the pages of *Planet Stories,* which featured work by Jack Vance, Ray Bradbury, A. E. Van Vogt, Poul Anderson, and many others, and which (unusually for a subgenre that had been heavily male-dominated) may have found its finest practitioners in two female authors, C. L. Moore and Leigh Brackett. Ray Bradbury published some of his famous *Martian Chronicles* stories in *Planet Stories,* and although Bradbury visited Venus there as well in stories like "The Long Rain" and "All Summer in a Day," he remained mostly best known for his Martian stories. Although both wrote about Mars as well, Venus belonged to Moore and Brackett. C. L. Moore's hard-bitten spaceman Northwest Smith adventured there in company with his Venusian sidekick Yarol in stories like "Black Thirst," and Leigh Brackett's heroes quested for adventure and fabulous treasures across a swampy, sultry Venus full of decadent Venusian natives, dangerous low bars where the unwary might get their throats slit, lost civilizations, and forgotten gods, in stories like "Enchantress of Venus," "Lorelei of the Red Mist" (with Bradbury), and "The Moon That Vanished."

Venus also featured as a setting in somewhat more mainline science fiction as well, outside of the confines of the pure Planetary Romance story (which, truth to tell, was looked down upon as somewhat raffish and déclassé by the core science-fiction fans), being visited by Olaf Stapledon in *Last and First Men*, C. S. Lewis in *Perelandra*, John W. Campbell in "The Black Star Passes," Henry Kuttner in *Fury*, Jack Williamson in *Seetee Ship* and *Seetee Shock*, Isaac Asimov in the YA series of *Lucky Starr* books, A. E. Van Vogt in *The World of Null-A*, Robert A. Heinlein in "Logic of Empire," *Space Cadet, Between Planets*, and *Podkayne of Mars*, Fredrick Pohl and C. M. Kornbluth in *The Space Merchants*, Poul Anderson in "The Big Rain" and "Sister Planet," and no doubt in hundreds of other stories, most long forgotten.

Then, abruptly, the Venus bubble burst.

On December 14, 1962, the American *Mariner 2* probe passed over Venus, and the readings from its microwave and infrared radiometers were dismaying for anyone holding out hope for life on the planet's surface, showing Venus to be much too hot to support life. These findings were later confirmed by the Soviet *Venera 4* probe, and by other probes in both the *Mariner* and *Venera* series, and the picture they painted of Venus was very far from salubrious. In fact, far from being a planet of world-girdling oceans or vast swamps and jungles, far from being a home for mysterious alien civilizations, Venus was revealed as being one of the places in the solar system that was the most hostile to life: with a surface temperature averaging 863 degrees Fahrenheit, it was the hottest planet in the solar system, hotter even than the closest planet to the Sun, Mercury; the famous permanent cloud cover was composed of clouds of sulphuric acid, not water vapor; the atmosphere was composed of 96.5 percent carbon dioxide, and the atmospheric pressure at the planet's surface was ninety-two times that of Earth, as severe as on the bottom of the Earth's oceans.

There couldn't possibly be any life on Venus. No dinosaurs. No web-footed amphibious natives. No ferocious warriors to have swordfights with or beautiful green-skinned princesses in diaphanous gowns to romance. It was just a ball of baking-hot rock and scalding poisonous gas, duller than a supermarket parking lot.

Almost at once, science-fiction writers lost interest.

There was one last great Venus story published, the nostalgic and deliberately retro (since the author certainly knew better by then) "The Doors of His Face, The Lamps of His Mouth," by Roger Zelazny, published in 1965.

By 1968, Brian W. Aldiss and Harry Harrison had edited a retrospective anthology called *Farewell, Fantastic Venus!*, bidding a nostalgic farewell to the Venus story.

And after that, the Venus story effectively disappeared.

For a while.

Few if any stories set on Venus—or, for that matter, on Mars, or on any of the other planets of the solar system—were published in science fiction in the seventies. By the eighties, though, and in an accelerating fashion throughout the nineties and the oughts, science-fiction writers began to become interested in the solar system again, as subsequent space probes began to make it seem a much more interesting and even surprising place than it had initially been thought to be. They even returned to Venus, as the idea of terraforming Venus to make it conducive to life—something first suggested, as far as I know, in Olaf Stapledon's *Last and First Men* in 1930—began to be explored by writers like Pamela Sargent and Kim Stanley Robinson. Dome cities armored against the heat, intense pressure, and poisonous atmosphere of Venus began to appear in stories like John Varley's "In the Bowl," as did even more popular options, huge space stations in orbit around the planet or floating cities that hover permanently in the cooler upper layers of Venus's atmosphere.

So there have been plenty of stories about the New Venus in the last couple of decades. One of them, using the floating-cities model, Geoffrey A. Landis's "The Sultan of the Clouds," won the Theodore Sturgeon Memorial Award in 2011.

But some of us missed the Old Venus, the Venus of so many dreams over so many years.

So why not write about it?

After all, as my coeditor George R. R. Martin pointed out in his introduction to this anthology's companion volume, *Old Mars,* science fiction is and always has been part of the great romantic tradition in literature, and romance has never been about realism. After all, as Martin says, "Western writers still write stories about an Old West that never actually existed in the way it is depicted; 'realistic Westerns' that focus on farmers instead of gunslingers don't sell nearly as well. Mystery writers continue to write tales of private eyes solving murders and catching serial killers, whereas real life PIs spend most of their time investigating bogus insurance claims and photographing adulterers in sleazy motels for the benefit of divorce lawyers. Historical novelists produce stories set in ancient realms that no longer exist, about which we often know little and less, and fantasy writers publish stories set in lands that never did exist at all."

So why not rekindle the wonderful, gorgeously colored dream of Old Venus?

So we contacted some of the best writers we know, both established names and bright new talents, and told them that we weren't looking for pastiches or postmodern satire, or stories set on the kind of terraformed, colonized modern Venus common in most recent science fiction, or orbital space colonies circling the planet high above, or domed cities set in hellish landscapes with poisonous atmospheres, but for stories set in the kind of nostalgic, habitable Venus found in the works of writers like Leigh Brackett, Edgar Rice Burroughs, C. L. Moore, Otis Adelbert Kline, Poul Anderson, Robert A. Heinlein, and so many others, before the hard facts gathered by space probes blew those dreams away. Stories set in the old-style Venus of vast swamps and limitless oceans and steaming jungles and wallowing dinosaurs. And Venusians, another sentient race to interact with, one of the great dreams of science fiction, whether that interaction involved swordfights or romance or close scientific observation or exploitation or uneasy coexistence.

The results of those newly hatched dreams of Venus are to be found in this anthology, stories that will take you to places that you've never been—but will not regret having visited.

ALLEN M. STEELE

In the suspenseful story that follows, we accompany a tough PI to Venus on a risky mission that takes him down some very Mean Streets indeed—even if, on Venus, there *aren't* any streets.

Allen Steele made his first sale to *Asimov's Science Fiction* magazine in 1988, soon following it up with a long string of other sales to *Asimov's*, as well as to markets such as *Analog, The Magazine of Fantasy & Science Fiction,* and *Science Fiction Age.* In 1989, he published his critically acclaimed first novel, *Orbital Decay,* which subsequently won the Locus Poll as Best First Novel of the year, and soon Steele was being compared to Golden Age Heinlein by no less an authority than Gregory Benford. His other books include the novels *Clarke County, Space, Lunar Descent, Labyrinth of Night, The Weight, The Tranquillity Alternative, A King of Infinite Space, Oceanspace, Chronospace, Coyote, Coyote Rising, Spindrift, Galaxy Blues, Coyote Horizon,* and *Coyote Destiny.* His short work has been gathered in three collections, *Rude Astronauts, Sex and Violence in Zero-G,* and *The Last Science Fiction Writer.* His most recent books are a new novel in the *Coyote* sequence, *Hex,* a YA novel, *Apollo's Outcasts,* an alternate history, *V-S Day,* and the collection *Sex and Violence in Zero-G: The Complete "Near Space" Stories: Expanded Edition.* He has won three Hugo Awards, in 1996 for his novella "The Death of Captain Future," in 1998 for his novella ". . . Where Angels Fear to Tread," and, most recently, in 2011 for his novelette "The Emperor of Mars." Born in Nashville, Tennessee, he has worked for a variety of newspapers and magazines, covering science and business assignments, and is now a full-time writer living in Whately, Massachusetts, with his wife, Linda.

Frogheads

ALLEN M. STEELE

THE SHUTTLE FELL THROUGH THE CLOUDS—CLOUDS as dense as grey wool, separating purple sky and sun above from perpetual rain below—for what seemed like a very long time until the windows finally cleared and Venus's global ocean lay revealed: dark blue, storm-lashed, endless.

Engines along the spacecraft's boatlike underbelly fired, forming a concentric circle of white-peaked wavelets that spread outward upon the ocean surface. Gradually the shuttle made its final descent until its hull settled upon the water. As careful as the pilots were, though, the splashdown was rough. A swift, violent jolt passed through the passenger compartment, shaking everyone in their seats, causing an overhead storage compartment to snap open and spill a couple of carry-on bags into the center aisle. Through the compartment, people cursed—mainly in Russian although a few American obscenities were heard as well—and someone in the back noisily threw up, an involuntary act that was greeted by more foul language.

Ronson wasn't happy about the landing either. This wasn't the first time he'd traveled off-world, but landing on Mars was mild compared to this. He couldn't blame the guy a few rows back for getting sick. Although the shuttle was no longer airborne, it still remained in motion, slowly bobbing up and down as it was rocked by the ocean. He'd been warned to take Dramamine before boarding, and he was glad he'd heeded the advice.

Clutching the armrests, Ronson gazed through the oval porthole beside his seat. Rain spattered the outer pane, but he could still see where he was. Not that there was much to look at: ocean for as far as the eye could see—the Venusian horizon was about three miles away, nearly the same as Earth's at sea level—beneath a slate-colored sky bloated by clouds that had never parted and never would. The shuttle was supposed to make planetfall at Veneragrad, but the floating colony must be on the other side of the spacecraft. Unless, of course, the pilots had miscalculated the colony's current position and had come down—*landed* wasn't the proper word, was it?—in the wrong place.

That was a possibility. Ronson had spent the last four months in hibernation, but his waking hours aboard the *Tsiolkovsky* had shown him that Cosmoflot's reputation for ineptitude was well deserved. He'd just begun to consider the possibility that the shuttle was lost at sea when a tugboat came into view. Smoke belching from its funnel, the rust-flecked craft circled the shuttle until it passed out of sight once again. Several minutes went by, then there was a thump as its crew attached a towline to the shuttle's prow. The shuttle began to move forward again, the tug hauling it toward its final destination.

Everyone on his side of the passenger compartment peered through the windows as the shuttle pulled into Veneragrad, including the middle-aged Russian in the aisle seat who unapologetically leaned over Ronson as he craned his head for a look at the man-made island. Veneragrad was as utilitarian as only a Soviet-era artifact could be: a tiered hemisphere a kilometer in diameter, a shade darker than the ocean it floated upon, the long, wooden piers jutting out from its sides giving it the appearance of an enormous, bloated water spider. Rickety-looking platforms, also constructed of native timber, rose as irregularly spaced towers from the outside balconies; they supported the open-top steel tanks that caught the rain and distilled it as the colony's drinking water. Radio masts and dish antennae jutted out at odd angles from near the top of the dome; a helicopter lifted off from a landing pad on its roof. An ugly, unwelcoming place.

"Looks bad, yes?" The man seated beside him stared past him. "Better than nothing . . . it's dry."

Ronson had already learned that his traveling companion spoke English, albeit not very well. His breath reeked of the vodka he swilled from a bag-wrapped bottle on the way down from orbit; he'd opened it as soon as the shuttle entered the atmosphere. "Is this where you live?" he asked, if only for the sake of being polite. "Is this your home, I mean?"

The other man barked sullen laughter. "This hellhole? No! My home, St. Petersburg. Come here to make money. Sell . . . um . . . ah"—he searched for the right word—"computers, yes? Computers for office."

Ronson nodded. He wasn't much interested in making friends with the businessman, but it appeared that conversation was unavoidable. "Whole colony, built in space above Earth, sent here by rockets," the businessman continued, telling Ronson something he already knew. "Dropped from orbit by para . . . para . . ."

"Parachutes."

"Parachutes, yes. Come down"—he lifted his hands—"*sploosh!* in water." He waved the bag toward the window. "People then build onto it. Wood from floating . . . um, forests, yes? Floating forests on moss islands."

"Yes, I see." Again, the businessman wasn't telling him anything new.

"Yes, you see." The Russian took another swig from his bottle, then offered it to Ronson. "So why you come here?"

Ronson shook his head at the bottle. There were several

ways he could get out of this unwanted conversation. He opted for the easiest approach. "I'm a detective," he said, and when the businessman gave an uncomprehending look, he rephrased his answer in simpler, if inaccurate, terms. "A cop."

"A cop. Yes." The businessman gave him the distrustful look Ronson anticipated, then withdrew the bottle and settled back into his seat.

Ronson didn't hear from him again for the rest of the way into port. Which suited him well. He didn't want to talk about why he'd come to Venus.

The heat hit him as soon as he stepped through the hatch. It was like walking into a sauna; the air was hot and thick, hard to breathe, humid beyond belief. The sun was larger and warmer here than on Earth, yet little more than a bright smear in the sky that heated up the atmosphere. Ronson began to sweat even before he reached the end of the wooden gangway that led from the hatch to the pier where the shuttle had been berthed. A fine, almost misty rain was falling, and it too was warm; he didn't know whether to take off the denim jacket he'd worn on the way down or keep it on. The dockworkers didn't seem to mind. Most of them wore only shorts, sneakers, and sometimes a rain hat, with the women wearing bikini tops or sports bras. They unloaded the bags from the cargo bay, and Ronson took a few moments to find his suitcase before walking the rest of the way down the pier to the spaceport entrance.

There were only a couple of customs officers on duty, bored-looking Russians in short-sleeve uniform shirts who regarded the line of passengers with bureaucratic disdain. The officer Ronson approached silently examined his passport and declaration form, gave his face a quick glance, then put his stamp on everything and shrugged him toward an adjacent arch.

No one had asked him to open his bag, but he knew what was about to happen. Sure enough, bells rang from the arch as soon as he walked through it. Its weapons detector had found the gun he was carrying.

Just as well. It only meant that he'd meet the police sooner than he had planned.

An hour of sitting alone in a detention area, another half hour of angry interrogation by a port-authority officer whose English wasn't much better than the businessman's, then Ronson was loaded onto an electric cart and spirited to police headquarters. Along the way, he got what amounted to a nickel tour of Veneragrad. The colony seemed to consist mainly of narrow corridors with low ceilings and low-wattage light fixtures, their grey steel walls decorated with grime, handprints, and stenciled Cyrillic signs, then the cart passed through a broad doorway and Ronson suddenly found himself in the city center: a vast atrium, its skylight ceiling a couple of hundred meters above the floor, with interior balconies overlooking a central plaza. As the cart cut across the plaza, Ronson caught glimpses of Veneragrad's daily life. Residents in shorts, vests, and T-shirts resting on park benches, hanging laundry on balcony clotheslines, standing in line in front of fast-food kiosks. A group of schoolchildren sitting cross-legged near a fountain, listening as their young teacher delivered a lesson. Two men in a heated argument; another couple of men watching with amusement.

A statue of V. I. Lenin stood in the center of the plaza. Incongruously dressed in a frock coat and high-collar shirt no Venusian colonist would be caught dead wearing—even inside the city, the air was tropically warm—he pointed toward some proud socialist future just ahead. But the statue was old and stained, and a broken string that might have once been a yo-yo dangled from the tip of his finger. The Communist Party was just as dead on Venus as it was on Earth; it was just taking the locals a little longer to get rid of its relics.

The cart entered another dismal corridor, then came to a halt in front of a pair of battered doors painted with a faded red star. The port-authority officer who'd questioned Ronson ushered him through the crowded police station to a private office, and it was here that he met Arkandy Bulgakov.

Veneragrad's police chief was about Ronson's own age, short and broad-chested, with the short-banged Caesar haircut that never seems to go out of style with European men. Seated at a desk piled with paperwork, he listened patiently while the officer delivered a stiff-toned report of the visitor's offense, punctuated by placing Ronson's Glock on the desk along with its extra clips, then Bulgakov murmured something and waved the officer out of the room. He waited until the door was shut, then he sighed and shook his head.

"You're the same guy who e-mailed me a while ago about the missing kid?" His English was Russian-accented but otherwise perfect.

"That's me." Ronson motioned to an empty chair in front of the desk; Bulgakov nodded, and he sat down. "Sorry about the gun. I was going to tell you about it when I reported in, but . . ."

"We don't allow private ownership of firearms. Didn't you know that?"

"I figured that my license might exempt me."

"No exemptions here. Only police are allowed to carry lethal weapons." Bulgakov's chair squeaked as he leaned forward to pick up the Glock; he briefly weighed it in his hand before opening a drawer and dropping it in. "I won't fine you, but you may not carry this. I'll give you a receipt. You may reclaim it when you leave."

"All right, but what am I supposed to use until then? I might need a sidearm, you know."

"To find a missing person? I doubt it." Catching Ronson's

look, the chief shrugged. "You can buy a Taser if it makes you feel better, but only if you're going outside the city. And if that's the case, then your chances of finding this fellow . . ."

"David Henry."

". . . David Henry alive are practically zero. At any rate, he's not in Veneragrad, I can tell you that right now."

"That's what you told me five months ago," Ronson said, "and that's what I told my client, too. But the old man isn't satisfied. His kid was last seen here nearly a year ago, when he came to Venus on a trip his dad bought him as a college-graduation gift."

Bulgakov raised a querulous eyebrow. "His father must be rich."

"The family has a few bucks, yeah, and the kid likes to travel. He's already been to the Moon and Mars, so I guess Venus was next on his list. Personally, if he was my boy, I would've given him a watch, but . . ."

"We don't have many tourists, but we do get some. His kind is not unfamiliar. Privileged children coming to see the wonders of Venus"—a brief smirk—"such as they are. They go out to the vine islands, take pictures, collect a few souvenirs. Now and then they get in trouble . . . a bar fight, dope, soliciting a prostitute . . . and they wind up here. But they eventually go home and that's the end of their adventure."

"That's not how it ended for him. He didn't come home."

"So it appears." Bulgakov turned to the antique computer on one side of his desk. He typed something on the keyboard, then swiveled the breadbox-size CRT around so that Ronson could see the screen. "This is him, yes?"

Displayed on the screen was a passport photo of a young man in his early twenties: moonfaced, arrogant blue eyes, sandy hair cut close on the sides and mousse-spiked on top. Good-looking but spoiled. The same boy in the picture his father had given Ronson when he'd visited the family home in Colorado Springs. "That's him."

Bulgakov turned the screen back around, typed in something else, paused to read the information that appeared. "He was registered at the Gastinitsa Venera," he said after a few seconds, "but failed to check out. When my detectives went there to investigate, they were told that his luggage was found in his room, which apparently he hadn't visited for several days before his scheduled departure aboard the *Gagarin*. My men visited all the restaurants, shops, and bars, and although he'd been noticed in some of them, no one who worked in those places had seen him recently. And, of course, he failed to appear at the Cosmoflot departure gate to make his shuttle flight."

"You told me this already, remember? In your e-mail." This was a waste of time. Which was what he'd expected; local police were seldom much help in missing-person cases. Still, he always made a point of checking in with the cops. Professional courtesy, mainly, but there was always the chance that he might learn something he could use.

"So I did, and I imagine that you shared the information with *gospodin* Henry. And when he contacted the Russian consulate in Washington . . . he did this, yes? . . . he told them this as well." Bulgakov leaned back in his chair. "Very well, let me tell you what I didn't say in my e-mail, because the government back home doesn't like to admit certain things and would be upset with me if I stated them in an official letter. On occasion . . . not often, but every once in a while . . . a young man like David Henry disappears while visiting Venus. Sometimes he wanders down the docks after he has been drinking all night, falls off a pier, and drowns, and his body is devoured by scavenger eels. That has happened. Sometimes he goes out on a boat tour with an unlicensed operator who's actually a criminal, who robs him, murders him, and leaves his body to rot on an island. That's happened, too. And sometimes . . . well, worse things happen."

"Such as?"

Bulgakov hesitated. "You've heard of *vityazka*, haven't you?"

"Yaz? Who hasn't?"

"That's the street name back home. *Vityazka iz kornia* is what it's called here." Bulgakov warmed to the subject. "It's derived from the same slickbark trees that grow on some of the vine islands and from which the pharmaceutical industry has bioharvested *korenmedicant*, a clinical analgesic used in hospitals. But while *koren* comes from tree bark, *vityazka* comes from the roots. A narcotic as addictive as heroin . . ."

"And tastes just as bad when you smoke it," Ronson finished. "Know all about yaz. It's all over America and Europe."

Bulgakov scowled. He clearly didn't like being interrupted. "What you probably *aren't* aware of is exactly how the smugglers are getting it. Their growers . . . yaz croppers, we call them . . . go out to islands where slickbark trees are found. On the islands the drug companies have already harvested, they recover the tree roots left behind and process them for yaz. But everything that goes into this . . . cutting, boiling, curing . . . is hard work, not something anyone willingly wants to do. So sometimes they'll abduct some poor tourist who was in the wrong place at the wrong time and force him into hard labor."

"And you think that's what happened to David Henry? He was shanghaied?"

"I'd say that's a strong possibility."

Ronson slowly let out his breath. His job had just become much more difficult. "If you're right, then how do I find him? I understand those islands can drift quite a long distance . . ."

"There are thousands of them being carried by the ocean currents, and the croppers do a good job staying hidden. My people have always had trouble tracking them down. Locating the boy on one particular island will be difficult." Bulgakov paused. "However, there may be a way. As you Americans say, it's a long shot, but . . ."

"As we Americans say, I'm all ears."

"Talk to a froghead."

"A what?"

"Frogheads. The native aborigines. No one calls them Venusians . . . sounds like a bad movie. Anyway, they're intelligent"—another smirk—"although I wouldn't call them good company. And they see a lot of what goes on here."

"I can't even speak Russian. How am I supposed to talk to . . . ?"

"I know someone who does. Mad Mikhail. You can find him down on the docks. Bring lots of rubles." Bulgakov smiled. "And chocolate, too."

"Chocolate?"

"You'll see."

Mad Mikhail hung out on the waterfront. Everyone who worked there knew who he was; all Ronson had to do was follow their pointing fingers to a small shack set up on the dock where the tour boats were moored.

Mad Mikhail made sushi from whatever he'd been brought by local fishermen, which he then sold to tourists. When Ronson found him, he was sitting on a stool inside his open-sided shack, cutting up something that looked like a cross between a squid and a lionfish and wrapping the filets around wads of sticky rice. He was a squat old man with a potbelly and fleshy arms and legs, his dense white beard nearly reaching his collarbone. His skin was wrinkled and rain-bleached, and he wore nothing but a frayed straw hat and baggy shorts; when he looked up at Ronson, it was with eyes both sharp and vaguely mystical.

"Sushi?" he asked, his rasping voice thickened by a

Ukrainian accent. "Fresh today. Very good. Try some."

Bulgakov had warned Ronson not to eat anything Mad Mikhail offered him; whatever he failed to sell today, he'd simply keep until tomorrow even if it had been spoiled by the heat and humidity. At least he spoke English. "No thanks. I've been told you can help me. I want to talk to a froghead."

Mikhail's eyes narrowed. "They are not frogheads. They are the Water Folk, the Masters of the World Ocean. You do not respect them, you do not talk to them."

"I'm sorry. I didn't know they . . ."

Mikhail slammed the long knife he'd been using down on the counter before him. "No one knows this! They call them frogheads, make jokes about them. Only I"—he jabbed a scarred thumb against his bare chest—"make friends with them when I came here over thirty years ago! Only Mikhail Kronow . . . !"

"You've been on Venus thirty years?" Ronson seized the chance to change the subject. "That means you would have belonged to one of the first expeditions."

"*Da.*" He nodded vigorously, not smiling but at least no longer shouting. "Second expedition, 1978. Chief petty officer, Soviet Space Force." A smile appeared within the white nest of whiskers. "The others went home, but I stayed. No one in Veneragrad been here longer . . . !"

"Then, Chief Petty Officer Kronow, you're the person I need to see." The best way to handle Mad Mikhail would be to appeal to his vanity. "I'd like to speak with the Water Folk . . . or rather, have you speak with them on my behalf since you know them so well."

Mikhail's gaze became suspicious. "About what? If it's only a picture you want . . . *pfft!* Fifteen hundred rubles, they come up, you stand next to them, I take your picture. Take it home, put it on the wall. 'See, there's me with the frogheads.'" Disgusted, he spat over the side of the dock.

"I'm not a tourist, and I don't want a picture." Ronson

reached into the pocket of his trousers—he'd have to buy shorts soon; his Earth clothes were beginning to stick to him—and produced the snapshot of David Henry his father had given him. Holding it beneath the shack's awning so that the rain wouldn't get it wet, he showed it to Mikhail. "I'm looking for this person. He came here almost a year ago, then disappeared. His family sent me here to find him."

Mad Mikhail took the photo, closely inspected it. "I do not know this boy," he said at last, "but the Water Folk would. If he went out to sea, they would have seen him. They see everyone who goes out into the World Ocean. You have chocolate?"

Ronson had purchased a handful of Cadbury bars at the hotel shop. He pulled them out and showed them to Mikhail. The old man said nothing but simply gave him a questioning look. Ronson found his money clip, peeled off several high-denomination notes, held them up. Mikhail thought it over for a moment. "Very well," he said at last, easing himself down from his stool. "Come with me."

He emerged from the shack wielding a cricket bat, the sort an Englishman would carry to a sports field. Taking the money and the chocolate bars from Ronson, he led the detective down the dock, passing the boats tied up alongside. Captains and crew members lounging on their decks watched him with amusement; someone called to him in Russian and the others laughed, but Mad Mikhail only scowled and ignored them.

He and Ronson reached the end of the dock. A wooden light post rose above the water slurping against the dock's edge. The former cosmonaut raised the cricket bat and, with both hands, slammed it against the post: two times, pause, then two more times, another pause, then two more times after that. Mikhail stopped, peered out over the water, and waited a minute. Then he hit the post six more times, two beats apiece.

"This is how you summon fro . . . the Water Folk?" Ronson

wondered if he was wasting his time.

"Yes." Mikhail turned his head back and forth, searching. "They hear vibrations, come to see why I call them. They do this for no one but me."

He'd barely completed his third repetition when, one at a time, three dark blue mounds breached from the rain-spattered surface just a couple of meters from the dock. With a chill, Ronson found himself being studied by three pairs of slitted eyes the color of tarnished pewter. Those eyes were all he could see for a few moments, then Mikhail held up the chocolate bars and the creatures swam closer.

"Move back and give them room," Mikhail said quietly. "Do not speak to them. They will not understand you."

One by one, the Venusian natives emerged from the water, climbing up onto the dock until they stood before Ronson and Mikhail. Each stood about a meter and a half in height, the size of a boy, and were bipedal, but their resemblance to humans ended there. They looked like a weird hybrid of a frog, a salamander, and a dolphin: sloping, neckless heads, broad-mouthed and lipless, with protruding eyes; sleek hairless bodies, streamlined and mammalian, their slender arms and legs ending in webbed, four-fingered hands and broad, paddlelike feet; short dorsal fins running down their backs, away from blowholes that vibrated slightly with each breath and tapered off as reptilian tails that barely touched the wet planks of the dock.

Ronson couldn't see any anatomical differences between males and females even though he knew that the natives had two genders. Each were naked, their light blue underbellies revealing no obvious genitalia; only subtle splotches and stripes upon their wine-colored skin distinguished one individual from another.

And they smelled. As they came out of the water, his nose picked up a fetid, organic odor that reminded him of an algae bloom in summer. The stench was offensive enough to make him step back, and not just because Mad Mikhail had asked him to do so. If they came any closer, he was afraid he'd lose his lunch.

Ronson had recently read a magazine article about how an Egyptian-American scientist, who'd perished during a dust storm on Mars, had discovered just before his death certain genetic evidence linking *Homo sapiens* to the native aborigines of the Red Planet. He wondered if much the same link might exist between the people of Earth and the Water Folk of Venus, and was both intrigued and disgusted by the thought he might be related, in some distant way, to these . . . frogheads.

Mikhail unwrapped the chocolate bars and offered them to the natives. As he did so, he addressed them in a low, warbling croak: *"Wor-worg wokka kroh woka."* It sounded like nonsense to Ronson, but the Water Folk apparently understood him. The ones on the left and right bobbed their heads up and down and responded in kind—*"Worgga kroh wohg"*—and moved toward him in a waddling, forward-hunched gait that might have been clumsy if it hadn't been so fast.

Only the native in the center remained where it was. It watched its companions with what seemed to be disdain as they each took a chocolate bar from Mikhail. When they opened their mouths, Ronson was startled to see that they contained rows of short, sharp teeth, with slightly longer incisors at the corners of the upper set. He was even more startled by the way they gobbled down the chocolate bars. Repulsively long tongues snatched the candy from their webbed hands; chocolate bars that even a hungry child might have taken a couple of minutes to eat were devoured in seconds. And yet the third froghead—Ronson couldn't help but to think of it that way—refused the bar that Mikhail held out to it.

"Why doesn't it take it?" Ronson whispered.

"I do not know," Mikhail murmured; he was a bit surprised himself. "They have never done that before." He raised his voice again. *"Wagga kroh?"*

"Kroh wogko!" The third froghead's tail swung back and forth in what seemed to be an angry gesture, its dull silver eyes narrowing menacingly. *"Kroh wogko wakkawog!"*

"What did it say?"

Mikhail didn't respond at once. He held out the bar for another moment or two, then slipped it in his pocket. The other two Water Folk made hissing noises that sounded like protests, but the third one stopped thrashing its tail and appeared to calm down a little. "The one in the middle is the leader," Mikhail said softly. "She . . ."

"You can tell it's a she?"

"Their leaders are always females. She refused the chocolate because . . . I think . . . she said it's poisonous." He shrugged. "I am not sure. I speak their language, yes, but some words of theirs I do not know well."

"But this is the first time you've seen any of them refuse chocolate?"

"Oh, yes. I've been giving it to them for many years. They love *kroh*. Nothing else like it on Venus. This is how I have made friends with them, learned how to talk to them." A thoughtful pause. "I do not know why one of them would refuse to take it. Very strange."

"Well, that's interesting, but I've got a job to do." Ronson pulled out David Henry's photo again. "Show this to them," he said as he handed it to Mikhail, "and ask if they've seen him."

The reaction was immediate. The moment Mikhail held up the photo, all three frogheads became agitated. Their tails swished back and forth, sometimes slapping the dock boards, as their heads bobbed up and down. They hissed, the leathery tips of their tongues slipping in and out of their mouths, and air whistled from their blowholes. Then the clan leader pointed to the photo and spoke in a rapid stream of angry-sounding croaks.

"Oh, yes . . . they recognize him, all right." Mikhail was just as surprised as Ronson. "And I do not think they like him very much."

"I kinda figured that. Ask if they know where he is."

Mikhail addressed the frogheads again, and once more they responded with head bobs and tail slaps. Then the leader bent almost double, shifted slightly to the left, and raised her tail to point to the left. Mikhail listened as she spoke to him at length, then he turned to Ronson.

"She knows where he is . . . on a moss island that's now some distance from here. She said she will lead us to him, but only if we will take him away."

"That's exactly what I want." Then he darted a look at Mikhail. "You said 'we'?"

Mad Mikhail smiled at him. "Unless you think you can speak to them, I will have to go with you, yes? And I will have to hire a boat, yes?"

Ronson knew without asking that the fee was going to be considerable. But he'd brought plenty of rubles with him, and he could always recoup his expenses from his client. "All right. Tell them that we . . ."

Mikhail didn't have a chance to translate. With no more conversation, the three frogheads suddenly turned and dove off the dock. Their bodies barely made a splash as they disappeared into the dark water. In an instant, they were gone.

"That was fast," Ronson muttered.

"We have an understanding. They will come back tomorrow morning." Mikhail turned away from the dock's edge, started walking back toward his shack. "Be here then. I will hire a boat and pilot to take us where they lead us. *Dasvidan'ye.*"

"See you later." At least he'd have time to buy new clothes and the equipment he'd need—namely a Taser, seeing that was the only kind of weapon he was permitted to carry. Yet he couldn't help but notice the guarded expression on Mad Mikhail's face and wonder if there was something the old man wasn't telling him.

The *Aphrodite* was a beat-up fishing boat with rain-warped deck planks and a wooden hull that appeared to have been patched many times. To Ronson's surprise, its captain was an American: Bart Angelo, middle-aged and a bit warped himself, smelling of fish and with ivory hair thinning at the top of his head. Forty thousand rubles was a lot to pay for the charter of a weathered old tub, but Ronson had little choice in the matter. He talked Angelo down to thirty-five thousand, and was grateful that he wouldn't have to also pay for a crew that the captain had decided to leave behind.

The frogheads returned, just as Mikhail said they would. Ronson assumed they were the same three he'd met yesterday, but he couldn't tell for sure. They didn't climb on the dock again, though, but instead lingered in the water beside the *Aphrodite,* half-submerged eyes steadily watching the men as they prepared to leave. Ronson wondered how they'd known which boat they'd use; Mikhail told him that they'd simply waited until they spotted him and Ronson again, then followed them to the *Aphrodite.*

"They are not animals," Mikhail added, giving him a stern look. "The Water Folk are intelligent . . . never forget that."

Hearing this, Angelo laughed out loud. "If they're so damn smart, then how come they keep getting tangled in my nets?"

"And what happens when they do?" Mikhail asked.

"They chew their way out." The captain finished counting the wad of money Ronson had just handed him and shoved it in his shorts pocket. "Goddamn critters cost me a repair bill whenever they do that."

Mikhail smiled knowingly. He didn't reply, though, but instead went aft to loosen the stern line. Ronson heard him murmur something in Russian; he had no idea what he'd said, but it sounded rather amused.

The frogheads joined the *Aphrodite* as it chugged out of Veneragrad's harbor. They swam alongside until the boat passed the outer buoys, then moved out front and surfed its bow wake as the boat picked up speed, occasionally breaching the surface just as if they were dolphins. Ronson was concerned at first that the captain would run them down, but once Angelo throttled up the diesel engines to twenty knots, the Water Folk returned to their previous positions. They had no difficulty keeping up with the boat; never once did Ronson or Mikhail completely lose sight of them.

Veneragrad gradually disappeared behind them, becoming smaller and smaller until it faded into the misty, perpetual rain. Long before it vanished over the horizon, though, they saw other signs of the human presence on Venus. They passed fishing schooners and tour boats heading out for the day, and at one point crossed the wake of one of the massive sea-dragon trawlers that prowled the global ocean for weeks on end. In the distance, they made out a tall structure erected on stilts: an oil derrick, probably owned by a Russian-Arab consortium, positioned just above a sea mount. Small, single-mast sailboats took advantage of the mild weather and fair winds, but only a couple; Venus was not a planet for pleasure boating, and amateur sailors were the kind who often vanished and were never seen again.

By early afternoon, though, all other vessels had disappeared, and *Aphrodite* was the only boat on the ocean as far as the eye could see. Yet it wasn't alone. The first of the vine islands had come into view, and the Water Folk were leading the boat straight to them.

Ronson had never been a good student—he'd dropped out of college to join the NYPD, which in turn eventually led him to become a PI—but he remembered enough from his high-school science classes to recall the planet's natural history. Billions of years ago, Venus had been Earth's twin sister, and even similar enough to Mars to make the panspermia hypothesis a possible explanation for a shared genetic heritage among humans, the Martian *shatan,* and frogheads. At some point in the planet's early eras, though, the Sun had raised the average global temperatures enough to cause a catastrophic greenhouse effect, which melted the polar ice caps and formed the permanent cloud layer with its incessant rain. Eventually the entire planet was flooded, its landmasses inundated before tectonic shifts could keep them above the rising waters.

All that remained was a global ocean, yet beneath the watery surface were the old continents with their canyons and mountain ranges, like some vast Atlantis that would never again see the light of day. In some places, the ocean bottom lay only a dozen or so fathoms down, and it was here that underwater vegetation grew in abundance. One of the most common forms of marine plant life was a thick, ropy kind of seaweed that, once it grew large enough to become buoyant, tended to break free and float to the surface. Ocean currents gradually caused these weeds to clump together and form floating islands, some kilometers in length.

Over countless millennia, life evolved on these drifting isles. The frogheads were one kind; the slickbark trees that were a harvestable source of everything from timber to pharmaceutical drugs to yaz were another. And once humans learned how to travel between planets, the people of Earth discovered that Venus was a world rich with resources just waiting to be exploited.

Not everyone was happy about this.

"We are raping this planet." Mad Mikhail leaned against the starboard rail, watching the frogheads as they swam toward a vine island not much larger than a house. One of them had approached the boat and told Mikhail, in its croaking native tongue, that they needed a rest, so Angelo had grudgingly complied and dropped sea anchor near the next island they came upon. Now the Russian was in a reflective mood, breaking the pensive silence he'd maintained since leaving Veneragrad.

"Rape?" Angelo sat beneath the tarp strung as a canopy across the aft deck, eating a sandwich he'd made in the galley. "Don't talk about your sister that way . . . it's not nice."

Mikhail ignored him, as did Ronson. The captain had an ugly sense of humor; Ronson had discovered this when he'd joined him for a while in the wheelhouse, only to have Angelo start telling him jokes that grew progressively more disgusting until he found an excuse to leave. "Why do you say that?" he asked, turning his back to the captain.

"We come here," Mikhail said, "and we take and we take and we take, but we give nothing back." He nodded toward the frogheads; they lay prone upon the island's matted weeds, vines, and moss, dozing in the midday heat. "They suffer the most. We steal their forests, pollute their water with oil, ruin their islands . . ."

"And then they hang around Veneragrad so they can mooch candy bars from you." Angelo shrugged. "Sounds like a fair trade to me."

"No. Not fair." Mikhail cast a cold glare at him. "Chocolate for a world . . . not a fair trade at all."

"Yeah, well . . . look who got 'em hooked on it in the first place." Noticing Ronson's quizzical look, Angelo sneered. "You mean you don't know? Chocolate is addictive to frogheads. Like cocaine, maybe even worse. Once they've had a taste, they gotta get more. And guess who got 'em started on it?"

"You lie!" Mikhail's face was red. "I was not the first to do this! One of my shipmates . . ."

"O, sure. Maybe it wasn't you, but you're their number one pusher." Angelo tossed the remnant of his sandwich overboard, wiped his hands against his shorts. "And if you're not, then why don't you toss over those candy bars you brung?"

Mikhail looked away, avoiding the accusation Angelo had made. Ronson wondered if it was true. "One day, we will pay for what we have done here," he said quietly.

"Yeah, well . . . you're paying me for this trip and the day ain't getting any shorter." Angelo stood up from the barrel, headed for the wheelhouse. "Tell the froggies to rise and shine. I want to find this place and go home."

The captain didn't get his wish. At the end of the day, the frogheads still hadn't reached their destination, forcing *Aphrodite* to seek another island where it could anchor for the night. Again, the frogheads found a place to rest on its mossy, vine-covered banks.

As darkness fell on the ocean, Angelo opened a locker on the aft deck and pulled out a large net. Ronson thought at first that he intended to go trawling, but instead Angelo told him and Mikhail to rig the net above the boat, from the wheelhouse roof to poles erected at the stern, until the deck was completely covered. Angelo then switched off the deck lamps, and once the three of them went below he closed the curtains in the cabin portholes.

They'd barely finished dinner when Ronson discovered the reason why the captain had taken such precautions. From somewhere outside came the sound of wings flapping, punctuated by high-pitched shrieks. Mikhail explained that they belonged to one of Venus's few avian species: night shrikes, nocturnal raptors not much larger than the pelicans they vaguely resembled but dangerous nonetheless. The shrikes hunted in flocks, seeking prey near the islands where they nested; they had little fear of humans, and had been known to gang up on unwary sailors who ventured out on deck after dark. The nets would keep them away, and if that didn't work, a Taser shot was sufficient to drive them off. Still, the best defense was to remain inside until daybreak.

Through the night, long after the three of them had crawled into their bunks, Ronson heard the shrikes prowling around the boat. Distant thunder and lightning flashes glimpsed around the edges of the porthole curtains told of an approaching storm. It came in around midnight, and although it only rocked the boat a bit and threw rain against the portholes, it kept Ronson awake for a while. He lay in his bunk, Taser beneath his pillow, listening to the shrikes and the storm.

Venus was a dangerous world.

Yet the morning was calm. The rain had slackened to a mild drizzle, the sun a hot splotch half-seen through the clouds. The frogheads were croaking impatiently beside the boat when Ronson and the others emerged from the cabin. Mikhail gave chocolate bars to two of the aborigines—as before, their leader refused to accept any—while Angelo and Ronson took down the net and hoisted the anchor. Then the captain started the engine and *Aphrodite* set out again, the frogheads once more taking the lead.

The floating isles had become bigger and less far apart by then, and for the first time, Ronson saw forests on the larger ones. Slickbark trees looked like palmettos but grew in dense jungle clusters, their broad trunks strangled by vines, their broad, serrated leaves casting shadows across the surrounding water.

Around midmorning, *Aphrodite* came within sight of a larger vessel going the other way: a lumber ship the size of a small freighter, its deck loaded with cut and trimmed tree trunks. The lumber ship blew its horn as it went by, but Angelo didn't respond to the hail.

"A yaz runner wouldn't do that," the captain explained.

"Yaz runner?" Ronson asked. "You mean, like someone who's . . ."

"Out to purchase yaz, uh-huh." Angelo gave him a sidelong

look. "That's what we're going to pretend to be once we get to this place . . . because, believe me, there ain't no way they're gonna let us live if they don't think we're here to buy dope."

Ronson was still coming to grips with this when the frogheads suddenly turned to the right and started heading for a large island only a kilometer away. As *Aphrodite* approached the island, the three men spotted thin lines of smoke rising from its forest. Angelo handed a pair of binoculars to Ronson, and through them he saw a couple of boats about *Aphrodite*'s size tied up at a floating dock.

"It's a yaz camp, all right," Angelo said, then he looked off to the side. "Hey! What the hell are they doing?"

Ronson followed his gaze. The three frogheads had suddenly turned and were swimming back toward the boat. "I think they want to talk," Mikhail said.

Angelo throttled down the engines. "So talk to 'em," he muttered with an annoyed shrug.

As the boat came to idle, the Russian walked back to the stern. By then, the frogheads were dog-paddling along the starboard side, their faces visible above the water. The leader warbled something to Mikhail; he listened for a few moments, then turned to Ronson.

"She says this is the place where we will find the man we are looking for," Mikhail said, "but they refuse to go any farther. They will remain here until they see us leave, then they will follow us."

Ronson was puzzled as to why the Water Folk wouldn't escort them the rest of the way to the island, but he wasn't about to argue. As the boat began moving again, he went below, where he found the Taser he'd left beneath his bunk pillow. He had just slid its holster on his belt, though, when Mikhail followed him into the cabin.

"Leave that behind," the Russian said. "If the yaz croppers

see you wearing it, they'll think we mean trouble."

Ronson stared at him. "Then how the hell am I supposed to rescue the kid?"

Mad Mikhail hesitated. "We will think of something," he said at last. "Let me do the talking, yes?"

Again, Ronson didn't have a choice. As the boat came closer to the island, though, he came out on deck with the Taser beneath the nylon rain jacket he'd put on. When no one was looking, he carefully hid the weapon behind the net locker where it couldn't be seen yet could be easily reached.

Men on the island had seen *Aphrodite* coming. Two yaz croppers were waiting on the dock as the boat glided up beside it. They grabbed the lines Mikhail and Ronson tossed to them and pulled the fishing boat alongside their own craft, then a thickset man with grey, brush-cut hair rested a foot on *Aphrodite*'s gunnel, arms folded across his bare chest.

"Priv'et," he said, gruff yet not entirely hostile. *"Kak vas tibut?"*

"Mikhail Kronow," Mad Mikhail replied. *"Vy gavarti pa angliski?"*

The other Russian looked over at his companion, a younger man with a shaved head and a goatee beard. "I do, mate," he replied, an Australian accent to his voice. "So who the hell are you, eh?"

"He is *gospodin* Ronson, an American friend." Mikhail barely glanced at Ronson. "Thank you for speaking English . . . his Russian is very bad." The Aussie laughed but the Russian remained silent, apparently not understanding a word they were saying. "We are here to do some business, yes?"

"What sort of business?"

"I think you know what kind." A smile and sly wink. "May we speak to your leader? Someone we can . . . um, how do you say . . . negotiate, yes?"

"Vityazka iz kornia," Ronson said. Mikhail gave him a sharp

look, but he saw no need to dance around the subject. There was only one reason why a boat would be all the way out here. "I'm looking to buy yaz."

The Aussie looked at the older man and spoke to him in his own language. The Russian cropper studied Ronson and Mikhail for a few moments, dark eyes sizing them up. Then he slowly nodded, and the Aussie turned to the visitors. "Sure, c'mon . . . this way."

Ronson glanced back at the wheelhouse. Angelo was standing at the door. He shook his head, silently telling Ronson that he was going to stay behind. Ronson nodded, then followed Mikhail off the boat. With the two croppers leading the way, they walked onto the island.

The ground was soft and spongy. Until he reached the crude walkway of wooden boards laid down by the croppers, Ronson's shoes sank a bit with each step he took, making squishy sounds. The forest closed in around them as he and Mikhail were led away from the dock until they couldn't see *Aphrodite* anymore, and he fought an impulse to hold his breath against a pungent reek that permeated the humid, chlorophyll-laden air. It got stronger the farther they walked, and at first he thought it came from the jungle around them, but then they reached the middle of the island and he saw what was causing it.

A clearing had been hacked out amid the trees and tangled underbrush, and it was here that the croppers had set up camp. Wooden shacks and canvas tents surrounded an open area. Nets were suspended from tall poles erected around the periphery, doubtless to ward off night shrikes but probably also to provide camouflage from any aircraft that might pass overhead. The camp had the basic amenities—a cook tent, a cluster of satellite dishes, outhouses—and might just as well have belonged to a wilderness expedition were it not for what was in its center.

Vats made from discarded fuel drums had been set up above iron braziers. Brackish water slowly boiled over wood coals, emitting stinking fumes that made his eyes weep. The men and women stirring the vats wore bandanas around the lower parts of their faces, and Ronson wished he'd known enough to take the same precautions. Lumpy brown scum floated on top of the bubbling water; as he watched, one of the croppers dipped a large, long-handled spoon into a vat, carefully scooped out a dripping mass, and placed it on a tray, which was then carried to a wooden platform set up beneath a tarp and laid out to dry.

"Yaz," Mikhail murmured, nodding toward the platform.

"Yeah, here's where we make it." The Aussie—his name was Graham, Ronson had learned during the trek through the forest—proudly pointed to the vats. The Russian, whose name was Boris, had left them as soon as they entered the camp. "We drop the roots in there, boil off the resin, scoop it out, cure it . . . that's how we get the good stuff." His finger moved to an open-sided shed, where a couple of women were using a grocery scale to weigh bundles of *vityazka iz kornia* before wrapping them in paper and twine. "Each of those is half a kilo," Graham went on, indicating a nearby shack where a large stack of bricks could be seen through the door. "From this island alone, we'll probably get . . . oh, I'd say, five hundred kilos at least."

"And then you move on," Ronson said.

"Uh-huh . . . another island, another crop, another big pile of rubles." Graham laughed, clapped him on the back. "Your pot farmers back in the States got nothing on us. They're stuck in one place, but we're a mobile operation."

Ronson only half listened to Graham as he searched the faces of the men and women around them, trying to spot David Henry. No one here looked like him, though, even allowing for the bandanas covering the faces of the men stirring the vats.

Indeed, no one in the camp looked like they were being forced to do anything. Some smiled and joked as they worked, and there were no armed guards keeping them in line. If anyone here had been shanghaied, they didn't seem to be upset about it.

Bulgakov might have been wrong, and the frogheads . . . Ronson felt annoyance growing in him. How could he have been so stupid as to trust those things? Masters of the World Ocean, his soaked ass. Animals, really, despite what Mikhail claimed. No wonder he was called Mad Mikhail . . . Someone tapped him on the shoulder. Ronson looked around, saw that Boris had returned. And standing beside him, wearing a jungle hat and a sweat-stained Coldplay T-shirt, was David Henry.

"Hello," David said, offering a handshake. "I hear you'd like to buy some yaz."

It was only his brief experience working undercover for the NYPD vice squad that kept Ronson from showing the surprise he felt. In an instant, he realized why David Henry had disappeared without a trace. Perhaps he hadn't come to Venus intending to become a drug lord. Perhaps the opportunity presented itself only after he'd been here awhile. Yet he wasn't a captive of these yaz croppers; he was their boss.

"That's what I'm looking to do." Ronson shook his hand. "Nice little operation you've got here. Never knew how this stuff was made."

David grinned, shrugged nonchalantly. "Not many people do until they see it themselves. No harder than weed . . . or even crack, for that matter. And out here, it's a little easier to get away with." He motioned to the nets strung above them. "That's really just to keep out the birds. The law's just about given up trying to find us. I don't think they even give a shit anymore."

Ronson silently agreed. Bulgakov had just about told him as such. "Must be a hassle getting the roots, though," he said, trying to find something to talk about while he gave himself a chance to figure out how to play this. He looked around the camp. "I mean, it doesn't look like you're cutting down any trees."

"Well, I've got my own . . ." David's voice trailed off. His gaze had fallen on Mikhail, who stood quietly nearby. "Hey, I know you!" he exclaimed. "You're"—he snapped his fingers a couple of times, trying to summon a memory—"that guy! The one who hangs out on the docks in Veneragrad and gets the froggies to pose for pictures!"

"Mikhail Kronow." Mikhail's eyes shifted nervously back and forth.

"Yeah! Mad Mikhail!" David was both surprised and happy to see him. "I guess you don't remember me. We never talked or anything, but . . . man, do I remember you! I owe you a lot, dude!"

Mikhail stared at him. "You do?"

"Uh-huh." David looked at Ronson again. "You got him as your translator, right? I mean, he couldn't have known how to find us, so I guess the dude who's driving your boat must have done that."

"That's pretty much it, yeah." Ronson let David make his own assumptions. "Mikhail hooked us up when I told him what I was looking for, so . . ."

"Cool." David returned his attention to Mikhail. "Like I was saying, that trick you have? Getting the froggies to come running for chocolate?" He waved an expansive hand around the camp. "That's made all this possible. C'mon, lemme show you . . ."

Another boardwalk led away from the camp. It ended at a smaller clearing not far away, where two croppers stood around a hole. It appeared to have been cut straight down through the vines and moss that made up the floating island, forming a deep well. A wheelbarrow stood nearby; the two men watched the hole, as if waiting for something to emerge.

"When I first came here," David explained, as they approached the hole, "croppers were using roots of slickbark trees cut down by the lumber operators. Which is okay, except that by the time our people got to them, the roots were all dried out, and that meant the yaz they got from them had lost much of its potency. Everyone knew that fresh roots make better yaz, but since slickbark roots grow underwater, you'd have to use scuba gear and trained divers to swim beneath the islands to get to them. And that's dangerous as hell . . . something might eat you while you're down there. Then I had an idea . . ."

"Coming up," said one of the men watching the well.

The water bubbled for a moment, then a froghead came to the surface. Its silver eyes regarded the men standing around the well for a couple of seconds; they stepped back from the hole to give it room, and the aborigine came the rest of the way up. A nylon bag was harnessed to its chest; once the froghead was standing on dry ground, one of the men unfastened the harness, carried the bag over to the wheelbarrow, and upended it. A couple of wet, fibrous objects that looked like large knots fell into the wheelbarrow: slickbark roots.

The man who'd collected the bag from the froghead picked up a root, inspected it, then held it out for his boss to see. He said something in Russian; David frowned a little but nodded anyway. The other cropper reached into his pocket, pulled out a Hershey bar, and held it out to the froghead.

Surprisingly, the aborigine didn't immediately take it. "Wurgo wogka kroh," it croaked, looking down at the hole from which it had just emerged. "Krokka kow wok-wokka."

Mikhail hissed, an angry sound that only Ronson heard. He didn't say anything, but from the corner of his eye, he could see that Mikhail's mouth was drawn into a tight line. "Oh, c'mon," the man with the candy bar said; he was an American, a Southerner judging by his accent. "Take it and git back down there." When the froghead didn't accept the chocolate, he yanked a cattle prod from his belt. "This or this," he said, holding up both the prod and the Hershey bar. "Your choice."

The froghead flinched at the sight of the cattle prod. Ronson realized then that this creature was different from the three Water Folk who'd escorted *Aphrodite* from Veneragrad. Thinner, its head slumped forward and its eyes dulled, there were dark, bruiselike marks on its flanks that could have only been caused by electrical burns. He was looking at a slave.

"*Kroh,*" it said softly, then it reached for the Hershey bar.

"Yeah, *kroh* this, you ugly mother." The cropper broke the bar in half and tossed the froghead the smaller part. "Now git back down there . . . and next time, make 'em bigger!"

The froghead put the chocolate in its mouth, swallowed it slowly. Then, as if resigned to its fate, it turned and jumped feetfirst down the hole.

"Pretty slick," Ronson said softly. Mikhail remained quiet.

"I kinda think so." David grinned, proud of himself. "I mean, it's just regular, ordinary chocolate, but they're totally addicted to it. So all we have to do is find a few froggies, give them a couple of bars, then don't give 'em anymore until they learn to chew off slickbark roots and bring 'em to us."

"Hell, I don't think they want anything else now *but* chocolate." The man with the cattle prod started to take a bite from the other half of the bar, then stopped himself. "Running low, boss," he added, his voice becoming worried. "I don't think we've got but a few bars left."

"Really?" David frowned. "Well, we're going to have to do something about that. Next time we send someone to Veneragrad for supplies . . ."

"We got some on the boat," Ronson said.

"Oh, yeah?" David looked at him again, his face brightening again. "How much?"

"Whole bag full. Couple of dozen bars at least." Ronson was exaggerating—he knew that Mikhail had brought only a few—

but an idea had occurred to him. "C'mon back to the boat, and I'll give 'em to you. We can work out a deal on the way . . . I've got the cash there, too."

A smile stretched across David Henry's face. "Sounds like a plan." He turned to walk back toward the camp. "I like a man who comes prepared. Let's go."

Ronson followed him, consciously avoiding Mikhail's angry glare.

Capturing David Henry was almost ridiculously easy. The kid was so confident that the Russian authorities would never catch him, he'd become trustful of anyone who offered to buy yaz from him. He didn't even take any of his crew with him when he followed Ronson and Mikhail back to the dock.

Ronson kept up the pretense on the way to the *Aphrodite*. He had to guess how much a runner might offer for a hundred kilos of yaz, but it appeared that he was close to the mark when he bid 500,000 rubles. David tried to talk him up to 600, and by the time they reached the boat, they'd settled on 550. Plus the bag of chocolate bars, which David laughingly called "a sweetener."

He was still chuckling at his own joke when they stepped onto the boat. Ronson was smiling, too, as he casually bent down beside the net locker and found the Taser he'd hidden there. He straightened up, turned around, and fired it at David before he knew what was happening. The charged prongs hit him in the chest; the kid collapsed with little more than a grunt, and he was still twitching on the aft deck when Ronson and Mikhail hastily cast off the lines and Angelo started up the engine.

By the time David regained his senses, his wrists and ankles were bound, and he'd been deprived of the jackknife Ronson found in his pocket. He rolled over on the deck and glared at the detective. "What the fuck are you . . . ?"

"Your father hired me to come find you." Ronson was sitting beneath the tarp, watching the island as it receded behind them. "If you're lucky, I'll be taking you home to him. But I know a certain cop who might have a say in that, so . . ." He shrugged.

"Dude, you're so screwed. When my guys figure out what you've done . . ."

"They'll come after you?" Ronson shook his head. "Don't count on it. No one's following us. I imagine that, even if they put two and two together, they're not going to risk everything trying to rescue you. My guess is that they'll pack up and move out as fast as they can, and someone will take over as the new boss." He glanced at David, gave him a knowing smile. "Hate to break it to you, kid, but with guys like that, you're expendable. And easily replaced."

David Henry glowered, but didn't reply. He must have realized the truth of what Ronson was saying. Ronson cracked open a beer he'd found in the galley. "So how did you fall into all this, anyway? Did you come here looking to get into the yaz business, or was it just something you stumbled into and . . . ?"

"Slow down!" Mikhail was standing at the bow, searching the waters ahead. "Stop! The Water Folk are just ahead!"

"Oh, for God's sake . . ." Angelo was reluctant to stop for the frogheads who'd led them to the island, but he throttled down the engines and the boat coasted to a halt. "Make it quick, okay? I want to put distance between us and the croppers."

The three aborigines floated just beneath the surface, their protuberant eyes the only things visible. As the boat idled, its engine still throbbing, Mikhail leaned over the rail and called to them. He spoke for nearly a minute, but the frogheads didn't respond. When he was done, they silently submerged, vanishing as if they'd never been there. Angelo waited a few seconds to make sure he wouldn't run over them, then started up the boat again.

"What did you say to them?" Ronson asked once Mikhail came back to the aft deck.

Mikhail didn't reply at once. He stood over David Henry, hands clenched at his sides, regarding the kid with cold and murderous eyes. David tried to return his gaze but quickly looked away. "I told them we found the man we were looking for," Mikhail said at last, his voice low, "and thanked them for their help."

"That's all?" Ronson didn't believe him. Mikhail had spoken a long time for something as simple as that.

Mikhail nodded, then went below, closing the cabin door behind him.

Aphrodite continued westward, chasing the shrouded sun as it gradually dipped toward the horizon. It was beginning to slide into the ocean when Angelo called a stop for the night. There were no islands around, so he simply stopped the engines, allowing the boat to drift. With no nearby islands, there was little chance they'd attract the shrikes who haunted them. The captain left the nets in the locker, and since it was a mild evening, Mikhail suggested that they have dinner on the aft deck beneath the tarp.

Time to relax a bit. All the same, Ronson took the precaution of scanning the ocean with the binoculars. Aside from a distant logging ship, they'd seen no other boats since escaping the yaz camp. As he'd predicted, the croppers had apparently decided that pursuing the people who'd abducted their chief—their former chief—was more trouble than it was worth. And although he'd occasionally glimpsed Water Folk breaching the surface, they'd kept away from the boat. He couldn't tell whether they were the same ones they'd met before, but he doubted it. Their task was done; no reason for them to have anything further to do with the humans.

He was wrong.

Darkness had fallen when a froghead rose to surface just behind *Aphrodite*'s stern. By then, the four men were seated in folding deck chairs beneath the awning. Ronson had removed the ropes around David's ankles but left his wrists tied; he was eating canned stew from the paper plate Angelo had placed in his lap when Ronson happened to glance behind the boat and spotted a pair of eyes that reflected the light of the deck lamps like silver coins.

"Company," he said.

Angelo turned around in his chair, followed his gaze. "Oh, hell," he muttered, annoyed by the distraction. "What does it want?" He looked at Mikhail. "Give it a candy bar and tell it to go away. It's putting me off my food."

Mikhail had been quiet all afternoon, saying little to anyone. Now he put down his plate, pushed back his chair, and stood up. Instead of turning to the froghead—no, Ronson realized, there wasn't just one pair of eyes, but two . . . and now three—he looked at David.

"You remember when we were at your camp and you were showing us how you got the Water Folk to bring you tree roots?" he asked. "You remember that one of them said something to you and your people?" David said nothing and Mikhail went on. "I know you did not understand what it was saying, but I did. It said that it did not want any more chocolate, and then it begged you to let it go."

"Yeah, well . . ." The kid was watching the frogheads. They were coming closer to the boat. Ronson counted six pairs of eyes, and it seemed like more were coming. "That's really tough, but I don't think . . . I don't think . . ."

"No. You don't think, do you?" Mikhail stepped away from the circle of chairs, out from under the tarp. "And now you pay the price."

A thump against the stern, then a froghead reached over the side. With surprising speed and agility, it pulled itself aboard. Its feet had barely touched the deck when another one followed it. And then a third.

"Hey, what're you . . . ?" Angelo was out of his chair, staring at the creatures. "Tell these goddamn things to get off my boat!"

"They will be gone soon." Mikhail was calm, hands at his sides. "They will leave as soon as they have taken what they want from us." A faint smile. "And no, it isn't chocolate."

"Mikhail, this has gone far enough." Ronson stood up, felt for the Taser he'd clipped to his belt. His hand fell upon an empty holster. Sometime in the last half hour or so, it had disappeared. He remembered Mikhail's bumping against him just before they sat down for dinner, and immediately knew what he'd done. "Mikhail . . . !"

Frogheads were climbing over the starboard and port gunnels. Ronson could hear more coming over the bow. Eight, ten, twelve? He had no idea how many. Now it wasn't just their eyes that were reflecting the light, but also the teeth within their open mouths. Wet, sharp teeth . . .

"Get 'em away from me!" The plate fell from David Henry's lap as he leaped to his feet. His eyes, when they swung toward Ronson, were wide and utterly terrified. "Get a gun or something and get 'em the fuck away from me!"

Ronson looked at Mikhail. Frogheads were standing on either side of the Russian now, advancing toward the other three men beneath the tarp. "Don't do this. Mikhail, don't let them do this . . ."

"Go below," Mikhail replied. "You too, Captain. If you do not interfere, they will not . . ."

All at once, the Water Folk attacked.

Ronson saw little of what happened next. It was swift, it was violent, and by the time he and Angelo reached the cabin and threw themselves inside, it was over. Almost. The screams were still coming as the captain slammed the door shut and they put their weight against it.

The frogheads hadn't come for them, though. They'd come for David Henry.

And for Mikhail, too.

Both men put up a fight, but it didn't last but a few seconds. The boat rocked back and forth, and there were the sounds of a struggle from the other side of the door. A series of loud splashes. And then the night was quiet again.

Ronson waited a minute or so. Not just to make sure that the frogheads had left, but also to give his heart a chance to stop hammering against his chest. Then, with Angelo fearfully peering over his shoulder, he inched the door open and peered out.

Overturned chairs. A ripped tarp. Blood on the deck, already mixing with puddles of seawater. No bodies.

The two men stood on the aft deck, feeling the warm rain against their faces. In the far distance, lightning flashes briefly delineated the horizon, painting the clouds with shades of purple and silver, silver the color of the Water Folk's eyes. A soft rumble of thunder. A storm was approaching.

"I really hate this fucking planet," Angelo whispered.

"Yeah," Ronson said. "Me too."

LAVIE TIDHAR

Here's a vivid pulp adventure of the old-fashioned kind, full of slam-bang action, that pits a hard-bitten spaceman against a vengeful god from a Lost Civilization in the depths of the steaming Venusian swamps . . .

Lavie Tidhar grew up on a kibbutz in Israel, has traveled widely in Africa and Asia, and has lived in London, the South Pacific island of Vanuatu, and Laos. He is the winner of the 2003 Clarke-Bradbury Prize (awarded by the European Space Agency), was the editor of *Michael Marshall Smith: The Annotated Bibliography,* and the anthologies *A Dick & Jane Primer for Adults* and *The Apex Book of World SF.* He is the author of the linked story collection *HebrewPunk,* the novella chapbooks *An Occupation of Angels, Gorel and the Pot-Bellied God, Cloud Permutations, Jesus and the Eightfold Path,* and, with Nir Yaniv, the novel *The Tel Aviv Dossier.* A prolific short-story writer, his stories have appeared in *Interzone, Clarkesworld, Apex Magazine, SCI FICTION, Strange Horizons, ChiZine, Postscripts, Fantasy Magazine, Nemonymous, Infinity Plus, Aeon, The Book of Dark Wisdom, Fortean Bureau,* and elsewhere, and have been translated into seven languages. His latest novels include *The Bookman* and its sequel *Camera Obscura, Osama: A Novel,* and, most recently, *The Great Game. Osama: A Novel* won the World Fantasy Award as the year's Best Novel in 2012. His most recent books are novels, *Martian Sands* and *The Violent Century.* After a spell in Tel Aviv, he's currently living in England again.

The Drowned Celestial

LAVIE TIDHAR

I.

COLT WAS PLAYING CARDS WHEN TROUBLE CRAWLED in through the door in the shape of a dead man who didn't yet know he was dead.

This was on old Venus, ancient and most decadent of planets. Make no mistake, as the blind poet said: man has conquered space before. Woman, too, though in fairness, Colt thought, what women had come to this planet in aeons past had not seemed to make it as far as Port Smith. It was a dismal Earth outpost, stranded somewhere on a solid strip of land amidst Venusian swamps. Violet clouds capped it like a forest of mushrooms, and the thick, green-leafed jungle sprouted at the edges of the swamps on all sides, enclosing the port in its relentless grip.

The Earthmen called the place Port Smith; what the Venusians called it, Colt didn't know.

Colt was playing a mixed Martian Wild Card Stud. He was in for all he was worth, which, admittedly, at that precise moment, wasn't a hell of a lot. Colt was out of cash and out of luck, and he needed a boost of both if he were ever to get off this wretched planet. Neither seemed likely to materialize.

In the corner, Old Ishmael, the blind musician, brought his

instrument to his lips and began to haltingly play. It was a dream-flute, and, as he blew, gently, into its mouthpiece, ghosts rose into existence around the bar. Colt's breath was caught in his throat, for they were Venusian dancers, from some long-vanished Atlantean temple, perhaps: bold and free, with their long, flowing black hair, their eyes in which ships sailed in the infinity of space. Slowly, they grew solidity and shape, gliding in a dance through the bar, amidst the tables and unoccupied chairs: and the eyes of all men in that place turned to them, in fascinated enchantment, even Colt's. All but the musician's blind eyes.

It was hot. The humidity wore you down, after a while. The other men sweated, though Colt kept his cool. Outside the windows of the Medusa's Head, the cloud cover stretched from horizon to horizon, covering the sky in an impenetrable dome: it was the same weather that, on Earth, heralds the coming of a hurricane. From time to time, a distant explosion could be heard, as one of the ships took off into the sky. Glancing out of the window, Colt was startled anew, each time, by a flash of silver as a rocket rose, disappearing beyond the clouds. He downed his glass of local *arkia,* squinted at his cards, and waited for his luck to change, for better or for worse.

There was a rumble in the distance, and the other players looked up. Colt kept his eyes on the table and his free hand on the butt of his gun. He was playing a four-hander: the others were two short, scaly Venusians, and an Earthman who called himself Carter. The sound, as of a distant explosion, sounded again, followed a moment later by a rumble that, this time, shook the ground. "That ain't the sound of no rocket ship," the other Earthman, Carter, said. The two Venusians exchanged uneasy glances, but kept their own counsel. "All-in," Colt said, and pushed what remained of his money, a bag full of gold Martian ingots, into the pot. For a moment, there was a silence.

"I'm out," one of the Venusians said, and the Earthman immediately followed suit. Colt found himself staring into the other Venusian's eyes. The Venusian's mouth curled in a smile Colt did not like. "Well?" he demanded.

Slowly, the Venusian laid down his cards.

Colt stared at the Venusian's cards and felt his heart sink.

He had lost.

The Venusian had the Queen of Despair, the Jack of Despair, and a ten of the same. On the table, the community cards were the Seven of Love, the Two of Surrendered Bliss, the Nine of Love, and the Shambleau: the wild card.

The Venusian had a Royal Straight. Colt had nothing—nothing but a gun.

"Don't," the Venusian said. There was the unmistakable sound of a weapon being charged.

At that moment, a third explosion erupted outside. This time it was almost directly overhead. The aftershock rocked the foundations of the bar and toppled the unoccupied chairs; it smashed glasses to the floor and made the cards fly into the air. Colt's hand closed on his bag of ingots and made it disappear. Already, he was rising, the gun in front of him, aimed at the door. The blind musician put his dream-flute down. The dancing girls flickered, then faded away, and Colt felt a momentary sense of loss.

"What—" the Earthman, Carter, began to say. The door to the bar blew open inward and a man came crawling into the room. He lunged forward, in one desperate, terrifying last desire to live, and fell by Colt's feet. He was badly hurt. "Get down!"

A ray-gun blast followed the man through the open door and the Earthman, Carter, fell down, screaming, as his face melted beyond recognition. Not taking his eyes off the door, Colt reached across the table and swept the man's remaining money into a pouch by his side. The Earthman would not, now, need it—but Colt did. Mercifully, the other man's screams shortly died, and with them, the man himself. They were now three against the unknown menace—the two Venusians, and Colt. The blind musician had disappeared, taking his dreams with him.

"Roog!" one of the two Venusians—the one who had folded early—said. Looking wildly in all directions, he ran to the door and outside. Colt could hear him shouting, but whether he was pleading, or threatening, or both, he could not tell. There was a fourth rumble of an explosion, shaking the walls and the floor, and Colt could hear the man scream, outside, then fall silent.

Colt and the one remaining Venusian were left alone in the bar: them, and the unknown men at their feet. "What's your name, Earthman?" the Venusian said.

"Colt. You?"

"Sharol. And that money belongs to me."

"We can fight over it later," Colt said. "When we get out of this mess."

Amusement crinkled Sharol's face. "If we get out, surely," he said. Colt shrugged. "Any idea what's out there?" he said.

"Roog, evidently."

"What is Roog?"

"I don't know." Sharol looked uneasy. "My money is on something bad."

"It . . ." It was the dying man at their feet. Colt took a close look at him, and was surprised to see it was an Earthman. He was badly scarred, and suffering from malnutrition. Burns, oozing puss, covered his hands. "It is . . . treasure."

"Treasure?" Sharol said. He had a purplish, mottled skin and small, near-translucent ears close to his skull. They are a more delicate-looking breed, on Venus, smaller than Earthmen and seemingly fragile, but never underestimate them, for it will be the last thing you ever do. "You have my interest, stranger."

"The temple lies . . ." The dying man's eyes fluttered closed. In a heartbeat, Colt was kneeling, though he kept his eyes and his gun trained on the door. "Where?" he said, shaking the dying man roughly. *"Where?"*

"The Roog . . ." the stranger said. "The Roog!" with horror and revulsion clear in his voice; and then his breath stilled. "Damn you!" Colt said. Sharol's cold chuckle made him glance up: the Venusian was looking at him in amusement. "Death is not the end, Colt of Earth," he said. "But let us hope this man's pursuers do not know that."

"Let them come!" Colt said, and felt the cold, savage fury burn through him, as clean and as pure as a knife. The Venusian merely gestured, silently. He and Colt separated, one to each side of the door. "Ready?"

"Is this a gun?"

"It certainly appears to be one, yes."

"Then I'm ready."

They turned, together, and burst through the doors, outside.

The sun was low over the horizon, behind the clouds; it painted them fantastical shades of violet and red and oozing green. Directly ahead, Colt saw the enemy—just as the enemy saw *them*.

Colt rolled, firing. He preferred a projectile weapon. Beam weapons were fine for dry worlds, for the sterility of space. But on a swamp world such as Venus, Colt felt better with an honest, Earth-made gun, the sort that fired bullets. You knew where you were, with bullets. It was almost like being back home.

The bullets certainly took the attackers by surprise. Colt did not know what they were. He gleaned impressions as he rolled and fired: tall, ungainly creatures, metal-plated, skinny: two purple antennae moved sinuously above their heads. He had no doubt they were communicating silently. They moved as one: they were made for war.

But so was Colt, who had survived worse odds on a dozen rough and wild planets. To the other side of him, the Venusian, Sharol, was firing steadily, his beam weapon flashing, but it merely glanced off the armor plating of the attacking, antlike creatures. "Aim for their antennae!" Colt called, and felt rather than saw the Venusian's grin. Sharol swept his weapon high, and a terrible hissing sound emanated from the attackers as their fragile communication fronds were seared off. Colt continued to fire, his bullets snapping the attackers' armor. He saw one, two, three drop. Clearly, whatever make or design these things were, they had not been prepared for an Earthman's old-fashioned weapon.

But then—he saw! Rising behind the antlike creatures, the source of the explosions that had rocked the bar, a fire burning bright in the sky, dispelling clouds, casting a deathly glow over the swamps and the spaceport itself. Within its glow, Colt could dimly make out a sinuous body, a reptilian head with large diamond eyes, and thin, graceful wings ... "What *is* that?" he said— whispered—and heard Sharol's choked reply, "It's a Sun Eater."

The attackers parted, and through the open swathe of space, Colt could see the creature soaring high above, a sleek, beautiful being flying on wings of—so it seemed—pure song; and whose exact dimensions it was too difficult to make out, so brightly did it burn.

Graceful it might have been. Yet it was not free.

The antlike creatures had, somehow, tethered the Sun Eater to ropes of a metallic hue, and, like children flying a kite, were controlling it from the ground. "We cannot fight it!" Sharol said, and Colt said, "It's beautiful . . ."

"We will die here, Earthman," Sharol said, sounding resigned. But inside Colt, the coldness of battle was replaced with the heat of rage. Whatever these things were, however much they wanted to kill him—these were things he understood.

Yet to enslave such a creature—such a spirit!—was to sin against nature itself.

And he could not—would not!—allow it.

He threw Sharol his gun. The Venusian caught it. "Take care of the advance party," Colt said. "Then follow me."

"What are you going to do?"

"Set it free," Colt said, and with that he was running, the rifle strapped to his back now in his hands. It was a Martian Corps carbine, manufactured for an old war in which Colt had once been a soldier, though it was unclear, to this day, on which side.

He came upon them like a Martian dust devil, a Fury as of some lost legend out of Lemuria or Mu, those continents of Earth now lost to the mists of time. The rifle barked, spewing fire. He watched one enemy fall, then another. Blaster fire singed the air and a pain crawled over Colt's arm, a burning that made him cry out, but he did not drop the gun. Then he was in their midst, battering, kicking, slamming the butt of the rifle into the strange creatures' featureless faces. They were machines, he thought, and memory returned, but he had no time for it, not now: he fired and punched, paying no heed to his own safety, watching only as the thin streaks of silver rope were let drift, one by one. Above him, slowly, the Sun Eater was rising higher into the air. It cried out then, a voice as pure as the water of a glacier. The remaining attackers came at Colt then with renewed fury, and he knew he was done for. They had surrounded him, they had beaten him down to the ground, in the Venusian mud he lay, looking up into a sky illuminated with an artificial sun. Is this how I die? he thought, not bitterly, but with a certain disappointment: he had always seen himself dying, at last, amidst the rolling green hills of Earth.

But then, as from afar, he heard the renewed sound of fire, and, turning his head so that his cheek rested against the muddy ground, saw the Venusian Sharol come running, firing with

Colt's own gun. Colt reached out, grabbed one of the ant-thing's legs, and pulled, unbalancing it. He would not die without a fight, he thought, and he set on the metallic creature, prying open its armor with his bare hands, until its plates parted, and inside it, a violent green and vociferous purple, like congealing blood. The inside of the creature was indeed organic, it was alive! Colt reached for the dagger strapped to his leg, raised it with the last of his power, and plunged it into the ant-thing's gelatinous flesh. A terrible shock ran up his arm from the creature's body as it convulsed and died. Overhead, the Sun Eater roared, finding its tethers suddenly unmanned. Colt heard the beating of wings and felt the heat of the sun blast down around him. He covered his head with his hands, his fingers slimy with the ant-creature's blood, and waited to die.

A moment later, still alive, he opened his eyes. All about him was a ring of ash where an unbearable heat had touched down. The ant-things were charred bodies of molten metal and bubbling ichor. Colt raised his eyes to the sky. Above his head, the Sun Eater hovered, its diamond eyes looking into Colt's. Its wings beat gently, almost lazily, against the air, raising a hot dry wind. For a long moment, they held each other's gaze. Then, with a final cry, in which gratitude or triumph, Colt never knew which, intermingled, the majestic being rose into the sky like the dawning sun.

"Colt? Colt!" It was Sharol, kneeling beside him, one arm dangling uselessly by his side: white bone jutted out of the flesh. "You're alive!"

Colt winced. "Your arm is broken," he said. "It's nothing," Sharol said. He threw Colt his gun back. Colt caught it one-handed. His own arm was badly burnt. "Come on!"

"Where?"

"Back to the bar. Before spaceport security or more of these creatures show up."

"You want a drink that badly?"

But Colt was rising, following the Venusian. His rifle was back in its place, his gun back in its holster. He felt good. It felt good to be alive, on Venus or any other world.

"Wait," he said, as they approached the bar. The bodies of ant-things littered the ground here, where Colt and Sharol had killed them. He knelt beside one, examined it cautiously. "What are they?" Sharol said.

"ReplicAnts . . ." Colt said. He turned one armored foot over, squinting. Imprinted into the metal, as he had expected, was a serial number. The memory returned. He had never seen them, until now . . . "They were manufactured back in the Jovean Wars," he said. "The bodies of human conscripts, embalmed alive into machine bodies. They were meant for war in space, not on the ground. I had thought that all of them were decommissioned and destroyed years ago."

"So how did they come to be here?" Sharol asked, and Colt said, "I have no idea."

"Come on," Sharol said, losing interest. He pushed into the dark interior of the bar and Colt followed. The bottle of *arkia* miracu-lously remained undamaged, though it had fallen to the floor. Sharol picked it up, took a long swig, and handed it to Colt. The drink burned pleasantly as it slid down his throat. The corpse of the man who had begun all this lay on the floor. "Roog," Sharol said thoughtfully.

"Treasure," Colt said. They traded glances. "Well," Colt said, "I guess we'll never know where he came from."

Sharol laughed. It was a surprisingly deep sound, and it echoed around the silent room. "I told you, Earthman," he said. "Death is not the end. Here. Fetch me your knife."

So the Venusian had noticed Colt's concealed dagger. He had proven himself a man of action, as good as any Earthman, if not better. He was worthy of grudging respect. And so Colt drew the knife, still slimed with the ReplicAnt's goo, its blood, and tossed it to the Venusian, who caught it easily with his good hand. "What are you going to—" Colt began, but the Venusian merely grinned cheerfully as he knelt by the dead man. Sharol applied the sharp knife to the dead man's throat and began to saw off the head, whistling cheerfully as he worked. Colt took another swig of *arkia*. In moments, it was over, and Sharol straightened up, tossed Colt back the knife, and picked up the dead man's head by the hair. The face stared sorrowfully at Colt.

"Was that really necessary?" Colt said. Sharol paid him no mind. "Let's get out of here," he said.

"Where are we going?"

"We need to find some mud," Sharol said.

"Mud?"

"And we need," Sharol said, and grinned again as he swung the head back and forth, back and forth with his good hand, "to find ourselves a witch."

2.

THE MUD STANK. IT REEKED OF FETID WATER AND decomposing plant and animal matter. Colt and Sharol were nestling in the shallow of the swamp. Their clothes lay in an untidy heap on the bank nearby, though Colt kept his gun near. The dead man's head was in a sack drawn with a string. Overhead the sky was a violent shade of purple and lightning flashed in the distance, heralding the coming of yet another storm.

They were two days away from Port Smith, deep into the Venusian jungles. The mud itched where it covered Colt's burns. It was healing them. Sharol, beside him, was peacefully puffing on a cigar, his arm entirely encased in thick, grey mud. Colt's toes stuck out of the water. Beyond them he could see the reeds of the swamp, and, here and there, the water predators circling, unseen. Sometimes a tentacle broke the surface, thick and veined, before dropping into the depths again. "If you don't bother them, they won't bother you," Sharol said. His naked chest was scarred with old wounds, much like Colt's. His nipples were small and hard. Colt looked away. When he peeled the mud off, new skin was forming over the burns. "Remarkable."

"Venus," Sharol said, "has many depths." Colt eyed the swamp as another tentacle rose to the surface. It was immense, and he did not like the thought of the underwater creature it belonged to. "I'm sure," he said.

"Relax!" Sharol replied. "Here, give me your back." Colt turned, and Sharol began to apply mud to Colt's skin. The water was as warm as a bath, and Sharol's fingers dug deep into Colt's skin, releasing a pressure Colt hadn't even realized was there. He sighed in satisfaction. "Don't stop," he said.

They remained in the water for some time. When they were done, they washed off the mud and dried themselves on the banks of the swamp. The sun was setting, the sky awash with blood-red hues. In the swamp, a majestic creature was rising to the surface, as large as a ship. Its domelike head had a beak and enormous red eyes. Around the creature, tentacles rose up to the surface, moving sinuously, creating waves. The beak opened and a forlorn cry sounded, piercing the night. "It is the cry of the Dwellers," Sharol said. There was a sadness, as well as love, in his voice. "Listen." Colt did, and became aware of other, distant cries rising into the air in answer. "They are calling to each other, as they do, each night, across the world. But each year there are fewer and fewer to answer the call."

Colt stared ahead. The creature, this Dweller, raised its massive bulbous head toward the unseen stars, crying in a language Colt could not understand. He cleared his throat, embarrassed, perhaps, at the Venusian's naked display of emotion. "Earth's colonial policy is not my prerogative . . ." he began, awkwardly.

"I know, Earthman," Sharol said, and there was bitter mockery in his voice. "You mean well, you all do, children of Earth, reaching for the stars. So enthusiastic, so sure of yourselves. Like overgrown toddlers, you mean us well . . . and yet, you continue to come."

Colt flexed his arm. His new skin tingled. There was a fortune to be made in Venusian mud, if it could be exported off-world. There were other places like Port Smith all around the continents of Venus, now. New Earth colonies on this once-grand world, existing on the sufferance of Venus's ancient, decaying civilization. One day the swamps would be drained, their Dwellers processed into dried-up delicacies for the enjoyment of the off-world rich, their mud packaged and sold in minute quantities for those who could afford its healing properties . . . He clapped Sharol on the back, for those days were not yet, and perhaps, he thought, would never come to be. "Believe me," he said, "I have no desire to stay on this stinking mudball of a planet any more than I have to. I'm light of funds, I've been shot at and nearly killed and I don't even know why, and we're carrying a dead man's head in a pouch. Where is this damned witch?"

Sharol laughed. Overhead, the sky darkened as the unseen sun sank beyond the clouds. "Oh, Earthman," he said, but not without genuine fondness. "Like a toddler, you look, but you do not *see*."

"See what?" Colt said.

Sharol, wordlessly, pointed.

Colt squinted. In the dim light, the Dweller seemed to grow more immense, rising higher, like a lotus flower opening at night. And then he saw her—a lighter shade against the monster's own. A female figure, nude and lithe, hairless and smooth, her skin the same shade of violet as Sharol's own. She was perched on the Dweller's mantle, and her long, reddish-violet hair caught the rays of dying sunlight through the clouds and momentarily shone. For a moment, Colt forgot to breathe. With a graceful movement, the female Venusian dove, headfirst, into the water of the swamp. With strong, economical strokes, she swam toward them and soon climbed on shore, her body shining with droplets of water like tiny diamonds. He had expected a witch—he had not expected to be bewitched instead! The swampwoman smiled, revealing small, sharp teeth. "Welcome back, Sharol," she said. "You bring strange friends."

The Venusian inched his head in reply. "An empty head, and a dead one," he said, grinning. "This is Colt, the Earthman. Who our companion is, I do not yet know."

"And so you came seeking me." She turned her attention away from him, abruptly, transferring her gaze to Colt's. Her eyes were fever-bright; her scrutiny discomfited Colt. "I would have come to you earlier," she said, "but I was observing your proclivities in the shallows, and, well . . . I thought it best to wait."

Colt found himself blushing. Sharol grinned harder. "This," he said, "is my sister, Yaro."

"A pleasure," Colt said. "Ma'am."

But again her attention snapped away, this time to the sack in Sharol's hand. "A dead man walking, who yet did not know it . . ." she said. "Who of us, walking around, alive under the scarlet skies, can ever truly name the time of our demise?"

"We were hoping," Sharol said, "to find out where he came from."

"Still hunting for treasure, brother?"

"Sure," Sharol said, easily. "Only this time, I have a partner."

Again, she cast that quick, mayfly glance at Colt, and away. She turned abruptly. "Come," she said. She led them through a narrow trail, away from the swamp, into the jungle.

There was nothing for them to do but follow.

3.

THE WITCH'S HOUSE SAT DEEP IN THE WOODS. BEYOND the forest, far in the distance, rose a range of volcanic mountains. At their base stood Earth's last settlement on this Venusian continent, which the Earthmen had called Lucille Town, perhaps named by its founder for some long bygone sweetheart. Beyond it lay only the unknown of the primeval Venusian wildlands.

"There is no Sunday west of Lucille Town," so the colonists said, "and no God west of Port Smith."

Though in that, as Colt and Sharol were soon to find out, the colonists could not have been more wrong . . .

"So, brother," Yaro said. "What do you have for me?"

They were in her house. It was simply but tastefully decorated, and a fire burned violet in the hearth, sending plumes of scented smoke into the air. Sharol opened the string and drew the dead man's head from the bag. "It stinks," Colt said. The head looked bad. The Venusian weather had not been kind to it, and it was beginning to decompose. Yaro said, "You should have brought it to me sooner."

Sharol shrugged. "Can you speak with it, still?"

"I can try." She took the head from him. She was dressed now, in a plain shift that rippled around her. She held the head in both hands, staring into its dead, glassy eyes. At last, Yaro shook her head. "Perhaps," she murmured. "Though he is long gone down the Dark Path."

She gestured for them to follow her. Colt moved sluggishly, the smoke making his senses dull and pleasant. Yaro opened the door to a second room. The air was colder there. A curious contraption stood in the middle of the room. It was as if it had grown out of the ground, a blunt trunk surrounded by many twisting branches that spread out and in again upon themselves like tentacles. Yaro placed the dead man's head on the trunk. She began to bend the branches, attaching them, one by one, to the head, pushing them deep into the melting skin and reluctant bone. Colt gritted his teeth but did not look away. When it was done, the head had been penetrated multiple times by the branches, and Yaro took a position in the tangle of branches. This time it was as though the tree itself was responding to her. The branches moved, snaking under Yaro's shift, attaching themselves to her. She began to murmur words in a language Colt did not understand. Her eyes closed and a faint blue light began to glow along the branches of the tree, spreading out from Yaro to the disembodied head. Colt stared in horrified fascination as the air began to fizz and hiss with a powerful discharge. Yaro began to shake, engulfed by cold fire.

The dead man blinked.

Colt stared. This could not be happening, surely.

The head blinked again. Then it opened its mouth and screamed.

Colt took an involuntary step back and bumped into Sharol, who held him steady. Yaro made a sharp gesture and the dead man immediately fell silent. "There is not much there," Yaro said.

"Try," Sharol said, gripping Colt's arm. Yaro closed her eyes. The head opened its mouth again. It began to speak.

"Drowned. In the swamp. Roog. Roog! See him come. The man from the stars has a whip for a heart. Heart of a star! The fire burns, he promised us wealth but made us into slaves. I alone escaped, but they follow, they follow! Untold treasure, all you desire. But the treasure is death. Do not seek your fortune! On the steps of the temple, north by northwest."

"Make it focus! Give us a route!" Sharol cried, his excitement infecting Colt. Treasure! he thought. He pushed out of his mind the dead man's warnings. Dead men could not be trusted at the best of times. Yaro was shaking, sweat pouring down her face, turning her shift damp. It clung to her body. Colt was aware of the curve of her backside, of her nipples, small and hard like her brother's. The blue flames shot upward, and over the dead man's head a picture began to form, hazy at first but gaining definition. It showed the volcanic peaks of the nearby mountain range, and beyond it, a mighty river snaking through marshland and swamps. Here and there, through the thick canopy of the trees, Colt could see smoke rising from unseen villages, Venusian settlements no Earthman had ever seen. The picture rushed forward, and suddenly he saw an ancient temple rising out of a clearing in the jungle, on the banks of a great swamp into which the river fed as it passed. "There!" Sharol said. At the sound of his voice, Yaro dropped her arms. She fell to her knees, the branches making slick wet sounds as they detached from her. The image faded away, and the disembodied head was silent once more.

"Yaro!" Sharol went to her, kneeling by her side. Yaro shuddered. Her eyes fluttered open, but what horrors she saw neither of them could see.

"Roog . . ." she said, and her voice was a pitiful howl of pain and rage and fear. "Roog . . . !"

4.

THERE IS A SPECIAL MONOTONY TO TRAVEL ON VENUS. You who have sampled, perhaps, the volcanic isles of Earth's South Pacific Ocean, or the thick jungles of that planet's interior, may think you understand something of its nature, but you would be wrong. There is something crushing to the soul in the ever-present cloud cover, never a release from the humidity and heat, never the sight of blue skies or the rolling green hills, of which the blind poet Rhysling famously wrote. He had not been fond of Venus, if Colt correctly recalled, writing of it as rotten, wretched, foul, and filled with death.

Well, what do you expect from a drunken old poet? was Colt's take on it. For, traveling for days through jungle and swamp, and sailing the majestic river, which the Venusian swampmen call the Mukhtar, and some worship as a god, Colt began to see Venus through his companion's eyes.

This was not the planet that the Earthmen, God-fearing administrators and colonists, ever saw. Through Sharol's eyes, Colt saw the beauty hidden in the interaction of clouds, for which the Venusians have as many as fifty or a hundred different names; he saw the swirl of hidden currents in the river and smelled the smoke of hidden villages, and that earthy, if unearthly, stink of the swamps, which the Venusians savor like a fine wine. Venus was a planet of secrets and hidden depths, of mysteries beyond recall. And as they traveled, their affinity deepened, his and Sharol's, and in the privacy of their small, leaflike boat, they consummated that special bond that only men can share with other men.

Sometimes, in the dark hours, it seemed to Colt that he saw a brightness in the sky, like a false sun in the distance, followed by the inevitable sound of a distant explosion. He did not comment on it, and neither did Sharol, but he had noticed it, ever since they had left Port Smith, and it made him think of the Sun Eater that he had inadvertently saved.

"Sharol?" Colt said. It was night, and in the distance the Dwellers called to each other across the swamps. The night was thick with humidity and the buzzing of flying insects, drawn to the boat's dim light.

"Yes?"

"What is that sound?"

Sharol went very still. His small, keen ears moved in a manner no Earthman's could. Scanning. Colt listened, too. The sound of the water had changed. It was deeper, quicker. A rumble in the distance, growing closer—

"Rapids!" Colt cried, just as Sharol's smaller body hit his, sending both of them overboard. The water was surprisingly cold, sending a shudder up Colt's spine. Sharol was a shadow beside him. "Hold on to me!" Sharol called. The current took their boat away. Ahead, white foam rose into the air and a roar entered Colt's ears. The falls were close—too close!

The current dragged them, fast. Colt began to panic when he felt Sharol's hand tightening on his arm, pulling him with force. They had stopped! He turned and saw a thick tangle of dark roots rising out of the water, Sharol a shadow amidst them. They were the roots of a natongtong tree, which spread out underwater. The current pulled, pulled at them! Colt held fast to Sharol's hand, then on to one of the roots. They began to drag themselves, laboriously, along the thick, slimy roots, holding on for their lives.

At last, they made the bank. They lay on the wet mud, breathing deeply and hoarsely. Colt stared out at the thundering smoke overhead. A mere hundred feet farther and they would have plunged to their deaths. He smiled, weakly. "Well, that was a close call," he said.

Sharol said nothing.

"Sharol?"

He turned his head, but Sharol wasn't there.

Colt pushed himself up, alarmed. The mud clung to his skin. Footprints on the ground. He scrambled up the slope from the river, hands and feet clawing for purchase. He came over the rise when a hand grabbed him roughly by the shoulder and forced him down. "Hush, you fool!"

Colt lay bellydown in the mud, next to Sharol.

And saw!

It rose out of the bank, more immense than anything Colt could have imagined. What vanished race had once possessed such advanced technology as to erect this temple complex? Vast stone pillars rose high into the sky, each the size and height of many men; giant statues were erected amidst them, of fantastical, vanished beings, the Shambleau and the Thag and the Nameless. And towering above all, a chain of vast pyramids, starkly illuminated against the violet sky, amidst which dark shapes flittered and fled, rising and soaring through the air.

"What *is* this place?" Colt whispered, awed. But Sharol's reply never came. In its stead there came the unmistakable sound of multiple energy guns, all charging in unison. Colt glanced wildly sideways. Dark shapes rose all around them, enclosing them in a trap from which there was no escape.

"What is this *place*?" It was a voice with the twang of Earth in it, a rich and melodious voice, in which amusement and contempt intermingled. A small, round shape stepped forward, revealing itself as a small, rotund man with round glasses and a soft, not unpleasant face. "It is *mine*."

Beside Colt, Sharol was reaching desperately for a gun. Colt grabbed his hand, stopped him. They were outnumbered and outgunned.

The small man laughed. There was something familiar about him, about his face and voice, his mannerisms . . . Colt's eyes opened wide as realization dawned, old memory returned. "Van Huisen . . . ," he said.

He knew that name—that face! The mining magnate, the rich playboy son of an Earth dynasty who had become the worst despot and warlord the solar system had ever seen. The Warlord of Jupiter, they had called him, and the Butcher of Europa. No wonder those ReplicAnt soldiers had seemed familiar—it was Van Huisen who had employed them, in his insane war to become the emperor of the Jovean moons!

But surely the man was dead? He had been indicted for countless crimes postmortem, including for xenocide (against the peaceful ocean-dwellers of Europa), his army scattered, his

ReplicAnt soldiers destroyed. Of his Five Year Reign, nothing remained, no statue, no memorial. The most evil man in the solar system, they had called him. Surely, surely he was *dead*?

"Van Huisen? Yes, yes . . . I remember that name," the man in the round glasses said, thoughtfully. "And who might you be?"

"Kill him, Colt! Kill him!" Sharol was shaking, sweat poured down his face: Colt had never seen him this way. He restrained his friend as best he could, afraid for his life. "Ah," Van Huisen said, smiling pleasantly. "You have heard of me?" He turned back to Colt, shaking his head. "Venusians," he said. "Such an emotional race, don't you think? They are like children, they need the firm hand of an adult to guide them. I could use you, yes. One does not waste labor. Bring them," he ordered his ReplicAnt, sharply. Colt and Sharol were pulled up to their feet. They were led away, deep into the temple complex, into the shadows of the pyramids.

5.

IN THAT WAR, COLT WAS BUT A YOUNG SOLDIER. HE still remembered landing on Europa, after the massacre. Remembered the corpses of the gentle, whalelike creatures, stranded on the ice, their enormous eyes unseeing. Once Europa had sang with the mind-song of its peaceful, telepathic inhabitants.

But the war had turned that icy moon into a wasteland.

6.

A HATRED HE HAD THOUGHT FORGOTTEN, BURIED deep, frozen, had erupted in him. Captive, helpless, he and Sharol were led into the complex. From within, all signs of grandeur were gone, and he could see the place for what it truly was: a ruin.

Make no mistake: man has conquered space before. And out of what strange, vanished race did *this* place come? Atlantis? Mu, of which only hints and myths remain?

Now the jungle encroached freely into the complex; the trees sent roots to break the stones, upend the statues. Once it must have sat on a raised plateau, but the ground had eroded and the river had come in, swamping the once-grand courtyard, turning the earth into fetid pools of stagnant water. They trudged through and around the main pyramid.

Beyond, an enormous part-lake, part-swamp spread out as far as the eye could see. The water reached up to the lowest level of the pyramids, leaving a black line along the ancient stone. All around the shore, amidst the pyramids, stood Venusian swampmen and -women. Colt heard Sharol's indrawn breath, the hiss of his anger and disgust.

Slaves.

They were slaves.

Chains linked the Venusians' legs, binding them together. Scattered among them were armed ReplicAnts, keeping order. The linked chains of slaves were sent into the water, wading, deeper and deeper. Lights hovered over the surface, and Colt saw a massive, floating platform, on which a giant crane stood, extending far over the water. Divers came and went from the platform.

It was a salvage operation.

"What is under there?" Colt said. Van Huisen smiled in evident satisfaction. "Treasure, boy!" he said. "Treasure the likes of which the solar system has not seen in aeons! And you, boys, will help me recover it."

Roog . . .

"What was that?"

For a moment, Van Huisen looked uncomfortable, confused.

Then the glint returned to his eyes, and Colt realized, with a cold, sickening feeling, that the man was quite, quite insane.

"Now get to work!" Van Huisen roared. The ReplicAnts dragged Colt and Sharol toward the nearest chain gang. Chains were fastened to their feet. A ReplicAnt overseer flicked an energy whip over them with casual contempt, and Sharol screamed as a strip of skin was burned clean off his back. Colt shuffled along with the Venusians. Into the shallows of the water, then deeper. What they were searching for, he didn't know. He knew, only, that they must find it—or die trying.

7.

ROOG . . .

8.

HOW LONG THEY HAD BEEN THERE, COLT DIDN'T KNOW. He had lost track of the passage of time. The voices were the worst, after a while. The incessant murmuring of the mad voice in the lake, calling, always calling to them to bring it out. *Roog. Roog!*

It was need and demand, hunger and hate, loathing and desire. It was a command, and they could do nothing but obey. They slept fitfully, and, rarely, were fed a thin gruel. Van Huisen and his ReplicAnt soldiers had enslaved the swampmen of the nearby villages and now ranged farther and farther, returning each day with new captives. *Roog!* It was a weapon, it was a prayer: in time, it almost became Colt's sole reason to live.

Almost. But not quite. For he was not alone. Sharol was with him, Sharol of the warm skin and the easy laugh, Sharol of the quick draw: they were partners. And the treasure would be theirs, and revenge with it. They just had to bide their time.

Colt was not the only Earthman in the salvage site. There were others there, and Martians, and the men of half a dozen other moons and planets. How they had come to be there he did not know. They were the dregs of the solar system, easily missed, easily lost. And every day he watched them give their lives to the swamp, and with each agonized death, each beating or drowning, he could feel the thing in the swamp grow stronger, hungrier, and heard its call echoing louder in his mind: *Roog!*

"It is near," he heard Sharol say, as though from far away. They were standing on the floating platform, illuminated by the harsh glare of floodlights. "It is rising."

"Yes," Colt said, and, "Yes."

Roog!

A numbness had spread through him. For three days and three nights, they had dived from the platform, into the depths of the swamp. Dredging, searching, knowing they were getting close. It had been easy to be promoted to the platform. No one survived up there long.

They were unchained, up here. They had to be, to dive and return. Colt had never been so tired. There was no escape from the platform, in the glare of floodlights and the shadows of the ancient pyramids. There was only one way out. Perhaps he had always known that.

He adjusted the mask on his face and dove headfirst into the water, and felt Sharol, a bullet shape beside him. Together they dove deep, their torches illuminating the murky depths. There were others down there, little mechanical submersibles and naked Venusian divers, nets and hooks and rope. And then there were the dead.

They were everywhere. They floated in a thick glow of decomposition and decay, staring at Colt with white, milky eyes. Venusians and Earthmen and Martians, sacrificed each day for the crazed god at the bottom of the swamp, this Roog, and with each death, it had grown stronger and more insane.

It was close.

He could feel it now, feel its relentless, hungry pull. How had it taken so long for them to find it, when it was so obviously *there*, a beacon calling out, warping minds, infecting their dreams? He dove, deeper and deeper, Sharol's muscular body moving beside him with fluid, economic grace. A rising shoal of divers, converging on this one place.

There!

In the mud, half-buried, ghostly in the half-light of their lamps. It was an enormous stone statue: a savage face like a ritual mask, eyes gouged deep into the stone, shining with bioluminescence. There was both savagery and beauty etched into that stone idol, a hunger, a desire. It was a thing out of Atlantis or Lemuria, the last remnant of its race, found here in the last place on or off Earth. A little lost god. The divers converged on the idol. Nets engulfed it. Ropes wrapped over it, carefully. Colt watched the first of the divers, a small Venusian woman, reach the idol. Perhaps curious, perhaps, in her tiredness and despair, lacking caution, she reached out a hand and touched it. For a moment, a dreamy look entered her face, palely visible through her mask. Then she simply burst open, like fungal spores or dust, a coalescence of blood and brains, intestines and ovaries. The idol seemed to *glow*, it sucked in the cloud as if the Venusian had never existed, and it exulted, screaming out in savage joy across all of their minds: *I ... am ...* Roog!

Still they heaved and secured, and overhead the giant crane began to pull, and slowly, slowly, the idol was pulled free of the mud. It rose through the water, an inhuman figure and yet, somehow, carved by humans long gone, whose science had become myth and superstition. Colt stared at it in horrified awe and disgust: this was the treasure they had come to find.

And now they were its captives.

He turned his head and saw Sharol looking at him, and a shared thought passed through their minds, and they began to rise, swimming to the surface. On the platform, Van Huisen himself, surrounded by his ReplicAnts, was standing, "Well?" he demanded, "Well, is it here? Is it here?"

He reminded Colt at that moment of an ill-tempered, spoiled child, one who had received too many presents and yet still bullied away those of others. To Van Huisen, the idol was just another toy.

Colt emerged fully out of the water and caught his breath, shuddering with cold and tension. A moment later Sharol, too, rose. He looked ill in the floodlights. Overhead the crane strained against the weight of the idol. Slowly, the line rose. The divers emerged like a dark cloud in the water.

The idol rose. Its great domed head broke the surface of the water. There was a silence all across the swamp and the old ruined temple. Roog. Roog was rising again.

And no one was paying attention to Colt and Sharol.

Again, they exchanged glances. They knew each other's minds. Quietly, they rose. The idol, pulled entirely out of the water, hung suspended in the air above the swamp. It was magnificent—magnificent and grotesque! The mud and water sluiced off it, hissing from some immense heat emanating from within the stone. The idol whispered of blood sacrifice and dark rituals, of death-magic and the science of pain. Van Huisen's eyes were shining, he seemed as enraptured as a child.

Colt and Sharol made their way unobtrusively behind the control unit of the crane. On the deck Van Huisen stood with his arms wide open, the waves lapping at his feet. The idol was being lowered toward him. It must have been a weapon, once, Colt thought, the ancient remnants of the wars that had torn

Lemuria and Atlantis apart and left their children stranded on this and other planets. What could Van Huisen do, being in control of it?

Colt raised his face to the sky. He missed the stars badly, at that moment. Then, far in the distance, but coming closer—something like dawn, like the sun. He heard a distant explosion. Sharol turned to him, a swift glance. "I've been hearing that sound ever since we left Port Smith," he said. Colt shook his head, pointed: a ReplicAnt had wandered a short way away from the others, was just turning toward them, its gun beginning to rise.

They took it front and back, Sharol grabbing the cyborg's gun as Colt kicked its legs out from under it and broke its neck, cleanly, with a twist. He lowered the ReplicAnt gently to the ground, leaning it against the control booth's metal wall. No one had noticed. Their chance of escape was now. Colt liberated a beam pistol from the creature's armor. They were armed, and, for the moment, they were free. Again, they exchanged looks. The water was near . . . all they had to do was swim for it.

Colt grinned. Sharol, after a moment, grinned back and hefted his gun. It felt good, Colt thought, to have a gun again. You always knew where you were, with a gun.

"Welcome, Roog of Lemuria, risen again after millennia!" They stepped around the control unit. The idol had been lowered onto the deck. Its eyes had not lost their weird, ethereal glow. In the distance, a false sun, growing closer. Van Huisen spread open his arms. "You who were worshipped as a god," he said, "will now meet one who has lived as one!" And so saying, he stepped forward, and embraced the monstrous stone statue, placing his lips on the idol's own in a lustful, obscene kiss.

"Now?" Sharol said.

"Now!" Colt said.

They stepped out in unison and began to fire.

The ReplicAnts were taken by surprise if such creatures can

be said to be capable of surprise. The beams hissed through the air, agitating water molecules as they passed. The air filled with steam. ReplicAnts dropped. Others turned, firing. Colt knew they could not win, that this was suicide, yet a savage joy sang through him as he fired, rolled, grabbed a weapon from the hands of a downed cyborg, and continued to mow down Van Huisen's guard. This was revenge, and revenge was a dish best served with guns.

Van Huisen still had his arms wrapped around the statue. Now he turned his head back, to look at them, an irritated frown crossing his face. That was what Colt always remembered, afterward: that petulant look on the Butcher of Europa's face, a moment before it changed forever. At first, it was simple confusion, then a nameless terror entered the man's eyes, and milky clouds began to pour into his retina. His body shuddered, spasming uncontrollably, and he began to scream.

Colt was cornered by two ReplicAnts, his arm and face bleeding and burned: he faced them, ready to die.

But no shot came. Colt stared at the ReplicAnts, but they were unmoving. Just ahead Van Huisen was still screaming, fused into the rock. Colt said, "Sharol?"

"Yes?" came the reply, from the other side of the platform.

"Are you still alive?"

"Yes." There was a short silence. "You?"

"I . . . yes?"

"Sure?"

Colt shrugged. He grabbed the beam gun from the nearest ReplicAnt, smashed in the creature's face, then fired in a long beam, low and wide, turning, leaving around him a circle of corpses.

"I'm pretty sure!" he said.

In the distance, there was the sound of an explosion, like thunder, but it was not thunder. Colt thought that he could see the sun, but that was impossible, on Venus. In the water, the Venusian swampmen and -women stared up at the two of them, mutely. "Sharol?"

"Yes?"

"They're staring."

"Right."

Sharol came and joined him, cutting a swathe of dead and broken ReplicAnts in his wake. "You!" Colt said, addressing the Venusians in the water. They looked up at him in mute incomprehension. "Shoo!" Colt said. "Shoo!"

"Get out of here!" Sharol said. Still they did not move. He sighed, adjusted the setting on his gun, and began to fire into the water. "Go away! Get back to your villages! Hurry!"

A panic broke in the water, and the Venusians, as one, began to swim to shore. Colt and Sharol, standing side by side in the glare of the one remaining floodlight, watched them come ashore like a dark tide. Soon they were gone amidst the pyramids.

The sudden silence was broken by a human laugh, the sound of hands, clapping. "Bravo," the voice said. Colt turned, slowly. Van Huisen was standing beside the idol, but the idol's eyes no longer shone, and there was something indescribably alien and disgusting in Van Huisen's face: something that used to be his eyes. "Bravo!"

"It's still here?" Sharol said.

"Shoot it," Colt said.

The face that had belonged to Van Huisen smiled. Colt and Sharol opened fire. Van Huisen staggered back, still smiling. Then he stopped and breathed deep. His chest inflated. He seemed to grow bigger and meaner in that time.

He took a step forward.

He was unharmed.

"Roog . . ." he said, softly. His tongue snaked out, red and fleshy like a Martian cactus. He licked his lips. His teeth were like stone, and there was mud leaking from his eyes and ears. He opened his mouth wide. *"Roog!"* he roared. His tongue snaked out and continued to emerge, a vast red snake. It looped around Sharol and pulled him to the ground. Colt fired, but the beams bounced harmlessly off of the monster. "Sharol!"

"Run! Save yourself!"

There was the sound of an explosion, closer this time. Waves lashed the platform, almost upending Colt. Van Huisen grew bigger, and bigger still. His tongue, a red pulsating tentacle, tightened over Sharol's helpless body. Van Huisen's weight was making the platform lean; the crane was tilting alarmingly, swinging as the platform rocked. Colt fired, helplessly, sweat pouring down his face. He threw down the gun and ran to his friend.

"Roog! Roog! Roog!"

"Go . . ." Sharol whispered. He reached out a hand, stroked Colt's cheek. "Colt . . . go."

"I'm not leaving you."

"Save yourself."

Colt shook his head. There was sweat in his eyes. He blinked. The Roog was by now enormous. Van Huisen's body bloated outward, muscles and skin and blood vessels stretched. He towered over them, as tall as the crane now. "I am Roog! Lemuria," he cried, "shall rise again!" Red tongues lashed out of his enormous mouth, tentacles reaching out for Colt, sinking into the lake, questing, hungering . . . Colt was going to get taken, the ancient god was going to devour them both. He squeezed Sharol's hand. "At least we found it," he said, trying to smile. "The treasure."

"Fool," Sharol said. The breath was leaving him. The monster's tongue wrapped itself around Colt. There was no escape. It was slimy and wet and hot. He felt its pull, tried to fight against it. Overhead, the giant risen god's laugh boomed across the sky.

No, Colt realized. It was a different sound, intruding on his consciousness. It was the sound of explosions, and the air felt hot and dry. The Roog stopped laughing, its head turned this way and that. It looked annoyed.

"Who dares disturb the mighty Roog?" he said. His voice had the petulance of Van Huisen still in it. His tentacle eased the pressure on Colt; just a little. He looked up.

The sun burned in the purple Venusian sky. It dispelled clouds and illuminated the night, casting shadows and reflections on the water. It was the sun the blind poet Rhysling had spoken of when he described feeling its warmth on his skin and knowing that he was back home, amidst the green hills of Earth.

And it cried. It cried out in song. It was not the sun, but . . .

"Sun Eater . . ." Sharol whispered. Colt's eyes filled with tears as he stared into the glare, saw, amidst the flames, the lizardine body, the leathery wings of the Sun Eater. It turned enormous diamond eyes on Colt as though it could see every part of him, which perhaps it could. Then it gave a cry of anger and rushed at the bloated god.

The tentacles eased off Colt and Sharol as the Roog turned to his attacker, his mouth opening in rage. Tentacles whipped through the air, trying to wrap around the Sun Eater, but the heat from the flying creature burned them clean off and the Roog cried with anger and pain. Chunks of tongue fell down to the water, red and hissing. The Sun Eater flew at the Roog, gouging deep chunks of meat out of its grotesque human shape, which splashed down into the water, as large as pyramid blocks. Colt grabbed Sharol's shoulders. The Roog's attention was off them. Sharol had lost consciousness. Colt began to drag him to the edge of the platform.

Overhead, the Sun Eater was a ball of flame, but the Roog

had stretched his massive lips into a nasty smile, and a new tongue appeared and licked his red flesh. His giant hands reached for the crane and tore it free. The Sun Eater, turning in a graceful swirl, was coming back at the Roog. The Roog screamed incoherent laughter and rage and swung the giant crane like a bat.

Colt could only watch, in horrified incomprehension, as the crane connected with the Sun Eater's body with a sickening crunch. For a moment, there was silence, and the sun seemed suspended in the air. Then it fell, like dusk, slowly and inexorably, and hit the deck. The platform shook and the water rose and fell on Colt and Sharol. The swamp water found the Sun Eater and extinguished it. It was dying. Without its light, it was just a beast, one no longer even capable of flight. It turned its diamond eyes on Colt and blinked, once. Colt crawled toward it. Above his head, the Roog was laughing, laughing, growing bigger and bigger into the sky. Soon his head was level with the clouds, his legs extended down into the swamp floor. He had forgotten them.

"I'm sorry," Colt whispered. He reached out, stroked the Sun Eater's reptilian head. It felt warm but no longer burning. He withdrew his hand.

Then the Sun Eater imploded.

9.

IT WAS A SILENT THING. THE CREATURE'S ENTIRE MASS compressed inward, eyes and scales and wings broke up and shrank, inward.

Colt stared at the death of the Sun Eater.

Where it had been, there remained a softly glowing egg.

* * *

10.

HE CARRIED SHAROL ON HIS BACK, SWIMMING TO THE shore. Sharol had recovered enough to walk, by then. They leaned on each other as they walked away from the temple complex. Behind them the giant Roog was smashing up the ancient pyramids. It was like a child, playing with its toys. Soon, if it weren't stopped, it would take over the world.

"What . . . happened back there?" Sharol asked.

"I saw a god rising," Colt said. "And a Sun Eater die. Come. We must hurry."

Sharol did not ask why. They walked away from the ancient temple, along the riverbank, before departing from it into the jungle.

"I can't . . . go any farther," Sharol said.

"You have to. Just over the next hill."

And Sharol would comply, and Colt would make him go over just one more hill. They were not like the green hills of Earth, but they were hills, all the same, and hard to climb. Hills often are.

"You need medical help," Colt said. "Lucille Town is three days away, by my estimate."

"What difference does it make?" Sharol said. "We lost."

Colt shrugged. "We are still alive," he answered.

At the top of the next hill they stopped and rested. They had a view over the jungle and the river, and in the distance they could see the swamp and the ruined temple. The Roog's head was lost in the clouds now. Soon he would be visible from space.

"No wonder the Atlanteans died out," Sharol said.

"Yes," Colt said.

He smiled, a private smile. "Look," he said.

They saw it before they heard it. The sound traveled slower than the light, so that, when they saw it, it was in total silence.

It was hard to say, afterward, exactly what it was they saw.

Certainly, there was a flash of terrible brightness.

The Roog's legs seemed to give way under him, suddenly.

It was the brightness of the sun, turning everything white. And then the Roog was no longer there. Sound followed, a rolling thunder, traveling for miles. The light dimmed, only slightly. The flames rose upward, smoke erupting in a vast towering mushroom cloud. Make no mistake, humanity has conquered space before; and out of that prehistory there came to us the ancient myths of the phoenix, resurrected in fire from ash, for such a creature could never have evolved on Earth.

It seemed to Colt afterward that before the cloud dispersed he saw a brightness, as beautiful as a bird, born out of the flames, rise and take off, into the air. The Sun Eater, being reborn in flame, like the phoenix.

They sat on the hilltop and watched the sun rise over the Venusian skies.

11.

IN THE DISTANCE, FAINT AND FADING, A FINAL WHISPER in their minds.

Roog . . .

Then silence.

12.

COLT WAS PLAYING VENUSIAN HI-LO AND WINNING when Sharol came into the bar. He was limping, holding on to a crutch, but he was smiling all the same. Colt smiled back.

They had traveled through swampland and jungle to Lucille Town, under the shadow of the volcanoes. Neither was in good shape when they finally made it. But they *had* made it. That was the important thing.

The city prospered. A lumberyard was operating at one end of the town, and the men were busy clearing away the trees. The houses were slowly being converted into permanent structures, surrounded by clean, white picket fences. A new road was being built, linking the settlement to Port Smith. Everything seemed orderly, prosperous, and safe.

One day, Colt thought, all of Venus would be like this. The colonists would drain the swamps, chop down the forests, build roads and towns all over the planet. Such a world would have no room in it for Dwellers or Sun Eaters, the old temples would become roadside attractions, the old gods would die—and such a world would have no place in it for a man like Colt.

One day, Colt thought. But not today.

"Got room for one more?" Sharol asked. Colt moved his chair and the man beside him, a gruff marine, did the same. Sharol pulled over a chair and sat down. He put his hand, briefly, on Colt's.

"Deal me in," he said.

PAUL McAULEY

Born in Oxford, England, in 1955, Paul McAuley now makes his home in London. A professional biologist for many years, he sold his first story in 1984, and has gone on to be a frequent contributor to *Interzone*, as well as to markets such as *Asimov's Science Fiction, SCI FICTION, Amazing, The Magazine of Fantasy & Science Fiction, Skylife, The Third Alternative, When the Music's Over,* and elsewhere.

McAuley is at the forefront of several of the most important subgenres in SF today, producing both "radical hard science fiction" and the revamped and retooled widescreen Space Opera that has sometimes been called the New Space Opera, as well as dystopian sociological speculations about the very near future. He also writes fantasy and horror. His first novel, *Four Hundred Billion Stars,* won the Philip K. Dick Award, and his novel *Fairyland* won both the Arthur C. Clarke Award and the John W. Campbell Award. His other books include the novels *Of the Fall, Eternal Light,* and *Pasquale's Angel, Confluence*—a major trilogy of ambitious scope and scale set 10 million years in the future, comprised of the novels *Child of the River, Ancients of Days,* and *Shrine of Stars—Life on Mars, The Secret of Life, Whole Wide World, White Devils, Mind's Eye, Players, Cowboy Angels, The Quiet War,* and *Gardens of the Sun.* His short fiction has been collected in *The King of the Hill and Other Stories, The Invisible Country,* and *Little Machines,* and he is the coeditor, with Kim Newman, of an original anthology, *In Dreams.* His most recent books are a new novel, *In the Mouth of the Whale,* a major retrospective collection, *A Very British History: The Best Science Fiction Stories of Paul McAuley, 1985–2011,* and a new novel, *Evening's Empires.*

Here he takes us to a remote mining station on the rugged

coast of Venus's mysterious, fog-shrouded equatorial continent, where the well-armed miners are on guard for an attack by monsters—for all the good it will do them.

Planet of Fear

PAUL McAULEY

ACROSS THE GLISTENING SLICK OF THE SUBTROPICAL sargasso, amongst shoals and archipelagos of bladderweed, several thousand sunfish floated in intersecting circles of churning foam. They were big, the sunfish, big humped discs ten or fifteen or even twenty meters across, patched with clusters of barnacles and thatched with purple-brown thickets of strapweed and whipweed, and all around them soldier remoras flailed and fought, flashing and writhing in frothing, blood-blackened water. A quadrocopter drone hung high above this shambles like a lonely seabird, avid camera eyes transmitting images to the ekranoplan anchored several kilometers beyond the sargasso's southern edge.

In the close warmth of the fire-control bay, bathed in the radiance of three big flatscreens, Katya Ignatova asked the petty officer piloting the drone to lock its cameras on a particular pair of sunfish. They were matched in size, each about twelve meters in diameter, and the fringes of their feeding tentacles had interlaced and fused and were now contracting, drawing them together. Dead and dying soldier remoras bobbed around them: slim, silvery torpedoes with chunks torn out of their flanks, shovel jaws gaping, eye clusters filmed white. Venusian fish were armored in bony chain mail, had external gills and horizontal tail fins resembling whale flukes, but they possessed swim bladders. Like terrestrial fish, their corpses floated.

The drone pilot said, "Such fury. Such waste."

"Soldiers attack everything that gets too close to their sibling," Katya said. "Including other sunfish. They can't mate until their soldiers have been neutralized. But the dead aren't wasted. Their flesh feeds the ecosystem where the next generation develops."

She hunched forward as the pair of sunfish began to jab at each other with the spears of their spermatophores, and asked the drone pilot if he could get a close-up of the action.

"No problem," he said, and made delicate adjustments to the joystick that controlled his little craft.

The views on the screens tilted and shifted, stabilized again. Katya prompted the pilot to zoom in on the tip of a calcified spear that scratched amongst drifts of purple-brown weed before abruptly driving forward.

"I believe they call that the money shot," the pilot, Arkadi Sarantsev, said.

He was a slender, cynical fellow in his midtwenties, a few years younger than Katya. She had noticed that he kept apart from the companionable clamor in the mess, reading a vivid paperback thriller as he forked food from his tray. Sitting close to him in the television light, she could smell the cola-nut oil he'd used to sleek back his black hair.

"It isn't sex as we know it," she told him. "Sunfish are hermaphrodites, both male and female. If you could zoom out now ... Yes. You see? Each has speared the other. They are exchanging packages of sperm. Injecting them into special areas of haploid epithelial cells that will develop into egg masses."

She planned to collect some of those egg masses in a day or two, when the mating battles were over, to test the hypothesis that they contained both fertilized eggs that produced juvenile sunfish and unfertilized eggs that produced haploid soldiers.

She hoped that she would be able to examine the rich and varied biota of the sargasso, too. The swarms of isopods and shrimp and thumb jellies on which sunfish larvae fed; the tripod octopi and fish which fed on them.

They really were amazing creatures, sunfish. They were eusocial, like ants, bees, and mole rats, with sterile, neotenous soldiers and fertile queens which not only lost their bilateral symmetry, like flatfish or the sunfish of Earth, but also lost their digestive systems, their eyes, and most of their nervous systems. And they were also symbiotic associations, like corals or lichens. The dense fringes of feeding tentacles of the queens, which filtered and digested plankton and extruded strings of nutrient-rich nodules which the schools of soldier remoras devoured, were derived from symbiotic ribbon jellies; the strapweeds and whipweeds rooted in their dorsal shells pumped sugars and lipids into their bloodstreams. Amazing creatures, yes, and really not much like anything at all on Earth.

Usually they led solitary, pelagic lives, drifting everywhere on the shallow seas of Venus, but every seventeen years they migrated to the sargassos where they had hatched, possibly following geomagnetic and chemical cues (another theory that needed to be tested), and mated, and spawned the next generation, and died. Katya's observations and data would contribute to a multidisciplinary research program into their life cycle, part of the International Biological Year, a milestone in the growing cooperation and rapprochement between the Venusian colonies of the People's Republic, the United States, and the British Commonwealth.

On the central screen, the two sunfish slowly revolved on the blood-black swell. On the screens to the left and right, a wider view showed other sunfish pairs ponderously locking together and surviving soldiers spending their fury on each other or on ripping apart smaller, unsuccessful sunfish.

Katya asked Arkadi Sarantsev to take his machine higher, was watching intently as it circled the entire area, trying to make sure she captured a good image of every pairing, when the ekranoplan's turbofans started up with a shuddering roar. A few moments later a seaman leaned into the hatch of the little room and told Arkadi to bring in his drone.

"Captain Chernov's orders," he said when Katya protested, and couldn't or wouldn't answer her questions.

She pushed past, hauled herself along the pitching companionway, and climbed to the teardrop cockpit that, with its pale wood and polished brass trim, the diffuse overcast of the cloudroof gleaming through its canopy, always reminded her of the luncheon room of the Engineers' Union where her mother, the architect I. V. Ignatova, took her every birthday for a ritual meal of beefsteak and cultivated wild mushrooms. The pilot and navigator were hunched in their horseshoe of switches and dials and computer screens; Captain Vladimir Chernov was enthroned behind them, sipping from a glass of black tea; all three wore bulky headsets. The ekranoplan had made a cumbersome turn away from the sargasso, and now the pilot gripped the throttle levers by his thigh and eased them forward. The roar of the big turbofans, mounted on canards behind the cockpit, ramped up as the ekranoplan began to accelerate.

Katya grabbed a spare headset to muffle the incredible noise and braced herself in the hatchway during the shuddering lurch of takeoff. She had learned the hard way that she could not speak to the captain in the cockpit until he acknowledged her, and he didn't acknowledge her until the ekranoplan was under way.

An adaptation of the famous curable-maket, the Caspian Sea Monster, it resembled a gigantic airplane but was really a wing-in-ground-effect machine that rode on the cushion of air generated by its turbofans and square, stubby wings: a long-range, lightly armed beast capable of speeds of up to three hundred knots. It was making top speed now, skimming some five meters above long, rolling waves, skimming over breakers frothing across sea-lily reefs. On its way to investigate an emergency at the People's Republic's most northerly outpost, Makarov Mining Station, according to Captain Chernov.

"I am sorry about the abbreviation of your studies," he told Katya, "but the station sent a disturbing message two days ago and has not responded since. Although we are not the nearest vessel, we can reach it before anyone else."

He did not look at all sorry: he appeared to be enjoying himself. A burly, broad-shouldered, bullet-headed man dressed in the Navy's tropical uniform—blue shorts and a blue, short-sleeved jacket over a striped telnyashka shirt—whose cool condescension reminded Katya of the sadistic anatomy lecturer who liked to pluck a student from the ranks and hand her a random bone and demand that she name it and identify the animal it came from.

Captain Chernov was scrupulously polite to Katya but did not bother to hide his scorn for her work, and the collaboration with the Americans and their British allies. He was a war hero who, during the campaign against American libertarian pirates ten years ago, had devised and carried out a daring, spur-of-the-moment raid that had ended with the capture of a particularly bloodthirsty warlord. Popular acclaim meant that the Navy couldn't cashier him for disregarding the chain of command, so he had been given a medal and promoted sideways to the Survey Corps, where he'd been chafing ever since.

When Katya asked him what kind of problem he was responding to, he studied her with remote amusement, then said, "It is something you might find interesting, if true. The miners claimed that they were being attacked by monsters."

"Monsters? What kind of monsters?"

"Most likely the American kind," Captain Chernov said. As

usual, he was speaking to a spot somewhere behind her left shoulder, as if addressing the ghost of an authority she herself did not possess. "If there really are monsters, if this is not some Yankee trick, you may be of some help. Until then, do your best to stay out of the way. My men must prepare for trouble."

The ekranoplan made the two-thousand-kilometer trip in just under five hours. Katya studied the images captured by the drone, sorted them into categories, and made a few preliminary measurements. She ate a sparse lunch alone in the long tube of the mess room (which could double as a field hospital if the need arose), composing a bitter complaint to the IBY committee, the Marine Biology Institute, and the Ministry of Defense, which she knew she would never send. Pick your battles carefully and fight them only in your head, her mother liked to say. No one remembers the righteous who go to war and lose.

The vibration of the turbofans created standing rings in her tumbler of water.

She wondered about the monsters that had supposedly attacked the miners at Makarov Station. The shallow seas of Venus teemed with an extravagance of macrofauna—sunfish, cornet squid, mock turtles, and so on—but only a few large animal species had been discovered on the northern continent settled by the Americans, and the thousands of islands and sea mounts and atolls of the southern hemisphere. So finding a species of carnivore capable of killing a man would be a considerable coup. A swarm of pack-hunting reptiloids. Some kind of super crocodilian. Or perhaps, just perhaps, something as rare and strange as a tiger or a wolf.

She went back to work, counting sunfish, measuring them, tracking the paths of individuals . . . Trying to squeeze as much data as possible from the truncated observations. At some point, she noticed that the deep drone of the turbofans had diminished to a gentle throbbing. The ekranoplan was afloat again, driven by its auxiliary engine as it nosed through dense billows of fog. Captain Chernov was outside, on the little railed observation deck behind the cockpit, with the chief petty officer. The two men wore pistols on their hips and were watching the long shadow of a shoreline resolve out of the fog: the shore of the mysterious equatorial continent.

Two billion years ago, the last great resurfacing era, vast quantities of molten rock from Venus's mantle had risen to the surface through long, vertical cracks in the crust. Injections of lava and differential crystallization of minerals had formed an enormous geological basin with distinct layered strata, including reefs of titaniferous magnetite gabbro, and vast quantities of tin and iron. The basin had tilted and eroded and half drowned, leaving only one edge exposed, a long, narrow continent that wrapped around half of Venus's equator. Most of its volcanic ranges and salt flats and deserts were scorching, waterless, and utterly uninhabitable, but a cold sea current rose at its southern coast, feeding banks of fog that grew during the long day and sustained an ecosystem found nowhere else on Venus. The People's Republic had established several mining stations there to exploit deposits of titanium and tin ore, copper and silver, platinum and bismuth, and to lay claim to the deserts to the north.

This was the coast that the ekranoplan was approaching, drowned in fog and mystery.

An even, pearlescent light, streaming with particles and tiny transient rainbows in whichever direction Katya happened to look. The close, clammy heat of a Turkish bath wrapping around her like a wet towel. The puttering of the auxiliary motor and the slap of waves unnaturally loud in the muffled hush. And something echoing in the distance: faint, staccato, persistent.

"I see no monsters," Captain Vladimir Chernov said, turning to Katya. "But I definitely hear something. Do you hear it, too, Doctor? Could you give your professional opinion?"

"It sounds like dogs," Katya said. "Dogs, barking. Do they have dogs?"

"I don't believe so. Pigs, yes. To eat their kitchen waste and supply them with fresh pork. They are Ukrainian, the miners here. And all Ukrainians love pork. But if the records are correct, there are no dogs."

"Well, it sounds more like dogs than pigs. Someone smuggled in their pets, perhaps. Or watchdogs were assigned to this place, and the paperwork was lost or mislaid."

"Perhaps. Or perhaps it is monsters that kill and eat men, and bark like dogs," Captain Chernov said. A fat pair of binoculars hung from his neck, a symbol of his status, perhaps: they were of no practical use in the fog.

"It would be something new to science," Katya said, refusing to rise to his bait.

"Science does not yet know everything," Captain Chernov said. "Isn't that why you were studying the sunfish, Doctor? Not just to be friends with the Americans, but because you wished to learn something. We are at the edge of an unexplored continent. Perhaps you will learn something here."

"Or perhaps they are really dogs. American running dogs," the chief petty officer said.

He was a stocky, grizzled fellow with a scornful gaze who had even less time for Katya than Captain Chernov did. But at least they were direct about their dislike, unlike the chauvinist fossils at the Marine Biology Institute, and it had nothing to do with her being a woman—a woman who asserted her own opinions and refused to recognize her inferiority. No, they resented her presence because the IBY had many enemies in the government, and if its unstable mixture of science and peacenik appeasement blew up, the fallout would contaminate everyone associated with it. Which was why, of course, Katya had been assigned to the sunfish project by her bosses, and why she wanted to make a success of it.

"Dogs, pigs, monsters: we will find out. And we must do it soon," Captain Chernov told Katya, for once addressing her directly. The ice age of his contempt had somewhat thawed. He was relaxed, almost cheerful. This was Navy work: he was no longer answerable to Katya and the IBY. "If the Americans are not already here, hiding from us or lying in wait, they will be here soon. They claim to have intercepted the distress call. They claim to want to help. There is no airstrip here. The terrain is rough. Too many steep hills and ridges. So everything comes in and goes out by sea. One of our frigates will be here in three days, but one of the American so-called research ships will be here tomorrow."

Makarov Station, strung along the edge of a natural harbor sheltered by a sandbar, was entirely obscured by the fog: it wasn't possible to survey it and the surrounding area with drones or lidar. Infrared imaging showed that the buildings, usually air-conditioned, were at ambient temperature. Apart from a man-sized trace perched on a dockside crane there was no sign of the twenty-six people who lived and worked there, or of the monsters that supposedly had attacked them.

The ekranoplan dropped anchor, sounded its siren, sent up a flare that burst in a dim red star high in the fog. There was no answer from the shore, no response on the radio, no reply when the chief petty officer called to the miners through a loudhailer, and no one was waiting at the edge of the long quayside as the landing party motored toward a floating stage in a big inflatable.

Captain Chernov sprang onto the stage and galloped up the

steps, pistol drawn, followed by the chief petty officer, the drone pilot Arkadi Sarantsev, and seven seamen—most of the ekranoplan's crew. Katya followed, her heart hammering in anticipation. When she reached the top of the stairs, sweating in the damp heat, the men had already spread out in a semicircle, menacing the fog with their pistols and carbines. The skeletal outline of a crane, heaps of dark ore, the outlines of a string of small, flat-roofed buildings and a tall radio mast faintly visible beyond. The persistent barking in the distance, tireless as a machine.

Captain Chernov paid no attention to it. He was standing with his hands on his hips, looking up at the crane's scaffold stem. The jut of its long jib was veiled in misty streamers, but it was just possible to make out the shadow of a man at its end. He did not respond when Captain Chernov ordered him to come down and he did not respond when the chief petty officer put a bullet into the steel plating a meter behind his feet. The sound of the shot whanged off across the muffled, fog-bound quay.

Captain Chernov cupped his hands to his mouth. "Next one he puts in your damn leg!"

No response. They all stood looking up at the man. The monotonous barking had not let up, hack-hack-hacking away deep in the fog.

"Take another shot," Captain Chernov told the chief petty officer.

"I'll go up there," Katya said.

"I distinctly remember telling you to keep out of the way," Captain Chernov said mildly.

"I am medically qualified," Katya said. It was technically true: she had been given basic first-aid training at Young Pioneer camp. "The poor fellow may be hurt or wounded. He may not be able to climb down without help."

"He may be an American for all we know," the chief petty officer said.

"You can bring him down?" Captain Chernov said.

"I can assess him, talk to him. Whether he comes down, that will be up to him," Katya said, with that airy feeling just before a dive, before she toppled over backward into unknown water. As her mother so often observed, she had a knack of talking herself into trouble.

"No, whether he comes down will be up to you, Doctor," Captain Chernov said, turning now, favoring her with his thin cool smile. "Don't disappoint me."

The steel rungs of the ladder, dripping with condensed moisture, slipped under Katya's fingers as she climbed, slipped under the tread of her boots. When she reached the little glass-and-metal box of the operator's cabin, she clung to the handrail and called out, asking the man if he needed help, trying to sound encouraging, friendly. The man did not respond. He lay prone at the far end of the jib, arms wrapped around a steel beam as if around a long-lost lover. There were only ten meters between them, but he did not even turn his head to look at her.

She swore and swung up the steel framework to the top of the jib, trying to ignore the dizzying plunge to the antlike cluster of people below. She called to the man again, asked him to tell her his name, and now he moved, rolling awkwardly to look at her without letting go of the beam. His eyes, sunk deep in dark hollows, seemed to be all pupil.

"You're safe now," Katya said, trying to project a confidence she did not feel. "Come toward me. I'll help you down."

The man's mouth worked, but no words emerged. He was young, younger than Katya, and wore blue coveralls and heavy work boots.

"I'll come to you, then," Katya said.

But soon as she started to crab toward him, the jib shivering uneasily beneath her, the man humped backward, like a demented caterpillar. She stopped, told him that everything was all right, that he was safe, and he closed his eyes and shook his head from side to side. He was crouched at the very end of the jib now, beside the cable wheel.

Captain Chernov called out, asking why this was taking so long. The man looked down, then looked back at Katya, and slowly rose to his feet, arms outstretched like a tightrope walker, balancing at the edge of the foggy void.

"Wait!" she said. "Don't!"

He did.

Katya closed her eyes. A moment later there was a hard wet sound and a shout of dismay below.

When she reached the ground, Captain Chernov said, "Your treatment worked, Doctor, but unfortunately it killed the patient."

The son of a bitch must have been working on that quip while he watched her climb down. She said, "He was scared to death."

"Of you?"

"Of his worst nightmare, I think."

She was staring at the captain because she did not want to look at the splayed body.

"The crane is twenty meters high," the chief petty officer said. "Whatever he was scared of, it must have been very big."

"And it's still here," Katya said, pointing in the direction of the distant barking that had not, in all this time, let up.

"You are eager to make a famous discovery. But first we must secure the station," Captain Chernov said, and detailed two seamen to stay by the boat, told the rest to stick together.

"Look after the doctor, lads," the chief petty officer said. "She isn't armed, she can't run as fast as we can, and she's probably a lot tastier than your salty hides."

"There were twenty-six people here," Katya said. "All men?"

"Of course," the chief petty officer said. "They were here to work. They didn't need distraction."

"All men," Katya said. "And they didn't do too well, did they?"

* * *

They swept through the buildings. Dormitories. A mess hall. Offices. Stores. Two generators purring in a shack constructed from concrete blocks and corrugated iron. An assay lab and a small clinic. A cold store with three bodies wrapped in black plastic sheeting. One had been badly mangled in some accident; the other two looked like suicides—a ligature of electrical cable around the neck, slashed wrists. Five more dead men were sprawled behind one of the dormitory huts, hands bound, chests torn by what appeared to be gunshot wounds, bullet holes in the hut's plank wall. Another body sprawled at the foot of the radio mast. His neck was broken, and Katya suggested that he had fallen while climbing.

"Climbing to escape from monsters, like your patient on the crane?" Captain Chernov said. "Or perhaps trying to escape from Americans who shot his friends."

"Perhaps they all went stir-crazy in this damn fog," the chief petty officer said. "There was a quarrel. It got out of hand . . ."

"Something drove them mad, perhaps," Captain Chernov said thoughtfully.

The prefab buildings were empty although there were signs that people had left with some haste. Plates of food rotting on tables in the mess, papers scattered on the floor of the office, a record rotating on a gramophone in one of the dormitory huts, making an eerie scratching click until Captain Chernov lifted the needle. The gun locker was open and empty, but apart from the five men who had been lined up and shot there was no sign of any struggle, no blood spray, no bullet holes anywhere else. And no sign of the sixteen men still unaccounted for.

"They ran off, or they were taken prisoner," Captain Chernov said. "If they ran off, we will find them. If they were taken prisoner, we will find the Americans who did it."

"With respect, I don't think this was anything to do with Americans," Katya said.

"The so-called libertarians took hostages for ransom when they attacked our trawlers and merchant ships," Captain Chernov said. "And executed them when no ransom was paid. What happened here, perhaps, was caused by some kind of psychological-war weapon. A gas, a volatile drug. After the men were driven mad by it, the Americans walked in, shot the few still able to resist, and took the rest prisoner. I see you do not like this story, Doctor. Well, if you have a better idea about what happened here, I should like to hear it."

"I don't have enough evidence to form a hypothesis," Katya said, and realized that it sounded stiff and priggish and defensive.

The captain smiled. He was having fun with her. "You hope to find monsters. You hope for fame. Very well. Let's go look for them."

Katya trailed after the party of seamen as Captain Chernov and the chief petty officer led them along the quayside, past pyramidal heaps of ore, past a row of articulated dump trucks: powerful machines with six-wheel drive and rugged tires as tall as a person. They moved slowly and cautiously through the fog, checking under the trucks, checking shipping containers and stacks of empty crates. Arkadi Sarantsev hung back with Katya, asking her if she really thought monsters had attacked the station, if they were right now feeding on men they had killed.

"That's what the captain thinks I think," Katya said.

"Do you think he is wrong, about something driving the men crazy?"

"If I had to guess, I'd say it was something to do with the isolation," Katya said. "That, and the fog."

"But not, you think, Americans," Arkadi Sarantsev said.

He had a nice smile and a cool attitude, had knotted a red handkerchief at the throat of his telnyashka shirt. He plucked a pack of cigarettes from the pocket of his jacket and offered it to Katya; when she refused with a shake of her head, he put the pack to his lips, plucked out a cigarette, and lit it with a heavy petrol lighter fashioned from a .50 cal cartridge case.

"If I didn't know better, I'd think that your captain was looking for an excuse to take on the American research ship," she said.

"The captain's father was one of the pioneer settlers," Arkadi said. "We all resent the capitalists, with their nuclear rockets and supercomputers and frontier mentality, but the pioneer families especially resent them. As far as the captain is concerned, their offer of help is a personal insult."

Katya had once sort of dated a Navy diver, who one drunken night had told her how a friend of his had come to the surface too quickly because his dive computer had malfunctioned. He had been stricken with the bends, screaming with the pain of nitrogen bubbles in his joints, fed vodka by his mates because they had no way of treating him. Their patrol boat had been making a hopeless dash to the nearest port when an American frigate which had intercepted its call for help had caught up with it and had taken off the stricken man and treated him in its decompression chamber. Katya's boyfriend had tried to make it into a joke, saying that his friend had not only beaten the bends but had discovered a tremendous hangover cure into the bargain, but it was the usual sad story of crazy Russian machismo combined with a massive inferiority complex.

She said to Arkadi, "I know your captain took things very personally in the war against the libertarians."

"He disobeyed orders when he staged that raid, yes. But he captured an important warlord and his entourage, and also rescued more than twenty hostages."

She had to smile at Arkadi's sudden passion. "You think he's a hero."

"One time, two years ago, we had the job of visiting a small island close to the South Pole," Arkadi said. "Very remote, very desolate. No one lives there, but it is important we have a claim on it. A previous expedition set up a beacon and also landed goats there. The idea was that they would breed and provide a source of fresh meat to any ships that passed by. We were tasked to clean the beacon's solar panels and replace its storage battery, and also to find out how the goats were doing."

"I can imagine what Captain Chernov thought about that."

"He believed that he was keeping the borders of the People's Republic safe," Arkadi said. "That is what he told us, at any rate. Well, a small party of us land. We cannot find any trace of the goats. Not so much as a bone. There are pancake crabs everywhere, though, so we think the goats died and the crabs ate them. The island is a volcanic cone, extinct. Black rocks, tangles of thorny bushes, and everywhere pancake crabs. Watching us from under stones, creeping close to us whenever we stop as we climb to where the beacon was placed.

"All the way around the top of the island's cone there is a thick belt of feather palms. Smaller than the ones on the Big Island, but still much taller than anything else growing there. And there are pancake crabs in the palms. As we make our way through them, the crabs drop on us. They stick to our skin with those suckers they have, we have to prize them off. It is disgusting, but we do not think it dangerous. At the top, there is a caldera, a deep funnel with a lake at the bottom. We find the beacon and do our work. We rest up, and a couple of idiots roll a boulder over the edge. It drops into the lake far below and makes a big splash. And after the ripples die away, there is another splash, more ripples. As if something had woken down there."

"You found a monster?"

"We did not see anything. Just the splash and the ripples. And we did not have any way of climbing down. So we start back down, and the wind changes direction, and it begins to rain. And then two of us become sick. An allergic reaction to the pancake crabs, we find out later. It rains harder. Rain blowing sideways on the wind. And when we get to the inlet where we left the boat, we find big waves rolling in and the boat has floated off, is riding on the waves at the mouth of the inlet. Captain Chernov strips off and swims out to the boat, but he can't bring it near the rocks where the rest of us are waiting because the waves are too fierce. And by now the two sick men are very sick indeed, and they can't swim out. So he motors off to the ekranoplan and comes back with a rocket line, shoots it from boat to shore, and uses it to swing the sick men above the waves to the boat, and everyone is saved."

"What about the monster?"

"We didn't go back to look. But while we wait to be rescued, we have some bad thoughts about it. Imagine it creeping up the cliffs inside the caldera, creeping toward where we are sheltering ... But the point is, whatever they say about the captain, he is not a monster. He did the right thing, in the war, and the brass punished him because he made them look bad. Listen to that. It isn't dogs, is it? It is in no way any kind of dog."

"It doesn't sound like pigs, either," Katya said.

The monotonous barking was loud and close now, coming from somewhere beyond a low rise crowned with a clump of bottlebrush trees. Katya and Arkadi watched as Captain Chernov and three seamen made a forking run, passing left and right around the trees, disappearing into streaming whiteness.

Two minutes passed. Three. No shots. No shouts. Katya's heart beat high as she strained to see into the fog. She badly wanted to know what was making that noise, but her hindbrain was telling her to run far and run fast. Arkadi lit another cigarette, and Katya pretended that she didn't see the flame of his lighter trembling when he applied it. The barking continued without pause. Eventually one of the seamen appeared on top of the ridge, a shadowy figure in the haze, scissoring his arms over his head to indicate the all clear.

There was a vegetable garden on the other side of the ridge, neat rows of potatoes and cabbage enclosed by a double fence of wire mesh to keep out pancake crabs, green leaves vivid and alien against the purples of the belt of native scrub beyond. And there was a paddock of bare earth inside a fence of wooden stakes and wire where two pigs lay in a muddy wallow, flanks heaving as they hacked and barked. Each time they coughed, bloody froth burst from their muzzles. The bodies of three other pigs lay swollen and rotting nearby, avid crowds of pancake crabs jostling and burrowing into them. Katya caught a strong whiff of ripe decay as she leaned against the fence. It seemed to tint the fog with the monochrome hue of grief.

"Here are your monsters, Doctor," Captain Chernov told her. "Would you care to examine them?"

The chief petty officer wanted to put the pigs out of their misery. Katya said that they should try to find out what had infected them first and was surprised when Captain Chernov agreed.

"This sickness could be a reaction to a nerve agent," he said.

"Or something they caught from the local biota," Katya said.

"Native diseases do not infect people," Captain Chernov said. "Or pigs."

"It hasn't happened yet," Katya said. "But life on Earth and Venus shares the same genetic code and presumably the same common ancestor. As far as Venusian viruses and bacteria are concerned, people and pigs are no more than new sets of mucous membranes to be penetrated, new masses of cytoplasm to be exploited and subverted."

"First you hope to find monsters," Captain Chernov said. "Now you hope to find the Venusian flu. Your expectations are dwindling, Doctor. If you want to make yourself useful, help Mr.

Sarantsev search the offices for diaries, logs, any records that might reveal what has happened. Meanwhile, I must look for the missing miners although I am pretty sure I will not find them."

"Because the Americans took them?"

"I am sure that like all scientists, you believe in logic. And logic tells us that if they are not here, they must be somewhere else," Captain Chernov said, and told Arkadi to make sure that Dr. Ignatova did not get into any trouble, and roared off with the rest of his men toward the open-cast mine in two trucks.

Katya found a log in the station's small clinic, found an entry three weeks old that noted two men displaying symptoms of a flulike infection: high temperatures, involuntary movements of the arms and legs, night sweats, recovery within twenty-four hours. By then, more men had become infected. It had swiftly passed through the camp, and everyone appeared to have succumbed, including the station's chemist, who doubled as its medical officer. In the assay lab, Katya found a photograph showing him standing with his two teenage daughters in front of the First Footstep monument on Big Island: a gangling, sandy-haired man with heavy-framed glasses and a high forehead. She had seen him before. He was one of the men who had been shot to death. His name was Georgi Zhzhyonov.

For a week after the last men came down with what he called twenty-four-hour flu, he'd made only routine notes in his log. Then there was a terse entry about a suicide—a man had hanged himself. Another man walked in front of a truck. More entries: fistfights, a nonfatal stabbing, broken bones due to drunkenness. Two men disappeared one night; three the next. One was found clinging to the top of a tall tree and brought down. The next day he was found dead, his wrists slashed open. A man hanged himself; four others disappeared. The last note, in Georgi

Zhzhyonov's neat, slanting script, read *I suffer from the most vivid and peculiar dreams.*

Katya found the forms certifying the deaths of the suicides, with notes on bloodwork. Georgi Zhzhyonov had run samples through his gas spectrometer, looking for heavy metals and toxins, finding only trace levels of tin and titanium, well within expected limits. He had also examined the blood of two pigs. Katya felt a chill at the base of her spine. The men had become ill; the pigs had become ill; Georgi Zhzhyonov had been trying to find a link. And because he was a metallurgist, he had used the tools of his trade.

There was a geological map on one wall of his little lab. Katya studied it carefully. The broad curve of the shoreline with sandbars running parallel to it. A black rectangle marking the site of the station. A series of steeply contoured ridges rising behind, with red stipplings indicating known deposits of ore. The site of the open-cast mine was marked on the first ridge by a crosshatched rectangle. She ran her finger along the top of the ridge, noting the high spots.

Arkadi Sarantsev, searching the disordered office of the mining station's commandant, had made his own discovery.

"Fish," he told Katya.

"Fish?"

"A lot of fish." Arkadi waggled a video disc. "Luckily for us, the commandant liked to make home movies."

It was short, choppily edited. Panning shots across windrows of black fish on a sandbar that faded into fog, black fish rising and falling on shallow waves. A zoom shot closing on fish shimmying and leaping out of the water, landing on fish already dead or dying. Skinny, armor-plated fish with pale gill ruffs and bulbous eyes. A close-up that included the cameraman's boots, showing several fish writhing in circles, snapping at their own tails. Men scooping fish into buckets, tipping the buckets into oil drums in the well of a skiff. Men shoveling fish into the water, men throwing fish at each other. A small bulldozer rolling back and forth in the fog, turning up combers of sand and fish and pushing them into the water. Waves rolling in, black with blood, agitated by the splashing of scavengers come to feed.

Katya insisted on replaying the scenes of the men at work. Ten men, twenty, twenty-five. And the cameraman, the commandant, made twenty-six. Everyone in the mining station had joined in the macabre beach party, and none of them had worn protective clothing. Most were dressed in bathing trunks and flip-flops; several were buck naked.

"When was this?" she said.

"Four weeks ago," Arkadi said.

"And a week later, the men started to become sick," she said, and gave a quick account of Georgi Zhzhyonov's notes. The suicides, the disappearances, the cryptic note about dreams.

Arkadi showed her the commandant's diary. Notes on patrols sent to search the forest behind the station, of sightings of men or man-shaped animals, of strange noises. Toward the end, the commandant's handwriting degenerated to a jagged scrawl. The last entry consisted of a few indecipherable words and drawings of skulls, fanged devil faces, daggers dripping blood.

"So you think it was the fish," Arkadi said. "The fish infected them, or they ate the fish and it made them sick. Sick in the body and in the head."

"It may be slightly more complicated than that," Katya said. "I think they fed the pigs with some of the fish. I need to examine them."

She found boxes of vinyl gloves in the little lab and face masks she soaked in bleach. It wasn't much protection, but it was the best she could manage. She didn't want to get close to the pigs, not without wearing a full contamination suit, so she and Arkadi rigged a sampler from a scaffold pole and a cup taped to the end, and, after some maneuvering, managed to collect a draft of froth from one of them. She treated it like plutonium, carefully tipping it into a plastic bottle and double-bagging the bottle.

She had noticed no less than six microscopes stacked in unopened boxes in the lab. No doubt the result of the same kind of supply error in central stores that had packed the ekranoplan's stores with tins of no other kind of soup but pumpkin. She set one up on the knife-scarred butcher's table in the kitchen of the mess, then used a rolling pin to knock out a window.

"Six microscopes," she told Arkadi, "but not one microscope slide."

She plucked a small splinter of window glass, put on a fresh set of vinyl gloves, adjusted her mask, smeared a drop of pig sputum on the splinter and set it on the platform of the microscope, and bent over it and adjusted the focus knob until the smear swam into focus.

Nothing.

She swept the platform on which the splinter was clamped back and forth, fingertips sweating on the vernier knobs, on the fine-focus knob, feeling a touch of the funk she remembered from undergraduate practical classes when she'd failed to see the thing she was meant to see.

"What do you see?" Arkadi said.

"Nothing. But it doesn't mean anything."

She had explained her idea on the way to sample the stricken pig's sputum, explained that Georgi Zhzhyonov had been on the right track but he had been looking in the wrong place. On Earth, she told Arkadi, there were diseases passed from animals to humans. Zoonoses. It was possible that the brain-burning flu was one such. The miners had fed their pigs with raw fish—all that free protein, willingly throwing itself ashore—and an infection carried by the fish had flourished in the animals. They had become reaction vessels, growing ill, coughing up infected sputum. Perhaps the man who fed the pigs had become ill first, then had infected everyone else. Or perhaps the men had become infected after eating undercooked pork. Katya had been hoping that it was some kind of parasite. Something she could see under the microscope. Worms. Fungal cells. Spores. Cysts.

"Something you could show the captain," Arkadi said.

He was a quick study.

"It could be a bacterium," Katya said. "Or a virus. Viruses are generally not much bigger than the wavelength of visible light, so hard to see with a conventional microscope like this. I'll find out exactly what it is when I get the samples to a fully equipped lab, but it has to be something native. Something that affects the behavior of its host. It made the fish beach themselves. It made the miners hallucinate. Made them believe that they were being attacked. Made some of them kill themselves. Made some of them kill their friends. I think the rest ran off into the countryside."

"But you can't prove it."

"Not here. Not yet. Unless Captain Chernov has found the missing men."

He hadn't. His search party had scoured the strip mine from one end to the other and returned to the station with two bodies they had found at the base of a vertical rock face, but there was no sign of the rest—six by Katya's count. Captain Chernov was convinced that they had been captured or killed by raiders, but listened to Katya's précis of Georgi Zhzhyonov's notes and watched the video.

At the end, he said, "The pigs became sick, the men became sick. And you want to link them with this—what did you call it?"

"A zoonosis," Katya said.

"But you have no proof."

"There is the timing. The men started to become sick a

week after the fish washed up. If they fed some of the fish to the pigs, it's long enough for an infection to develop."

"The man on the crane, was he coughing? No: he was crazy. And the dead men we found—they died from their own hand, or from bullets. Not some parasite."

"Men and pigs are similar but not identical—"

"The pigs might have caught some illness. Maybe from the fish, why not? But what happened to the men is different. It is clear that their minds were affected."

"On Earth, there are many examples of parasites that alter the behavior of their hosts," Katya said.

"We are not on Earth," Captain Chernov said. "And this is nothing to do with parasites. The men were driven mad, that is clear. But by what? I think it could very well be the result of the testing of some kind of psychological-war weapon. A poison gas, perhaps. A gas that does not kill but alters the mind. The Americans deployed it here, in this remote place, observed the results, then captured the survivors. And now they return, pretending to help, but really wanting to capture us, in case we have discovered evidence of what they did. And your talk of a disease could help them, Doctor. Have you thought of that? Suppose the Americans claim that this was due to a native disease that infects people? Suppose they present false evidence to back up their story? We would have to quarantine this station and perhaps evacuate the others. Leave the coast open for the Americans to claim. Well, we will not run. We will defend this place. We will engage the enemy. We will uncover the truth about the atrocity they committed here. Do that for me, Doctor. Find the truth. Not fairy tales."

He would not look at the map, would not listen to Katya's idea about where the last of the miners could be hiding. He had worked up a story that satisfied his prejudices, and he was not going to change his mind. The enemy had done this; they were returning to the scene of the crime; they must be punished.

The chief petty officer and two seamen were left to guard the station; everyone else went back to the ekranoplan. Katya wasn't confined to her cabin, but the hatches to the observation deck and the wings were locked down, and Captain Chernov made it clear that the bridges were off-limits. She spent a little time writing up a report, trying to keep it as dispassionate as possible. She wasn't sure if anyone would read it, but she had to put down the facts and her own conclusions.

Overhead, something rumbled and whined. She wondered if it was something to do with the missile launch tubes mounted on the top of the ekranoplan.

When she was finished, she couldn't stay in her cabin. The ekranoplan was full of restless activity. Men clattering up and down ladders, along companionways. Loud voices. A general excitement. Three seamen cleaning carbines in the mess hall ignored Katya as she pottered in the galley, ignored her when she left, carrying two mugs of tea.

She found Arkadi Sarantsev in the fire-control bay, handed him one of the mugs. He told her that Captain Chernov had reported to Central Command in Kosmograd, and they had taken him seriously. A three-hundred-kilometer exclusion zone had been declared along the coast, and all American and British vessels had been ordered to leave it. The Americans had lodged a formal protest and were sending two frigates to back up their research vessel, which had turned around fifty kilometers from shore, and was heading away. Arkadi brought up the missile guidance system's radar on the big central screen: the long line of the coast, the hard green dot of the research vessel with a little block of white figures beside it.

"We are waiting for clearance to engage," he said.

Katya felt a fluttering agitation in her blood. "To fire missiles at it?"

Arkadi sipped from his mug of tea. "To head out and capture it. The captain believes that it carries evidence of a psy-war attack on the station, and Central Command is discussing that idea."

"He'll attack anyway, won't he? Like he did before. Except this time he could start a war."

"He will do the right thing."

"You know there was no American plot. You know that the miners became infected with something that drove them crazy. You know the survivors are hiding, like the poor man up in the crane."

Arkadi studied her for a moment, with a look of regret. "We are friends, you and I. But I am also an officer of the Navy of the People's Republic, and I serve under the man who saved my life," he said, and pulled aside the collar of his striped telnyashka shirt to show a white wheal on his shoulder. "I was one of those who had an allergic reaction to pancake-crab spit, on that island."

"So you won't help me," Katya said.

"I advise you to let us do our work."

"That's what I thought," Katya said. "But I had to ask because I'm not sure if I can do this alone."

Arkadi's eyes widened and he dropped his mug of tea and raised his hand. Too late. Katya whacked him on the side of his head with the sock stuffed with dried beans, whacked him again, and his eyes rolled back and he slid out of his chair and fell to the floor. She ransacked his pockets and found a set of keys, then laid him on his side, in the recovery position, and headed toward the nearest hatch.

No one saw her drop from one of the wings into the cool water—a drop higher than she'd expected, plunging her a good meter below the surface. And although her entire skin tingled with anticipation as she swam to shore, no one raised the alarm or shot at her. She was a strong swimmer: she had met the Navy diver when he had noticed her in the pool of the spa in the Druzhba sanatorium, high in the mountains of Big Island. Wearing only her underwear, she crested confidently through the cool, calm water, her clothes and shoes in a bag belted to her waist. The fog's vaporous ceiling hung about a meter over the surface; fog drew a veil all around her. It was as if she were swimming in a private bubble.

As she neared the quay, she heard the barking of the pigs, and, with a pang of regret, wished that she had asked Arkadi to shoot them after she had taken her sample. But he would have probably refused because Captain Chernov wanted to keep them alive to prove his ridiculous theory.

She hoped Arkadi wouldn't get into trouble because she had stolen his keys. She hoped he would understand why she'd done it. She hoped he would forgive her.

No one challenged her when she climbed onto the quay. She ran past the heap of ore to the parked trucks and paused, breathing hard, listening. Nothing but the labored bark of the poor pigs. No shouts or sirens, no warning shots. She squeezed water from her hair and knotted it in a loose ponytail, pulled on her shirt and cargo pants and shoes, and climbed into the cab of the truck at the far end of the row. She'd driven heavy vehicles like it when, in the long vacation at the end of her first university year, she'd worked at the construction site for the sports center her mother had designed. Power steering, synchromesh gears, no problem. No one challenged her when she pressed the start button and the big engine coughed into life, but as she drove off she saw in the side mirrors a man chasing after her, waving frantically as he fell behind and vanished into the fog.

The truck rode easily and smoothly up a winding, graded road. Perched in the high, roomy cab, cool air blasting out of the air-conditioning, her clothes drying stiffly, Katya drove as fast as she dared in the fog, navigating by the GPS map in the dashboard screen and red lights set on posts at twenty-meter intervals on either side of the road. A never-ending chain of stars appearing out of the fog, drifting past, vanishing.

She imagined men running for the trucks, speeding after her. Nothing showed in the side mirrors, but visibility was down to less than twenty meters. She wouldn't know she was being chased until they were right on the tail of the truck's hopper.

The road grew steeper. She shifted down, shifted down again, and at last it topped out. Trying to match the GPS map with reality, she drove past a pair of bulldozers, some kind of mobile conveyer belt, and a string of prefab huts before a terraced cliff horizontally striped with dark ore deposits loomed out of the fog. She turned right, driving across packed dirt, skirting around a spoil heap that rose into streaming whiteness, past the tower and hoppers of a screening plant. Then a faint red light appeared to her left and she turned toward it, realizing with tremendous relief that she had found the road that led to the top of the ridge.

It switchbacked up steep, wooded slopes. Trees grew on either side, stabbing up into the fog. Some were a little like conifers, or a child's drawing of conifers: stiff radial branches strung with puffballs of fine needles that condensed water droplets from the fog. Others were hung with what looked like tattered sails, or bunches of ragged, velvety straps that sparkled with condensation in the truck's headlights. Puffballs and straps and sails were tinted deep purple—Venusian plants used a pigment similar to rhodopsin to capture light for photosynthesis. Fat cushions of black moss saddled between the trees. Everything was dripping wet.

A shape loomed out of the fog: a yellow, articulated dump truck exactly like the one she was driving, tipped nose down in the deep ditch at the side of the road. She slowed as she went past, craning to look inside the truck's cab, seeing that it was empty and feeling a measure of relief: feeling that she was on the right track.

The oppressive shroud of the fog began to lift and break up into streamers caught amongst branches and sails, and she drove on in pewter light, trees thinning to scattered clumps with rough scrub between. The road turned, and gave out abruptly, and a truck was slewed at its end.

The men had come here, all right. Trying to escape the monsters in their heads by driving out of the fog to the place they came to play and relax.

Katya drove past the truck, drove across a rough meadow, past a barbecue pit and picnic tables, jolting on up a steepening slope until even in its lowest gear the truck could climb no farther.

She switched off the motor and swung out of the cab, looked back at the way she had come. A pure white sea stretched toward the horizon, seamlessly melding with the ivory dome of the planet's permanent cloud cover. The sun was a bright smear low in the east. In less than twenty days, it would set at this latitude, and the long night—117 days long—would begin. Forty kilometers above, a lightning storm flashed and flickered under the cloudroof: she heard the distant, dull percussion of thunder, saw thin, shadowy twists of falling rain that would evaporate before they hit the ground.

There was still no sign of pursuit, but she did not doubt that she was being followed and began to climb toward the top of the ridge. Steep, stony slopes sparsely stubbled with purple vegetation. Squat vases, skull-sized puffballs, clumps of stiff, thorny whips or tall plumes. The air was very still, weighted with sultry heat. Long shadows tangled everywhere.

She was sweating hard, out of breath, her pulse hammering in her ears, when at last she reached the top of the ridge and saw the crests of further ridges rising above the fog, parallel rakes stretching toward the distant prospect of a stark mountain range, the beginning of the desert interior. Ahead of her, the broad ridge ran out toward a high prow crowned with a copse of trees.

A horn blared far below. She felt a spike of alarm, saw a yellow dump truck draw up beside hers, saw three men spill from it.

As she jogged toward the copse of trees, a speck materialized in the distance, scooting above the shadow it cast on the restless sea of fog, cutting through wisps of drifting vapor, rising as it tracked toward her. It was one of the ekranoplan's drones, a chunky quadrocopter like a garbage-can lid pierced by a cross, with a caged rotor at the end of each bar of the cross. Its cluster of cameras glinted as it buzzed past her and turned and came back, flying low and fast, a homicidal Frisbee aimed at her head.

She dropped flat, felt the backwash of the drone's fans blow over her, pushed to her feet as the quadrocopter curved around and shot toward her again, and ran toward a clump of thorns at the edge of a steep drop. She broke off one of the dead canes in the core of the clump and swung it at the drone, and the machine veered sideways and made a wide turn and came back toward her, moving in cautious, erratic spurts, halting a few meters away.

There was a metallic clatter and a voice said, "Stay where you are, Doctor. Wait for my men."

"Is that you, Captain? If you care to follow me, I'll lead you to the missing miners."

"You disobeyed a direct order, Doctor. But if you come back now, I'll overlook your transgression."

"They climbed up here, looking for a place where they'd be safe," Katya said, and pointed toward the trees.

The quadrocopter drone tilted and shot forward, and she jumped over the edge and plowed down the steep slope in a cloud of dust and small stones, fetching up breathless and bleeding in a clump of stiff purple plumes. She had lost the thorn cane. The drone was falling toward her, and she snapped off a plume and thrust it like a spear into one of the machine's fans.

There was a grinding noise and a stinging blizzard of shards and splinters sprayed around her and the drone spun past, canted at a steep angle. It tried to turn back toward Katya, and the mismatched thrust of its fans spun it in a death spiral and it struck a shelf of rock and clattered away down the slope, bouncing and shedding parts.

The three men climbing toward her paused as the wreckage of the drone spun past, then started to climb again.

It took all of Katya's strength to scramble back up the slope. She paused at the top, her pulse drumming in her skull, and blotted sweat and blood from her eyes—flying splinters had badly cut her face. The men were much closer now. The chief petty officer shouted something to her, and she turned and limped along the crest of the ridge, hot pain knifing in one ankle. Hot air clamped around her like a fever sheet; the world contracted to the patch of stony dirt directly in front of her feet. She scrambled up a steep gully, mostly on all fours, only realized that she reached the top when the shadows of the trees fell across her.

They were rooted amongst black boulders, upright trunks soaring skyward, stiff horizontal branches clad in bunches of purple needles. A man lay on his back on a dry litter of fallen needles, eyes shrunken in their sockets, cracked lips flecked with froth. Katya thought he was dead, but then he turned his head toward her and started to tremble and whimper.

Both his legs were broken. She could see bone sticking out of the shin of his torn trousers. A rifle lay some way off. She supposed that he'd dropped it when he'd fallen.

She knelt beside him and took one of his hands and asked him where his friends were. His eyes rolled back. She thought he had fainted, then she understood, and looked up. And saw small shadows high up in the jutting branches, half-hidden by puffball clusters of needles. Atavistic apes clinging to the safety of their perches.

Katya held on to the man's hand as the chief petty officer and two seamen stepped toward her.

"I don't know why he didn't have you killed," her mother said.

"Chernov didn't have a plan," Katya said. "He had a fixation, a belief that everything that he saw was the result of some fiendish American plot. He was trying to stop me, yes, but he was also trying to rescue me from what he believed to be my own foolishness. When his men saw that I had found the miners, that was the end of it."

"I suppose we should for once be grateful for the rigid code of honor men value so highly."

"Arkadi called him a hero. And he acted like one."

"And now *you* are the hero. My daughter, who saved the world from war."

"From a stupid skirmish created by that rigid code of honor. And I was wrong about too many things to qualify as any kind of hero. I was wrong about what infected the miners, to begin with."

They were talking over lunch. Katya and the crew of the ekranoplan had just been released from quarantine, and her mother had whisked her away from the scrum of reporters and onlookers and a crew from the state TV news to the calm of the luncheon room of the Engineers' Union, with its views across the simmering basin of Kosmograd and the blue curve of Crater Bay.

The other diners were openly staring at them, and not, for once, because they were the only two women in the room. Katya wore the shirt and cargo pants in which she'd been released; her mother wore a severely cut white suit that emphasized her slim figure, and her trademark, red-framed glasses.

"You weren't wrong, dear," she said. "The men had been

infected by something that drove them mad."

"But it wasn't a bug or a parasite. And it didn't have anything to do with the pigs. And we have only circumstantial evidence that it had anything to do with the fish."

It had taken several weeks of tests in the naval hospital to determine that the miners had been infected by a kind of prion: an infectious agent that closely resembled a misfolded version of a protein found in neurons in the amygdala, the small subcortical structure in the brain that regulated both fear and pleasure responses. The prion catalyzed the misfolding of those proteins, creating an imbalance of neurotransmitters and triggering an exaggerated version of the fight-or-flight reaction and release of massive amounts of adrenaline and other hormones. The psychotic breaks and hallucinations suffered by the miners had been attempts to rationalize uncontrollable emotional thunderstorms.

Katya wanted very much to prove that the prion had been present in the blood of the fish which had beached themselves. As for the pigs, they had been infected by a parasitic threadworm, but it had only affected their respiratory systems and did not seem to be transmissible to humans. She had been right in thinking that the miners' madness was due to an infection, but had gotten every detail wrong because she had based her ideas on terrestrial examples. She had made the mistake of arguing from analogy, of trying to map stories from Earth on the actuality of Venus, and the fit had been imperfect.

"I saw two different things," she told her mother, "and tried to make them part of the same story. Captain Chernov was right about that, at least."

"He was wrong about everything else. And you are too hard on yourself," her mother said fondly.

"I wonder where I got that from?"

"Can the poor men you rescued be cured?"

"They're under heavy sedation and undergoing cognitive

therapy. They're no longer scared to death, but purging the prions from their brains won't be easy."

"It sounds as if you have found a new project."

"I'm wondering if it's a general problem," Katya said. "This particular prion caused a gross behavioral change, but there may be others that have more subtle effects. We think that we are separate from the biosphere of Venus, yet it is clear that we are not. All of us, Russians, Americans, British, we have more in common with each other than with the people from our homelands. We came from Earth, but we are all Venusians now. Venus is in our blood, and our minds."

"So you have a new research topic, and a new way of getting into trouble," her mother said. "What about this new man of yours?"

"We're taking it slowly. He forgave me, at least, for giving him a bad concussion and injuring his pride."

Although Arkadi had said, the first time they had met in quarantine, that if he had been piloting the drone, he would have had no problem returning the favor.

"A man who puts love before pride," her mother said. "Now there's a lovely example of a new way of thinking."

MATTHEW HUGHES

Matthew Hughes was born in Liverpool, England, but spent most of his adult life in Canada. He's worked as a journalist, as a staff speechwriter for the Canadian Ministers of Justice and Environment, and as a freelance corporate and political speechwriter in British Columbia before settling down to write fiction full-time. Clearly strongly influenced by Jack Vance, as an author Hughes has made his reputation detailing the adventures of rogues like Henghis Hapthorn, Guth Bandar, and Luff Imbry, who live in the era just *before* that of *The Dying Earth,* in a series of popular stories and novels that include *Fools Errant, Fool Me Twice, Black Brillion, Majestrum, Hespira, The Spiral Labyrinth, Template, Quartet and Triptych, The Yellow Cabochon, The Other,* and *The Commons,* with his stories being collected in *The Gist Hunter and Other Stories.* His most recent books are the novels in his Urban Fantasy *Hell and Back* trilogy, *The Damned Busters* and *Costume Not Included,* and *Hell to Pay.* He also writes crime fiction as Matt Hughes and media tie-in novels as Hugh Matthews.

In the deliciously sly tale that follows, he takes us to Venus, the Planet of Love, to show us that while Love might be an irresistible force, sometimes it's a good idea to give resisting it your very *best* shot.

Greeves and the Evening Star

MATTHEW HUGHES

I THREW BACK THE COVERS AND SAT UP. "GREEVES," I said, "I had the most bally awful dream."

"I am sorry to hear it, sir."

He handed me the morning cup and saucer and I took the sip without which the Gloster day cannot begin. The ordinary day, that is, in the common run of things, not the kind of day that follows a night of revelry and riot at the Inertia Club, when one awakes with the sense that death is not only imminent but cannot arrive soon enough.

"I dreamt that Baldie Spotts-Binkle had lured me onto Slithy Tove-Whippley's homemade rocket ship, battened down the hatch, if battened's the word I want . . ."

"It is, sir."

"Right ho . . . and then we'd blasted off for Venus—not the statue, mind, but the evening star itself—and that we'd slept like that Winkle chap for months on end before pitching up at Baldie's estate in the middle of the most dismal swamp imaginable."

Greeves inclined his head in a manner I recognized as conveying sympathy. I plowed on, the dream as real to me as the vital oolong of which I now took a second, fortifying draught. "It was a place steeped in gloom where the sun never shows its face, all stagnant pools and sluggish streams, with only the occasional dab of what we might call solid earth."

"Oh, dear, sir."

"Ah well," I said, motioning with my unencumbered hand to indicate that the unpleasant figments were fast dwindling in life's rearview mirror. "Draw the curtains, will you, Greeves, and admit the smiles of rosy-fingered—"

"Sir, you must prepare yourself for a disagreeable prospect," he said.

"Rain?" I hazarded a guess. "Stiff winds?"

"Not the winds," he said, throwing aside the heavy cloths to reveal panes streaked with rivulets whose flows were perpetually interrupted by the impact of freshly arrived droplets the size of marbles.

I rose from the bed and went to the window. It can justly be said that while Bartholomew Gloster may occasionally be surprised, and now and then, when circumstances so conspire, even awestruck, it is rare that he is actually staggered.

Yet I was staggered by the view from the window. The cup and saucer fell unnoticed from a nerveless hand, though not unnoticed by the ever-vigilant Greeves, who deftly caught them without the spilling of a drop.

"I say, Greeves," I said, "I mean to say." Though what I meant to say, I did not know. It was scarcely a moment for the *mot juste*.

"Indeed, sir."

As far as the eye could stretch, whatever wasn't gray was green, and whatever wasn't green was gray. Even so, every green was well tinged by the gray. And all was being relentlessly battered from above by unending bucketloads of rain.

"This," I declared, "will not do."

Greeves agreed. "Most disturbing, sir."

There sprang into my mind, like Athena springing from the brow of Zeus, only the other way round, a plan. First, a bath; then breakfast; then a brisk and businesslike dialogue with

Baldie, leading to the earliest possible embarkation on Slithy's contraption; and so to home.

I gathered myself and issued instructions. Greeves moved out of view, and, an instant later, I heard water running in the bathroom. "Right," I said, shedding the pajamas like a snake with a pressing agenda while figuratively girding myself for strife. "And off we go."

"Baldie," I said, over the remains of a remarkably large kipper and an even larger than remarkable egg, "we must speak."

"Agreed, Bartie," he said. "It's why I had Slithy bring you."

I should pause briefly to furnish a sketch of Archibald Spotts-Binkle, the better to focus the reader's inner eye on the proceedings. Imagine a fish in a fairy-godmother tale, magically transformed into a man afflicted with horn-rimmed specs, except that the f-g in question has skimped on the incantation, so that the transmogrification was only nine parts out of ten. Bulbous eyes, protruding lips that are ever moist, glabrous skin with just a hint of scaliness. Now add a voice that sounds like the product of a child's first involuntary sawings at the violin, and you have Baldie taped and targeted. Thus it would come as no surprise to discover that the sole abiding passion of his existence has been a fascination with newts.

This was the pallid apparition that blinked dully at me across the breakfast table as I unburdened myself of a few trenchant observations on the damage done to a lifelong friendship by a "ruddy shanghaiing off to a sodden planet one wouldn't wish on one's direst foe."

When in distress, it was Baldie's habit to draw his neck into his meager shoulders to a depth greater than ought to have been anatomically possible. The effect was rather like that of a fish trying on an impression of a turtle. He performed this maneuver now, and I formed the view that once I ceased beleaguering him, he would advance a suitably penitent apology, allowing me to be magnanimous in victory, as befits my nature.

I therefore softened my tone and relinquished the floor, although as we were sitting I'm not sure exactly what I was relinquishing. But, instead of tendering his regrets, my old chum thrust his narrow neck back out of concealment, and said, "Oh, fie, Bartie!"

"Fie?" I said. I am often taken aback when confronted by raw injustice.

"Yes, fie!" he returned. "And double fie at that!"

"Steady on, Baldie," I said. "Bear in mind that some fies, once launched, can ne'er be recalled."

He elevated his negligible chin. "I don't care, Bartie," he told me. "It's all meaningless, else."

"Else what?"

"What do you mean?" he said.

"What do you mean?" I said.

The bulging eyes blinked several times. "Stop repeating what I say!" he snapped. "This is no time for childish games!"

"Childish games?" I said. "Well, I must say, that's a bit over the top, coming from a fellow who would have a dashed hard time demonstrating that he's reached man's estate!"

His pale skin grew even paler and flecks of spittle appeared on his lower lip. I experienced a sudden memory of the only time Baldie Spotts-Binkle, in our long-ago school days, had lost his rag while being bullied by Roderick Bass-Humptingdon, a thug in an Eton collar who reigned over the junior form in much the same way Tiglath-Pileser, if that's the bloke I want, had lorded it over the Ten Lost Tribes. I remembered piercing shrieks and a flailing of stick-thin limbs, like a stringed puppet whose master is overcome by a fit of apoplexy. All ending, of course, in tears, Bass-Humptingdon's schoolyard sobriquet of Basher being well earned.

But, here in Baldie's breakfast room, the anticipated frenzy did not occur. Instead, he burst into tears, then buried his snuffles in his cold, long-fingered hands. It was a good thing I had already breakfasted since here was a sight to quell the appetite of a Cyclops.

"Steady on, Baldie," I said for the second time, in mere moments, but my tone was now softer. Bartie Gloster might be able to summon the stern eye and the censorious word as warranted, but when an old pal breaks down and blubs across the breakfast table, the better angels sit up and seize the reins. Admittedly, I waffled a bit as to whether I should bluffly encourage the stiff upper lip or offer the consoling pat on the shoulder. In the latter department, Spotts-Binkle's specimens were not such as to invite contact, being more in the line of the Carpathian Mountains—sharp, hard, and like to bruise the tender flesh.

But a decision was soon reached, and I extended a hand to pat the upthrust bony protrusion, adding the traditional, "Now, now," "there there," and "what's all this?" as indicated.

The result was a fresh gusher, leading me to believe that I'd taken a wrong turn. I reviewed my stock of consoling phrases and realized that I had already emptied the store. I was considering a tactical shift toward the stiff u l when the door opened and Slithy Tove-Whippley entered the breakfast room with only slightly less swagger than your average pirate exhibits when boarding a prize.

"What ho, Bartie!" he said, sashaying over to the sideboard to survey the goods.

I welcomed the change of focus. For it was he who, while purporting to show me the rocket ship he'd assembled on the lawn, had led me into its cramped saloon and asked for my views on a new cocktail he'd devised. An "atom-smasher" he'd called it. I took a first sip, and said, "I say, Slithy," as the brew's potency made itself felt. But no further words passed the numbed Gloster lips. Instead, the lights went out and I was plunged down a rabbit hole from which I did not emerge until I awoke in the depths of space.

"Don't you 'what ho' me," I said, rising and casting aside a furious napkin. The phrases "unmitigated gall," "dastardly trick," and "absolute stinker" were jostling one another in my brain to see which would be first out of the gate. I was also considering "sharper than a serpent's bosom," though I wasn't quite sure it scanned well.

But Slithy showed me the backs of his fingers, moving in a way suggestive of crumbs that were swept aside. "Come on, Bartie," he said, helping himself to scrambled eggs and a rasher of bacon I had thought looked a bit dodgy, it being an odd shade of green, "can't you take a joke?"

"A joke? Well, that takes the biscuit!" I had now marshaled gall, trick, and rotter into a single devastating phalanx and was about to send it crashing into Tove-Whippley's line. But just then, Baldie gave forth with another freshet of woe, and it seemed somehow not the done thing to be offering battle when there were wounded in need of comforting.

Comfort, though, was not Slithy's style. "Buck up, there, Baldie!" he said, in a parade-ground tone, before sitting down and addressing himself to his plate in a manner that put one in mind of a wolf that had mastered the rudiments of wielding cutlery. I recalled that, at school meals, the other boys had always left a clear space around Tove-Whippley; hands other than his that penetrated the pale risked sudden and not inconsiderable injury.

While I was thus briefly immersed in reminiscence, Baldie Spotts-Binkle rose from the table and, dashing tears from his eyes, fled the room. Slithy detroughed himself long enough to grunt an ambiguous comment—or he might just have been loosening some morsel lodged in his throat—then returned to the clashing of silver on porcelain.

Concern for Baldie drove my anger to the rear. I said, "I say, Slithy, what has cast Spotts-Binkle into the slough of despond?"

He looked up at me, and, around a mouthful of egg, said, "Newts."

Well, of course, it would be newts. I should have seen that right away. Since his formative years, Archibald Spotts-Binkle had been entranced by the slimy little wrigglers. At school, in his study, he kept a covey of them in a glass tank, and would spend hours considering their ways, often dangling flies on strings before their muzzles.

The rest of us boys, busy with our own interests, gave scant thought to Baldie's odd fascination. If we had, I suppose it would only have been to give thanks that he hadn't settled on some even less wholesome pursuit. And there lay our error. For as our boyhood interests gradually blossomed, if that's the word I want, into more manly fields, Baldie's traipsed off in the other direction.

He grew ever more engrossed in his study of newts, to the point where it became his life's work. If he had ever mastered spelling, I am sure he would have written a book about the little blisters. As it was, he launched learned papers at some journal that concerned itself with newtdom; its editor, one Hudibras Gillattely, FRS, routinely sent back these epistles with stinging comments, igniting a long-simmering feud that may well have enlivened whatever gatherings drew newt fanciers together.

Through all this, Baldie stuck to his ancestral pile in the country, where he was mostly content, as the estate contained a pond that fairly seethed with newts. And there he would have remained had he not, while on a newt-seeking ramble along bosky bucolic lanes, happened upon one Marilyn Buffet, with whom he fell precipitously in love.

Theirs was a stormy courtship, on one moment, off the next, into which I was unwillingly drafted as a patcher and restorer. At one time, a left-handed twist of fate had seen me engaged to Marilyn myself, a situation that chilled the Gloster blood until it lay inert in the veins. In the end, thanks to a brilliant stroke by Greeves, who is rather deft in such matters, Baldie and Marilyn were delivered safely to the altar to become as one flesh.

The thought of the large-eyed yet somewhat droopy former Miss Buffet now raised a question in the penetrating Gloster mind. It was not like her to be hanging back in the shadows. She was a girl who liked to make her presence felt—not the sort to dominate a room but certainly able to pervade it. So it struck me as curious that the room in which I stood, and the bedroom in which I had awakened, betrayed no trace of the Marilyn Spotts-Binkle oeuvre: their respective wallpapers were not cloyed with flowers, the tablecloth was not embroidered with flocks of cheerful bluebirds, nor did every available surface bear a cluster of porcelain rabbits and mice colorfully attired in the habits of rustic folk of a bygone age.

For all the depth of my cogitations, no more than a moment had passed since Tove-Whippley had voiced his one-worded explanation as to what was wrong with Baldie. I now advanced a new and possibly more pertinent question. "Where's Marilyn?"

He raised his eyebrows in a meaningful way. "Earth."

A shiver passed through. This news was not good. In his salad days, before Marilyn had hove into view and taken him in tow, Baldie could have posed for a likeness of monomania. The realization that he was here on his own, and with newts in the picture, boded ill. I sat down again at the breakfast table and lit a meditative cigarette, blew out a peal of smoke, and said, "Out with it, Slithy. The full chronicle."

I won't reproduce his exact words, nor the several questions I had to put to elicit them. Conversation was never Slithy Tove-Whippley's métier; he got by mostly on grunts and monosyllables. But the story that we together unfolded revealed that Baldie, after a lifetime of newt studies, had come to the melancholy conclusion that the field would henceforth offer him no new worlds to conquer. He had exhausted all that newts could offer him, and the realization caused him to fall into the aforementioned *s* of *d*.

But then he had read in the papers of the emergent craze for rocketing off to Mars and Venus. The former did not interest him, being a dry place; but the descriptions he read of the planet named for the goddess of love—its vast swamps, its rain-sodden jungles, its mosses and lichens—could not help but to ring the one bell in Baldie's lightly furnished belfry: here must be newts; and not just any newts, but *new* newts waiting to be discovered, newts that languished unobserved, loitering about in their watery lairs until a bulbous Spotts-Binkle eye should fall upon them and make them known.

And then he'd heard that his arch foe Gillattely had upped stakes from Warwickshire to build himself a house in the middle of a Venusian swamp. There he was beavering away at winning the acclaim that warmed Archibald Spotts-Binkle's dreams. He cast about for an early passage on a Venus-bound rocket, but was rebuffed at all the entrances; jaunts to the evening star were this year's version of a season in Monte Carlo: all ships were booked solid. There was not a chance of an empty berth before next year.

But then a conversation overheard by chance in the Inertia Club opened the way before him. Slithy Tove-Whippley, marked for eccentricity in a club that included the likes of Barking Mondeley-Spriggs and Flinders Bunchup, had caught the Venus infection—not the newt variant, but the whiz-bang bug. He had already built a one-man rocket and flown it to Venus and back, and now he was seeking funds to build a more capacious model, which he would offer for charters.

Gripped by manic energy, Baldie began sending telegrams. In short order, he became the major shareholder of the Tove-

Whippley Rocketry Company. He also sent several peremptory missives to Professor Gillattely, recommending that he cease all inquiries until a Spotts-Binkle was on the scene. These telegrams were returned as undeliverable.

Baldie redoubled his efforts to spur on Slithy Tove-Whippley, writing a blizzard of checks. And soon the silvery dart was ready to rise on its tail of fire. Baldie, equipped with nets, rubber Wellingtons, and a yellow sou'-wester, stepped aboard and blasted off in quest of newts.

"And did he find them?" I asked the rocket man.

"And how!" He chewed a piece of the local bacon. Apparently it was tough sledding, as it took him a while to clear the passages. "Pond. Middle of the estate. Newts abounding." He raised both hands, crumbs dropping from fork and knife. "Big uns!"

Another conundrum. A Spotts-Binkle who had sought newts and found them in abundance ought to be dancing on moonbeams, not weeping over the kipper bones. There was little point in quizzing Slithy Tove-Whippley. His last peroration had probably temporarily exhausted a year's supply of words. It would take hours for the cistern to replenish itself.

I had a momentary inclination to seek out Greeves and lay the mystery before him. Greeves comes equipped with a prodigious brain, whose powers he augments by frequently dining on fish. But a Gloster is also not without a neuron or two, and I resolved to pursue the matter myself. I went in search of Baldie.

It was a fair-sized house—it appeared to have been brought over in prefabricated sections—but experience told me that if the grounds contained a pond that contained newts, on its shores would be the first place to look for a newt fancier. I first had to find boots and an oilskin; my plus fours and tweed jacket, though eminently fashionable in Belgravia, would not have served. I sloshed my way from the rear of the house, down what would have been a sloping lawn had it not been ankle deep in moss. I found my old schoolmate on the banks of a dark pool whose surface was continually stippled by the ceaseless downpour.

The pond was not self-contained, but more of a widening in a sluggard of a river that separated the island on which stood the house from another bit of high ground where Slithy Tove-Whippley had parked the rocket. A stone bridge arched across a narrow stretch of the waterway to connect the two bits of *terra firma*.

While I was taking in the lay of the land, I also noticed that a short distance from the house, someone had stuck a short, white wooden stake in the ground. A little farther on was another, then two more, leading down to the water. Near the bank, a few more bits of wood were scattered about, as if someone had been marking out a playing field for a game but had grown tired of it and gone in to tea.

Rambling down to where Baldie stood and letting the bygones fall where they may, I offered a cheery, "What ho!"

He had been inspecting the water. I saw that he must have still been in a state of distress when he exited the premises because he had neglected to clothe himself against the elements. His suit was drenched, as was he. His narrow shoulders hunched and the rain ran down his collar. One would have to fare far and turn over many a rock to uncover a more morose specimen.

He gave my greeting no answer nor raised his eyes from the pond. *Once more unto the breach,* I counseled myself, and said, "I say, this looks a dashed fine *locus in quo* for the odd lizard or two, what?"

He turned his mournful gaze my way. The downturn of his mouth put me in mind of a croquet hoop. "Just the one," he croaked, "but what a one, Bartie!" And then came a fresh flood of tears.

I again applied the consoling hand to the shoulder. "Come on, Baldie," I said, "out with it, there's the stout fellow. What's it all about?"

He snuffled and shook his head, droplets flying unnoticed in the downpour. "Love, Bartie," he said. "It's about love."

I looked about, like that fellow on that peak in Darien. "Do you mean to say Marilyn's given you the cold mutton? Easily fixed, I should say. Fly to her side with a bouquet of the best and tell her she's the apple's eye. Throw in a sonnet or such like. Can't miss. Girls like Marilyn are easy prey to a well-turned quatrain."

"It's not *Marilyn*, you oaf!" He drew himself up though he still reached no great heights. "I love another."

"Another?" I goggled, or boggled, or whatever it is one does when confronted by life's absurdities. "Another what?"

"A goddess!" he said. "She walks in beauty like the something something . . . I can't remember the rest, but she's the real McCoy, Bartie."

I took an involuntary step back, then a voluntary one for good measure, and said, "I mean to say, old chum, it's not on, is it? A broken engagement, that's one thing, but a putting asunder? Besides which, an enraged Buffet is not a factor to be left out of one's plans. Disemboweling's not out of the question."

"I don't care, Bartie," he said. "The heart has its imperatives."

"Oh, it does, does it?" I said. "Well, Marilyn has the aspect of the tiger. Not the imitation, the real thing."

He had deflated again. "It doesn't matter," he said. "For though I love with a passion to shake the ages, the goddess does not smile on me."

Light dawned—not the real thing, of course; the sun would have needed a trowel to penetrate the clouds that lowered over us—but the figurative glimmer of comprehension. "Hold on, there, Baldie. Are you saying that you love another, but she does not care to return the serve?"

"I am," he said, brightening a little. "You always have the right phrase at your fingertips, don't you, Bartie? That's why I asked Slithy to bring you."

"You want me to tell you what to say to win her heart?" It seemed a rum business. One doesn't go around helping chums to overturn the marital applecart. Besides, there was the prospect of an unmarried Marilyn Buffet just over the horizon. When she and Baldie had been on the outs, during their tortuous courtship, the blue Buffet orbs had fixed on Bartholomew as her second string in the matrimonial target shoot. The idea of exposing myself once more to the predatory aims of the Buffet turned my knees to water and my bowels to jelly. Or perhaps it was the other way round. Either way, it was not a fate that invited a forward rush.

"I won't advise you," I said. "My lips are sealed."

"I don't want you to advise me," he said.

"Oh, well, good." I heaved a sigh of relief. Rather a heavy one.

"I want you," he said, "to speak to her."

"To her?" I said, water and jelly galloping back into the picture. "To Marilyn?"

"Not to Marilyn. Stop talking about Marilyn! She is past and forgotten, one with Nineveh and Tyre. I want you to speak to *her*."

His pale fingers fluttered in the general direction of the dark pond. I turned in the direction indicated, peering through the curtain of rain to see if there was someone standing on the other side of the water. I could see nothing.

"Where is she?" I said. "And, a salient point, who is *she*?"

Instead of answering, he squatted by the edge of the water. Then he extended a hand and patted the surface of the pool with his fingertips, in what appeared to be a deliberate rhythm, though Baldie couldn't have kept a beat in a jam jar. After a moment, apparently satisfied, he rose and stood back.

"I'm sorry, Baldie, but I don't quite see—"

"Shh," he said, gesturing toward the pond. "Look!"

Out in the center, a circular ripple appeared. Then it became a vee, making toward where we loitered on the shore. It seemed a very determined sort of vee, the kind one sees in films that feature brawny-chested types in loincloths who have nothing better to do with their afternoons than wrestle crocodiles that leap upon them from gray, greasy rivers. Gray and greasy, incidentally, made a pretty good description of the color and texture of Baldie's pond.

I took a judicious step back, leaving Baldie to remain in *status quo,* drooped over the water's edge like a willow mourning the loss of its will to live. The vee continued to close upon him.

"Baldie," I said, meaning to add a warning. But, at that moment, the surface at the point of the vee broke. From it emerged a green triangular head, roughly the size and shape of a ditch digger's spade, except that it had two large and golden eyes about where you'd expect to find them. As the head rose from the water, I saw that from under the lower jaw protruded branchlike organs. I had a vague memory of a much younger Baldie Spotts-Binkle pointing to some little lizard in a tank and inviting me to notice its gills—an invitation that I am glad to say I succinctly declined.

The head was now well clear of the surface. Below it were two narrow shoulders that sat above a slim and sinuous torso. As the apparition reached the shore and emerged from the water, it produced a pair of slender arms and a matching set of pins, both ending in webbed digits. A long, glistening tail, sporting a kind of fin that actually began at the nape of the creature's longish neck, provided the denouement.

Words failed. I emitted a sound that began with a "guh" and ended in an "ack," with a kind of hiccup to bridge the two. Baldie shot me the sort of look an aunt gives a fellow who's just spilled tea on the best Persian, and said, "For God's sake, Bartie! Stop gawking and say how do you do to Shilistrata."

I closed my mouth, opened it, still found nothing of use in it, and closed it again. But then I managed to rally the routed remnants of my vocabulary. "How do you do?" I said. "Shilistrata, is it? Charming. Unusual."

"Don't be an ass, Bartie," said Baldie. "I doubt it's at all unusual on Venus." He turned to the—and let's not beat around the shrubbery; *she was a newt*—and said, "You'll have to forgive my chum. He can be a touch provincial, don't you know."

That was a bit stiff coming from a fellow who'd spent most of his life messing about in rural puddles, and who, to my certain knowledge, had not shown his piscine phiz in London more than once in ten years. But I let it pass, because the creature from the pond had now turned her remarkable eyes—round, amber with flecks of silver—on me and at the same time a voice spoke in my head, saying, "You are the Bartie? The Gloster?"

"Well, yes," I said. "So to speak. And you are the Shilistrata, I believe. How do you do?"

"It is what the Archibald calls me," the voice said.

"It's a perfectly good name," said Baldie. I had a passing recollection that Shilistrata might have been the moniker he had bestowed on one of his tank denizens, back in our school days.

"Would you like to call me something else?" said the voice, which, now that I focused on it, I realized was rich and warm, calling up an image of honey being stirred into cream.

"No, no," I said. "Shilistrata's just the ticket."

She smiled at that. I should clarify that assertion on two points. Point the first: although Shilistrata showed none of the anatomical bits and pieces associated with the divine female form, still less any fripperies of feminine fashion, being clad only in her mottled green skin, every aspect of her bespoke the fairer sex. Not least the voice, which had the sort of mellifluosity, if that's the word I want, that would have set a troubadour to swooning.

Point the second: when she opened her mouth, exhibiting more pearlies than one is used to—indeed two needlish ranks of them, above and below—along with a tongue that put me in mind of a pink bonnet ribbon, the only gentlemanly response was to receive the action as a smile and to send one back across the net.

"Well," I said, then "well" again. I realized that I was rocking back and forth on toe and heel, something I'm prone to do when conversation sails into the doldrums. As one does when a rear tire becomes surrounded by mud, a gentle rocking eases the old two-seater up and out and back to cruising the byways.

On the heels of that realization came another. Someone was hissing. At first, I thought it might be Shilistrata. Then, realizations now coming thick and fast, I grasped that the sound was coming out of Baldie. He was saying, "Hist," in a stage whisper, obviously to get my attention.

I turned to him, and he said, "For goodness sake, Bartie, speak up!"

At first I thought that he was trying to tell me that the talking newt was a little hard of hearing—no shell-like ears were in evidence—but then he made the back of the fingers gesture in her direction, and the final realization of the occasion now made its entrance: Baldie wanted me to speak up—for *him*, and to *her*.

A Gloster is always willing to come to the aid of an old school pal. It's what we're bred for, after all. But in this instance, a clear path to the goal was lacking. I turned Baldie's way, put up a hand to shield my lips, and said, "About what, exactly?"

I was rewarded with the sight of Baldie impersonating an exasperated fish. "About *me*, of course!"

"About you?" I said, then the penny hit the bottom of the chute. "You don't mean as a *suitor*?"

"I mean nothing else!"

"But, Baldie, she's a . . ." I threw an apologetic glance Shilistrata's way and lowered my voice to a whisper. "A newt! Or at least a newtess!"

"I am aware of that, Bartie," he said.

"Well, then," I said, "how exactly would you expect matters to work themselves out? I mean to say, what is your goal?"

Now I saw an exasperated fish dealing with an obtuse interlocutor. "Matrimony, of course!"

"But, Baldie, she's a *newt*!"

"Stop saying that!" he said. "There is nothing wrong with my organs of perception! And I should think that if either one of us is likely to recognize a newt on sight, it would be I!"

There was clearly something wrong with at least one of Archibald Spotts-Binkle's organs, and I would have taken odds on its being the one stewing behind his fish eyes. I made one last attempt. "A newt, Baldie! You're not even the same order, or genius, or whatever it is!"

"Oh, that," he said, with a roll of the eyes, "we're above all that. This is a marriage of souls, a union of essences. We will conjoin on a spiritual plane, in an exalted merger of the spirit." He fluttered those dismissive fingers again. "It's beyond your comprehension, Bartie."

It certainly was. I found myself blinking, at a loss as to how to make further headway. It came to me that now would be a suitable moment to enlist the cerebral powers of Greeves. If ever there was a fellow who could think his way—or mine, for that matter—out of a tight spot, Greeves topped the list. I turned and looked about, hoping that that well-stocked head might be somewhere in view. But that recourse was not on offer. And now Baldie seized my arm and hissed, or *histed*, at me once more.

"Tell her, Bartie!"

"Tell her *what*?"

"About me, you fathead! About my . . . qualities."

"Oh," I said. "Rather. Right ho, Baldie." I turned to the sinuous green form, which had been swaying before me like one of those cobras summoned from baskets by near-naked flautists on the subcontinent. "Um," I began, then followed with a "well" and a "here's how it is," but then the spring ran dry.

I turned to Baldie, and said, "I say, Spotts-Binkle, it would be a dashed sight easier to praise you in your absence. One feels constrained when the subject of the paean is hanging about, snagging every word."

Now it was his turn to blink. "Really?" he said. "It hadn't occurred."

More likely, he'd had so little experience of being lionized, in his absence or presence, that the ins and outs eluded him. But now he nodded, and said, "Right ho, Bartie. I'll leave you to get on with it." And with a nod and a bow to the newtess, he shuffled off toward the house.

Shilistrata gave no sign of having noticed his departure. Instead, her lambent eyes remained fixed on yours truly and her swaying became even more pronounced. There certainly didn't seem to be much wrong with her backbone, assuming she had one. She would have won the first-in-class ribbon for limberness. I had an odd passing thought: Baldie had used to go one about how newts courted each other by wriggling and tail-shaking. I suppressed the query as nongermane.

"Well, Shilistrata," I said, "you've caught yourself a first-rater in our Archibald. Why, when it comes to knowledge of the ways of pond-dwellers, you couldn't have struck more lucky. Backed a sure winner, so you have."

Her motions now became alarmingly fluid. There was something almost hypnotic about the side-to-siding, and it seemed as if a song was humming in my brain—and not to any toe-tapping Charleston or Black Bottom rhythm, but more on the louche and languid side of the dance floor.

Nonetheless, there was a job to be done. "I doubt," I pressed on, "that there's a better newt man in all of England than Archibald Spotts-Binkle. My advice is to snap him up, and sharply, before some other newtess tosses a lasso around his angular form."

I paused there, expecting some kind of rejoinder. Instead, all I got was more swaying and humming. I found that my own head was moving in concert with her motions, and that the song she was humming was growing more and more entrancing. I was thinking that that was just the song I'd always wanted to hear though I hadn't known it until now.

And now her voice was speaking. I thought it was quite a good trick, to be able to speak and hum at the same time. It beat the pants off Flinders Bunchup's celebrated turn at the Inertia Club Christmas saturnalia, two years back, when he sang "The Darktown Strutters' Ball" while juggling an entire set of condiment dishes.

"Come to me," she was saying. "You are the one."

"The one what?" I managed. But now it was not just my head that was moving in a mysterious way. My whole body was in syncopation with hers.

"Come," she said, "it is the time. You are chosen."

Still bonelessly undulating, she was backing toward the dark pond. Yet somehow the distance between us had not grown. That puzzled me for a moment, until I realized that I was swaying along after her. It seemed to be exactly the right thing to do.

I had the vaguest inkling that I was supposed to be engaged in some other task, something to do with Baldie. The word "qualities" tried to make itself known, but the humming and the swaying played trump upon trump.

I took another step. At that moment, a blast of icy cold liquid slapped against my face, instantly sobering me.

"I beg your pardon, sir," said Greeves. "I was bringing you a glass of refreshment and stumbled on the uneven ground." A firm hand took my arm, as he said, "Please let me lead you to the house, where we will locate a towel and undo the damage."

The strong grip now drew me steadily away from the pond. The humming and speaking faded to a dwindle, then suddenly the Gloster head was once more illuminated by its customary clarity. I looked at Greeves and saw him regarding me with what I took to be a judgmental eye. I withdrew my arm from his grasp.

"A towel, Greeves?" I said, then added, "Pshaw! The occasion requires not less but more liquid, preferably brown, well aged, and with a splash of soda." I strode toward the house.

"Indeed, sir," he said, matching me step for step. "I will be pleased to prepare it for you."

"Do so, Greeves," I said as we crossed the threshold, shedding my rain gear, "and be not parsimonious in the dispensing."

"As you wish, sir."

Moments later, in the drawing room, he handed me a beaker of the best. I quaffed half in one swallow, took a breath, then downed the rest. I extended the glass to Greeves, and said, "Another is called for, I think."

"Indeed, sir," he said, gliding over to the drinks cabinet to repeat the miracle.

"And then," I said, "some thinking must ensue."

He returned with the whiskey. "Yes, sir. If I may say so, I have taken the liberty of examining the records stored in the library, and I believe I can provide grist for the mill."

I might have mentioned before that Greeves is a great one for the information-gathering. Little that has happened since Adam was a ball of clay has escaped his attention. "Say on, Greeves," I told him, taking a seat and doing justice to the drink. I was surprised that Baldie should have bothered to stock a decent single malt; carrot juice was more his line of country. But Greeves soon cleared up that minor point along with some more salient issues.

It seemed that the house in which we stood—actually, I sat

while Greeves paced and recounted the fruits of his researches—had been built by none other than Hudibras Gillattely, a newt boffin. Baldie, arriving to give the professor the benefit of his views, had found it empty and simply moved in.

"I take it that, once he was exposed to the climate, this Gillattely fellow realized that the game was not worth the candle?" I said. "He departed for sunnier climes?"

"Apparently not, sir," was the answer. "It seems that Professor Gillattely mysteriously disappeared while still in the midst of a research project focused on the pond outside. But he published his initial observations in the *Journal of Salamandidrae Studies,* of which he was the editor. Mr. Spotts-Binkle read the article and immediately wrote to the author. When his telegram was returned as undeliverable, he took umbrage and came to Venus to make his points in person."

A picture was beginning to emerge, though I could not quite bring it into focus. "Is there more, Greeves?" I said.

"Indeed there is, sir." His face took on a cast that I recognized. There was not only more, but the more was a pip. I bid him say on and braced myself for the fall of the other shoe.

"Professor Gillattely's notes were written in a gentlemanly hand—" he began.

"In other words, nearly unreadable?" I offered.

"Very nearly, sir. But I was able to decipher much of them. His work was focusing on a new species he had named *veneria salamandidrae sireni,* especially on the creature's reproductive habits."

"I say," I said, remembering Shilistrata's limberness, "something saucy?"

"No, sir. To the contrary: the species is parthenogenetic."

I grasped at a passing straw. "Persians?"

"No, sir. If I may presume to correct you, the term comes from the Greek word for a maiden, *parthenos,* and denotes a method of reproduction in which the female plays all the necessary roles, without benefit of male participation."

"Oh," I said, "not very sporting, if you ask me."

"Indeed, not. No sport at all, sir."

We seemed to have wandered down a byway. I sought to bring us back to the main thoroughfare. "What's this got to do with Baldie?"

"Mr. Spotts-Binkle has taken up the torch where Professor Gillattely let it fall, sir," Greeves said. "He has continued to study reproduction among the *v. salamandidrae sireni*. He has been fortunate not to suffer the same fate as his predecessor."

"Eh?" I said. "I thought that was a mystery?"

"It was, sir," he said, "until I examined the evidence."

"Well, well done, Greeves," I said. "They haven't yet devised the plot you can't fathom. That Christie woman should put you on a retainer."

"Very kind of you to say, sir."

"Not at all. Credit where credit's due. So, what's it all about, then?"

"The crucial clue, sir, was in the creature's name, specifically the *sireni* cognomen."

The term rang a faint bell. "Something to do with that Ulysses chap and beeswax?" I said.

"Indeed, sir. Ulysses put wax in the ears of his fellow Argonauts, then had them chain him to the mast while they rowed the *Argo* past the Isles of the Sirens, whose irresistible song drew hapless mariners onto wave-washed rocks."

"Irresistible song, Greeves? You mean like that catchy little ditty Shilistrata was humming?"

"Exactly like, sir."

The picture was becoming clear now, and a dire vista it made. "She was trying to lure me?"

"Into the pond, sir. Where she would have, if you'll pardon

my plain speaking, immersed you in the ooze and laid her eggs in every available orifice."

"Oh, I say, Greeves! A fate worse than death!"

"I'm sorry to contradict you, sir. Death would have come before the egg-laying. By drowning, as it no doubt did for Professor Gillattely."

"You haven't seen any beeswax lying about, have you, Greeves?" I looked around, as if some might be conveniently to hand.

"Again, sir, I must correct you," Greeves said.

"Blaze away, Greeves! The floor is yours."

"Wax will not serve, sir, because the creature Mr. Spotts-Binkle has named Shilistrata communicates by mental telepathy."

"Reads minds, you mean?"

"I cannot vouch for the reading, sir," he said. "Her mentation is not like ours. But certainly she broadcasts a strong signal."

"That humming," I said. "Rather compelling."

"Indeed, sir."

I dwelt upon the matter for a few moments while allowing more of the flavor of peat and heather to do their salutary work. Then a thought struck. "But, you, Greeves, were not affected. It was as if your mental ears were stuffed with wax."

"My mind was on other things, sir," he said, "most particularly your safety."

"Ah," I said, and, "well." After a moment, I added, "Thank you, Greeves."

"Not at all, sir."

"Is there more?"

"A little, sir. It would seem that Shilistrata, having fulfilled her biological destiny with Professor Gillattely, again came into season and began seeking a new host for her young. Mr. Spotts-Binkle presented himself and she began the process of, if I may speak bluntly, reeling him in. But then she decided, for reasons only she could know, that he was unsuitable. She decided to wait for a better prospect."

"Slithy Tove-Whippley wouldn't do?" It seemed to me that there was more than a meal or two to be made of Slithy's meaty frame.

"The gentleman does not go near the pond," Greeves said, "and has not been aboard the rocket ship since we landed."

"Probably just as well," I said. I finished my whiskey and rubbed decisive palms together. "Well," I said, "I suppose we'd better go break the bad news to Baldie."

"I'll give you bad news," said Baldie from the doorway. "And you can have a broken bone or two while I'm at it."

"Ah, Baldie. What ho," I said.

"Don't you 'what ho' me!" he said, advancing into the room. I had an odd sense of déjà-vu, as if I'd recently heard just those words, though I couldn't quite place where. But Spotts-Binkle's next utterance drove the question from my mind. "You conniving hound! You treacherous cheat! You cad!"

I raised an eyebrow, then another. "I say, Baldie, steady on!"

"I'm steady enough," he answered. For the first time in our long acquaintance, I saw color in Archibald Spotts-Binkle's countenance: two bright red spots at about the height of his cheekbones; like an aging actress who has dipped once too often into the rouge pot. "Steady enough to break your eye and blacken your nose!"

"I think you'll find you mean—" I began, but he spoke over me, in a most un-Baldie-like way.

"I mean to batter you into a shapeless mass, then trample you into the carpet!" he said.

"But I'm just about to save your life!"

"Save your own!" he said. "If you can!" He had balled his knobbly hands into fists and now he raised one as if he knew how to use it. I remembered again the short, sharp set-to with Basher Bass-Humptingdon in the junior boys' cloakroom, and recalled that though Baldie had been deficient in the technical aspects, he had not lacked for energy. I moved to put an obstructing sofa between us.

But he was not to be stayed by sofas. He leapt onto the cushions, still brandishing his fist, and now he did so from the advantage of greater height. Suddenly the likelihood of Baldie's doing actual damage grew less remote.

"I say, Spotts-Binkle," I said, "what's this all about?"

"It's about treachery and double-dealing! And a man I thought was a friend behaving like a worm!"

Greeves, who had been standing by, quiet as a statue, now spoke. "May I inquire, sir, if it concerns the person you have named Shilistrata?"

"He knows it does!" Baldie said, without taking his feverish eyes from mine. "He was supposed to speak to her for me! Instead, he spoke for himself!"

"I praised you to the skies!" I protested. "I called you a winner and a first-rater among newt men. I counseled her to seize the day before some other newtess claimed you for her own!"

He still loomed over me, but the homicidal mania had lost some of its pep. He resembled a Viking berserker who had paused to take thought. His gaze slid toward Greeves.

"Is this true, Greeves?"

"It is, sir."

"But when I went to her, just now," Baldie said, climbing down from the cushions, "she spurned me. 'Bring me Bartholomew' she said. 'I must have *him*.'"

"Well, she's not getting me, nor any part thereof," I said. "One shudders to think—"

"That's enough of that sort of talk!" said Baldie, his color, however localized, rising again. "One does not speak thus of the woman I intend to wed!"

"Baldie . . ." I said, casting about for a clear avenue of

approach, "it's not a stroll down the petal-strewn aisle she has in mind."

Again, the dismissive digits. "Oh, I know there are differences between us," he said. "Know them better than most, I'd say. But with goodwill and growing affection, I'm sure they can be overcome."

"Baldie—"

"I won't hear any more against her!"

I made a silent appeal to Greeves, via eyebrows and corners of the mouth. Baldie has always had a high regard for his acumen.

As good souls will, Greeves filled the gap in the line. "Mr. Spotts-Binkle," he said, "it grieves me to be the bearer of unhappy tidings, but the lady in question is not seeking a mate. Rather, she is thinking in terms of, shall we say, support for her children."

"I understand that, Greeves," Baldie said, "and I've assured her that my resources will be at their disposal. I mean, what's the use of having a bob or two if you don't use it to do some good?"

"It is not *wealth*, sir, that is sought," Greeves said. "It is the candidate's more immediate assets that the *sireni* has in view."

"Baldie," I said, "she means to drown me and bury me in the ooze at the bottom of the pond while her grubs, or whatever they are, feast upon my rotting carcass."

As Greeves and I fed him the true gen, he once again defaulted to that pop-eyed, slow-blinking Baldie that is the classic model. After a pause to take it all in, he said, "I don't believe it!"

"She prefers Mr. Gloster," Greeves said, "because, as with Hudibras Gillattely, who suffered the same fate, his form is more fleshy"—he turned to me—"if you will permit my saying so, sir."

"Not at all, Greeves. There is more on the Gloster bones than on the Spotts-Binkles. Luck of the draw in the parentage department, probably."

There ensued another period of Baldie's blinking, accompanied by the up-and-down course of his Adam's apple as he metaphorically, if that's the word, swallowed the bitter pill of truth.

Then he spat it out. "I don't believe a word of it!" He dismissed me with a curl of the lip and rounded on Greeves. "For once, Greeves, you've misread the cues, followed the tracks up the wrong path."

"I am sorry, sir, that you think so. Professor Gillattely's notes were quite detailed."

"Pah! Him!"

Greeves produced a bound notebook. "He wrote, sir, and I quote, 'I will endeavor to ascertain the range of the creature's mesmeric influence, placing a series of white stakes in the turf. I will begin with the distance at which I feel the first mental itch, then proceed to the point at which it becomes almost irresistible.'"

Greeves offered Baldie a view of the page. "As you'll see, sir, that was his last entry."

"That could mean anything, Greeves!"

"I think you'll find, sir, that it means the professor advanced a stake too far."

"By Jove, Baldie," I said, "Greeves has cinched it again! I saw those stakes in a line down toward the water, with the last few all in a higgle and piggle! That must be the *locus delecti* or whatever the Latin is for the spot where she did the dirty on old Gillattely."

"That was my surmise, too, sir," said Greeves.

The two of us had clearly hung Baldie on the horns of a dilemma. Clearly, he did not want to wave in the news that his inamorata was an aquatic Nosferatu, if that's the fellow I'm thinking of, but Greeves's air of quiet confidence, coupled with the evidence of the stakes, was undermining his defenses.

"If I may make a suggestion, sirs," Greeves now said, "we should depart at the earliest opportunity. Professor Gillattely's notes also indicate that there are several other females of the species in the vicinity, some of them considerably larger than the one we have been discussing. I fear that our presence has drawn them toward the house. Mr. Tove-Whippley went to see if he could launch the rocket and bring it to this side of the stream. The fact that he has not done so indicates that our situation grows dire."

Baldie, by this point, had lost the knack of taking action. He seemed to be contemplating some bleak inner vista—probably involving his inevitable homecoming conversation with Marilyn Spotts-Binkle, née Buffet—that was robbing him of whatever was needed to cause him to buck up and soldier on. It was time for a Gloster to take charge.

"Would you see about the packing, Greeves?"

"If I may, sir, I would advise a more precipitous departure. Night is falling, and the creatures grow more restive in the hours of darkness."

"Right ho, Greeves! All hands, abandon ship!" Then a thought occurred. "If we've lost Slithy, who will operate the rocket?"

"I closely observed Mr. Tove-Whippley's activities on the outward voyage, sir," Greeves said. "I believe the task is not one that would pose difficulties to an agile mind."

"You think I'll be able to manage a takeoff, Greeves?" I said.

"I was thinking rather, sir, that you would minister to Mr. Spotts-Binkle."

"Ah, yes," I said, regarding the proposed object of my tender care. "Baldie? Are you with us?"

But Baldie was present in name only. He had even stopped blinking. Greeves proposed that we each take an arm and walk him toward the rocket ship. I agreed, and we took up our stations and proceeded toward the door. But then Greeves bid us stop and went to the drinks cabinet, where he snaffled up a large bottle of something.

"Good thinking, Greeves," I said. "I'm sure we'll need a stiffener somewhere along the line."

"Indeed, sir," he said. "Now, sir, if I may advocate a certain rapidity of gait?"

"Advocate away, Greeves. I'm with you." Then, as we went through the door onto the mossy lawn, I let out a short note of laughter.

"Sir?"

"I just thought, Greeves, well . . . what we're doing with poor old Baldie."

"The situation excites humor, sir?"

"Well," I said, savoring the moment to come, "it's a frogmarch, isn't it? I mean to say: frogs, newts; march, marsh. It works on many levels."

"Indeed, sir. Most droll. Now, we are coming within range. If I may recommend that you concentrate your mind in a way that will resist the female's siren call. A brick wall, perhaps. Or large earmuffs."

"Oh, for beeswax, eh, Greeves?" I said.

"Oh, indeed, sir."

But then his voice faded into the background cacophony that was rising all around us, the swamp dwellers letting the night know that they were all present and open for business. We struggled on, with Baldie doing a rather convincing impression of a sack of potatoes between us, angling our course away from the pond toward where the little bridge spanned the stream that trickled through the marsh. Beyond the stone arch, on the swamp's only other elevation, I could see the dull sheen of Slithy's rocket ship. Its hatch was open, with a bit of a ladder leading up to it.

As we neared the crossing, I felt a tickling between my ears. I'd been expecting another rendition of the slow and sultry number Shilistrata had been playing at our earlier tryst, but it seemed that, in the presence of other anglers, she had gone for a straightforward gaffing of the Gloster fish. The tickle grew quickly into an unbearable itch; I would have gladly torn off the top of my skull just for a chance to scratch it. Accompanying the maddening sensation was the certain knowledge that it would stop the moment I turned toward the pond.

"I say, Greeves," I said, "I've got this awful—"

"Itch, sir?" he said, and I saw that his face was almost registering a strong expression, rather like one of Hesiod's Titans acknowledging an earache.

"An itch to end all itches," I said.

"Very apt, sir, inasmuch as giving in to it would soon bring about the end of existence."

"I believe I'll put it out of my mind, Greeves."

"Do endeavor to do so, sir," he said, "although I fear it is about to become more difficult." He had only his chin to point with, like Achilles before the walls of Troy, and he used the appendage to indicate that Shilistrata had come out of the pond to take up a position at the near end of the bridge. She had spread her arms wide to bar our passage while narrowing her eyes to slits. She was also giving us an uninhibited view of those rows of glistening needles along her pale, pink gums.

"Sirening be dashed," I said, the itch in my brain having suddenly ceased, "she's going for brute force!"

"More than that, sir," Greeves said. "Professor Gillattely believed that the creature's bite is poisoned."

"Um," I said, "so simply booting her out of the way will invite peril?"

"Hence this, sir." He raised his free arm, which contained the item he'd picked up from the drinks cabinet.

"Planning to render her squiffy?" I said.

"No, sir," he said, advancing on the newtess, with Baldie and me perforce marching in his train. When we neared the hissing creature, Greeves let fly. It seemed that he had not brought along a flagon of Gillattely's hooch, but the full soda bottle. He now depressed its lever and sprayed Shilistrata from her head to her nonexistent navel with a stream of clear, bubbly liquid.

One often sees soda bottles thus used in the cinema, where, along with the tossing of custard pies, they are a staple of Mr. Sennett's comedies. On the newtess, however, the effect was more in a tragic vein: where the sparkling water touched her, her green skin turned first a pale yellow, then bleached to a leprous white. Her hiss became a yawp. She scrubbed at her front with her paws, and the contact made her paws exhibit the same color change.

She bent over, emitted a series of yips, and abandoned her bridge-blockading strategy in favor of a quick plunge back into the pond. Greeves and I, with Baldie still hung between us like an oddly shaped rug on a clothesline, tramped onto the bridge.

But at the far end we saw a new obstacle: another newtess, big enough to make Shilistrata look like the runt of the litter, had dredged herself up from the creek and was giving us the same dentist's-eye-view of her pointed gnashers.

"Onward, sir, if you please," Greeves recommended, and we thundered down the slope of the arch like a three-man version of the Scots Greys' charge at Waterloo, a painting of which my aunt Dahlia had over her bed. Greeves gave the enemy a thorough dousing with soda water, with much the same effect as on the first occasion. In a moment, the way lay clear and we crossed to dry—well, dryish—land and struggled up the slope to where the rocket stood.

"That's the spirit, Greeves," I said.

"I regret, sir, that the curtain is not yet down," he said, waving the bottle to indicate that a passel of newts were rising from the water to pursue us. "May I again counsel speed, sir?"

"No need," said I, putting on the best I was capable of. Together, we slogged up to the top of the knoll and thrust

Baldie bodily through the hatch.

"After you, sir," Greeves said, as he turned to play Horatio at the bridge.

"Never you mind that," I said, taking the soda bottle from him. "Go in and get the engine warmed up or whatever one does."

A gape-mouthed newtess hove into view and I let her have a splash of soda large enough to have ruined a snifterful. Another one came right behind her, and I let fly again. The same color change and expression of horror came over both of them, and they beetled off to wherever they'd come from.

"Don't care for it at all, do they, Greeves?" I called over my shoulder. I could hear clicks and flicks from behind me as he did things with the ship's controls.

"Their skins are covered in an acidic slime," he said as he continued to work. "The bicarbonate of soda neutralizes the acidity, causing them much the same discomfort as you and I would feel if someone poured acid on us."

I gave another comer a faceful of fizz. "I say, Greeves," I said, "we're running low on soda."

I heard a fresh series of switch-snappings, then I felt two strong hands under my arms. "Please forgive my manhandling you, sir," he said as he hoisted me backward through the hatch and kicked the door closed. He led me to a sort of chaise longue fitted with straps and buckles and made me secure, then did the same for Baldie.

Something banged on the hatch. "If I may, sir?" he said, gesturing to the control console.

"Please, Greeves," I said. "Venus has lost whatever charms it may once have held."

He sat in a chair and moved a lever. The ship began to vibrate. Then I began to feel strangely heavy.

* * *

Sometime later, Greeves hove into view with a pot of tea and the necessary accoutrements. He undid my buckles, then informed me that he had administered a draught of the sleeping potion to Baldie, who would now lie in the arms of that Morpheus chap throughout the long journey home.

"Would you care to sleep, too, sir?" he asked.

"Wouldn't that leave you all alone for, I don't know, weeks?"

"Months, sir, in fact."

"Good grief in garters, Greeves. I couldn't let you do that all alone."

"Very good of you, sir."

I took a sip of the brew and thought for a moment, then said, "Greeves, I came to Venus because Slithy Tove-Whippley slipped me a mickey. But how did he trick you?"

"The gentleman did not trick me, sir. When I saw that he meant to abscond with you, I insisted that he take me, too."

"Wide-awake, Greeves?"

"Indeed, sir."

"Must have been a dashed boring trip, though, eh?"

"Mr. Tove-Whippley was kind enough to teach me a card game called pinochle. He learned it while working with Mr. Ford in America."

"Good game, Greeves?"

"Quite engaging, sir. And even when played for small stakes, the winnings from several months of constant pinochle-playing can add up."

"Won a packet, did you, Greeves?"

"I won the *Lulu*, sir."

"The *Lulu*?"

"It is the name of this rocket ship, sir." He took thought for a moment. "Though I may change it."

"Good for you, Greeves," I said. "Now, how about one more cup of tea, then we'll cut the cards."

"Very good, sir."

"And Greeves?"

"Yes, sir."

"Thank you for . . ." I made a gesture that took in all of Venus and its manifold trials.

"Not at all, sir."

GWYNETH JONES

Here's the story of an intrepid explorer who volunteers to be the test subject for a radical new scientific experiment, and finds himself very far away from home—and up to his hips in trouble!

One of the most acclaimed British writers of her generation, Gwyneth Jones was a cowinner of the James Tiptree, Jr., Award for work exploring genre issues in science fiction, with her 1991 novel *The White Queen,* and has also won the Arthur C. Clarke Award, with her novel *Bold As Love,* as well as receiving two World Fantasy Awards—for her story "The Grass Princess" and her collection *Seven Tales and a Fable.* Her other books include the novels *North Wind, Flowerdust, Escape Plans, Divine Endurance, Phoenix Café, Castles Made of Sand, Stone Free, Midnight Lamp, Kairos, Life, Water in the Air, The Influence of Ironwood, The Exchange, Dear Hill, The Hidden Ones,* and *Rainbow Bridge,* as well as more than sixteen Young Adult novels published under the name Ann Halam. Her too-infrequent short fiction has appeared in *Interzone, Asimov's Science Fiction, Off Limits,* and in other magazines and anthologies, and has been collected in *Identifying the Object: A Collection of Short Stories.* She is also the author of the critical study, *Deconstructing the Starships: Science, Fiction and Reality.* Her most recent books are a new SF novel, *Spirit: Or the Princess of Bois Dormant* and two collections, *The Buonarotti Quartet* and *The Universe of Things.* She lives in Brighton, England, with her husband, her son, and a Burmese cat.

A Planet Called Desire

GWYNETH JONES

I. JOHN FORREST, ADVENTURER

THE LABORATORY WAS ON AN UPPER FLOOR. ITS WIDE windows looked out, across the landscaped grounds of the Foundation, to the Atlantic Ocean. One brilliant star, bright as a tiny full moon, shone above the horizon, glittering in the afterwash of sunset.

"My grandfather's people called her *Hawa*," said the scientist.

"Is that a Dogon term, PoTolo?" asked John Forrest: a big man, fit and tanned, past forty but in excellent shape. He wore a neatly trimmed beard and moustache; his vigorous red-brown hair brushed back and a little long; his challenging eyes were an opaque dark blue. "You're Dogon, aren't you?"

They were alone in the lab: alone in the building aside from a few security guards. Dr. Seven PoTolo, slight and dark, fragile and very young-looking beside the magnate, was uncomfortable with the situation, but there was nothing he could do. Mr. Forrest, the multibillionaire, celebrity entrepreneur/philanthropist, environmentalist, lover of life-threatening he-man stunts, owned the Foundation outright. His billions financed PoTolo's work, and he was ruthless with any hint of opposition.

PoTolo shook his head. "I'm afraid my ancestry is mixed:

Cameroon is a melting pot. My maternal grandfather spoke one of the vanishing languages of the Coast. But *'hawa'* is a loan-word. I think it's Arabic, and means desire."

"Sensual desire, yes," agreed Forrest. "The temptation of Eve."

He turned to survey the untried experimental apparatus.

"What will conditions be like?"

"Conditions on the surface could be remarkably Earthlike," said PoTolo. "The tectonic-plate system hasn't yet broken down, the oceans haven't boiled away, atmospheric pressure hasn't started to skyrocket, the atmosphere is oxygenated. Rotation should be speedier too. Much longer than our twenty-four-hour cycle, but a day and a night won't last a local year . . ."

Forrest studied the rig. Most of it was indecipherable, aside from the scanning gate and biomedical monitors introduced for his benefit. A black globe with an oily sheen, clutched in robotic grippers inside a clear chamber, caught his eye: reminding him somehow of the business part of a nuclear reactor.

"But no guarantees," he remarked, dryly.

"No guarantees . . . Mr. Forrest, you have signed your life away. Neither your heirs, nor any other interested parties, will have any legal recourse if you fail to return. But the risks are outrageous. Won't you reconsider?"

"Consider *what*?" Forrest's muddy blue eyes blazed. "Living out my life in some protected enclave of a world I'd rather go blind than see? The trees are dying, the oceans are poisoned. We're choking on our own emissions, in the midst of a mass extinction caused by our numbers, while sleepwalking into a Third World War! No, I will not *reconsider*. Don't tell me about risk. I *know* about risk!"

PoTolo nodded carefully, more physically intimidated than he liked to admit by this big rich white man, disinhibited by great power and famous for his reckless temper.

"My apologies. Shall we proceed?"

"I take nothing? No helmet full of gizmos, no homing beacon?"

"Only the capsule you swallowed. If conditions are as we hope, the probe will be retrieved, bringing you along with it. There'll be an interval, I can't tell you exactly how long, the variables are complex. You don't have to do anything. You can move around, admire the scenery, then suddenly, you'll be back here."

"Amusing, if I'm in the middle of a conversation . . . One more question. You've staked your career on this, PoTolo, as much as I'm staking my life. What's in it for you?"

"Habitable zones," said the scientist. "Ancient Venus is, in effect, our nearest accessible exoplanet. If we can confirm the existence in space-time of the Venusian habitable zone we've detected, that's a major confirmation of our ability to identify viable alternate Earths. We may not be able to use this method to send probes across the light-years, to distant systems; there may be insuperable barriers to that, but—"

"Bullshit. Your motive was glory, and the glory is mine now." Forrest grinned. "You lose, I win. That's what I do, PoTolo. I see an opportunity, and I *take* it."

"Are you quite ready, Mr. Forrest?"

"I am."

Forrest assumed the position, standing in the gate, arms loosely by his sides. He turned his head for a last glance at that bright star. The world disappeared.

He stood in a rosy, green-tinged twilight, surrounded by trees. Most seemed young, some had boles thicker than his body. Fronds like hanging moss hung around him; the ground underfoot was springy and a little uncertain, as if composed entirely of supple, matted roots. No glimpse of sky. The air was still, neither warm nor cold; the silence was absolute, uncanny.

He looked at himself, checked the contents of belt loops and pockets. He was dressed as he had been in West Africa, complete with a sturdy, familiar, outdoors kit. This struck him as very strange, suddenly, but why not? What is a body but a suit of clothes, another layer of the mind's adornment? And his body seemed to have made the trip. Or the translation, or whatever you called it. No pack. PoTolo had told him he couldn't carry a pack.

PoTolo!

The name rang like a bell, reminding him just what had happened. What an extraordinary feat! He took a few steps, in one direction, then another: keeping himself oriented on the drop zone. Pity he didn't have a ballpark figure for the "interval." Ten minutes or ten hours? How far was it safe to stray? Grey-green boles crowded him, the hulk of a dead giant or two lurking, back in the ranks. He suddenly wondered if he was dreaming. Yes, probably he was. The PoTolo narrative, the apparatus, the act of standing in that gate, feeling absurd in his wilderness kit, folded up like a telescope, became implausible as a dream. Only the twilit jungle remained concrete, but how did he get here?

He heard nothing. He simply became aware of a rush of small, purposeful movement, closing in. The creatures were highly camouflaged, about the size of ground squirrels: long, flexible snouts, shaggy, apparently limbless bodies. Their swift appearance seemed uncanny, *the dream turned to nightmare,* but of course they had smelt his blood. He fled, grabbing at appropriate defense, spun around and pepper-sprayed them. Which did the trick. Hell, they weren't armor-plated, and they liked the taste of their own kind, a useful trait in aggressive vermin. Inevitably the drop zone was now out of sight, but before he could think about that, a new player arrived. Shaggy four-legged things: bigger than the first guys and smart, organized pack-hunters. He ran, but they had him outflanked. Forced to climb, he shot up the first three or four meters of his chosen refuge in seconds, and went on climbing, easy work, to a knot of boughs high above the ground. There he perched, assembling his pellet gun, thrumming with adrenaline and almost laughing out loud.

An exhilarating place, this planet called Desire!

No pack, and no effective firearms, a lack he might come to regret. He was equipped for the wilderness, but not for slaughter. How do you say "I come in peace" to a pack of Venusian hyenas? He saw formidable teeth, and hoped his armory was sufficient. But apparently Venusian hyenas couldn't climb. The brutes circled, panting in frustration, then retreated, vanishing into the dim ranks of the trees.

Not worth it, muttered Forrest. *Or I smell wrong, unappetizing.*

He took stock of his situation: treed in a trackless forest full of hungry predators, some 2 or 3 billion years and around 38 million kilometers from home, and noticed that his secret burden of depression—the Black Dog mood that had haunted him for years—had vanished. Savoring PoTolo's crowning moment, he wondered if he might be here for days. He'd need food; water; shelter; some way to defeat beasts that could tear him apart! The challenges he might face, possibly fatal, possibly insurmountable, delighted him.

He was debating whether to take the gun apart or carry it down assembled, when a severe, numbing pain alerted him to the tree's behavior.

He bared his right leg and saw grey noduled strands tightly wrapped around his calf. The knot of boughs had produced suckers and sent them to feed, stealthily creeping inside his pant leg. Forrest grabbed his knife and slashed. The pain was unmistakably deep and compelling: there was venom involved and no time to lose. The suckers fell away. He slashed again at a row of puckered wounds, like scribbled smiley faces, opening a long gash, in the hope of bleeding the poison out. Too late. In the act of securing a tourniquet below the knee, he stopped being able to breathe, lost consciousness, lost his balance, and fell.

He woke on his back, lying on some kind of bed, a very warm coverlet confining him. He smelled foul meat and remembered being dragged through darkness, maybe in the teeth of those hyenas, in a red mist of pain . . . The pain was still intense, and there were other discomforts, possibly broken bones, but hyenas hadn't brought him here—wherever *here* was. Flickering light showed a hollow, interior space, crudely furnished. There was someone with him, a figure squatting by a firebowl, poring over small objects on a slab. Silvery fingers rearranged the items, a sleek bent head pondered the pattern. He was sure he'd seen the same thing before, far away, in another world—

She's telling my fortune, he thought, though how he knew the figure was female he had no idea. The items were swept away and vanished. The figure sat back, murmuring, looking down into upturned palms, seeming to engage in a dialogue with the Unseen.

He slept again. The pain burned low, like a smothered fire.

When he next woke, she was by his couch, in a very unhuman posture.

"Good," she said. "You're awake. Your head is clear?"

He nodded, staring. He had been rescued by a glistening, greenish woman with a muscular, sheeny tail, which she was using as a third lower limb, a hairless head, and bird- or snakelike features (green eyes that filled the face, a long mouth with an eerie curl, glint of needle teeth). She spoke and he understood her. He must be dreaming, after all.

"Your fall saved your life, at a cost. I have set your broken bones, the venom is overcome, but the *nibbler* bite itself is now urgent. Rotten flesh must be excised, regeneration triggers implanted. You should know: I can immobilize you, I can give you analgesics, but I can't put you out." She showed him her palm: he saw moving symbols. "I can read your *cell signature* on this, but not the details of its expression, and anesthesia is complex. I might kill you."

"You are a medicine woman," said John Forrest slowly.

"Yes." Her eerie mouth curled further, until he thought her jaw would split from her face. "I am indeed. The procedure will be very painful."

"Go ahead and operate, Doctor. Do I need to sign anything?"

"Not necessary."

The operation was a success. When pain was once more a smothered fire, she told him all was well and he would soon mend. She asked him where he'd come from.

"From the sky," said Forrest, "does it matter?"

"Not to me," said Lizard Woman, her long mouth curling.

He noticed, at last, a spidery transparent headset, and a mic by her mouth, catching gleams of firelight. He raised an arm, the one that wasn't still immobilized by the heated coverlet.

"What's that?" he muttered, incredulous. "Some kind of *babelfish*?"

"Yes, sir, it's a *translation device*. It may look old-fashioned and clumsy, but it converts my language into yours, and yours into mine, adequately enough. Mr. From-the-Sky, I have business that cannot wait. When you can walk, I'll take you to a better-equipped refuge, where you may rest and recover in safety."

Forrest decided that he wasn't dreaming. He was on Ancient Venus, and his rescuer was a sophisticated Venusian, an unexpected bonus! She had some rationale to account for his odd anatomy and strange arrival: fine, he would let her be. He had no urgent need to explain himself. He couldn't gauge how long he'd been in this cave, not even by the growth of his beard, which she had kept close-trimmed. But he could assume the retrieval had failed; probably he was too far from the drop zone.

He wasn't overly concerned. PoTolo would certainly keep trying. All Forrest had to do was get himself back to the zone, before the orbits of the two planets veered too wildly apart.

She walked him up and down. She showed him the "wellspring," a water supply tapped from the root system of the trees, and explained how to operate a firebowl (the flames were natural gas, from the same source), how to use the gourdlike ration packs. Her tone was always frosty, if translated emotional nuance could be trusted, her conversation minimal. Forrest surmised, amused, that whoever he was supposed to be, in local terms, was a bad guy in her reckoning—temporarily protected by her Venusian Hippocratic Oath.

They left the cave via a twisting, crawl-space passage—waking nightmare memories for Forrest—and emerged from a hole in a huge dead root. Her "refuge" was the hollow under a giant tree stump. She led the way, Forrest stumped behind, favoring his lame leg. He'd tried to convince her to take him back where she'd found him, to no avail, and he was angry. But not such a fool as to strike out on his own, against her will. If Lizard Woman had dragged him below herself, she was extremely strong. Or had confederates he hadn't met; or both, of course. She was alone, living on gourds of mush but implanted with impressive tech. What was the story? Who was Forrest supposed to be? So many unknowns, and he'd have relished them except that he was so annoyed.

But her pace started to tell. She had the pack, he carried nothing, which he found galling. If there were trails, she didn't use them; if she had transport, she preferred to hike. What was she? Some kind of Venusian Backwoods Survivalist, humiliating a hated city slicker? He refused to be outdone. When she handed him one of those sappy-gruel gourds, he emptied it without breaking stride. But it got to be desperate work. She wore a floating grey robe; under it a shirt, and pants that accommodated the tail by having no back side. When the robe lifted, as she crossed some obstacle, he saw the big gleaming root of her tail, and it was sexy in a weird way.

Before long, her tail was the only thing that kept him moving.

Dizzy with exhaustion, he picked at his itching fingertips, trying to extricate a tiny, wriggling, brown worm or caterpillar from under one of his fingernails. He didn't know he'd stopped until Lizard Woman was in front of him, taking hold of his wrist.

She pulled out her headset and donned it. "Your head swims," she suggested, a cool, contemptuous light in her huge eyes. "Disoriented, can't think straight? Your skin creeps?"

"All of that," mumbled Forrest. "Well done, *Doctor*. You said you would *help* me."

"I don't believe I did say that, and yet I will."

She was lying, things only got worse. Now they *really* went off the piste. Forrest was dragged through virgin thickets, thrown into ditches, forced over madsastrugi of upheaved root mass . . . until they reached a small clearing where a new kind of tree, reddish and gnarled, grew with no near neighbors. Stumbling and confused, he was ordered to strip, and hustled onto a natural platform among its roots. The lower part of the bole was scarred. She stuck something in his hand, forced him to grip, and shouted at him.

"Stab the tree! *Stab* it! Over your head. Cover your eyes. Okay?"

He was holding a knife. He reached up, and stabbed the tree. A huge gush of stinging hot liquid burst out, and pounded on him.

A hot shower! My God!

The itching that had been driving him mad, a vile, active

sensation over his whole body, leapt to a crescendo. He looked down and saw a nest of little dark worms on his chest. More of them, over his belly, his arms. They were wriggling out of his pores, his anus, they were *everywhere*, there were *hundreds* of them. The hot, scouring liquid diminished. Frantically he stabbed the tree again, and again, oh blessed relief—

The first time he left the platform, she sent him back. The second time, she was satisfied, and slapped a new kind of soft-walled gourd into his hands.

"Hold that. Whatever they gave you, Mr. From-the-Sky, it doesn't last. You'll have to do as we do, in here. Depilate and use barrier methods, or the *sippers* will overwhelm you in hours. I'm going to fix you up, before you collapse."

She made him sit on the ground, massaged a grainy goop into his hair, his beard, his arms and legs, his chest, his pubes: sent him to rinse off, then helped to apply a cream that left his skin shining like her own. There was also breathable gel, she said, as she sleeked his every crevice, for nostrils, mouth, and eyes: but it wasn't necessary in the short term. The "sippers" wouldn't block airways, or endanger sight, until their host was actually dying. The erection she provoked along the way didn't bother her, she ignored it and so did he. But there was something between them, when he was hairless, purged, and dressed again, that had not been there before.

"Since we're talking, sir. What about a name?"

"Forrest. My name is John Forrest, and you?"

"Sekρool."

"*Sek*. That means the woods, doesn't it?"

"You know my humble language?"

He shook his head. "In the cave, I sometimes heard you talking to someone. Or communing with your gods? I listened. I figured out that *sek* meant woods, frequency of occurrence." He gestured around them. "Since here we are."

"I have no gods," she said, and added, "*Ool* means song. The ρ̇ is a separating sound, my name is Woodsong. *Sekool* without the ρ̇ means something different."

The distinction was obviously important: but he wasn't sure how to respond.

"Woodsong, okay. Er, John means *gift of God*."

She laughed, at least the sound she made felt like laughter. His eyes burned, he'd forgotten to cover them, but the world was in focus. He was awake, alive, firing on all cylinders again, maybe for the first time since he'd touched down. He looked at the gouged tree bole, and the shower platform: a natural formation, smoothed by long use.

"There are people living around here?"

"There are the indigenes, primitive surface-dwellers: you won't see them. A few others: you'll see them even less. Let's go. It's not much farther."

Soon they crossed a really large clearing, and he was able to gauge the height of the frondy canopy at last: impressive but not extraordinary, sixty or seventy meters. Only mosses grew on the open ground, but the springy, uncertain feeling stayed the same.

Sekρ̇ool kept to the margin of the trees. Up ahead, a shadow moved, between the canopy and a ceiling of bright cloud; a grey curtain falling under it, defined like a rainstorm, seen from afar on a wide plain. Forrest thought they were heading into rain until they crossed the shadow's trajectory, and he stared in amazement at the tangled, mighty underbelly—then flinched and ducked, as vagrant shining strands actually brushed his naked skull.

"Don't worry," she said. She'd kept the headset on since his shower-bath, a concession he appreciated. "They're just eating air. It doesn't know we're here."

They reentered the woods, and almost at once she halted, gesturing for him to step well back. A knotted growth, a tumor on a root, stood knee high in their path. Sekḉool crouched, her tail balancing her, and cut herself between the fingers of her right hand with the knife he'd borrowed. Was her blood red? He couldn't tell in this everlasting rosy-green twilight—

"Wait. Don't move from where you stand."

Following her with his eyes, he saw the same ceremony performed again, farther into the trees on his right. What was she doing? Placating demons? Having met some of the demons, he didn't move a muscle until she reappeared from the left. She'd circled round something big. They walked on and stood in the precinct of a truly vast dead giant: a tree stump tall as a house and broad as a barn. Forrest looked it over with respect.

"I hope *this* guy doesn't feed on flesh."

"Actually he does, but the heartwood is inert."

The last section of the entrance tunnel was vertical. They descended a ladder into a room rounded and domed like the first cave, but far more spacious and better furnished. There were covered couches, low tables, domed chests, a firebowl at one focus of the ellipse, a wellspring bubbling at the other. Doorways (closed off) seemed to lead to other areas.

Forrest's appetite had returned. He longed for steak, fries, and a good malt, but he made do with another sappy-gruel gourd (he should stop calling them "gourds," since they were obviously manufactured), fell onto a couch, and plunged into oblivion.

In his dreams, the snouted things chased him, limbless bodies covered in worms. The hyenas circled under the venom tree, shaggy with their freight of bloodsuckers. The tiny worms that filled the sek's air, and had invaded his pores, had smaller worms to bite them. He woke with a shuddering start. *Nibblers, sippers*: cute names for unappeasable horrors. *Wee folk, good folk, trooping all together* ... Parasites are everywhere, far too many of the bastards on Earth, but if Sekp̆ool hadn't found him, what an appalling fate! But she didn't find me, he thought. She was watching me. *"Your fall saved your life, but at a cost—"*

He opened his eyes. She was beside him, in her tripod pose: wearing the headset. She smiled at him. He'd come to like that eerie, too-wide smile very much. But it had an edge to it, on which he feared to cut himself.

"I must return your gear."

She handed over everything, including the pellet gun, which he'd assumed was lost or confiscated. "That is not a lethal weapon," she remarked. "You carried none. What if you'd run into trouble, Johnforrest?"

What kind of trouble, he wondered. Friends of yours? "What if I did? Thou shalt not kill. I'm on a fact-finding mission, I'm not at war with anyone."

"A fact-finding mission," she repeated. "Indeed. I see."

"What about you, Sekp̆ool? I'm deeply in your debt, of course, but what are *you* doing in this hellhole? How did you happen to turn up like that?"

"The surface is a source of raw materials, Johnforrest. We come here to make deals with the indigenes and squabble with each other over the spoils. I was researching tree venoms that can be weaponized, if you must know."

"That's no work for a doctor."

"We live in the dark as well as the bright, Mr. From-the-Sky, and though I chose medicine, I was born to something else. I saw you run from the vermin, I saw you climb, then fall, it was pure chance."

Now I know too much, thought Forrest. And whatever the hell's going on, I get the feeling I'm in serious trouble. But you'd spare me if you could, for which I thank you—

He said nothing, just nodded gravely.

"I'll be leaving soon," she said. "Here you have everything

you need, and no *sippers* or *nibblers* can reach you: the hollows under the *great hearts* are our safe houses. I'll give you a homing beacon, since you have none, to guide you back to the spot where I found you. But you were very ill. Please wait: eat, rest, and exercise awhile before leaving. I'm not happy about the way you keep falling asleep in the daytime—"

"Oh, that? We call it *jet lag*. It's nothing, it's just taking me a while to adjust to a different time zone—"

Forrest liked to wear a wristwatch; he collected them. Before leaving for West Africa he'd had one specially made for this trip. An ingenious, expensive toy; instead of hours and seconds, it followed the intricate dance of the orbits of the two planets. Sekpool had returned this device. He didn't think she could have tampered with it. As he spoke he read the time, the only time that mattered to him, and his heart skipped a beat.

He wanted to ask her *just how long was I "very ill"? How long is your world's "day," right now*? He had no idea how to frame the question, and it didn't matter. He knew enough of PoTolo's complex requirements to be sure he'd missed his window. His next chance wouldn't be coming around for . . . for quite a while.

"But Johnforrest, I have a proposal. It suddenly struck me. Why not come to the clouds? You're on a fact-finding mission: I could introduce you to interesting people, and later we could surely set you down wherever you need to be."

Forrest slipped the orrery watch into an inside pocket. Her big green eyes were limpid with lies, her smile had that bleak, warning edge, and he didn't care.

"What a wonderful idea, I'd be delighted. When do we leave?"

If he was stranded, for a year and a half or forever, he might as well see the world. Stir things up, in this story he didn't understand. Why not? If Lizard Woman feared for his life, maybe

she just didn't know John Forrest very well! But that pouch on
the cord around her neck, where she kept her oracle bones, what
was going on there—?

She was making arrangements for his visit: Forrest had
"fallen asleep in the daytime" again. The room was dim, the
lights that stood in wall niches were at their lowest setting. He
heard Sekpool's voice, but she was nowhere in sight. She'd
screened off an area at the end of the room, the way she used to
screen his bed sometimes when he was sick. The headset lay on
a table. Intrigued, he donned it and sneaked up to the screens,
creeping around until he could peer between them. He saw
himself, standing naked, quivering, full frontal.

The shock was momentary. He was looking as if into a full-
length, freestanding mirror, but it was a mirror that didn't
reflect the room he was in. The naked figure was a hologram. A
stranger, a Lizard Man (though he couldn't see a tail) stood by
the holo, dressed in black and white. Sekpool, her back to Forrest,
spoke rapidly in a language that crackled and fizzed like
fireworks: but reached him as English (mostly)—

"No. He's an original, not any kind of *flishatatonaton*. But
he's carrying an implant, attached to his stomach wall. I haven't
touched it, and I don't know what it's for—"

Good to know I'm still a walking interplanetary probe,
thought Forrest. Lizard Man's contribution, over the videolink,
was incomprehensible.

"Deniable is good, but how long could it stand up? This is
better. Far better than a . . . a *kinsnipping*, Esbwe! We want to
avoid reprisals, don't we?"

Her tail, he thought, should be lashing. He'd have liked to
see that. He retreated, replaced the headset where he'd found it,
and lay down again: his thoughts racing.

Feigning sleep, he must have dozed. He woke when he
heard something crawling.

The globes were still dim, the screens had been dismantled. Sekρool sat by the firebowl, tail around her feet. Nothing moved, but the sound of crawling was closer. Puzzled, Forrest turned on his side, as if in sleep, and saw something come through the wall of the room.

It crossed the floor. A male human figure, slender and juvenile, naked and very battered, hauling himself along on one hand and one knee, back, ribs, and shoulders marked with livid weals. Bruises blotted out his eyes. No sign of a tail, which made Forrest think he was asleep and dreaming of a human boy except that the whole thing was too complete, too coherent. The kid's hair was dark, his greenish skin unnaturally pale—until he reached the firelight. Then he was more than pale: he was translucent, transparent.

A mangled corpse, but moving, the apparition crept into Sekρool's arms.

Another hologram? Not the way Sekρool responded. Not the way she held the kid, rocked him and murmured to him, stroking his shadow-hair from his swollen, battered shadow-brow, then somehow Forrest made a sound.

She looked up: instantly, the ghost was gone.

"What was *that*?" he breathed.

Enormous eyes unblinking, she calmly left the fire and picked up the "translation device."

"My son, Gemin. He comes to me when it's quiet. Usually I'm alone; you've never woken before. He died under torture. Don't die under torture, Johnforrest. It's not a good way to go."

She removed the headset and turned away; the subject was closed. Forrest got up and joined her by the firebowl, collecting the headset on the way. He held her gaze, deliberately settling the flexible web around his skull.

"Tell me, Sekρool."

She looked into the flames, drawing her tail more closely around her.

"There's not much to tell. He was caught up in the secret war and taken hostage; we failed to negotiate his release. He was mistreated, our protests achieved nothing; we learned that he'd died. There's nothing to be done. I only comfort him, and quiet him as best I can . . . Death is not the end, Johnforrest, as we all know, because our dead *return*. They speak to us and know us, *in dream and in the waking world*. But when they depart at last, we don't know what happens next. We don't know if the unquiet ones, trapped in the way they died, escape from suffering at last. It's cruel."

"I know you're a *shaman*," he said. "There must be something you can do."

Her long fingers closed on the bag of bones.

"No. Let's say no more about it. I can't help my boy. He'll fade, that's all, and he'll be gone, and I won't know where."

2. OUT OF THE FRYING PAN, INTO THE FIRE

ON THEIR WAY OUT, SEKP'OOL HAD TO PLACATE THE demons again. Forrest kept his distance and didn't stir until she'd made her circuit. She seemed self-conscious, something he'd never seen in her before, and he liked it. He had no doubt that, if he'd asked, she'd tell him that of course she'd planned to disarm the venom-spitting fence, if she'd been leaving him behind (to await those kinsnippers!). He said nothing. He just followed her, as before, grinning to himself: no longer helpless baggage. In charge of his own destiny again, and it felt good.

But surely, subtly, *everything had changed*? Had the trees actually *moved*? Surely the spaces between the ranks were different, the uncertain ground had new contours—

"Happens all the time," said Sekρool, catching his bewildered glances. "The *sek* is a single organism: it shifts about as it pleases. That's why there are no trails. The indigenes have their own ways to get around. We use our beacons, and come in on foot. It's simpler."

"What a world. It's like *a circle in Dante's hell*."

"Indeed. All death in life is here, eating its own tail. Yet somehow I love it."

There was a wind blowing outside the wood, they could hear it. Sekρool gave Forrest a robe like her own: he wrapped himself, the folds settling firmly round his head and face, and they emerged from tepid stillness into a dust storm. Well protected but half-blind, he felt a hard surface under the skidding grit and glimpsed big squared and domed shapes. Fighting the wind to look behind him, he saw the sek: rising like a grey-green mirage, on the edge of a desert-devoured town. She headed for an intact building and used a touch pad to open massive double doors. In a covered courtyard, a welcome silence, she bared her face—

"I have a call to make. It won't take long."

The room they entered made Forrest think of a chapel: a podium for the minister, benches for the congregation. Images of lizard-people, animal, and vegetable flourishes, in colored metals or enamel, covered the walls. She approached the podium, Forrest took a seat. His legs were too long. Sekρool was tall, but like a Japanese woman, her height was in her pliant body ... Expecting a videolink, he saw, to his astonishment, powdery matter begin to whirl inside a clear cylinder: building something from the platter upward. The cylinder withdrew, and there stood a solid, masculine-seeming human figure, Venusian style: a Lizard Man. Not the guy Forrest had seen in the mirror-screen: someone new. He had scanty head hair, he wore some kind of dress uniform; he seemed authoritative but old; or maybe sick.

Sekρool spoke, Lizard Man mainly listened. At one point, he

looked over her shoulder, and Forrest, disconcerted, felt eyes on him: a presence in the instant simulacrum. Finally, Sekρool bowed, the old guy did the same. The body crumbled and vanished.

She walked past Forrest, resuming her headset as she headed for the doors.

"Who was that?"

"My husband. Excuse him if he seemed rude, you'll meet him properly up above. Do you have wives, Johnforrest?"

"I've had two. Then I gave up."

"Wise man . . . I did what was expected of me. I gave a powerful old man my baby's name, his futurity for our security. A fair trade on both sides: we didn't expect it would be forever. I have no complaints, none at all. But oh, he's a long time dying!"

She flashed him that eerie smile. "Now we need to hurry. The wind usually eases at nightfall, but I want to be far from here by then."

In the covered yard, Sekρool left him, and swiftly reappeared, leading an extraordinary animal: a low-slung, big-haunched, tan-hided, wrinkly camel, with bulbous cat's-eyes, a sinuous neck and tail, a muzzle thick with stiff, drooping whiskers—

"Johnforrest, meet Mihanhouk. I don't take him into the *sek*, but we need him now. You'll have to ride behind me, I'm afraid. I wasn't expecting to bring home a guest."

Who had harnessed Mihanhouk? He listened. Not a footstep, not a voice.

"Are we alone? Where is everybody?"

"Only the indigenes live permanently on the surface, and around here they don't leave the haunted woods. Let's go, it's a long ride to the Sea Mount Station."

If anybody asks, he thought, the ground staff never saw me—

The cat-camel's paces were challenging. He loped like a hare, pushing off from his big haunches, landing with an insouciant bounce on his forepaws. So far, so uncomfortable, then he put on speed. At every leap, Forrest (with muttered curses) nearly lost his seat; at every touchdown, his tailbone tried to send his cervical vertebrae through the top of his head. Sekρool rode with her tail tucked up, stirrups high as a jockey's. She glanced around, green eyes vivid between folds of grey and the whipping dust, registering his discomfort. She faced ahead again, and he felt a curious, thrilling, muscular movement.

She was wrapping her tail around him.

"Is that better?"

"Yes," he breathed. "That's . . . fine."

Gradually, the howling died and the dust cleared. Mihanhouk seemed to feel he'd done enough. He ambled along a rudimentary trail, uphill, between eroded boulders that blocked the view, to a bluff like a wave crest. Sekρool tapped his shoulder with the knotted end of her reins: the beast knelt, and they dismounted.

They climbed the last few meters to a viewpoint and suddenly faced a staggering gulf. Red-gold cliffs plunged, *way* deeper than the Grand Canyon, into the haze of a basin that stretched forever. To their left, far below the bluff, Forrest saw the trail continuing to another complex of buildings, and skeletal bridgework that reached out, over the abyss, to a rocky, conical pillar. Narrowing his eyes, he saw the sequence repeated: a string of rocky cones, rising from unseen depths, and the bridgework linking them, becoming tiny and vanishing.

Directly ahead, but far off, brilliant whiteness reflected the pale clouds.

"Is that the ocean out there?"

"Once upon a time," said Sekρool. "It's mostly a big salt pan now. We live in the clouds and in the skies, Johnforrest, where everything is fine. Only fanatics think it matters that we *can't* live on the surface anymore if we wanted to. Which is just as well. The situation down here is beyond repair, anyway."

"So what's the use of worrying? It never was worthwhile."

"Indeed. I'd like to learn your language. From what I can tell, it has a fine turn of phrase, many interesting concepts. *Thou shalt not kill*. There's another of them!"

Forrest nodded, his thoughts very far away. Out of the frying pan, into the fire ... Our beautiful neighbor planet *before* she ran into trouble? Your calculations are slightly out, PoTolo!

"What caused the devastation? Do your scientists have an explanation?"

She thought about it, measuring her words. "Long ago, we lived in a dangerous world and didn't know it. Everything was kind, plenty was all around. One day, we stepped on a hidden switch, we pulled the wrong lever, we unknowingly tipped a balance, and destruction was set in motion, click, clack, like a child's toy: sly and comical and relentless. Or so I understand it. But we took that wrong step a *very* long time ago, Johnforrest. The damage was done before we moved to the clouds, let alone the skies. It's nonsense to apportion blame."

The stillness after the wind, the somber majesty of the scene held them in silence.

"I didn't bring you up here to accuse you of anything, Mr. From-the-Sky. There's something I wanted you to see, a trick of this landscape. Look to the east."

He felt the chill before he saw the cause. Far away and very distinct, like a bold line on a child's drawing, a dark ellipse appeared, stretching from horizon to horizon. It grew, like the shadow of the moon across the sun in a solar eclipse, contained, yet seeming liquid as ink. No flashes of radiance, no sunset colors heralded the change. The transition from light to shadow was perfectly abrupt, pure as a note of music.

It was the dark.

Forrest thought of a world without a visible sun. No moon, no stars. A horror ran through him; he wanted to run. At his shoulder, the Venusian sighed in delight, as perfect night, velvet night, rose to the zenith and hurried down to engulf them.

"*There,*" she murmured, when blackness lapped their vantage point.

"Thank you," whispered Forrest.

They rode to the Sea Mount Station as if descending under miles of dark water. She'd fastened lights to Mihanhouk's bridle, although he didn't seem to need them: he was sure-footed and at ease. The Station was lit, and as deserted as the town by the *sek*. Their cable car, swinging from frictionless chains, black sides hung with rosy lights, reminded Forrest of an Egyptian ship of the dead, on a temple frieze. It rode silently down to their platform; they embarked.

Mihanhouk had a compartment to himself. Sekpool made him comfortable, then joined Forrest in the stateroom, where a buffet offered store-cupboard foods: pickles, spreads, and tough breads, savory cakes of pressed beans (or insect larvae?), crystallized fruit. A fine change from sappy gruel. They moved on, having eaten, to an observation car, taking along a carafe of spirits. The couches were soft and wide: they settled side by side.

"Here's another sight not to be missed, Johnforrest. We're passing over the Trench."

In fathomless blackness, way down under them, he saw a vivid, active red line.

"What's that?"

"A rent in the world's hide, close to the old coastline, where the fires of renewal pour out, and worn-out flesh is devoured. It's shrinking . . . My city takes pictures. All the *healthy wounds,* as our scientists call them, are healing. It's not a good sign."

"I've heard about that."

"When the fire stops flowing, when the wounds are gone . . . then even the clouds and the skies may fail us. But that's a long way off. Neither you nor I need worry!"

Forrest filled two tiny cups, she emptied hers and held it out for more. Like-for-like translation, he thought, turned them into a medieval knight and his lady, speaking of eldritch secret dooms known only to the wise. She tossed her cup aside, and took his hand. Four-fingered, both outer digits opposable: she gripped like a chameleon.

"This is a great favor you're doing for me."

"A trip to the clouds?" Forrest smiled to himself. "It's my great pleasure!"

"Still, I feel I owe you. Let me give you some return."

"There's no need."

"Myself?"

"Well, now. That would be an unexpected bonus."

"An interlude, I mean nothing more."

"Of course not!"

Romantic overtures would have been in poor taste, but his lust was honest, and however she squared it, her offer seemed honest too. Seeing no reason to refuse, he reached around and took the splendid root of her tail in a forthright, determined grip.

The tongue that met his when they kissed was slender, strong, active, and probing. The gulf behind her smile could have swallowed him whole. They shucked out of their clothes and embraced, her tail lashed itself around him, and he probed in turn, deeper and longer than he'd have thought possible. Blissfully spent, he fell asleep, and woke still held in her grip, a silky, powerful frottage undulating up and down his thighs, his buttocks—

He wondered if he would survive this dark journey or die happy?

Unmeasured riches followed, an engrossing, fabulous *interlude*, only interrupted by the briefest of briefings for Forrest, about her city. They hardly ate or drank, they slept coupled and entwined. But once, when he woke, he was alone.

Sekþool was on the opposite couch, limned in faint light, head bent over the oracle bones: the way he'd first seen her. He went over. She looked up, accepting, and drew back to let him see. Just four items—no bones. The "slab" he remembered was a paper-thin tablet, lit from within, marked in a grid of four by four. Plenty for a tribal shaman, still living at the dawn of time. Not much of an apparatus to model the fate of a complex, high-tech society.

But four by four is a powerful number.

The tokens are relics from your own life, he said. *You've invested them with meaning, for telling the fortunes of your people: that I understand. Will you explain how it works?*

A fragment of patterned textile, wrapped around three small flat sticks: *what was*.

A shiny feather or fish scale, set in silver wire: *what might have been*. Or, better: *the conditional, the always possible*.

A shriveled coil of brown, veiny material, probably a root fragment: *what is*.

A black stone, glossy as obsidian, was *The Truth*.

The headset was nowhere in this exchange. He asked and she answered in gesture, the timeless, universal language of this other trade of hers—

Does what you read come true?

If you know so much, you know that's a fool's question.

Then she smiled. The black stone in one fist, she laid her free hand on his breast, where his heart was beating. *But when I know I'm right, however unbelievable, I'm right . . .*

Forrest felt suddenly very confused.

Sekþool returned her tokens to the pouch and slipped the

cord over her head. She was soon deeply asleep, but he lay awake. *Sekpool Sekool,* Woodsong the Sorceress. Had he really understood her? It didn't seem possible.

Their arrival at Tessera Station was as dramatic as darkfall, in its way. Her city, a sky raft the size of Manhattan Island, had come to meet them. Moored by mighty hawsers, it stood at the sheer edge of the Tessera Plateau, beside the cable-car buildings. Forrest watched the underbelly as they came in: a mass of swollen, membranous dirigibles, layered and roped together in a gargantuan netted frame.

"Unlike the upper-atmosphere habitats," Sekpool remarked, "our cities were developed from life. The original bladder-raft colonies, which provide our germ material, still flourish: small as tables, big as mountaintops. We harvest and data mine them for improvements."

"Fascinating," said Forrest, making her laugh.

"About Gemin. You will be discreet?"

"Of course."

She had told him that her city, Lacertan, led an alliance of liberal and independent cloud-cities known as The Band. The other major bloc was an empire, run on military lines, centered on a vast sky raft called Rapton. Empire and Band were currently, technically, at peace, but the covert maneuvering was vicious: this was the situation that had cost Gemin his life. The dirty story hadn't been released, it was too inflammatory. The official line was that he'd been killed in a caving accident, on an expedition to one of the old ocean beds; and tragically it had been impossible to recover his body.

It *was* a prospecting expedition, said Sekpool. In disputed territory, where there are rich pickings, and they ran into trouble. He shouldn't have been there at all, of course.

They disembarked, smiling for the welcoming committee, in their desert robes and battered wilderness clothes. The Man From-the-Sky was instantly surrounded by officials and Venusian-style media folk. He didn't speak to Sekρool again for a while.

Forrest didn't get to watch the return of the bright: Lacertan was riding strong winds and everyone was indoors, sleeping or not. But after that, the city—which had been quiet as an Arctic night—began to bustle. Washed, brushed, and dressed in Venusian formal style; provided with fine accommodation and service, he was swept from reception to reception. He ate high-class delicacies, no better or worse than the same absurd fancywork in New York or London. He talked (in like-for-like translation) with many interesting Venusians, and had no trouble passing for a denizen of the upper atmosphere. Contact between the realms was minimal, he was their first actual visitor: a Marco Polo at the court of Kublai Khan.

Perhaps the most personally interesting fact he picked up was that Lizard Men, like the naked ghost boy, had no tails. Which explained a couple of things.

He met Sekρool again at his private audience with the Master of the City.

The simulacrum he'd seen had been a flattering portrait. In life, the Master was a wraith in a medicalized cocoon, though his eyes, appraising Forrest with great interest, were still sharp. Sekρool was at the bedside, in a dark blue formal gown: the first time he'd been close to her since the cable car. Raised on pillows, the Master offered greetings translated by an aide wearing a headset. Forrest had arranged for the orrery watch to be boxed and wrapped, in suitable style. He offered it with misgiving, hoping that the gift at least *looked* impressive, but the old man fizzed and crackled with a connoisseur's delight.

"The Master is pleased," reported the aide. "He says the orbits of our planet and our near neighbor present a pretty problem. He has never seen the puzzle worked in craft with such elegance and charm. He suggests you must twin your soul with my lady's brother, our Chief Scientist, who is also fascinated by the third world."

Then the Master was tired, and they were both dismissed.

She donned a headset as soon as they were clear of the Master's apartments. "I think you have no engagements just now, sir. Let me show you a view over the city."

The view from the terrace was not dazzling, they were hemmed by blank walls and the defensive redoubt that protected the Residence. But there was a glimpse of bright cloud above, and more rosy greenery than he'd seen elsewhere.

"So that's my marriage," she said, pacing. "He was a good leader, now he's old, and deathly sick. But he's not senile and he doesn't want to let go, so that's that. He's just forgotten how he's paralyzing me: paralyzing the whole city—"

Her hair, grown out, ran in natural, feathery cornrows to her nape. She wore classy makeup, there were jewels at her throat. The gown was daringly décolleté in the back, at the swell of her tail's root. But he missed her jungle pants.

"You think I'm speaking very freely? Don't worry, everyone knows how I feel. Including the Master. Nobody's going to blab indiscretions in your company, Johnforrest. These things." She tapped her headset. "Are notoriously easy to *hack*."

"What does the Master think about what happened to your son?"

"That the accident was in disputed territory, and anything's better than war. That I can marry again when he dies and have other children. Or adopt, it's been done before. That he'll negotiate, when he's stronger (which will never happen, he's dying). I can't bear to tell him *how real my son's suffering still is to me*. So I just have to wait."

The people of Lacertan, Forrest had learned, were a godless lot of sophisticated animists, like Sekpool herself. They were liberal, they were easy, but the idea of their prince lying untended, "trapped in his death," at the bottom of some hole, gave them the horrors. And *they* weren't visited by that crawling corpse.

He knew he was talking to a desperate woman and forgave her many things.

"What about my twin soul? Your brother, the Chief Scientist?"

"Esbwe? Who knows? He's an eccentric genius, he lives in a world of his own."

The smile he loved fought with the pain. "Enjoy the rest of your visit. You may not have been following the reckoning, we've come a long way since you boarded. We'll soon pass over the spot where you and I met, then I suppose you'll leave us."

That's it, thought Forrest. He'd been wondering when he was due to disappear.

So be it.

The Chief Scientist worked in a surprisingly shabby old building, in a heritage area close to the Residence. He didn't seem overburdened with staff, either. Possibly "Chief Scientist" was a courtesy title? The *Minister* for Science—who had escorted Forrest, only to be left twisting her tail in an anteroom—had been reticent on the subject.

Forrest was ushered into a big, shiny laboratory, full of expensive-looking equipment. A Lizard Man, in a black smock and white pants (Venusian-style professional clothing) stood peering into a clear tank, affecting to be unaware of the visitor. They were alone, and Esbwe definitely *was* the guy Forrest had glimpsed in the mirror-screen—

"Come and look at this, sir. Look into the *visor* and keep your hands to yourself."

Forrest walked over, and obeyed. The tank seemed empty. Then tiny moving dots appeared, and took on form: became twisting strands that divided and recombined—

"What do you see?"

"Er, the *living material of cell signatures?*"

"*Life,* sir! On our world all life is doomed, that is beyond doubt. But I have calculated that the third world has a biosphere, and my great project is to *infect* it. As soon as I've perfected my delivery system, those *animacula* will be injected through the clouds, they will cross the airless deeps. And something of us may survive."

"A noble dream," said Forrest politely.

"You don't believe me. How could one of *us* be an Interplanetarian? You gave the Master that orbit-tracking toy for a joke, I'm sure. You forget that the skies above our levels were often clear, *before our habitats were launched.* You overlook the fact that we cloud-dwellers hold a wealth of astronomical knowledge; observations many thousands of years old—"

"I find Lacertan science very impressive."

The scientist stared unpleasantly, curling his lip in an ugly shadow of her smile.

"How generous! I'm not one of the idiots who've been fawning over you, Mr. From-the-Sky. To me, the sky habitats are the enemy, the Rapt are our natural allies. The sooner we can join the empire, the better I'll be pleased, and I don't care if you take that message home."

"My headset is malfunctioning," said Forrest, mugging puzzlement. "I can't understand a word. I must try to come back another time. So sorry."

* * *

Forrest didn't need her to know he was a willing victim. Regrettably, he'd be safer if she didn't. But now he felt they had to have a frank discussion. Maybe it was a fatal, irresistible temptation: be that as it may, luckily or unluckily, he knew the right venue for a meeting—in this city where she'd warned him everything he said and heard was monitored.

He placed a personal call to Esbwe and left a message confirming his second visit to the lab, naming a time after Lacertan office hours.

"Falling asleep in the daytime" was discouraged by incessant bursts of public music. A loud and melodious call to quiet relaxation was fading, as Forrest entered the shabby old building. Nobody about. He stationed himself around the corner from the lab and waited.

Sekpool arrived. He was right behind her as she unlocked the doors.

"I thought that would smoke you out."

"*Excuse me?* I was expecting to meet my brother."

"I don't think he's going to turn up," said Forrest, following her inside.

He'd chased his spoken message with an automated cancellation, which she wouldn't have seen. Not that he cared if Esbwe came along. A frank exchange of views would be *fine*!

"Sekpool, we need to talk, and I know this room is safe. I don't think even your crazy brother would have risked the kind of open sedition I heard from him earlier, if *Homeland Security* were listening in. I knew this lab was firewalled, anyway," he added, deliberately. "You made a videocall, from the *great heart* refuge. I saw him in here, when the two of you were planning how to use me in a hostage exchange—"

Her big green eyes got bigger, but she kept her head. No panic, no fluster. "So you know. All right . . . I was desperate, I decided to take matters into my own hands. I went hunting for a suitable opposition candidate, I ran into you, and the plan changed—"

"Yeah. I was to be *kinsnipped,* after you left . . . But then you had a better idea. I'm clear with all that. I just don't know *why the hell* Esbwe's involved. That arrogant idiot is going to *destroy* you, Sekρool. Did you know he's seriously planning to sell this city to the Rapt? How do you think the Master, how d'you think *your people,* would like the sound of that?"

"Esbwe talks a lot of nonsense, nobody listens. I needed his expertise."

But suddenly it was personal. They were two people who had been intensely intimate, but *not very talkative.* Here they were alone again, and the silence was falling apart—

"And he has a right," said Sekρool, her big eyes shamed and defiant. "An inalienable right, to help me recover our son's body."

"My God . . . Are you saying your brother is, is your boy's *father*?"

She recoiled. "I know. I know how it sounds, but Johnforrest, I *couldn't* marry him. He was erratic even then. He had no reputation, he's no leader, he was totally unsuitable. I let myself get pregnant, but I married the Master. It made sense to me. My husband would die. I could never *marry* Esbwe. But he'd be beside me, our son would inherit—"

You learn something new every day, thought Forrest . . . So, talent gets courted and rewarded, dynastic power stays with the blood royal—

"Maybe not such good sense to Esbwe."

"Maybe not . . . I asked his help, I owed him that. It's illegal, of course: a simulacrum isn't supposed to have a life span, but the deal is acceptable, it's been accepted. What I did to you, to get what we needed, was theft, and I'm sorry—"

"A simulacrum," repeated Forrest, stunned. "A *flishatatonaton*—"

"Yes? A short-lived fleshly automaton, for a dead boy. A fair trade, I thought, and we have a good chance of getting away with it. The Rapt refuse to admit they're holding Gemin, and they'd love to know more about the sky habitats, even what little they can learn from an ephemeral puppet, but they won't want to admit that side of the deal, either—"

So much for my heroics, thought Forrest. And she was bold, she was crazy-reckless, his Woodsong, but maybe Forrest was the one who needed forgiving—

"Sekρool, it's not going to work. I'm not, er, what you think I am."

"I know."

"You *know*—?"

"Of course. Esbwe's convinced you're a sky-dweller, but he makes puppets: I'm a doctor. In my world, boy babies' tails are excised, at birth or soon after; the nonexistent gods only know why. Yours has never been excised, it's vestigial and internal. That's what I first noticed, but then, your entire skeleton is *different*. Not deformed, *different*; organs too. Your cell signature is legible, and obviously functional, but I've never seen anything like it. Maybe I took a mad risk, but I did you no harm and I thought you'd be far away, and never know." Her long smile broke out, uncertainly. "I'm sure you have resources I can't imagine, hidden somewhere in the *sek* where I found you—"

"No, I don't," said Forrest. "No resources, ma'am. I'm a *shipwrecked sailor*."

Her hand went to the pouch at her throat, she stared at him in amazement—

Then a man screamed. A hideous sound: high-pitched, jagged, and brutal. Forrest looked wildly around the empty lab. But Sekρool leapt across the room, and slapped her palm on a touch pad. The wall beside her opened silently. Within the space revealed, a naked man sat strapped to a chair: flushed and dripping sweat, a headset clasping his skull, tools of torture attached to his body. The Chief Scientist stood by, thoughtfully adjusting his instruments.

The naked man was Forrest.

Sekρool went up and stood over the chair. "The Rapt would have been kinder. Esbwe, you are *disgusting*. This was not in the bargain."

"What's *he* doing here?" snarled Esbwe, backing away and glaring at Forrest. "Now we'll have to eliminate the bastard, and *that* wasn't in the bargain."

"I've been living under a madman's heel," said Sekρool, in dawning wonder, taking out her knife. "I did you a cruel injustice once, Esbwe. I can't undo it. But enough is enough."

Esbwe howled in fury. "Don't touch it! It's *mine!*"

A lash of her tail sent him skidding into a wall. The knife plunged, violent and precise, into the hollow of the doll's collarbone. She stared at the wet ruin.

"I don't know why I never realized," she murmured. "I don't have to wait. I can seize power, I can make my own rules, give myself in place of Gemin if I must."

"Don't talk like that," said Forrest. "Sekρool, when I thought you were going to hand me over in person, I was willing. I'm still willing. I'll handle the hostage crisis. I've done the work before. Trust me, I'll bring your son's body home, and I'll be fine—"

"Why would you do that, *man from somewhere else?*"

Forrest, smiling with his eyes, drew her close, and kissed her brow—

But something was happening. Were the palace guards rushing in? No, it was his hands, they were breaking up, vanishing. He felt a shock, strangely familiar, this had happened to him before . . . It was PoTolo's *method*. The sky raft must be over the drop zone.

"Sekρool! Wait for me! I can't stop this, but I'll come back!"

She laid her hand against his heart. "I know."

3. THE BLACK STONE

WHEN THE ORBITS WERE ALIGNED ONCE MORE, JOHN
Forrest returned to West Africa to repeat his stunt for a select
group of scientists. He arrived before the guests and joined Dr.
PoTolo, alone in the lab. Nothing much had changed, in the
room with the big windows looking out to the sunset horizon.
John Forrest, dressed as before in wilderness kit, also seemed
unchanged; except that he was in a better temper.

"That thing," he said, nodding at the oily black globe in its
chamber. "Your time-travel gizmo. Does it have to be held like
that, in the container?"

"No, it just has to be in the room."

"What happens if I touch it? Sudden death? Radiation
sickness?"

"You can *touch* it. I wouldn't advise you to keep it in your
pocket for a week," said PoTolo, a little bolder, a little less
intimidated, this time.

"You're dispatching me to *the exact place and time* where you
picked me up?"

"As requested, I'll be using the complex of space-time values
recorded during the successful retrieval. But you should know,
Mr. Forrest, it isn't that simple."

On the previous occasion Forrest had disappeared at sunset
and reappeared, mysteriously bedraggled, an hour before dawn.
The interval (in local time, West Africa) did not, necessarily,
indicate the length of his stay, or even prove that Forrest had
arrived on the surface, and Forrest was no help. It was puzzling.
But the *proof* that the probe had visited a habitable Ancient Venus
was safely recorded in the data, and it was very, very convincing.

"You still remember nothing?"

Forrest puckered his lower lip and shook his head. "Nothing
at all, alas."

"We'll do better this time. We have a memory-retrieval brain scanner on hand, we'll pluck the images straight from your head before they can vanish."

Forrest smiled politely, thinking of Sekρool, the sorceress.

Her promise, which he was about to put to the test.

The guests assembled. There was some chatter, some flattery. He stood in the gate.

All eyes were on the human element in the apparatus. Nobody noticed that the globe had gone from its place. Hands in his pockets, he looked to the west, where Hawa herself was lost in cloud, but the stars that he would never see again were beginning to shine out.

The world disappeared.

JOE HALDEMAN

Here's a pilot on a desperate rescue mission after a disaster on Venus who soon finds that he might need rescuing himself ... and who makes a discovery that changes everything we know about life.

Born in Oklahoma City, Oklahoma, Joe Haldeman took a B.S. degree in physics and astronomy from the University of Maryland, and did postgraduate work in mathematics and computer science. But his plans for a career in science were cut short by the U.S. Army, which sent him to Vietnam in 1968 as a combat engineer. Seriously wounded in action, Haldeman returned home in 1969 and began to write. He sold his first story to *Galaxy* in 1969, and by 1976 had garnered both the Nebula Award and the Hugo Award for his famous novel *The Forever War,* one of the landmark books of the seventies. He took another Hugo Award in 1977 for his story "Tricentennial," won the Rhysling Award in 1984 for the best science-fiction poem of the year (although usually thought of primarily as a "hard-science" writer, Haldeman is, in fact, also an accomplished poet, and has sold poetry to most of the major professional markets in the genre), and won both the Nebula and the Hugo Award in 1991 for the novella version of "The Hemingway Hoax." His story "None So Blind" won the Hugo Award in 1995. His other books include a mainstream novel, *War Year,* the SF novels *Mindbridge, All My Sins Remembered, There Is No Darkness* (written with his brother, SF writer Jack C. Haldeman II), *Worlds, Worlds Apart, Worlds Enough and Time, Buying Time, The Hemingway Hoax, Tools of the Trade, The Coming,* the mainstream novel *1968, Camouflage* (which won the prestigious James Tiptree, Jr., Award), *Old Twentieth, The Accidental Time Machine, Marsbound,* and *Starbound.* His short work has been gathered in the collections *Infinite Dreams, Dealing in Futures, Vietnam and Other Alien Worlds, None So Blind, A Separate War and Other Stories,* and an omnibus of fiction and nonfiction, *War Stories.* As editor, he has produced the anthologies *Study War No More, Cosmic Laughter, Nebula Award Stories 17,* and, with Martin H. Greenberg, *Future Weapons of War.* His most recent books are a new science-fiction novel, *Earthbound,* a big retrospective collection, *The Best of Joe Haldeman,* and a novel *Work Done for Hire.* Haldeman lives part of the year in Boston, where he teaches writing at the Massachusetts Institute of Technology, and the rest of the year in Florida, where he and his wife, Gay, make their home.

Living Hell

JOE HALDEMAN

MAYBE I SHOULD HAVE STAYED ON MARS.

That's a sentiment repeated so often here on Venus it's right up there with "I should have read the fine print." About a third of the people here first did a stint on Mars, and I guess we thought that Venus had to be better. Wrong as rain.

And Venus is rain.

There are dry periods up by the poles, but we don't go there—no plants. And the equator is wind-driven steam that would flay the flesh from your skeleton. Only girls went there, heavily armored. And robots, and telepresence.

They could employ robots up here in the so-called temperate zone, too, but people are supposedly cheaper in the long run. Made with unskilled labor, as the saying goes, but more or less teachable.

Plus the advantage of unquantifiable factors like imagination and initiative, and the supposition that a team is more than the sum of its parts. Versatility and initiative. You can program a machine to solve a thousand different problems, and you hope it becomes a machine for finding the thousand-and-first.

This team found more than it bargained for.

Humans as individuals are fallible in their own ways, with errors less predictable than those of machines, but the other side of that is being able to see problems that didn't appear to be problems and, once in a great while, solutions that don't appear to be solutions.

We were almost killed by that virtue, back when humans were new here. People call it the Second Wave now, which is a little grandiose and hopeful, since if there was a First Wave, it consisted of only eight people, five of them eventually buried under the planet's muddy soil.

"Buried" is kind of a euphemism, since anything edible is dug up immediately and integrated into the lively Venusian ecology. But cremation's not a real option, not with everything wringing wet, surrounded by hardly enough oxygen to keep a match lit. Did I mention that it's not a garden spot? Though it *is* full of plants.

I wrote into my will that if I die here, they should just put my body outside with a nice ribbon tied around some appendage. Use the ribbon from my Ph.D. diploma, finally giving it a useful purpose.

(On the way to and from Mars I accumulated thirty credit hours and wrote a dissertation on anomalies in heat-transfer models in extreme environments. Like the one I was going to enjoy on the planet of steam 'n' stink.)

The girls who work down toward the equator have to stalk around in heavy plastic armor, but the air in their suits is cool and sweet. I applied for that assignment, but I think was automatically disqualified, not really for being male but for not weighing less than a hundred pounds. They're all tiny and cute, and when you talk to them on the cube, they're not wearing too much.

My friend Gloria, who works down there, lamented that it smells like a women's locker room with no perfume. I imagined that I could handle that, compared to *eau de* rotting greenhouse, but was smart enough not to say anything.

I wouldn't have any reason to go down there, anyhow. You might ask why someone with a physical-science doctorate finds himself with a job collecting biota on an alien planet, but that would prove that you didn't know a lot about the intersection of science and bureaucracy. Half a lifetime ago, I got a bachelor's in environmental engineering because that's where the jobs were, but then went on to aero/astro. So of course when the wheels of the gods ground out this assignment for me, they saw the "EnvEng" and ignored the fact that I did go on to the physics doctorate, and have forgotten more biology than I ever learned.

The transfer orbit we took from Mars to Venus lasted six months, and I did take two biology courses en route. But I also wanted to finish my dissertation before I forgot all my thermophysics. So I absorbed just enough xenobiology to avoid touching plants that would kill me. You don't need any course work to avoid the animals that would.

While I was up in orbit, we got a message from a movie guy asking about doing a Venus-based remake of the classic *Jurassic Park*. Much hilarity ensued. Someone remembered a joke about the difference between a producer in science and one in Hollywood: a producer in science needs decades of education, not to mention intelligence and dedication—so he or she can *produce* something. A producer in Hollywood just needs a phone.

Oh, and no one was ever eaten by a special-effects monster.

In fact, when we studied the macrofauna of Venus, it was with the understanding that for every animal that had a name, there were two or three that hadn't yet made their presence known. Some *very* "macro," and either good at hiding or so macro they wouldn't even notice killing you.

My favorite is the flying carpet, both big and almost invisible underfoot. It looks like a large rug that's contracted a skin disease—which means that it doesn't look that different from most of the ground. You can stroll right over it, and it doesn't move until you're in the middle of its several square meters. Then it tries to roll itself up with you inside. Your warning is an enzyme that smells like rotten apple juice: if you smell that, you have about half a second to jump back the way you came. Because that enzyme ain't apple juice.

The microfauna have had less success in incorporating us into the food chain; except for whatever the crotch-eaters like, our body chemistry isn't compatible. The creatures who eat us get very sick, which seems only fair.

I supposed that they would eventually develop an aversion to us, but Hania, our only actual xenobiologist, says that's not likely. Too many monsters and too few of us for them to eat and throw up. Thus not enough learning opportunities.

She would remind me that *humans* are the monsters here. I'll persist in species chauvinism and call a monster a monster.

I remembered a point that my high-school biology teacher made: a prey animal that's taken by a predator obviously can never communicate the knowledge of having been killed that way to the next generation. But a prey animal that does survive the encounter may communicate the thrill of the chase. Presumably the abstraction "that was close; better not do that again" is too complex for their ungulate brains.

But they do observe and learn. A complex example on Earth was a "tribe" of burrowing creatures, meercats, who would dive into their holes if humans approached carrying guns, but would ignore humans carrying shovels. (That was language behavior as well as perception and discrimination: the meercat who was the lookout had different sounds for armed and unarmed humans.)

There's nothing as innocent as ungulates or meercats here. If there were cute fuzzy little burrowing animals, they would drink blood or give off a poison gas, or both.

The little disaster that led to the current trouble was the local space elevator's falling down. Earth's space elevator is as safe as the one at Macy's, but Earth doesn't have Venusian weather. One cable unraveled, then another, and it's a good thing they'd put the equatorial station to the east of the damned thing, or it might have flattened all the human females on the planet. One of them did die in the storm of whipping cables and metal shreds. Two storage modules were destroyed, one with most of their food, and their shuttle was sliced in two.

They couldn't survive for long on the planet, and they had no way off. So the wisdom of redundancy was made clear: each base had the wherewithal to keep both crews alive for longer than it would take for help to arrive from Earth. Most of those resources were duplicated again up at Midway, the unmanned synchronous satellite that was the nexus for the space elevator.

Midway probably wasn't hurt when the elevator took its little trip. But it was suddenly a very expensive destination in terms of fuel.

My shuttle craft is "bimodal," as an economy measure. It can fly around in the atmosphere of Venus or in the vacuum of outer space. In the miserly atmosphere, it concentrates oxygen from the planet's thin "air" soup as it sputters along, but it's nothing like a terrestrial turbojet. A lot of the energy from the engine goes right back into extracting oxygen. And if I fly too high, the oxygen concentrator seizes up.

The first-person pronoun there is unfortunately accurate. When the storm hit, there was nobody else pilot-certified at the "temperate" base. There wouldn't really be room for a copilot, anyhow, once I picked up the women.

So my trip south was solo, slow, and tense. Most of the time I was flying low over ferocious electrical storms, so the ride was bumpy until I got high enough, and the radio was useless with static.

I did sporadically get through enough to know that the surviving women were safe for now, inside the living module of their shuttle, but of course it wasn't flyable.

We didn't discuss the other dangers. There were thunder lizards big and strong enough to tear through the light metal skin of the ship—it was great for keeping vacuum out and protecting against micrometeoroids, but even I, with merely human strength, could tear a hole into it with a crowbar and tin snips. The biggest lizards were half the size of the ship. If they thought there was something good to eat inside, they wouldn't need to look around for a can opener.

The women had guns, as we did. But they wouldn't have much value, even as noisemakers; the environment was full of dangerous-sounding noises. You can shoot at the native life all day, and it's just target practice. Dumb as rocks. They don't know somebody's shooting at them. If you hit them, they don't even know they're dead.

They did shoot three or four of the beasts when they first landed. All that meat lying around rotting kept the other creatures occupied for a while, and most of them grew cautious enough to stay away from the ship, at least during the day. At night, there would be a lot of feeding and fighting, but during the day the larger meat-eaters mostly slept.

The women were doing fine in their way, and the men in theirs, for about a Venusian year, nine Earth months. And then the Sun decided to misbehave.

It's not as if we hadn't had solar flares before. They screw up everything for a couple of days, but you basically power down and play cards until the storm is over.

This was a superflare, though, the largest one recorded this century. It even shut down communications on Mars, let alone Earth and Venus.

Mercury Station had time to broadcast three words, or two and a half: "LOOK OUT—FLA . . ." It was not a warning for Florida.

Ten hours later, the coronal mass ejection from the flare hit us. Quantum electronics went south. Solid-state circuits became *really* solid, as in fused. Switches welded shut. Radios became paperweights.

The shuttle had been designed with a fallback manual mode that required no electronics. Of course, I'd never used it except in a training simulator.

The ship even had a paper-print manual, which gave off a whiff of mildew when I opened it. I'd studied it well enough to be certified, twenty years ago. And I could read the parts that were English. Most of the math was gibberish to a normal person.

Could I navigate well enough to find the women? Yes and no.

Venus does have a pole star, but you might have to wait a few years for a break in the clouds to align with it.

Or go above the clouds.

There was a manual fuel feed by a forward-facing port, along with an airspeed indicator and a visual fuel gauge. Of course, the gauge only told you how many liters of fuel you had left, not how far you could get on them.

The manual had appendices in the back that told you how much fuel the tub burned per second at full throttle, half throttle, and stall. The calculator bucky-printed on the page was useless without power, but luckily someone had had a sense of humor— there was an old-fashioned slide rule in a wall module like a fire alarm: IN CASE OF EMERGENCY BREAK GLASS. Ha, ha. I used the butt of my pistol to gain access to lower mathematics.

There were several blank pages in the back of the manual, and in a MISC drawer, I found an old pencil with an eraser.

I couldn't make the eraser work; I guess the battery was dead. But with the tables in the back of the manual, and the slide rule, I figured we had twenty-seven minutes of full acceleration, more than enough to get to Midway and refuel for Earth transfer.

Of course, the electronics on Midway would be useless. I could fly to it and dock by the seat of my pants. But could I get inside? Take care of that when we get there, I guess.

The most economical Hohmann transfer would get us to Earth orbit in as little as six months. I packed four and a half crates of freeze-dry in the shuttle, all I had at the one-man base. Buckled up and took off.

I took a suborbital trajectory up high enough to be in space, kind of, and found the south celestial pole in between Ursa Minor and Draco. Oriented the ship to be pointing nose south, and dove back down.

The equatorial station was fortunately at the intersection of an Amazon-sized river and a big brown sea, so I could just follow the sea's coastline down to the river and look around. That would be simple if it were a nice clear day.

Venus never has one.

Buffeted by storm winds, I had my hands full keeping visual contact with the coastline while the ship pitched and yawed through driving rain. Too-frequent lightning glared every few seconds.

I didn't expect to see the space elevator cable, less than a meter thick, until it's close to the base. But you could easily see where it had fallen, a straight brown line of dead vegetation. When the map showed I was near the base, I dropped to treetop level and crawled along dead slow.

They damned near shot me down! A signal flare exploded just off my port wing, and by reflex I slapped the smart-descend. In the absence of electronics, that was not smart. It killed the engine, and I was a very heavy glider for about eight seconds.

I tried for the beach and almost made it. Branches slapped and scraped and did break my fall. I gouged up about thirty meters of sand and came to a stop just before finding out whether the thing would work as a submarine.

Or an anchor.

In fact, I wasn't too badly situated, pointed seaward with the shuttle's nose slightly elevated. I eased the throttle forward a fraction of a millimeter and it did fire up and move me a little nudge. So if I had to, I could get away fast.

In a bin marked SURVIVAL GEAR, I found a web belt with two canteens and a holstered pistol. Filled the canteens and put a full magazine in the pistol. There were ten more full magazines in a cardboard box; I dumped them into a camo knapsack along with some food bars.

There was also a heavy machine gun, too big to lift comfortably with one hand. Overkill, unless I was attacked by an infantry platoon.

The pistol was an old-fashioned powder type, flash and smoke and big boom. Maybe it would startle some monster enough to give it indigestion after it ate my arm.

Actually, as a usually observant vegetarian, I didn't feel good about the prospect of blasting away at innocent animals. But I didn't want to become part of the food chain myself, either.

I hoped I was within a few miles of where the girls had called from. The radio was all white noise and crackle, but I shouted a description of my situation into it anyhow.

They had probably heard the shuttle come screaming in and crash. Would they come toward the sound? I supposed I would, in their situation. Or maybe split into two groups, one staying put and the other going off to search for my smoldering remains. In any case, my most obvious course was to stay put myself, for at least as long as it would take for them to get here.

So of course I went outside. Or, to be fair, I did sit in the semidarkness of the emergency lighting for as long as I could stand it, maybe five minutes.

I drew the heavy pistol and opened the door just wide enough to see outside. Nothing slithered into the ship, so I opened it wide enough to exit and studied the jungle for several minutes. The ripe and rotten smell conquered the shuttle's air-conditioning pretty thoroughly, but there was no sign of life bigger than an insect—though that might mean the size of your foot, on Venus.

It was a short jump to the ground. My boots sank two inches

into the mud. I aimed around for targets of opportunity, a cheerful and optimistic phrase. None appeared, so I pulled the rain hat down tight and made a careful circle around the ship.

It didn't appear to be greatly damaged. The leading edge of its wings had a couple of dents, which would limit reentry speed for atmospheric braking, but once I got off this blasted planet, I didn't really plan on returning. When I got back to Earth, I'd just take the elevator down. Leave this tub in orbit for Solar System Enterprises to sell for salvage.

A snake I hadn't seen reared up to about belt level. I fired reflexively and it flew away. A flying snake? Maybe it was just gliding, technically. Bad enough.

The snake had a face, sort of smiling, and bright yellow antennae, or horns. What a charming planet.

I hadn't hit it, but the noise made my ears ring and the pistol's recoil had smacked my palm like a baseball bat. I wasn't going to be blasting away like some hero in a cowboy movie.

I almost didn't hear the girls' answering shot, surely less than a mile away. I fired again, and listened carefully while I reloaded two fat cartridges. I yelled "Hello?" a couple of times at the top of my lungs.

I went back to the shuttle's stern. The primary blast nozzle was wider than I am tall, so nothing was likely to sneak up behind me. It was still radiating heat and creaking as it cooled, which might also discourage animals.

Unless they thought *That thing is lying still and squeaking helplessly* . . .

A voice I almost recognized shouted hello back to me. "Gloria?"

She came out of the jungle and I stepped toward her and stopped.

She looked like a very accurate cartoon. Sexy short-shorts and a halter top and bare feet. Bare feet? Walking in this jungle?

Her clothes looked painted on and her hair was perfect, solid.

"Gloria?"

She repeated "Hello." But her grinning mouth was full of long yellow spikes. Her muscles bunched to spring, and I fired twice.

One bullet hit her knee, and the leap turned into a sprawl, that covered half the distance. She snarled at me, a hair-raising sound like a sheet being torn, and staggered back into the jungle—changing, as she went, into a creature that looked like a large cat crossed with an armadillo, armored shoulders and back. She left behind a spatter trail of bright blue blood.

The xenobiologists were going to love this. Of course there were Terran animals that used mimicry, but I think in a more timid way, trying not to be eaten. I don't think any of them try to talk.

Getting back inside the shuttle sounded like a really good idea. Not an easy one to accomplish, though, without a ladder. The bottom of the door was almost at eye level, and I had last done gymnastics about thirty years ago. But with the help of healthy fear, I did manage on the second try to swing my right leg up high enough to hook a heel around the corner of the door and scramble up gracelessly, pulling a big muscle on the inside of my thigh.

I limped straight back to the survival-gear bin and hauled out the big machine gun. Four heavy magazines that held fifty rounds each. It was set up to fire bursts of four. So I could tap the trigger fifty times. Or just hose it around until the noise stopped. Reload and hose some more.

Up in the temperate-zone base, they had a noisemaker that made loud random bangs every minute or so, which kept the fauna away from the perimeter pretty well. Should I do that here? It might have the opposite effect, attracting curious flesh-eaters.

I sat there listening to the jungle and trying to access the young and foolish man I had been thirty years ago. Man-eating creatures with big yellow teeth? Hey, just give me a gun.

Now it's sort of "give me a transfer." We grow too soon old, my grandmother used to say, and too late smart.

There was a noise at the edge of the clearing. I raised the weapon and realized that I didn't know what the drop was set for. Aim high or low? Well, I wasn't that good a shot anyhow.

The woman who came out was not half-naked and was not Gloria. She took one look at me and screamed.

I lowered the rifle. "Sorry!" Waved at her. "Get in the ship! There's a wounded animal out there."

Three of them followed her, sprinting across the sand; the others hobbling along as one five-legged limping beast. Gloria was trying to hop on one good leg, supported by two other women. Her leg gave out while I was watching.

I slid down, keeping the rifle pointed at the jungle. "What happened?" Gloria didn't respond.

"Some goddamned thing bit her," another of the women said. Gloria was barely conscious, pale as snow except for the leg, angry red up past the knee, puffy with streaks of black. "Is it gangrene?" the woman whispered. She had a Texas accent and her name patch said LARAMIE.

I shook my head. "I don't know." Gangrene was just a word to me, something that happened to people in old novels. This was probably something worse, something Venusian.

In novels, the choice was always between amputation and death.

"I have a diagnostic suite," I said, "but I'm pretty sure it wasn't designed to survive a crash landing."

"You weren't, either," a tiny woman said, "but here you are. Let's get her up there."

It was a clumsy business, me hauling from above while the two taller women pushed from below. She cried out, then moaned and passed out, her eyes rolling up.

Laramie was tall enough to lever herself aboard the way I had, and together we laid Gloria down gently on the cot that unfolded under the diagnostic machine. She was some sort of medical specialist, a caduceus patch on her blouse. She rapped on the two output screens and they stayed dark, ignoring her authority.

Its ON switch didn't do anything, even though it was properly set in the auxiliary-power position. Well, the lights on the same circuit were dim. Maybe the machine required full power or nothing would happen.

I got a neomorphine pad out of the kit, but the nurse Laramie stopped me from tearing it open. "Better not," the short one said. "She's had more than a double dose already. Doesn't seem to do anything."

They tried to undress her, but the swelling made it impossible. I found some shears in the toolbox that could just barely cut through her suit fabric, which was reinforced by some strong plastic thread.

Taking turns, the three of us managed to cut a ragged line around the leg of her suit just below the crotch, and then snip down from there to the swelling. She woke enough to moan, shaking her head from side to side. I tried to say reassuring things, but she wasn't hearing them.

Her jaws clenched against screaming, she squeezed my hand hard enough to make the knuckles pop.

We snipped down far enough to relieve the local swelling, but that didn't seem to reduce the pain.

"She's fighting something our bodies have no defense against," the medic said. "I don't know . . ."

Gloria cried out, back arched, then her body suddenly relaxed. Her eyes closed and she sagged into stillness.

"Shit," the medic said quietly. She pressed two fingers under Gloria's chin. "She does have a pulse." She rapped the machine again, harder.

I got a multimeter out of the tool kit and checked a couple of connections. Exactly half of the power-cell elements were dead. I unscrewed the top of the battery box and ducked away from the sharp smell of formic acid.

"Here's the problem." I pointed to where the bottom three elements shared a wide crack, which oozed purple solute.

"You can't fix them?" the small woman said.

"Not even in a shop, no," I said. "On Earth, you'd just switch out the ruined elements. Even on Mars." I picked up a dirty shirt and wiped the acid away from the crack with it and stared and thought. "Your own electrical system is out, completely out?"

"I don't know about 'complete.' The ship's dark," the medic said.

"What about this part?" I tapped with the wrench. "The fuel cells?"

"I guess it's pretty much junk," she said. "It's all crushed and . . . and . . ."

"Julie's body's in there," Laramie said. "Stuck there. We couldn't get her out."

"We didn't really try," the short one said. "No chance she survived."

Sounded grim enough. "No chance at all?"

"Head crushed," Laramie said, her voice husky. "And a lot more."

"Could you see the control console? I mean . . . is it possible the power cells are intact?"

They looked at each other and shook their heads. "Couldn't see in," the medic said. "Didn't go too far in."

"She was . . . all over the place," the little one said. "We had the communicator out, and the canteens, and didn't want to go back in if we could help it. We called you guys and they said you'd get here in an hour or so."

In their dreams. But I checked my watch and was surprised to see that only a couple of hours had passed since I took off.

I looked down in the direction they'd come from. "How far is the ship?"

"Maybe ten minutes down the trail," Laramie said.

"It's an actual trail?"

She nodded. "Easy going."

"You didn't cut it?"

"Huh-uh . . . it was just there."

That wasn't good. In the absence of people, it had to be a game trail. The planet had lots of herbivores, harmless enough in themselves. But the animals they were game *for* could be a problem. Probably one's last problem.

I rummaged through the toolbox and selected the biggest screwdriver and some heavy metal shears, the kind that uses a heavy spring to magnify its force. A flashlight. Still one empty pocket in my fatigues. I wished for a grenade.

"What, you're going back there?" the medic said.

"Guess I have to. You see an alternative?"

"I'll come with you," Laramie said. "You don't have eyes in the back of your head."

"I can't—"

"Just give me the damned pistol and let's get going."

No place for chivalry here. I handed it to her and picked up the machine gun with an extra magazine. "You all stay inside here." As if anyone would go out for a stroll without a handy machine gun. I hopped to the ground and jacked a round into the chamber. Scanned the jungle line and gave Laramie a hand down.

"Back the way we came?" she said.

"Might as well." If we tried to beat a new way through the jungle, the noise might draw attention. Though the rain was pounding down pretty hard.

We were about a minute down the trail when we ran into our first fauna. It might have been a big green rock, to a casual observer. But six stubby, scaled legs appeared underneath it, and a large head craned out, bigger than a human head and sporting a bright yellow beak and bulging sky-blue eyes. A black wattle on the sides of the beak, and a crown of unruly black hair. Gills flaring, bright pink.

It hissed and tipped back, reaching out with two front legs—arms—that sported glittering black talons.

I fired once and the bullet spanged off its shell, apparently to no effect. I aimed for the head, but by then it was gone. Moving way too fast, for a turtle-ish thing the size of a small car.

It left behind a smell like burned chocolate.

"Ever see one of those?"

"Not so close," she said in a small voice. "Sometimes we'd see them watching from a distance, smell them. But we never caught one."

"Probably a good thing. It's aquatic?"

"We first saw them in the ocean."

"Wish they'd stay there." The sound of the shot, though, might have chased them away, back to the water. Or they were hiding, lying in wait.

We hustled down the path, swatting at bugs occasionally, but the biggest animals we saw were about cat-sized. Or armadillo-sized; they all had shells. They didn't attack, but they didn't run away, either.

I smelled the wreck before I saw it. A wartime smell no one ever forgets. I swallowed back bile and Laramie bent over and puked.

She coughed a few times. "God. We haven't been gone that long."

The scientist in me followed the same thread. How long does it take for a hundred-some pounds of meat to decompose that much? I knew from a unit in forensic medicine that it should take all day, or more, even in this heat. Even with a body that had been squashed? That would speed things up.

"Probably some Venusian microorganism," she said hoarsely. That made me feel queasy. Whatever it was, I was breathing it. We went around a long curve and found the wreck.

This ship was never going anywhere again. A big tree had crushed it between its reactor and fuel tanks, faint smell of hydrazine on top of the stench.

The ramp up was twisted and it creaked under our weight. We went up slowly, deliberately, not eager to get there.

Julie had been beautiful. Now her face was gone. Every place skin had been exposed was a mass of red and orange cilia, wriggling. Her body smelled of molasses and decay. Laramie edged around it without comment.

The smell was different from my memory of corpses on Earth, when I'd been an unarmed medic in a short war. Burial detail. This was less pungent, perhaps sweeter, perhaps more like mold. Most of mine had been dead for some while, though.

My feet didn't want to move. I couldn't take my eyes off the nightmare. I hadn't known her that well, but we had flirted in a joking way back at Farside a couple of years ago. The mouth I'd kissed good-bye was grey bone now and too-white teeth.

"We don't have all day," Laramie said gently.

There were no lights inside the wreck, but I had a small penlight. Fortunately, the pilot controls were old-style, almost identical to the ones I'd trained on.

I unscrewed the access panel and held my breath when I touched the fuel-cell terminals with the two multimeter probes. Twenty-three volts, plenty.

"Think we're okay." I had to use the shears to free the fuel cell, doing maybe ten thousand credits' damage. Send the bill to fucking Venus.

It weighed less than thirty pounds, clumsy rather than heavy. But I only had one free arm now. "Take this," I said, and traded her the rifle for the pistol. "You better lead."

By the time we inched past, the corpse was totally covered with the colorful worms, writhing more slowly. Nothing human visible. You couldn't even see bones anymore.

The smell was gone.

"Same way?" she asked as we stepped carefully down the ramp.

"Yeah. What happened to the smell?"

"Nothing left to generate decomposition gases, I suppose." She shook her head. "In just a few minutes, Jesus. Fast work."

We had company before we reached the bottom of the ramp. A crawling horror about the size of a man was waiting patiently. A chimera with head and arms but no legs, just a long, tapering body, shiny with bright yellow scales. Three eyes that looked old and wise, over a red mouth dripping saliva. A grin full of sharp teeth. We both fired and missed, and it squirmed away. My second shot hit its tail. It wailed like an oboe with a bad reed, and it rose up to stare back at us malevolently before it ducked under my third shot.

"Get back in the ship?" Laramie said in a quavering voice.

"I don't think so. If we can't raise the ramp or close the door, we're gonna just be dinner, as soon as it gets dark. Have to get back to *my* ship."

We were at the edge of the ramp when something moved in the brush in front of us. "Christ!"

It also looked about man-sized, but then raised itself up on a combination of arms and tentacles. Dark blue and shiny and higher than my head.

I fired and missed; fired again and hit it square. It opened its mouth—bright red tongue and shark teeth—and said "Oh! Oh!" in a loud bass growl.

Laramie was pulling the trigger over and over, to no effect. "Arming lever!" I said. "Cock it!"

"No!" the beast said. "No! Don't cock!" Two spindly arms, like a tyrannosaurus, raised up. My last bullet took an arm off at the elbow.

It howled in pain. "I said No! Don't! Don't shoot. Me."

A pink tentacle wormed out of the arm stump. It turned dark blue, curling, then flexed and became a new arm. "See?"

Laramie lowered her weapon. "Are you . . . talking to us?"

"Yes! Trying! Talk! To talk."

I left my finger on the trigger but didn't pull it. I looked at the beast over the pistol sights. "You can talk?"

"Yes! Not good!" The new arm had completely regrown. The creature studied it from a couple of angles. "Don't do that again! That hurts!" It picked up the severed limb and sniffed it, and then swallowed it in two horrible bites.

"Taste," it said. "A man should taste . . ." It shook its head violently. "A man should share, no." It looked at its new hand. "Pain. Peril. A man should share the passion and action of his time at peril of being." It opened its jaws wide, with a loud cracking sound, then sat back and cleared its throat.

"'A man should share the passion and action of his time, at peril of being judged not to have lived.' Oliver Wendell Holmes, 1884 Old Style. May 30."

"How do you know that?" she asked.

"D-juh, d-joo, Julie. I know what Julie had. Has. In her brain." It nodded slowly. "Had in her brain at the time that she joined me."

"Because you *ate* her?" I said. "Ate her *brain*? Jesus!"

"No, no!" It shook its head violently, spraying tendrils of saliva. "Because . . . 'because' is hard. Itself."

"Riddles," I said, and tightened my grip on the gun.

"Wait," Laramie said. "You mean 'because,' like, *causality*? That's hard?"

"Yes." The beast's gaze swiveled to her. "Causality is not simple. I am her. When Julie died here, she became part of here. Part of Venus. And so part of me. She will always be."

It looked back at me, huge blue eyes. "Everything. Every worm, every microorganism that ever died on Venus is part of Venus, forever. It's different from Earth and Mars, I think." I heard a step behind me, and turned.

It was Julie, my Julie. Naked, whole, unharmed. Next to her,

Gloria. Also naked, leg completely healed.

"Dying is not the same here, darling," Julie said, and shrugged. "Not so permanent."

I fainted dead away.

The science of it is still not clear, to put it mildly. If it even is science.

The Venusian I tried to kill had "sort of" died dozens of times, in the centuries of life it remembered. For a Venusian to actually die, for keeps, it takes something catastrophic, like a fire. Otherwise, it will go through a rejuvenating process like the grisly transformation we had seen starting with Julie's body. "Food for worms" doesn't mean the same thing as on Earth.

There's a lot that doesn't mean the same thing anymore. Astronomy, biology, cosmology, just to start down the alphabet. If a planet can be sentient, what do you redefine? Planets or sentience? It has to be both, and everything.

It's an existential headache, and not just existential.

The main thing Julie suffered was a profound career change, from explorer-scientist to laboratory animal. Or perhaps a new kind of explorer.

As far as researchers have found, all she lost was a portion of long-term memory. She could still do calculus and higher math, but had to relearn the multiplication tables and long division for them to work.

We spent many hours picking up where we had left off, on Farside a few years ago. At first I was helping her to reclaim her memory. Then we started making new memories of our own.

So now I'm living with a woman who is, I suppose, technically not human. That hasn't stopped us from making a couple of copies.

So far they seem to work all right.

STEPHEN LEIGH

In the tense story that follows, a man who lost almost everything on Venus returns to the planet that had nearly cost him his life, and to the woman who had urged him on to destruction, to give them both another shot at finishing the job . . .

Stephen Leigh is the author of the *Neweden* series, which consists of *Slow Fall to Dawn, Dance of the Hag,* and *A Quiet of Stone.* He's also the author of the *Mictlan* series, consisting of *Dark Water's Embrace* and *Speaking Stones,* and has contributed six novels to the *Ray Bradbury Presents* series, some with John L. Miller, including *Dinosaur World, Dinosaur Planet, Dinosaur Warriors,* and *Dinosaur Conquest.* His stand-alone novels include *The Bones of God, The Crystal Memory, The Woods,* and *The Abraxas Marvel Circus;* he has also contributed to the *Wild Cards* series and the *Isaac Asimov's Robot City* series, and has written as S. L. Farrell and Matthew Farrell. His short stories have been collected in *A Rain of Pebbles* and *A Tapestry of Twelve Tales.* His most recent novel is *Assassins' Dawn,* a book in the *Neweden* series. Leigh lives with his family in Cincinnati, Ohio.

Bones of Air, Bones of Stone

STEPHEN LEIGH

TAKE A SMALL ROCK, TOSS IT INTO A ROTATING cylinder, and pour in abrasives. Tumble the mess for several days, while the grit gnaws at the hard edges and scrubs the rounding surfaces. What eventually emerges from the harsh chrysalis of the tumbler is rock subdued and transformed, shimmering and polished like molten glass, all the hidden colors and veins revealed . . .

Somewhere in my early teens, my parents gave me a rock-polishing kit. I went pretty quickly through the provided assortment of pebbles, pleased with what came from my growling, slow cylinder but bored with the tedious, long hours needed for the result. Like most kids that age, I preferred instant gratification. I would almost certainly have set the polishing kit aside like every other hobby of the month I'd owned, except that my grandmother, Evako, came up to my room one evening not long after.

"Here, Tomio," she said, handing me a drab, ordinary piece of dark rock. "Run this through your noisy machine for me."

"Sure," I said—we were all used to the brusque demands of the Norkohn Shuttles matriarch, just as she was used to obedience. I tossed the rock up and down in my hand. It was nothing I'd have chosen: a chunk of undistinguished granite. "Why don't you get some opal from the gardener, Obaasan," I suggested, not wanting her to be disappointed with what I was certain would be mediocre results. "It'd look a lot better."

She sniffed, taking the rock back from me and holding it in her fingers. I remember that her fingers were thin and wrinkled already, with knuckles swollen and large with arthritis that would only worsen as the years went on. "Obviously you don't know what this is," she told me.

"It's granite," I told her. "And it's about as common as dirt."

She shook her head at me. "This is Akiko. *My* obaasan."

I could feel my brow wrinkling. "I don't understand, Obaasan."

"So I see." Obaasan Evako sighed and sat on my bed, twirling the rock in the afternoon sun coming through the window. "Akiko had a wonderful garden in our villa in Chincha Alta. I grew up there, and that's where I always came back to visit her. On my last visit, just before she died, I took this stone from the garden—not an important stone, not any different from a thousand others there. Yet . . . every time I look at it, I can see Akiko again, and that garden. As long as the rock lasts, so will that image in my mind." She had been speaking more to the sunlight and the rock than to me; now she turned and fixed her gaze on me, as sharp as the flaked edges of the rock. "How can this rock be less than beautiful, with the truth and memories it holds?"

She didn't say anything else, just placed the pebble on the cover of the bed and left the room, knowing that I'd do what she asked. And, of course, I did. It took several days to give the rock the right sheen, to take all the edges from it. When I finally took it from the tumbler, a pointillistic swirl of colors rolled in the palm of my hand and I found myself turning it over and over, marveling at the complex play of hue and shade.

Obaasan Evako, when I gave it to her, nearly smiled. "Now it looks more like her than ever," she said. "Now I can see the true beauty of her that was hidden in the stone."

Ever since then, for many years, I would take common pebbles from places that were important to me at the time and try to uncover whatever gift they held. Many times the results were disappointing, an utter waste of time. But a few of them I've kept with me, wherever I've gone:

—a pale pink crystal shot with fractures that comes from the garden of the Norkohn estate on Cape Hinomisaki near Izumo—a piece of home that pulls Nippon and especially Shimane Prefecture up from its resting place in my mind . . .

—a thick needle of dark gray granite from the hills of New Hampshire, where I went to university, the subtle, rich satin of its surface never failing to conjure autumn on the east coast of North America . . .

—a nearly round ball packed with fine, crazed white lines from Tycho Crater on the moon: my first trip offworld, the quick panic of stepping outside unprotected from vacuum except by my space suit, the euphoria of bounding in one-quarter gravity across dusty plains . . .

—a red-orange marble with streaks of rich brown: I plucked that from Olympus Mons on Mars during my ascent with Avariel. I thought then that I'd met the one true love of my life with her . . .

—an ebony, glassy spheroid speckled with blue-black highlights: the beach at Blackstone Bay. That stone was also Avariel.

That stone was Venus.

I'd not expected to be back on Venus ever again. I thought that all I would ever retain of Venus and Avariel was that fragment of polished lava.

The single, precipitous main street of Port Blackstone was raucous and loud, and more crowded than I remembered. There were even a few shreeliala on the streets, too, something that when I was last here—a decade and a half ago—wasn't common. Back then, if you saw shreeliala—the sentient Venusian race who lived under the waves of the Always Sea, the endless and shallow ocean that covers their world—it was either down at Undersea Port or if you were out on the Always Sea. I could smell their cinnamon-laden exhalations as I passed them, sucking in seawater from the bubblers strapped between the double line of fins down their backs.

The buildings I passed on the way, clinging like limpets to the steep side of the volcanic island that was the single landmass on Venus, seemed weary and exhausted. The fresh paint that had been smeared on them seemed like the too-thick makeup on an ancient whore, enhancing rather than hiding age.

The smell was the same, though. The winds that smeared the low ranks of the clouds over Port Blackstone smelled of the Always Sea: an odor of sulfurous brine, a stench of rotting vegetation; the cinnamon of the shreeliala. The air was as thick as I remembered its being, heavily oxygenated and laden with moisture. There was no sun; there was never a sun during Venus's day, only the smeared, unfocused light that the clouds allowed through.

And the rain . . .

If the Eskimos have a hundred words for snow, the humans who live on Venus have nearly as many words for the types of rain that the eternal clouds spew down on them. It was raining now, as it usually did—what the locals called a *sheeter*: a needlelike, wind-driven spray that was part rain and part foam ripped from the ocean waves. The sheeter hissed and fumed against my rainshield as it pummeled the buildings on either side of me. Lightning shimmered blue-white through the clouds overhead, sending brief, racing shadows across the street; the thunder followed a half second later, crackling and loud enough to rattle the windows in the nearest buildings.

I walked down Blackstone's lone, rain-slick street from the flat plateau, where the supply shuttles landed on the shoulder of the volcano, toward the port proper, my luggage rolling along behind me on its autocart. At the far end of the street, amongst the piers and jetties and the eternal wave-spray, the street finally plunged under the long, racing swells: Undersea Port, where the human world met that of the shreeliala.

Maybe it was the relentless and grim dimness of the day, maybe it was my expectations, maybe it was the oppressive heat—have I mentioned the heat yet?—but Venus and Blackstone seemed less than enthusiastic in welcoming me back from Earth after over a decade. A group of youths, dressed in thin laborer's clothing, ran by me in the rain, shouting half-heard words in their thick Venusian accents that might have been curses; shopkeepers leaned in the doorways of their businesses, staring at me like the intruder I was.

I knew why they stared . . .

It's not often that you see a person with field prostheses, especially not in an age where limbs can usually ("usually" . . . such a comforting word unless it doesn't apply to you) be regrown. The emptiness between my hips and shoes were twin-shaped fields, the controls implanted along my spine. The shoes—the far end of the field—moved as if attached to bone, sinew, and flesh, which showed my years of practice. In the correct light, you can see the heat-waver of the fields; an imaginative person can sense the flexings and almost glimpse the transparent legs.

Almost.

I would wear long trousers and have it appear that my body is whole, albeit somewhat stiff, but why play that charade? Obaasan Evako always scolded us for telling unvoiced lies, for pretending to be something we weren't. Besides, no one wears much clothing on Venus: it's too damned hot and too damned wet for that. So instead, I wore shorts which just covered the stumps of my thighs, which means that I looked like the torso of a dismembered body floating ghostlike a meter above the ground. I wondered how many of those here would think back fifteen years and remember my face from the newscasts of the time. Probably none of them looked at my face at all.

Fifteen years ago, I'd left my legs behind on Venus. I'd left behind a lot more, as well. I ran fingertips over the cool, smooth surface of the stones in my pocket, and when I found a familiar shape, I pulled it out. The stone, polished and about as big as the tip of my little finger, was satin black and glassy, flecked with a blue that was almost black itself. I turned it in my fingers, looking at all the familiar swirls of its polished surface, then shoved it back in my pocket.

My last stop had been the Blackstone Library and the data terminals there. Avariel was here, somewhere. When the Green Council announced that Blackstone would be reopened to offworld traffic, I'd known she would come here. I'd been afraid she would. Now I'd seen the permits from the Green Council, and I knew what she was planning to do.

And that scared me . . .

The night was strained with some invisible tension, and those outside glanced up at the eternal clouds of the planet as if they might see some doom about to descend on them. I'd probably find my own, I was certain, before too much longer. I left the streets gladly.

As I entered the hostel's lobby, the owner opened one eye and blinked at me from behind the desk. From the shifting blur of color in his left eye and a haze of tinny sound around him, I knew he was watching something on his implant. He'd also "gone native"—those who had decided to make Venus their permanent home often had surgical modification, and I could see the healing tracks of gill covers along the proprietor's neck.

He snarled something in my direction.

"What was that?" I asked.

"Oh yeah, spread those legs, you bitch . . ."

Not having legs, I assumed that wasn't directed to me and waited as he grumbled to his feet. His grimy fingers (new webbing set between them) scrabbled on the grimier plastic of the registration desk. "You need a room?" he mumbled, only slightly louder this time. He reached below the counter, then slapped down a registration pad. His hand stayed on it, fingers splayed so that the speckled webbing was prominent. "Usually, we're closed by now," he stated. "I stayed up past my usual time 'cause I knew there was a passenger on the shuttle."

His right eye stared, vague shapes moved in his left. A chorus of insects moaned around him. "Nice of you to do that," I ventured.

"I'm missing the best part of my favorite show now." A forefinger tapped the pad.

I fumbled in my pocket—the one without stones—and fished out the coins I found there. I placed them alongside the pad. His hand spider-crawled over to the money, and I put my hand on the pad. It beeped and chirped. "Room's just down the hall," the hostel owner said.

I nodded to the owner; his duty accomplished and tip secured, he was already lost in his entertainment; he didn't even notice my lack of legs. His eyes were closed, his lips moved with the verse of some unheard song.

I went down the hall to my room.

I stayed long enough to unpack a few things, then hobbled out of the hostel toward the lone Blackstone tavern, fumbling with anxious fingers at the five or six polished stones in my pocket. Fifteen years ago, the establishment had been called "By The Sea," and Avariel and I had eaten and gotten drunk there a few times before we left the port. The sign outside the establishment proclaimed that it was now "Venus Genetrix"—Mother Venus. I doubted that anyone here either knew or cared. I was just glad to leave the wet, steep streets and the suspicious stares for the bar.

"Fuck, look at *that*," someone said as I entered, in an inebriated stage whisper. Half the patrons of the tavern glanced around at me with that, and in the blur of faces, I saw her. In an alcove to the back, she sat in the dim light. Seeing Avariel reminded me of too many things. I wanted to hide. I wanted to run.

Running is one thing I'm no longer capable of; walking's the best I can manage.

Instead, I smiled, rattled the stones in my pocket, and walked toward their alcove.

Next to her was a shreeliala, the tubes of a bubbler wrapped around its purple-and-green neck over the gill slits, its long, webbed fingers lifted as if it were in midspeech with Avariel though its mouth was closed, and it, too, was looking my way. Its huge eyes blinked once: the transparent underlids sliding sideways, the translucent overlids sliding up from their pouch under the eyes. The shreeliala had the slash of an overseer tattooed on the lilac scales of the crown of its head; beneath it was the emerald dot that said that it was a member of the Council. There was another mark, too: a short, yellow-white bar, bulging slightly at either end: this shreeliala possessed "bones-of-air"—a mutation that caused some shreeliala to have lightweight, air-pocketed bones, which meant it could never sink into the Great Darkness to rest with its own kind, the normal shreeliala with what they call "bones-of-stone." Instead, this shreeliala would be burned here on the island when it died, in the caldera at the summit of Blackstone—the place the shreeliala call the Pit.

Avariel watched my approach with a careful almost-smile on her face; the Venusian watched as well, but I knew that attempting to read any human emotion into that face would be a mistake. "Avariel," I said when I reached their table. "I thought I might find you here."

She looked . . . older. Somehow, I hadn't expected that. There were severe lines around her eyes and at the corners of her mouth that hadn't been there before, and creases around her neck. Gray had settled in the dark brown hair of her temples. Her arms were covered with white patches of scars, some of them new. But she was still muscular and fit. Still the athlete, ready to conquer any physical task to which she set herself.

Her smile flickered. Settled. "Tomio," she answered flatly. The shreeliala's huge eyes swiveled in their sockets as it looked from her to me. Bubbles thrashed their way through the clear plastic pipes connecting its gill bubbler to the tank on its back. "I have to admit that I didn't expect to see you here."

"Really?" I answered, returning her meaningless smile. "After the Green Council's decision? I thought you'd *expect* me to come here—if only because I knew *you'd* be the first one here."

"Tomio . . ." A sigh. Her fingertips tapped an aimless rhythm on the tabletop near her ale. "There's no going back to what we were. I'm sorry. You really shouldn't have come here."

I raised my hand. "Uh-uh," I said. "Our relationship isn't at issue. You know, despite everything, I would have come if you'd asked, if you'd stayed in touch after . . ." I gestured at the empty space below the stumps of my legs and the floor.

"Don't lay that guilt at my door, Tomio," she said. "I won't accept it."

The shreeliala seemed to hiss, spraying a fine mist of water from its mouth; it adjusted the bubbler. The salty droplets pooled on the varnish of the table; we all looked at it. "The humans know one another?" *Heh hoomanths noah won hunover?* It had been a long time since I'd heard the shreeliala accent; I had to replay the comment in my head before I understood what it had said, by which time Avariel had already answered.

"Tomia was here with me the last time, Hasalalo," she said. "We went down into the Great Darkness together." The shreeliala nodded. *The last time . . . The water going from green to blue to black. I'd thought it would be easy. I thought we'd just swim down and down until we reached the bottom . . .*

Avariel's comment was all that was needed; Hasalalo seemed to know immediately what she referred to, even if for the short-lived shreeliala the events of fifteen Earth years ago were a generation removed. Hasalalo, who looked to be in his prime years, probably hadn't been alive then, or was just a newly sprouted bud.

"Will it . . . ?" Hasalalo stumbled over the pronoun, and spat water again. "I mean, *he* be going with you this time?"

"No," Avariel answered. Her gaze was on me, and the smile had seemingly vanished. "He won't. In fact, he shouldn't be here now."

She started to get up; I reached out and found her arm.

"Avariel, I'm sorry. Really. Please, don't go." In the dim light, her eyes were bright with reflections. "The Great Darkness took my legs," I said. "I think that's all the motivation I need. Avariel, you knew you were coming back as soon as the Green Council would allow it, but you weren't sure that I would. I wasn't the one who left the relationship as soon as possible after I was hurt." I saw a trail of moisture on her face, and I suddenly hated myself. "I'm sorry," I said. "That was unfair."

"No," she answered, very softly. "I don't think that was unfair at all."

"Then we could still do this together?" Optimism rose like a bird . . .

"No." . . . and plummeted stricken back to the floor. "But I understand why you had to ask."

Neither of us said anything for long seconds after that. Avariel sighed and reached down below her chair, pulling up a backpack. She put the straps around her shoulders and cinched the left side tightly, muscles knotting along her jaw. "Getting to the bottom of the Great Darkness was the only time I failed at something I tried," she answered finally. "That's why I'm here." Avariel adjusted the other strap and got to her feet, hefting the pack. "People sometimes need something so badly that they'd sacrifice nearly anything to attain it," she said. "I wouldn't want to be any other way. Not for me."

I thought it was you, I wanted to tell her. I thought it was you that I needed like that. Now, I just don't know, and I thought if I saw you again, I might find out. "I understand," was all I said.

"I hope you do," she said, slinging the pack over her shoulder, then her voice and her face softened. "I never wanted to hurt you, Tomio—I hope you can believe that, at least. I'm sorry I wasn't the type of person who could share her life with you, and maybe that was more my fault than yours."

I shrugged back at her. "If you had been that person, I probably wouldn't have wanted you so much," I told her.

She lifted her chin at that, then her gaze slid over to Hasalalo. "Make the arrangements, Hasalalo," she told the Venusian. "I'll come to you tomorrow with the final part of the fee, and we'll do this."

"Yes, Avariel." Yessh ... With a hiss and a lisp. The liquid affirmation came wafting over the table laden with the odor of cinnamon. Avariel nodded once before turning and leaving.

After Avariel had gone, I looked at Hasalalo; it looked at me. "So you were the other human who descended with her," it said, halfway between question and statement. "You were the reason she never reached the bottom of the Great Darkness, and saw the ancestor-bones or the Lights-in-Water."

"Yeah," I told it. "It was my fault." The words tasted far more bitter than I intended, and I tried to temper them with a smile that I wasn't sure the shreeliala would understand. It only nodded.

"I'll never see the Great Darkness or the Lights-In-Water either," it said, and it touched the pale bar tattooed on its head. Its gill bubbler hissed; it sounded like a sigh.

I didn't quite know what to say to that. I knew from my time on Venus that when a shreeliala dies anywhere on this world, no matter how far away the colony might be, its body is carried out to the Great Darkness—a deep canyon just off the shore of Blackstone Mountain—with great ceremony by a group of shreeliala dedicated to that task: "priests" might be the best term, but given that the shreeliala don't have organized religions in the sense that we think of them, it's also a very *wrong* term. (Hell, I wasn't entirely certain how the shreeliala even reproduced, though I'm certain some of the scientists stationed here could have told me.) The body is released over the Great Darkness with a prayer—or maybe it's just a ritual statement—and, shreeliala bodies with bones-of-stone being heavier than water, the dead one drifts steadily down through the blackness of the waters into the depths toward . . .

. . . well, toward whatever's at the bottom, which no human has ever seen. We know what the Great Darkness is: once a long, vertical hollow in the volcanic rock, perhaps a lava tube reaching up from the plumes far, far below. But the thin roof of the vertical cavern collapsed under the corrosion and weight of the water above it, leaving the Great Darkness. Beyond that, the shreeliala are closemouthed about it, and they refuse to allow any of our cameras or robotic instruments to accompany any of the bodies on its journey: as sentient beings, we have to respect that, and we have. To them, it's a sacred place, and not to be violated.

But they did, once, allow Avariel and myself to undertake the journey, on our own. And we failed. Or, rather, I failed and therefore Avariel also failed.

I saw a flash, or thought I did, and something like an undersea wave pummeled me and I hit the side of the canyon. Rocks began to fall, and I shouted for Avariel, but then I felt the crushing pain, and ... When I awoke again, I was back in Blackstone, in the hospital. Or, at least, half of me was ...

I must have spent too long in reverie, because Hasalalo's bubbler hissed again as it spoke. "You and Avariel were ... *lovers?* That's not a relationship we can understand."

"Neither can we, most of the time," I told it.

Hasalalo burbled more to itself, its large eyes blinking and its hands spreading so that I could see the translucent, speckled webbing between the long fingers. The skin glistened with the gel the shreeliala use to retain moisture when they're on land. "Why did you want to see the Great Darkness and the Lights-in-Water?" it asked. "Before."

"I didn't, particularly."

Hasalalo blinked. It seemed to be thinking through the English. "It ... If ... How ..." It stopped. Breathed. "Then why?" it asked.

"Avariel wanted it. And I wanted Avariel."

Hasalalo shivered. I seemed to remember that was the Venusian equivalent of a human shrug. "That is the explanation?"

I grinned at the shreeliala. "It's all I got," I told it. "Maybe my grandmother could explain it better for you—if you ever meet her."

The memories flooded back with that.

The affair was more or less in honor of Avariel. I say "more or less" because back then Obaasan Evako arranged gatherings every month or so whether there was an excuse or not. Avariel had just completed the ascent of the previously unconquered eastern cliffs of Olympus Mons on Mars, an expedition sponsored by the family company Norkohn Shuttles—our PR department was already churning out ads trumpeting our involvement. I'd been on the support team, my own climb confined to a leisurely ascent of the lower lava flows. I had shivered a lot in the shelter of Base One while Avariel and her support team of genuine climbers went on; they'd go to Base Two, and Avariel would finish the climb solo—as she always did.

She and I were lovers already; I'd wondered about that at first, suspicious that the primary reason she'd come to my bed was because I'd been the one who had talked Obaasan Evako into parting with the grant for the climb. Still, we were good lovers, comfortable with each other. We were friends. I was well on the way to considering making the relationship more permanent, in love with the idea of being in love.

Mobile fabrics were the fashion that season. Most of the people wearing them shouldn't have been, though I thought Avariel looked fine. Her blouse, restless, crawled slowly over her shoulders. I'd be talking to her, but my gaze would be snagged by her neckline slipping suggestively lower: that was a good time for voyeurs.

The evening was turning cool and I was getting tired of smiling at people I really didn't like that well. I found Avariel in the garden and detached her from the gaggle of admirers around her. The hoverlamps had just turned themselves on, flickering like huge fireflies around the lawn while Mount Fuji turned golden on the horizon. Touching her arm, I inclined my head to the blaze of lights that was the house. "Let's go inside. I've a few people you should meet."

She nodded and made polite noises to her crowd, but when we were away from them, she sighed. "Thanks. I've been trying to lose them for the last half an hour. I have to say that sometimes I miss being all alone up on Olympus Mons. Shame on you, Tomio, for leaving me to those wolves."

"Part of the bane of being the host."

The party was noisier and brighter and more crowded inside: lots of glitter, meaningless laughter, and full glasses. As we stood watching in the doorway, Obaasan Evako waved to us from where the caterers were setting the buffet. "Tomio!" she called loudly. "You've been hiding the guest of honor from me all evening. I refuse to be neglected any longer. Bring her here."

An imperious gesture accompanied the command. Those nearby tittered and smiled before turning back to their drinks.

I grinned. Avariel, glancing from me to my grandmother, smiled uncertainly in my direction. Obaasan could be intimidating to those who didn't know her; I could feel Avariel's fingers digging into the skin of my arm. Obaasan Evako was a small, thin woman; half Japanese and half northern European, with short, white hair, and a well-wrinkled face. She exuded energy and purpose, carrying a habitual frown on her lips. To those she wanted to leave with the impression, she was hard, brittle ice; most of the family knew better. "Don't worry," I whispered to Avariel. "She's really a lamb."

Avariel's glance told me that she didn't believe me. We made our way over to my grandmother, who stood waiting, one foot tapping the carpet. "Counteffia no Regentia Norkohn," Avariel said, using Obaasan's full title from the Asian Liánméng, and bowing as proper etiquette required.

Obaasan looked Avariel up and down as if she were a piece of furniture. Then she glanced at me. She spoke in Mandarin, not Japanese or English. "I'm surprised at you, Tomio. She's not your type. When you talked about this Olympus Mons business, I expected to see one of the usual pieces of pretty fluff you drag down here."

"I'm not fluff, Counteffia"—that from Avariel, who had straightened and now looked more irritated than flustered—"I can talk and I even understand what people say about me," she answered in heavily accented Mandarin.

That snapped Obaasan's head around. She stared at Avariel with line-trapped eyes, then nodded. "Good. See that you manage to stay unfluffy. It's too damn easy to become comfortable. By the way, I assume you realize that your outfit doesn't flatter you at all. Stay away from fashions unless they enhance your image. I'd use simpler and more classic clothing with that body."

Avariel blinked. "Counteffia—" she began, but Obaasan cut her off with a wave of a thin hand. "Call me Evako. Anybody who can make Tomio behave sensibly deserves the courtesy of familiarity—he's been paying more attention to the business lately, if only because I told him that he needed to pay back the sponsorship of your climb."

"I want to thank you for that."

"It was a waste of money."

Another blink. "I'm sorry you feel that way . . ."

"Let me finish, child. It was a waste of money unless it's finally taught Tomio what can be accomplished when you want something badly enough. He's had everything too easily, and it's ruined him. I told his parents it would."

Avariel glanced back at me and saw that I was still grinning. She managed to look puzzled and faltered into a defense. "Tomio was a great help to me. Without him—"

"*Bah!*" With another wave of her hand. "Without him, you'd still have managed the climb, one way or another. You'd have found some other funding. Don't delude yourself on that. Having Norkohn's backing was convenient, but the loss of it wouldn't have stopped you." Then she gave her the briefest of smiles; it smoothed her face. "Gods, child, if you don't allow us elders our bluntness, how am I ever going to convince the idiots around here that I'm not someone they can walk over?"

"I . . . don't think that's anything you need to worry about."

"Oh, you'd be wrong. You'll need to do the same. Let me tell you another truth. What you do is ultimately meaningless. You climb a thing or attempt things so that you'll be the first one to accomplish it, so you'll get to engrave your name in the record books. But that's emptiness. You also climbed Rheasilvia's central peak on Vesta, four years ago, and two years ago were the first person to take a submersible down through Europa's ice pack to the liquid ocean below. But beyond that, do you *know* either Europa or Vesta? You climbed Olympus Mons, yes, but do you *know* Mars as a result? No—you made your climb and you left. You've no *relationship* with the places you've gone. Just like you have no real relationship with my Tomio."

It was my turn to protest at that. "Obaasan," I began, but she lifted her hand toward me without taking her gaze from Avariel. "I can tell that you'd be pretty if you wanted to make the effort," Obaasan said to her. "You're neither beautiful nor stunning, mind you, and I'm sorry if that bothers you, but you really don't want false flattery. Still, you'd be easily as attractive as most of the people here tonight if you'd taken the hours they did to get ready. Yet you didn't bother: very little cosmetics, no gloss, no fakery except that mistake of a blouse, which you probably chose because you thought it was expected. All that's good. You look like someone out of the ordinary the way you are, while if you tried for looks, you'd just be one within the multitude. Well, I'm like that, also. I act just differently enough that no one makes the mistake of treating me like all the people I'd resemble otherwise. It's a good trick. Keep it. Teach it to Tomio, too, while you're about it. He'll try to learn if only because he's in love with you."

"Obaasan—" I tried again, and this time I got a glance.

"Oh, she already knows it, Tomio. She's too smart not to

have seen it, and you're just damned lucky that she's not taken more advantage of your vulnerability. You should try to keep her, if you can, but it'll take some doing. I don't know if either of you are up to the task. You're another little cliff she needed to scale, and though I love you, Tomio, you're still trying to figure out what it is you want in life."

Obaasan Evako gave a little start then, her mouth twisting back into a frown. "I've forgotten to check with the caterer about the wine. He'll try putting it on ice again, and it should be served chilled, not cold. I want to talk to you later, Avariel; you can tell me how Norkohn's going to get its money's worth from this Venus expedition. Tomio, play host while I convince the caterer that it's his decision to serve food the proper way."

With that, she left us, moving away with her quick, unstoppable stride, already calling out loudly for the head caterer. Avariel laughed once, more in relief than anything else. "Good God. You might have warned me," she said, staring at Obaasan's wake.

"Hey, she likes you."

"What does she do when she hates someone?" I saw her face scrunch into a scowl. "She doesn't know me as well as she thinks she does."

"You'd be surprised at what she probably knows."

"Uh-huh." Avariel glanced toward the bar and the restless tide of people around it. I couldn't tell if she believed me or not. "After that, I think I need a drink," she said.

I waved the bartender over to our table as thunder from outside rattled the windows and Hasalalo burbled in its gill bubbler. "What do you have that passes for Scotch?" I asked her. She was another adapted human native: even though her skin was brown, there was still a sense of pallor to her that only came with the eternal lack of sunlight here; her eyes had been surgically altered, the iris and pupil widened and a protective underlid added much like that of the shreeliala. There was webbing between her long, extended fingers also, and the twin lines of gills were on her neck, with long, scarlet fronds that said they'd been there a long time.

"If you want genuine, it's expensive," she told me. "If you'll take the local variety, it's cheap enough."

"Expensive," I told her. "I've had the local."

She sniffed and glanced at Hasalalo. "Hasalalo?" she asked—which told me that she knew it fairly well. Hasalalo didn't reply immediately, and I prodded its arm.

"Nothing?" I asked the shreeliala. "I'm buying. Or rather, my pension fund is buying." Hasalalo shook its head, and the bartender left. "You're sure?" I asked it. "I know you shreeliala don't care for our particular poisons, but I knew a few of you who could slam back sugar water like crazy."

It ignored what I said entirely. Staring at me, it said, "You didn't care if you saw the Lights-in-Water or the bones at the bottom of the Great Darkness? That's what I want, more than anything. That's why I pushed the Green Council to let Avariel come back. She said she would tell me what she saw in the Great Darkness, what my body will never experience with bones-of-air."

"Bones-of-air," I mused. "That's all I have, now."

I meant it as a joke. Hasalalo's hissing was louder this time, more emphatic, and its voice had a timbre I'd rarely heard in shreeliala before. "I thought you would understand," it said, though I wasn't sure if that was agreement, sarcasm, or denial. "Have you seen the Pit, where those of us with bones-of-air go?"

I hadn't, though sitting with Hasalalo, I wondered why. I knew about the Pit, the cauldron at the top of Blackstone Mountain, but Avariel had only glanced at the Blackstone's paltry heights—no challenge to someone with her athletic ability—

and shrugged. She'd had no interest in a walk to the heights, only in her descent to where no human had gone before, so therefore *I* had expressed no interest either. But that seemed too much to explain to Hasalalo, so I only shook my head.

It burbled some more, and, pushing away its chair, rose to its feet: twin scaled, long flippers with webbing extending down between the legs past the knobs of knees, far more suited to water than to land. On the land, shreeliala waddled rather than walked. "Come," it said, and gestured. I rose from my own seat.

"It's a long walk to the Pit," I told it, "and on the steep side." I gestured at the space where my legs should have been. "Do you think . . . ?"

It stared at me with huge eyes that blinked wetly. From the tank on its back, a nozzle hissed and sprayed thick, gelid water over the shreeliala. "Come," it said again. The command in its voice reminded me of the way Obaasan Evako spoke.

I came, calling to the bartender that I'd be back for that Scotch later. She grimaced, clearly annoyed, though whether it was with me or Hasalalo or both of us, I couldn't tell. She shook her head as we left.

I shouldn't have worried about the walk. As we left the bar, an open-topped scooter hurried quickly over through the rain from somewhere farther down the street, driven by another shreeliala, illuminated by flashes of lightning and accompanied by thunder. Hasalalo entered the small cab behind the driver, then gestured to me. "Come," it said again. As I slid into the seat alongside it, Hasalalo leaned forward and said something to the driver in English: the shreeliala never spoke anything but English while on land. The driver nodded; the scooter whined and complained as it made its way away from the harbor. We moved back up Blackstone's single road toward the plateau on which the port sat, and beyond it—now along an unpaved, potholed trail—toward the caldera that sat near Blackstone's summit. The hot spot in the crust that had created both Blackstone and the Great Darkness had moved on millennia ago and was undoubtedly building up a new island somewhere to the northwest. Once, this place would have been a steaming, hissing hell where the eternal rain hammered at sputtering lava flows. No more; the volcano of Blackstone was long dormant and cold. The driver stopped near the rim of the crumbling crater, and we got out into a driving rain, with lightning crackling around us. I'd thumbed on my rainshield as soon as we'd left the bar; Hasalalo seemed to relish the wetness.

Here, on the highest mountain that Venus had to offer, modest as it was, I could look out at the unbroken sweep of the Always Sea—at least to what the storm allowed me to see. I thought that, out past Blackstone Bay, where the long ocean swells started, I could glimpse a darker green-blue against the lighter gray-green: the Great Darkness.

I could smell the caldera long before I could see it. We made our way slowly over the broken, eroded volcanic rock to where we could look down, and I wished that the rainshield could keep out odors as well as rain.

The caldera stank of rotting flesh. Shreeliala bodies, in various stages of decomposition, were scattered down the sides of the caldera in front of us, some of them half-draped over the slope just in front of us, as if they'd been tossed aside like so much unwanted trash. The floor of the crater was littered with their bones, flashing white in the erratic lightning flashes. Wrigglers—the blue-green, maggotlike worms that were one of Venus's few land creatures—fed on the decaying matter. I gagged at the smell of rotting flesh and had to fight to keep my last meal in my stomach.

Hasalalo was staring down with me, though I couldn't read the expression on its face to see if it matched the horror on mine. I looked more closely at the closest skeletons to us. Nested in the bones, I saw small clusters of rounded pebbles, rocks unlike any of the volcanic variety on Blackstone. Little groups of them were plentiful, almost as plentiful as the bones. I crouched down to look more closely: the stones were smoothed on their ridges though the rest of the rock was rough, as if they'd already been in a tumbler for a few hours. I glanced at Hasalalo and pointed to the nearest pile: four or five of the stones caged under the curve of a shreeliala's ribs. "May I . . . ?" I asked Hasalalo, who gave me an almost perfect human shrug. I hoped it meant the same thing and reached down for one of the stones, carefully trying to avoid touching the bones that enclosed it. I managed to fish one out between two fingers and stood up, looking at it closely. In my hand, rain no longer varnished its surface; it dried quickly almost as if the stone was absorbing the water. The stone was reddish, with light gray veins marbling it; the higher surfaces were almost polished, the lower ones still had lots of surface irregularities. I turned it in my fingers, looking at the black, glassy highlights and wondering how it would look after I ran it through my tumbler. *Blackstone Mountain. The Pit. Venus.* "Can I keep this?" I asked Hasalalo.

Its bubbler hissed. Hasalalo was watching me. Its underlids slid over its eyes and remained there as the rain started to pelt down harder: no longer a sheeter, but now what the locals called a "pounder." "Why?" it asked.

I reached into my pocket with my free hand and pulled out my little collection of polished rocks, displaying them to Hasalalo in my palm. "It's amazing what a rock looks like when you polish it like this. They become little jewels: the essence of the stone. Or maybe it's the truth inside the stone. It's something I do, everywhere I go. See, this one: it's a rock I took from the beach the last time I was here." Blue-black glass, so finely polished that you could see the darker imperfections floating inside like planets nested in a dark nebula.

Hasalo leaned over my hand and stretched out a web-snaggled finger to touch it. "This is one of the black stones?"

I nodded. "Pretty, isn't it? I'd like to do the same with this stone from the pit, just to see how it comes out, to see what beauty it's hiding."

"Do you know what you hold?"

I shook my head.

A hiss from the bubbler. "You know what happens to those of bones-of-stone when they die?"

"Yes. You release the bodies over the Great Darkness. There's something about reincarnation for a few, and, well, your gods . . . umm, the Lights-in-Water are down there and, uh . . ." My voice trailed off. The truth was that while I knew the shreeliala had a complex mythology that revolved around the Great Darkness, all that Avariel had cared about was that no human had ever been all the way to the bottom of the Great Darkness and that she'd be the first. Therefore, that was all I cared about, too. Just as I hadn't bothered to learn how the shreeliala reproduced, I'd also ignored their beliefs. I figured the way they dealt with death was like our own tales of death and afterlife: ancient myth and fantasy, with none of it real.

"Those with bones-of-stone fall into the Great Darkness," Hasalalo continued. If it was annoyed at my bumbling narrative of their beliefs, I couldn't tell. "The Lights-in-Water feed on their flesh, leaving behind their bones, and among the bones are also their stomach-stones. Sometimes, the Lights-in-Water find a particularly beautiful stomach-stone, and they take that stomach-stone back up out of the Great Darkness and place the stone where a bud-mother can find it, and when the bud-mother swallows it, it sprouts a new shreeliala, so that each shreeliala may come back to life again. That's the possibility that awaits most shreeliala in the Great Darkness, but not those of bones-of-air. I've talked to the Eldest of us, and they say that the Pit has always been the same. The Lights-in-Water can't come here, so the stomach-stones left here never leave, and those who rot here are never reborn."

Hasalalo gestured to encompass Blackstone Mountain. "All this came to be because those of bones-of-air went into the Great Darkness by tying rocks around their bodies against all warnings, and the Lights-in-Water of the Always Sea grew angry and vomited up the bones-of-air in a fury of glowing rocks, until the sea bottom rose above the Always Sea as a sign to never do that again. Since then, all of us with bones-of-air have been placed here and are forbidden the Great Darkness. I know Avariel believes this is just superstition, and so you probably think the same. The Lights-in-Water, their choosing of the stomach-stones, everything about the Great Darkness is only myth. Maybe it is. Maybe there's no difference between what happens to those with bones-of-air and bones-of-stone. This is why I worked with the Green Council to allow Avariel to come back. She said she would tell me what she finds at the bottom of the Great Darkness. If she does, I will know. We will *all* know."

That was by far the longest speech I had ever heard a shreeliala make. Through most of it I was staring at the stone I was holding: a "stomach-stone," a gastrolith, I knew now. Part of me wanted to drop it: this had been in the gizzard of one of the dead shreeliala, which explained how it had been partially polished, grinding the sea plants that the shreeliala ate.

"Take the stone and find the truth inside it," Hasalalo told me as I hesitated. "I wish to see it afterward."

I rubbed the stone between my fingers, thinking I could almost feel slime coating it, as if it had just been vomited up. I shivered, but I closed my fingers around it as Hasalalo stared at me. "All right," I told it. "I'll get it started tonight. It'll take a week or more, though. It takes a lot of time to get to the truth, as you put it."

Hasalalo seemed to sniff. "If that is so, then why does Avariel never stay anywhere very long? Why do you do the same?"

To that echo of what Obaasan Evako had once said, I had no answer at all.

After I left Hasalalo back at *Venus Genetrix*, after I stopped at my hotel room and removed the rock tumbler I kept in my luggage and started the gastrolith's polishing, I went to see Avariel. I knew where she'd be: down Blackstone's single street to where it plunged into a tunnel of Plexiglas and steel and down under the slow waves to Undersea Port proper.

There, the light was dim and green—more suited to shreeliala eyes than ours—and the odor of brine and fish dominated, mingling with the cinnamon exhalations of shreeliala. Here were the markets for the fish and kelp and other niceties that formed the trade between shreeliala and human; here were the water-filled chambers where human delegates and negotiators could meet with shreeliala officials. Here was the interface between two worlds and two species.

Avariel and her support crew had taken one of the subs docked there. The street hatch was open, so I went in. I found her in the lower chamber, checking out the diving equipment with a man who'd been part of our support crew last time: Mikhail. ". . . the fiddling I did with the CCR should give you at least another two hours if you need it. You bought the best rebreather on the market, I know, but now it's better," he was saying to her.

"I hope so," Avariel said, then she saw me. She gave me the expression of someone suffering from severe acid reflux. "Mikhail," she said, "why don't you check with Patrick on the com unit?"

Mikhail raised a dark eyebrow toward me, the brow rising

higher and his mud-brown eyes widening slightly as he noted my missing legs. "Sure," he said. He was trying not to stare at me. "I'll do that. Hey, Tomio."

"Mikhail. Good to see you again." The polite thing you say when you're really saying nothing at all.

"You, too," he answered, words equally as empty. Then he glanced at Avariel, shrugged, and left, climbing the ladder to the upper compartment. I watched his legs disappear, but Avariel's voice pulled me back.

"What do you want, Tomio? I'm rather busy right now."

"You already know."

"And I already gave you the answer. No, you can't go with me. Not this time." I saw her gaze fall down past my waist to the emptiness there.

"I can still swim," I told her, stomping the foot end of the prosthetic field for emphasis. The sole of the shoe was rubber; there wasn't much sound, even in the hard-walled chamber. "That's not the problem."

"No," she answered quietly, "that's not the problem at all."

"You're taking Mikhail? Or Patrick?"

She was already shaking her head. "I'm doing this alone."

"That's ridiculous. And foolish."

She gave a cough that might have been a laugh. "Is it? Were you there when I climbed the last cliffs at Olympus Mons? That final ascent . . ."

"I know," I told her. "You did it on your own. Doesn't make it any less—" I stopped. "Stupid" was the word on my lips. I could see from her face that she knew it, too. I could also see that the more I argued, the more her answer to me wasn't going to change, and I could also tell from the release of tension in my gut that I'd *wanted* her to tell me "no"—because the ghost that I was chasing didn't involve returning to where the Great Darkness had taken my legs. That ghost was standing in front of me.

Avariel took a long breath, closing her eyes momentarily as if composing words in her head. Then she looked at me again, her eyes bright. "Look, Tomio. I know what I am: an adrenaline junkie, someone who likes to push the envelope, to do things that no one else has done. And yeah, I like the attention that gets me, too. Your grandmother had me tagged pretty well, and I know myself well enough to admit it now. You—I don't think you *ever* knew what you wanted. After your accident in the Great Darkness . . ." She caught her upper lip in her teeth momentarily, as if biting back something. Mikhail told me afterward that when Avariel came for me, my legs were already gone, crudely guillotined from my body by the rocks. She managed to put tourniquets around the stumps and take me back up to the sub before I entirely bled out. When I came back to consciousness, several days later, she'd already left Venus. "I'm not proud that I left you. But you and me . . ." Her head shook. I waited. "It wasn't going to work. I think you knew that as much as I did."

"I don't know," I told her. "At the time, I had other things on my mind, like wondering when I'd ever walk again."

She sucked in her breath, a hiss like Hasalalo's bubbler, and I was suddenly repentant. "All right," I told her, "can I at least be there tomorrow when you dive? I could help Mikhail and Patrick up top."

I thought she was going to say no once more. She looked away from me, and down to the dive equipment on the floor. Her head was still shaking, but she took a step toward me, grabbing my hands and looking up into my face. I could see the lines on her face, carved deeper than I remembered, the brown puffiness under her eyes, the small scars on her skin from the burn regeneration. Her fingers pressed mine, tightly.

It was the closest we'd been since the night she'd left me, in the hospital here.

"If that's what you want," she said, "then all right, for what we once were, for what happened last time." Then she let go of my hands and stepped back. "If you're going to be here, then at least help me stow this crap," she said.

The sub was stationed over the broken rim of the Great Darkness, seemingly perched on great legs of blue-white spotlights, as insubstantial as my own. The Always Sea was deepening here, sloping down the submerged flanks of the volcano that was Blackstone Mountain. Staring out the wide, transparent ports of the sub, I could see several shreeliala gathered at the rim of the Great Darkness below us, with the rounded, woven structures of the shreeliala's Blackstone Village (our name for it, not theirs) receding away into the green-blue distance toward where its seaweed-draped outskirts met the human buildings of Undersea Port.

On the rim of the Great Darkness, a great and wide forest of blue-black kelp undulated in the slow currents of the Always Sea. The shreeliala were gathered above the canopy of kelp, and I could see the bubbling forms of shreeliala speech as they spoke amongst themselves. The words of the shreeliala language are essentially shaped water-and-air-bubble structures (which is why they resort to English when out of the water), as much visual as audible. The scientists studying their language are still trying to discern the grammar and construction and putting together a dictionary, but I doubt that any human is ever going to be able to "speak" or understand shreeliala without mechanical help.

Smelling cinnamon, I spoke aloud. "I wonder what they're saying?" Hasalalo, aboard the sub with us, peered over my shoulder to the scene below.

"They're not pleased that this is happening," it said. "Many of us, especially those of bones-of-stone, weren't pleased with the Green Council's decision. They say it is bones-of-air stupidity to permit this." A long finger stroked the marking on its skull, reflexively.

"They're not going to try to stop us, are they?" Mikhail asked from his console. Mikhail's finger hovered above the com button. On the screen in front of him, we could see Avariel in the dive chamber, with Patrick helping her fit on the last of her gear.

Hasalalo's eyes widened. "They don't think they'll have to. The Lights-in-Water will do that for them."

Mikhail laughed at that, and his finger moved away from the com. "The Lights-in-Water haven't met Avariel. That woman's got a nasty mean streak for people who get in her way." He chuckled again, then glanced at me. The chuckle died.

"Is that what you think?" I asked Hasalalo. "The Lights-in-Water will stop Avariel?"

It looked at me placidly. The bubbler gurgled and spat water. "They stopped *you*."

Movement. A flash of brilliance accompanied the pain. Then nothing until I woke up in the hospital. "It was a rockfall that stopped me. I got too close to the edge and hit something unstable," I told it.

"I wonder," Hasalalo answered, "what truth was buried inside those rocks that took your legs?"

I started to answer it, but Avariel's voice came over the com and the holoscreens lit up around the compartment. "Going live," she said, her voice muffled through the rebreather. "Do you have the feed, Mikhail?"

"Got it," Mikhail answered. "Everything looks good here."

"Fine. I'm going down, then. Wish me luck."

Luck, I whispered under my breath. "No luck needed," Mikhail told her. "You got this. Piece of cake."

The image on the holoscreens bounced and swirled, then filled with bubbles as the dive hatch filled with water and opened for her. Avariel swam out into the haze of the sub's lights, the view on the screen swaying dizzily as she looked up and the camera on her mask picked up the sub above her. Our lights overloaded the camera until it dimmed, then opened up again as she glanced over at the shreeliala gathered at the lips of the canyon, watching her and speaking to each other in a rush of half-glimpsed water shapes. Behind us, we heard Patrick clamber up the metal ladder into our chamber and settle down by the com unit.

"Hey, Avariel, you're green across the board here," Patrick said. "Ready?"

She looked down, and we saw the blue-black below that the sub's light could not penetrate. Her arm came into view, laden with her dive watch and depth instrumentation. "Everything looks green here, too," she said. "Patrick, Mikhail, I'm heading down."

I tried not to feel insulted by the lack of any reference to me.

On the screens, we watched the water around her slowly darken and the readout from her depth gauge climb just as slowly. She stayed near the edge of the canyon wall, as we had both done the last time, but not—I noted—as closely as I had clung to it. As the sub's light faded, she switched on the mask's headlamps, and we could occasionally catch glimpses of the jagged, volcanic rock of the lava tube that was the Great Darkness, adorned with Venusian kelp and the creatures who lived there amongst the rocks and vegetation.

I remembered that much myself: *the walls of the Great Darkness had been alive in front of me. I saw anglerworms dangling their fish-shaped heads outward into the water, enticing the snaggle-mouthed puffers to come close enough to be speared by the poisoned lance of their tongues. I watched a wave of green painters undulate past me, the inky dye from their bodies leaving swirling trails of purple as they passed. Snorting shells, with their long spires and carapaces swirled with brilliant blues, yellows, and reds belched air as they made their way along the ledges of the Great Darkness. The shallow waters of the Always Sea teemed with life, everywhere. There were species unseen by any human to be discovered everywhere we looked and we could have spent days cataloging and describing them, but Avariel was intent only on going down into the blackness . . .*

Down, and down. I knew that Avariel would be starting to feel the pressure building against her flexible suit, which would be hardening against the weight of the water. The suit she wore was a hybrid: self-contained and powered only by Avariel's legs, but also a miniature "vessel" that would allow her to reach depths that an individual diver would not be able to reach. Because for religious reasons, the shreeliala had refused to allow us to probe the Great Darkness with remote-controlled vehicles, we had no idea of the actual depth of the lava tube though indirect estimates suggested that it was no more than eight hundred meters.

The hissing of the rebreather would be loud in her ears, and the canyon wall she followed down became stripped of the kelp, which needed the faint, cloud-shielded sunlight that was mostly nonexistent below seventy-five to one hundred meters. Instead, the rocks were dotted with the gray-white tubes of puff-worms and the lacy, swollen cells of prison-crabs, laden with the bones of the fish they'd snagged with their long, prehensile tails.

"I'm at 210 meters," Avariel said, her voice becoming distorted in pitch as the rebreather added more helium and neon to the air she was breathing. I knew why she mentioned it: that's where I'd had my accident, where she'd been forced to abandon the quest the last time. She was well away from the canyon wall now, the lights on her mask illuminating only dark, empty water. She wasn't going to repeat my "mistake."

The dive meter display showed 280 meters when it happened.

"There's something . . ." they heard Avariel say. "Coming up from below. Lights . . ." In the viewscreen, the camera swayed as she looked down, and we saw a swarm of firefly lights, green and cold, swirling below like a flock of phosphorescent birds, and rising, rising as they grew larger. "I can feel them . . ."

The sense of something approaching . . . then the pain, the terrible pain that sent me whirling into unconsciousness . . .

"Avariel," I said, leaning over Patrick's console, "be careful . . ."

"I don't believe—" she began, but the lights rushed inward: too bright, too huge, and the camera view tumbled wildly as they heard Avariel cry out. "No! Don't . . ."

Then the screens all went dark at once, the readouts went to flatline, and there was only the hiss of static in the speakers. "Avariel!" I shouted, though I knew already that it was too late. "Avariel!"

Silence. I heard Mikhail cursing at his console. "I'm taking us down," he said. "We'll go and get her."

"No!" That was Hasalalo, its voice shrill through the bubbler. "That is not permitted. The Green Council forbids it. *I* forbid it."

"Fuck both you and the Green Council!" Mikhail ranted. "We have to do something. Patrick, give me her last position."

I put my hand on Mikhail's shoulder; he pushed it away. "You can't," I told him. Patrick hadn't moved, staring at all of us. "Avariel knew the risks."

"And last time, she brought *you* back," Mikhail answered.

"Not all of me," I answered. "Some of me is still down there. She knew the risks," I repeated. He stared at me. He cursed again, punching a closed fist on the console. A screen sparked in static at the punishment. Then he let his hands drop to his side.

We waited, hovering above the Great Darkness, until an hour after her air should have run out. Then, in furious silence and grief, we headed back to Undersea Port.

* * *

I stood at the shore of the Always Sea. The rain was a bare drizzler, fat drops falling from scudding, gray-black clouds as the wind frothed the tips of the low rollers coming in. Lightning from a storm near the horizon licked bright tongues into the sea. I'd left the rainshield behind in my room; if Venus wanted me to get wet, I'd oblige her and allow it to happen. I imagined the gods of Venus spitting on me from the eternal cloud banks, and laughing when one of the droplets hit me. I stared out toward the Great Darkness, half-believing I could see the darkness of it even though I knew that was impossible.

Avariel's body never came back up. I imagined her bones, down there with all the others. With a few of mine, as well.

I heard the scrape of a flippered foot on the rocks and the hiss of a bubbler behind me, and glanced over my shoulder to see Hasalalo there. It stood alongside me, silent except for the noise of the bubbler. "The Green Council has closed the Great Darkness to all further human exploration," it said. "None of your kind will ever do what Avariel attempted."

It was staring at me. I took a long breath, then plunged my hand into my pocket. I pulled out the stomach-stone I'd taken from the pit. It shone in the rain and the diffuse light from the eternally clouded sky: marbled blue highlights in a swirling, orange-red matrix—gorgeous, and oddly heavy. "Here," I told it. "You wanted to see the truth hiding in the stone. Here it is." I took its hand and put the finished piece on its scaled flesh, the polished surface glinting like a wet jewel.

Hasalalo's bubbler burbled as it stared, prodding the stone with a webbed finger. Its huge eyes looked up. "There was great beauty inside," it said. "How could the Lights-in-Water not love such a thing if they could see it, if someone gave it to them?"

I nodded. I thought it would keep the stone, but Hasalalo handed the stomach-stone back to me; I put it in my pocket to nestle with the other stones: *Avariel. Venus. The last time . . .*

Neither of us said anything for a time, just watching the rain-pocked rollers coming in off the Always Sea. "You'll be leaving," Hasalalo said finally.

I shook my head. "No," I told it. "I think I'll stay here for a while. Maybe you were right about seeing truth. I've always moved around. For once, I think I'll try staying long enough to see what's underneath the surface. Maybe I'll even figure out what the Lights-in-Water are."

Hasalalo seemed to contemplate that. "You will live longer than me," it said finally, slowly. "When I die, if you're still here . . ." It stopped. It was staring out at the misty horizon, where the Great Darkness lay.

"If I'm still here . . . ?" I prodded.

"They will throw my body into the Pit. After the wrigglers have taken my flesh, would you come for my stomach-stones? Would you find the truth inside them? And would you . . ."

Hasalalo didn't finish, but it looked out toward the Great Darkness through the rain, and I knew what it wanted. I nodded. "I will," I told it. "I promise."

ELEANOR ARNASON

Eleanor Arnason published her first novel, *The Sword Smith,* in 1978, and followed it with novels such as *Daughter of the Bear King* and *To the Resurrection Station.* In 1991, she published her best-known novel, one of the strongest novels of the nineties, the critically acclaimed *A Woman of the Iron People,* a complex and substantial novel that won the prestigious James Tiptree, Jr., Award. Her short fiction has appeared in *Asimov's Science Fiction, The Magazine of Fantasy & Science Fiction, Amazing, Orbit, Xanadu,* and elsewhere. Her other books are *Ring of Swords* and *Tomb of the Fathers,* and a chapbook, *Mammoths of the Great Plains,* which includes the eponymous novella, plus an interview with her and a long essay. Her most recent book is a collection, *Big Mama Stories.* Her story "Stellar Harvest" was a Hugo finalist in 2000. She lives in St. Paul, Minnesota.

Here she takes us along with a National Geographic safari headed out of Venusport to the wildest part of the Venusian Outback in search of dramatic wildlife footage, and where they find something much more dramatic than they had anticipated.

Ruins

ELEANOR ARNASON

OF COURSE, THE STORY BEGAN IN A LOW DIVE IN Venusport, in the slums up on the hillside above the harbor. The proper town was below them: grid streets with streetlights, solid, handsome concrete houses, and apartment blocks. The people in the apartments—middle-class and working folks with steady jobs—had their furniture volume-printed in one of the city's big plants. The rich folks in their houses patronized custom printing shops, where they could get any kind of furniture in any style.

> The rich man in his castle,
> The poor man at his gate,
> God printed out the both of them
> And ordered their estate

Not that it mattered up on the hill. The people here scraped by without regular jobs that could be relied on. There were always layoffs, when construction was cut back or the equipment from Earth did not arrive. If there were God-given rules for their lives, they didn't know them.

The bar Ash was in had beat-up, previously owned chairs and tables. A dehumidifier–heating unit glowed against one wall because it was winter, and the usual winter rains fell heavily outside. It wasn't cold that was a problem. No place on Venus was really cold, except the tops of a few tall mountains. But the damp could get in your bones.

Ash sat in a corner, her back against a wall. On the table in front of her was a glass of beer and a tablet. She was playing solitaire on the tablet. The game occupied her mind just enough to keep out old memories but left her with attention for the bar. It could be dangerous on payday nights, when people were flush and drunk, or after big layoffs, when people were angry and spending their last money. Tonight it was mostly empty.

The guy who walked in—there was always someone walking in at the start of a story—did not belong. He was short and neatly dressed, with a fancy vest full of pockets; and his head was shaved, except for a few tufts of bright blue hair. It was the kind of haircut that required upkeep. Most people in Hillside didn't bother.

He stopped at the bar and spoke to the bartender, who nodded toward Ash. The man bought a glass of wine, which was a mistake, as he would find when he tasted it, then walked over.

She had no chance of winning the current game and turned the tablet off.

"Hong Wu," he said in introduction. "I'm an editor with *National Geographic*."

"Yes?" She nodded toward the chair opposite. The man sat down, took a sip of his wine, and made a face. "You are Ash Weatherman."

"Yes."

"We want to do a story about the megafauna on Venus, and we want to hire you."

"The story's been done," Ash said.

"We think another look at the megafauna is worth it. We did a thousand stories about wild animals in Africa, until they were gone. People could never get enough of elephants and lions. They still can't. Look at zoos."

She had grown up on *National Geographic* videos: all the lost wilderness of Earth, the charismatic megafauna of land and ocean. Most had been mammals, of course, and near relatives to humanity. Nothing on Venus was as closely related although pretty much everyone agreed that life on Venus had come from Earth, most likely via a meteorite that hit Earth a glancing blow, then landed on the inner planet, bringing Terran organisms scraped up in the first collision. Geologists thought they had found the crater on Earth and the final resting place on Venus. Both craters were eroded and filled in, not visible on the planetary surface. The great plain of Ishtar and something whacking big in Greenland.

There were people who thought it had happened twice, with the second meteorite bringing organisms from a later era; and they had found another pair of craters. But whatever had happened was long ago, and the organisms that came to Venus were single-celled. They had their own evolutionary history, which had ended in a different place, with no cute, furry mammals.

"The fauna here are certainly big enough," she said out loud. "Though I don't know how charismatic they are." She tapped her tablet, and a new game of solitaire appeared. "What do you know about me?"

"You grew up in Hillside, graduated from high school here, and got a degree in the history of evolutionary theory at Venusport College. According to the police, you were involved with a student anarchist group but did nothing illegal.

"You worked in a printing plant while you were in college and after—until your photography began to sell. For the most part, you do advertising. Fashion, such as it is on Venus, furniture and real estate, and nature shots for the tourism industry. On the side, you do your own work, which is mostly images of the Venusian outback. That work is extraordinary. We have our own first-rate videographer and a thoughtful journalist, but we think it would be interesting to have a Venusian perspective."

Interesting that they'd seen her photos. They had shown at a small gallery downtown: 3-D blowups on the walls and a machine in back to print copies with a signature: Ashley Weatherman, 2113. She'd made some money. People safe in Venusport liked to have the Venusian wilderness on their walls: cone-shaped flowers two meters tall, brilliant yellow or orange; amphibianoids that looked—more or less—like giant crocodiles; and little, rapid, bipedal reptiloids.

"You're going to need someone to organize your safari," Ash said. "Do you have anyone?"

"We thought we'd ask you."

"Arkady Volkov. You're going to want to go to Aphrodite Terra. That's where the best megafauna are, and you won't want to deal with any corporations. Most of Ishtar Terra is company land. Believe me, they protect it."

Hong Wu nodded. "Rare-earth mining and time-share condos."

"Arkady knows the territory," Ash said. "I've worked with him before."

Hong Wu nodded a second time. "We know. The police here say he's reputable even though he comes from Petrograd."

The last Soviet Socialist Republic, which remained here on Venus long after the collapse of the USSR, an enclave of out-of-date politics on the larger of the two Venusian continents. She liked Arkady, even though he was a Leninist. *The heart hath its reasons that reason knoweth not.* "Are you willing to hire him?"

"Yes," Hong Wu said.

The rest of the conversation was details. Hong Wu left finally. Ash ordered another beer.

The bartender asked, "What was that about?"

"Work."

"He looked like a petunia."

"He is an employer, and we will be respectful."

"Yes, ma'am." The bartender grinned, showing metal teeth.

She finished the beer and walked home through winter rain, not hurrying. Her parka was waterproof, and the streets were covered with mud that had washed down from eroded hillsides. Half the streetlights were out. It would be easy to slip on the badly lit, uneven surface. She hated getting muddy. Even more, she hated looking vulnerable.

The buildings she passed were concrete and low: row houses for families and barracks for single workers. Graffiti crawled over them, most of it dark and slow moving. Here and there were tags written in more expensive spray that jittered and sparkled. "REVOLUTION NOW," one said in glowing red letters. "F U, F U, F U," another said in flashing yellow. The tags wouldn't last downtown, where the ambiance cops would cover them, but here—

There were shanties and tents in the supposedly empty lots, mostly hidden by vegetation. You could see them if you knew how to look. Some folks did not like living in barracks, and some didn't have the money to pay bed-rent.

She turned a corner next to a lot full of tall, feathery pseudograss. In daylight, it would have been deep green, edged with purple. Now it was as black as the graffiti on the nearest building. In the street ahead, a pack of piglike amphibianoids nosed around a Dumpster. Mostly not dangerous, in spite of their impressive tusks and claws. Ash paused. The matriarch of the pack eyed her for a moment, then grunted and lumbered away. The rest followed, leaving heaps of dung.

Her place was past the Dumpster: a two-floor row house. A light shone over the door, making it possible for her to see the land scorpion resting on the step. More than anything else, it looked like the ancient sea scorpions of Earth: broad, flat, segmented, and ugly. Instead of swimming paddles, it had many legs. This one was dull green and as long as her foot. Most likely it wasn't venomous. The toxic species advertised the fact with bright colors. Nonetheless, she stepped on it firmly, hearing the crack of its exoskeleton breaking, then scraped her boot on the edge of the step.

She unlocked the door and yelled a greeting to the family on the first floor. Bangladeshi. The smell of their curries filled the house; and if she was lucky, they invited her to dinner. Tonight she was too late. Ash climbed the stairs and unlocked another door. Lights came on. Baby, her pet pterosaur, called, "Hungry."

She pulled off her boots and put a stick of chow in Baby's cage. The pterosaur dug in.

Of course, the animal was not a real pterosaur. Life on Earth and Venus had been evolving separately for hundreds of millions—maybe billions—of years. But it had skin wings stretched over finger bones, a big head, and a small, light body. Pale yellow fuzz covered it, except around its eyes, where its skin was bare and red. A crest of feathers adorned Baby's head, down at present. When up, the feathers were long and narrow, looking like spines or stiff hairs; and they were bright, iridescent blue.

Some people—mostly middle-class—used the Latin names for the local life. But people on the hill called them after the Earth life they most resembled.

"Bored," the animal said.

"We're going into the outback," Ash said. "Flying, Baby. Hunting. Food."

"Fly!" Baby sang. "Hunt! Food!"

She scratched the pterosaur's muzzle, which was full of needle teeth. The head crest rose, expanding into a brilliant, semicircular array.

Venus was surprising, she had learned in school. No one had expected flying animals as intelligent as birds. Famous words, repeated over and over—No one had expected.

She pulled a beer out of the electric cooler, sat down in the chair next to Baby's cage, and unfolded her tablet. One tap brought up Arkady's address. As usual, it was irritating. A glowing red star appeared on her screen. "You have reached the home of Arkady Volkov. He is out at present, making plans for a new revolution, but if you leave a message—"

"Cut it out, Arkady," Ash said. "You are down at the local bar, getting pissed."

The star was replaced by Arkady: a swarthy man with a thick, black beard and green eyes, surprisingly pale given his skin and hair. "Do not judge others by yourself, Ash. I am sitting at home with a modest glass of wine, trying—once again—to understand the first three chapters of *Capital*."

"Why bother?"

"Education is always good. The ruling class denies it to workers because it's dangerous to them. As a rule, one should always do what the ruling class finds dangerous."

Easy for him to say, living in Petrograd, where his opinions were tolerated because a ruling class did not officially exist. Even there, most people found his ideas out-of-date. Oh, silly Arkady, he believes the old lies.

"Did you call to banter?" Arkady asked. "Or to argue politics? In which case I will find something offensive to say about anarchism."

"Neither," Ash said, and told him about the job.

He looked dubious. "I wasn't planning to go out in the near future. There are things in Petrograd that need to be dealt with. Do these people pay well?"

Ash gave him the figure.

Arkady whistled. "Who are they?"

"*National Geographic*. They want to do a story on charismatic megafauna. I want to take them into a real wilderness, where they won't run into surveyors or test plots or mines."

"I will do it," Arkady said, and lifted his glass of wine to her. "Capitalists have so much money. How many people?"

She gave details, as she had learned them from Hong Wu.

"Two vehicles," Arkady said. "Ural trucks modified for passengers. Rifles. I can provide those. We'll need two drivers and a cook, all of whom should be good with guns. That means we will have to hire the cook in Petrograd. Your cuisine is better, but your shooting is worse, and most of you do not know how to handle a Pecheneg."

In theory, a rifle could take down anything on Venus, but only if the shot was well placed. There were times when the best thing to do was to rip the animal apart, and a Pecheneg could do that. Arkady was fond of them. They were solid and reliable, like the legendary AK-47 and the Ural 6420, the last version of the truck made before the USSR fell. It had been designed for use on Venus as well as in Siberia; and it could go through almost everything.

"I know someone here in Petrograd who does an excellent borscht—a man could live on borscht and bread—and can make more than adequate Central Asian food. She was in the police force and can both fire a Pecheneg and fieldstrip it."

"It's a deal, then," said Ash.

She met the *National Geographic* team in the Venusport airport. The journalist was as expected: a tall, lean man in a jacket with many pockets. His dark eyes had a thousand-kilometer stare. The videographer was a surprise: a round sphere that rested on four spidery metal legs. Its head was atop a long, flexible neck—a cluster of lenses. "You are Ash Weatherman?" the machine asked in a pleasant contralto voice.

"Yes."

"I am an Autonomous Leica. My model name is AL-26. My personal name is Margaret, in honor of the twentieth-century

photographer Margaret Bourke White. You may call me Maggie."
It lifted one of its legs and extruded fingers. Ash shook the cool
metal hand.

"And I am Jasper Khan," the journalist said, holding out his
hand, which was brown and muscular.

More shaking. This time the hand was warm.

"Baby," said Baby.

"And this is Baby. Don't try to shake. He nips."

"A pseudorhamphorynchus," Jasper said.

"Not pseudo," Baby said.

"How large is his vocabulary?" Maggie asked.

"More than five hundred words. He keeps picking up new
ones."

Maggie bent its neck, peering into the cage. "Say cheese."

"Not in vocabulary," Baby replied, then opened his mouth
wide, showing off his needle teeth.

"Excellent," said Maggie. A bright light came on, and the Leica
extended its—her—long neck farther, curling around the cage,
recording Baby from all sides. The pterosaur did not look happy.

"You will be famous, Baby," Ash said.

"Want food."

The plane took off on time, rising steeply into the almost-
always-present clouds. Ash had a window seat, useless after the
clouds closed in. Baby was next to her on the aisle; and the
National Geographic team was across the aisle.

Six hours to Aphrodite Terra. Ash fed a chow stick to Baby.
The pterosaur held it in one clawed foot and gnawed. Ash felt
her usual comfort in travel and in getting away from Venusport.
Petrograd might be retrograde and delusional, the last remnant
of a failed idea. But she liked Arkady, and nothing on the planet
could beat a Ural 6420.

She dozed off as the plane flew south and rain streaked her
window, then woke when the descent began. A holographic

steward came by and warned them to fasten their seat belts. She had never unfastened hers, but she checked the one around Baby's cage.

She looked out as the plane dropped below the clouds. Another grid city like Venusport, but smaller, with no tall buildings. A failure, slowly dying according to people on Earth and in Venusport. Cracked, gray runways crossed shaggy native grass.

They landed with a bump and rolled to a stop in front of the terminal. Ash undid her belt and Baby's, then stood, feeling stiff.

Arkady was at the gate. On Earth there was security, which grew more intense as violence grew. Here on Venus, people were less desperate; and it was possible to wait at a gate with an AK-47 over one shoulder. It wasn't the original version, of course, but a modern replica with some improvements, but not many. It remained as simple and indestructible as a stone ax and as easy to maintain. The best assault weapon ever made, Arkady said.

Baby opened his wings as far as he could in the cage. "Arky!" he cried.

The Russian grinned and waved.

Introductions followed. The two men were wary of each other, in spite of vigorous handshakes and broad smiles. Arkady was warmer toward the robot. "A pleasure," he said, clasping the extruded fingers. "The Urals are waiting. We can head out at once."

"Excellent," the Autonomous Leica said.

They picked up the rest of their baggage at the carousel, then went into the rain. The Urals were across the drop-off-pick-up road. Two massive vehicles, each with four sets of wheels. The front truck had a box. The one in back was a flatbed, with a Pecheneg fastened to the bed. A tarp covered it, but Ash knew what it was.

Arkady escorted Maggie and Jasper to the flatbed, then

pointed at the truck in front. Ash climbed into the backseat. The driver made a friendly, grunting sound.

"This is Boris," Arkady said as he climbed in. "Irina and Alexandra are in the second truck."

The trucks pulled out. Rain beat on the windshield, and wipers flashed back and forth. They bumped out of the airport and along rough, wet streets. Petrograd was around them: low, dreary-looking, concrete buildings, dimmed by the rain.

Arkady opened a thermos of tea and handed it back to Ash. She took a swallow. Hot and sweet.

"Do you want to show them anything special?" Arkady asked.

"They want charismatic megafauna and maybe something else. I keep wondering why they hired me. Do they want to write about Venusian culture as well?"

"The replica of America on Ishtar Terra, and the remains of the USSR on Aphrodite Terra," said Arkady in a genial tone. "It might make a good story. At least they did not ask for mostly naked natives. We don't have any, except in saunas and swimming pools."

The city was not large. They were soon out of it and rolling through agricultural land: bright green fields of modified Earth crops. The rain let up though the cloud cover remained. By midafternoon, they reached the forest. The fields ended at a tall wire fence. Beyond were trees. Green, of course. Chlorophyll had evolved only once—on Earth—and been imported to Venus. But the native forest's green always seemed richer, more intense and varied to her. Purple dotted the ragged foliage of the low bottlebrush trees. The foliage of the far taller lace-leaf trees was veined with yellow, though this was hard to see at a distance.

The trucks stopped. Arkady climbed down and opened the gate, then closed it after the trucks were through, climbed back into the cab, and flipped on the radio. "Large herbivores can break through the fence and do sometimes," he told the truck in back. "Fortunately for us, they do not like the taste of Terran vegetation, though they can metabolize it. Unfortunately for us, the only way for them to learn they don't like our food is to try it."

"Ah," said Jasper.

"I got images of your opening the gate," Maggie said. "Bright green fields, dark green trees and you with your AK-47. Very nice."

The trucks drove on. The road was two muddy ruts now, edged by an understory of frilly plants. The air coming in her partly open window smelled of Venus: rain, mud, and the native vegetation.

Animals began to appear: pterosaurs, flapping in the trees, and small reptiloid bipeds in the understory. Now and then, Ash saw a solitary flower, cone-shaped and two meters tall. Most were a vivid orange-yellow. The small flying bugs that pollinated them were not visible at a distance, but she knew they were there in clouds. Now and then Maggie asked for a stop. Ash had her camera out and did some shooting, but the thing she really wanted to capture—the robot—was invisible, except for the lens head, pushed out a window at the end of Maggie's long, long neck.

Midway through the afternoon, they came to a river. A small herd of amphibianoids rested on the far shore. They were larger than the street pigs in Venusport, maybe five meters long, their sprawling bodies red and slippery-looking. Their flat heads had bulbous eyes on top—not at the back of the head, where eyes usually were, even on Venus, but in front, close to the nostrils and above the mouths full of sharp teeth.

Maggie climbed out her window onto the flat bed of the second truck. She braced herself there, next to the Pecheneg, and recorded as the trucks forded the river. The water came up to the trucks' windows, and the riverbed was rocky, but the trucks kept moving, rocking and jolting. Nothing could beat a Ural!

"A gutsy robot," Arkady said.

Alexandra answered over the radio. "She has four sets of fingers dug into the truck bed, right into the wood. A good thing. I don't want to fish her out of the river."

Ash aimed her camera at the amphibianoids as the animals bellowed and slid into the river, vanishing among waves. Maggie was more interesting, but she still couldn't get a good view.

The trucks climbed the now-empty bank and rolled onto the road. The Leica climbed back into the cab. "Not mega, but very nice," Maggie said over the radio.

An hour or so later, they reached the first lodge, a massive concrete building set against a low cliff. Vines hung down the cliff, and pterosaurs—a small species covered with white down—fluttered among the vines.

There was a front yard, protected by a tall fence. Once again, Arkady climbed down and opened the gate. The trucks rolled in. Arkady locked the gate behind them. Boris shut down their truck and grabbed an AK-47, climbing down to join Arkady. They looked around the yard, which was full of low vegetation, mashed in places by previous safaris. Nothing big could hide here, but there were always land scorpions.

An AK-47 seemed excessive to Ash. Good boots and stomping worked just as well. But the citizens of Petrograd loved their guns; and there was no question that the experience of crushing a land scorpion, especially a big one, was unpleasant.

Finally, Boris unlocked the lodge's door, which was metal and so heavy it could be called armored, and went in. She knew what he was doing: turning on the generator, the lights—ah, there they were, shining out the open door—the air, the temp control, the fence.

Baby shifted in his cage. "Want out. Hunt. Eat."

"Soon."

"Pterosaur chow is crap," Baby added.

She reached a finger through the cage's bars and rubbed his head. His large eyes closed, and he looked happy.

Boris came out and waved.

"All clear," Arkady called. "The fence is electric and on now. Stay away from it."

Ash opened the cage. Baby crawled out and rested for a moment in the open window. Then he flapped out, rising rapidly. The small pterosaurs in the vines shrieked. She felt the brief doubt she always felt when she let Baby go. Would he return?

"Did it escape?" Jason asked over the radio.

"He's going hunting." Ash climbed down. The air was damp and hot. By the time she reached the lodge, her shirt was wet.

"I want all the food inside," Arkady said. "Also all the weapons and any personal belongings you want to preserve. The fence will keep most things out, but it's not one hundred percent secure."

She put the cage down and went back to help unload the trucks. Irina was a broad, boxlike woman, as solid and useful as a Ural. Alexandra was surprisingly slim and elegant, the chef who'd been a cop and could fieldstrip a Pecheneg. She moved like a dancer, and Ash felt a terrible envy. Did women ever stop feeling envy?

Maggie recorded them as they worked, while Jason took notes on a tablet. Ash felt mildly irritated by this. Couldn't he help with the boxes? But he was a paying customer and an employee of a famous news source.

Once they were all inside, Boris shut the door, bringing down a heavy bar.

"Bathrooms are down the hall," Arkady said. "Paying customers go first. Dinner will be in an hour."

"An hour and a half," Alexandra said.

"I am corrected."

When she got back from her shower, Ash noticed that the

virtual wind
spotlights. Beyo
fire burned in the firepla
table in front of the fire.

She poured a glass, then went to help Alex
with dinner. It was sautéed vegetables and fish from
Petrograd fishponds.

They ate around the fireplace.

"Someone has been here," Boris said, as they ate.

"It must have been another safari," Arkady said mildly. "They all have the access code."

"I checked. No safaris have been this way since the last time we were here, and the security system has recorded nothing. But I know how I arrange canned goods. They are no longer in alphabetic order. I think it's the CIA."

"What?" asked Jason, and pulled his tablet out.

"There is a CIA post in the forest," Arkady said. "They spy on Petrograd, though we're barely surviving and no danger to the American colony or anyone. We ignore them because we don't have the resources to confront them. But they are present—and not far from here. Boris might be right. They could have tinkered with the security system. I don't know who else could have."

"Why do you hang on if you are barely surviving?" Jason asked. "The USSR fell, in part because it exhausted itself trying to settle Venus. All the republics have become capitalist states, but you remain here, stubbornly Soviet."

"Not all change is good," Boris said. "And there is more to life than selfishness."

"Surely you would do better if you had the assistance of the American colony on Ishtar."

Arkady said, "The capitalists on Earth are investing in what interests them, which is not the lives of ordinary people. We in Petrograd are a dream that has failed, or so we are told. Ishtar

a rare-earth
...ally decide that

...comfortable than life here,"

...survive."

"Be honest, Arkady," said the boxlike woman, Irina. "People get tired of shortages and go to Ishtar Terra. It's a slow but continual drain. In the end, Petrograd will fail."

"We don't know that," Boris put in. "Even our setbacks are not entirely bad. Our food shortages have brought our rates of heart disease and diabetes down; and our fuel shortages mean we walk more, which is healthy."

Irina did not look convinced. Nor did Jason Khan, though Ash could not be sure. He was an oddly opaque man. Maybe she would find out what he was thinking when the article finally came out. At present, the Leica was easier to understand.

"There," said Arkady. "You said you wanted charismatic fauna." He pointed at one of the virtual windows.

A flock of bipeds moved along the fence, illuminated by the spotlights. They were slender and covered with bright blue down, except for their chests, which were orange-red.

"The Americans call them robins," Arkady said. "Notice that they are following the fence, but not touching it. They know it's dangerous, if we are here, and the spotlights tell them we are here. If this were Earth in the Triassic, those little fellows would be the ancestors of the dinosaurs. But this isn't Earth. We don't know what they will become. They're bright, and they have hands capable of some manipulation. Maybe they will become us in time."

A second kind of animal joined the bipeds at the fence. Ten meters long or more, its body was hairless and black. It had a gait like a crocodile's high walk, and its lifted head was long and reptilian, the mouth full of ragged teeth. The bipeds ran off. The animal nosed the fence once and drew back with a roar.

"You see," Arkady said. "Not so bright. It doesn't have to be. It's big and nasty. If this were Earth in the Triassic, it would represent the past, a species that will vanish, unable to compete. But this is not Earth."

Something pale flew into the spotlights. Baby, Ash realized. The pterosaur flapped low above the pseudosuchus, taunting it. The animal roared and reared up on its hind legs, snapping at Baby and almost getting him. The pterosaur flapped up and over the fence, landing on one of the Urals. The pseudosuchus dropped down on all fours. Most likely Ash was reading in, but it looked frustrated. Baby looked frightened. The little fool. She'd have a talk with him.

"They are descended from bipeds," Arkady said. "As a result, their hind legs are longer and stronger than their front legs, and they can—as you see—rear up. They also move more quickly than you would suspect."

"I got it," Maggie said. "But the image won't be as good as I could have gotten outside."

"Go out," Boris said. "This fence is strong enough to hold."

Ash went out with the *Nat Geo* people. Of course, the pseudosuchus saw—or maybe smelled—them as soon as they went outside. It slammed into the fence and roared, then reared up, grasping the fence with its forepaws and shaking it. That must hurt. More roaring, while Maggie recorded, using a light so brilliant that Ash could see the glitter of the animal's scales. Ash got a lovely image of the robot and the monster. Light hit from different angles, cast by the lodge's spots and Maggie, creating areas of glare and shadow. Even in color, the image looked black-and-white.

Baby flapped to her, settling on her shoulder.

"Idiot," she said.

"Poop on you," Baby replied.

The fence bowed under the animal's weight. Behind them, Arkady said, "I'm not going to turn the current up. That is a protected species."

"Come in," Ash told Jason.

"The fence is supposed to hold."

"Most likely it will," Arkady said in a comfortable tone. "But if it doesn't—"

They piled back inside, and Arkady barred the door. Baby flew to his cage, opened the door and climbed in, pulling the door shut. Ash heard the lock click. The pterosaur huddled, looking thoroughly frightened.

"You shouldn't tease the monsters," Ash said.

"Poop! Poop!" Baby replied, and pooped on the floor of his cage.

She would have to clean that up, but not now. Let Baby get over being afraid.

She glanced at one of the virtual windows. The pseudosuchus was back on all fours, looking thoroughly pissed off. After a moment or two, it moved off. It was clear from the way it moved that its forefeet were injured.

"Not bright," Arkady said. "But a top predator. They do not need to be bright, as the history of America has shown."

"I'd like help in the kitchen," Alexandra put in.

Ash gathered glasses and followed Alexandra out of the room. The kitchen had a dishwasher from Venusport. Everything went in. Alexandra set the controls and turned the machine on.

"What is Venusport like?" Irina asked.

"Unjust," Ash replied. "Run from Earth for the benefit of mining companies and tourists and the rich."

"That sounds like a manifesto, not a report," Alexandra said. "What is life like for you? Do you have enough to eat? Can you buy glittery toys?"

Ash hesitated, then answered. "I have enough to eat. I can buy some toys. Hell, I make most of my living producing images of glittery toys."

"We see broadcasts from Ishtar Terra," Irina said. "Life there looks more attractive than life in Petrograd."

"Are you thinking of bailing out?" Ash asked.

"Maybe," Alexandra said. "I would like glittery toys."

Irina shook her head. "I don't think so. I have family and a lover, who is like Arkady. She believes in Petrograd."

Once the counters were wiped down, Ash went back into the living room. Jason and Arkady were lounging in chairs by the fire. Maggie had retracted her legs and neck and head, becoming a large, featureless, silver ball in front of the hologram flames. Red light played over her surface.

Baby was sitting on top of his cage, eating a stick of chow.

"You found nothing to eat?" Ash asked.

"Caught small pterosaur. Ate it. Still hungry."

She settled in a chair. There was a new bottle on the table, surrounded by fresh glasses. One of Petrograd's scary brandies. Ash poured and tasted. This one was raspberry. It burned in her mouth and down her throat, ending as a warm glow in her gut. "Where's Boris?" she asked.

"Looking around the lodge. He's still worried about his canned goods."

"He really arranged them alphabetically?"

Arkady nodded. "He is both compulsive and paranoid. But an excellent safari driver and a good drinking companion. A man as obsessed as he is needs ways to relax. He never drinks while driving, in case you are wondering."

Ash eased back in her chair, feeling content. Brandy, a fire, Baby chewing on chow, the prospect of charismatic megafauna and gigantic flowers. Life was good.

Jason had his tablet out, his fingers dancing over the screen.

She still didn't know what he was reporting on. Venusian wildlife? Petrograd? The American colony? Whichever it was, the pay was good, and she got a break from the glittery toys that Irina and Alexandra envied.

She should not judge them. She had the toys, or at least the toy makers, as clients. It was easy for her to feel indifferent to them.

Boris came into the room, holding a land scorpion, one hand behind the animal's head, the other on its tail. It was alive and twisting in his grip, trying to find a way to bite him or pinch him with its large front claws.

"Shit," said Arkady. "How did that get in?"

"I told you someone had been here." Boris stopped and displayed the creature to them. Jason looked horrified. Maggie, who must have been listening, extruded her head and neck. In a smooth motion, she rose on her legs, and the cluster of lenses she had instead of a face turned toward Boris.

The scorpion was about half a meter long, wide, flat, shiny, dark purple, and still twisting in Boris's grip. The mouth, with mandibles and fangs, was in continuous motion. Ash felt a little queasy. Damn! The things were ugly! She was pretty certain this species was poisonous. Arkady would know.

"Get me a pair of shears," Boris said.

Ash went to the kitchen, where Irina and Alexandra were still talking. "We have a problem. I need shears."

Alexandra found them. Ash took them to Boris.

He knelt carefully and placed the animal on the floor, holding it with one hand. With the other hand, he took the shears and cut the scorpion's head off, then stood quickly. The many-legged body thrashed around, and the head jittered on the floor, its mandibles still opening and closing.

"It was under the bed in the room that Jason picked as his bedroom," Boris said.

"What is it?" Jason asked in a tone of terror.

"One of the many species of land scorpion," Arkady said. "Many have poisonous bites. This species would not kill you, but it would make you sick."

Boris took one of the glasses on the table and used it to scoop the head up. "The body is not toxic. The fangs and the venom glands are in the head. Keep the rest as a souvenir, if you want."

"I have dramatic images," Maggie said. "That is sufficient. Our viewers will be horrified and disgusted."

"How did it get in?" Arkady asked again.

"I want to take a closer look at the head," Boris said, and went into the kitchen.

Alexandra and Irina were in the living room by now, watching the twisting, scrabbling, headless body with interest.

"Edible?" Baby asked.

"Wait," said Ash.

"Hungry," Baby complained.

"Have another stick of chow."

"Not tasty."

"Life is hard," Ash told him.

"Do not understand."

"Eat your chow."

The scorpion's body was slowing down though it still thrashed.

"I hate drama," Alexandra said.

"That is why you are a chef now, rather than a cop," Arkady told her.

"Yes, but it doesn't explain why I work for you."

"Money," Arkady said.

Boris came back, carrying the scorpion's head on a cutting board. He set the board on the table and Maggie leaned down to record it. He'd cut the head open. Some kind of dark matter, the brain most likely, was inside. In the middle of it was a tiny silver bead. Barely visible silver wires radiated out from it.

"Most likely it is a nano machine," Boris said. "It was injected into the circulatory system and migrated to the brain, then built itself. The animal has become an organic robot. It was planted on us as a spy."

Ash felt queasy. She had no trouble with ordinary robots, such as Maggie, who was recording the split-open head. But the idea of taking a living being and turning it into a robot bothered her. Even cockroaches, which had come to Venus with humans, deserved their own lives. The technology used to enslave bugs could be modified for other animals or humans, though that was illegal, of course.

"How did you know to look for it?" Arkady asked Boris.

"I looked at the security recordings. It was there though only in glimpses. I don't think there are any more."

"My images are excellent," Maggie said. "This will add drama to our story."

"Is it the CIA?" asked Jason.

"I believe so," Boris answered. "We live in their shadow."

"Well, if Boris thinks there are no more, we can enjoy the rest of the evening," Arkady put in.

"Can Baby eat the body?" Ash asked.

"No," said Boris. "We don't know what else might be in it. I'll toss it in the garbage."

"Sorry," Baby said.

Boris carried the head and body out. Ash drank more raspberry brandy.

"We grow the raspberries in greenhouses, along with other fruit," Arkady said. "Our crops may fail but we always have brandy."

Nothing more happened that evening or night. Ash slept badly, waking from time to time to listen for the rustling sound of a scorpion. She turned on the lights once but saw nothing except Baby sleeping in his cage.

The next morning, they drove on. The rain stopped, and

rays of sunlight broke through the cloud cover, lighting patches of the forest. There were lots of cone-shaped flowers. A group of large herbivores fed on one. Similar animals on Ishtar Terra were called forest cattle though they didn't seem especially cowlike to her, being larger than any cow she had ever seen, even in images from Earth, and green. A crest of hair went along their backs, and their large mouths had four big tusks. There were half a dozen of them around the bright red flower, ripping into it. Petals coated their muzzles and dripped from their mouths like blood.

Boris braked.

"Look to the right," Arkady said to the radio. "More megafauna."

"I would not call them charismatic," Jason replied over the radio.

"They are two meters high at the shoulder, and they can be dangerous," Arkady said. "If you don't believe so, I can let you off here."

"No," said Maggie. "I need Jason."

The trucks moved on. Ash had been on this route before, a loop that went from fortified lodge to fortified lodge, till it returned to Petrograd and dinner at one of several luxury hotels. A hospitality firm based in Venusport had built them and ran them, making sure that the tourists had a reliably luxurious experience.

"This is *National Geographic*," she said to Arkady. "Can't you show them something different?"

"We are thinking about that. But not today."

She set down her camera and drank tea. As usual, it was strong and sweet. She felt tired because of a bad night's sleep but mostly good. Baby was next to her in his cage, hunched up, his eyes closed. Was there anything cuter than a sleeping pterosaur?

There were more pterosaurs flapping in the trees, and bipeds scurrying through the undergrowth. Early in the afternoon, the clouds broke apart, and rays of sunlight slanted into the forest. A herd of forest cattle—twenty or more—crossed the track in front of them, forcing them to stop and wait till the loutish herbivores finally moved on. But they saw no large predators.

"Apex predators are always rare," Arkady said when Jason complained. "And this is not Earth in the Jurassic."

They reached the next lodge late in the afternoon. It was a concrete pillbox, surrounded by a high fence. Alexandra and Irina did the check this time, stepping on several small land scorpions. There was something lonely about the two women, stalking through knee-high vegetation. They both carried rifles but used them only for poking among the leaves. Beyond the fence was the forest, darkening as daylight faded and denser clouds moved in. Ash took photos, as did Maggie.

They went inside finally and Boris did another search. "My cans are in order," he announced. "And I have found no scorpions."

They unloaded the trucks and Alexandra made dinner. This time it was a pilaf and a mixture of spinach and chickpeas.

"Home food," said Arkady happily.

Heavy rain began to fall outside. Ash watched it through one of the virtual windows. It shone like a silver curtain in the lodge's spotlights. The low plants around the lodge bent under the weight of water, and a gusty wind made them flutter. Arkady got out plum brandy this time.

Jason looked unhappy. Maggie recorded the lodge's interior, and Ash took shots of the Leica, head tilted and lenses shining in the false firelight. She had the impression that Maggie was perfectly content, in spite of the lack of drama.

"Want outside," Baby said.

"The weather is bad," Ash replied.

The pterosaur hunched down, looking as unhappy as Jason.

Of course, the journalist wanted something exciting to happen. Ash was content to sit by the false fire and drink fruit brandy. What she liked about the outback was its strangeness, its inhumanity. Was that the right word? Being in a place without imported plants and animals, where people didn't fit in though they had made roads—a few, at least—and built lodges. Maybe what she liked about Arkady was his line of work. This was his turf. As much as anyone, he knew Aphrodite Terra.

In some ways, Venus was lucky. Earth did not have the resources to really settle the planet. The USSR had destroyed itself trying to win the Venus Race. The US had largely given up, in part because it no longer had a rival and in part because the problems on Earth kept getting worse. Venus provided some raw materials—not many; the shipping costs were ridiculous—and it was a tourist destination. Some people retired to the gated communities near Venusport. Others bought beachside condos against the time that Earth was no longer habitable. But most of the planet remained empty of humanity.

The next day, they moved on. The ground was rising and getting stonier, and the trees were all short, with big, drooping leaves. Small animals moved in the branches and the undergrowth. Midway through the afternoon, their truck turned off the rutted track into forest, mashing low plants and avoiding trees. The second truck followed.

"What?" asked Ash.

"We are going to show *National Geographic* a good time," Arkady said. "As you asked us to."

"And make a point," Boris added.

"Do you mind telling me what?" Ash asked.

"In good time," Arkady replied. "I'm tired of Jason's complaining about our fauna. It reminds me of other safaris I have led, full of rich tourists who want dinosaurs. I tell them that Venusian fauna is similar to fauna on Earth, but not identical, and we are not in the Jurassic. I've had the bastards ask for money back because we couldn't show them an allosaurus. I wanted to feed them to a pseudosuchus, which might not impress them but could certainly eat them."

Arkady was usually even-tempered, but he sounded angry now. Well, she got angry at some of her work. The fashion shoots could be fairly awful.

They crunched through more undergrowth. There were rocks here, making the driving chancy: outcroppings of a creamy yellow stone.

"Limestone," Arkady said. "This used to be underwater. There ought to be good fossils, though Jason does not strike me as a fossil man."

"I'm not one," Boris said, guiding the truck between two good-sized chunks of stone. A pair of pterosaurs rested on top of one. They were big, with impressive crests.

"Stop!" said Ash.

Boris did. She photographed the animals, which looked damn fine, their crests like orange sails.

"Don't like," Baby muttered. Of course not. These guys were big enough to eat him. They would if given the chance. The pterosaurs were not cannibals, but they happily ate related species, as humans once ate monkeys when there were monkeys in the wild.

They went on, coming finally to another track, this one much less used than the one they had been following. Boris turned onto it.

"I don't remember this," Ash said.

"It's good country," Arkady said. "Interesting. But the damn, gutless executive committee has decided the area is off-limits."

"Are you breaking rules?" Ash asked.

"Yes. This is the perfect time to explore, with a *National Geographic* videographer along."

"And with the CIA putting poisonous spies in our lodge," Boris growled.

Ash had a bad feeling. But Arkady ran the most reputable tours on the continent.

They bumped among more outcropping of cream-yellow rock.

"This looks right," Boris said, glancing at his GPS, which was in Cyrillic. Ash could not read it.

"For what?" she asked.

"An impact crater," said Arkady. "Or something else."

Boris hit the brakes.

Next to the road was a low wall made of yellow limestone. It curved gently, apparently part of a huge circle. The section in front of them had been dug out. Heaps of dirt lay in front of it. Off to either side, the soil had not been excavated, and the wall was a mound, covered with low plants and vines.

"I wasn't expecting the excavation," Arkady said. "I suppose we have the CIA to thank."

"Who built this?" Ash asked.

"Not us," Arkady replied. "And not the CIA. It shows up in early satellite surveys, along with three other circles, all in this area and all arranged in a broad arc. One circle is broken, only half there. The rest are complete. None has been investigated. In theory, they are impact craters from a body that broke apart before it hit.

"Remember that our colony was run from Earth. The apparatchiks in Moscow said exploration could wait. This wasn't a scientific settlement. It was military and economic. By the time we were ready to look around, the CIA was in the area. The government decided to leave them alone. We didn't have the power to confront the Americans."

They all climbed out and walked to the wall. It looked to be made of the same stone as the outcroppings. But it was a single piece, as far as Ash could tell, and the surface was slick. Ash ran her hand along it. As smooth as glass. When she pulled her hand away, she saw blood. The edge of the wall was knife-sharp.

"Here," said Arkady, and handed her a red handkerchief.

"What's that for?" Ash asked. "The revolution?"

"At the moment, it's for your hand. Use it."

Ash wrapped the handkerchief around the bleeding fingers. Maggie was recording her, she noticed.

The wall—the part aboveground at least—was more than a meter high, too tall to sit on comfortably, if one was human, and too tall to step over comfortably.

"Amazing," Jason said. "If humans did not build this, then it is proof of intelligent life on Venus."

"There isn't any," Ash put in. "The brightest things on the planet are animals like Baby. He's bright, but he doesn't build walls."

"It can't possibly be natural," Jason said.

"I agree," Arkady replied. "I also agree with Ash. I do not think this was built by anything native to Venus."

Maggie was panning, making a record of the entire length of the wall.

In back of them, a voice asked, "Who the hell are you?"

Ash turned, as did the others. A soldier in full body armor stood in the road between the two trucks. He was carrying a terrifying-looking, very-high-tech rifle. Ash saw that first, then she noticed that he was standing above the road, his boots not touching the surface.

"You are a hologram," Boris said.

"Yes. But there are gun emplacements all around you. Take a look."

Ash did. Red lights, sighting lasers, shone on top of neighboring rocks. As far as she could tell, they were aimed at her.

"If you doubt me, I can melt something," the hologram said. "Your robot."

"She is autonomous," Jason replied quickly. "A citizen of the

United States and an employee of *National Geographic*."

"Shit," said the hologram. "Stay put. I have to consult. If you move, the guns will fire." The soldier vanished.

"Are you still recording?" Jason asked Maggie.

"Yes, and I'm uploading my images to the nearest comsat. This place is about to become famous."

"That will make life uncomfortable for the CIA," said Arkady in a tone of satisfaction.

"And the useless Petrograd executive committee," Boris added.

"And for us," Ash put in. "You have just pissed off the most dangerous organization in the solar system."

The hologram reappeared. "I have backup coming. Stay where you are. I've been informed that your robot is emitting radio signals. Stop that!"

"Very well," Maggie said. She didn't add that it was too late.

They waited, staying where they were, even though a fine rain began to fall. Inside the truck cab, Baby squawked for food.

"Later," Ash called.

"Hungry!"

At last, a car appeared, bumping down the track. It stopped, and a pair of men climbed out, dressed entirely in black, with shiny black boots. They wore computer glasses with opaque lenses and dark, thick frames.

"Who are you?" one asked.

"Arkady Volkov Wildlife Tours," Arkady said.

"*National Geographic*," Jason added.

"Ashley Weatherman Fashion Art," Ash put in.

"Shit," the man said, then added, "Follow us, and don't try anything funny. There are guns in the forest. Any trouble, and they will melt your trucks."

They climbed into the trucks. Arkady handed Ash a first-aid kit, and she sprayed a bandage on her fingers. The antiseptic in it made the cuts sting. Venusian microbes did not usually infect humans, but there were Earth microbes spreading across the planet, and some of them were nasty.

The car turned and went back the way it had come. The trucks followed. As they began to move, Ash looked back. The hologram soldier was still in the middle of the road, rifle in hand, watching. Then the second truck rolled through him, and he was gone.

"I apologize," Arkady said. "I thought we could look at one crater and get out safely, with a few images that might—I hoped—endanger the CIA's control of this region."

"Were you expecting to find an alien artifact?" Ash asked.

"The longer we looked at the craters the more suspicious they have looked," Boris said. "We were looking at the CIA, of course. We would not have examined the satellite images so closely otherwise."

Ash leaned back and drank more tea. Next to her, Baby gnawed on a chow stick. Of course she was worried, but she couldn't imagine the CIA taking out *National Geographic*. Even monsters had their limits.

The rain grew heavier. Looking out, Ash saw a group of fire scorpions resting on a tree trunk, sheltered by foliage. They weren't large, but their exoskeletons were bright red, a warning of serious poison.

"I don't think I will draw Maggie's attention to them," Arkady said. "The CIA might not want us on the radio. A pity. They look handsome, and they are very poisonous. Tourists always enjoy deadly animals."

A half hour later, they reached a cliff made of the same yellow stone as the outcroppings. It rose above the forest, running as far as she could see in both directions. The road ended in front of it. The car stopped, and they stopped as well. Everyone climbed down.

"Leave the rifles in the trucks," one of the men said. "And

you can leave that thing too." He waved at Baby in his cage.

"He gets lonely," Ash said.

One man went ahead of them, opening a door in the cliff face. It looked human-made, but Ash was less sure of the opening it closed. Rectangular, very tall and narrow, it didn't look like the kind of doorway humans would cut. They filed through, followed by the second man, who closed the door and locked it. Inside was a corridor, as tall and narrow and rectangular as the opening. Lights were stuck along the walls. These were clearly human. As for the corridor itself—the stone was polished and as slick as glass. There were fossils in it. Ash made out shells, gleaming behind the glossy surface, as well as long things that might be worms or crinoids, though this world did not have crinoids. If she'd had another life to live, she would have been a biologist or paleontologist, though she had a low tolerance for the finicky work required of both. Maybe it was a better idea to shoot fashion models and megafauna.

Baby muttered in his cage.

The corridor ended in another narrow doorway, this one without a door. Beyond it was a rectangular room with polished-stone walls. Like the hall, it was narrow and tall. It contained a table and chairs, all 3-D-printed. Ash recognized the style. Human Office Modern.

"Okay," said one of the men. He took off his glasses, showing pale blue eyes with dark, puffy skin below them. "What is this about? We have a deal with the executive committee of the Petrograd Soviet." He looked at the other man, who still wore glasses. "Mike, get coffee, will you?"

"Sure," Mike answered. "Don't say anything exciting till I get back." The voice was contralto.

Ash took another look. Mike was either a woman or an FTM, though it was well hidden by the boxy suit and heavy-rimmed computer glasses. Not that it mattered. A female CIA agent was as dangerous as a male.

Mike left, and they sat down. Arkady and Boris looked grim. Irina and Alexandra looked worried. The *Nat Geo* journalist had an expression that combined fear and excitement. Maggie's gleaming lens face revealed nothing.

"Who built this?" Arkady asked.

"We don't know," the man replied. "We found it."

"Are there artifacts?" Arkady asked.

"Aside from the circles and these tunnels? Nothing we have found."

"This is a site of systemwide historical importance," Boris said. "Evidence that someone, not human, was on Venus before we came. You sat in it, keeping the people of Petrograd—and the scientists on Venus and Earth—from investigating. Not to mention the tourists we could have brought in, improving our economy."

"It meant we didn't have to set up camp in the forest," the man said. "It's dry in here, and there's a lot less animal life—or was, till recently. Believe me, this place isn't interesting. Just corridors and rooms, going a long way back into the cliff. All empty, except for the debris left by animals. Bones and dry leaves and dried-out feces."

Mike came back with a tray, carafe, and coffee cups. He or she poured coffee. There was a slight chill in the room, and it was pleasant to hold the warm cup and sip the hot coffee. Ash's cut fingers still stung a little.

"The question is, what will we do with you?" the first man said.

"*National Geographic* will be concerned if we vanish," Jason said. He sounded anxious.

"Accidents happen in the outback," Mike said in his or her high voice.

"I was recording and uploading my images, until your hologram told me to stop," Maggie put in. "The material went to the nearest comsat, which belongs—I believe—to Petrograd. I assume the comsat sent it on to our office in Venusport. The message was encrypted to prevent piracy. But our office can decode it. They will have done so by now."

"They know about the circle," Jason added. "And the robot you put in the lodge."

"What robot?" the man asked.

"The bug. The scorpion. It had wires."

Mike was leaning against a wall, cup in hand. The nameless man looked over, frowning.

"Not ours," Mike said. "Petrograd must be spying on itself."

Baby stirred in his cage. Ash reached a finger to scratch him and—in the same movement—undid the lock on the door. No one seemed to notice except Baby, who looked interested and alert.

She wondered about ventilation and ways to escape, looked around and saw a rectangle cut in the stone of one wall just below the ceiling. It was long and narrow with vertical bars made of the same stone as the wall. As she watched, a pair of antennae poked out between two of the bars. The animal followed. A scorpion, of course. The pale gray body suggested it was a cave scorpion, as did the lack of obvious eyes.

She watched as its front legs scrabbled to get a grip on the slick stone. It failed and fell, landing with an audible "tock." The nameless man spun in his chair, then was up and stamping the scorpion over and over. It wasn't even that big, Ash thought. No more than twenty centimeters.

The man remained bent over for several moments. "Oh God, I hate them."

"They are carrion eaters," Arkady said. "Living off the debris of pterosaur colonies that nest on cliffs and in shallow caves. Their bite does little harm to humans."

"I hate them," the man repeated.

"He has a phobia," Mike said. "Cave scorpions don't bother me."

The nameless agent straightened up. "The tunnels connect

with caves. The damn things have discovered they can live off us. They're all over."

"But hardly a serious problem," Arkady said.

"We also have fire scorpions," Mike put in.

The nameless agent twitched at the name. Mike smiled slightly. Ash had the impression he enjoyed his colleague's fear.

"That is a problem," Boris said. "But you shouldn't have them. They live in the forest, not in caves."

"They've bred with the cave scorpions," the nameless man said. His voice sounded constricted, as if fear had robbed him of breath.

"They can't have," Arkady said. "They are different species, living in different environments."

The two men exchanged glances and were silent.

After a moment, Boris said harshly, "You were not satisfied with robot scorpions. You have played with DNA and created a new species in violation of numerous laws."

"Not the laws on Earth," Mike said.

"You are on *Venus*," Boris pointed out. "And in Petrograd."

"I don't think we need to talk about this."

"Yes, we do," Arkady replied. "And not just here. You are in very serious violation of several treaties. Venus and Earth need to know about this."

The nameless agent pulled out a handgun, aiming it at Arkady. The gun was shaking. Ash could see that clearly. The gun, the shaking hand, the room, the other people were all unnaturally sharp and clear.

"Go," she said to Baby. The pterosaur was out in a moment, flapping onto the agent's head and clawing. The gun went off with a loud—very loud—sound. Arkady dove at the man, taking him down. The gun spun across the floor, away from Arkady and the nameless agent.

"Stop that," Mike said.

Ash looked toward him. His coffee cup lay on the yellow floor, in the middle of a brown pool of coffee, and he had a gun out, pointing it at Arkady.

Never mix with the CIA. But it was too late for that warning.

"No," said Alexandra. Ash was trying not to move, but she could see the ex-cop from the corner of her eye. The woman had a gun, held steadily and pointed at Mike. This was ridiculous.

"Get the damn animal off Brian," Mike said.

The nameless agent was on the floor, Arkady lying across him, and Baby still on his head, biting and clawing.

"Stop," Ash called. "You can stop now, Baby."

The pterosaur flapped back to his cage, settling on top and folding his downy wings.

"This is stupid," Mike said. "I'm not going to shoot anyone in here, and I hope to God this lovely lady is not going to shoot me. You guys look like idiots on the floor. Get up."

The two men did. Arkady looked rumpled, which was his usual condition. Blood ran down the face of the nameless agent. He wiped it with one hand, making a smear.

"We're pulling out," Mike added. "Petrograd knows this."

"Why?" asked Boris.

"Why do they know? We told them."

"Why are you pulling out?"

"The scorpions. The things are deadly, and Brian's right. They're all over."

"Am I right?" Boris said. "Did you create them?"

Mike was silent.

"They must have wanted something that could live in sewers and the crawl spaces of buildings," Arkady put in. "And that was toxic. It sounds like a weapon that could be used against Petrograd."

"They are telling us too much," Boris said. "They must be planning to kill us."

"Not while I hold this gun," Alexandra said.

"We're pulling out, as I told you," Mike said. "And there is no proof that we made the scorpions or intended to use them for anything. You Soviets are way too paranoid."

"How many people are left here?" Arkady asked.

"Dozens," said the agent named Brian.

"Don't be a fool. We saw no one coming in, and no one has responded to the sound of gunfire. Either you are alone, or your colleagues are not close."

"Three," Mike answered. "They're in the back rooms, destroying the equipment. When they're done, we'll take the last VTL."

Boris pulled a roll of duct tape from his vest. He tossed it to Arkady. "Tape them up."

"No," said Brian. "What if more scorpions come?"

"Too bad," Boris said.

The man bolted for the room's doorway. Baby flapped onto him, clawing and shrieking, "Bad! Bad!"

Brian stumbled. Boxlike Irina grabbed his arm and pulled him around, then drove a fist into the man's midsection. He bent over, coughing, and collapsed onto his knees. Fortunately, because Ash hated vomit, he did not throw up.

"That's some punch," Mike said in his or her pleasant voice.

"She used to be a stevedore," Arkady said. "Now I will tape you up, and you will hope that none of your new, mutant scorpions arrive."

"I'm not phobic," Mike replied. "And I'm not going to shoot it out with you. We don't know what these walls are made of, but you can't scratch them. Anything that hits them is going to bounce off." He put his gun on the table. "We've been lucky so far. The last ricochet didn't hit anyone. I think the bullet went out the door. There's no reason to think we'll be lucky a second time."

Arkady and Irina taped the two men while Alexandra kept her gun leveled.

"Are you recording?" Arkady asked after they were done.

"Yes," Maggie said. "But I'm having trouble with my radio signal here. As soon as we are outside, I will send the photos to Venusport."

Arkady set a knife on the table next to Mike's gun. "It will cut the tape," he said to Mike. "Even if your comrades don't come looking for you, you'll be able to get free."

"That may be a mistake," Boris said.

Arkady nodded. "We all make them. Let's get out of here."

They left the room and retraced their way through the mazelike stone corridors. No one appeared though they did encounter a scorpion, crawling over the floor. It was dirty pink with tiny eyes, thirty centimeters long and the ugliest land scorpion Ash had ever seen. Boris stepped on it hard, crushing its exoskeleton. The many legs kept scrabbling, and the mandibles twitched back and forth, but the animal's body could not move. It was broken. "This is why we wear tall boots," he said.

They found the trucks where they had left them. Rain still fell heavily.

"I can send the recordings now," Maggie said.

"Do it," Jason said. "I am going to write an exposé that will rip those guys apart. They were ready to kill us."

They ran for the trucks, climbed in, and pulled out, going along the track away from the ruins.

Ash could feel her heart beating rapidly. Her mouth was dry, and she was shaking. Fear fighting with amazement. She had been inside ruins built by aliens, and she had escaped from the CIA. What a day!

Baby was in his cage, shivering and repeating "bad, bad" over and over in a quiet voice.

"Okay," Ash said after her heart slowed down. "What was that about?"

Arkady leaned forward and checked the truck radio, which was off. "We knew the CIA was here and that they had some kind of agreement with the Petrograd executive committee. We knew about the circles. And we had this." He handed her a tablet. On the screen was a piece of sculpture, deeply worn and barely recognizable as a person. It had two arms and two legs, all long and thin, the legs together and the arms folded across the chest. The person's torso was short and wide, its neck long and narrow, its head wedge-shaped.

"This might be expressive distortion," Arkady said. "Or it might be an alien. It is only ten centimeters long. It was found in the outback in the early days of settlement, and it ended in the Petrograd Museum. The curators thought it was fake. It remained in the collection but was never investigated."

"We learned about it and put it together with the circles," Boris said. "Do you have any idea how much money Petrograd could make from tourism if we had authentic alien ruins?"

"Who are you?" Ash asked.

"People who want to embarrass the executive committee," Arkady said. "Can you imagine what Lenin would have said about that collection of petty bureaucrats? Now *National Geographic* will publish its exclusive. With luck, there will be a huge stink. The Petrograd Soviet will decide to remove the executive committee, and the CIA will be so embarrassed that it will leave Aphrodite Terra."

"That's too much to hope," Boris growled.

"Maybe," Arkady replied. "In any case, we couldn't pass up the chance. The entire solar system pays attention to the *National Geographic*."

"What about the bug in the lodge?" Ash asked. "Mike said it wasn't one of theirs."

"It was CIA, but they didn't put it in the lodge. Some of our farm workers found it crawling in the fields, heading toward Petrograd, and sent for the police. They captured it. I brought it with us," Boris said. "We wanted *Nat Geo* to see what we had to put up with. Poisonous robot spies! They are a crime against nature and peaceful coexistence!"

The truck was bumping over the rough road, among dripping trees, while rain beat on the windows. Looking back, she saw the other truck, dim in the rain.

"I feel as if everything has been fake," she told the two men. "You set up the robot scorpion and you set up discovering the circle."

Arkady said, "The circles are real, and they are not impact craters, though we don't know what they are. Ball courts? Fishponds? Temples?

"And the tunnels are real. We didn't know about them, but now they will be famous."

Boris added, "Those idiots on the executive committee were so afraid that they let the CIA camp on a site of systemwide historical importance. We have been slowly dying when we could have made a fortune from tourism. Why would anyone go to Venusport when they can come here and see alien ruins?" He was silent for a moment, then added, "We'll have to get rid of their damn pink scorpions. That won't be easy. And then take a serious look. Who knows what may be in the caves and circles? More statues like the one in the museum? Maybe even a skeleton?"

"Who are you guys?" Ash asked.

Arkady laughed. "I am myself. Arkady Volkov of Volkov Tours. Boris is a part-time employee."

"What else does he do?"

"I'm an analyst for the political police," Boris replied. "But my hours have been cut because of the Soviet's cash flow problems—which we would not have if we had more tourists."

"Or if the executive committee stopped listening to American economists," Arkady added.

"I don't want a lecture on economics," Boris said. "I needed a second job. Arkady gave me one."

"And Irina and Alexandra?" Ash asked.

"Ordinary working people," Arkady said.

"Could the CIA really have been stupid enough to create a new kind of scorpion?" Ash asked.

"Remember that no one has ever gone broke by underestimating the intelligence of Americans," Arkady said.

"This seems way too Byzantine," Ash added.

Boris gave a rasping laugh. "Arkady's ancestors came from some damn place in Central Asia. But I am Russian, and Russians are the heirs of Byzantium."

They made it back to the pillbox lodge at nightfall. Arkady and Boris checked the parking space with flashlights and called all clear. They went in through the rain.

Arkady turned on the fire, as the rest of them pulled off their wet jackets and hung them up to dry.

"I'll start dinner," Alexandra told them. "Irina, will you help?"

The ex-cop and the ex-stevedore went into the kitchen. Ash sat down in front of the fire, Baby's cage on the floor next to her. Baby climbed on top of the cage. "Hungry."

She found a piece of chow and gave it to him.

"Hunt," he said.

"Not now."

Jason and Maggie joined her, the journalist settling into a chair, the Leica standing on her four silver legs, her long neck stretched out, head turning as she made another recording.

"I think we can call the trip successful," Jason said. "We have discovered the first evidence of intelligent aliens, and I have a dramatic story about fighting the CIA."

"I suspect the CIA part of the story will vanish," Arkady said. "But you will have the alien ruins."

"I'll fight for the entire story," Jason said. "It's outrageous that we were threatened by our own government."

"We'll go back to Petrograd," Arkady said. "I will show you a piece of sculpture at the museum, and you might be interested in talking to the Soviet's executive committee. Ask them what they were thinking to let the CIA perch in the most important piece of archeology in the solar system. God knows what kind of damage they might have done! War—overt or covert—is not good for art or history."

Boris set a bottle of fruit brandy on the table, along with four glasses. "I'll go back. I have worked as an exterminator. I want to know what's in the tunnels and the caves, aside from vermin; and I will enjoy getting rid of those damn pink scorpions."

After dinner, in her bedroom, Ash considered the journey. She was a little buzzed from alcohol and shaky from adrenaline. But nothing was happening now. She could finally think.

The circles and tunnels could not have been faked. She was less certain about the figurine. It didn't have the glassy surface of the stone in the circle and the tunnels; and even if the government in Moscow hadn't been interested in science, it would have been interested in an alien figurine. That had to have some kind of propaganda value. Unless they were afraid of it. Would fear have made them put it in a museum and forget it?

It would be easy to fake something as small as the figurine. Arkady said it was in the Petrograd Museum, but he could have brought it with him, planning to plant it near the circle for Jason to find. That and the toxic scorpion in the lodge would have given *National Geographic* its big story. With luck, the story would have forced the CIA out and brought down the executive committee.

She could imagine Arkady learning who the client was and hurriedly putting together an elaborate con. Never trust a Leninist entirely. And she could imagine him as completely honest. As far as she knew, he always had been.

Well, if the figurine was fake, that would be discovered, probably quickly.

But the ruins had to be real. She lay there, her light still on, considering the possibility that humanity was not alone. Where were the aliens now? In the solar system? Or had they moved on? And what difference would knowledge of them make to Earth, shambling toward destruction? Or to Venus, tied to Earth and maybe unable to survive on its own? Ash had no idea. But the world—the two worlds—had suddenly become more interesting and full of possibility.

"Turn light off," said Baby, hunched in his cage. "Sleep."

THE END

Note: Our Venus rotates backward compared to most planets in the solar system, and its day is longer than its year. The current theory is it was dinged by something big early in the development of the system. The ding turned it backward and slowed its rotation. In my alternative history, this ding did not happen. My Venus rotates forward and has a day about as long as that of Earth or Mars. This rotation gives it a magnetic field, which our Venus does not have. The field prevents—at least in part—the development of the planet's current toxic greenhouse atmosphere. In addition, there was a ding that didn't happen in our history, at least as far as we know. A body—possibly two—hit Earth after life had developed there, then went on to hit Venus, depositing Earth microbes. As a result, my Venus has blue-green algae, and this over time gave it an atmosphere comparable to Earth. The similarity of Venusian life to life on Earth is due to the shared genetic history.

The history of Earth is the same as in our time line, until Soviet probes discover that Venus is habitable. Then a serious space race begins. The cost of the race helps to destroy the Soviet Union and helps to distract the United States from dealing with global warming.

As you may have noticed, the Pecheneg machine gun was never used. Chekhov was wrong. You can put a gun on the wall in the first act and never use it.

DAVID BRIN

Change may not be good, but it's often unavoidable—especially when it's your whole world that's about to change . . .

David Brin entered the science-fiction field in the late 1970s, and has been one of the most prominent SF writers in the business ever since, winning three Hugo Awards and one Nebula Award for his work. Brin is best known for his *Uplift* series, which started in 1980 with *Sundiver,* and subsequently has continued in *Startide Rising,* which won both a Hugo in 1984 and a Nebula in 1983, *The Uplift War,* which won a Hugo in 1988, and then on through *Brightness Reef, Infinity's Shore, Heaven's Reach,* and *Gorilla, My Dreams.* There's also a guide to the *Uplift* universe, *Contacting Aliens: An Illustrated Guide to David Brin's Uplift Universe,* by Brin and Kevin Lenagh. He won another Hugo Award in 1985 for his short story "The Crystal Spheres," and won the John W. Campbell Memorial Award in 1986 for his novel *The Postman,* which was later made into a big-budget film starring Kevin Costner. Brin's other novels include *Kiln People, Kiln Time, The Practice Effect, Earth, Glory Season, Sky Horizon,* and, with Gregory Benford, *Heart of the Comet.* His short work has been collected in *The River of Time, Otherness,* and *Tomorrow Happens.* He edited the anthology *Project Solar Sail* with Arthur C. Clarke, and has published several nonfiction books such as *The Transparent Society, Through Stranger Eyes,* and *King Kong Is Back!: An Unauthorized Look at One Humongous Ape.* His most recent book is a new novel, *Existence.*

The Tumbledowns of Cleopatra Abyss

DAVID BRIN

1.

TODAY'S *THUMP* WAS OVERDUE. JONAH WONDERED IF it might not come at all.

Just like last Thorday when—at the Old Clock's midmorning chime—farmers all across the bubble habitat clambered up pinyon vines or crouched low in expectation of the regular, daily throb—a pulse and quake that hammered up your foot soles and made all the bubble boundaries shake. Only Thorday's *thump* never came. The chime was followed by silence and a creepy letdown feeling. And Jonah's mother lit a candle, hoping to avert bad luck.

Early last spring, there had been almost a *whole week* without any thumps. Five days in a row, with no rain of detritus, shaken loose from the Upper World, tumbling down here to the ocean bottom. And two smaller gaps the previous year.

Apparently, today would be yet another hiatus . . .

Whomp!

Delayed, the *thump* came *hard,* shaking the moist ground beneath Jonah's feet. He glanced with concern toward the bubble boundary, more than two hundred meters away—a membrane of ancient, translucent volcanic stone, separating the paddies and pinyon forest from black, crushing waters just outside. The barrier vibrated, an unpleasant, scraping sound.

This time, especially, it caused Jonah's teeth to grind.

"They used to sing, you know," commented the complacent old woman who worked at a nearby freeboard loom, nodding as gnarled fingers darted among the strands, weaving ropy cloth. Her hands did not shake though the nearby grove of thick vines did, quivering much worse than after any normal *thump*.

"I'm sorry, grandmother." Jonah reached out to a nearby bole of twisted cables that dangled from the bubble habitat's high-arching roof, where shining glowleaves provided the settlement's light.

"*Who* used to sing?"

"The walls, silly boy. The bubble walls. Thumps used to come exactly on time, according to the Old Clock. Though every year we would shorten the main wheel by the same amount, taking thirteen seconds off the length of a day. Aftershakes always arrived from the same direction, you could depend on it! And the bubble sang to us."

"It sang . . . you mean like that awful groan?" Jonah poked a finger in one ear, as if to pry out the fading reverberation. He peered into the nearby forest of thick trunks and vines, listening for signs of breakage. Of disaster.

"Not at all! It was *musical*. Comforting. Especially after a miscarriage. Back then, a woman would lose over half of her quickenings. Not like today, when more babies are born alive than warped or misshapen or dead. Your generation has it lucky! And it's said things were even worse in olden days. The Founders were fortunate to get any living replacements at all! Several times, our population dropped dangerously." She shook her head, then smiled. "Oh . . . but the music! After every midmorning *thump* you could face the bubble walls and relish it. That music helped us women bear our heavy burden."

"Yes, grandmother, I'm sure it was lovely," Jonah replied,

keeping a respectful voice as he tugged on the nearest pinyon to test its strength, then clambered upward, hooking long, unwebbed toes into the braided vines, rising high enough to look around. None of the other men or boys could climb as well.

Several nearby boles appeared to have torn loose their mooring suckers from the domelike roof. Five . . . no six of them . . . teetered, lost their final grip-holds, then tumbled, their luminous tops crashing into the rice lagoon, setting off eruptions of sparks . . . or else onto the work sheds where Panalina and her mechanics could be heard, shouting in dismay. *It's a bad one,* Jonah thought. Already the hab bubble seemed dimmer. If many more pinyons fell, the clan might dwell in semidarkness, or even go hungry.

"Oh, it was beautiful, all right," the old woman continued, blithely ignoring any ruckus. "Of course in *my* grandmother's day, the thumps weren't just regular and perfectly timed. They came in *pairs*! And it is said that long before—in *her* grandmother's grandmother's time, when a day lasted so long that it spanned several sleep periods—thumps used to arrive in clusters of four or five! How things must've shook back then! But always from the same direction, and exactly at the midmorning chime."

She sighed, implying that Jonah and all the younger folk were making too much fuss. You call *this* a thump shock?

"Of course," she admitted, "the bubbles were *younger* then. More flexible, I suppose. Eventually, some misplaced thump is gonna end us all."

Jonah took a chance—he was in enough trouble already without offending the Oldest Female, who had undergone thirty-four pregnancies and still had *six* living womb-fruit—four of them precious females.

But grandmother seemed in a good mood, distracted by memories . . .

Jonah took off, clambering higher till he could reach with

his left hand for one of the independent dangle vines that sometimes laced the gaps between pinyons. With his right hand he flicked with his belt knife, severing the dangler a meter or so below his knees. Sheathing the blade and taking a deep breath, he launched off, swinging across an open space in the forest . . . and finally alighting along a second giant bole. It shook from his impact and Jonah worried. *If this one was weakened, and I'm the reason that it falls, I could be in for real punishment. Not just grandma-tending duty!*

A "rascal's" reputation might have been harmless, when Jonah was younger. But now, the mothers were pondering what Tairee Dome might have to pay, in dowry, for some other bubble colony to take him. A boy known to be unruly might not get any offers, at any marriage price . . . and a man without a wife-sponsor led a marginal existence.

But honestly, this last time wasn't my fault! How am I supposed to make an improved pump without filling something with high-pressure water? All right, the kitchen rice cooker was a poor choice. But it has a gauge and everything . . . or, it used to.

After quivering far too long, the great vine held. With a brief sense of relief, he scrambled around to the other side. There was no convenient dangler, this time, but another pinyon towered fairly close. Jonah flexed his legs, prepared, and launched himself across the gap, hurtling with open arms, alighting with shock and painful clumsiness. He didn't wait though, scurrying to the other side—where there *was* another dangle vine, well positioned for a wide-spanning swing.

This time he couldn't help himself while hurtling across open space, giving vent to a yell of exhilaration.

Two swings and four leaps later, he was right next to the bubble's edge, reaching out to stroke the nearest patch of ancient, vitrified stone, in a place where no one would see him break taboo. Pushing at the transparent barrier, Jonah felt deep ocean pressure shoving back. The texture felt rough-ribbed, uneven. Sliver flakes rubbed off, dusting his hand.

"Of course, bubbles were younger then," the old woman said. *"More flexible."*

Jonah had to wrap a length of dangle vine around his left wrist and clutch the pinyon with his toes, in order to lean far out and bring his face right up against the bubble—it sucked heat into bottomless cold—using his right hand and arm to cup around his face and peer into the blackness outside. Adapting vision gradually revealed the stony walls of Cleopatra Canyon, the narrow-deep canyon where humanity had come to take shelter so very long ago. Fleeing the Coss invaders. Before the life spans of many grandmothers.

Several strings of globelike habitats lay parallel along the canyon bottom, like pearls on a necklace, each of them surrounded by a froth of smaller bubbles . . . though fewer of the little ones than there were in olden times, and none anymore in the most useful sizes. It was said that, way back at the time of the Founding, there used to be faint illumination overhead, filtering downward from the surface and demarking night from day: light that came from the mythological god-thing that old books called the *sun,* so fierce that it could penetrate both dense, poisonous clouds and the ever-growing ocean.

But that was way back in a long-ago past, when the sea had not yet burgeoned so, filling canyons, becoming a dark and mighty deep. Now the only gifts that fell from above were clots of detritus that men gathered to feed algae ponds. Debris that got stranger every year.

These days the canyon walls could only be seen by light from the bubbles themselves, by their pinyon glow within. Jonah turned slowly left to right, counting and naming those farm enclaves he could see. *Amtor . . . Leininger . . . Chown . . . Kuttner . . . Okumo . . .* each one a clan with traditions and styles all their own. Each one possibly the place where Tairee tribe might sell him in a marriage pact. A mere boy and good riddance. Good at numbers and letters. A bit skilled with his hands, but notoriously absentminded, prone to staring at nothing, and occasionally putting action to rascally thoughts.

He kept tallying: *Brakutt . . . Lewis . . . Atari . . . Napeer . . . Aldrin . . . what?*

Jonah blinked. What was happening to Aldrin? And the bubble just beyond it. Both Aldrin and Bezo were still quivering. He could make out few details at this range through the milky, pitted membrane. But one of the two was rippling and convulsing, the glimmer of its pinyon forest shaking back and forth as the giant boles swayed . . . then collapsed!

The other distant habitat seemed to be *inflating*. Or so Jonah thought at first. Rubbing his eyes and pressing even closer, as Bezo habitat grew bigger . . .

. . . or else it was rising! Jonah could not believe what he saw. Torn loose, somehow, from the ocean floor, the entire bubble was moving. Upward. And as Bezo ascended, its flattened bottom now reshaped itself as farms and homes and lagoons tumbled together into the base of the accelerating globe. With its pinyons still mostly in place, Bezo Colony continued glowing as it climbed upward.

Aghast, and yet compelled to look, Jonah watched until the glimmer that had been Bezo finally vanished in blackness, accelerating toward the poison surface of Venus.

Then, without warning or mercy, habitat Aldrin imploded.

2.

"I WAS BORN IN BEZO, YOU KNOW."

Jonah turned to see Enoch leaning on his rake, staring south along the canyon wall, toward a gaping crater where that ill-fated settlement bubble used to squat. Distant glimmers of glow lamps flickered over there as crews prowled along the Aldrin debris field, sifting for salvage. But that was a job for mechanics and senior workers. Meanwhile, the algae ponds and pinyons must be fed, so Jonah also found himself outside, in coveralls that stank and fogged from his own breath and many generations of previous wearers, helping to gather the week's harvest of organic detritus.

Jonah responded in the same dialect Enoch had used. Click-Talk. The only way to converse, when both of you are deep underwater.

"Come on," he urged his older friend, a recent, marriage-price immigrant to Tairee Bubble. "All of that is behind you. A male should never look back. We do as we are told."

Enoch shrugged—broad shoulders making his stiff coveralls scrunch around the helmet, fashioned from an old foam bubble of a size no longer found in these parts. Enoch's phlegmatic resignation was an adaptive skill that served him well, as he was married to Jonah's cousin, Jezzy, an especially strong-willed young woman, bent on exerting authority and not above threatening her new husband with casting-out.

I can hope for someone gentle, when I'm sent to live beside a stranger in a strange dome.

Jonah resumed raking up newly fallen organic stuff—mostly ropy bits of vegetation that lay limp and pressure-crushed after their long tumble to the bottom. In recent decades, there had also been detritus of another kind. *Shells* that had holes in them for legs and heads. And skeleton fragments from slinky creatures that must have—when living—stretched as long as Jonah was tall! Much more complicated than the mud worms that kept burrowing closer to the domes of late. More like the fabled *snakes* or *fish* that featured in tales from Old Earth.

Panalina's dad—old Scholar Wu—kept a collection of

skyfalls in the little museum by Tairee's eastern arc, neatly labeled specimens dating back at least ten grandmother cycles, to the era when *light* and *heat* still came down along with debris from above—a claim that Jonah still deemed mystical. Perhaps just a legend, like Old Earth.

"These samples . . . do you see how they are getting more complicated, Jonah?" So explained old man Wu as he traced patterns of veins in a recently gathered seaweed. *"And do you make out what's embedded here? Bits of creatures living on or within the plant. And there! Does that resemble a bite mark? The outlines of where teeth tore into this vegetation? Could that act of devouring be what sent it tumbling down to us?"*

Jonah pondered what it all might mean while raking up dross and piling it onto the sledge, still imagining the size of a jaw that could have torn such a path through tough, fibrous weed. And everything was pressure-shrunk down here!

"How can anything live up at the surface?" He recalled asking Wu, who was said to have read every book that existed in the Cleopatra Canyon colonies, most of them two or three times. *"Did not the founders say the sky was thick with poison?"*

"With carbon dioxide and sulfuric acid, yes. I have shown you how we use pinyon leaves to separate out those two substances, both of which have uses in the workshop. One we exhale—"

"And the other burns! Yet, in small amounts it smells sweet."

"That is because the Founders, in their wisdom, put sym-bi-ants in our blood. Creatures that help us deal with pressure and gases that would kill folks who still live on enslaved Earth."

Jonah didn't like to envision tiny animals coursing through his body even if they did him good. Each year, a dozen kids throughout the bubble colonies were chosen to study such useful things—biological things. A smaller number chose the field that interested Jonah, where even fewer were allowed to specialize.

"But the blood creatures can only help us down here, where the

pinyons supply us with breathable air. Not up top, where poisons are so thick." Jonah gestured skyward. *"Is that why none of the Risers have ever returned?"*

Once every year or two, the canyon colonies lost a person to the hell that awaited above. Most often because of a buoyancy accident; a broken tether or boot-ballast sent some hapless soul plummeting upward. Another common cause was suicide. And—more rarely—it happened for another reason, one the mothers commanded that no one might discuss, or even mention. A forbidden reason.

Only now, after the sudden rise of Bezo Bubble and a thousand human inhabitants, followed by the Aldrin implosion, little else was on anyone's mind.

"Even if you survive the rapid change in pressure . . . one breath up there and your lungs would be scorched as if by flame," old Scholar Wu had answered yesterday. *"That is why the Founders seeded living creatures a bit higher than us, but beneath the protective therm-o-cline layer that keeps most of the poison out of our abyss . . ."*

The old man paused, fondling a strange, multijawed skeleton. *"It seems that life—some kind of life—has found a way to flourish near that barrier. So much so that I have begun to wonder—"*

A sharp voice roused him.

"Jonah!"

This time it was Enoch, reminding him to concentrate on work. A good reason to work in pairs. He got busy with the rake. Mother was pregnant again, along with aunts Leor and Sosun. It always made them cranky with tension, as the fetuses took their time, deciding whether to go or stay—and if they stayed, whether to come out healthy or as warped ruins. No, it would not do to return from this salvage outing with only half a load!

So he and Enoch forged farther afield, hauling the sledge to another spot where high ocean currents often dumped interesting things after colliding with the canyon walls. The algae ponds and pinyons needed fresh supplies of organic matter. Especially in recent decades, after the old volcanic vents dried up.

The Book of Exile *says we came down here to use the vents, way back when the sea was hot and new. A shallow refuge for free humans to hide from the Coss, while comets fell in regular rhythm, thumping Venus to life. Drowning her fever and stirring her veins.*

Jonah had only a vague notion what "comets" were—great balls drifting through vast emptiness, till godlike beings with magical powers flung them down upon this planet. Balls of *ice*, like the pale blue slush that formed on the cool, downstream sides of boulders in a fast, underwater current. About as big as Cleopatra Canyon was wide, that's what books said about a comet.

Jonah gazed at the towering cliff walls, enclosing all the world he ever knew. Comets were so vast! Yet they had been striking Venus daily, since centuries before colonists came, immense, precreation icebergs, pelting the sister world of Old Earth. Perhaps several million of them by now, herded first by human civilization and later by Coss Masters, who adopted the project as their own— one so ambitious as to be nearly inconceivable.

So much ice. So much water. Building higher and higher till it has to fill the sky, even the poison skies of Venus. So much that it fills all of creatio—

"Jonah, watch out!"

Enoch's shouted warning made him crouch and spin about. Or Jonah tried to, in the clumsy coveralls, raising clouds of muck stirred by heavy, shuffling boots. "Wha—? What is it?"

"Above you! Heads up!"

Tilting back was strenuous, especially in a hurry. The foggy faceplate didn't help. Only now Jonah glimpsed something overhead, shadowy and huge, looming fast out of the black.

"Run!"

He required no urging. Heart pounding in terror, Jonah

pumped his legs for all they were worth, barely lifting weighted shoes to shuffle-skip with long strides toward the nearby canyon wall, sensing and then back-glimpsing a massive, sinuous shape that plummeted toward him out of the abyssal sky. By dim light from a distant habitat dome, the monstrous shape turned languidly, following his dash for safety, swooping in to close the distance fast! Over his right shoulder, Jonah glimpsed a gaping mouth and rows of huge, glistening teeth. A sinuous body from some nightmare.

I'm not gonna make it. The canyon wall was just too far.

Jonah skidded to a stop, raising plumes of bottom muck. Swiveling into a crouch and half moaning with fear, he lifted his only weapon—a rake meant for gathering organic junk from the seafloor. He brandished it crosswise, hoping to stymie the wide jaw that now careened out of dimness, framed by four glistening eyes. Like some ancient storybook *dragon,* stooping for prey. No protection, the rake was more a gesture of defiance.

Come on, monster.

A decent plan, on the spur of the moment.

It didn't work.

It didn't have to.

The rake shattered, along with several ivory teeth as the giant maw plunged around Jonah, crashing into the surrounding mud, trapping him . . . but never closing, nor biting or chewing. Having braced for all those things, he stood there in a tense hunker as tremors shook the canyon bottom, closer and more spread out than the daily thump. It had to be more of the sinuous monster, colliding with surrounding muck—a long, long leviathan!

A final ground quiver, then silence. Some creakings. Then more silence.

And darkness. Enveloped, surrounded by the titan's mouth, Jonah at first saw nothing . . . then a few faint glimmers. Pinyon light from nearby Monsat Bubble habitat. Streaming in through holes. *Holes* in the gigantic head. Holes that gradually opened wider as ocean-bottom pressure wreaked havoc on flesh meant for much higher waters.

Then the smell hit Jonah.

An odor of death.

Of course. Such a creature would never dive this deep of its own accord. Instead of being pursued by a ravenous monster, Jonah must have run along the same downdraft conveying a corpse to its grave. An intersection and collision that might seem hilarious someday, when he told the story as an old grandpa, assuming his luck held. Right now, he felt sore, bruised, angry, embarrassed . . . and concerned about the vanishing supply in his meager air bubble.

With his belt knife, Jonah began probing and cutting a path out of the trap. He had another reason to hurry. If he had to be rescued by others, there would be no claiming this flesh for Tairee, for his clan and family. For his dowry and husband price.

Concerned clicks told him Enoch was nearby and one promising gap in the monster's cheek suddenly gave way to the handle of a rake. Soon they both were tearing at it, sawing tough membranes, tossing aside clots of shriveling muscle and skin. His bubble helmet might keep out the salt sea, but pungent aromas were another matter. Finally, with Enoch tugging helpfully on one arm, Jonah squeezed out and stumbled several steps before falling to his knees, coughing.

"Here come others," said his friend. And Jonah lifted his gaze, spying men in bottom suits and helmets, hurrying this way, brandishing glow bulbs and makeshift weapons. Behind them he glimpsed one of the cargo subs—a string of midsized bubbles, pushed by hand-crank propellers—catching up fast.

"Help me get up . . . on top," he urged Enoch, who bore some of his weight as he stood. Together, they sought a route onto the massive head. There was danger in this moment. Without clear ownership, fighting might break out among salvage crews from different domes, as happened a generation ago, over the last hot vent on the floor of Cleopatra Canyon. Only after several dozen men were dead had the grandmothers made peace. But if Tairee held a firm claim to this corpse, then rules of gift-generosity would parcel out shares to every dome, with only a largest-best allotment to Tairee. Peace and honor now depended on his speed. But the monster's cranium was steep, crumbly, and slick.

Frustrated and almost out of time, Jonah decided to take a chance. He slashed at the ropy cables binding his soft overalls to the weighted clogs that kept him firmly on the ocean bottom. Suddenly buoyant, he began to sense the Fell Tug . . . the pull toward heaven, toward doom. The same tug that had yanked Bezo Colony, a few days ago, sending that bubble habitat and all of its inhabitants plummeting skyward.

Enoch understood the gamble. Gripping Jonah's arm, he stuffed his rake and knife and hatchet into Jonah's belt. Anything convenient. So far, so good. The net force seemed to be slightly downward. Jonah nodded at his friend, and jumped.

3.

THE MARRIAGE PARTY MADE ITS WAY TOWARD TAIREE Bubble's dock, shuffling along to beating tambourines. Youngsters—gaily decked in rice flowers and pinyon garlands— danced alongside the newlyweds. Although many of the children wore masks or makeup to disguise minor birth defects, they seemed light of spirit.

They were the only ones.

Some adults tried their best, chanting and shouting at all the right places. Especially several dozen refugees—Tairee's allocated share of threadbare escapees from the ruin of Cixin and Sadoul settlements—who cheered with the fervid eagerness of people desperately trying for acceptance in their new home rather than mere sufferance. As for other guests from unaffected domes? Most appeared to have come only for free food. These now crowded near the dock, eager to depart as soon as the nuptial sub was on its way.

Not that Jonah could blame them. Most people preferred staying close to home ever since the thumps started going all crazy, setting off a chain of tragedies, tearing at the old, placid ways.

And today's thump is already overdue, he thought. In fact, there hadn't been a ground-shaking comet strike in close to a month. Such a gap would have been unnerving, just a year or two ago. Now, given how awful some recent impacts had been, any respite was welcome.

A time of chaos. Few see good omens even in a new marriage.

Jonah glanced at his bride, come to collect him from Laussane Bubble, all the way at the far northern outlet of Cleopatra Canyon. Taller than average, with a clear complexion and strong carriage, she had good hips and only a slight mutant mottling on the back of her scalp, where the hair grew in a wild, discolored corkscrew. An easily overlooked defect, like Jonah's lack of toe webbing, or the way he would sneeze or yawn uncontrollably whenever the air pressure changed too fast. No one jettisoned a child over such inconsequentials.

Though you can be exiled forever from all you ever knew if you're born with the genetic defect of maleness. Jonah could not help scanning the workshops and dorms, the pinyons and paddies of Tairee, wondering if he would see this place—his birth bubble— ever again. Perhaps, if the grandmothers of Laussane trusted him with errands. Or next time Tairee hosted a festival—if his new wife chose to take him along.

He had barely met Petri Smoth before this day, having spoken just a few words with her over the years, at various craft-

and-seed fairs, hosted by some of the largest domes. During last year's festival, held in ill-fated Aldrin Bubble, she *had* asked him a few pointed questions about some tinkered gimmicks he had on display. In fact, now that he looked back on it, her tone and expression must have been . . . evaluating. Weighing his answers with *this* possible outcome in mind. It just never occurred to Jonah, at the time, that he was impressing a girl enough to choose him as a mate.

I thought she was interested in my improved ballast-transfer valve.

And maybe . . . in a way . . . she was.

Or, at least, in Jonah's mechanical abilities. Panalina had suggested that explanation yesterday, while helping Jonah prepare his dowry—an old cargo truck that he had purchased with his prize winnings for claiming the dead sea serpent—a long-discarded submersible freighter that he had spent the last year reconditioning. A hopeless wreck, some called it, but no longer.

"Well, it's functional, I'll give you that," the Master Mechanic of Tairee Bubble had decreed last night, after going over the vessel from stem to stern, checking everything from hand-wound anchor tethers and stone keel weights to the bench where several pairs of burly men might labor at a long crank, turning a propeller to drive the boat forward. She thumped extra storage bubbles, turning stopcocks to sniff at the hissing, pressurized air. Then Panalina tested levers that would let seawater into those tanks, if need be, keeping the sub weighed down on the bottom, safe from falling into the deadly sky.

"It'll do," she finally decreed, to Jonah's relief. This could help him begin married life on a good note. Not every boy got to present his new bride with a whole submarine!

Jonah had acquired the old relic months before people realized just how valuable each truck might be, even junkers like this one—for rescue and escape—as a chain of calamities disrupted the canyon settlements. His repairs hadn't been completed in time to help evacuate more families from cracked and doomed Cixin or Sadoul Bubbles, and he felt bad about that. Still, with Panalina's ruling of seaworthiness, this vehicle would help make Petri Smoth a woman of substance in the hierarchy at Laussane, and prove Jonah a real asset to his wife.

Only . . . what happens when so many bubbles fail that the others can't take refugees anymore?

Already there was talk of sealing Tairee against outsiders, even evacuees, and concentrating on total self-reliance.

Some spoke of arming the colony's subs for war.

"These older hull bubbles were thicker and heavier," Panalina commented, patting the nearest bulkhead, the first of three ancient, translucent spheres that had been fused together into a short chain, like a trio of pearls on a string. "They fell out of favor, maybe four or five mother generations ago. You'll need to pay six big fellows in order to crank a full load of trade goods. That won't leave you much profit on cargo."

Good old Panalina, always talking as if everything would soon be normal again, as if the barter network was likely to ever be the same. With streaks of gray in her hair, the artificer claimed to be sixty years old but was certainly younger. The grandmothers let her get away with the fib, and what would normally be criminal neglect, leaving her womb fallow most of the time, with only two still-living heirs, and both of those boys.

"Still." Panalina looked around and thumped the hull one last time. "He's a sturdy little boat. You know, there was talk among the mothers about refusing to let you take him away from Tairee. The Smoths had to promise half a ton of crushed grapes in return, and to take in one of the Sadoul families. Still, I think it's *you* they mostly want."

Jonah had puzzled over that cryptic remark after Panalina left, then all during the brew-swilled bachelor party, suffering crude jokes and ribbing from the married men, and later during a fretful sleep shift, as he tossed and turned with prewedding jitters. During the ceremony itself, Mother had been gracious and warm—not her typical mien, but a side of her that Jonah felt he would surely miss. Though he knew that an underlying source of her cheerfulness was simple—*one less male mouth to feed.*

It had made Jonah reflect, even during the wrist-binding part of the ceremony, on something old Scholar Wu said recently.

The balance of the sexes may change, if it really comes down to war. Breeders could start to seem less valuable than fighters.

In the docklock, Jonah found that his little truck had been decked with flowers, and all three of the spheres gleamed, where they had been polished above the waterline. The gesture warmed Jonah's heart. There was even a freshly painted name, arcing just above the propeller.

Bird of Tairee.

Well. Mother had always loved stories about those prehistoric creatures of Old Earth who flew through a sky that was immeasurably vast and sweet.

"I thought you were going to name it after me," Petri commented in a low voice, without breaking her gracious smile.

"I shall do that, ladylove. Just after we dock in Laussane."

"Well … perhaps not *just* after," she commented, and Jonah's right buttock took a sharp-nailed pinch. He managed not to jump or visibly react. But clearly, his new wife did not intend wasting time once they were home.

Home. He would have to redefine the word, in his mind.

Still, as Jonah checked the final loading of luggage, gifts, and passengers, he glanced at the fantail one last time, picturing there a name that he really wanted to give the little vessel.

Renewed Hope.

* * *

4.

THEY WERE UNDER WAY, HAVING TRAVELED MORE than half of the distance to Laussane Bubble, when a *thump* struck at the wrong time—at the worst possible time—shaking the little sub truck like a rattle.

The blow came hard and late. So late that everyone at the wedding had simply written off any chance of one today. Folks assumed that at least another work-and-sleep cycle would pass without a comet fall. Already this was the longest gap in memory. Perhaps (some murmured) the age of thumps had come to an end, as prophesied long ago. After the disaster that befell Aldrin and Bezo two months ago, it was a wish now shared by all.

Up until that very moment, the nuptial voyage had been placid, enjoyable, even for tense newlyweds.

Jonah was at the tiller up front, gazing ahead through a patch of hull bubble that had been polished on both sides, making it clear enough to see through. Hoping that he looked like a stalwart, fierce-eyed seaman, he gripped the rudder ropes that steered *Bird of Tairee* though the sub's propeller lay still and powerless. For this voyage, the old truck was being hauled as a trailer behind a larger, sleeker, and more modern Laussanite sub, where a team of twelve burly men sweated and tugged in perfect rhythm, turning their drive-shaft crank.

Petri stood beside her new husband, while passengers chattered in the second compartment behind them. As bubble colonies drifted past, she gestured at each of the gleaming domes and spoke of womanly matters, like the politics of trade and diplomacy, or the personalities and traditions of each settlement. Which goods and food items they excelled at producing, or needed. Their rates of mutation and successful child-raising. Or how well each habitat was managing its genetic diversity . . . and her tone changed a bit at that point, as if suddenly aware how the topic bore upon them both. For this marriage match had been judged by the Laussane mothers on that basis, above all others.

"Of course I had final say, the final choice," she told Jonah, and it warmed him that Petri felt a need to explain.

"Anyway, there is a project I've been working on," she continued in a lower voice. "With a few others in Laussane and Landis Bubbles. Younger folks, mostly. And we can use a good mechanic like you."

Like me? So I was chosen for that reason?

Jonah felt put off and tensed a bit when Petri put an arm around his waist. But she leaned up and whispered in his ear.

"I think you'll like what we're up to. It's something just right for a *rascal*."

The word surprised him and he almost turned to stare. But her arm was tight and Petri's breath was still in his ear. So Jonah chose to keep his features steady, unmoved. Perhaps sensing his stiff reaction, Petri let go. She slid around to face him with her back resting against the transparent patch, leaning against the window.

Clever girl, he thought. It was the direction he had to look, in order to watch the *Pride of Laussane*'s rudder, up ahead, matching his tiller to that of the larger sub. Now he could not avert his eyes from her, using boyish reticence as an excuse.

Petri's oval face was a bit wide, as were her eyes. The classic Laussane chin cleft was barely noticeable, though her mutant patch—the whorl of wild hair—was visible as a reflection behind her, on the bubble's curved, inner surface. Her wedding garment, sleek and formfitting, revealed enough to prove her fitness to bear and nurse ... plus a little more. And Jonah wondered— *when am I supposed to let the sight of her affect me? Arouse me?* Too soon and he might seem brutish, in need of tight reins. Too late or too little, and his bride might feel insulted.

And fretting over it will make me an impotent fool. Deliberately,

Jonah calmed himself, allowing some pleasure to creep in, at the sight of her. A seed of anticipation grew . . . as he knew she wanted.

"What *project* are you talking about? Something involving trucks?" He offered a guess. "Something the mothers may not care for? Something suited to a . . . to a . . ."

He glanced over his shoulder, past the open hatch leading to the middle bubble, containing a jumble of cargo—wedding gifts and Jonah's hope chest, plus luggage for Laussane dignitaries who rode in comfort aboard the bigger submersible ahead. Here, a dozen lower-caste passengers sat or lay atop the stacks and piles—some of Petri's younger cousins, plus a family of evacuees from doomed Sadoul Dome, sent to relieve Tairee's overcrowded refugee encampment, as part of the complex marriage deal.

Perhaps it would be best to hold off this conversation until a time and place with fewer ears around, to pick up stray sonic reflections. Perhaps delaying it for wife-and-husband pillow talk—the one and only kind of privacy that could be relied upon in the colonies. He looked forward again, raising one eyebrow, and Petri clearly got his meaning. Still, in a lower voice, she finished Jonah's sentence.

"To a *rascal*, yes. In fact, your reputation as a young fellow always coming up with bothersome questions helped me bargain well for you. Did you intend it that way, I wonder? For you to wind up *only* sought by one like me, who would *value* such attributes? If so, clever boy."

Jonah decided to keep silent, letting Petri give him credit for cunning he never had. After a moment, she shrugged with a smile, then continued in a voice that was nearly inaudible.

"But in fact, our small bunch of conspirators and connivers were inspired by yet another *rascal*. The one we have foremost in our minds was a fellow named . . . Melvil."

Jonah had been about to ask about the mysterious "we." But mention of that particular name stopped him short. He blinked hard—two, three times—striving not to flinch or otherwise react. It took him several tries to speak, barely mouthing the words.

"You're talking about . . . *Theodora Canyon?*"

A place of legend. And Petri's eyes now conveyed many things. Approval of his quickness . . . overlain upon an evident grimness of purpose. A willingness—even eagerness—to take risks and adapt in chaotic times, finding a path forward, even if it meant following a folktale. All of that was apparent in Petri's visage. Though clearly, Jonah was expected to say more.

"I've heard . . . one hears rumors . . . that there was a *map* to what Melvil found . . . another canyon filled with Gift-of-Venus bubbles like those the Founders discovered here in Cleopatra Canyon. But the mothers forbade any discussion or return voyages, and—" Jonah slowed down when he realized he was babbling. "And so, after Melvil fled his punishment, they hid the map away . . ."

"I've been promised a copy," Petri confided, evidently weighing his reaction, "once we're ready to set out."

Jonah couldn't help himself. He turned around again to check the next compartment, where several smaller children were chasing one another up and down the luggage piles, making a ruckus and almost tipping over a crate of Panalina's smithy tools, consigned for transshipment to Gollancz Dome. Beyond, through a second hatchway to the final chamber, where sweating rowers would normally sit, lay stacked bags of exported Tairee rice. The refugee family and several of Petri's subadult cousins lounged back there, talking idly, keeping apart from the raucous children.

Jonah looked back at his bride, still keeping his voice low.

"You're kidding! So there truly *was* a boy named Melvil? Who stole a sub and—"

"—for a month and a week and a day and an hour," Petri finished for him. "Then returned with tales of a far-off canyon filled with gleaming bubbles of all sizes, a vast foam of hollow, volcanic globes, left over from this world's creation, never touched by human hands. Bubbles just as raw and virginal as our ancestors found, when they first arrived down here beneath a newborn ocean, seeking refuge far below the poison sky."

Much of what she said was from the Founders' Catechism, retaining its rhythm and flowery tone. Clearly, it amused Petri to quote modified scripture while speaking admiringly of an infamous rebel; Jonah could tell as much from her wry expression. But poetry—and especially irony—had always escaped Jonah, and she might as well get used to that husbandly lack, right now.

"So . . . this is about . . . finding new homes?"

"Perhaps, if things keep getting worse here in Cleo Abyss, shouldn't we have options? Oh, we're selling it as an expedition to harvest fresh bubbles, all the sizes that have grown scarce hereabouts, useful for helmets and cooking and chemistry. But we'll also check out any big ones. Maybe they're holding up better in Theodora than they are here. Because, at the rate things are going—" Petri shook her head. And, looking downward, her expression *leaked* just a bit, losing some of its tough, determined veneer, giving way to plainly visible worry.

She knows things. Information that the mothers won't tell mere men. And she's afraid.

Strangely, that moment of vulnerability touched Jonah's heart, thawing a patch that he had never realized was chill. For the first time, he felt drawn . . . compelled to reach out. Not sexually. But to comfort, to hold . . .

That was when the *thump* struck—harder than Jonah would have believed possible.

Concussion slammed the little submarine over, halfway onto its port side, and set the ancient bubble hull ringing. Petri hurtled into him, tearing the rudder straps from his hands as they tumbled together backward, caroming off the open hatch between compartments, then rolling forward again as *Bird of Tairee* heaved.

With the sliver of his brain that still functioned, Jonah wondered if there had been a collision. But the Laussanite ship was bobbing and rocking some distance ahead, still tethered to the *Bird,* and nothing else was closer than a bubble habitat, at least two hundred meters away. Jonah caught sight of all this while landing against the window patch up front, with Petri squished between. This time, as the *Bird* lurched again, he managed to grab a stanchion and hold on, while gripping her waist with his other arm. Petri's breath came in wheezing gasps, and now there was no attempt to mask her terror.

"What? What was . . ."

Jonah swallowed, bracing himself against another rocking sway that almost tore her from his grasp.

"A thump! Do you hear the low tone? But they're never this late!"

He didn't have breath to add: *I've never felt one outside a dome before. No one ventures into water during late morning, when comets always used to fall.* And now Jonah knew why. His ears rang and hurt like crazy.

All this time he had been counting. Thump vibrations came in sequence. One tone passed through rock by *compression,* arriving many seconds before the slower *transverse* waves. He had once even read one of Scholar Wu's books about that, with partial understanding. And he recalled what the old teacher said. That you could tell from the difference in tremor arrivals how far away the impact was from Cleopatra Canyon. . . . *twenty-one . . . twenty-two . . . twenty-three . . .*

Jonah hoped to reach sixty-two seconds, the normal separation, for generation after generation of grandmothers.

. . . twenty-four . . . twenty-f—

The transverse tone, higher pitched and much louder than ever, set the forward bubble of the *Bird* ringing like a bell, even as the tooth-jarring sways diminished, allowing Jonah and Petri to grab separate straps and find their feet.

Less than half the usual distance. That comet almost hit us! He struggled with a numb brain. *Maybe just a couple of thousand kilometers away.*

"The children!" Petri cried, and cast herself—stumbling—aft toward the middle compartment. Jonah followed, but just two steps in order to verify no seals were broken. No hatches had to be closed and dogged . . . not yet. And the crying kids back there looked shaken, not badly hurt. So okay, trust Petri to take care of things back there—

—as he plunged back to the tiller harness. Soon, Jonah was tugging at balky cables, struggling to make the rudder obedient, fighting surges while catching brief glimpses of a tumult outside. Ahead, forty or fifty meters, the *Pride of Laussane*'s propeller churned a roiling cauldron of water. The men inside must be cranking with all their might.

Backward, Jonah realized with dismay. Their motion in reverse might bring the *Pride*'s prop in contact with the towline. *Why are they hauling ass backward?*

One clue. The tether remained taut and straight, despite the rowers' efforts. And with a horrified realization, Jonah realized why. The bigger sub *tilted* upward almost halfway to vertical, with its nose aimed high.

They've lost their main ballast! Great slugs of stone and raw metal normally weighed a sub down, lashed along the keel. They must have torn loose amid the chaos of the *thump*—nearly all of them! But how? Certainly, bad luck and lousy maintenance, or a hard collision with the ocean bottom. For whatever reason, the *Pride of Laussane* was straining upward, climbing toward the sky.

Already, Jonah could see one of the bubble habitats from an

angle no canyonite ever wanted . . . looking *down* upon the curved dome from above, its forest of pinyon vines glowing from within.

Cursing his own slowness of mind, Jonah let go of the rudder cables and half stumbled toward the hatch at the rear of the control chamber, shouting for Petri. There was a job to do, more vital than any other. Their very lives might depend on it.

5.

"WHEN I GIVE THE WORD, OPEN VALVE NUMBER ONE *just a quarter turn!*"

It wasn't a demure tone to use toward a woman, but he saw no sign of wrath or resentment as his new wife nodded. "A quarter turn. Yes, Jonah."

Clamping his legs around one of the ballast jars, he started pushing rhythmically on his new and improved model air pump. "Okay . . . now!"

As soon as Petri twisted the valve they heard water spew into the ballast chamber, helping Jonah push the air out, for storage at pressure in a neighboring bottle. It would be simpler and less work to just let the air spill outside, but he couldn't bring himself to do that. There might be further uses for the stuff.

When *Bird* started tilting sideways, he shifted their efforts to a bottle next to the starboard viewing patch . . . another bit of the old hull that had been polished for seeing. Farther aft, in the third compartment, he could hear some of the passengers struggling with bags of rice, clearing the propeller crank for possible use. In fact, Jonah had ordered it done mostly to give them a distraction. Something to do.

"We should be getting heavier," he told Petri, as they shifted back and forth, left to right, then left again, letting water into storage bubbles and storing displaced air. As expected, this had an effect on the sub's pitch, raising the nose as it dragged on the tether cable, which in turn linked them to the crippled *Pride of Laussane*.

The crew of that hapless vessel had given up cranking to propel their ship backward. Everything depended on Jonah and Petri now. If they could make *Bird* heavy enough, quickly enough, both vessels might be prevented from sinking into the sky.

And we'll be heroes, Jonah pondered at one point, while his arms throbbed with pain. This could be a great start to his life and reputation in Laussane Bubble . . . that is, *if* it worked. Jonah ached to go and check the little sub's instruments, but there was no time. Not even when he drafted the father of the Sadoul refugee family to pump alongside him. Gradually, all the tanks were filling, making the *Bird* heavier, dragging at the runaway *Pride of Laussane*. And indeed . . .

Yes! He saw a welcome sight. One of the big habitat domes! Perhaps the very one they had been passing when the thump struck. Jonah shared a grin with Petri, seeing in her eyes a glimmer of earned respect. *Perhaps I'll need to rest a bit before our wedding night.* Though funny, it didn't feel as if fatigue would be a problem.

Weighed down by almost full ballast tanks, *Bird* slid almost along the great, curved flank of the habitat. Jonah signaled Xerish to ease off pumping and for Petri to close her valve. He didn't want to hit the sea bottom too hard. As they descended, Petri identified the nearby colony as Leininger Dome. It was hard to see much through both sweat-stung eyes and the barely polished window patch, but Jonah could soon tell that a crowd of citizens had come to press their faces against the inner side of the great, transparent bubble wall, staring up and out toward the descending subs.

As *Bird* drifted backward, it appeared that the landing would be pretty fast. Jonah shouted for all the passengers to brace themselves for a rough impact, one that should come any second as they drew even with the Leininger onlookers. A bump into bottom mud that . . .

. . . that didn't come.

Something was wrong. Instinct told him, before reason could, when Jonah's ears popped and he gave vent to a violent sneeze.

Oh no.

Petri and Jonah stared at the Leiningerites, who stared back in resigned dismay as the *Bird* dropped below their ground level . . . and kept dropping. Or rather, Leininger Bubble kept ascending, faster and faster, tugged by the deadly buoyancy of all that air inside, its anchor roots torn loose by that last violent *thump*. Following the path and fate of Bezo Colony, without the warning that had allowed partial evacuation of Cixin and Sadoul.

With a shout of self-loathing, Jonah rushed to perform a task that he should have done already. Check instruments. The pressure gauge wouldn't be much use in an absolute sense, but relative values could at least tell if they were falling. Not just relative to the doomed habitat but drifting back toward the safe bottom muck, or else—

"Rising," he told Petri in a low voice, as she sidled alongside and rested her head against his shoulder. He slid his arm around her waist, as if they had been married forever. Or, at least, most of what remained of their short lives.

"Is there anything else we can do?" she asked.

"Not much." He shrugged. "Finish flooding the tanks, I suppose. But they're already almost full, and the weight isn't enough. *That* is just too strong." And he pointed out the forward viewing patch at the *Pride of Laussane*, its five large, air-filled compartments buoyant enough to overcome any resistance by this little truck.

"But . . . can't they do what we've done. Fill their own balls—"

"Ballast tanks. Sorry, my lady. They don't have any big ones.

Just a few little bottles for adjusting trim."

Jonah kept his voice even and matter-of-fact, the way a vessel captain should, even though his stomach churned with dread, explaining how external keep weights saved interior cargo space. Also, newer craft used bubbles with slimmer walls. You didn't want to penetrate them with too many inlets, valves, and such.

"And no one else has your new pump," Petri added. And her approving tone meant more to Jonah, in these final minutes, than he ever would have expected.

"Of course . . ." he mused.

"Yes? You've thought of something?"

"Well, if we could somehow cut the tether cable . . ."

"We'd sink back to safety!" Then Petri frowned. "But we're the only chance they have, on the *Pride of Laussane*. Without our weight, they would shoot skyward like a seed pip from a lorgo fruit."

"Anyway, it's up to them to decide," Jonah explained. "The tether release is at their end, not ours. Sorry. It's a design flaw that I'll fix as soon as I get a chance, right after repainting your name on the stern."

"Hm. See that you do," she commanded.

Then, after a brief pause, "Do you think they might release us, when they realize both ships are doomed?"

Jonah shrugged. There was no telling what people would do when faced with such an end. He vowed to stand watch though, just in case.

He sneezed hard, twice. Pressure effects were starting to tell on him.

"Should we inform the others?" he asked Petri, with a nod back toward *Bird*'s other two compartments, where the crying had settled down to low whimpers from a couple of younger kids.

She shook her head. "It will be quick, yes?"

Jonah considered lying and dismissed the idea.

"It depends. As we rise, the water pressure outside falls, so if air pressure inside remains high, that could lead to a blowout, cracking one of our shells, letting the sea rush in awfully fast. So fast, we'll be knocked out before we can drown. Of course, that's the *least* gruesome end."

"What a cheerful lad," she commented. "Go on."

"Let's say the hull compartments hold. This is a tough old bird." He patted the nearest curved flank. "We can help protect against blowout by venting compartment air, trying to keep pace with falling pressure outside. In that case, we'll suffer one kind or another kind of pressure-change disease. The most common is the bends. That's when gas that's dissolved in our blood suddenly pops into tiny bubbles that fill your veins and arteries. I hear it's a painful way to die."

Whether because of his mutation, or purely in his mind, Jonah felt a return of the scratchy throat and burning eyes. He turned his head barely in time to sneeze away from the window, and Petri.

She was looking behind them, into the next compartment. "If death is unavoidable, but we can pick our way to die, then I say let's choose—"

At that moment, Jonah tensed at a sudden, jarring sensation—a *snap* that rattled the viewing patch in front of him. Something was happening, above and ahead. Without light from the Cleopatra domes, darkness was near total outside, broken only by some algae glow bulbs placed along the flank of the *Pride of Laussane*. Letting go of Petri, he went to all the bulbs inside the *Bird*'s forward compartment and covered them, then hurried back to press his face against the viewing patch.

"What is it?" Petri asked. "What's going on?"

"I think . . ." Jonah made out a queer, sinuous rippling in the blackness between the two submarines.

He jumped as something struck the window. With pounding heart, he saw and heard a snakelike thing slither across the clear zone of bubble, before falling aside. And beyond, starting from just twenty meters away, the row of tiny glow spots now shot upward, like legendary rockets, quickly diminishing, then fading from view.

"The tether," he announced in a matter-of-fact voice.

"They let go? Let *us* go?" A blend of hope and awe in her voice.

"Made sense," he answered. "They were goners anyway." *And now they will be the heroes, when all is told. Songs will be sung about their choice, back home.*

That is, assuming there still is a home. We have no idea if Leininger Dome was the only victim, this time.

He stared at the pressure gauge. After a long pause when it refused to budge, the needle finally began to move. Opposite to its former direction of change.

"We're descending," he decreed with a sigh. "In fact, we'd better adjust. To keep from falling too fast. It wouldn't do, to reach safety down there, only to crack open from the impact."

Jonah put the Sadoulite dad—Xerish—to work, pumping in the opposite direction, less frantically than before, but harder work, using compressed air to push out and overboard some water from the ballast tanks, while Petri, now experienced, handled the valves. After supervising for a few minutes, he went back to the viewing port and peered outside. *I must keep a sharp lookout for the lights of Cleo Canyon. We may have drifted laterally and I can adjust better while we're falling than later, at the bottom.* He used the rudder and stubby elevation planes to turn the little sub, explaining to Petri how it was done. She might have to steer, if Jonah's strength was needed on the propeller crank.

A low, concussive report caused the chamber to rattle and groan. Not as bad as the horrid *thump* had been, but closer, coming from somewhere above. Jonah shared eye contact with Petri, a sad recognition of something inevitable. The end of a gallant ship—*Pride of Laussane.*

Two more muffled booms followed, rather fainter, then another.

They must have closed their inner hatches. Each compartment is failing separately.

But something felt wrong about that. The third concussion, especially, had felt deep-throated, lasting longer than reasonable. Amid another bout of sneezing, Jonah pressed close against the view patch once again, in order to peer about. First toward the bottom, then upward.

Clearly, this day had to be the last straw. It rang a death knell for the old, complacent ways of doing things. Leininger had been a big, important colony, and perhaps not today's only major victim. If thumps were going unpredictable and lethal, then Cleopatra might have to be abandoned.

Jonah knew very little about the plan concocted by Petri's mysterious cabal of young women and men, though he was glad to have been chosen to help. To follow a *rascal's* legend in search of new homes. In fact, two things were abundantly clear. *Expeditions must get under way just as soon as we get back. And there should be more than just one, following Melvil's clues. Subs must be sent in many directions! If Venus created other realms filled with hollow volcanic globes that can be seeded with Earthly life, then we must find them.*

A second fact had also emerged, made evident during the last hour or so. Jonah turned to glance back at a person he had barely known, until just a day ago.

It appears that I married really well.

Although the chamber was very dim, Petri glanced up from her task and noticed him looking at her. She smiled—an expression of respect and dawning equality that seemed just as pleased as he now felt. Jonah smiled back—then unleashed another great sneeze. At which she chirped a short laugh and shook her head in fake-mocking ruefulness.

Grinning, he turned back to the window, gazed upward—
then shouted—

"Grab something! Brace yourselves!"

That was all he had time or breath to cry, while yanking on
the tiller cables and shoving his knee hard against the elevator
control plane. *Bird* heeled over to starboard, both rolling and
struggling to yaw-turn. Harsh cries of surprise and alarm erupted
from the back compartments, as crates and luggage toppled.

He heard Petri shout "Stay where you are!" at the panicky
Xerish, who whimpered in terror. Jonah caught a glimpse of
them, reflected in the view patch, as they clutched one of the air-
storage bottles to keep from tumbling across the deck, onto the
right-side bulkhead.

Come on, old boy, he urged the little sub and wished he had
six strong men cranking at the stern end, driving the propeller
to accelerate *Bird of Tairee* forward. If there had been, Jonah
might—just barely—have guided the sub clear of peril tumbling
from above. Debris from a catastrophe, only a small fraction of it
glittering in the darkness.

Hard chunks of something rattled against the hull. He
glimpsed an object, thin and metallic—perhaps a torn piece of
pipe—carom off the view patch with a bang, plowing several
nasty scars before it fell away. Jonah half expected the transparent
zone to start spalling and cracking at any second.

That didn't happen, but now debris was coming down in a
positive rain, clattering along the whole length of his vessel,
testing the sturdy old shells with every strike. Desperate, he
hauled even harder, steering *Bird* away from what seemed the
worst of it, toward a zone that glittered a bit less. More cries
erupted from the back two chambers.

I should have sealed the hatches, he thought. But then, what
good would that do for anyone, honestly? Having drifted laterally
from Cleo Canyon, any surviving chambers would be helpless,

unable to maneuver, never to be found or rescued before the stored air turned to poison. *Better that we all go together.*

He recognized the sound that most of the rubble made upon the hull—bubble stone striking more bubble stone. Could it all have come from the *Pride of Laussane*? Impossible! There was far too much.

Leininger.

The doomed dome must have imploded, or exploded, or simply come apart without the stabilizing pressure of the depths. Then, with all its air lost and rushing skyward, the rest would plummet. Shards of bubble wall, dirt, pinyons glowing feebly as they drifted ever lower . . . and people. That was the detritus Jonah most hoped to avoid.

There. It looks jet-black over there. The faithful old sub had almost finished its turn. Soon he might slack off, setting the boat upright. Once clear of the debris field, he could check on the passengers, then go back to seeking the home canyon . . .

He never saw whatever struck next, but it had to be big, perhaps a major chunk of Leininger's wall. The blow hammered all three compartments in succession, ringing them like great gongs, making Jonah cry out in pain. There were other sounds, like ripping, tearing. The impact—somewhere below and toward portside, lifted him off his feet, tearing one of the rudder straps out of Jonah's hand, leaving him to swing wildly by the other. *Bird* sawed hard to the left as Jonah clawed desperately to reclaim the controls.

At any moment, he expected to greet the harsh, cold sea and have his vessel join the skyfall of lost hopes.

6.

ONLY GRADUALLY DID IT DAWN ON HIM—IT WASN'T over. The peril and problems, he wasn't about to escape them that easily. Yes, damage was evident, but the hulls—three ancient, volcanic globes—still held.

In fact, some while after that horrible collision, it did seem that *Bird of Tairee* had drifted clear of the heavy stuff. Material still rained upon the sub, but evidently softer materials. Like still-glowing chunks of pinyon vine.

Petri took charge of the rear compartments, crisply commanding passengers to help one another dig out and assessing their hurts, in order of priority. She shouted reports to Jonah, whose hands were full. In truth, he had trouble hearing what she said over the ringing in his ears and had to ask for repetition several times. The crux: one teenager had a fractured wrist, while others bore bruises and contusions—a luckier toll than he expected. Bema—the Sadoulite mother—kept busy delivering first aid.

More worrisome was a *leak*. Very narrow, but powerful, a needle jet spewed water into the rear compartment. Not through a crack in the shell—fortunately—but via the packing material that surrounded the propeller bearing. Jonah would have to go back and have a look, but first he assessed other troubles. For example, the sub wouldn't right herself completely. There was a constant tilt to starboard around the roll axis . . . then he checked the pressure gauge and muttered a low invocation to ancient gods and demons of Old Earth.

"We've stopped falling," he confided to Petri in the stern compartment, once the leak seemed under control. It had taken some time, showing the others how to jam rubbery cloths into the bearing, then bracing it all with planks of wood torn from the floor. The arrangement was holding, for now.

"How can that be?" she asked. "We were *heavy* when the *Pride* let us go. I thought our problem was how to slow our descent."

"It was. Till our collision with whatever hit us. Based on

where it struck, along the portside keel, I'd guess that it knocked off some of our static ballast—the stones lashed to our bottom. The same thing that happened to *Pride* during that awful thump quake. Other stones may have been dislodged or had just one of their lashings cut, leaving them to dangle below the starboard side, making us tilt like this. From these two examples, I'd say we've just learned a lesson today, about a really bad flaw in the whole way we've done sub design."

"So which is it? Are we rising?"

Jonah nodded.

"Slowly. It's not too bad yet. And I suppose it's possible we might resume our descent if we fill all the ballast tanks completely. Only there's a problem."

"Isn't there always?" Petri rolled her eyes, clearly exasperated.

"Yeah." He gestured toward where Xerish—by luck a carpenter—was hammering more bracing into place. Jonah lowered his voice. "If we drop back to the seafloor, that bearing may not hold against full-bottom pressure. It's likely to start spewing again, probably faster."

"If it does, how long will we have?"

Jonah frowned. "Hard to say. Air pressure would fight back, of course. Still, I'd say less than an hour. Maybe not that much. We would have to spot one of the canyon domes right away, steer right for it, and plop ourselves into dock as fast as possible, with everyone cranking like mad—"

"—only using the propeller will put even more stress on the bearing," Petri concluded with a thoughtful frown. "It might blow completely."

Jonah couldn't prevent a brief smile. *Brave enough to face facts ... and a mechanical aptitude, as well? I could find this woman attractive.*

"Well, I'm sure we can work something out," she added. "You haven't let us down yet."

Not yet, he thought, and returned to work, feeling trapped by her confidence in him. And cornered by the laws of chemistry and physics—as well as he understood them with his rudimentary education, taken from ancient books that were already obsolete when the Founders first came to Venus, cowering away from alien invaders under a newborn ocean, while comets poured in with perfect regularity.

Perfect for many lifetimes, but not forever. Not anymore. *Even if we make it home, then go ahead with the Melvil Plan, and manage to find another bubble-filled canyon less affected by the rogue thumps, how long will that last?*

Wasn't this whole project, colonizing the bottom of an alien sea with crude technology, always doomed from the start?

In the middle compartment, Jonah opened his personal chest and took out some treasures—books and charts that he had personally copied under supervision by Scholar Wu, onto bundles of hand-scraped pinyon leaves. In one, he verified his recollection of Boyle's Law and the dangers of changing air pressure on the human body. From another he got a formula that—he hoped—might predict how the leaky propeller-shaft bearing would behave if they descended the rest of the way.

Meanwhile, Petri put a couple of the larger teen girls to work on a bilge pump, transferring water from the floor of the third compartment into some almost full ballast tanks. Over the next hour, Jonah kept glancing at the pressure gauge. The truck appeared to be leveling off again. *Up and down. Up and down. This can't be good for my old* Bird.

Leveled. Stable . . . for now. That meant the onus fell on him, with no excuse. To descend and risk the leak becoming a torrent, blasting those who worked the propeller crank . . . or else . . .

Two hands laid pressure on his shoulders and squeezed inward, surrounding his neck, forcefully. Slim hands, kneading tense muscles and tendons. Jonah closed his eyes, not wanting to divulge what he had decided.

"Some wedding day, huh?"

Jonah nodded. No verbal response seemed needed. He felt married for years—and glad of the illusion. Evidently, Petri knew him now, as well.

"I bet you've figured out what to do."

He nodded again.

"And it won't be fun, or offer good odds of success."

A headshake. Left, then right.

Her hands dug in, wreaking a mixture of pleasure and pain, like life.

"Then tell me, husband," she commanded, then came around to bring their faces close. "Tell me what you'll have us do. Which way do we go?"

He exhaled a sigh. Then inhaled. And finally spoke one word.

"Up."

7.

TOWARD THE DEADLY SKY. TOWARD VENUSIAN HELL. IT had to be. No other choice was possible.

"If we rise to the surface, I can try to repair the bearing from inside, without water gushing through. And if it requires outside work, then I can do that by putting on a helmet and coveralls. Perhaps they'll keep out the poisons long enough."

Petri shuddered at the thought. "Let us hope that won't be necessary."

"Yeah. Though while I'm there I could also fix the ballast straps holding some of the weight stones to our keel. I . . . just don't see any other way."

Petri sat on a crate opposite Jonah, mulling it over.

"Wasn't upward motion what destroyed Leininger Colony and the *Pride*?"

"Yes ... but their ascent was uncontrolled. Rapid and chaotic. We'll rise slowly, reducing cabin air pressure in pace with the decreased push of water outside. We have to go slow, anyway, or the gas that's dissolved in our blood will boil and kill us. Slow and gentle. That's the way."

She smiled. "You know all the right things to say to a virgin."

Jonah felt his face go red. He was relieved when Petri got serious again.

"If we rise slowly, won't there be another problem? Won't we run out of breathable air?"

He nodded. "Activity must be kept to a minimum. Recycle and shift stale air into bottles, exchanging with the good air they now contain. Also, I have a spark separator."

"You do? How did ... aren't they rare and expensive?"

"I made this one myself. Well, Panalina showed me how to use pinyon crystals and electric current to split seawater into hydrogen and oxygen. We'll put some passengers to work, taking turns at the spin generator." And he warned her. "It's a small unit. It may not produce enough."

"Well, no sense putting things off, then," Petri said with a grandmother's tone of decisiveness. "Give your orders, man."

The ascent was grueling. Adults and larger teens took turns at the pumps expelling enough ballast water for the sub to start rising at a good pace ... then correcting when it seemed too quick. Jonah kept close track of gauges revealing compression both inside and beyond the shells. He also watched for symptoms of decompression sickness—another factor keeping things slow. All passengers not on shift were encouraged to sleep—difficult enough when the youngest children kept crying over the pain in their ears. Jonah taught them all how to yawn or pinch their noses to equalize pressure, though his explanations kept being punctuated by fits of sneezing.

Above all, even while resting, they all had to breathe deep as their lungs gradually purged and expelled excess gas from their bloodstreams.

Meanwhile, the forechamber resonated with a constant background whine as older kids took turns at the spark separator, turning its crank so that small amounts of seawater divided into component elements—one of them breathable. The device had to be working—a layer of salt gathered in the brine collector. Still, Jonah worried. *Did I attach the poles right? Might I be filling the storage bottle with oxygen and letting hydrogen into the cabin? Filling the sub with an explosive mix that could put us out of our misery at any second?*

He wasn't sure how to tell—none of his books said—though he recalled vaguely that hydrogen had no odor.

After following him on his rounds, inspecting everything and repeating his explanations several times, Petri felt confident enough to insist, "You must rest now, Jonah. I will continue to monitor our rate of ascent and make minor adjustments. Right now, I want you to close your eyes."

When he tried to protest, she insisted, with a little more of the accented tone used by Laussane mothers. "We will need you far more in a while. You'll require all your powers near the end. So lie down and recharge yourself. I promise to call if anything much changes."

Accepting her reasoning, he obeyed by curling up on a couple of grain sacks that Xerish brought forward to the control cabin. Jonah's eyelids shut, gratefully. The brain, however, was another matter.

How deep are we now?

It prompted an even bigger question: *how deep is the bottom of Cleopatra Canyon nowadays?*

According to lore, the first colonists used to care a lot about measuring the thickness of Venusian seas, back when some surface light used to penetrate all the way to the ocean floor. They would launch balloons attached to huge coils of string, in order to both judge depth and sample beyond the therm-o-cline barrier and even from the hot, deadly sky. Those practices died out—though Jonah had seen one of the giant capstan reels once, during a visit to Chown Dome, gathering dust and moldering in a swampy corner.

The way Earth denizens viewed their planet's hellish interior, that was how Cleo dwellers thought of the realm above. Though there had been exceptions. Rumors held that Melvil, that legendary rascal, upon returning from his discovery of Theodora Canyon, had demanded support to start exploring the great heights. Possibly even the barrier zone, where living things thronged and might be caught for food. Of course, he was quite mad—though boys still whispered about him in hushed tones.

How many comets? Jonah found himself wondering. Only one book in Tairee spoke of the great Venus Terraforming Project that predated the Coss invasion. Mighty robots, as patient as gods, gathered iceballs at the farthest fringe of the solar system and sent them plummeting from that unimaginably distant realm to strike this planet—several each day, always at the same angle and position—both speeding the world's rotation and drenching its long-parched basins. *If each comet was several kilometers in diameter . . . how thick an ocean might spread across an entire globe, in twenty generations of grandmothers?*

For every one that struck, five others were aimed to skim close by, tearing through the dense, clotted atmosphere of Venus, dragging some of it away before plunging to the sun. The scale of such an enterprise was stunning, beyond belief. So much so that Jonah truly doubted he could be of the same species that did such things. *Petri, maybe. She could be that smart. Not me.*

How were such a people ever conquered?

The roil of his drifting mind moved onward to might-have-beens. If not for that misguided comet—striking six hours late to wreak havoc near the canyon colonies—Jonah and his bride would by now have settled into a small Laussane cottage, getting to know each other in more traditional ways. Despite, or perhaps because of the emergency, he actually felt far *more* the husband of a vividly real person than he would have in that other reality, where physical intimacy might have happened ... Still, the lumpy grain sacks made part of him yearn for her in ways that—now—might never come to pass. That world would have been better ... one where the pinyon vines waved their bright leaves gently overhead. Where he might show her tricks of climbing vines, then swing from branch to branch, carrying her in his arms while the wind of flying passage ruffled their hair—

A *twang* sound vibrated the cabin, like some mighty cord coming apart. The sub throbbed and Jonah felt it roll a bit.

His eyes opened and he realized *I was asleep.* Moreover, his head now rested on Petri's lap. Her hand had been the breeze in his hair.

Jonah sat up.

"What was that?"

"I do not know. There was a sharp sound. The ship hummed a bit, and now the floor no longer tilts."

"No longer—"

Jumping up with a shout, he hurried over to the gauges, then cursed low and harsh.

"What is it, Jonah?"

"Quick—wake all the adults and get them to work pumping!"

She wasted no time demanding answers. But as soon as crews were hard at work, Petri approached Jonah again at the control station, one eyebrow raised.

"The remaining stone ballast," he explained. "It must have been hanging by a thread, or a single lashing. Now it's completely gone. The sub's tilt is corrected, but we're ascending too fast."

Petri glanced at two Sadoulites and two Laussanites who were laboring to refill the ballast tanks. "Is there anything else we can do to slow down?"

Jonah shrugged. "I suppose we might unpack the leaky bearing and let more water into the aft compartment. But we'd have no control. The stream could explode in our faces. We might flood or lose the chamber. All told, I'd rather risk decompression sickness."

She nodded, agreeing silently.

They took their own turn at the pumps, then supervised another crew until, at last, the tanks were full. *Bird* could get no heavier. Not without flooding the compartments themselves.

"We have to lose internal pressure. That means venting air overboard," he said, "in order to equalize."

"But we'll need it to breathe!"

"There's no choice. With our tanks full of water, there's no place to put extra air and still reduce pressure."

So, different pumps and valves, but more strenuous work. Meanwhile, Jonah kept peering at folks in the dim illumination of just two faint glow bulbs, watching for signs of the bends. Dizziness, muscle aches, and labored breathing? These could just be the result of hard labor. The book said to watch out also for joint pain, rashes, delirium, or sudden unconsciousness. He did know that the old dive tables were useless—based on Earth-type humanity. *And we've changed. First because our scientist ancestors modified themselves and their offspring. But time, too, has altered what we are, even long after we lost those wizard powers. Each generation was an experiment.*

Has it made us less vulnerable to such things? Or more so?

Someone tugged his arm. It wasn't Petri, striving at her pump. Jonah looked down at one of the children, still wearing a stained and crumpled bridesmaid's dress, who pulled shyly, urging Jonah to come follow. At first, he thought: *it must be the sickness. She's summoning me to help someone's agony. But what can I do?*

Only it wasn't toward the stern that she led him, but the forwardmost part of the ship . . . to the view patch, where she pointed.

"What is it?" Pressing close to the curved pane, Jonah tensed as he starkly envisioned some new cloud of debris . . . till he looked up and saw—

—light. Vague at first. Only a child's perfect vision would have noticed it so early. But soon it spread and brightened across the entire vault overhead.

I thought we would pass through the therm-o-cline. He had expected a rough—perhaps even lethal—transition past that supposed barrier between upper and lower oceans. But it must have happened gently, while he slept.

Jonah called someone to relieve Petri and brought her forth to see.

"Go back and tell people to hold on tight," Petri dispatched the little girl, then she turned to grab Jonah's waist as he took the control straps. At this rate they appeared to be seconds away from entering Venusian hell.

Surely it has changed, he thought, nursing a hope that had never been voiced, even in his mind. *The ocean has burgeoned as life fills the seas . . .*

Already he spied signs of movement above. Flitting, flickering shapes—living versions of the crushed and dead specimens that sometimes fell to Tairee's bottom realm, now undulating and darting about what looked like scattered patches of dense, dangling weed. He steered to avoid those.

If the sea has changed, then might not the sky, the air, even the highlands?

Charts of Venus, radar mapped by ancient Earthling space probes, revealed vast continents and basins, a topography labeled with names like Aphrodite Terra and Lakshmi Planum. Every single appellation was that of a female from history or literature or legend. Well, that seemed fair enough. But had it been a cruel joke to call the baked and bone-dry lowlands "seas"?

Till humanity decided to make old dreams come true.

What will we find?

To his and Petri's awestruck eyes, the dense crowd of life revealed glimpses—shapes like dragons, like fish, or those ancient *blimps* that once cruised the skies of ancient Earth. And something within Jonah allowed itself to hope.

Assuming we survive decompression, might the fiery, sulfurous air now be breathable? Perhaps barely, as promised by the sagas? By now, could life have taken to high ground? Seeded in some clever centuries delay by those same pre-Coss designers?

His mind pictured scenes from a few dog-eared storybooks, only enormously expanded and brightened. Vast, measureless jungles, drenched by rainstorms, echoing with the bellows of gigantic beasts. A realm so huge, so rich and densely forested that a branch of humanity might thrive, grow, prosper, and learn—regaining might and confidence—beneath that sheltering canopy, safe from invader eyes.

That, once upon a time, had been the dream, though few imagined it might fully come to pass.

Jonah tugged the tiller to avoid a looming patch of dangling vegetation. Then, ahead and above, the skyward shallows suddenly brightened, so fiercely that he and Petri had to shade their eyes, inhaling and exhaling heavy gasps. They both cried out as a great, slithering shape swerved barely out of the sub's way. Then brilliance filled the cabin like a blast of molten fire.

I was wrong to hope! It truly is hell!

A roar of foamy separation . . . and for long instants Jonah felt free of all weight. He let go of the straps and clutched Petri tight, twisting to put his body between hers and the wall as their vessel flew over the sea, turned slightly, then dropped back down, striking the surface with a shuddering blow and towering splash.

Lying crumpled below the viewing patch, they panted, as did everyone else aboard, groaning and groping themselves to check for injuries. For reassurance of life. And gradually the hellish brightness seemed to abate till Jonah realized, *It is my eyes, adapting. They never saw daylight before.*

Jonah and Petri helped each other stand. Together, they turned, still shading their eyes. Sound had transformed, and so had the very texture of the air, now filled with strange aromas.

There must be a breach!

With shock, still blinking away glare-wrought tears, Jonah saw the cause. Impact must have knocked loose the dog bolts charged with holding shut the main hatch, amidships on the starboard side—never meant to open anywhere but at the safety of a colonial dock.

With a shout he hurried over, even knowing it was too late. The poisons of Venus—

—apparently weren't here.

No one keeled over. His body's sole reaction to the inrushing atmosphere was to sneeze, a report so loud and deep that it rocked him back.

Jonah reached the hatch and tried pushing it closed, but *Bird of Tairee* was slightly tilted to port. The heavy door overwhelmed Jonah's resistance and kept gradually opening, from crack to slit, to gap, to chasm.

"I'll help you, Jonah," came an offer so low, like a rich male baritone, yet recognizably that of his wife. He turned, saw her eyes wide with surprise at her own voice.

"The air . . . it contains . . ." His words emerged now a deep bass. ". . . different gases than . . . we got from pinyons."

Different . . . but breathable. Even pleasant. Blinking a couple of times, he managed to shrug off the shock of his new voice and tried once more to close the hatch before giving up for now. With the boat's slight leftward roll, there was no immediate danger of flooding, as seawater lapped a meter or so below. The opening must be closed soon, of course . . .

. . . but not quite yet. For, as Jonah and Petri stood at the sill, what confronted them was more than vast, rippling-blue ocean and a cloud-dense firmament. Something else lay between those two, just ahead and to starboard, a thick mass of shimmery greens and browns that filled the horizon, receding in mist toward distant, serrated skylines. Though he never dreamed of witnessing such a thing firsthand, they both recognized the sight, from ancient, faded pictures.

Land. Shore. Everything. And overhead, creatures flapped strange, graceful wings, or drifted like floating jellyfish above leafy spires.

"It will take some time to figure out what we can eat," his wife commented, with feminine practicality.

"Hm," Jonah replied, too caught up in wonder to say more, a silence that lasted for many poundings of his heart. Until, finally, he managed to add—

"Someday. We must go back down. And tell."

After another long pause, Petri answered.

"Yes, someday."

She held him tight around the chest, a forceful constriction that only filled Jonah with strength. His lungs expanded as he inhaled deeply a sweet smell, and knew that only part of that was her.

GARTH NIX

Here's an ex-soldier who's dragooned into joining an expedition attempting to penetrate the deepest, most deadly, and most impenetrable part of the Venusian swamps, and who finds that he must "go native" in the most profound and fundamental of ways if he's to have any chance to survive . . .

New York Times bestselling Australian writer Garth Nix worked as a book publicist, editor, marketing consultant, public-relations man, and literary agent before launching the bestselling Old Kingdom series, which consists of Sabriel, Lirael: Daughter of the Clayr, Abhorsen, and The Creature in the Case. His other books include the Seventh Tower series, consisting of The Fall, Castle, Aenir, Above the Veil, Into Battle, and The Violet Keystone, the Keys to the Kingdom series, consisting of Mister Monday, Grim Tuesday, Drowned Wednesday, Sir Thursday, Lady Friday, Superior Saturday, and Lord Sunday, as well as stand-alone novels such as The Ragwitch and Shade's Children. His short fiction has been collected in Across the Wall: A Tale of the Abhorsen and Other Stories. His most recent books are two novels written with Sean Williams, Troubletwisters: The Mystery and Troubletwisters: The Monster, a new stand-alone novel, A Confusion of Princes, and a new collection, Sir Hereward and Master Fitz: Three Adventures. Born in Melbourne, he now lives in Sydney, Australia.

By Frogsled and Lizardback to Outcast Venusian Lepers

GARTH NIX

THE MARTINI GLASS IN ITS SPECIAL BRACKET NEAR Kelvin's left hand shivered as the shuttle's wheels touched the plascrete runway. For a moment, it looked like the blood orange, gin, and vermouth mixture would splash over the side before it settled down as the shuttle eased into its long, whining run down Venusport's shortest, cheapest, and busiest landing strip.

"Didn't spill," said Kelvin. Without taking his eyes off the strip ahead or his right hand from the control yoke, he reached over and picked up the martini to take a delicate sip. "That's two-fifty you owe me now."

"I'll be checking the black-box vid," said a disembodied woman's voice through the cockpit speakers. "Besides, it could still spill when we brake."

"Nope," said Kelvin. A holographic display had popped up in front of him, advising him to apply reverse thrust and wheel brakes, and several other pop-ups were flashing amber alerts about systems not working as expected, but they were the ones he expected, so that was OK. "Drinking it now. First touchdown, that's always the rule. Everyone OK back there, Suze?"

"Sure. Only had to stun two so far. Early starters, on some kind of energizer. Got a bit overexcited about the fabled Venusian attractions, wanted to get out early. Like at ten thousand meters."

"Miners!" said Kelvin. He put the martini back and worked

the controls, briefly applying himself to bringing the shuttle to a complete stop before immediately taxiing off the strip toward the terminal. There was another shuttle a minute and a half behind him, and twelve more in various stages of approach. The six-month shift change from Mercury Incorporated was on, the leave ship—a converted megaliner—was in orbit, and ten thousand miners who couldn't afford to get all the way back to Earth were raring to come down to sample the delights and diversions of the excessively humid, permanently cloud-shrouded city of Venusport and its surrounds.

"Venusport, Venusport," said Kelvin. "Drop Baker Seventeen rolling in to Gate Twenty-Five, looking for a fast turnaround. What's my slot on the catapult?"

There was no immediate answer, which was unusual. Shuttle traffic was controlled by an expert system with a voice synthesizer some joker had tweaked to make it sound like an old Venus hand with lung-husk problems. It usually snapped back immediately, wasting no time.

"Venusport, Venusport, I say again, this is Drop Baker—"

"Drop Baker Seventeen make gate, Pilot in Charge stand by for further instructions."

"Stand by?" asked Kelvin. He recognized the voice of Chief Controller Kandis, who was very rarely to be found in the tower. Venusport Traffic was easygoing, with few rules about anything other than safety, and the expert systems ran that well enough. "You kidding me, Kandis? I got to pay for this crate, you know, I can't be sitting on the ground when there are miners to move."

"Stand by for orders, Kel," said Kandis wearily. "Terran Navy will meet you at the gate."

"What? *Navy* to meet *me*? Why?"

"Don't ask me. Now leave me alone. I'm busy today."

"You done something bad?" asked Suze over the insystem.

"Nothing that would involve the Terran Navy," said Kelvin,

mystified. Venusport was a treaty city, administered by a complicated tripartite council from the Terran World Government (which wasn't really the whole world, as it excluded several pariah states), MBU (Mars and Beyond United, not including Ceres), and Mercury Incorporated (corporate dictatorship at its best). In practice, local interests dominated Venusport and everything was pretty freewheeling unless something major came up and one of the interplanetary governments decided to shove their oar in.

"I think."

"Sort it out quick," said Suze. Kelvin owned 63.7 percent of the shuttle *Lightheeled Loafer*, but the rest was held by Suze's family on Venus Above, the orbital station. Suze was aboard to protect their interests as much as manage passengers and cargo, and her many clone brothers and sisters handled all the back-end office and engineering tasks.

"I will, I will," vowed Kelvin. He handed over to the robot docker, fingers running through the shutdown sequence even as his mind wandered over years of sometimes shady dealings and borderline illegal activities. He could think of plenty of reasons why the usually somnolent Venusport Customs Service might want to talk to him with the aim of extracting further payola. But he couldn't think of anything he'd done recently that would get the Terran Navy on his back.

Despite not being able to come up with anything specific, Kelvin still had a niggling feeling of disquiet. He kept thinking about it as he knocked back his antifungal booster tablets with the last of the martini, unstrapped and got out of his seat, unsealed his helmet and racked it, smeared some antifungal cream on his face and hands, then put on his planetside belt with holstered heat-beam (for Venusian ambulatory fungus and the like), stunner (for ambulatory human lowlifes and the like), and bush knife (for when the options got really limited). He eyed the bar at the back of the cockpit for a moment, considering a second martini, but decided against it. Time enough for that when the *Loafer* was back in orbit.

"Cabin secure?" he asked Suze, though as always he also checked the somewhat mildewed viewscreen next to the hatch. Miners were exiting to the gate in an orderly fashion, doubtless encouraged by the sight of Suze, huge in her armored vacuum suit, a stunner held tight in her right gauntlet, her left hand entirely encased in the ball of a field-lightning projector, for those exciting moments when the occupants of the entire front six passenger rows needed to be shocked into better behavior.

"Yeah, all OK."

Kelvin palmed the hatch, then repeated the gesture several times until it opened, letting in a wave of warm, moist air. Like everything else on the shuttle, the sensor was affected by too much moisture and by Venusian molds that had a liking for plastic. Only so much could be done with regular cleaning and decontamination, the life of even "Venerified" tech was always much shorter than the manufacturers claimed.

"Go and get whatever it is sorted out," said Suze. "I'll do the ground admin and clear us to go back up."

"Thanks, Suze," said Kelvin. He smiled, trying not to show his apprehension. He hoped it *would* be both of them going back up. Suze could fly the shuttle if she had to, though she wasn't anywhere near as experienced as Kelvin, having learned on the job, whereas he had been through the full orbital-atmosphere school at Fort Atherton, then flown ten years operational with the Pan-Pacific Collective Combined Forces on Earth before somehow living through the Third PPCCF Intervention, flying assault shuttles to and from the beachhead on Deimos to Mars . . .

"Oh shit," he said, as his previous vague apprehension solidified into a more certain dread. His Navy service was twenty years ago, and with a different navy, but he was still getting a derisory pension and there had been some small print attached to that when he demobbed . . .

"What?" asked Suze.

"I just remembered something," he said grimly, a memory made more concrete by the sight of a thin-faced chief petty officer in a Terran Navy coverall sidling down the side of the gate tube, the miners edging across to give her room when they saw the razorgun on her hip and the lit-up SP brassard on her arm. Venusport Police were inclined to turn a blind eye and could be bribed, but everyone knew that you didn't want to cross the Terran Navy Shore Patrol, the MBU Law Enforcement Detachment, or the Mercury Inc. Compliance Facilitation Division, the three organizations that took turns in policing the spaceport.

"Commander Kelvin Kelvin 21, formerly of the PPCCF?" asked the petty officer. She didn't wait for Kelvin to nod, already holding up a field identification unit, taking a snap of his eyes before proffering its waiting orifice.

"Yeah, that's me," said Kelvin because there was no point trying to pretend he was someone else. He put his hand in the unit and waited for the prick of the tester, which would sample his DNA, specifically looking for the encoded sequences spliced there long ago by the PPCCF to identify him from his clone siblings, and, later still, to note various information and secrecy access levels as he was promoted or when he got assigned to Special Forces.

The ID unit reported positively to the petty officer, who collapsed it and returned it to a thigh pocket. Then she conjured a blue flimsy from somewhere, possibly inside her sleeve, handed it to Kelvin and saluted him.

He almost saluted back out of long-lost habit, but the blue flimsy was in his hand, and it was squawking only slightly more slowly than he could read the printed words.

"Nonsecret. Commander Kelvin Kelvin 21 OFC HPPC

Second Class, under the terms of the amalgamation of the PPCCF in Terran World Government Treaty Part Seven Section Three Paragraphs Four through Twenty 'Absorption of Existing Active and Reserve Military Forces' your Sufficient Service Exemption from Recall to Active Service Exemption Type 23A is revoked and under the TWG Emergency Requirements Activation Act (New) you are hereby required to report immediately and without delay to Commanding Officer Venusport Treaty Obligation Detachment, TN for service not to exceed three standard Terran years and of this moment your salary, Venusian supplements, Pilot Bonus, and War service gratuity will commence at the rate of Commander Step Three (Special Forces) Terran Navy. Thank you and have a nice day."

"Shit," said Suze. "Three years!"

"What's this about, Chief?" asked Kelvin. "Did a war start and no one tell us?"

"Not so as I've heard, sir," replied the CPO. "If you'd just follow me, sir?"

Kelvin nodded and turned to Suze.

"Take the *Loafer* back up as soon as you can. You and Sal fly together, take turns as pilot in charge, and have Sim and Saul in the cabin—better to double up just in case. I'll be back as soon as I see what this is about. Uh, tell Susan Senior not to worry."

"You just going to go along?" asked Suze.

Kelvin shrugged. "You heard it. I forgot the PPCCF kept all of us Mars Intervention vets on the reserve list and World Gov just took that over, I guess. Nothing I can do about it. But I can't see them needing a clapped-out fifty-year-old shuttle pilot for long."

"I was told to hurry, sir," reminded the petty officer. "If you wouldn't mind."

"Lead on," said Kelvin. "See you, Suze."

The terminal was crowded with miners trying to expedite themselves ahead of one another through the rudimentary automatic arrival system, but instead of joining one of the jostling queues, the CPO led Kelvin to a VIP exit, where two Venusian Police agents checked her pass and waved them to a moving walkway that ran through a prep tunnel that misted them with antifungal agents, performed an automated ID check, then extruded them out through some slowly yawning armored doors of great antiquity into the vehicle park, where the full soggy warmth of Venus hit. Kelvin took a handkerchief out of the sleeve pocket of his coveralls, mopped the instant sweat off his forehead, and tied it around his nose and mouth to help keep out the airborne spores. The booster tablets were supposed to take care of anything inhaled or digested, but Kelvin figured that cutting down the ingestion in the first place was always worth a try.

"So what can you tell me now that there are no civs listening, Chief?"

"Nothing, sir," replied the CPO. She held up a hand and a waiting groundcar popped its doors. Two more Shore Patrol types got out of the front, putting paid to any notions that Kelvin might have had to do a runner. Not that he had any. There was nowhere to run *to* on Venus, not long-term anyway. At least, nowhere he *wanted* to run to, that was for sure.

While the spaceport was somewhat ordered, the rest of Venusport was pretty much a shambles. Along a notional grid pattern that had been bent, twisted, and ignored over the last hundred years there rose the massive domes from the First through Fifth Expeditions, each now containing hundreds of homes, businesses, and small industries. Sprinkled between the domes were buildings of every possible style, from single-box prefab plasteel instahuts to six-story mansions of local phlegm-colored brick, abandoned ships repurposed as factories or dwellings, and the ever-popular yurts of local lizard-hide over steel frames that could be quickly moved if circumstances required it.

As Kelvin expected, the groundcar was not headed for any of these places but drove at the customary top speed of twenty kilometers an hour along Central Avenue toward the imaginatively named stone frigate TNS *Aphrodite,* trusting that its bright yellow flashers and spark-tipped feather feelers would clear the road of walking miners, prostitutes, panhandlers, prophets, pickpockets, and whoever else was walking, shambling, or staggering around, there being no other vehicular traffic at all.

But the groundcar didn't keep going to *Aphrodite.* Just before they reached the main gate, the car left the road, turned to the right, and followed the rough track that ran around the outside of the ten-meter-high perimeter fence.

"Oh, don't tell me," said Kelvin, craning his neck to look out through a windscreen that was already dappled with splattered orange spore bodies. "Some totally black operation, right?"

"Nope," said the CPO. "You got to meet someone who won't submit to the antifungal cleansing routine of the base. Easier to meet out here."

Kelvin thought about that as the groundcar continued around the perimeter. There was a five-hundred-meter exclusion zone around the fence, but it was hardly needed, as most of Venusport sprawled in the opposite direction. There were just a few shanties nearby. Constructed from very mixed materials, they were almost lost in a jungle of three-meter-tall green tops, the fortunately innocuous fungi that grew everywhere it was not slashed, burned, or sprayed back.

He expected that they were heading now for one of those shanties but was surprised again when the car slanted off and he saw a temporary camp up ahead in the middle of the bare red earth of the exclusion zone: an array of five small domes laid out in approved fashion around a tracked armored command vehicle, with sentries in place some ways out.

There was also a riding lizard tied up outside one of the

domes, its head hooded, its blue midsection wrapped with a rather incongruous tartan-colored heater blanket that was hooked up to a big Navy power unit that had been wheeled up next to it.

Kelvin twitched when he saw the lizard, not because of some racial fear of dinosaurs, though it did strongly resemble an allosaurus, but because of what its presence meant.

Venusport was built on the Huevan Plateau, a good five thousand meters up from what was usually called the Deep Swamp, a swamp that stretched for thousands of kilometers in every direction, getting hotter and weirder as it headed toward the distant equator. The lizards inhabited the closer parts of the Swamp and never came up to the relatively cooler plateau unless under human direction, and the humans who farmed the lizards—and other things—only came to Venusport when they needed to trade for something. There was a whole human society out in the Swamp that had at least partially detached itself from modern civilization, trying to fit in with Venus rather than trying to force Venus to become Earth-like. Beyond those settlers, there were humans who had gone even further in their attempts, adapting to Venus in ways that made Kelvin extremely uneasy.

The groundcar stopped, the doors popped, and the CPO pointed to the dome with the lizard tied up outside it.

"Just go in there, Commander. All will be explained."

"Just like that, huh?" asked Kelvin. "*All* will be explained."

"All you need to know, sir," said the CPO with a wink. "However much that is."

"Yeah," said Kelvin sourly. "Thanks, Chief."

He climbed down, noting that apart from the sentries there was no one moving outside the domes. But there was no real attempt at secrecy, the whole camp was visible from the fringe of Venusport, any passerby outside the secure zone could see it, and more important, could see Kelvin arrive. So it wasn't likely he was going to disappear into the maw of some black operation that would later be claimed as never having existed in the first place. That was highly encouraging, as was the fact no one had bothered to take his heat-beam or stunner.

The dome was new, sprung straight out of the container, and surprisingly, both its air-lock doors were open, allowing the Venusian humidity, airborne spores, and general discomfort free access, which was odd, considering that the whole point of the domes was to provide a lovely scrubbed and air-conditioned environment.

Kelvin went in, and immediately understood why the doors were open. There were three women gathered around a map-display table. Two were Terran Navy officers: a captain in Terran Navy planetside blues, probably the commanding officer of *Aphrodite;* and a lieutenant in Venus outdoor camo, sporting a heat-beam in a shoulder holster and a belt festooned with pouches, no doubt containing the latest useless Venusian survival gear developed on Earth.

The third person was the reason the doors were open. She wore a singlet, shorts, and boots of tanned lizard-skin; a broad hat of woven shongar reeds hung on her back from a cord of lizard gut around her neck, keeping company with a breathing mask made of cross-layered sponge-bracken. A pair of goggles fashioned from whisky-bottle glass and a kind of fungal rubber equivalent were pushed back on her shaved head; and she had a heat-beam on one hip and an old-fashioned explosive-projectile pistol on the other, next to a long bush knife.

There were broad blue patches of what the locals called swamp lichen growing on her forearms and up her thighs. More grew on her face, here carefully guided by the sparing use of antifungal agents to grow in concentric circles on her cheeks, across her forehead, and around her neck.

Her face was instantly recognizable to Kelvin. He knew it as

well as his own, swamp lichen notwithstanding, because it *was* his
own face. Even though the woman was half a head taller and much
broader in the shoulders, she was a variant of the same clone line,
and, like all the Kelvin Kelvins, was a veteran of the PPCCF, though
in her case, her service had been with the elite commando drop
troopers colloquially known as ASAP, which legend had it stood for
Air-Space-Any-Fucking-Place. The "F" was silent in the acronym,
and so were they, at least until they wanted to be noticed.

"Kel," said the woman, inclining her head. "How are you?"

"Vinnie," answered Kelvin. "I'm OK, apart from being drafted
again, or whatever's just happened. And kind of puzzled . . ."

"You're wondering why on Earth . . . or Venus . . . we need
both you and your clone sister here," said the captain. She came
around the table and saluted. This time, Kelvin responded,
though not with what could be called parade-ground exactitude.
The captain was half a meter taller than he was, and he almost
jinked his neck looking up at her. "I'm Captain O'Kazanis, this
is my communications officer, Lieutenant Mazith. I'm sorry
about the draft business, that came from HQ. I said we could
just hire you, but it was felt that it would be better to put this
on . . . ah . . . more official grounds."

"Hire me to do what, sir?"

"Go on a damn-fool mission into the Deep Swamp to rescue
a bunch of inbred morons who shouldn't be there," said Vinnie.

"That does just about sum it up," admitted O'Kazanis. "But
perhaps we might go into the details . . . Mazith."

"Yes, sir," said Mazith. Unlike O'Kazanis, whose height and
Greek-Irish name almost certainly indicated an origin in one of
the former Pan-European L5 colonies, Mazith had the made-up
name and blended appearance of a World Government
gengineered new person, of no particular ethnic, racial, or
geographic origin. She was probably a clone, too.

"Approximately sixty-three hours ago," she began, "a private yacht named *Jumping Jehosophat,* on charter to a fraternity/ sorority house of the University of Luna, made an emergency planetfall 312 kilometers southeast of Venusport—"

"Right in the middle of the Roar," interrupted Vinnie. "Like I said, morons."

The Roar was a particularly disturbed part of Venus, an almost permanent, swirling cyclone several hundred kilometers in diameter that not only interdicted any atmospheric traffic but also messed up radio transmissions and generally was not somewhere anyone sensible ever wanted to go to voluntarily.

"Actually, we don't think anyone was in charge, not even a moron. Available data points to the yacht landing on automatic, using some kind of least-fuel algorithm that meant that it went for closest landfall regardless of atmospheric factors," said Mazith. "Certainly neither of the two hired pilots were on board and though we have only limited intel on the passengers, none appears to have had any pilot training."

"So what actually happened?" asked Kelvin.

"The yacht was on a celebratory graduation tour from Luna. It was docked at Venus Above and the crew and passengers debarked for a visit, with a flight plan filed for the yacht to land here at Venusport when a slot became available—"

"What kind of yacht?" asked Kelvin.

"A civilian variation of what you would know as a Brindi Patrol Corvette," said Mazith. "Winged, VTOL, with a one-shot orbitmaker so she doesn't need a catapult. As far as we can figure out from the surveillance at Venus Above, the passengers went back on the ship for some reason and somehow activated an emergency protocol that blew the ship from dock and sent it down."

"I'm surprised no one took it out," remarked Kelvin. "You guys, or the Martians, or even MercInc. What are those picket ships up there for anyway?"

"We asked them not to," said Captain O'Kazanis. "It was

clear within the first few minutes the ship was not on a trajectory that would offer either a launch solution at Venusport or a suicide ramming attack."

"And . . ." suggested Kelvin. "There's got to be a better reason than a momentary act of kindness and beatitude. The passengers, I'm guessing?"

Captain O'Kazanis nodded.

"Twenty-four students from U-Luna, including the son of a Mercury Corp board member, twin daughters from two World Government Senators, and the younger clone brother of a Martian Perpetual Chairperson."

"But they're dead now," said Kelvin. "Right?"

"We think they're alive," said O'Kazanis. She looked at Mazith, who nodded.

"The ship was tracked most of the way down and we have reason to believe that a successful landfall was made. That being so, and considering who is on board, a rescue mission is indicated. Which is where you and your clone sister come in."

"They're dead," said Kelvin. "An autopilot drop into the heart of the Roar? No chance. It'd be incredibly risky even with a gun pilot. Besides, it was probably some kind of assassination deal, someone lures them back on to the yacht, fiddles the emergency protocols, dumps them in the shit. So I bet there was a bomb or something as well just to make sure. End of story, sorry Senators, sorry Board member, Sorry Perpetual Chairperson. 'Even golden lads and lasses must, as chimney sweepers, come to dust.'"

"Shakespeare," said Vinnie to the puzzled naval officers. "He only quotes the Bard when he's stressed. Kel, they want us to go and have a look, and if the ship is there and spaceworthy, they want you to take it up again. Easiest way to get anyone who is still alive back to safety."

"Go into the Roar?" asked Kelvin. "*No one* goes into the Roar—"

"Well, that's not quite true," said Vinnie.

"Don't tell them that!" exclaimed Kelvin.

"There *are* people who go in," continued his clone sib. "It's kind of a religious thing, for the Lepers, they go into the eye of the storm—"

"Excuse me?" asked O'Kazanis. "We don't have anything on . . . did you say *Lepers?*"

"Not actual lepers, as in Hansen's disease lepers," said Kelvin sourly. "Just people who've gone loopy for Venus, let all sorts of shit grow on themselves, they reckon they're adapting or transmogrifying or something. I didn't know you hung out with the Lepers, Vinnie. Or that they went into the Roar."

"The Lepers go for a far more extreme version of what we local settlers do with the lichen," said Vinnie, sending a quelling glance at Kelvin. "Which, it has to be recognized, is extremely effective. The lichen keeps the malignant spores off far better than any manufactured antifungal agent."

"Yeah, and then the lichen takes six months to remove," said Kelvin. "Like after the last time I was dumb enough to get talked into a walk in the Swamp."

"You offered to help," said Vinnie. "I didn't make you come along."

"Well . . . *Loafer* was in dock for repairs anyway," said Kel. "I didn't have anything better to do. But this is miner season, I'm flat-out busy. I haven't got time to go and rescue a bunch of plutocratic larvae who are probably already dead anyway. Not to mention trying to launch a damaged Brindi into orbit through a fucking cyclone, I mean I'd have to wind it up with the storm to forty thousand meters, zip out into the eye for the vertical ascent, light up the orbitmaker, and keep her true without getting sucked back into the cyclical system . . ."

"I told you he'd know how to do it," said Vinnie to O'Kazanis.

"You've got a dozen pilots who could do it!" said Kelvin.

"In theory, perhaps. Not one that's done anything like it before," said O'Kazanis. "*You* have, though, and survived the Swamp as well. So you're overqualified."

"Seriously, there's no point," said Kelvin. "They're dead."

"We think even a slim chance is worth pursuing," said O'Kazanis, with another sideways glance at Mazith. "Major Kelvin Kelvin 8 has been briefed more comprehensively on the predicted landing point. She will be in charge until or if you lift off in the *Jumping Jehosophat,* when you will assume command. Lieutenant Mazith will go with you to provide communications—"

"Radio doesn't work in the Roar," interrupted Kelvin. "Lasers, masers, no good. Perpetual cloud, rain, high winds, magnetic rocks, you name it, it's got it."

"Mazith is a special communicator," said O'Kazanis.

"OK, all right then," said Kelvin, raising an eyebrow. Special communicators were paired clone telepaths, capable of instantaneous communication over interplanetary distances, and were very rare. Mazith was quite possibly the only one the Terran Navy had on Venus, which indicated that this mission was being taken very seriously indeed. More seriously than seemed warranted to Kelvin, no matter how important the lost passengers.

"You leave immediately," continued O'Kazanis. "Understood?"

"I understand I just got shafted and my big sister dumped me in it," said Kelvin. "With all due respect."

"Personnel spat us both out," said Vinnie. "I didn't volunteer; you know I would never volunteer. I was just coming into town to pick up some stuff. Wrong place, wrong time . . . I don't know why our clone line has all the good luck. Let me know when you're ready to quit whining and go ride a lizard."

"*And* I have to ride a lizard," complained Kelvin. "We picking up equipment at your place, Vinnie?"

"Yep."

"What about extra help? Osgood and Jat?"

Osgood and Jat were both former ASAP commandos turned lizard ranchers like Vinnie. Or more accurately, Osgood had turned rancher. Jat had earned her peculiar name not by being an omnicompetent jack-of-all-trades, though she actually *was* one, but by being teed off with anything involving work. She could do nearly anything practical if she put her mind to it, but that hardly ever happened. However, she was absolutely deadly with all, any, or no weapons and was also Vinnie's life partner, so Kelvin, like everyone else, cut her a lot of slack.

"Nope, too busy," said Vinnie. "Ranch has got to be run. Besides, we don't need them."

"*Jat's* too busy?"

"Says she is," said Vinnie, with a quelling look. "As for the lizard ride, enjoy it while you can, 'cos when we get toward the Roar we're going to have to ask the Lepers for a frogsled."

Kelvin shuddered.

"I hate frogsleds even more than the lizards!"

"What's a frogsled?" asked Mazith.

"You'll find out, Ms. Mazith," said Kelvin. "You ever ridden a lizard?"

"No, sir," said the lieutenant. A slight tremor in her voice gave away the fact that special communicators didn't expect to be sent on potentially deadly planetside missions on lizardback, accompanied by what could only be described as extremely irregular forces.

"Just think of it like a paid holiday to the parts of Venus the tourists never see," said Vinnie.

"There's a good reason for that," muttered Kelvin.

"Oh, stop with the whining, Kel. Anyone would think you were six again."

"Yes, considerably older sister," said Kelvin.

"Carry on," said O'Kazanis, poker-faced. "I'll see you in Venus Above, with the rescued students."

"I hope," she added, under her breath, as Mazith saluted and followed the bickering clone siblings out of the dome.

Outside, Vinnie dialed up the power pack to give the lizard an extra burst of warmth before its blanket came off, then quickly rigged an extra saddle between its third and fourth bony plate, a somewhat smaller space than between the first and second, where she would ride double with Kelvin.

"Hop up there," she said to Mazith. "Put your feet through the stirrups, there are a couple of handholds welded onto the plate, there. You all lotioned up?"

"The latest all-defense formula, sir," confirmed Mazith. She grabbed hold as the lizard shifted, feeling her weight.

"That'll work for now," said Vinnie. "But we'll have to do you and my idiot brother over with the lichen when we get to the ranch, get you proper masks, and so forth. Nothing Terran-made will work in the Roar, and I'm guessing you don't want to turn into a giant mess of mushroom flesh?"

"No, sir!" said Mazith. She hesitated, then added, "But does it really take six months to get the lichen off again?"

"Nah," said Kelvin. He vaulted easily up into the forward saddle, and eased back to make room for Vinnie, who gathered the reins and mounted up before using the quick-release pull to unhood the mount, who reflexively snapped at the air in front of it. Even though its teeth had been filed down, it would have delivered a nasty bite. "I was exaggerating. It only took four months."

Mazith was silent as they rode out of Venusport and began the slow descent down the quaintly titled Road to Hell, the clouds thickening with every kilometer and the temperature ratcheting up several degrees. Kelvin unsealed everything he could unseal on his flight suit and was still too hot. He and Vinnie exchanged a few words, mostly just catching up on various family news, his complicated relationship with Susan Susan 5 on Venus Above and so forth, before relapsing into the comfortable silence of close relatives who also happen to be good friends.

It was only when they started splashing through the first pools of steaming water and the green tops began to overhang the track that Mazith asked how far it was to the ranch, and then how long it would take to reach the crash—or hopefully landing—site beyond.

"Ranch by nightfall, or just before," said Vinnie. "We'll head out again at first light. Lizardback for three days, I guess, to get to Leper territory. Then we have to find some Lepers, borrow a frogsled, I guess another day after that. Five days there say, five days back."

"But we'll fly back, won't we?" asked Mazith. "In the yacht?"

Vinnie glanced back over her shoulder, sharing a look with Kelvin.

"It really is unlikely the ship is intact enough to take off again," said Kelvin. "And even more unlikely anyone survived. Apart from the crash and the high probability of sabotage, a bomb or something, there's just . . . Venus. The farther you get into the Swamp, the more weird shit there is, of all kinds. We'll probably end up taking a look to confirm the situation, then have to just slog back again."

"I . . . we're fairly certain there are survivors," said Mazith, followed by a sudden exclamation as a small herd of tumblers rolled out of the green-cap jungle around them and across the track, the lizard straining at the reins to go after them, the small rolling reptiles being one of its main sources of food in the wild.

"Tumblers," said Vinnie. "Harmless. But if you see something that looks the same, only light purple, that's not. A fungal mimic. Nasty. Beam it if it's closing in, let them go if not."

"OK," said Mazith. "Uh, I don't get a lot of practice with small arms usually . . ."

"You'll get plenty this trip," said Vinnie, deliberately misunderstanding her concern. "Don't worry."

"So how does this special communication work?" asked Kelvin. "We didn't have any back in the day. Are you communicating all the time? You know, your sib sees and hears what you see kind of thing?"

"No," said Mazith. "It's not that straightforward. We sense each other all the time, but to communicate takes a lot of concentration. If it works, then I can speak through . . . Lyman's mouth. And he can speak through mine."

"So where's Lyman?" asked Vinnie.

"Uh, he's on the *Rotarua*," replied Mazith. "I . . . um . . . drew the short . . . the straw for the planetside assignment."

"*Rotarua?*" asked Kelvin. "That's a battle cruiser, isn't it? I thought the treaty limited visiting warships to nothing bigger than a heavy cruiser?"

"Apparently under the treaty terms she is a heavy cruiser," said Mazith easily. "Besides, we aren't exactly visiting, just a kind of touch and go. We were on patrol and got called in when the shuttle went down."

"I see," said Kelvin. She was lying about something, he thought, but he couldn't figure out exactly what, or why. The business with the *Rotarua* was strange. If the battle cruiser had been in anything like a regular approach and orbit, he would have seen it on the traffic scans on the way down that morning, but nothing had shown up apart from the usual picket ships, familiar icons on the screen. A "touch-and-go" approach could mean anything from literally dropping a boat while en route to somewhere else, or a long, irregular orbit that might be designed to keep the ship off the scans of both traffic control and the picket ships, but still put the ship close enough once every

Venusian day or so for a brief window to fire ordnance or otherwise conduct military operations.

But why would they want to do that, mused Kelvin . . .

As predicted, they reached the ranch just as the light faded, the cloud lowering and thickening into a dense fog, as it always did at nightfall. The lizard quickened its pace, keen to get into a warm huddle with its fellows, Vinnie having to hood it to slow it down long enough for the saddle-sore Kelvin and Mazith to dismount and hobble up into the ranch house, a high-stilted building constructed from gorretwood, the valuable fungus-resistant hard timber that only grew on the highest points of the plateau.

Vinnie opened the door with an old-fashioned bronze key in a massive bronze lock that would have suited a Terran house of four hundred years before. There was no one inside, but a note was on the table of the common room.

"Osgood is rounding up some strays," said Vinnie. "And Jat's gone on ahead to line up things with the Lepers."

"How did she know to do that?" asked Kelvin. "I thought the Navy picked you up in town? And besides, since when has Jat done anything anyone asked her to?"

"The Navy did pick me up in town," said Vinnie. "We've got a landline here now, at least for the dry season. I called and told Jat about the mission, and asked her to ask *Osgood* to go to the Lepers while she stayed back to look after the ranch."

"Smart," said Kelvin.

"Nah, she knew what I was doing. It just gave her an excuse to say no to my request, then do what I wanted while pretending not to."

"You guys have a very complicated relationship."

"And you don't?"

"Uh, I don't suppose there is any chance of a shower, sir?" asked Mazith. Her formerly nicely pressed camo uniform was looking quite bedraggled now, and was splashed with mud and speckled with multicolored spores.

"Through there," said Vinnie. "It'll be the last one for a while. Scrub off all your lotion, let me know when you're ready, and I'll apply the lichen. It'll need overnight to get established. Kel, you can use the decon shower. You want to apply your own lichen? There's a pot there."

"Yeah, yeah," grumbled Kelvin. "Can I borrow some clothes?"

"Help yourself," said Vinnie. "I'll see if they left us anything ready for dinner."

They had, and after lizard steaks with breadfungus and several classic martinis, Kelvin felt considerably better than he had, despite the creeping sensation of the lichen spreading along his arms and legs, around his groin and armpits, and across his face. In a fit of whimsy, he'd applied antifungal ointment to constrain the lichen in tiger stripes, with some whiskers out either side of his nose. It was already coming into effect, judging from the sidelong glances from Mazith. Her facial lichen matched Vinnie's spirals and she had adopted a lizard-skin singlet while retaining her camo trousers, all of it indicating an effort to fit in.

"Time you hit the hay, Lieutenant," said Vinnie, when the clearing up was done. "We'll be getting up at first light. Bunkhouse through the red door, take any bunk. See you in the morning."

As soon as she'd left, Vinnie checked that the door was firmly shut before the clone siblings made each other another drink. Martini for Kelvin, and a local Venusian whisky for Vinnie.

"So what did smooth Captain O'Kazanis not tell us?" asked Kelvin. "And what's Lieutenant Mazith lying about?"

"It could be just the kids *are* that important," replied Vinnie. She paused and added thoughtfully, "If there *are* any kids . . ."

"Yeah," said Kelvin. "A bunch of veep maggots take off by

themselves? Sounds pretty thin to me. What happened to their bodyguards, conducting officers, babysitters . . ."

"I don't get sending Mazith with us, either," said Vinnie. "Why do we need instant comms? And how do we even know she is a special communicator?"

"You think she might not be?"

"I dunno. There's something not right . . ."

"She's definitely lying about something to do with the special communication," said Kelvin.

"Yeah," mused Vinnie. "Got to wonder why they're using us, too, our megaskills notwithstanding. Pretty deniable, couple of old-timers from a pre–World Gov Navy."

"Maybe the Navy wanted that yacht crashed and whatever indication they've got that it didn't crash is bad news," said Kelvin. "Negative kill. So they have to send an operator to make sure, only its being where it is, they need local help."

"You got a suspicious mind, brother."

"Could be, could be something else again," said Kelvin. He scratched his head, frowned, and carefully inspected his fingernail. Itches on Venus were not to be ignored. "I figure whatever it is, it'll come clear enough when we get close to the yacht."

"I'll have a word with Jat when we catch up with her," said Vinnie. "Get her to watch over us, hey?"

"Will she do it?" asked Kelvin.

Vinnie gave him the look that had quelled many a junior officer and NCO.

"You ride the rear saddle tomorrow, too. Keep an eye on our young looie."

It was raining when they set out the next day, warm rain that came down in sudden, smothering deluges that lasted a few minutes before easing off, only to deliver another barrage ten or fifteen minutes later. Within a few hours, they were into the Swamp proper, and finding a way with ground solid enough and water not too deep for the lizard became a full-time task for Vinnie, even with the tall bronze way markers that had been hammered deep into the soft ground to show the path to the Lepers' territory.

Only a few kilometers into the Swamp, the treelike green caps gave way to a profusion of clusters of smaller fungi, in many different colors, some of them mobile. There were also rabbit-sized lizard-things, and insectoid critters that swam and jumped and chattered, and early on the afternoon of the first day, something shadowy and huge loomed ahead in the fog. Vinnie backed the lizard off and all three of them readied their heat-beams before it continued on its way. There were only two known Venusian life-forms that big. One was a truly monstrous lizard and the other the Devil's Tower, an ambulatory fungoid terror with fruiting spore-arms six meters long.

Two sweaty, itchy days later—broken by two long, hot nights spent on too-small islands that, while not actually underwater, were astonishingly damp—they came to what Vinnie described as the "Leper Trading Post," a massive, cube-shaped pink fungus at least fifteen meters a side, that had either naturally solidified into something approaching concrete or been somehow encouraged to, with windows and doors and rooms excavated out of it as if it were a small, rocky hill.

"There's nearly always a Leper here," said Vinnie. "There'd better be. I can't navigate us any farther into the swamp."

"They live inside that fungus cube?" asked Mazith. She pointed to the top corner, where the fog was swirling and discolored, a strain of grey through its normal bilious green. "And is that smoke?"

"Yeah, they use fires for drying out, cooking, and so on," said Vinnie. "Some of those dark purple, kind of chicken-shaped fungi burn slow, they're good fuel. Smoke is good, it means someone's home. Come on, let's go say hello. Remember, they can look a bit . . . confronting. Keep your hand off your heat-beam."

The Leper who came to the front door was *extremely* confronting. Kelvin considered Vinnie's advice to keep his hand off his heat-beam very wise, for if he'd seen the Leper out in the swamp, he would have burned first and investigated afterward.

Still roughly human-shaped, with two arms and two legs, the Leper wore no clothes and was instead clad in outgrowths of different-colored and -textured fungus from its body. It—for it was impossible to tell if it was a man or a woman—had a hard, bulbous carapace over its chest and back, extending down to its thighs, and rippled, corded growths along its arms and legs. Its feet were now more like flippers, the big toes still visible, the other toes buried beneath layers of a rubbery, bright yellow fungus reminiscent of duck feet.

Its head was almost entirely encased in a fuzzy ball of many thousands of black filaments, which were in constant motion. Only its face was free of this growth, and even then only around the eyes, nostrils and a narrowed mouth, lips replaced by puffy orange growths.

"Howdy," said the Leper, the depth and timbre of his voice indicating that he was probably male. Or had been male before his fungal transformation, which presumably went well beyond the visible indications. He raised his hand, which had only three fingers and a kind of wound-up sprung tendril in place of the pinkie.

"Afternoon," said Vinnie. "I'm Vinnie, and this is my brother Kelvin, and an associate, Mazith. Maybe you heard about us coming through from Jat?"

"Oh, yeah, Jat said you'd be by. My name's Theodore, by the way. You folk want a drink, bite to eat?"

"We're kind of eager to keep going while there's light, thank you all the same," said Vinnie. "We're going into the Roar to see if anyone's survived a spaceship crash. Time might be kind of short if someone has."

"Yeah, I heard about that," said Theodore. "You need a frogsled, too, and a driver?"

"We do," said Vinnie. "I was hoping we could work something out with your people, maybe Terran credit, or lizard steaks or hides, whatever."

"Sure, sure, we'll take your credit," said Theodore. "Or the Navy's, I believe."

"And I heard tell that you . . . your people—"

"Call us Lepers, that's what we call ourselves," said Theodore, with a laugh that set the filaments on his head all quivering.

"I heard tell that you Lepers can find your way in the Roar," said Vinnie. She pulled out a paper map—map tablets died faster than treated paper would rot on Venus—unfolded it across her arm, and pointed out the likely position of the yacht. "We got a rough planetfall, probably give a search area of a couple of kilometers, but I sure as shit can't navigate us there, not in the Roar."

Theodore leaned close to look at the map and nodded.

"That's not far off a marked trail, and it's in the eye," he said. "Tell you what, I might drive that frogsled for you folks myself. Been a while since I went into the Roar. Might be kind of unsettling going through the storm, but it's very nice in the eye. Calm, and you get less cloud. I even saw the sky once."

"Get out of here!" protested Kelvin. In thousands of shuttle flights, he'd never seen the sky. Not as such, not from anywhere even close to ground level. The cloud cover extended from twenty thousand meters to ground level, and never cleared. Not anywhere near Venusport, anyway.

"Just for half a minute or so, the clouds were sucked back by the storm," said Theodore. "Beautiful! Now, you all lichened up, all parts? Because you don't want to be on a frogsled with me, nor go into the Roar, unless you are. We don't do conscription, you know. Got to volunteer to be a Leper. Like an ASAP, huh, Vinnie?"

"I never volunteered for anything," said Vinnie sternly. "That was propaganda bullshit. We were *made* to be ASAPs. Variation D12 of only six clone lines, most of us Kelvin Kelvins or Oscar Goodsons."

"Well, *we're* honest about the volunteering," said Theodore. "Truth is, it don't work out unless it's voluntarily. Fungus grows wrong otherwise, don't know why, but that's what happens. So if you get to be interested, just let me know."

"Will do," mumbled Kelvin, with something like a nod from Mazith. Vinnie didn't answer.

"When was Jat here, by the way?" asked Vinnie. "Did she say where she was going?"

Theodore laughed.

"She was kind of here, then she wasn't," he replied. "Yesterday. Dunno where she went, or even how she was traveling. Didn't see a lizard."

"That's Jat," said Kelvin. Annoying as hell but often useful. He hoped she was going to be around. The more he saw of Lieutenant Mazith, the more he doubted she was a straightforward special communicator, and if she wasn't a communicator, then what was she?

"Let's go get on the sled," said Theodore. "Got a bunch of frogs raring to go, we should make good time."

The frogsled was a kind of punt drawn by four of the jumping Venusian batrachian analogues that were similar to Terran frogs, being a nice bright green with big back legs for jumping and smaller ones at the front. They were also the size of small hippos and on closer inspection they turned out to have hard carapaces and an additional set of vestigial legs, so the comparison was not very scientific. When harnessed to a frogsled, they moved the vehicle in a series of jerking, sliding, bucking movements that Kelvin had always found horribly like a spacecraft about to suffer a catastrophic thruster explosion.

The first day's travel was relatively uneventful, at least by the standards of the Swamp. For a while, Kelvin thought that Theodore was changing direction erratically, just for the fun of alarming his passengers, but after some careful observation he recognized that the Leper was avoiding potential dangers, and not just danger to the humans, but also the other way around, where their passage might disrupt the careful balance of the Swamp's ecosystem. This included taking a long diversion around a huge mass of early stage breadfungus that would have been torn apart by the frogsled and not come to maturity, depriving many of the higher life-forms of their sustenance.

They had to sleep on the sled that night, no islands being in evidence, with the frogs circled round and two of them on watch at all times. Toward dawn Kelvin woke Theodore to point out something he didn't recognize, a slow-moving luminous carpet of something that was either a fungus or a gestalt entity of tiny insects that mimicked the look of spores, floating across the water.

Theodore knew it, and swam around cursing while he quickly harnessed the frogs.

"Glowpile," he explained, as they started out again, the frogs swimming rather than jumping, taking it slow. "Absorbs everything in its path, spits what it doesn't want out the back. Highly resistant to heat-beams, chemicals, and the defensive spores we use. But at least it's slow and we can get out of its way."

When they stopped for breakfast on a welcome islet of rare rock, Mazith suddenly stopped chewing and her eyes went blank for half a minute. Kelvin watched her carefully, presuming that he was witnessing a communication from her telepathic sibling. Which meant a message from the battle cruiser.

When her eyes focused again and she started chewing,

Kelvin asked her what that communication had been.

"Just routine," she said. "Like a radio check. They want to know if we're getting close."

"We are," said Theodore. "Can't you hear it?"

"Hear what?" asked Mazith.

"The Roar," answered Theodore, the tendrils on his head making a waving motion, all in the same direction, though the ever-present fog was so thick there was no knowing what he was pointing out that way.

"I'm not . . . sure," said Mazith. She tilted her head, listening intently. "There is something."

They could all hear it, now that they were listening. It was slight, for the moment, like a faint clearing of the throat noise overheard through a closed window, but constant.

"It will get louder," said Theodore. "Much louder."

He was right. The noise got much louder and louder still with every kilometer they zigzagged and backtracked and meandered toward the Roar.

With the noise, there later came a breath of wind, welcome at first, simply because it made a change. The fog moved and shifted, and after a few more hours transformed into scudding cloud at surface level, sometimes even breaking up enough so that they could see more than the twenty meters they'd got used to in the other parts of the Swamp.

This too, was welcome at first. But the wind speed continued to increase as they lurched and skipped onward, soon drenching them in muddy spray mixed with spores, with the frogsled making a crabwise course, constantly having to be angled diagonally across the wind, for it was impossible to go against it. The frogs were not jumping now but rather crawling and paddling, their pace slowed to something not much better than a human could wade.

"Worse higher up," shouted Kelvin to Vinnie, as they lay flat on the frogsled, drenched, mud-spattered, and windblown, gripping on for dear life. "Wind's about eighty kilometers an hour down here, double that at two thousand meters, double again at ten thousand meters."

"It's bad enough here," yelled Vinnie. The frogsled had almost gone over several times, and would have if Theodore had not already deployed a kind of gripping keel that provided greater stability, again at the cost of slowing their speed even more.

"We are getting close to the eye," Theodore called back to them. He was strapped in at the front of the sled, the reins in whatever he called his hands. "Would've been there hours ago if we could have cut straight across. But we're getting close."

How Theodore knew this was impossible to fathom, but an hour later he lifted the keel. The frogs began to jump again, short jumps that made the sled lurch forward with a sucking pop as the surface tension was broken. Kelvin raised himself up slightly, grimacing as the wind cut at the skin on his face that wasn't protected by mask and goggles. But the wind was definitely weakening. The rushing clouds were slower ahead too, some breaking up and being sucked back behind them, into the eternal circular motion of the storm. He hadn't noticed before, but it was getting quieter too, the noise of the Roar subsiding as they continued deeper into the eye of the storm.

"The calm center," said Theodore. He sat up straighter and breathed in deeply, the air no longer quite so full of spray, mud, and particulate fungus. "Beautiful, isn't it?"

Kelvin and Vinnie did not remove their masks to take a breath. They looked at each other, then at Mazith. She was lying at right angles to them, behind Theodore, pressed as flat as she could make herself on her stomach, with her head turned toward the clone siblings. Her eyes behind her mud-smeared goggles were shut, her breathing mask tight around her mouth.

Kelvin reached across and tapped her on the shoulder,

repeating the movement a second later. Mazith stirred and sat up, grimacing as the wind smacked her wetly in the face. At that same moment, Vinnie snatched Mazith's heat-beam from her shoulder holster and pointed it at the young officer's head, finger next to the firing stud.

"We've got a few questions, Lieutenant," said Vinnie.

"Are you really a special communicator?" asked Kelvin.

"Yes," said Mazith. "Of course I am!"

"Why do we need a special communicator?" asked Vinnie.

"Uh, I guess, Navy HQ thought I could be useful," replied Mazith. "I mean, there are VIPs who want to know what's happened to their children, without delay."

"Maybe true," said Vinnie harshly. "But I bet there's more to it. What's the *Rotarua* doing?"

"I don't know," said Mazith. "Just a patrol. I'm only a lieutenant, I don't know anything."

"We know that's true in general," said Kelvin kindly. "But we think you might be an exception and actually know *something*. So why are you really here?"

"To communicate," said Mazith. "That's all."

"How many special communicators has the Terran Navy got?"

"That's top secret," said Mazith. "Of course."

"There are not that many, are there?" asked Kelvin. "Because they can't be gengineered, right?"

"No," said Mazith.

"So why send one of these incredibly rare special communicators into the wilds of Venus, into the Swamp, into the Roar?" asked Vinnie. "Please tell us why you're *really* here, because otherwise I am—with great regret—going to shoot you, then Kelvin and I will turn around and go back right now and report that the ship was a write-off and you got killed by something along the way."

"No!" exclaimed Mazith. "We have to keep going!"

"Why?" asked Kelvin.

"Because she . . . they . . . there *are* survivors."

"Who is *she*?" asked Vinnie quickly. "And how do you know?"

"I . . . I can't tell you," said Mazith.

"Lieutenant Mazith," said Vinnie. "You know that Kelvin and I are veterans of the Third Martian Intervention. You know I was an ASAP. I really will kill you if I'm not satisfied with your answers, and we definitely will not bother going any farther."

"I'm . . . I'm one of a triplet," said Mazith. "It's top secret. Everyone thinks there can only be telepathic pairs, but there are three of us."

"Let me guess," said Kelvin. "Your third is on that downed ship."

"Yes," sobbed Mazith. "Jezeth's in one of the survival pods. When they landed, they opened the air lock, and something got in, she said the others were careless, and now they're . . . they're . . . she doesn't know what they are, not exactly dead, but not alive, there's a fungus, she saw a little before she locked herself away . . . she's hurt, she can't send very much . . ."

"But why put you in a rescue party?" continued Vinnie. "Sure, they lose one communicator but then they've still got a pair like everyone else. Why risk that to try and rescue this Jezeth?"

Mazith didn't answer for a moment.

"Remember what I said about answering my questions," said Vinnie. Her voice was calm and matter-of-fact.

"Jezeth's a made communicator," whispered Mazith. "She's younger than Lyman and I, eight years younger, gengineered to link up with us, and it worked. Sort of worked . . . there are . . . problems. So we have to get her back."

"Why was she on the ship?" asked Kelvin. He paused, a nasty thought creeping into his brain. "And were there really any VIP kids on board?"

Mazith shook her head.

"All triplets," she whispered. "Made ones. But they're kind of . . . unstable, I guess . . . they do dumb stuff. Like steal the *Jehosophat*."

"They stole the yacht?"

"Yes," said Mazith. "I don't know, Jezeth didn't send to me until they were going down and they realized that they didn't have a pilot. They had a crazy idea that they could defect to Mercury Inc., their genetic material would get them executive positions—"

"It'd get them vivisected most likely," interrupted Vinnie. "I've seen some stupid young folk in my time, but . . ."

"Jezeth's only fifteen," said Mazith. "The oldest is . . . was . . . sixteen."

"So you think we've really been sent here to rescue survivors?" asked Kelvin.

"Of course!" said Mazith. "What else . . ."

Kelvin and Vinnie looked at each other. They were thinking exactly the same thing, and it wasn't about World Government trying to *rescue* a bunch of created telepaths. Far more likely that they'd want to make sure that any genetic information that could enable anyone else to duplicate the feat was destroyed. But to do that, they needed to know exactly where the ship had gone down.

"Tell me," said Kelvin. "You said that telepathic communicators are always 'aware' of each other. Does that mean that you know where the others are? I mean in specific terms, like you could supply coordinates?"

"We always know where our partners are," said Mazith. "In terms of a direction and distance. But Jezeth is injured or just too scared; I can't link up with her properly. Otherwise, I could just tell you exactly where to go."

"It wasn't Jezeth I was thinking about," said Kelvin. "Do you know where Lyman is right now, on the *Rotarua*?"

Mazith shut her eyes and was still for a moment. Then she

pointed up at the sky at an acute angle.

"There," she said. "About 1.2 million kilometers out, coming toward us."

"So Lyman knows where you are too?" asked Vinnie, catching on.

"Direction and distance," said Mazith. "But he can extrapolate that on a chart, he can use the . . . well, there's a visualization system, to help us plot, that's one of the experiments with the triplets, because you can triangulate so much better . . ."

"I reckon they're on the return path of an elongated planetary orbit perpendicular to the standard plane," said Kelvin, looking up where Mazith had pointed. "Can you tell if they're accelerating on that course?"

"I can only sense the direction and velocity," said Mazith. "Is this important? I could send to Lyman and ask him."

Kelvin did a mental calculation of attack paths, ordnance speed, and launch windows. It seemed extremely probable to him that the *Rotarua* was on a sneaky approach pathway to launch something targeted by courtesy of the unaware Lieutenant Mazith, and after doing that, it would then continue on into the obscurity of deep space.

"I think we'll keep communication silence for a while," said Kelvin. "Don't send anything unless I say so, all right?"

"Yes, sir," said Mazith.

"You say the young triplet, Jezeth, she's not sending properly," said Vinnie. "What is she sending?"

"After she locked herself in the lifeboat, it's just been flashes of emotion. It's common in the made triplets; if they get unbalanced, they can't focus properly, and I have to block out most of the terrified stuff that she does send. It's like someone screaming all the time. Please, Major. I don't know all the ins and outs of the program or anything, but I do know my little sister is on that ship. I'll do whatever you say, but can we please go on and help her?"

Vinnie looked at Kelvin.

"How long have we got if they do launch something once they've got the target from the lieutenant here?"

"What!" exclaimed Mazith, her back suddenly rigid, her neck tensed.

"At 1.2 million klicks out, they're probably coming in at two gees, a spread of the latest-generation tactical multis launched half a mill out . . ." Kelvin figured it out in his head as he talked. "I reckon we might have just short of an hour once they confirm the target."

"But . . . but my orders . . . we're meant to rescue the survivors and take the yacht back up!" protested Mazith. "Why would they launch missiles?"

"Figure it out," said Vinnie. "World Gov doesn't want anyone else to get the technology to make telepaths. They know most of them are dead already because you told them so. Better to waste a couple of communicators and some reactivated old grognards than to risk someone else's finding the genetic trove."

"But I wouldn't give them my location to be a target!"

"They don't need to ask you," said Kelvin wearily. "Won't your mate on the cruiser just point and say 'There she is' when the XO looms over him and asks? I bet you've been told to report in when you sight the yacht, right?"

"Yes," said Mazith. She was quiet for about twenty seconds, then she said, "I . . . I suppose you're right. What are . . . what are you going to do? Shoot me and go back?"

"Nope," said Kelvin. "I think we're going to do what they don't expect."

"Which is what?" asked Vinnie.

"Find that damn yacht and fly it back up," said Kelvin. "As soon as we clear the Roar, we start squawking to Venusport, Venus Above, and everyone else about how we've successfully carried out the rescue. That'll bring the picket ships over, the

Rotarua won't attack if anyone's watching. They'll sheer off—with all the publicity, Terran Navy has to call us heroes, we sign a few secret forms, and go back to normal life."

"You hope!" said Vinnie, with a snort. "We have to find the ship in the first place and sort out whatever—"

"The ship's over there," said Theodore, who made no attempt to hide the fact he had been listening intently the whole time. "Leastways, I reckon it is, judging from the look of things."

He did something complicated with the reins, tugging on the secondary nerve ganglions that lined the frogs' ridged backs. They slowed, then stopped, paddling gently in the shallow water. Theodore slipped over the side and immersed his head completely underwater, the fungal filaments on his scalp waving. When he came back up, he nodded.

"There's something over in that direction," he affirmed. "A current of destruction flowing . . . a burn-off where the ship came down, I guess."

"I don't know . . . ," said Vinnie. "You reckon the *Rotarua* will be in a launch position an hour from when they know we're at the location, Kelvin?"

"Yeah, give or take five minutes."

"But I won't report we've found it," said Mazith urgently. "I promise."

"What if Lyman checks in with you?" asked Kelvin. "Could you hold it back? You mentioned receiving emotions, images . . . he could tell probably, right?"

"Yes, he might," said Mazith. "But I could ask him not to tell—"

"Don't be stupid, Lieutenant," said Vinnie. "He's up there, on the bridge, surrounded by superior officers. He'd tell them. So would you if you were in his position. He won't know why they want the location fix."

"So we'll have say fifty-five minutes to get into orbit and start shouting from when we see the ship and Mazith gets pinged from the *Rotarua*," said Kelvin.

"Doable?" asked Vinnie.

"Yes," said Kelvin. "*If* she's not too damaged. *If* we can deal with whatever fungus offed the rest of the triplets. *If* we can—"

"Don't break out into Kipling," warned Vinnie. "Shakespeare's bad enough."

"It *would* be easier to shoot the lieutenant and just go back," offered Theodore.

Kelvin and Vinnie looked at the Leper, who shrugged not so much with his shoulders but with a curious undulating movement of his fungal carapace.

"I'm just saying. It's not a recommendation or anything."

"You'd better come with us if we try to lift the yacht," said Kelvin.

"Nope," said Theodore. "I'm a Venusian now, got no business in space. I figure if there's an hour going, I'll hightail it on the sled. You mentioned multis, but I'm presuming low-yield microfusion, maybe a hand of eight. I reckon there's a reasonable chance I can get clear of that."

Vinnie gave him the look.

"Commissioned Engineer," said Theodore. "Syrtis Spaceforce, before the amalgamation, MBF for a while afterward. Long time ago."

"Hell of a long time!" exclaimed Kelvin. "Syrtis got subsumed, what, back in '21 or '22. That's ninety years!"

"Lepers live longer," said Theodore. "Didn't you see the bumper sticker on the back of the sled?"

"What's a bumper sticker?" asked Mazith, Kelvin, and Vinnie, all at the same time.

"Ancient history," said Theodore, with a sigh. "So what are we doing?"

"Lay on, McTheodore and damned be him who first

cries 'Hold! enough!' " said Kelvin.

"What does that mean?" asked Mazith.

"I know," growled Theodore, and whipped up the frogs.

They found the *Jumping Jehosophat* three hours later, in the quiet heart of the eye of the Roar. The ship had landed well considering the circumstances, a better landing than Kelvin expected any autopilot to make. The ship was still in one piece, and was only slanted into the swamp at a gentle angle, the nose buried in mud and water some five meters or so, just past the cockpit escape hatch. Looking at it, Kelvin figured that the ship must have been flung out of the storm into the eye high enough to be able to make a series of corkscrewing turns within the calm center, and had then landed on its VTOL fans, only to discover that the apparently solid island beneath it was really loosely compacted mud.

As they sighted it, Mazith's eyes glazed over. Vinnie had been watching for this, and immediately pushed the young woman over the side into the water, dragging her back onto the sled a moment later.

"Does he know you've found it?" asked Vinnie.

"Maybe," coughed Mazith. "I . . . I just haven't been trained to block, I couldn't help answering—"

"Doesn't matter," said Kelvin. He looked at his watch, a locally made automatic winding timepiece that had no electronics at all. "We have to presume they know we've found it, have the position, and will fire on it. Fifty-five minutes to get into the ship and get out of here. Theodore, you'd better leave now."

"In a few minutes," said Theodore. "I'm kind of curious as to what's got inside that ship."

"Main air-lock outer door *is* open," confirmed Vinnie, as they drew closer. She slipped over the side of the sled into the waist-deep water, heat-beam in her hand. Kelvin followed suit, and a moment later, so did Mazith. "Not good."

"Nope," agreed Theodore.

He snapped the reins, and the frogs turned quickly, pulling the sled into position for a quick getaway. But he didn't leave.

Kelvin looked around. Here in the center, the fog settled like it usually did, but it was thin and he could see at least fifty meters. There was no visible threat, nothing was coming out of the air-lock door, nothing moving around the ship.

"Is Jat around?" he whispered to Vinnie. "Because I don't particularly fancy going in there myself."

"Wimp," said Vinnie. "She's here. Don't know how close."

"Maybe I could contact Jezeth," said Mazith eagerly.

"No!" Kelvin and Vinnie spoke together. "No contact with anyone, OK?"

"So what are you going to do?" asked Theodore with interest, from several meters back.

"We have to go in," said Kelvin. "Time's getting away."

"Someone's coming out!" exclaimed Mazith, pointing. "It's one of the other triplets, not dead after all!"

She started to wade forward as a figure appeared in the air-lock door. A teenaged boy in a bright gold-and-black civilian flight suit, without a helmet. He stood in the air lock and waved one arm jerkily.

"Stay back," ordered Vinnie. "Lieutenant Mazith! Halt!"

Mazith didn't obey. She thrashed vigorously through the water toward the open air lock, calling out, "Hey!"

Vinnie cursed and dashed after her, reaching out to pull her back by the harness of her Terran Navy webbing belt. But it broke, the fabric having rotted away in just the few days of exposure. Mazith floundered on.

In the air lock, the man waved again but he also rose up, feet dangling, a huge pink spore mass suddenly visible behind him. Fungal creepers ran beneath the man's feet and splashed out into the water, racing toward Mazith with frightening speed.

Kelvin and Vinnie fired together, heat-beams sizzling over Mazith's head as they targeted the spore body in the air lock and its human puppet. But unlike most Venusian fungi the thing didn't burst into flames. The pencil-thin beams just drilled smoking, blackened holes and more and more spore creepers kept spewing from it, the leading ones rushing toward the frantically reversing Mazith.

She only made it a few meters back before they latched on to her, drilling through lizard-skin and artificial fibers and straight through skin, following blood vessels and nerves and muscles, holding her upright as she screamed. Then she stopped screaming, and her arms lifted up and down, as if the fungus was testing its control of its new puppet.

"Back and sweep," ordered Vinnie tersely, firing in broad arcs across the water only ten meters ahead, trying to stop the creepers. Kelvin followed suit, backing and shooting and swearing, but the creepers were going wide and there were so many of them, dozens and dozens of tendrils that would encircle them both in a matter of seconds, and Theodore and the frogsled too—

Something erupted from the water just behind Kelvin. He began to turn, and it smashed into him and pushed him deep underwater. Panicking, he reached up to claw his way to the surface—and everything above went white, the white of utmost brilliance that marked the detonation of a tactical plasma grenade.

Even facedown under a meter of dirty water and wearing goggles, Kelvin was blinded for a few seconds. He thrashed and fought in dark fear as something dragged him out of the water, till he realized it was a human hand and not fungal tendrils about to bore into his flesh.

"Brace your feet!"

Kelvin dug his feet in and leaned back as water rushed around him. His vision cleared, apart from some dancing spots of darkness. He briefly saw a deep, smoking crater between himself and the *Jumping Jehosophat*, before it was once again filled as the waters rushed back in. Theodore was whipping his frogs into a frenzy of paddling and jumping to keep the sled from being sucked back, while Vinnie was bulling her way against the current toward him and the woman who was still holding him up.

"A hit, a very palpable hit," muttered Kelvin, shivering. Not from cold, for it was as warm as ever, the water still steaming and boiling twenty meters away, the final aftereffects of the grenade.

There was nothing left of Lieutenant Mazith and the fungus tendrils. She might never have existed at all.

"Never seen anything like that puppeteer," said Jat, slotting the snout of the Mark XXII Plasma Grenade projector over her back into its harness, the whine of its protective shield generator slowly fading as the weapon went into standby mode. She was an Oscar Goodson clone, small and wiry, and apart from the grenade-launcher harness and several other weapons, she wore only a kind of lizard-skin swimsuit, and the rest of her body, face and hairless scalp included, was covered in swamp lichen grown in a splinter pattern mimicking ASAP Terran equatorial jungle camouflage. A particularly large frog paddled placidly in a circle behind her, trailing a rig rather like the travois of the Plains Indians of Earth. "You reckon there's more inside?"

Kelvin spat out some water, rinsed his goggles, and took a look at the air lock. The plasma blast had scoured out the air lock and the fungal mass that he'd seen there, doubtless along with all the electronics and who knew what else. They'd be lucky if they could get it to close manually now. But he wasn't particularly worried about that. The thought of more puppeteer fungus was of much more immediate concern.

"Probably not," called out Theodore. "I've seen them puppeteers before. Single spore body always, no groups or clusters. They always keep one life-form to use as a decoy and absorb the rest. Interesting fellers."

" 'Probably not' doesn't sound all that convincing," said Kelvin. He looked at his watch. "Forty-eight minutes."

"Shit," said Vinnie, raising her heat-beam. Kelvin's head flashed up. There was another jerking, twisting figure in the air lock, another puppet raised by the bright pink threads of the fungus behind it.

"Turn and brace!" ordered Jat tersely, unlimbering the launcher. Kelvin felt a crawling sensation across his skin as the force shield extended outward. He had already spun about and was hunching down, with his eyes closed, when the second grenade went off.

A minute later he was blinking and hopping backward to avoid a stream of very hot water that had rushed past as the shield came down. The launcher's power pack could only maintain the shield for two or three seconds, to protect a squad from the initial blast. It wasn't designed for the aftereffects of detonation close to water.

The yacht's air lock was now definitely out of operation, the outer door hanging at a slight angle, scorch marks and pockmarks of melted alloy visible on the inside.

"So what are the chances of there being more than two?" asked Jat.

Vinnie shrugged and looked at Kelvin.

"Too risky to go in," she said. "We'd better hightail it out of here with Theodore."

"I guess so," said Kelvin heavily. He looked up at the clouds above, visualizing the sky beyond and the missiles that would be streaking in sometime in the next thirty-eight minutes or thereabouts. "What about if I go in? The ship's been venerified; they'll have a deluge system of antifungals operated from the bridge."

"You'd have to get to the bridge, and you know most of those antifungals aren't worth shit for the stuff out here," said Vinnie.

"I'll go have a look," said Theodore. He got off his sled and started to wade ahead toward the ship. He didn't bother drawing his heat-beam.

"Hey!" called out Vinnie. "Wait up!"

"Lot of the local fungi leave me alone," called out Theodore. "I'll have a look around. If I'm not back in five minutes, help yourself to the sled."

He gingerly tested the half-melted lip of the air lock but it had already cooled enough, so he hauled himself aboard, disappearing inside.

"I fucking hate Venus sometimes," said Kelvin.

"It is what it is," replied Jat with a shrug. "You got to admit, it's an improvement on Mars."

"Anything is an improvement on Mars," said Kelvin. He looked at his watch again. "Anyone know the exact kill radius of whatever Terran Navy uses for tac nukes these days?"

"Got to be five kays each warhead, and they'll overlap a bunch," said Jat. "Also, the Roar will deflect them some, so the spread will be uneven. We could get lucky."

"I haven't noticed a lot of luck in the last little while," said Kelvin.

"So we're due some," said Vinnie. "Quit with the whining."

"I wasn't whining," protested Kelvin. "Just pointing out a fact."

"Movement," said Jat, raising the grenade launcher. "I only got one shot left with this, by the way."

"It's Theodore . . ." said Kelvin. The Leper appeared in the air lock, but there was something strange . . . he was holding up a bluish figure that might be another differently colored puppeteer or something equally dangerous . . .

"Hold your fire till my command," ordered Vinnie tersely.

"It's all clear!" called out the Leper. "A few minor things growing here and there, nothing serious."

He lifted the blue-encrusted shape, which moved of its own accord a little, revealing a head and limbs.

"This is Jezeth! The triplet, Mazith's 'little sister,'" he called. "She escaped the puppeteer but has what we call the blue blanket. I'll have to take her with me, she'll die under any Terran treatment."

"I thought Lepers had to volunteer!" called out Vinnie.

Theodore gave his strange, rippling shrug.

"You could say she has," he said. "The blue blanket hasn't killed her, and she'll come back to consciousness and a good life in time, I would say."

Kelvin looked at his watch. Thirty-four minutes.

"We have to take off and get the word out," he said.

"I don't think I can just leave that girl with Theodore," said Vinnie. She looked at Jat, who nodded. "You take the ship up, Kel. We'll go with Theodore."

"You sure?" asked Kelvin.

"Yeah, I'm sure," said Vinnie. "To tell you the truth I was never keen on leaving the planet anyway. I haven't been off Venus since we were demobbed. I guess the place has grown on me."

Kelvin didn't laugh at the old joke.

"Take care, then," he said, giving her a quick one-armed hug. "I'll do my best to make sure the *Rotarua* doesn't launch anything. I'll get the rescue story out."

"Here," said Jat, handing over a flame pistol, the bigger military version of the heat-beams Kelvin and Vinnie carried. "You never know; Theodore might have missed something."

Kelvin took the weapon and made as if to hug Jat as well. She ducked under his arm in a lightning move and punched him very lightly on the side of the head, which for Jat was pretty much an extreme show of affection.

Theodore carried the girl out of the air lock, lifting her high as he waded over to the waiting frogsled. Kelvin raised a hand as he passed, but not too close.

"Thanks, Theodore," he said. "Stay leprous."

As Kelvin expected, the outer door of the air lock wouldn't shut under power and he didn't have time to wrestle with the hydraulic system. The inner door did shut, however, and he closed every hatch behind him as he made his way cautiously to the bridge, flame pistol ready. There were patches of mold all over the place, but nothing that moved, sent out tendrils, blew spores into the air, or otherwise seemed immediately inimical.

The bridge was sealed, which was good and bad. Good because it meant it should be relatively unaffected by anything Venusian and bad because it took Kelvin five minutes of his precious time to circumvent the security lockout using old military override codes that, as he had hoped, were grandfathered into the ship's operating system.

The bridge *was* fungus-free. Lights winked here and there, indicating the presence of standby power and dormant systems, another sign that the landing had been much more successful than it deserved to be. Kelvin hurried forward past the rear seats for the nonexistent bridge crew, checked the command pilot's chair to make sure there wasn't anything nasty waiting in its highly padded interior, and sat down, his hand sliding easily into the authorization glove. This was the real test.

A holographic screen flickered in the space in front of his eyes.

"Commander Kelvin Kelvin 21, Terran Navy, assuming emergency command in potential disaster situation," rasped Kelvin. He felt the slight prick of the sampler. The screen flashed amber, then red, then finally the green of acceptance. Other holographic screens blinked into bright existence, the authorization glove slid away and a control stick rose up under his hand.

Kelvin scanned the screens. The layout was familiar enough. There were various small malfunctions, a couple of big ones like the open exterior air lock, but on the whole he thought he could raise ship. The lifting fans in the wings were out of the water, and as the whole craft had been venerified, should work even if they weren't. The nose was probably dug into the mud a bit, but he could tilt his wings and edge backward and up.

He looked at his watch. Twenty-nine minutes.

Ignoring the holographic interface and its complicated expert system-ruled procedures that would take too long, he twisted open the emergency catches, folding down the direct control panel with its heavy-duty switches and dials. Lights lit up on the panel as he turned the switches. The ship shuddered as the power plant shifted from standby to ready use. The lifting fans began to slowly whir in the wings, telltales indicating that they were a bit bent up but still within the margins of military tolerance. The expert system would have shut them down immediately, of course.

Kelvin flicked an icon on the holograph and it wiped blank, then refreshed to show a panning view of the exterior. There were clouds of vapor coming off the wings, probably just churned up swamp water. He could just make out the frogsled, leaping into the distance, Jat's big frog its close companion.

Twenty-five minutes.

Kelvin ran over his mental checklist, flicking a few more switches. The lifting fans were slowly gathering speed. He had to push them ahead slowly, carefully watching the telltales, ready to shut down a fan if there was a problem. He could take off on two of the four fans, but not if one of them exploded and destroyed the wing.

What else? He got out of his seat and looked behind it, detaching the case with its emergency vacuum suit. He put it on but didn't expand the concertina-like soft helmet, setting it on the copilot's seat. Then he went to look at his watch, realized it was under the suit, and took a valuable thirty seconds to unseal at the wrist and strap the watch on the outside.

Twenty-two minutes.

"Plenty of time," muttered Kelvin to himself. "I could make a martini. If I had the makings."

He looked around again, and saw the bright green handle of the antifungal deluge system. Kelvin reached up and turned it to the right, a red-bordered holograph flicking up to offer numerous warnings, the most significant one being that no one could breathe the stuff that would be misted through every possible part of the ship.

Kelvin turned it to the right again and pulled it down. A Klaxon sounded a strident warning, very loud on the bridge. He sat back in his command chair and reached across for the emergency-suit helmet. Pushing it open, he fixed it over his head before connecting the external air supply. Then very deliberately he fastened his harness, double-checking every connection and point of attachment.

A yellow mist fell around him as he called up the weather radar, one small segment of the massive swirling storm of the Roar completely dominating the whole display. He looked at the airspeeds, rotating and moving the model across and up and down, his mind instinctively gauging how he would approach it, use it to lift him up, and when he was high enough, come slingshoting out of it and fire off the booster that would take the ship into orbit.

Eighteen minutes.

Kelvin's fingers twitched. The lifting fans howled. There was a horrible creaking, sucking sound as the ship lurched backward and upward. The crash screen over the forward viewports slid back as the nose came out of the swamp, but Kelvin hardly bothered to look. He was feeling every motion of the ship, every small vibration, watching the telltales for the power plant, the fans, the control surfaces.

He fed more power to the fans. The ship rose higher. Several audio alerts sounded, squawking about ground proximity and the open air lock and a dozen other things. Kelvin ignored them. One fan was running ragged, drawing too much power and providing little lift. He shut it down and flew on the remaining three, now tilting them forward a little, the ship climbing up in a corkscrew. But he couldn't keep it up all the way in the eye; there wasn't enough room, and the fans couldn't provide vertical lift for more than a thousand meters.

He had to go into the Roar. At exactly the right angle of attack.

The time was forgotten now, the closing cruiser on its attack run, his clone sister and friends trying to escape below. Kelvin's whole being was with the ship and the great storm, his mind and body remembering lessons learned from the terrible ascents out of the battlefield on Mars, climbing through the raging dust storms that spun as fast as the Roar, with enemy ordnance exploding all around, in ships worse damaged than this one, crowded with the dead and dying, the bridge itself packed so close he could barely move his elbows out and knowing that even if they made it, he'd have to go back down again . . .

The ship shuddered violently and pitched up, Kelvin correcting, tweaking, using all his skill to ease into the windstream. Clouds whisked past the viewports, so fast they were like flickers of shadow. There were more audible warnings, more amber- and red-bordered holographs glaring near his face.

The control stick shuddered under his hand and the ship rocked violently. The fans were tilted right back now for horizontal flight, but the number three fan wouldn't stay in that position. Kelvin shut it down, hesitated for a moment, hit two more switches, and pulled the short lever that emerged from the panel. A few seconds later, there was a deafening crack from somewhere aft and the ship jerked sideways. Kelvin's left hand flew across holographic controls and manual switches, as he flew with his right hand tight on the stick. The ship would not come level, but it still answered, was still climbing with the storm.

A schematic flashed red in Kelvin's peripheral vision. He glanced at it, seeing a hole where the number three fan used to be. He'd ejected it perhaps a second before it exploded, only just in time to save the wing, while still sustaining some damage.

The *Jumping Jehosophat* on two of four fans was only marginally controllable in the storm. Sweat poured down Kelvin's face under his helmet, no matter how high he dialed up the air circulating through the suit. Though he was only handling a tiny control stick, flicking holographs and turning smooth manual switches, his arms felt like he'd been carrying heavy cargo under high gravity for hours.

In a moment, he would have to slingshot out, but if he did it even slightly at the wrong angle or the wrong speed, the ship would be torn apart, the mangled pieces being strewn widely over the Venusian swampscape.

And without him to alert Venus to their presence, the *Rotarua* would undoubtedly fire on the last known position of their errant telepathic communicators, and that would very likely take out Vinnie, Jat, Theodore, and the poor girl under the blanket of blue mold.

The moment came. Kelvin took it, without any preparatory calculations or consultation of the ship's systems. He instinctively absorbed all the data on the screens in front of him, he felt the vibration, he sensed the speed, direction, and possibility.

The *Jumping Jehosophat* came catapulting out of the endlessly circling storm forty thousand meters high, pointing almost straight up. The fans began to lose their purchase in the thin air. For a moment the ship hung suspended, either to fall like a stone or rise to even greater heights.

Kelvin goosed the fans, made the slightest adjustment, and lined the ship up absolutely vertical for a straight ride to the stars. Then he hit the one-shot orbitmaker.

There was a second where he thought that the rocket booster wasn't going to activate, where he felt his stomach rise up before the fall.

Then there was a roar greater and closer than the storm. Kelvin was savagely thrust back into his chair and he blacked out.

He came to feeling intensely aggrieved. How could he have blacked out? He never blacked out. He'd been designed from birth to be a pilot! But the emotion only lasted the merest instant. Already, he was automatically taking stock of his situation. There was no massive pressure holding him back. The orbitmaker was off and . . . he wriggled in place . . . they were in zero G. In some sort of orbit, at least for the time being.

His eyes raced over the displays, his full senses returning. With them came a sudden shock. How long had he been out? Kelvin's arm jerked but his watch wasn't there, it had fallen off his suit and was floating somewhere. The ship's time was meaningless, the display set to Venus Above.

His fingers sped across controls, bringing up comms. Radio, laser-link, maser, every damn thing the ship possessed. At the same time, he activated scans, looking for his own position, the picket ships, Venus Above, and, most important, the *Rotarua*.

There she was, a massive blip coming around the curve of the planet, heading in fast and almost . . . almost but *not* quite . . . in attack range, either to take out him or launch on the crash site.

Automatic queries were coming in, answering the hails he had set in motion. Venusport Traffic Control, the familiar hoarse lungy voice of the expert system, emotionlessly asking where he had come from, what he was doing, why his transponder was off.

Kelvin used the manual board to flick on the backup

emergency transponder and plugged his suit into the comm system, to broadcast by all means across many channels.

"Anyone receiving, anyone receiving, this is Kelvin Kelvin 21, pilot in charge of the salvaged vessel *Jumping Jehosophat*. We have damage, comms issues, request relay from any receiving party to Venusport Traffic, Venus Above Orbit Control. Please relay position as per data blip, and relay following to Terran Navy NOIC Aphrodite. Vessel located planetside, no survivors. Lieutenant Mazith killed by fungal hostile. Despite damage, ship is maneuverable, I intend docking Venus Above Hazard Area, please be advised need high-level decon."

As his words went out, Kelvin settled back in his seat. On the scan, he saw the *Rotarua* change course and slow, as if it were never intending any kind of attack run anyway. A Martian picket ship was coming in over the pole, closely followed by a Mercury Corp patrol vessel and some small civilian craft that might well be a newshound.

Vinnie and the others would be safe, at least from an attack from space, and he figured they were good for anything else.

Beneath him, the clouds of Venus roiled, the Roar like some dark, unwavering eye looking up toward him, as if to get a good look for the next time he came to visit.

"Not a chance," said Kelvin, waving. "I am *never* going back to see you, buddy. I'm not stepping one meter outside of Venusport, no matter what!"

At that moment, the audible alerts that had diminished to a whisper grew raucous again, and a flashing holograph bigger and brighter than any before erupted in front of his face.

"Orbital decay! Orbital decay!"

Kelvin sighed, and reached for the controls.

MICHAEL CASSUTT

As a print author, Michael Cassutt is mostly known for his incisive short work, but he has worked intensively in the television industry over the past few decades, where he is a major Mover and Shaker. He was co–executive producer for Showtime's *The Outer Limits*— which won a CableACE Award for best dramatic series—and also served in the same or similar capacities for series such as *Eerie, Indiana* and *Strange Luck*, as well as having worked as the story editor for *Max Headroom*, as a staff writer on *The Twilight Zone*, and having contributed scripts to *Farscape, Stargate SG-1*, and many other television series. His books include the novels *The Star Country, Dragon Season, Missing Man, Red Moon, Tango Midnight*, the anthology *Sacred Visions*, coedited with Andrew M. Greeley, and a biographical encyclopedia, *Who's Who in Space: The First 25 Years*. He also collaborated with the late astronaut Deke Slayton on Slayton's autobiography *Deke!* His most recent books are the *Heaven's Shadow* series, written with David S. Goyer, and consisting of *Heaven's Shadow, Heaven's War*, and *Heaven's Fall*.

In the compelling story that follows, he demonstrates that dangers that you ignore are still dangers, and that some warnings had better be listened to, whether you think you know better or not.

The Sunset of Time

MICHAEL CASSUTT

"DON'T WORRY, YOUR GIRLFRIEND WILL BE HERE."

D'Yquem (Exile Quotient [1,2,3,4,5,6,7]) gestures with his brue, the cheap brand created by Petros ([1,3,4,6]), owner of the 13-Plus Tap, which is the least of the three bars that cater to the Terrestrian population of Venus Port. It is the one Jor ([2,4,7]) prefers, for its low prices, panoramic view, and especially the absence of Terrestrian Authority figures—or anyone whose EQ is under 12.

"You keep calling her my girlfriend."

"Suggest another name then," D'Yquem snaps. He emigrated to Venus from England, and his manner is still annoyingly upper-class, aristocratic. "We've already rejected 'tart,' and 'sweetie' is unbearably cloying. 'Impedimenta' is clearly inaccurate since she's more independent than you."

"Drink your brue," Jor snaps, turning so he can watch the entrance. Having fled Chicago and a suffocating Midwestern American existence, he is an unlikely friend to D'Yquem.

Yet they do share similarities. Both are tall and thin, though Jor's complexion is darker, and his stomach is beginning to expand, thanks to the nightly ingestions of brue. D'Yquem remains pale and almost skeletal.

Their other commonality is, according to D'Yquem, "We're both hereditary kicks. Horse-holders. Second-raters. Never heroes."

"What is that supposed to mean?"

"I'm the snarky one at every meeting," he says, which Jor knows to be true. "And you're the one who trails behind the boss but does all the work."

"But I'm a project manager!"

"But not the head of TA." Which is Harrison Tuttle (4,5), a dull, petty American from New York who controls every aspect of Terrestrian life, from the assignment of living quarters in the four towers to approved styles of clothing—but pays no attention to the progress of the Lens.

Unlikely friends or not, nine out of every tenday, Jor and D'Yquem can be found in 13-Plus . . . though normally at the bar, not at a table. In days past, they used the vantage point to evaluate newly arrived female Terrestrians.

But tonight Jor is anticipating the arrival of the Cherished Abdera, Golden Glowing of the Clan Bright Sea—"Abdera" for sanity's sake—the female Venerian with whom he has been friendly for a considerable time. Jor has pondered the nature of their relationship since its beginning two years past. "Girlfriend" is certainly not the correct term, not in his mind, and certainly not in hers. Venerians don't have unauthorized, prematrimonial associations among themselves . . . understandable given their five identified genders, bitter clannish rivalries, complicated inheritances, ridiculously long life spans, and uncertain periods of sexual activity.

Nevertheless, it is fair to state that Abdera—who, in the permanent twilight of the Twi-Land, and allowing for oddities of dress and her light green coloring, could pass for a human female of thirty—is indeed Jor's girlfriend.

And tonight, for the first time in their relationship, Abdera has not only volunteered to enter the 13-Plus—where Venerians of any gender are rarely present—she has fixed a rendezvous.

Which she has now missed! And by a considerable amount

of time. In all their time together, Abdera has never been late. "Tardiness," as D'Yquem frequently says, "is a Venerial sin."

(In addition to the labeling of Jor's relationship, D'Yquem's favorite topic is Foolish Terrestrian Terminology. His usual starting point is the Terrestrian name for natives of the second solar planet, frequently reducing it to a joke at Jor's expense, as in, "Wouldn't you rather have a Venusian girlfriend than a Venereal one?" Or similar.)

Jor feels that his friend is tiresome on the subject. But this is one of the topics that recurs under the influence of brue—which is vital to Terrestrian survival on Venus. "Maybe I should have gone to her."

"And risk being run down by a rogue skiff? Picked up by TA's curfew cops and brought before Tuttle? Sink in the mud and never be found? Don't be an idiot." D'Yquem grins again, tipping his half-empty glass (he is not a glass-half-full person) toward the window that looks north toward the Venus Port, and the human-built tower that looms above it. "Enjoy the view. It's almost clear this evening, and the Lens actually glows."

Venus Port lies in the northern third of the Twilight Lands, the broad band of habitable temperatures that circles Venus from pole to pole. Travel too far east, you broil in the Noon Lands if you don't drown in the Bright Sea, or vanish into the many jungles and swamps.

Too far west, and you freeze in the eternal darkness of Nightside.

Humans know that the sky and stars and sun can be seen from Nightside: the low temperatures freeze any open water and eliminate the otherwise-permanent cloud cover that shrouds the rest of the planet.

But the sky above Venus Port is generally uniform, gray, like Chicago on a dreary winter afternoon, changing colors only when it rains—which is frequently. Terrestrians have no day, no night, no seasons, all of which contributed to TA's adoption of the brutal ten-day workweek, not that the controlling organization needed additional means of exploiting its workers.

Now and then, however, due to some yet-to-be-understood dynamics in the Venerian atmosphere, the gloom lifts a bit, and some stray beams of sunlight brighten the upper reaches of the Lens.

From this distance, Jor can't see the rivets, the individual girders, the discolorations, the patchwork . . . just the giant glassy disc and its twin focal arms.

"Almost makes it all worthwhile," he says. The construction has been a struggle, consuming most of his energies for the fifteen years he has lived on Venus. The same for D'Yquem, who has been here even longer. "One year of tests . . ."

"And then," D'Yquem said, "everyone with the money can walk in a door on Earth and step out into this glorious Venerian landscape." He examines the bottom of his empty glass. "I do wonder, Jor, if we aren't working against our best interests here."

"When haven't we?"

D'Yquem laughs. He is capable of amusement at Jor's attempts at cynicism. "This is a new low, even for the TA." He belches. "We prosper here—"

"—If you call this prospering."

"—Because it takes real effort to get to Venus." D'Yquem's point cannot be argued. Interplanetary spaceships are crowded and unpleasant, the tickets expensive, the voyage long. "No one wants to follow us with a warrant, then haul us back."

Jor realizes that D'Yquem, in his fashion, has raised a legitimate point: with no exceptions worth noting, not even among the political leaders of the TA, no Terrestrian is free of an Exile Quotient . . . a public rating of his or her sins against the morals and behavioral standards of Earth, the headings being:

1   General maladjustment
2   Poor family relations
3   Substance abuse
4   Financial incompetence
5   Political unreliability
6   Sexual misconduct
7   Religious heresy

Each Terrestrian wears the EQ as a badge of honor—the denizens of 13-Plus glory in it; you can't enter unless your score is thirteen or higher.

D'Yquem reaches across to Jor's brue, takes it, drains it, a not-remotely-subtle signal to get the next round. "And by the way," D'Yquem says, in one of his famous conversational veerings, "she will show."

Jordan Lennox is the project manager for the Lens, a job he could not have imagined having when he first arrived at Venus Port. But politics, personalities, and the challenges of constructing an advanced technological facility on an alien world have seen the Lens run through eleven prior managers.

Now into his third year, Jor holds the record for tenure, largely—he believes—due to Charles D'Yquem.

The drunken aristo is a specialist in computing and calculating devices, tools that were banished from Earth a century past and rejected by Jor's predecessors on Venus. (Jor feels that the EQ should have an eighth category . . . some Terrestrians are sent to Venus because they are just too fucking stupid.) Having listened to D'Yquem touting the devices for the best part of a decade, Jor was willing to try them once he moved into the top job.

Thanks to them, and Jor's own relentless energy, the Lens now approaches completion.

Jor rises to head for the bar, a bit surprised by D'Yquem's encouraging remark. His friend's attitude toward Abdera usually starts out cold and judgmental, growing warmer only with increased alcoholic intake. Who knew D'Yquem was quite that drunk?

As he waits for a new pitcher of brue, Jor busies himself glancing from the entrance to the terrifying vista in the huge window: the blunt Terrestrian towers giving way to the more exotic—to human eyes, anyway—Venerian columns and galleries and mounds—all of them in the process of disassembly.

And, beyond both, the glittering thousand-foot diameter of the Lens shining in the perma-twilight.

He knows every foot of the Lens, of course. It feels as though he has personally lifted each I-beam, welded each structural plate, drilled each cable run, and even pulled each wire.

He has approved the design for all of these elements . . . while also ensuring quality control and integration. And he has seen the Lens grow from a stubby foundation formed from hardened Venerian slime to the tallest, broadest, most spectacular human structure this side of the Trans-Atlantic Tunnel.

One month away from its first tests . . . will it really work?

"Hey, Jordan!"

D'Yquem's voice from across the bar.

He realizes that the pitcher has been sitting in front of him for perhaps two minutes . . . an eternity to a drinker like D'Yquem.

He is on his way back to the table when Abdera enters, looking sick with worry. Jor knows that while Venerian facial features are much like humans, their expressions are more extreme. A grown Venerian who is happy will glow like a human infant being tickled . . . one who is unhappy would have the expression of St. John regarding the Opening of the Graves.

Abdera looks like that now. "Jordan," she says, as if she

only has strength to utter his name.

"You're late," he says, feeling stupid.

Which only seems to make Abdera feel worse. "I was trapped."

Jor moves her to the table, where D'Yquem helps her take a seat. Jor offers her a sip of brue, which she gulps in a single swallow. The beverage is designed to bolster human resistance to Venerian germs and other environmental factors; in small doses, it will not hurt Abdera.

But she downs Jor's drink before being able to speak. "My clan ordered us to stay indoors for a cycle." Cycle being the Venerian equivalent of thirty Earth hours.

"Why?"

"They never say. But this order came without warning, on a day that is usually devoted to business. There were many protests, none successful."

"Yet here you are."

And now she smiles. And in a less worried voice, says, "And here I am."

Although Abdera would strike most human males as attractive, it is not her looks that continue to inflame Jor's passion. Rather, it is her voice—throaty, articulate, versatile, capable of terrifying low anger and inspiring high laughter . . . a true Siren song.

Fluent in English, she has no accent, or none that Jor, a Midwestern American of the twenty-second century, can detect. (D'Yquem is merciless about Jor's "absurd nasal honk" and "questionable pronunciation.")

And now, D'Yquem, who occasionally exhibits a finely tuned set of social graces, excuses himself, leaving Jor and Abdera alone. The Venerian female watches him cross to the far side of 13-Plus. It's as if she has never seen him walk before.

"What do you think of the place?" Jor says.

"It's exactly as you described it though with fewer Terrestrians."

"It's a slow night." He feels the moment is right. "Why did you want to come here? After all this time, I mean."

There is a long pause, as if Abdera has a message, but can't find the words. "Your Lens is almost finished," she finally says.

"Months at most, yes." Then Jor realizes: *she thinks I am going to leave.* They have never talked about a future together . . . their relationship is unique in the Venus Port community, subject to so much gossip and speculation that their conversation has frequently been consumed by mutual sharing of same, and subsequent amusement.

A relationship of the moment.

"Would you ever consider leaving Venus Port?" he says, trying to sound casual in spite of the improvisation.

Casual or not, the question clearly surprises her. "And go where?"

"Elsewhere on the planet. There will be a second Lens in the southern hemisphere. Maybe a third."

She smiles faintly. "Southern clans aren't as welcoming to outsiders as your people." Which suggests outright hostility.

"Then how about Mars?" he says. "Lots of opportunities there."

"For you. But the adaptation—"

"—Would be a challenge, yes." Then he thinks, for the first time in fifteen years: "How about Earth?"

The sheer audacity of this suggestion makes Abdera laugh, and a Venerian laugh is always worth witnessing; it draws sympathetic laughter from Jor, as he imagines the look on Miller Lennox's face when confronted with his prodigal son. "I thought you couldn't!" she says, meaning the reverse adaptation, Venus to Earth.

"There are ways," Jor says, knowing of one experimental method—

"Am I interrupting?" D'Yquem is returning to his chair.

"A moment of speculation," Abdera said, her mood suddenly solemn. Jor notices that her flowing sarilike garment is torn near her left elbow.

He is beginning to form a question when the building shakes, a violent jolt that breaks glass at the bar and triggers shouts of alarm.

"What in God's name was that?" D'Yquem says.

"The Lens!" Petros calls.

Crunching on broken glass, Jor rushes toward the bar and its big view window—

The evening is still unusually clear, and it makes the sight all the more horrific: there is a hole in the big dish of the Lens.

By the time Jor, Abdera, and D'Yquem emerge from the ground floor of the 13-Plus tower, the situation at the Lens is more troubling: the evening marine layer has rolled in, obscuring the ground view of the top of the structure—except for flashes of light, which mean additional explosions. (*Any* flashes of light are anomalies.) Jor cannot hear explosions, of course. The dense, rolling fog damps distant sound. Nor can he feel the ground shaking, but that could be due to the mud.

Even after years on Venus, he has never gotten used to the fact that the evening mist is hot, not cold as it would have been in an Earthly port city.

It takes far too much time to reach the Lens. TA has always skimped on rescue equipment, naturally, preferring to reserve precious cargo volume on spaceships for prefabricated construction materials, not fire or rescue trucks.

So Abdera, D'Yquem, and Jor are forced to travel in a Venerian skiff, which means letting Abdera serve as pilot. Terrestrians have never learned to operate the raftlike machines, especially since—owing to the lack of Venerian mass production—none is like another.

It makes D'Yquem unhappy. "Don't we have more important things to worry about?" Jor says.

"We can fix the fucking Lens," he snaps. "When you lose social status, you lose everything." It is one of those passing remarks that makes Jor realize that D'Yquem's pre-Venereal life must have been far different from his own.

Grumbling and petty, he climbs aboard nonetheless, and the trio commences a glide toward the smoking, flashing Lens at a speed they could easily exceed by walking.

Not that walking is possible. Venus Port is built on a delta. Instead of real streets, it has shallow rivulets and streams—more water than land.

And on most open land, and all "streets" and even on water near the shores, lay piles of newly raw material awaiting shipment via skiff.

Venus Port is being taken apart. According to Abdera, the process, known by the Venerian world as "reloquere"—has been going on for the equivalent of two hundred Earth years. The first human explorers originally thought that the open pits and half-built buildings were signs of construction.

It was quite the other way around. They were what remained of residence towers and palaces and businesses and manufacturing facilities and libraries—whatever one would find in a city.

Reloquere is the prelude, Venerians say, to the great Sunset of Time, that moment each ten thousand or hundred thousand or one million (accounts vary, depending on which Venerian clan is asked) years when the clouds fade . . . the Sun is clearly visible.

And it sets as Venus creaks into a partial rotation, unleashing storms, floods, quakes.

Remaking the landscape. Where once was Twi-Land would now be Noon, or Nightside.

Or so the legend has it. Most Terrestrians dismiss the idea, either for lack of scientific backing or their own theological reasons. But the Venerians seem convinced: wars between the city-states have ceased in the past few years as reloquere spread throughout the Twilight Lands.

So, even as the Terrestrian Authority raises the Lens to the heavens, the Venerians continue to disassemble their city brick by vine.

The process isn't just a disassembly of structures . . . the individual *elements* of each structure are taken apart, too. Bricks are taken to a place to the north and east, where there is almost no dry land, and dissolved . . . returned to the mud whence they came.

Piping is melted down and returned to more solid ground. (TA's long-ago offer to buy this metal was rejected so thoroughly, Jor knows, that a second request was never made.) Glass, the same—transformed back to sand and spread on the shore.

Even the wiring of the Venerians' electronic grid has to be stripped out of structures, coiled, then melted down.

This strikes Jor as simply foolish: art and decorative items are also on the list. Venerians have statues though most are abstract rather than representational, and these are also victims of reloquere. Not long ago he happened to see the removal and disassembly of one obelisk from his Lens station over a tenday, and he was impressed with the care and even ceremony, like a state funeral.

Nevertheless, at the end of it a thirty-foot-tall piece of art had been reduced to a cooling vat of creamy goo.

He later asked Abdera how the artists felt about the death of their work, only to be told, "They are long gone." Which, given the Venerian life span, suggested that the artists had completed their work centuries ago . . . or something more sinister.

The Venerians also have great gardens filled with broad-leafed ferns and purple Twi-Land flowers with blossoms as big as a human head, so richly fragrant that spending too much time too close might result in suffocation. (For a human, that is: the Venerians thrive when surrounded by Twi-Land's blooms.)

What this means is that Jor's skiff is forced to avoid the "streets," since these are crowded with materials-to-be-shipped, in addition to Venerians now living in tents. There are also a few humans, stirred from their towers by the disturbance at the Lens.

It takes them an hour to cover a distance of less than five miles. Jor cannot speak to Abdera; she certainly does not turn and communicate with him or D'Yquem. Nor do Jor and D'Yquem have anything to say.

They finally reach the base of the Lens and are allowed inside the perimeter. "Someone tunneled under the fence on the Venerian side," one of the security team, Hollander ([2,4,7]) tells Jor, who does not bother to correct the man: *everything* outside the fence is the Venerian "side."

"Crawled up the Lens without using the lift or the backup ladder—"

"—Which explains why no one saw this," Jor snaps. There are observers, and even cameras, watching the gridlike tower, not for saboteurs, of course, but for damage . . . stray vines.

Hollander flinches, anticipating punishment. "They attached an explosive with a timer, then crawled back to the ground to watch what happened."

Jor has other orders to give Hollander, but there is a disturbance at the base of the Lens. Security wants to arrest Abdera.

"She's with me, you idiots," Jor snaps. There are three security shifts; the first two would know that Abdera and Jor are involved. The late shift, apparently not.

Then there is a problem with the lift: a security team has taken it to the top and won't let it return.

So Jor begins to climb up the girder itself. If the Venerian bombers can do it—

Physical exertion is not advised for Terrestrians, especially those soggy with brue. But Jor is determined to see what happened to his Lens.

D'Yquem and Abdera follow though more slowly.

The Lens reminds most Terrestrians of the Eiffel Tower. The two structures share a common shape though the Lens is slightly shorter (850 feet as opposed to over a thousand) and is topped by a rotating silvery disk that is itself 250 feet in diameter, and represents the greater engineering challenge. It is designed to gather, then focus, megahigh-frequency transmissions from the giant orbital Equatorial dish, opening a portal between Earth and the second planet.

Jor is aching, puffing, sweating heavily as he reaches the platform level. Pausing for breath, he takes in the view, the evening mist blanketing Venus Port as he hears Abdera and D'Yquem from below . . . the aural dampening effect of the fog making them seem closer than they are, as if all of them were in the cozy interior of 13-Plus, not hanging off the side of a tower.

Jor is quickly able to see that the saboteurs have blown a hole in the disk large enough to throw a skiff through.

He runs to the far end of the platform, which is still incomplete, with boards and slats instead of metal grilling. "Jor, be careful!" Abdera shouts.

He is not worried about falling. Although conflicted about the ultimate value of the Lens, Jor knows it is still his project, his life's work; any attack on it is an attack on him.

Once he has completed his circuit and examined the gear joints of the steering mechanism, he relaxes so thoroughly that he laughs.

"How is this funny?" D'Yquem says, barely able to utter words, he is so out of breath.

"All they did was poke a hole in the disk," Jor says. "We can fix that in a few days. If they'd really wanted to destroy the Lens, they should have put their bomb in the gears. That would not only take months to repair, it might have brought down the whole structure."

Perhaps it is the residual effects of the brue. Or the climb. Jor shouts into the Venerian night, "Idiots! Tear your city down! Leave the Lens alone!"

He turns and sees Abdera staring at him with what can only be disgust.

Back at the base of the Lens, Jor, Abdera, and D'Yquem fall into a crowd of confused security types. D'Yquem goes off in search of information. Abdera and Jor stand by her skiff in the roiling hot mist, so thick now that Jor can barely see Abdera ten feet away.

"I'm sorry about what I said up there." One lesson he has learned from his cruel father is, when necessary, be the first to apologize. (Because Miller Lennox never does.)

Among the many differences between Terrestrian and Venerian responses—they don't shrug. If uncomfortable and unwilling to engage, they just stare.

And so Abdera stares. Jor cannot fail to notice that, even in the thick mist, which coats his skin and clothing, Abdera appears cool and dry. Her garments, standard for a Venerian female of her clan, are largely a series of varicolored wraps and scarves that bind her hair while not really covering her head. She wears sandals that could easily have been found on Earth.

There is no differentiation in garments by male and female, but rather by age and status: postfertile Venerians wear more structured clothing, prematable Venerians much less.

"I was angry," Jor says. "Then I was overly elated because the Lens survived."

Still she stares.

"What was it you wanted to talk about?" he says, changing his tone and, hopefully, the whole conversation. "Why did you want to meet me tonight?"

Finally, he engages her. She takes a step toward Jor, actually touching his arm (a rare event in mixed public). "It is a painful admission—"

"Hey!" D'Yquem shouts as he suddenly appears out of the mist. "They caught them!"

"The bombers?" Jor says.

"They were still inside the compound, still carrying climbing tools and explosives." He shakes his head at the unlikelihood. "They didn't even try to get away."

He holds up an image. Jor and Abdera see five Venerians, two males and three pregendered youths.

Abdera is clearly upset, turning away. Jor reaches for her, but she runs off, disappearing into the mist.

"Now what?" he says.

"Maybe she knows them," D'Yquem says. "They're from her clan."

Jor has no contact with Abdera the next day. In a way, he's glad: he has no idea what to say to her. And too much other work.

His first eight hours are consumed by plans for repairs to the Lens, and five times the usual Venus–Earth–Venus message traffic, all of it reducible to two phrases: "Venerian damage to Lens." "Stay on schedule and punish the criminals!" (This last related with great sternness by Tuttle.)

"Amusing sidelight," D'Yquem says, as Jor emerges from the conference room, having applied classic team motivation to his own department heads ("Work faster, you fuckers!").

"Please share. Amusement is hard to find today."

"Your miscreants were up to other mischief."

"Such as?"

D'Yquem hands him a flimsy. "They, and some team of yet-to-be-identified accomplices, staged a raid on our garbage dump."

Jor cannot understand this; D'Yquem is amused. He nods toward the message. "They removed giant heaps of metal slag, soiled mud, vegetative matter, and took it somewhere."

"That was all?"

"They apparently failed to disturb anything mechanical, including what was left of my Mark III device." That had been D'Yquem's first attempt at bringing computational science to the Lens. The device had overheated and melted down. Mark IV had an improved cooling system.

"If they left your garbage alone, why do you care?"

"I don't, especially." He smiles. "I just happened to be lurking by your assistant's desk when the message arrived." Jor's secretary is a middle-aged Norwegian woman named Marjatta ([2,3,4]), now married after a brief and unsatisfactory affair with Jor a decade past. She is capable, but easily distracted, especially by D'Yquem, who seems to spend an inordinate amount of time hovering near her desk.

"Strange—" Jor suspects a connection. The attack on the Lens is such an outrageous action by the Venerians that every aspect must have meaning. But the alcohol, stress, and short night have left him fuzzy.

"If I were you, I would ask Security to track the theft. See where the material ends up."

"Don't we have better things to do? I know that Security feels quite stretched at the moment."

"If you want to know why the Venerians attacked, you'll press this." Then he smiled again. "Or you could just ask your girlfriend. You're both rebels."

Jor blushes at the memory. The #2 and #6 in his Exile

Quotient—as D'Yquem knows—are the result of a romance Jor had at college with a young woman from Sub-Africa.

Any sort of relationship, even a nonromantic one, would have made Jor and Njeri notorious . . . the fact that Jor's father was Miller Lennox, one of the most powerful business and religious figures in Illinois, made the couple into outright targets. And not just to the public . . . it was Miller Lennox who arranged for Njeri to be shipped home in disgrace—

And for Jor to join the ranks of exiled Terrestrians on Venus.

Where, if D'Yquem's analysis is correct, he resumed his old ways . . . becoming involved with an inappropriate partner. In self-defense, Jor would note that he lived at Venus Port for a decade during which he was involved with three human females, including Marjatta. His liaison with Abdera only began when she became the primary contact for the Lens team and her clan, which had some ancient rights to the air above the plot of marsh where the Lens was built.

It had happened quickly—from first handshake to intimacy, no more than a day, which was unprecedented in Jor's prior relationships. And, he later learned, in the Venerian equivalent.

One night in 13-Plus, Jor had dared to ask D'Yquem, "What do you think she sees in me?"

D'Yquem snickered. "Money and power."

"Besides that."

"Well, maybe it's because you look like a fucking Venerian male."

Jor knows that his complexion is darker than many of his fellow Terrestrians—not the handful from Africa, of course. He is taller than most, thinner, too.

But what D'Yquem almost certainly means is his face: all of the men in the Lennox family have prominent noses and close-set eyes. "We look like the business end of hatchets," Jor's older brother Karl once told him.

Of course, Jor also knows that physical resemblance, while key in initiating personal relationships, is not enough to sustain one. Especially a relationship that crosses social and biological and clannish lines.

"So it's mutual rebellion," he said, answering his own original question.

"More has been built on less." D'Yquem tips his glass. "Say, remember the pilings?" D'Yquem says.

"They still haunt my sleep." Sinking the pilings for the Lens almost broke the Lens project in its early going. In many places, Ve-neria's mud is little better than brown water. "Soup" is what D'Yquem calls it. Pilings had to be sunk repeatedly and to depths three or four times greater than they would on a comparable terrestrial location.

"We learned something from them."

"You mean, besides 'don't build a tall heavy structure on Venus'?"

"We got core samples."

"I recall Rostov saying that the Venerians would never allow that." Rostov ([2,3,5]) had been TA's staff geologist in those days. He had begged to be allowed to take core samples to prove or disprove Venerian legends of reloquere and the Sunset. Naturally, he'd been denied, just as human archaeologists were denied the chance to dig in Jerusalem because religious leaders feared what they might find—or not find.

"And they never did, as research. But for structural engineering . . ." D'Yquem grins, always a disconcerting image. (Those English teeth!)

"So Rostov found—"

"Nothing. No evidence at all that Venus had ever undergone radical, transformative geological or climactic shifts. Not in the past half a billion years, that is." He grins again. "Your girlfriend and her people live a long time, but not that long."

Jor has never truly really believed Abdera's stories—no more than he believed in the strict Christianity of the Lennox family.

Nevertheless, the work of reloquere has continued at a faster pace. When work on the Lens first commenced, Sunset was said to be far in the future—the equivalent of a human century.

But as the Lens neared completion, so, it seems, has the disassembly of Venerian civilization. Based on what Jor sees now, in the streets and mudflats, it could be a matter of weeks . . . possibly days.

He had asked Abdera: "Where will you go when reloquere comes?"

"With my clan."

"Where will they go?" Sometimes she is too literal. On the other hand, he realizes that she is the one speaking a different language.

"Into the Bright Sea."

"All of you?"

"There are many skiffs, most of them stored for a long time."

"And then?" He thinks she's joking.

"Return to the land wherever it forms."

"Sounds awful."

"It is. But it's necessary."

The subject changed then, and for some time thereafter Jor concentrated on Abdera's somewhat grim acceptance of reloquere.

Only now does he recall her hint that she *had been through it before*.

But there is no word. And he has no way of reaching her.

In the afternoon, Jor is called to TA headquarters, the oldest of the four towers in the Terrestrian compound, to see the five bombers in their holding cell.

Venerian premales are shorter, broader, brighter green than

females like Abdera. Unlike her, they wear the garb of sea farmers . . . clothing that seems to be fashioned from scales, like a knight's armor.

Jor begins to think of them as teenaged boys . . . mischievous, trying to prove themselves, not terrorists. This is silly, he realizes, and not just because he has fallen into D'Yquem's conceptual trap.

Even if these young creatures did try to harm the Lens, their questioning has been harsh: Jor can see signs of bruising and branding. It appears that one of them has a broken arm.

"Have they said why?" he asks Hollander.

"They just sing and pray," the security man tells him.

Jor is exhausted. He goes.

The next morning, Jor is up earlier than usual—and he always rises earlier than most, no matter how hungover—and upon arriving at his desk finds two flimsy documents, the coin of the realm in the Lens offices: first, a secret report that all five of the Venerian premales died in custody the night before.

Which is terrible news.

The relationship between TA and the Venerian council of clans is comfortably colonial—from Authority's point of view. After all, Terrestrians possess spaceships, therefore power.

In practice, however, the balance frequently shifts. Venerians are technologically savvy, armed, and, as their own recent history shows, willing to fight.

Why have they allowed Terrestrians to establish Venus Port at all, much less build the Lens—which surely suggested an even larger footprint? The official answer was technology transfer: Terrestrians were paying for time and territory with information—hence the colonial smugness.

This was another question Jor had put to Abdera in their

early days, only to receive what he could only describe as an amused shrug. "You gave us land near one of your largest cities," he had said.

"Not very much of it. And we use very little, as you've seen."

"What do you think of the Lens?" Jor had never asked her; when they met, the tower was already rising. Permissions had been obtained from the clans.

She had smiled—a humanoid gesture—and slithered up and down his body in a Venerian one, the total effect being quite . . . arousing. "If it will bring more attractive, rich human males, how could I dislike it?"

Jor wasn't ready to accept this glib answer. "It will bring all kinds of humans, and while many will be richer and more powerful than me, none will be more attractive. Some of them will be cruel and greedy and dangerous."

Now she was serious. "I know." Then she offered the Venerian equivalent of a shrug. "It really doesn't matter."

She did not need to say why: Sunset.

"Don't you think of us as invaders?"

"Some do."

"But not you."

And here he was rewarded with a smile of unrestrained Venerian amusement. "Only sexually."

Which is another aspect of their relationship that binds them—at least Jor to Abdera. Their lovemaking is frequent, satisfying, innovative . . . and frequently (by Jor's standards) almost public. Which adds to the excitement.

He was sexually experienced before meeting Abdera, of course, but entered that phase of their relationship as ignorant as a fundamentalist bride. He had heard nothing about Terrestrian-Venerian sexual relations beyond the usual ignorant rumors.

But, in the twilight, garments gone, the classic moves dominated. Abdera was more aggressive than women in Jor's past . . . but he found that he enjoyed it.

Jor believes that this intimacy gives him greater insight into Venerian character and customs. And while it is true that he has learned several phrases and knows more about Venerian food and drink . . . he realizes on this grim day that he is no better informed than Tuttle or the others in TA.

And with five premale Venerians dead in TA custody, he feels overwhelmed, unsure, and outnumbered.

Only then does he find a second message—from Abdera, in her charming, flowery style: "We must meet by midday or I will perish from the shame of my actions. The landing."

Although most Terrestrians, especially those newly arrived from Earth, argue the point, Venerians are more advanced than humans. The assumption that they are somehow equivalent to European civilizations of the late Middle Ages grows out of ignorance and xenophobia, and a mistaken belief that an advanced civilization requires a large population.

There are, Jor knew, fewer than 100 million Venerians. Naturally they have fewer, smaller cities. Their economy is largely directed toward sea farming in the Twi-Land waters, especially Bright Sea—which is why Venus Port was built where it was. (Venerian sea farming was so extensive, involving the actual herding of aquatic creatures we still did not truly understand, that the word "fishing" seemed inadequate.)

But they have electronics, their own communication system, weather forecasting, science, art, and wildly sophisticated politics, which one would expect from a clan-based society.

Their interpersonal relationships are immensely complicated by their proliferation of genders, from post-male/female (once they are no longer fertile and breeding, Venerians essentially lose their sexual identity and plumbing), to active male and female and the prepubescent versions of both, though Venerian puberty seems quite protracted, likely another result of the long life spans.

The only advantage Terrestrians truly seem to possess is space travel, and even here superiority is suspect: the antipodal clans dominating the southern hemisphere's Twi-Lands have smaller seas and a clear history of aviation and other technological development. It is rumored that these clans had developed space travel . . . many thousands of years in the past . . . and have even traveled to Earth! (This rumor led to dozens of wild speculations about shared Terrestrian-Venerian evolution . . . Jor always assumed the Venerians are a branch of the main Terrestrian trunk, but in truth it could just as easily have been the other way around.)

But they had abandoned the whole business, so the story goes. Abdera claimed that while it might be, she didn't know. "Our clans don't share."

Given that until shortly before they met those clans had been actively at war, Jor believes her.

And these are just the Venerians Jor knows, the clans of the Bright Sea.

Before he leaves for what he hopes will be a completely distracting several hours, Jor makes one final pass through his in-box, where he finds a plain note saying, *"Northern Jungle today."* It is just the sort of anonymous message he receives daily, some from his team or underlings, but just as frequently from Tuttle's inner circle.

During his first years on the second planet, he had largely worked with crews hoping to tame the Northern Jungle, to use another Terrestrian name that was wildly inadequate.

The Terrestrian Authority, in its master plan, had hoped to create a land route to the Highlands, the rounded, mineral-rich mountains to the north, unreachable by sea skiff. (Air transport was possible but uneconomical, given the size and number of cargo planes that would have to be built after their materials had been sent across interplanetary space; D'Yquem had once shown Jor the figures and the projected profit point was five hundred years in the future.) This meant a brute force assault on . . . trees with wood so rugged it broke saws.

The Northern Jungle did not want to be conquered. And it wasn't.

Then the Lens was approved and the TA happily attacked in a new direction. "No wonder the Venerians sat back and smiled as we hacked up their jungle," D'Yquem said.

Jor waits for his visiphone to warm up, feeling appreciative toward D'Yquem, who had lobbied hard with the TA staff and even with parties back on Earth to acquire six of the devices, planning to link them to his computational device.

Four of the machines had been scooped up by the TA, where, as far as Jor knew, they were being used as paperweights or dust collectors. D'Yquem had the fifth.

The material available on the visiphone is limited, primarily financial documents such as ledgers and budgets, but D'Yquem had equipped it with the ability to display images, too.

Jor searches for the Northern Jungle Road, finding half a dozen images that date back to his time as a tree-topper and 'dozer driver. But then a new one appears, showing a location much like those of a dozen years past.

He wishes for the ability to place two images side by side; lacking that, his eyes are good enough to tell him.

Every trace of the road has vanished. All the heaping mounds of chopped and rotted wood, leaves, and vines are gone. If not for the label on the image stating that it was Authority Roadway #1, and the fact that he recognizes a particular trio of peaks in the distance, Jor could believe that he is viewing some other part of the Northern Jungle—or the southern one.

A minor question . . . who took this picture? He looked at the logging data at the bottom of the screen: D'Yquem himself!

Jor realizes that if the Venerians are that serious about returning a remote location like Authority Roadway #1 to its original state . . . they must be serious about their Sunset of Time.

The final image shows him something even more surprising: Abdera.

Jor walks to the landing very slowly, though with the Terrestrian traffic light and the reloquere work largely complete, there is no reason.

Other than fatigue. Shock. Betrayal.

He reminds himself that seeing D'Yquem and Abdera together means nothing, even if the location is remote. Even if D'Yquem made it clear that he barely knew the Venerian female.

Jor's "girlfriend."

The landing was where Jor had first seen Abdera, and where they had spent most of their public time. It was a port to rival New Orleans or San Francisco, those being the two earthly equivalents best known to Jor, with skiffs of many shapes and differing sizes arriving to be unloaded with an elegance that suggested a ballet.

Surrounded by the aromas of sweet, then spicy, then unknowable cooking from small ancient shops lining the uneven quay, kelp and weed and sea beasts were swiftly transferred from skiff to warehouse to shop to land-bound transport with few words and optimum action from the teams of mature male and female Venerians.

It was always a setting that soothed Jor's mind, calmed his jittery nature. If only Earth had been like this—

This day, however, is different. Not only is he troubled by his suspicions about Abdera and D'Yquem, but the landing seems subdued, empty. The number of skiffs is perhaps a third what it should be. The buzz of activity—never high—seems nonexistent.

There are fewer Venerians.

"I long to go back to the skiffs." Abdera's voice, behind him. She has performed her usual trick of appearing by magic.

"I never knew you were on them," Jor says. "In them."

She links arms. "All of us work the skiffs at a certain stage in our lives. No matter our differences, we always have the Bright Sea."

"Sounds lovely."

"It is actually insanely difficult work that kills more of my clan than anything else." She turns to him. "But it binds us."

Jor cannot raise the subject of D'Yquem. He doesn't want to hear the answer. "Why did your clansmen try to destroy the Lens?"

"Why are you asking me?"

"You must have some information or insight."

"Jordan, you and I have more in common than I do with a Venerian male." It takes Jor a moment to realize that Abdera is talking about emotional commonality, not physical or biological.

"Don't you even know them?"

"Yes, they were members of my clan. Yes, I knew their names. Yes, I have farmed with them. But I had no interaction with them, no exchanges of words or gestures—we have not shared a skiff. I don't know what motivated them. And why does it matter? They're dead now."

"I had nothing to do with that—"

She puts her arms around him. "I know you better than that. I know you would be fierce in protecting the Lens, but you are not a killer."

"Is there anything I can do?"

"There is no need. Greater powers will balance the scale." Suddenly she is staring out to sea. A human woman would shade her eyes, Jor thinks. Of course, Abdera is Venerian—

and there is no sun to require shading. "And I could have warned you."

"You knew about the attack?"

"Not the specifics. But you can't keep secrets within the clan; I knew there would be an action at the Lens.

"Among the other secrets that can't be kept within the clan is my relationship with you . . ." She turns back to him. "The seniors locked me up."

"How did you get out? Oh." The torn sari.

"It was more humiliating than painful. It was also . . . difficult emotionally. I was betraying my clan."

"I wish you had. We'd have been saved a lot of pointless trouble."

"Yet your Lens survives."

"You disapprove? After all this time?"

"My clan welcomed you, allowed you to build. I made you a friend."

"So you don't disapprove. Then—"

"It's Sunset. It approaches." She indicates the flattened, empty waste that Venus Port is becoming. Her whole manner says: the Sunset changes everything.

"What about us?" Jor points to the four Terrestrian towers and, visible beyond that, the blunt noses of three ships at the spaceport.

Jor senses that Abdera is withdrawing. Nevertheless, he presses. "We're still going to be here. So . . . what about us?"

"I think," she says, "that our joy is ended."

And then she turns to walk away.

Jor could follow her. But he feels paralyzed.

He does not go to 13-Plus that night. He has no wish to confront D'Yquem, not without hearing Abdera's side of things.

And he cannot act as if he knows nothing.

Fortunately, he has a good supply of brue in his quarters in the third tower.

That night, thrashing in bed between drunken collapse and sleep—or in that darker moment after waking up, head throbbing, mouth dry, eyes aching—Jor thinks about those hours at the controls of a D-9 caterpillar, one of only three on Venus, attacking the brush and branches. Or even his time as a topper, climbing high on the giant trees armed only with a handsaw.

In spite of the crude, drunken, incompetent companions, the sizzling heat and humidity (the D-9 had a pressurized, climate-controlled cab); native Venerian animals that burrowed under the rudimentary road and undermined it when they weren't dropping things on it; vicious bugs the size of small aircraft that never seemed to move except in swarms the size of buildings; roots that seemed to grow back within minutes of being cut, and the mud . . . the endless, thick, sucking madness of the Northern Jungle's mud, the squalling rain—

Jor thinks of those days as free and happy.

He is a Lennox, Chicago-based engineers and builders for two centuries. He has many memories of his father Miller pointing from the front yard of their home on the North Shore to the city skyline, identifying seven different buildings from the Lennox shop. "There is room for more," he said then, offering the challenge to Jor's older brothers Liam and Karl.

As the third of three brothers, Jor's problems at school and his utter lack of interest in the family trade made him a candidate for emigration to Venus.

Where, finally away from his family, he had no expectations to fulfill . . . only a simple job to do, chopping, 'dozing, and adding to the vast heaps of green trash by the side of the road.

The next morning is spent personally supervising repairs to the Lens dish on the high platform. He also recalibrates the aiming and steering controls, confirming their functionality—Sunset of

Time be damned. The work is all-consuming, exhausting, and frustrating, driving all thought of Abdera from his mind.

On the plus side of the ledger, as always his hangover is vaporized by the exertion. By the end of the extended workday, Jor is spinning and sputtering as usual . . . and frantic to return to the 13-Plus and the inevitable confrontation with D'Yquem.

He prepares to descend from the instrument platform, where some riggers are grimly raising replacement panels while others totter precariously atop ladders and crude scaffolding trimming the jagged ends of the hole caused by the blast. Only then does he take a moment to look west, toward the endless swampy plains that lead to Nightside . . . at the mounds of excess material excreted (there is no better word) by the Terrestrian occupation.

They seem smaller. Squinting in the twilight, he thinks he can see humanoid figures moving near and even atop the heaps. At this distance, with his eyes, it is impossible to know whether they are Terrestrian or Venerian.

Surely not the latter, not after the attack—

"Oh no, TA's resolve popped like a soap bubble," D'Yquem says, twenty minutes later.

"They're letting the Venerians take *everything*?"

"Why not?" He drinks, and Jor notes that D'Yquem's hand shakes. "It's their garbage."

"Not all of it," Jor says. "A good percentage includes material from Earth."

"Who needs it? Let the Venerians have the, ah, metal shavings, torn fabric, odd bits of this and that, broken furniture, and, oh yes, food by-products, such as whatever our favorite bruemaster has left over when his alchemy is done." D'Yquem smirks. "I think it's also where the organic waste from the residence goes, if you're truly concerned—"

"Be serious."

"You are years too late in suggesting that." He has drained his glass and is already filling another. Jor sees again how shaky he is.

"Did you start without me?"

"What are you talking about?"

"You're trembling."

"Nonsense."

Jor knows that voice and chooses not to pursue the matter. He had arrived at 13-Plus and sat down with D'Yquem as he had for years, launching right into the latest TA stupidity.

Which must be pursued to its conclusion. Anything to postpone the painful conversation about Abdera. "Why would TA reward the Venerians for their bad behavior?"

"Perhaps to compensate for our own?" Jor thinks of the five dead premales. "Besides," D'Yquem says, "it is unsightly and unhealthy and better for the Venerians to take it off into the wilderness and bury it. Or remake it into jewelry or clothing . . . I don't care, as long as I don't have to look at it. Or talk about it anymore."

That is a clear message: change the subject. But, in addition to the Lennox family's emotional distance, Jor has the mulishness, too. It is difficult to move him when he isn't ready to be moved.

"What do you think about this whole Sunset business?"

D'Yquem smirks. "If it's good enough for your girlfriend—"

Jor lets that pass for now. "So you admit the possibility that Venus might rotate again."

"There's Rostov. Let's ask him."

D'Yquem nods toward a burly Terrestrian in his fifties, droopy-eyed, sad-faced, drinking alone at the bar.

With an EQ totaling 12, Serge Rostov is not technically eligible for entry into 13-Plus, but Petros isn't complaining, not with business down this day. Nor, in a departure from his normal role as EQ judge and jury, is D'Yquem.

"Rostov, my child," D'Yquem says, as he and Jor approach.

"Fuck off." Rostov doesn't even look at D'Yquem. Jor has no idea what has caused this hostility—beyond D'Yquem's noted ability to get people angry at him.

"Serge," Jor says. "Given all that's happened . . . this whole Sunset business."

Forgetting his anger, Rostov laughs. He is an impulsive man given to emotional outbursts, quickly forgotten. "What do you want me to tell you, Mr. Rational Engineer? The expected, the predictable? 'Our science shows no evidence that Venus ever turned. It is a world that has never seen a sunset.' You're a sensible man." Even though he no longer seems overtly angry at D'Yquem, Rostov addresses his remarks only to Jor.

"I hope so," Jor says. "But I thought the Venerians were sensible, too—"

"Some are, some are not." And here, if Jor is not mistaken, Rostov actually leers. "Some see us as invaders and take any excuse to strike back."

"So the attack is political. The religious business is just a cover."

"That is the sensible conclusion." Obviously eager to end the conversation, he turns to Petros to order another drink.

"Let me get that," Jor says. His reward is a dissatisfied sigh from D'Yquem.

But now Rostov is obligated. "Look," he says. "I was originally trained in astronomy. TA has encouraged me to broaden my interests and specialties to include geology or—"

"Venereology?" D'Yquem says brightly. He cannot stop himself, no matter the circumstances.

"We have taken core samples. We have done our surveys. We have mapped Venus from Equilateral—and created a radar map, too.

"The Venerians claim that there have been many sunsets in their recorded history. For that to be true, their recorded history would have to span 500 million years. Our fossil and geological record goes cold beyond that."

"Well, they *are* unusually long-lived," D'Yquem chirps. Rostov ignores him.

"So this is just another myth," Jor says. Like the Christianity of the Lennoxes.

"So it would seem. Though it is a powerful one that is uniform across all the clans and controls their actions." Like the Christianity of the Lennoxes!

Jor had begun to feel reassured. Now he's wavering. "What are you saying?"

"I am not an orthodox man," Rostov says, shrugging. "As you know from my EQ."

"Unorthodox enough to suggest that we should be worried?"

Now Rostov smiles, revealing jagged, steel teeth that make him look savage rather than sagelike. "Why worry about things you can't change? If the sunset happens, if the planet somehow magically begins to rotate . . . the damage would be indescribable. Earthquakes, tsunamis, eruptions. The only safe place would be Equilateral." He points to the ceiling.

"This is idiocy," D'Yquem says.

Rostov acts as though D'Yquem is addressing his remarks to someone else.

But Jor cannot resist. "Which part? His willingness to consider the possibility, or—"

"His description of the event is ludicrous. This worldwide catastrophe. He makes it sound biblical."

"Please, friend D'Yquem," Rostov says, engaging the computationist for the first time. "Share your vision of this hypothetical event."

D'Yquem glances at Jor, as if to say, this is all your fault. Jor notices that D'Yquem's hands are no longer shaking . . . and that he is ignoring his empty glass. "Stipulate that the Venerian myth is true, that every few thousand years their world moves. I've actually seen a paper—suppressed now, of course—that suggests that Venus isn't tide-locked, but that it merely has a very slow and irregular period—"

"—Which is nonsense," Rostov says. "Not the concept . . . the idea that the paper was suppressed."

"Perhaps not in your circles," D'Yquem says.

"I don't care about that," Jor says, growing angrier.

"Stipulating," D'Yquem says, "we must then accept the idea that the Sunset is not a world-wrecking catastrophe but far less damaging. After all," he says, "if it had the ability to rearrange the surface of the planet, to wipe out all life . . . why are the Venerians still here?"

At that moment everyone in 13-Plus feels the tower shudder. Jor fears that it's another attack on the Lens but soon realizes that it's the rain. A sudden squall has blown in from the Bright Sea, so strong it rattles the windows of the bar.

Conversation ceases. Even Petros pauses in his work, glancing, like Jor, toward the big window, where the view of Venus Port from on high has vanished, replaced by sheets of water and roiling black clouds.

Jor wants to leave. It isn't fear; he's not afraid that 13-Plus will be damaged. It's just the situation . . . the storm, the crowd, the growing sense of a sour smell all around him, which he blames on Rostov. He hates speculations, preferring facts. His emotions are confused, too. And all of this is likely due to last night's events, the lack of sleep, and the stress of the situation with Abdera and D'Yquem.

He thanks Rostov and abruptly heads for the door. He realizes that what is really driving him is a desire to be out of D'Yquem's presence. In fact, for the first time in fifteen years, he no longer wants to be a Terrestrian on Venus at all.

D'Yquem catches him before he reaches the elevator. "Where are you going?"

"My flat."

"Retreating is so unlike you." It is usually D'Yquem, veteran of ten thousand drunken evenings, who calls a halt to the festivities. Jor will sit there until staggering.

"I'm tired."

"Actually, you're angry. Not quite the same."

"Rostov—"

"Is a bore. Which I told you. Worse yet, he's a fairly stupid one. At least he could know his science."

"It doesn't seem that anyone actually knows the science."

"Of Sunset? There is no science, that's the problem."

Jor feels dizzy and nauseous. "What do you think?"

"Haven't I made that clear? I'm quite open to the idea."

"Your open-mindedness doesn't extend to, I don't know, making emergency plans."

"Jor, there can't be any plans, only evacuation. And then only at gunpoint. The flight here was so monstrous for most of us that getting back into those ships"—he points toward the spaceport, where three squat, shell-shaped vehicles wait—"is like being pushed off the top of a tower. Risking death only to escape certain death."

"So we can't do anything?"

D'Yquem grins. "Oh, we can resume drinking."

For the first time in their friendship, drowning in this tidal wave of betrayal, smugness, intransigence, Jor wants to punch D'Yquem. He grabs his shoulder, about to turn him. But D'Yquem sees what's coming and raises an arm to block it. "You're being tiresome."

"Then I've always been tiresome."

"No. You used to be *interesting* in a perfectly American

manner, treating your forced exile here as some kind of fresh start." D'Yquem is pointing at him now, accusing him like a prosecutor. "Given your background, that was not surprising—and part of the fun of knowing you has been watching to see if you might be correct. You've almost finished the Lens, and that will surely expand the Terrestrian presence—

"Or, well, it would have, except for the pesky Venerians and their superior knowledge of their own world . . . and their remarkable long-range planning, of which we suspect little and truly know nothing."

"You suspected, obviously."

"Only out of habit. Given my own family and its history, I would have had to be much stupider to fail to be suspicious of everything I see or to expect that everyone is keeping secrets."

"Or betraying a friend."

"Ah, well, yes. I can understand why you might see it that way."

"I realize it's too much to expect an apology," Jor says. "But can't you even acknowledge your mistake?"

D'Yquem takes an unusual amount of time to respond. When he speaks, his voice is harsh. "What makes you think I had any choice in the matter? Or that any Terrestrian has any control over his destiny on Venus? That we can take any action that will have any effect?" He laughs bitterly. "We are just being swept along like . . . like weed on the Bright Sea, my friend. Not just me: you, too."

He turns and staggers. Jor realizes that his former friend is drunker than he's ever seen him. Given the number of times they have shared brue, and the amounts, this is shocking.

Could he be telling the truth?

"Oh, by the way," D'Yquem said. "After you left, that idiot Russian confirmed it. The Sun is not only visible now, it's lower in the sky."

And then he enters the elevator. Jor lets the doors close. He doesn't want to go with him.

By the time Jor reaches the ground floor and prepares to leave, the storm has passed. The rain has returned to its expected state of hot drizzle. Emerging from the 13-Plus tower and heading toward his residence, he feels unusually alone.

And no wonder. There is no Terrestrian traffic at all—the immigrants from Earth are all tucked into their towers. And the Venerian presence is nonexistent, too, with shops largely gone or certainly abandoned . . . streets empty and, in fact, no longer streets but merely tracked areas between larger untracked ones.

The Lens tower looms even taller in the near distance. Jor is drawn to it, following the pathway toward it that takes him between the two residence towers.

Then he hears his name. "Jordan!"

Abdera steps forward. She has clearly been waiting some time; even her waterproof Venerian garb couldn't stand up to that storm. She is soaked, her hair plastered to her skull . . . making her look definitively alien.

Yet, the voice is the same.

"What do you want?" he asks. "To apologize?"

"No."

"To explain, then." He can't keep the sarcasm from his voice.

"Impossible."

"Then why are you standing in the rain?"

"To honor what we had," she says.

"I can't do that." He wants to recall their times together, but it's as if D'Yquem's shadow hides them.

"One day you will."

And, as if this is all she wanted to say, she turns. Now Jor grabs for her. "Is that it? You stood in the rain to tell me nothing?"

"No, to see you one more time."

"You're leaving."

"It's Sunset."

"You could have warned me."

And now she laughs. "I *have* warned you. *All* of us have warned you. Since the day Terrestrians arrived, we have been engaged in the reloquere! Yet you continued to build."

"Is that why you cheated with D'Yquem?" he says, struggling to find a motive. "Because I built the Lens?"

She gives him the Venerian stare. "I wanted you to build your Lens," she says. "And you should go to it."

Then she leaves, turning abruptly and without breaking into a run, moving so quickly that Jor couldn't possibly catch her.

She is headed for the landing, where skiffs still bob on the tide.

Jor watches her. He feels as he did when Njeri told him she must return to Africa—times ten. And yet, how foolish to think they had a future. Venerian and Terrestrian. This moment was inevitable; only the details remained to be determined.

He can't go back to his residence yet. So he will grasp for the last moment of his relationship with Abdera . . . will take her advice.

And go to his Lens.

By the time he has reached the top, he has worked himself into a proper Lennox-style rage. First, he finds that the security team is not on duty—called off by Tuttle? Or simply having deserted their posts due to a storm?

Jor would have returned to the towers to find them, but not before assuring himself that the Lens is secure.

And it is, controls caged and ready. Giant dish strong and steady, glistening from its recent bath.

Jor looks to the east, toward the Bright Sea. D'Yquem told the truth: not only is the Sun visible, it is notably lower in the sky.

The shallow water of the Venus Port delta is receding, too, carrying with it the last of the Venerian skiffs, Abdera's clan, and Abdera.

As it goes, so does Jor's spirit. He is enough of an engineer to know what this means . . . soon there will be a wall of water, how tall? It really won't matter. Even though he is hundreds of feet high, the violence of the crashing wave is likely to destroy the Lens tower.

And all of the Terrestrian quarter of Venus Port.

The evening is clear; he can see the four towers, their windows lit. Do those fools know what's happening? D'Yquem was right; no one believed. No one prepared. They would only head for the three ships at the spaceport if their towers fell on them.

Suddenly Jor has an idea.

He enters the control station and powers it up.

The Lens controls that are designed to focus transmission beams work just as well on the visible spectrum . . . and now, with the sun making its first appearance in the Venerian sky, Jor moves the Lens.

It takes precious minutes, but eventually he has it in the right position, taking the light from the new sun and focusing it on the four Terrestrian towers.

Then he narrows the beam, increasing the light and, more to the point, the heat.

He knows the materials used in the construction of the towers, how truly fragile they are. (TA's famed cheapness. Having the surface be waterproof was sufficient.)

The tops of two residence towers ignite, meaning that Jor's residence in one will soon be ablaze . . . and so will D'Yquem's in the other. Then the third tower, the oldest one, Tuttle's TA headquarters.

Finally the fourth, site of 13-Plus. Jor regrets that, but only for a moment.

The air must be changing, because he believes he can hear not only sizzling and crackling as the top floors begin to burn, but alarms.

He hopes for alarms.

He knows there is a chance he is injuring or killing Terrestrians, not motivating them to save themselves. At this moment, frankly, it doesn't really matter.

The water continues to recede, exposing a muddy sea bottom identical to the muddy plains Jor has crossed so many times on Venus. He tries to see, but clouds are forming to the east . . . soon they will boil high enough to cover the setting sun.

He looks up at the Lens, tweaks his aim. Then looks to the towers. There is a swirling layer of fog rolling in not from the sea, but from the west, obscuring Jor's view of the base of the towers. But shifting light and shadows there suggest that people are gathered . . . that they are in motion.

And now the wind kicks up from the west—quite strongly. A sudden gust rattles the platform so violently that Jor is knocked down.

He rises to reaim the Lens, thinking of the disappointment on Earth at the loss of the Terrestrian base . . . at the thousands or tens of thousands with high EQs who will not be shipped off-planet.

He is wondering why he has no sympathy for their plight when he sees the beginnings of a giant wave forming in the Bright Sea . . . and is struck by a piece of the Lens structure as it comes apart in the wind.

When he regains consciousness, he is in orbit, at Equilateral, strapped to the floor of a cabin whose four bunks are already filled with the injured. He feels cold, as if pulled from the ocean—and possibly he was. His head hurts. He is hungry.

"Welcome back," D'Yquem says from the open hatch. He, too, is injured, both hands bandaged. In spite of their last encounters, Jor is happy to see his friend.

Happy to see anyone, in fact.

"Some of us made it," he says.

"Most Terrestrians did reach the spaceport ahead of the wave," D'Yquem says. "Which was fortunately on higher ground than Venus Port. Everyone jammed in and took off so close to the waves that we generated a considerable amount of steam.

"But the tricky part was reaching Equilateral here. The station wasn't in position for rendezvous, so all the ships had to linger in orbit for two days until calculations could be made." And here he smiles his smug D'Yquem smile. "If they had one of my devices, they could have solved the problem in half an hour."

"How was I rescued? I was nowhere near the ships."

"We had to go back for you three days later. One ship was able to find dry land again and set down. Fortunately the Lens still stands. You were quite a mess, unconscious when you weren't delirious. But even Tuttle insisted that you had to be found."

"So the Lens—"

"Minimal damage, frankly. With a bit of work, it would be ready for transmissions from Earth on schedule." D'Yquem smiles. "Of course, it is now located in the middle of an inland sea that will soon, Rostov predicts, become an ice field in the new Nightside of Venus."

Jor thinks of Abdera, adrift in the fleet of skiffs. "What about the Venerians?"

"They were able to ride out the wave, as apparently they have done many times in the past."

Jor absorbs this news. "One more thing," D'Yquem says. "I regret not telling you before, but I wasn't sure until I had time to talk with Rostov again, and to examine the past—"

"Your injuries must have been severe."

He raises his bandaged hands. "It will be months before I can lift a glass again.

"Abdera's fling with me was deliberate. She went after me because of reloquere!" He can surely see the confusion on Jor's face. "The Venerians not only take apart their physical world before the Sunset of Time ... they also dissolve their relationships. We've already seen the clans and fleets realigning. We shouldn't be surprised that it extends right down to ... boyfriend and girlfriend."

Jor is in no mood to argue. Though it is close to comforting. "She could have told me."

"Yes," D'Yquem says, "but remember how long-lived the Venerians are ... how sophisticated they are in their choices and actions. I think she wanted you in a ... a dangerous frame of mind. Angry. Driven. Eager to prove yourself."

"Why?"

And here D'Yquem smiles with what might be genuine warmth, as if acknowledging a difficult truth.

"So you would be tempted to be a hero."

TOBIAS S. BUCKELL

Tobias S. Buckell is a Caribbean-born science-fiction author. His work has been translated into sixteen different languages. He has published some fifty short stories in various magazines and anthologies, and has been nominated for the Hugo, Nebula, Prometheus, and Campbell awards. He's the author of the *Xenowealth* series, consisting of *Crystal Rain, Ragamuffin, Sly Mongoose,* and *The Apocalypse Ocean.* His short fiction has been collected in *Nascence* and *Tides from the New Worlds.* His most recent novels are *Arctic Rising* and a sequel, *Hurricane Fever;* his most recent collection is *Mitigated Futures.* Much of his short work has recently been made available as Kindle editions.

In the harrowing story that follows, he shows us that some atrocities seem to repeat themselves down through history—even on another world.

Pale Blue Memories

TOBIAS S. BUCKELL

I.

I GRABBED THE ARMS OF MY ACCELERATION CHAIR AS we spun, our silver bullet of a rocket ship vomiting debris and air into the cold night of Venus's stratosphere. Commander Heston James, Sr., flung himself from control panel to control panel, trying to regain control of our craft, but the Nazi missile had done its nasty work well.

From a distance, the great pearly orb of Venus had been a comfort to us. Our exciting destination. A place that beckoned adventure.

We would land, for our country. And strike a great blow against the German Reich, proving that the war machine of the United States of America was more powerful. The great Space Race that grew out of the guttering stalemate of the Great War saw Nazi moonbases and stations matched by Allied forces in the final frontier. Now the race was on to claim a planet.

But the sneaky Nazi bastards, unable to beat us to the sister planet's surface, shot us out of the sky with a missile that had boosted behind us from Earth, hiding in our rocket ship's wake until right as we deorbited.

"Charles!" Commander James shouted at me, looking back over his shoulder. "Do we have communications?"

I'd been flipping switches and listening to static for the last ten minutes of terror. The faint, steady, reassuring pip from Earth was nowhere to be found. And our tumbling meant it would never be found until we stabilized.

Or it could mean all our antennas were snapped clean off.

"Charles!"

I shook my head at him. "No, Commander. Everything is off-line."

In radio silence, we continued to fall out of the sky.

Commander James strained against the g-forces snapping at us to continue working his panels, fighting for control of his ship all the way down. A hero to the last breath.

Out of one of the small portholes I watched the expanse of white clouds beneath us spin past again and again.

All this was a punishment, I thought to myself, as the blood continued to rush up against the inside of my head and dizzy me. Like Daedalus, I'd flown too high and been burned. Now I was falling.

And falling.

People from my kind of family didn't end up becoming astronauts. My kind of family had aunts and uncles who had to drink from the *other* fountains and couldn't order stuff from the front.

My dad came from Jamaica, towing behind the rest of his family. They came looking for jobs and ended up working out in the Illinois countryside. White folk could tell Dad wasn't white, but they weren't sure *what* exactly he was, due to his kinky hair and skin that browned when he worked outside too long.

Dad said that back home they called him "high yellow," which meant he was mixed race but looked more white than black. Folk up North were more uneasy about the idea of mixed-race people. In some ways, that made it harder for Dad. He was a living, walking example of miscegenation. A child of a white father and a black mother.

If you were one or the other, in America, he said, everyone knew exactly how to treat you. But being stuck somewhere in the middle left him pulled in directions that I couldn't fathom.

He married a white woman: an even greater sin. We wouldn't have been able to do that in the South, but in the North, as long as we kept to ourselves and didn't "flaunt" it, people pretended it didn't exist as long as my mother and father didn't go out together.

And as for me, I took after my mother.

I remember sitting in front of the window, looking at my reflection, trying to get my father's comb to stick in my hair like it did in his. But instead it would just slide out of my straggly, fine strands and fall to the floor.

My fair-skinned mother would find me crying in front of the mirror and ask me what was wrong. I never had the words to explain to her, and that would sometimes upset her more.

When I was five, my father sat me down. "I want to tell you where you came from," he told me, his face serious, his gray eyes piercing my fidgety five-year-old soul. "Because it's only once you know where we are from that you can understand who you really are."

I nodded, like I understood the wisdom he was dropping on me. Mostly I was excited to be let into this circle of trust he was drawing around us. Because these were things we had to keep close to us, as if they were horrible secrets. And yet, in fact, it was just the truth about how we'd gotten where we were.

Sometimes simple truth was radical.

"Your forefathers come from the Ivory Coast, in far-off Africa. From across the seas," he told me.

He taught me their names, and the name of the tribe his forefathers had once belonged to. "I once knew the dances, and some of the words, as they were passed on to me from my grandfather," he told me with sad eyes. "But I have forgotten them. But I have not forgotten where I came from. And you can't either. Your skin is pale, son, and that will be to your advantage in this world. You might go on to do great things here. But you have to know who we are."

"Will we go back?" I asked, excited.

He looked at me for a long time. "I don't know if there is a back to go back to, son. We live here. It is what we know. And what we need to know is how best to survive, and more importantly, thrive. Because a man should be able to live anywhere in the world and not suffer, do you understand? This is our home because we are here. And we are with each other."

I don't know if he believed it. But at five, looking up at his broad shoulders, the lesson embedded itself deep in me and took root.

Thirteen years later, I would be flying trainer aircraft and pushing myself to beat everyone around me. More kills, more daring stunts. I'd been training in languages while in school but left to help fight the Great War and Hitler's minions.

I'd heard about the squadron of negro-only fighters in the sky, heard that bombers were asking for the Red Tails because of their record of flying close and protecting.

The Red Tails were breaking records in their section of the sky. I was secretly doing it over here. And one day I'd reveal myself. And it would be known that I was as good as any other pilot.

Only I was a ghost. A shadow person. A secret with my one drop of different blood.

And now I, Charles Stewart with my mixed blood, would die on the surface of Venus in a spectacular crash and no one would ever know what I'd truly accomplished, would they? No one would know I'd been as good as any white astronaut, and they hadn't even known about me in their midst.

I'd flown too high.

No. That was the blood squeezing against my brain. I'd flown high. I was proud to have flown high!

We plunged through the thick clouds of Venus, and for a brief second I saw lush green vegetation and wide expanses of ocean.

Commander James cut himself free of his restraints, slamming into a bulkhead and cutting his head open.

"Keep calling out elevation, Davis," he shouted back at the navigator, Tad Davis.

Tad began shouting out the numbers as we fell. Heston pulled Shepard Jefferson out of his chair and dragged him back on hands and knees deeper into the heart of the craft. I could hear banging and swearing.

Eric Smith, our geologist and general scientist, grabbed my arm from his position strapped in on my left. "I know communications is down, but patch me in anyway." He stared out of the porthole. "I'm going to broadcast what I can make out as we go down, for the benefit of whoever might hear something."

The ears of the world might be straining to hear us. And Eric was a scientist to the last. I linked his microphone to the radio. "You're on, if we're able to transmit," I told him through gritted teeth.

"We're spinning wildly," Eric narrated, "but I'm sure I can see jungle out on the land we're far above. There are great oceans in between the main sections of land we're over, and there appear to be cloudbursts all around us. This is a rainy world. A wet world. A humid world."

He continued on in that manner as the details grew, and Eric described mountains rising toward us. A lake. Highlands, thick with jungle.

I had a wristband with a cyanide pill in it, in case things

went bad. I idly wondered if it made sense to take it before we hit the ground. I didn't want to feel the moment of impact.

"Shep: hold on!" Commander James shouted from back behind us.

We slammed in our restraints as the craft suddenly decelerated. For a moment I was cheered. We'd gotten the rocket back on and would descend on our tail in fire and triumph to the surface of this new world.

But that wasn't it, we still yawed and swung. The descent was slow, but the thundering roar of the rocket was absent.

"Parachutes!" Tad said. "They got the emergency parachutes open."

A wall of green flung itself at the portholes. My chair broke loose from its bolts and I spun across the cabin in a sudden cartwheel as the rocket ship struck trees and marsh in a grinding screech.

2.

THE AIR OUTSIDE WAS THICK WITH MOISTURE AND the smells of exotic, alien plants. Dark purple fronds filled the steep hills all around us, and just a few miles ahead stony mountains jutted up into the air.

We'd been just split seconds away from dashing ourselves against them, I realized.

All five of us gathered outside to walk the hull at Commander James's insistence. "We need to know how bad the damage is," he said.

I just wanted to stand outside. We'd been cooped in a metal tube for almost an entire month, eating pills and squeezing food out of tubes. I wanted to just stand in the open copse created when the rocket ship slammed through the palmlike fronds.

But we all nodded and followed orders.

"How bad is it, Shep?" Heston asked, once we'd all walked a circuit around the silvered ship. We'd all paused near the water tanks that had saved our lives. Had the Nazi missile struck anywhere else, we likely would have died right then and there.

"We didn't just lose water," Shepard reported. "We vented fuel, and the hull probably won't survive taking us back up into orbit. The stress of firing the engine might well just cause the whole thing to crumple."

Heston looked thoughtful. Thinking about all the variables. Working on a plan of action. He looked out over the vegetation around us with a grimace. "Then we're not here to explore and return. The mission parameters have just changed. We're here to survive until we can be rescued by another mission. Stewart: where are we with comms?"

I looked up from staring at massive yellow lily pad–like leaves on a nearby plant. "I sent out distress signals the moment we knew the missile was there, sir. And all the way down. But the equipment's broken. I can look at the spare parts, see what I can cobble up. But I can't do anything until Shepard gets the power back on."

Heston turned back to Shepard. "Shep?"

"I'll get to work on it. A couple hours?" Shep wiped his hands, then jumped back up to the doors and hauled himself into our broken ship.

"In the meantime," Heston said, "I need you and Eric to take some bottles and hunt for a clean source of water. Eric: get what you need to test the water, make sure it's safe."

"Yes, sir!" we said, and I moved to help Eric get a couple of machetes and some large containers.

We'd landed in the high foothills near a natural plateau. The ground was muddy, and at first the closest thing we found to water was several pools of swampy muck as we chopped through the jungle.

Eric was quiet, no doubt as a result of being a bit shook-up. But I was also out of sorts myself. I was happy to be by his side, though. A bookish type, Eric was the crew member I'd always liked the most. Of all the crew, he had yet to make a random comment about Italians, Jews, Poles, Blacks, or Hispanics that left me secretly angry but outwardly carefully neutral.

I could relax a little near him, not expecting some sudden verbal explosion that would wing me.

The heat and humidity caused me to sweat heavily as we hacked our way onward, and I pulled my long-sleeved shirt off to wrap it around my waist.

"I'd keep that on," he said.

"Why's that?"

Eric pointed the machete at fist-sized black marks on the feathered leaves of nearby fronds. "They're not exactly like mosquitoes, but they're giant bugs. Probably because of the denser air, I imagine."

I pulled my shirt back on. "Will a shirt stop a supermosquito?" I asked.

He shrugged. "Don't know, but maybe it'll help." There were large gnats, clouds of which burst out from the ground like jittery dark thunderclouds when we disturbed them.

Eric perked up after a while and began examining the vegetation, trying to pin down what it might be analogous to back on Earth. "Very Mesozoic," he kept saying. And all I knew about that was that it had something to do with dinosaurs.

We stopped at the edge of two fetid pools of water while Eric examined them. "Stagnant," he pronounced, and we kept on.

The ground grew muddier, but Eric found a ridge of rock to scramble on that poked over the worst of it, and we began to skirt over the jungle. Occasionally he stopped to draw landmarks on a pad of paper. "There's no sun, or stars, or compass we can use here," he said. "We have to be careful not to get lost."

He also stopped twice to make quick sketches of brightly colored, long-tailed, birdlike creatures that burst out of the treetops and glided through the air.

Eventually we took a break near another flat plain by more swamp. By now, Eric was grinning, our predicament taking a backseat to his scientific wonderment at the flora and fauna of an alien world. "There are tracks here. There seem to be large animals. And we should be able to follow them to a source of water," he said.

I sat with my back to him, looking toward the tall rocks we'd scaled down from, and took a long sip of water from my canteen.

And it was then that I felt Eric's back stiffen straight. "Charles," he hissed:

"Yes?"

"Don't. Make. A. Move."

The ground thudded. And again. I looked oh-so-slowly over my shoulder. A ten-foot-tall, six-legged beast with dappled green hide and a fiercely reptilian face hissed at us.

But that wasn't what made my stomach clench. A thin-limbed man, with skin so pale it looked almost transparent, stood up on leather stirrups and pointed what was unmistakably a long-barreled weapon at us.

From farther down the trail, three more mounted Venusians plodded along, their long rifles aimed right at us.

"They're bipedal," Eric breathed. "And humanoid. How graceful!"

"They have weapons," I murmured.

"This must be some form of parallel evolution. This is the sister planet, and these are sister peoples," Eric said to me out of the corner of his mouth. "Or maybe we all came from the same organisms . . ."

He didn't get to finish his thinking, because the four Venusians charged us. The heavy-footed beasts thundered as their long necks slinked forward with more eager hisses.

I grabbed Eric's shoulder and hauled him to his feet and we ran, but within seconds the thud of saurian beasts filled our world and nets with heavy weights slapped into our backs.

We fell to the ground, entangled and struggling to get our machetes out to chop at the netting. I managed first, sawing through and scrambling up. Eric followed.

He raised his machete, and a bright flash of light cracked out from one of the rifles. Eric screamed and dropped his blade, then raised his hands warily. "You'd better drop yours too," he said.

I let it fall to the ground.

The Venusians regarded us with large eyes and dark pupils, then dropped to the ground with loops of rope.

Within a minute, we were tied behind the beasts and being pulled along down the trail, through the jungle.

"I don't understand," Eric said, in shock. "We are visitors from another world. They must have seen the rocket ship. We must look alien to them. This is a First Contact situation, what are they doing?"

"I don't know," I said, and gasped as the rope yanked at me.

They pulled us into what looked like a village, with huts made out of long poles and woven with fronds. Wary Venusians sat around cooking pots. They began to shout and point at us with large smiles, while the Venusians who captured us responded with similar whoops.

"We. Come. In. Peace," Eric declared, but was rewarded with a strike to the head for his efforts. I grabbed him as he staggered and helped him stand as we were shoved into a set of cages at the center of the village.

I should have spent the next couple of hours paying attention and learning what I could about the Venusians, but instead I did my best to make Eric comfortable and keep him from falling asleep.

A blow to the head was never a good thing.

As a result, I almost didn't notice another party of Venusians returning in triumph with the rest of our crew. Cmdr. Heston James, shoved forward by gunpoint, Shepard by his side, both of them holding Tad up by an arm and looking exhausted, bruised, and shocked.

Inside the cage with us, Heston took a look at Eric briefly. "He should be okay," he said in a grim voice. "But Tad's in worse shape. He fought back. All the way. They shot him."

There was a burned hole in Tad's stomach. It was blackened with cauterization, but we all had enough medical training for the trip to know that it was fatal.

"Charles, you're the languages and communications expert, any read on these Venusians?" Heston asked.

I shook my head. I was the languages guy, which meant that I'd studied seven or so before the war while I was in college. The half-completed linguistics degree had helped edge me into the communications spot on the crew. "It's another planet. Another species. And I've been watching after Eric."

"Fucking savages," Heston spit. "Animal-riding, hut-living savages."

I said nothing.

Tad died a few hours later, gurgling out his last breath with a whimper of pain. Eventually, we all tried to get some sleep as the ambient, cloud-filtered sunlight faded away.

We woke early the next morning to Shepard's shouting at several tiny Venusians who were poking him with a sharp stick.

Eric was looking around, dazed and awake, thank goodness. His only comment on the situation was a bemused observation. "I think the superpale skin they have is an adaption," he murmured, almost to himself. "Not much sunlight gets to the surface of Venus. If you look at people on Earth, it's the same. The farther north, the less sun, the paler they get."

3.

WE WERE TAKEN DOWN OFF THE PLATEAU THE NEXT morning on a two-day-long, jolting cart ride to a fortress that looked like a giant sea urchin with black, spiked rock spurs radiating in all directions.

Under one of the spurs, the Venusians argued for fifteen minutes with another set of Venusians wearing fancy red silks.

Then more Venusians came out with a crate full of rifles.

"I think we just got traded for rifles," Shepard said. "Jesus Christ."

The hill Venusians turned and left us standing in front of the spiked fortress, heading back to their swampy home.

"They won't know we came from the sky," Eric said, his voice quavering slightly.

"Then we learn the local lingo," Commander James said quietly. "However long it takes us. And we tell them. They can see, with their own eyes, that we look different."

"For all they know," I said, speaking for the first time that morning, "we're strange Venusians from some unknown location on their planet."

"Stow that talk," Heston ordered.

The next week of travel blurred. More carts. Baggage trains. Often we were forced to walk along them, our hands bound, pale Venusians shouting at us. Shepard and Eric had been keeping shifts tracking our turns and directions, trying to keep an internal map of how to get back to our ship.

The humid air stopped feeling so strange in the second

week of walking. The feathery fronds of the vegetation began to stop looking so strange. Though every time something rustled from deep inside the vegetation, I still felt nervous.

We arrived at a coast in the second week. A great walled city sat half in the emerald forest and half projected out into the gray ocean. Docks stuck out like fingers from a hand, and a crude seawall protected it all from the ocean swells.

Rock houses leaned this way and that inside the walls. Warehouses painted in pastel shades leaked strange scents none of us could recognize. Was that cinnamon? With a bacony sort of vanilla?

We'd been fed Venusian food. A tasteless, pasty stew that caused me to spend the first night in agony with stomach cramps but that I'd adapted to in the days of walking. But smelling the scents, I realized we'd been given their equivalent of gruel.

We followed our captors down streets no more than four or five people wide, then into a central market. It was filled with Venusians selling flanks of meat, what looked like misshapen vegetables in unappealing colors, and the spices that we'd smelled passing the warehouses.

A short Venusian with scars advanced on us with a knife. We recoiled, but he used it quickly to cut our clothes away.

"Damn it!" Heston screamed, uselessly, as he stood in the air naked as the day he was born, his naturally ramrod straight back suddenly curved as he tried to cover himself.

Venusians threw buckets of water on us to clean the road dirt away and scrubbed us clean.

And we were marched over to a stone dais.

My stomach clenched as I stood there and watched Venusians cluster around to stare at us.

"We're visitors!" Shepard shouted at them. "Visitors from another world! Don't you understand? You should be giving us a parade!"

"Shep," Eric said quietly, and looked at me. "I think Charles is right. They've never seen outside the clouds. They might not know about other planets, stars. They probably think we're just strange-looking Venusians."

"But we came in a rocket ship!" Shepard protested.

"Is that anything like an airship?" Eric asked, and pointed over our heads.

We looked up. A massive lighter-than-air machine glided in over the ocean toward the city, slowly beginning to drop out of the air toward a large field.

"The Venusians that captured us might not even know much about such things," Eric said. "They didn't know how to make guns, and live in the hills. They sold us for the guns. They might not have even explained to these guys how we showed up."

He was right. And I was right.

And I knew how right I was when it began. It might have been in an alien tongue, but I knew the patter for what it was.

An auction.

I began to weep silently to myself, suddenly alone and cold in the humid tropical air of Venus, rescue millions of miles away.

Heston snapped at me. "Get ahold of yourself, Charles. We're going to figure a way out of this."

"Really?" I stared at him. "It took hundreds of years back home for people to figure a way out. And even then, they still live as second-class citizens. Even if we do communicate with them, judging by all this, we may end up being little more than scientific curiosities."

The crew stared at me like I'd grown a second head.

But we didn't have much time to debate further. We were ripped apart, the auction done. Heston and I were taken to a mansion with a vast cobblestoned courtyard on the edge of the city's walls. Men in silks and headdresses covered with snakelike patterns of gold led the way, while short, scruffy

Venusians poked and prodded us along.

Then they swarmed us, grabbing us by legs and arms and holding us down to the wet stones as we struggled and fought the sudden immobilization.

One of the silk-wearing Venusians kneeled next to us. He held a tiny slug in the grip of some tongs.

"What are you doing?" Heston shouted. "I demand . . ."

The Venusian shoved the slug into Heston's nose. For a moment, both slug and man lay still, somewhat stunned.

Then it began wriggling. All the way up into his nose.

Heston screamed.

The Venusian was handed another set of tongs, and turned for me. And I screamed and struggled to no avail.

It slithered into my nose, a slimy wetness moving upward. Mucus dripped down my lip, and my nasal cavity screamed as it was filled with a pushing, tearing sensation. I tasted blood as it dripped down the back of my throat and I gagged.

The Venusians closed great stone doors at the entrance. Some bored guards with rifles patrolled an elevated walkway and looked down at us. But we were left alone on the courtyard's stones to stare up at the clouds as our foreheads ached.

Dark, gray clouds. Always.

I'd never see a blue sky again, I realized, before I slipped into fever dreams. We vomited bile, bled through our noses, and curled into balls on the stones. Occasionally Venusians would come and yell at us. "Get up! Do you understand us yet?"

It wasn't until later in the day that I realized something. "Heston! Heston, I think I understand them!"

Heston groaned. "I thought it was you yelling insults at me, but I don't think you'd call me a *Kafftig*, whatever that is."

I could imagine Eric's telling us that our nasal cavities were the closest entrance in the body to our brains, and this slug would have crawled up there to . . .

I staggered up. "I can stand," I said. "Can you understand me?"

"Get up!" a Venusian demanded. "If you can understand me, get up!"

Heston held on to my shoulder. He was excited. "We're visitors! We're from another world." He pointed up at the dark, gray clouds that stretched from horizon to horizon. "We're from beyond the clouds."

The Venusians around us laughed. A yipping, barking sound. "There is nowhere else but the surface, and there is nothing beyond the clouds but more clouds and emptiness."

Heston wouldn't let it go. He kept arguing. And eventually his shouts led to warnings, then the Venusians clubbed him until he shut up. They forced me to carry him, dazed, across the courtyard and into a small, cramped common house.

It was dark, and damp, and the floor covered in straw. We huddled in the corner away from other Venusians who growled at us as the door was locked shut for the night.

The next morning we were all led out to the landing fields of the city, where the airships slowly eased in over the ocean and came to a rest. Under the eye of two armed Venusians, we unloaded the airship's wares. Packages of foods, jars filled with oils and spices. The sort of cargo that empires sent to far-flung cities at the periphery.

"I don't understand," Heston said. "They have technology. We're unloading airships. They have laser rifles. Why forced labor? This makes no sense. Maybe they don't have capitalism or democracy here. Maybe we'll have to bring it to them! Because I tell you what, a few good, red-blooded, American longshoremen would get this ship unloaded faster than any of these other poor creatures."

I must have snorted because Heston stared at me. "Capitalism and democracy included slavery until late last century, Commander. That was the American way until the Civil War. As far as I can tell, visiting the cotton fields, it is still the natural friend of slavery. You have family in West Virginia digging coal, right? Any of them in debt for life to the company store, being charged company rent for their home and company credit for their groceries? If you can force someone to work for free, isn't that the most profit ever? If all that matters to you is profit, then it's a natural endpoint."

Heston stopped working and glared at me. "Are you a communist?"

I had a retort, but one of the overseers waded in with a club. Heston stood up and shouted back at him but earned several smacks to the head.

By now I was surprised he could even think.

"Work!" we were ordered. "This is not the time for talking. Keep talking and we'll sear your skin off."

We got back to lugging stuff off the ship to the waiting carts with their six-legged beasts patiently holding steady in their harnesses.

"If we can just talk to the right people," Heston whispered, as we walked back. "We need to find a politician or a scientist. We need to talk to their leaders, not workers and overseers. Talk to just the right person in power, it will be okay."

The commander believed that. He believed that because for him it had always been true. His life had ups and downs, but for true injustices, he'd always been able to find the right person and set things right.

There was order and justice. He truly believed in those things. The world worked a certain way for him.

"If we get this over, and see if we can petition a judge, or someone, we might be able to talk to the right people."

Heston worked faster and faster, his mind set on the goal of getting the airship unloaded. I struggled to keep up with his newfound energy. The commander had a destination in mind, and now he had set himself to it.

"Commander," I whispered. "Slow down."

He blinked. "Why?"

"The other Venusians aren't working as fast. Think about it. They're slaves. There's no reason to kill themselves working harder, they're not getting paid. The only way for them to make this bearable is to work just fast enough to not be abused, see?"

"Their laziness isn't my problem," Heston growled.

That night the entire common house of Venusians beat us with balled fists. Heston gave as good as he could for the first ten minutes, but there were just too many of them.

The next day, we could barely keep up, our bruises and torn muscles were in so much agony we gasped as we worked and said nothing to one another.

"Welcome," one of the other Venusians had said after he broke my ring finger beneath his blue-veined heel. "To the city of Kish."

4.

COMMANDER JAMES GOT HIS CHANCE TO TALK TO THE right Venusian after a long, backbreaking week of labor. Before the sun faded away, the Venusians would let us relax in the purple grasses inside the walls.

I had settled near a reflecting pool, dipping my aching feet in it, when a retinue of colorfully dressed Venusians swept through the courtyard. In the center was the lord of the house, who we had come to learn from overhead chatter was a customs official for the city of Kish.

Heston threw himself into the Venusian's path. "My lord of the estate!" he shouted as Venusians turned in shock and horror. One of the overseers loitering around the edge of the courtyard raised a rifle, but the lord raised his hand to stop the killing shot.

I realized that Heston had faltered, as he didn't know the lord's name. He was only referred to as "the lord." A pronoun, *the* pronoun. The only one that mattered within these walls.

Heston stumbled forward. "My lord, I am a rocket man from above the clouds . . ."

That was as far as he got. The lord shook his head impatiently and gestured, and Commander James was hauled away. He might have been stronger than the slender Venusians, but there were more of them.

"Was he one of the new exotics?" the lord asked, and looked over at where I still sat.

"Yes, my lord," one of the overseers said, rushing to bow. "They work hard."

"Good. Worth the metal price. But do cut off their tongues if they ever dare babble at me again."

And in a flourish of silks and nutmeglike perfume, the retinue left for the sound of music and laughter somewhere deep in Kish.

"He is lucky they didn't take his tongue out as a first punishment," said a Venusian nearby. She sported knife scars up and down her arms, and I could tell she came from the northern hills by her cadence and the punctures in the webs of her hands, where she'd once worn gold rings.

"He's stubborn," I told her. "I bet he will lose it before we are done here."

I tended to a dazed Heston after his beating, trying to get him to drink water. I was trying to get him oriented because he was floundering. "You know free economies are rare, Commander. Even on Earth. It's not surprising, really. If aliens were to land on Earth and look vaguely like us, it might not have been good for them either, being different. Imagine if aliens had landed in the South, before the Civil War that we had to fight so bloodily to get rid of this stain . . ."

Through bruised lips and swollen eyes, Commander James said, firmly, "The War of Northern Aggression was fought over states' rights."

And with a grunt of pain, he picked up his blanket, his dog tags that he'd been allowed to keep, and dragged himself over to the other side of the common house.

I became an alien on another world, with the only other person I knew refusing to speak to me. I was annoyed at first, working out arguments in my head that I would have with the commander when we next spoke. But the work ate into me.

The moment the sun leaked through the clouds, Venusians beat us awake to head out to the fields where the large, silvered airships came to rest. And all day long we'd unload what the city of Kish needed to consume, and a lot of what its lords desired to spend their vast wealth on.

"Where do these goods come from?" I asked the Venusian with the scarred arms.

The first time I asked, she ignored me. But as we stood and waited for another airship to arrive and drank from waterskins, she spoke to me.

"Other cities, larger cities," she said, pointing off toward the ocean. "The lords of Kish cannot do without the spices and foods from their mother cities. And Kish is not big enough to grow its own."

"And Kish trades rifles and machines for minerals, ores, and work," I said.

"Yes."

The next airship we loaded with scared Venusian hill-tribe folk, possibly even some of the same ones who'd first captured us, now captured by some other group with laser rifles. We shoved and beat them aboard and tried not to meet their pleading eyes.

One late night, she came to my blanket.

"My name is Maet of Tannish," she told me.

"I'm Charles Stewart," I said.

"Where is Stewart?" she asked.

"Nowhere. It doesn't matter. I'm Charles of Earth. And Earth is beyond the clouds."

"There is nothing but void beyond the clouds," Maet told me with a pitying chuckle. "All that is important lies beneath the veil. There must be a reason we can't see beyond it, and that is most likely because there is nothing worth seeing."

I opened my mouth to argue with this, then realized that Maet was my only companion, and I was too tired to argue. I'd thought the weeks of training to be a spaceman intense.

I had no idea.

I'd had energy and verve my first few days. But as weeks became months, my back felt like it'd been set on fire by the constant bending. My fire to understand and study the world around me dampened every day. There were no weekends. No labor laws to limit being rushed out in the middle of the night to grab the ropes of an incoming airship, then unload it once it was tethered. No time to recoup. Just a slow, steady erosion.

Maet just lay next to me, and that was enough that first night, to feel someone breathing next to me.

I struggled to glean information about where Kish lay from her and what was out beyond its borders. The free lands of wild peoples. Hill tribes. What trails led where? I wanted to make a map of the world in my head before I made any decisions. I needed to find out how best to make my way in this world, and to understand its rules, no matter how horrific.

And I'd always had to play the game of their rules and my hidden face. I remembered my grandfather telling me once, "Never show anyone what you're really thinking, because then they might know what you're going to do." Even Maet, as we continued to huddle in our corner of the common house, didn't know what I thought about.

As Maet and I grew together, I saw Heston had started to talk to other Venusians. In the courtyard behind a tree. Near the corner of the common house.

I wasn't surprised when he crawled over to my blanket as I lay sweating in the tropical heat and humidity while Maet was off talking to someone else.

"Soldier, we may have our differences," he hissed to me, "but now it's going to be time to fight together."

"You're planning a revolt," I said, looking over at his crouched form. It was a shadow against a shadow in the city light that came in through the barred windows at the top of the walls.

I couldn't see surprise on his silhouetted face, but I could hear it in his voice. "Yes. There are others who want their freedom. I've been talking to them. Will you join us?"

Ever since I saw him whispering to others, I'd thought about it. And about what I would say. "You ever read much about slave history?" I asked. "Probably not, it's not a field many people study. But let me tell you something: all of the slave revolts except the one on Haiti were put down. And we're not on an island that we could defend. Even in South America, where they had great numbers, they still remained under colonial rule for many long ages."

"None of them had a US Marine in charge," Heston hissed.

"You think none of them had any war experience?" I asked calmly. He didn't know their names, or positions, because they'd been wiped out. But many early slaves had been captured in war.

My own family held at least two tribal leaders, according to legend. One of them had committed suicide after three years of being forced to work a sugar plantation.

"They need the *right kind* of leader," Heston said.

I put a hand out to him. "I wish you luck."

Heston hissed. No doubt disgusted with me and thinking me a coward, he ignored my hand and left as he saw Maet's silhouette coming toward us.

Was I a coward? I could hardly sleep that night, bile in the back of my mouth.

In the early gray light of dawn, I woke to Heston's screams. I remembered the sound of a cat that had been caught by a hunting dog one of my neighbors had penned up when I was a kid, and it was something like that. A high-pitched mewling that didn't stop, it snapped me out of my dreams about blue skies and no clouds.

Heston was in the courtyard, his hands and feet bound to a pole set into a notched hole in one of the flagstones.

Venusians didn't use whips. They hung pink-and-snow-feathered leeches from Heston's chest and back. As I got close I could hear a loud sucking crunch, and Heston screamed again.

When the creature was finished, one of the overseers pulled it away, leaving a deep and ragged hole that streamed blood and black ichor. It smelled of licorice and rot.

Venusians streamed past, darting sidelong glances as I moved to stand in front of Heston. He looked up at me through a haze of pain. "Charles . . ."

"Who betrayed you?" I asked sadly.

Heston coughed. "Thought it was you, at first. But it was a Venusian. Telkket. From one of the southern marshes. He stood here and announced to everyone what I'd done. Why? Why would someone do that?"

"The same reason it's always been done," I said, fiddling with my bracelet. "Even if your uprising had succeeded, most of our fellow workers in the common house stood a chance of dying from the repercussions. A slaver society reacts strongly to uprisings, they'd know that. By ratting you out, he's guaranteed a small improvement in his life. Most people go for the bird in the hand."

Heston began to cry. "They're going to drag this out. They're going to kill me."

"Or not," I said. "A living, crippled and broken slave is a good example to have as well."

"Oh God." That last was a faint whimper.

I thought for a long second, then continued. "You probably suspected this, given the things I've said. But some of my ancestors were slaves. My great-grandfather, he fought. Like you. Was whipped. Hobbled. Scarred by brands. But one day, after fighting so long, he up and cut his own throat rather than continue living under the whip. Not something I figured you'd appreciate before this morning, but something I've been thinking on ever since we were captured."

Heston looked up at me with lost eyes.

I cracked my wristband and removed the cyanide pill inside. "I know you didn't have time to use yours," I said. "Maybe they won't kill you. Maybe they'll keep hurting you. I don't know. But I want to give you this. Just in case."

I placed the pill on his tongue, like a priest giving someone a Communion wafer.

"Thank you," he hissed.

One of the overseers struck me, yelling at me to move on. I left as they were putting the leeches back on. This time they ate at his ankles, and Heston sagged at the pole as his feet failed.

By sunset he was dead, mouth foaming from the cyanide pill.

* * *

5.

"I'M PREGNANT," MAET TOLD ME ONE MORNING AS WE lined up for the fields.

The look on my face unnerved her. She squeezed my hand. "Don't be so sad, Charles of Earth."

"I didn't know," I said.

"Didn't know what?" Maet asked.

"That we could even have a child." She was Venusian. But we all were humanoid, as Eric had noted in our first days trapped together. He had talked about common evolution, or panspermia. Or even more fanciful reasons why the human form existed here.

And then the real horror of it all struck me. "What life will my child grow into?" I asked. I thought about myself at four, free and playing in the grass, ignoring my mother's call to come inside. I tried to imagine bringing my own child along to the fields to unload the ships. Seeing my child whipped and broken.

"There are many here who are generations old," Maet said. "We will adapt. All adapt." But there was a note of sadness and resignation in her voice.

I could hardly see the ground in front of me for days.

My world revolved around the stone street out to the field where the airships landed. I could count the stones on the walk to and from the common house with my eyes closed, half-asleep in the early morning shamble out, and the tired shuffle back to what I'd come to regard as home.

My dreams, when I was rested enough to dream now, turned from trying to remember what blue skies looked like to dreaming of flying. It took me a long while to understand what my subconscious mind had decided, as I had slipped into a dark place while thinking about bringing a child into this world.

But one day, watching the silvered airship approach and drop its single bowline, I knew how I would leave: I wouldn't run, I would fly.

I'd been walking in and out of the cabins of these ships for so long. I knew the layout, and although I couldn't read Venusian, I had some sense of the controls. I had been a pilot in the war, after all.

The Venusian airship designs were better than the old Nazi ones we'd seen in newsreels. The Venusians compressed the helium inside into tanks, letting the airships glide down onto the ground and unload cargo without shooting up into the air. The bowline was a formality, probably a holdover from when they'd been more like the airships on Earth and always lighter than air.

It took just a few minutes to pump the helium back into the airship's envelope. That, I thought, would be the trickiest segment of my plan.

But I wouldn't be able to fly it alone.

The longest stretch of work came as I worked to convince the overseers to bring Shepard and Eric over to our estate, promising them that the three of us would work harder despite the nightly beatings we would surely suffer for rising above the pack.

That took working extra hard. To get noticed by the overseers so I could sell them on the idea. And that meant barely sleeping in a corner with a small piece of metal I'd rubbed into a sharp blade against a stone edge to protect Maet, my unborn child, and myself.

When the lord approved the purchase, and the overseers shoved a very thin Eric into the common room, I barely recognized him. Emaciated, his hair unkempt, he collapsed by my blanket and slept.

"It was hellish," Shepard told me as I kept watch with my blade. "They were working us to death building a seawall for real ships. Knee deep in the water, moving rocks however we could.

Bit by bit. I kept telling them I was an engineer. We could do better with machines, and they beat me every time. I learned to shut up pretty quick."

"It is better here," I told him. And Shepard began to weep silently and thank me for getting them moved. They were not surprised by Maet, or to find that she was pregnant. Eric shrugged, and wasn't even fascinated by the fact.

How quickly our priorities could change! From heroes of a nation to weeping about being moved to a less servile state.

I told them about Commander James, and Shepard nodded. "They took our bracelets away and sold them as trinkets to the children. Sometimes I would lie awake hoping one of them ate the pill, and other times I hated myself for thinking it."

"I understand," I said. "Now get some sleep."

I watched over them that first night in the dark like a feral mother cat, until Shepard woke up and spelled me. In the days that followed, we set watch each night and got enough sleep to survive.

I waited for Eric to get his strength back before I began whispering my own plan to them. They blanched at first, thinking about Commander James's fate. "This is not a revolt, this is running off into the bush. There were a lot of people who managed it and built lives for themselves." I thought of the runaways who had lived in the mountains of Jamaica that my father would tell tall tales about.

"When do we make a run for it?" Shepard asked.

"When we're done unloading, and everyone is going back. We cut the moorings and leap aboard. We'll only ever have one chance. And we'll have to make sure there aren't armed Venusians aboard. I won't know the best moment to do this ahead of time, but if I call for you, do not hesitate."

The Venusians at my estate let us keep possessions, though the overseers ransacked through them on random occasions. I'd been storing cured meats that we'd been given and a kind of hard bread. A few water sacks hid the stuff that could get us in trouble.

Food, water, a handmade metal knife, some needles and thread that Maet kept hidden for herself, so she could mend her rough-spun clothes: this was everything we owned.

I hadn't told her what we planned though I began to suspect she knew.

We would head for the northern swamps, near the foothills we'd crashed at. Hike over the nearest pass we could find, and if we made it, off into areas few in Kish cared to visit on the other side.

And, then, maybe, we could figure out what to do. Eric spoke of rescue and scanning the skies. I thought about hacking a small farm out of the wilderness. Shepard knew how to build traps.

Even if we died, we reasoned, we would die once again free.

We just needed the right airship, and a little bit more food to hide in our water sacks, and we could make the run.

The Nazis, though, destroyed our careful plans by arriving one uncharacteristically chilly morning.

The three Nazis had been captured ten days ago, the overseers told us, on an island to the west. They still wore muddied, but tattered German uniforms with Nazi insignia on the shoulders. "You should be excited to have more of your tribe here to work alongside you," the proud overseer who had arranged the sale explained, and pointed at Eric and Shepard. "Just like these two."

"But they aren't like us," I explained. "They're from a different country, one we're at war with."

"War?" the overseer talking to me found that curious. "Well, there is no war for you here. Just more like you. You're the same. So you will work the same."

Left alone, we all eyed one another warily. I realized that Eric and Shepard looked to me for a decision.

I wanted to kill them, for blowing us out of the sky with a missile, but I knew that would only draw attention to us.

The Nazis took the first move, though, introducing themselves nervously. Their commandant, Hans, spoke in lightly accented English. "They captured us when we landed. We thought we were going to be the first Germans to liaise with their civilization, but instead they destroyed our rocket ship and captured us. They refused to believe we came from above the clouds and they put us and all our stuff in cages. They took us around by aircraft to manors and showed us off to royals and important people."

"Like animals," another Nazi, Yost, spit. "They put collars on us and chained us."

"We escaped, once, but they hunted us back down. We killed a few of them," Hans said, satisfied with himself.

"So they sold us off. We were too much trouble."

I stood impassively for a while, then held out changes of clothes. Rough-spun fabric, just like the gray clothes we wore. "Well, it won't be nice like that anymore," I said. "Now you will be working."

"That will give us more time to plan," Hans said.

"To do what?" I asked.

"Gather what tools we can to fight," the commandant said.

"It's been tried," I told him.

"What these creatures need is the *right* kind of leader. A decorated fighter, a strong strategist. I commanded a panzer squadron in Egypt," Hans said, his chest sticking out.

"Get dressed," I told him. "If you take any longer, the overseers will come at us."

As the Nazis changed clothes, Eric whispered, "Are we going to let them join us?"

I shook my head.

"But they're humans," he said. "The only other ones. Surely we have an obligation . . ."

"We were shot out of the sky by a Nazi missile, Eric," I

whispered back. "What makes you think they won't try to kill us again? Are you willing to bet everything on that?"

The Nazis would not speak around Maet and viewed her with suspicion. So I kept her close as we worked their first day.

"Will you run with me?" I asked her.

She showed me her scarred arms. "I was free once. They bound me to the pole and scarred my arms to teach me my lesson. But I would be free again, yes."

I would have hugged her there, but there was work to be done. That night I snuck my blade between Hans's blankets as he slept. Afterward we tiptoed over to a new place in the common house.

Before the Nazis woke up I found an overseer. The Nazis were enemy combatants, I told myself. Men who would see people like my grandparents eliminated from the world. That was what I had believed when I joined the army.

Yet, on some dark nights, I'd wondered. After all, what were the Nazis but the ultimate end point of European colonialism? Nazis were even white people who had told other white people they weren't white enough. They were white people who had invaded and colonized other white countries to spread their concept of a master race. Much like those invaded Europeans had once colonized other countries and told the brown people there that *they* were the master race. Was what the Nazis did to Europe different than what Belgians did to the Congo?

My family had experienced things close to Nazi beliefs on our own home front. Enough that I could shiver and wonder what the point of the fighting was, in darker moments.

But, I reminded myself, Nazism was purified European colonialism. A heady alcohol to the weak beer of American colonialism that was somewhat more survivable; despite the lynchings, there'd been no total ethnic cleansing. So I'd joined the world war and fought, and to my bitterness, seen the war continue on.

Seen the war spread even into outer space as we raced Hitler to other worlds.

No, it would not leave me sleepless to do what I planned, I thought, as I woke the overseer to tell them about the knife.

We woke, hours later, to the sounds of human screams. The Nazis hung bound from three poles. Outside we found Hans slumped forward, dead, my crude knife sticking out of his neck.

The other pair wailed and wept as the colorful leeches sucked and tore into their skin. The overseers had questioned the other Venusians about knife-waving humans, and they pointed to the corner of the common house. One human looked like the other to them, and I'd moved my small group away from the Nazis, who were wearing our old clothes. I'd told Maet to sleep somewhere else.

"We take an airship today if the chance is there," I said to my fellow remaining humans. "They'll all be focused on other things right now."

6.

THE NAZIS SCREWED THINGS UP FOR US. I'D HAD TO use my homemade knife, and now I didn't have anything to cut the airship's bowline with. So I stood by the tie-down point as casually as I could, a large sack of grain on my shoulders, and loosened the massive knot until it slipped free.

I left the line loose around the great sand-screw sunk ten feet into the ground. From a distance, I hoped it would look like it was still tied.

And then I nonchalantly returned after dropping the grain off.

I could hear Shepard swearing from inside as I loped back into the cabin. Two-thirds of the cargo had been shuffled out by the unloading crew. Six Venusians were inside with us, and one overseer lounged against the wall of the cargo bay, watching the unloading, shouting and smacking us with his club when he deemed us too slow.

Eric leaned over. "Do we wait for everyone to leave with their cargo?"

"Now," I hissed.

"And the Venusians?"

"Once we're off the ground they can jump out if they want to stay, or join us if they want freedom," I said.

We'd wanted a few more days to plan the exact attack on an airship, but we had our chance. Normally several overseers stood inside to watch us. Normally they were more vigilant. But they'd gotten their troublemakers this morning. They were sated from the violence and punishment.

Eric and I attacked the overseer from each side. We wrapped a ripped-open water sack around his head to muffle his cries. We yanked him beneath bags of grain and I crushed his neck with the heel of my foot repeatedly until the soles of my feet struck metal.

Shepard ran into the empty control room and triggered the helium-release valve, reversing the flow from the pressurized tanks.

The hiss was loud, and I glanced down the bay. No armies of overseers swarmed us yet though they were turning, their large, dark eyes opening in realization.

"Fellow people," I announced to the whole cargo bay. "We are stealing this ship. And if you would like to flee with us, you are welcome. If not, run for the ground!"

Two Venusians ran, jumping out of the bay. It was already three feet off the ground. They rolled on the grass, and for their loyalty were treated with kicks from enraged overseers.

One of them grabbed the lip of the open bay, struggling to get aboard. I kicked at his hands as we continued to rise into the air. He looked up at me, hanging from the edge, such hatred and astonishment in his eyes.

I stomped his fingers until he screamed and let go. He dropped ten feet to the ground, his legs folding awkwardly under him.

The other Venusians turned and ran back for their rifles as we rose higher. The violent lasers cracked and sizzled the air, but I ran forward with Shepard to jam the engines full on. When they droned to life the airship surged away even faster.

Later, I walked back to the open bay and looked back at the stone towers of Kish as they receded in the distance. We passed over the swamps and marshes that surrounded it. Something with a giant, saurapodian neck peeked its head out of the treetops and bellowed at us.

We were a craft of free people.

7.

WHEN MY SON TURNED FIVE, I SAT HIM DOWN. "IT IS time to tell you who you really are, and where you really came from," I said.

I told him that he was from the tribe of humanity, from the world of Earth.

"Where is that?" he asked.

"Far above the veil of gray." I pointed at the clouds.

"Will we ever go back?" he asked.

"Most likely not," I told him. Maybe war had consumed them all. I remembered the stories soldiers told of a new superweapon both sides had supposedly tested out in the deserts of Nevada and North Africa. A bomb that could unleash hell itself and destroy the world many times over. I hadn't heard of any new Earthmen being captured, or coming through the skies, so maybe the atom bomb had been used.

Or maybe Earth assumed that the surface of Venus was too

dangerous, as both missions there had failed to return.

But I told my son of the blue skies and beautiful places I'd seen. About his grandparents and great-grandparents. All the history I knew.

"One day, you, or your child, will stand tall among the Venusians," I told him. He looked more like his mother than me. And while it complicated our relationship, I knew at least some small part of what he was going through. "But always remember where you came from."

When he hugged me, his face showed that he didn't understand.

But I would continue to tell him anyway. Until the stories lodged deep and could be carried onward.

"I know I'm of the tribe of Earth," he said, and then left to play in the wading pool near the common house. It was hot, and the splashed water cooled him.

He never asked about the scars on my arms, but one day I would have to tell him I'd been branded as a runaway. That the overseers marked me, and would beat me for the slightest provocation.

I never told him his own mother, Maet, cut her throat when they finally caught us. They had followed a homing beacon still working in the wreckage of the airship. They found where we ditched it, and spent months tracking us through the fetid jungle.

I never told him that the mild-mannered scientist, Eric, threw himself in front of laser fire to save my son's life.

I never told him why his "uncle" Shep limped so horribly.

These things he would discover the truth of sooner or later, and I wanted it to be as late as possible.

On Earth, many slaves living in the very country I had risked my life to protect had in the past tried to run away, like I had. And been dragged all the way back across states, hundreds of miles, to the place they'd run away from. Some across countries.

Because a successful runaway was a precedent. They'd spent

resources to hunt us down and bring us back. And in some ways, I'd been no different than Heston. I'd assumed I was smart. Different. Special. That I would be the one to beat the odds.

I knew more now. More of the maps, and paths, and geographies out past Kish. I knew them better than ever before. But to risk the run was to risk my innocent child's flesh to torture, or worse, for being a runaway if caught.

When he was older, I thought, maybe he would want to try to escape with us. Or maybe not, and I would have to leave him to face life on his own. But I couldn't leave him now. This is how so many in the past must have gotten trapped, I realized, even as I continued to plan my escape.

I found myself apologizing to my own ancestors. Apologizing for getting caught again, after they worked so hard to free themselves.

There was a poem one of my aunts read to me by a poet named Paul Dunbar. I understood it, finally, though I wish I never had.

> When his wing is bruised and his bosom sore,—
> When he beats his bars and he would be free;
> It is not a carol of joy or glee,
>
> But a prayer that he sends from his heart's deep core,
> But a plea, that upward to Heaven he flings—
> I know why the caged bird sings!

Every night, in the common house, while I fell asleep, I dreamt of pale, blue skies.

ELIZABETH BEAR

Elizabeth Bear was born in Connecticut, and now lives in Brookfield, Massachusetts, after several years living in the Mojave Desert near Las Vegas. She won the John W. Campbell Award for Best New Writer in 2005, and in 2008 took home a Hugo Award for her short story "Tideline," which also won her the Theodore Sturgeon Memorial Award (shared with David Moles). In 2009, she won another Hugo Award for her novelette "Shoggoths in Bloom." Her short work has appeared in *Asimov's, Subterranean, SCI FICTION, Interzone, The Third Alternative, Strange Horizons, On Spec,* and elsewhere, and has been collected in *The Chains That You Refuse* and *New Amsterdam.* She is the author of three highly acclaimed SF novels, *Hammered, Scardown,* and *Worldwired,* and of the Alternate History Fantasy *Promethean Age* series, which includes the novels *Blood and Iron, Whiskey and Water, Ink and Steel,* and *Hell and Earth.* Her other books include the novels *Carnival, Undertow, Chill, Dust, All the Windwracked Stars, By the Mountain Bound, Range of Ghosts,* a novel in collaboration with Sarah Monette, *The Tempering of Men,* and two chapbook novellas, "Bone and Jewel Creatures" and "Ad Eternum." Her most recent books are a new collection, *Shoggoths in Bloom,* two novels, *Shattered Pillars* and *One-Eyed Jack,* and a novella, "The Book of Iron."

Here she paints a dramatic portrait of a scientist so determined to prove a controversial theory that she'll go to any length to do so—even if it kills her. Which, on Venus, it well might.

The Heart's Filthy Lesson

ELIZABETH BEAR

THE SUN BURNED THROUGH THE CLOUDS AROUND noon on the long Cytherean day, and Dharthi happened to be awake and in a position to see it. She was alone in the highlands of Ishtar Terra on a research trip, five sleeps out from Butler base camp, and—despite the nagging desire to keep traveling—had decided to take a rest break for an hour or two. Noon at this latitude was close enough to the one hundredth solar dieiversary of her birth that she'd broken out her little hoard of shelf-stable cake to celebrate. The prehensile fingers and leaping legs of her bioreactor-printed, skin-bonded adaptshell made it simple enough to swarm up one of the tall, gracile pseudofigs and creep along its smooth grey branches until the ceaseless Venusian rain dripped directly on her adaptshell's slick-furred head.

It was safer in the treetops if you were sitting still. Nothing big enough to want to eat her was likely to climb up this far. The grues didn't come out until nightfall, but there were swamp-tigers, damnthings, and velociraptors to worry about. The forest was too thick for predators any bigger than that, but a swarm of scorpion-rats was no joke. And Venus had only been settled for three hundred days, and most of that devoted to Aphrodite Terra; there were still plenty of undiscovered monsters out here in the wilderness.

The water did not bother Dharthi, nor did the dip and sway of the branch in the wind. Her adaptshell was beautifully tailored to this terrain, and that fur shed water like the hydrophobic miracle of engineering that it was. The fur was a glossy, iridescent purple that qualified as black in most lights, to match the foliage that dripped rain like strings of glass beads from the multiple points of palmate leaves. Red-black, to make the most of the rainy grey light. They'd fold their leaves up tight and go dormant when night came.

Dharthi had been born with a chromosomal abnormality that produced red-green color blindness. She'd been about ten solar days old when they'd done the gene therapy to fix it, and she just about remembered her first glimpses of the true, saturated colors of Venus. She'd seen it first as if it were Earth: washed-out and faded.

For now, however, they were alive with the scurryings and chitterings of a few hundred different species of Cytherean canopy-dwellers. And the quiet, nearly contented sound of Dharthi munching on cake. She would not dwell; she would not stew. She would look at all this natural majesty and try to spot the places where an unnaturally geometric line or angle showed in the topography of the canopy.

From here, she could stare up the enormous sweep of Maxwell Montes to the north, its heights forested to the top in Venus's deep, rich atmosphere—but the sight of them lost for most of its reach in clouds. Dharthi could only glimpse the escarpment at all because she was on the "dry" side. Maxwell Montes scraped the heavens, kicking the cloud layer up as if it had struck an aileron, so the "wet" side got the balance of the rain. *Balance* in this case meaning that the mountains on the windward side were scoured down to granite, and a nonadapted terrestrial organism had better bring breathing gear.

But here in the lee, the forest flourished, and on a clear hour from a height, visibility might reach a couple of klicks or more.

Dharthi took another bite of cake—it might have been

"chocolate"; it was definitely caffeinated, because she was picking up the hit on her blood monitors already—and turned herself around on her branch to face downslope. The sky was definitely brighter, the rain falling back to a drizzle, then a mist, and the clouds were peeling back along an arrowhead trail that led directly back to the peak above her. A watery golden smudge brightened one patch of clouds. They tore, and she glimpsed the full, unguarded brilliance of the daystar, just hanging there in a chip of glossy cerulean sky, the clouds all around it smeared with thick, unbelievable rainbows. Waves of mist rolled and slid among the leaves of the canopy, made golden by the shimmering, unreal light.

Dharthi was glad she was wearing the shell. It played the sun's warmth through to her skin without also relaying the risks of ultraviolet exposure. She ought to be careful of her eyes, however: a crystalline shield protected them, but its filters weren't designed for naked light.

The forest noises rose to a cacophony. It was the third time in Dharthi's one hundred solar days of life that she had glimpsed the sun. Even here, she imagined that some of these animals would never have seen it before.

She decided to accept it as a good omen for her journey. Sadly, there was no way to spin the next thing that happened that way.

"Hey," said a voice in her head. "Good cake."

"That proves your pan is malfunctioning, if anything does," Dharthi replied sourly. *Never accept a remote synaptic link with a romantic and professional partner. No matter how convenient it seems at the time, and in the field.*

Because someday they might be a romantic and professional partner you really would rather not talk to right now.

"I heard that."

"What do you want, Kraken?"

Dharthi imagined Kraken smiling, and wished she hadn't. She could hear it in her partner's "voice" when she spoke again, anyway. "Just to wish you a happy dieiversary."

"Aw," Dharthi said. "Aren't you sweet. Noblesse oblige?"

"Maybe," Kraken said tiredly, "I actually care?"

"Mmm," Dharthi said. "What's the ulterior motive this time?"

Kraken sighed. It was more a neural flutter than a heave of breath, but Dharthi got the point all right. "Maybe I actually *care*."

"Sure," Dharthi said. "Every so often you have to glance down from Mount Olympus and check up on the lesser beings."

"Olympus is on Mars," Kraken said.

It didn't make Dharthi laugh because she clenched her right fist hard enough that, even though the cushioning adaptshell squished against her palm, she still squeezed the blood out of her fingers. *You and all your charm. You don't get to charm me anymore.*

"Look," Kraken said. "You have something to prove. I understand that."

"How can you *possibly* understand that? When was the last time you were turned down for a resource allocation? Doctor youngest-ever recipient of the Cytherean Award for Excellence in Xenoarcheology? Doctor Founding Field-Martius Chair of Archaeology at the University on Aphrodite?"

"The University on Aphrodite," Kraken said, "is five Quonset huts and a repurposed colonial landing module."

"It's what we've got."

"I peaked early," Kraken said, after a pause. "I was never your *rival*, Dharthi. We were colleagues." Too late, in Dharthi's silence, she realized her mistake. "*Are* colleagues."

"You look up from your work often enough to notice I'm missing?"

There was a pause. "That may be fair," Kraken said at last. "But if being professionally focused—"

"*Obsessed.*"

"—is a failing, it was hardly a failing limited to me. Come *back*. Come back to *me*. We'll talk about it. I'll help you try for a resource voucher again tomorrow."

"I don't want your damned *help*, Kraken!"

The forest around Dharthi fell silent. Shocked, she realized she'd shouted out loud.

"Haring off across Ishtar alone, with no support—you're not going to prove your theory about aboriginal Cytherean settlement patterns, Dhar. You're going to get eaten by a grue."

"I'll be home by dark," Dharthi said. "Anyway, if I'm not— all the better for the grue."

"You know who else was always on about being laughed out of the Academy?" Kraken said. Her voice had that teasing tone that could break Dharthi's worst, most self-loathing, prickliest mood—if she let it. "Moriarty."

I will not laugh. Fuck you.

Dharthi couldn't tell if Kraken had picked it up or not. There was a silence, as if she were controlling her temper or waiting for Dharthi to speak.

"If you get killed," Kraken said, "make a note in your file that I can use your DNA. You're not getting out of giving me children that easily."

Ha-ha, Dharthi thought. *Only serious.* She couldn't think of what to say, and so she said nothing. The idea of a little Kraken filled her up with mushy softness inside. But somebody's career would go on hold for the first fifty solar days of that kid's life, and Dharthi was pretty sure it wouldn't be Kraken's.

She couldn't think of what to say in response, and the silence got heavy until Kraken said, "Dammit. I'm *worried* about you."

"Worry about yourself." Dharthi couldn't break the connection, but she could bloody well shut down her end of the dialogue. And she could refuse to hear.

She pitched the remains of the cake as far across the canopy as she could, then regretted it. Hopefully, nothing Cytherean would try to eat it; it might give the local biology a bellyache.

It was ironically inevitable that Dharthi, named by her parents in a fit of homesickness for Terra, would grow up to be the most Cytherean of Cythereans. She took great pride in her adaptation, in her ability to rough it. Some of the indigenous plants and many of the indigenous animals could be eaten, and Dharthi knew which ones. She also knew, more important, which ones were likely to eat her.

She hadn't mastered humans nearly as well. Dharthi wasn't good at politics. *Unlike Kraken.* Dharthi wasn't good at making friends. *Unlike Kraken.* Dharthi wasn't charming or beautiful or popular or brilliant. *Unlike Kraken, Kraken, Kraken.*

Kraken was a better scientist, or at least a better-understood one. Kraken was a better person, probably. More generous, less prickly, certainly. But there was one thing Dharthi *was* good at. Better at than Kraken. Better at than anyone. Dharthi was good at living on Venus, at being Cytherean. She was more comfortable in and proficient with an adaptshell than anyone she had ever met.

In fact, it was peeling the shell off that came hard. So much easier to glide through the jungle or the swamp like something that belonged there, wearing a quasibiologic suit of superpowered armor bonded to your neural network and your skin. The human inside was a soft, fragile, fleshy thing, subject to complicated feelings and social dynamics, and Dharthi despised her. But that same human, while bonded to the shell, ghosted through the rain forest like a native and saw things no one else ever had.

A kilometer from where she had stopped for cake, she picked up the trail of a velociraptor. It was going in the right direction, so she tracked it. It wasn't a real velociraptor; it wasn't even a dinosaur. Those were Terran creatures, albeit extinct; this was a Cytherean meat-eating monster that bore a superficial resemblance. Like the majority of Cytherean vertebrates, it had six limbs though it ran balanced on the rear ones and the two forward pairs had evolved into little more than graspers. Four eyes were spaced equidistantly around the dome of its skull, giving it a dome of monocular vision punctuated by narrow slices of depth perception. The business end of the thing was delineated by a saw-toothed maw that split wide enough to bite a human being in half. The whole of it was camouflaged with long, draggled fur-feathers that grew thick with near-black algae, or the Cytherean cognate.

Dharthi followed the velociraptor for over two kilometers, and the beast never even noticed she was there. She smiled inside her adaptshell. Kraken was right: going out into the jungle alone and unsupported would be suicide for most people. But wasn't it like her not to give Dharthi credit for this one single thing that Dharthi could do better than anyone?

She *knew* that the main Cytherean settlements had been on Ishtar Terra. Knew it in her bones. And she was going to prove it, whether anybody was willing to give her an allocation for the study or not.

They'll be sorry, she thought, and had to smile at her own adolescent petulance. *They'll rush to support me once this is done.*

The not-a-dinosaur finally veered off to the left. Dharthi kept jogging/swinging/swimming/splashing/climbing forward, letting the shell do most of the work. The highlands leveled out into the great plateau the new settlers called the Lakshmi Planum. No one knew what the aboriginals had called it. They'd been gone for—to an approximation—ten thousand years: as long as it had taken humankind to get from the Neolithic (agriculture, stone tools) to jogging through the jungles of an alien world wearing a suit of power armor engineered from printed muscle fiber and cheetah DNA.

Lakshmi Planum, ringed with mountains on four sides, was one of the few places on the surface of Venus where you could not see an ocean. The major Cytherean landmasses, Aphrodite and Ishtar, were smaller than South America. The surface of this world was 85 percent water—water less salty than Earth's oceans because there was less surface to leach minerals into it through runoff. And the Lakshmi Planum was tectonically active, with great volcanoes and living faults.

That activity was one of the reasons Dharthi's research had brought her here.

The jungle of the central Ishtarean plateau was not as creeper-clogged and vine-throttled as Dharthi might have expected. It was a mature climax forest, and the majority of the biomass hung suspended over Dharthi's head, great limbs stretching up umbrella-like to the limited light. Up there, the branches and trunks were festooned with symbiotes, parasites, and commensal organisms. Down here among the trunks, it was dark and still except for the squish of loam underfoot and the ceaseless patter of what rain came through the leaves.

Dharthi stayed alert but didn't spot any more large predators on that leg of the journey. There were flickers and scuttlers and fliers galore, species she was sure nobody had named or described. Perhaps on the way back she'd have time to do more, but for now she contented herself with extensive video archives. It wouldn't hurt to cultivate some good karma with Bio while she was out here. She might need a job sweeping up offices when she got back.

Stop. Failure is not an option. Not even a possibility.

Like all such glib sentiments, it didn't make much of a dent in the bleakness of her mood. Even walking, observing, surveying, she had entirely too much time to think.

She waded through two more swamps and scaled a basalt ridge—one of the stretching roots of the vast volcano named Sacajawea. Nearly everything on Venus was named after female persons—historical, literary, or mythological—from Terra, from the quaint old system of binary and exclusive genders. For a moment, Dharthi considered such medieval horrors as dentistry without anesthetic, binary gender, and being stuck forever in the body you were born in, locked in and struggling against what your genes dictated. The trap of biology appalled her; she found it impossible to comprehend how people in the olden days had gotten anything done, with their painfully short lives and their limited access to resources, education, and technology.

The adaptshell stumbled over a tree root, forcing her attention back to the landscape. Of course, modern technology wasn't exactly perfect either. The suit needed carbohydrate to keep moving and protein to repair muscle tissue. Fortunately, it wasn't picky about its food source—and Dharthi herself needed rest. The day was long and only half-over. She wouldn't prove herself if she got so tired she got herself eaten by a megaspider.

We haven't conquered all those human frailties yet.

Sleepily, she climbed a big tree, one that broke the canopy, and slung a hammock high in branches that dripped with fleshy, gorgeous, thickly scented parasitic blossoms, opportunistically decking every limb up here where the light was stronger. They shone bright whites and yellows, mostly, set off against the dark, glossy foliage. Dharthi set proximity sensors, established a tech perimeter above and below, and unsealed the shell before sending it down to forage for the sorts of simple biomass that sustained it. It would be happy with the mulch of the forest floor, and she could call it back when she needed it. Dharthi rolled herself into the hammock as if it were a scent-proof, claw-proof cocoon and tried to sleep.

Rest eluded. The leaves and the cocoon filtered the sunlight, so it was pleasantly dim, and the cocoon kept the water off except what she'd brought inside with herself when she wrapped up. She was warm and well supported. But that all did very little to alleviate her anxiety.

She didn't know exactly where she was going. She was flying blind—hah, she *wished* she were flying. If she'd had the allocations for an aerial survey, this would all be a lot easier, assuming they could pick anything out through the jungle—and operating on a hunch. An educated hunch.

But one that Kraken and her other colleagues—and more important, the Board of Allocation—thought was at best a wild guess and at worst crackpottery.

What if you're wrong?

If she was wrong . . . well. She didn't have much to go home to. So she'd better be right that the settlements they'd found on Aphrodite were merely outposts, and that the aboriginal Cytbereans had stuck much closer to the north pole. She had realized that the remains—such as they were—of Cytherean settlements clustered in geologically active areas. She theorized that they used geothermal energy, or perhaps had some other unknown purpose for staying there. In any case, Ishtar was far younger, far more geologically active than Aphrodite, as attested by its upthrust granite ranges and its scattering of massive volcanoes. Aphrodite—larger, calmer, safer—had drawn the Terran settlers. Dharthi theorized that Ishtar had been the foundation of Cytherean culture for exactly the opposite reasons.

She hoped that if she found a big settlement—the remains of one of their cities—she could prove this. And possibly even produce some clue as to what had happened to them all.

It wouldn't be easy. A city buried under ten thousand years of sediment and jungle could go unnoticed even by an archaeologist's trained eye and the most perspicacious modern mapping and visualization technology. And of course she had to be in the right place, and all she had to go on there were guesses—deductions, if she was feeling kind to herself, which she rarely was—about the patterns of relationships between those geologically active areas on Aphrodite and the aboriginal settlements nearby.

This is stupid. You'll never find anything without support and an allocation. Kraken never would have pushed her luck this way.

Kraken never would have needed to. Dharthi knew better than anyone how much effort and dedication and scholarship went into Kraken's work—but still, it sometimes seemed as if fantastic opportunities just fell into her lover's lap without effort. And Kraken's intellect and charisma were so dazzling . . . it was hard to see past that to the amount of study it took to support that seemingly effortless, comprehensive knowledge of just about everything.

Nothing made Dharthi feel the limitations of her own ability like spending time with her lover. Hell, Kraken probably would have known which of the animals she was spotting as she ran were new species, and the names and describers of all the known ones.

If she could have this, Dharthi thought, just this—if she could do one thing to equal all of Kraken's effortless successes—then she could tolerate how perfect Kraken was the rest of the time.

This line of thought wasn't helping the anxiety. She thrashed in the cocoon for another half hour before she finally gave in and took a sedative. Not safe, out in the jungle. But if she didn't rest, she couldn't run—and even the Cytherean daylight wasn't actually endless.

Dharthi awakened to an animal sniffing her cocoon with great whuffing predatory breaths. An atavistic response, something from the brainstem, froze her in place even as it awakened her. Her arms and legs—naked, so fragile without her skin—felt heavy, numb, limp as if they had fallen asleep. The shadow of the thing's head darkened the translucent steelsilk as it passed between Dharthi and the sky. The drumming of the rain stopped momentarily. Hard to tell how big it was from that—but big, she thought. An estimation confirmed when it nosed or pawed the side of the cocoon and she felt a broad blunt object as big as her two hands together prod her in the ribs.

She held her breath, and it withdrew. There was the rain, tapping on her cocoon where it dripped between the leaves. She was almost ready to breathe out again when it made a sound—a thick, chugging noise followed by a sort of roar that had more in common with trains and waterfalls than what most people would identify as an animal sound.

Dharthi swallowed her scream. She didn't need Kraken to tell her what *that* was. Every schoolchild could manage a piping reproduction of the call of one of Venus's nastiest pieces of charismatic megafauna, the Cytherean swamp-tiger.

Swamp-tigers were two lies, six taloned legs, and an indiscriminate number of enormous daggerlike teeth in a four-hundred-kilogram body. Two lies, because they didn't live in swamps—though they passed through them on occasion, because what on Venus didn't?—and they weren't tigers. But they *were* striped violet and jade green to disappear into the thick jungle foliage; they had long, slinky bodies that twisted around sharp turns and barreled up tree trunks without any need to decelerate; and their whisker-ringed mouths hinged open wide enough to bite a grown person in half.

All four of the swamp-tiger's bright blue eyes were directed forward. Because it didn't hurt their hunting, and what creature in its right mind would want to sneak up on a thing like that?

They weren't supposed to hunt this high up. The branches were supposed to be too slender to support them.

Dharthi wasn't looking forward to getting a better look at this one. It nudged the cocoon again. Despite herself, Dharthi went rigid. She pressed both fists against her chest and concentrated on not whimpering, on not making a single sound. She forced herself to breathe slowly and evenly. To consider. *Panic gets you eaten.*

She wouldn't give Kraken the damned satisfaction.

She had some resources. The cocoon would attenuate her scent, and might disguise it almost entirely. The adaptshell was somewhere in the vicinity, munching away, and if she could make it into *that*, she stood a chance of outrunning the thing. She weighed a quarter what the swamp-tiger did; she could get up higher into the treetops than it could, theoretically. After all, it wasn't supposed to come up this high.

And she was, at least presumptively, somewhat smarter.

But it could outjump her, outrun her, outsneak her, and—perhaps most important—outchomp her.

She wasted a few moments worrying about how it had gotten past her perimeter before the sharp pressure of its claws skidding down the rip-proof surface of the cocoon refocused her attention. That was a temporary protection; it might not be able to pierce the cocoon, but it could certainly squash Dharthi to death inside of it, or rip it out of the tree and toss it to the jungle floor. If the fall didn't kill her, she'd have the cheerful and humiliating choice of yelling for rescue or wandering around injured until something bigger ate her. She needed a way out; she needed to channel five million years of successful primate adaptation, the legacy of clever-monkey ancestors, and figure out how to get away from the not-exactly-cat.

What would a monkey do? The question was the answer, she realized.

She just needed the courage to apply it. And the luck to survive whatever then transpired.

The cocoon was waterproof as well as claw-proof—hydrophobic on the outside, a wicking polymer on the inside. The whole system was impregnated with engineered bacteria that broke down the waste products in human sweat—or other fluids—and returned them to the environment as safe, nearly odorless, nonpolluting water, salts, and a few trace chemicals.

Dharthi was going to have to unfasten the damn thing.

She waited while the swamp-tiger prodded her again. It seemed to have a pattern of investigating and withdrawing—Dharthi heard the rustle and felt the thump and sway as it leaped from branch to branch, circling, making a few horrifically unsettling noises and a bloodcurdling snarl or two, and coming back for another go at the cocoon. The discipline required to hold herself still—not even merely still, but limp—as the creature whuffed and poked left her nauseated with adrenaline. She felt it moving away then. The swing of branches under its weight did nothing to ease the roiling in her gut.

Now or never.

Shell! Come and get me! Then she palmed the cocoon's seal and whipped it open, left hand and foot shoved through internal grips so she didn't accidentally evert herself into free fall. As she swung, she shook a heavy patter of water drops loose from the folds of the cocoon's hydrophobic surface. They pattered down. There were a lot of branches between her and the ground; she didn't fancy making the intimate acquaintanceship of each and every one of them.

The swamp-tiger hadn't gone as far as she expected. In fact, it was on the branch just under hers. As it whipped its head around and roared, she had an eloquent view from above—a clear shot down its black-violet gullet. The mouth hinged wide enough to bite her in half across the middle; the tongue was thick and fleshy; the palate ribbed and mottled in paler shades of red. *If I live through this, I will be able to draw every one of those seventy-two perfectly white teeth from memory.*

She grabbed the safety handle with her right hand as well, heaved with her hips, and flipped the cocoon over so her legs swung free. For a moment, she dangled just above the swamp-tiger. It reared back on its heavy haunches like a startled cat, long tail lashing around to protect its abdomen. Dharthi knew that as soon as it collected its wits it was going to take a swipe at her, possibly with both sets of forelegs.

It was small for a swamp-tiger—perhaps only two hundred kilos—and its stripes were quite a bit brighter than she would have expected. Even wet, its feathery plumage had the unfinished raggedness she associated with young animals still in their baby coats. It might even have been fuzzy, if it were ever properly dry. Which might explain why it was so high up in the treetops. Previously undocumented behavior in a juvenile animal.

Wouldn't it be an irony if this were the next in a long line of xenobiological discoveries temporarily undiscovered again because a scientist happened to get herself eaten? At least she had a transponder. And maybe the shell was near enough to record some of this.

Data might survive.

Great, she thought. *I wonder where its mama is.*

Then she urinated in its face.

It wasn't an aimed stream by any means, though she was wearing the external plumbing currently—easier in the field, until you got a bladder stone. But she had a bladder full of pee saved up during sleep, so there was plenty of it. It splashed down her legs and over the swamp-tiger's face, and Dharthi didn't care what your biology was, if you were carbon-oxygen-based, a snoutful of ammonia and urea had to be pretty nasty.

The swamp-tiger backed away, cringing. If it had been a human being, Dharthi would have said it was spluttering. She didn't take too much time to watch; good a story as it would make someday, it would always be a better one than otherwise if she survived to tell it. She pumped her legs for momentum, glad that the sweat-wicking properties of the cocoon's lining kept the grip dry, because right now her palms weren't doing any of that work themselves. Kick high, a twist from the core, and she had one leg over the cocoon. It was dry—she'd shaken off what little water it had collected. Dharthi pulled her feet up—standing on the stuff was like standing on a slack sail, and she was glad that some biotuning trained up by the time she spent running the canopy had given her the balance of a perching bird.

Behind and below, she heard the Cytherean monster make a sound like a kettle boiling over—one part whistle, and one part hiss. She imagined claws in her haunches, a crushing bite to the skull or the nape—

The next branch up was a half meter beyond her reach. Her balance on her toes, she jumped as hard as she could off the yielding surface under her bare feet. Her left hand missed; the right hooked a limb but did not close. She dangled sideways for a moment, the stretch across her shoulder strong and almost pleasant. Her fingers locked in the claw position, she flexed her biceps—not a pull-up, she couldn't chin herself one-handed— but just enough to let her left hand latch securely. A parasitic orchid squashed beneath the pads of her fingers. A dying bug wriggled. Caustic sap burned her skin. She swung, and managed to hang on.

She wanted to dangle for a moment, panting and shaking and gathering herself for the next ridiculous effort. But beneath her, the rattle of leaves, the creak of a bough. The not-tiger was coming.

Climb. Climb!

She had to get high. She had to get farther out from the trunk, onto branches where it would not pursue her. She had to stay alive until the shell got to her. Then she could run or fight as necessary.

Survival was starting to seem like less of a pipe dream now.

She swung herself up again, risking a glance through her armpit as she mantled herself up onto the bough. It dipped and twisted under her weight. Below, the swamp-tiger paced, snarled, reared back and took a great, outraged swing up at her cocoon with its two left-side forepaws.

The fabric held. The branches it was slung between did not. They cracked and swung down, crashing on the boughs below and missing the swamp-tiger only because the Cytherean cat had reflexes preternaturally adapted to life in the trees. It still came very close to being knocked off its balance, and Dharthi took advantage of its distraction to scramble higher, careful to remember not to wipe her itching palms on the more sensitive flesh of her thighs.

Another logic problem presented itself. The closer she got to the trunk, the higher she could scramble, and the faster the adaptshell could get to her—but the swamp-tiger was less likely to follow her out on the thinner ends of the boughs. She was still moving as she decided that she'd go up a bit more first and move diagonally—up *and* out, until "up" was no longer an option.

She made two more branches before hearing the rustle of the swamp-tiger leaping upward behind her. She'd instinctively made a good choice in climbing away from it rather than descending, she realized—laterally or down, there was no telling how far the thing could leap. Going up, on unsteady branches, it was limited to shorter hops. Shorter . . . but much longer than Dharthi's. Now the choice was made for her—out, before it caught up, or get eaten. At least the wet of the leaves and the rain were washing the irritant sap from her palms.

She hauled her feet up again and gathered herself to stand and sprint down the center stem of this bough, a perilous highway no wider than her palm. When she raised her eyes, though, she found herself looking straight into the four bright, curious blue eyes of a second swamp-tiger.

"Aw, crud," Dharthi said. "Didn't anyone tell you guys you're supposed to be solitary predators?"

It looked about the same age and size and fluffiness as the other one. Littermates? Littermates of some Terran species hunted together until they reached maturity. That was probably the answer, and there was another groundbreaking bit of Cytherean biology that would go into a swamp-tiger's belly with Dharthi's masticated brains. Maybe she'd have enough time to relay the information to Kraken while they were disemboweling her.

The swamp-tiger lifted its anterior right forefoot and dabbed experimentally at Dharthi. Dharthi drew back her lips and *hissed* at it, and it pulled the leg back and contemplated her, but it didn't put the paw down. The next swipe would be for keeps.

She could call Kraken now, of course. But that would just be a distraction, not help. *Help* had the potential to arrive in time.

The idea of telling Kraken—and *everybody*—how she had gotten out of a confrontation with *two* of Venus's most impressive predators put a new rush of strength in her trembling legs. They were juveniles. They were inexperienced. They lacked confidence in their abilities, and they did not know how to estimate hers.

Wild predators had no interest in fighting anything to the death. They were out for a meal.

Dharthi stood up on her refirming knees, screamed in the swamp-tiger's face, and punched it as hard as she could, right in the nose.

She almost knocked herself out of the damned tree, and only her windmilling left hand snatching at twigs hauled her upright again and saved her. The swamp-tiger had crouched back, face wrinkled up in distaste or discomfort. The other one was coming up behind her.

Dharthi turned on the ball of her foot and sprinted for the end of the bough. Ten meters, fifteen, and it trembled and curved down sharply under her weight. There was still a lot of forest giant left above her, but this bough was arching now until it almost touched the one below. It moved in the wind, and with every breath. It creaked and made fragile little crackling noises.

A few more meters, and it might bend down far enough that she could reach the branch below.

A few more meters, and it might crack and drop.

It probably wouldn't pull free of the tree entirely—fresh Cytherean "wood" was fibrous and full of sap—but it might dump her off pretty handily.

She took a deep breath—clean air, rain, deep sweetness of flowers, herby scents of crushed leaves—and turned again to face the tigers.

They were still where she had left them, crouched close to the trunk of the tree, tails lashing as they stared balefully after her out of eight gleaming cerulean eyes. Their fanged heads were sunk low between bladelike shoulders. Their lips curled over teeth as big as fingers.

"Nice kitties," Dharthi said ineffectually. "Why don't you two just scamper on home? I bet Mama has a nice bit of grue for supper."

The one she had peed on snarled at her. She supposed she couldn't blame it. She edged a little farther away on the branch.

A rustling below. *Now that's just ridiculous.*

But it wasn't a third swamp-tiger. She glanced down and glimpsed an anthropoid shape clambering up through the branches fifty meters below, mostly hidden in foliage but moving with a peculiar empty lightness. The shell. Coming for her.

The urge to speed up the process, to try to climb down to it was almost unbearable, but Dharthi made herself sit tight. One of the tigers—the one she'd punched—rose up on six padded legs and slunk forward. It made a half dozen steps before the branch's increasing droop and the cracking, creaking sounds made it freeze. It was close enough now that she could make out the pattern of its damp, feathery whiskers. Dharthi braced her bare feet under tributary limbs and tried not to hunker down; swamp-tigers were supposed to go for crouching prey, and standing up and being big was supposed to discourage them. She spread her arms and rode the sway of the wind, the sway of the limb.

Her adaptshell heaved itself up behind her while the tigers watched. Her arms were already spread wide, her legs braced. The shell just cozied up behind her and squelched over her outstretched limbs, snuggling up and tightening down. It affected her balance, though, and the wobbling of the branch—

She crouched fast and grabbed at a convenient limb. And that was more than tiger number two could bear.

From a standing start, still halfway down the branch, the tiger gathered itself, hindquarters twitching. It leaped, and Dharthi had just enough time to try to throw herself flat under its arc. Enough time to try, but not quite enough time to succeed.

One of the swamp-tiger's second rank of legs caught her right arm like the swing of a baseball bat. Because she had dodged, it was her arm and not her head. The force of the blow still sent Dharthi sliding over the side of the limb, clutching and failing to clutch, falling in her adaptshell. She heard the swamp-tiger land where she had been, heard the bough crack, saw it give and swing down after her. The swamp-tiger squalled, scrabbling, its littermate making abrupt noises of retreat as well—and it was falling beside Dharthi, twisting in midair, clutching a nearby branch and there was a heaving unhappy sound from the tree's structure and she fell alone, arm numb, head spinning.

The adaptshell saved her. It, too, twisted in midair, righted itself, reached out and grasped with her good arm. This branch held, but it bent, and she slammed into the next branch down, taking the impact on the same arm the tiger had injured. She didn't know for a moment if that green sound was a branch breaking or her—and then she did know, because inside the shell she could feel how her right arm hung limp, meaty, flaccid—humerus shattered.

She was dangling right beside her cocoon, as it happened. She used the folds of cloth to pull herself closer to the trunk, then commanded it to detach and retract. She found one of the proximity alarms and discovered that the damp had gotten into it. It didn't register her presence, either.

Venus.

She was stowing it one-handed in one of the shell's cargo pockets, warily watching for the return of either tiger, when the voice burst into her head.

"Dhar!"

"Don't worry," she told Kraken. "Just hurt my arm getting away from a swamp-tiger. Everything's fine."

"Hurt or broke? Wait, *swamp-tiger?*"

"It's gone now. I scared it off." She wasn't sure, but she wasn't about to admit that. "Tell Zamin the juveniles hunt in pairs."

"A *pair* of swamp-tigers?"

"I'm fine," Dharthi said, and clamped down the link.

She climbed down one-handed, relying on the shell more than she would have liked. She did not see either tiger again.

At the bottom, on the jungle floor, she limped, but she ran.

Four runs and four sleeps later—the sleeps broken, confused spirals of exhaustion broken by fractured snatches of rest—the brightest patch of pewter in the sky had shifted visibly to the east. Noon had become afternoon, and the long Cytherean day was becoming Dharthi's enemy. She climbed trees regularly to look for signs of geometrical shapes informing the growth of the forest, and every time she did, she glanced at that brighter smear of cloud sliding down the sky and frowned.

Dharthi—assisted by her adaptshell—had come some five hundred kilometers westward. Maxwell Montes was lost behind her now, in cloud and mist and haze and behind the shoulder of the world. She was moving fast for someone creeping, climbing, and swinging through the jungle, although she was losing time because she hadn't turned the adaptshell loose to forage on its own since the swamp-tiger. She needed it to support and knit her arm—the shell fused to itself across the front and made a seamless cast and sling—and for the pain suppressants it fed her along with its prechewed pap. The bones were going to knit all wrong, of course, and when she got back, they'd have to grow her a new one, but that was pretty minor stuff.

The shell filtered toxins and allergens out of the biologicals it ingested, reheaving some of the carbohydrates, protein, and fat to produce a bland, faintly sweet, nutrient-rich paste that was safe for Dharthi's consumption. She sucked it from a tube as needed, squashing it between tongue and palate to soften it before swallowing each sticky, dull mouthful.

Water was never a problem—at least, the problem was having too much of it, not any lack. This was *Venus*. Water squelched in every footstep across the jungle floor. It splashed on the adaptshell's head and infiltrated every cargo pocket. The only things that stayed dry were the ones that were treated to be hydrophobic, and the coating was starting to wear off some of those. Dharthi's cocoon was permanently damp inside. Even her shell, which molded to her skin perfectly, felt alternately muggy or clammy depending on how it was comping temperature.

The adaptshell also filtered some of the fatigue toxins out of Dharthi's system. But not enough. Sleep was sleep, and she wasn't getting enough of it.

The landscape was becoming dreamy and strange. The forest never thinned, never gave way to another landscape— except the occasional swath of swampland—but now, occasionally, twisted fumaroles rose up through it, smoking towers of orange and ochre that sent wisps of steam drifting between scalded, yellowed leaves. Dharthi saw one of the geysers erupt; she noticed that over it, and where the spray would tend to blow, there was a hole in the canopy. But vines grew right up the knobby accreted limestone on the windward side.

Five runs and five . . . five *attempts* at a sleep later, Dharthi began to accept that she desperately, *desperately* wanted to go home.

She wouldn't, of course.

Her arm hurt less. That was a positive thing. Other than that, she was exhausted and damp and cold, and some kind of thick, liver-colored leech kept trying to attach itself to the adaptshell's legs. A species new to science, probably, and Dharthi didn't give a damn.

Kraken tried to contact her every few hours.

She didn't answer because she knew if she did, she would ask Kraken to come and get her. And then she'd never be able to look another living Cytherean in the face again.

It wasn't like Venus had a big population.

Dharthi was going to prove herself or die trying.

The satlink from Zamin, though, she took at once. They chatted about swamp-tigers—Zamin, predictably, was fascinated, and told Dharthi she'd write it up and give full credit to Dharthi as observer. "Tell Hazards, too," Dharthi said, as an afterthought.

"Oh, yeah," Zamin replied. "I guess it is at that. Dhar . . . are you okay out there?"

"Arm hurts," Dharthi admitted. "The drugs are working, though. I could use some sleep in a bed. A dry bed."

"Yeah," Zamin said. "I bet you could. You know Kraken's beside herself, don't you?"

"She'll know if I die," Dharthi said.

"She's a good friend," Zamin said. A good trick, making it about her, rather than Kraken or Dharthi or Kraken *and* Dharthi. "I worry about her. You know she's been unbelievably kind to me, generous through some real roughness. She's—"

"She's generous," Dharthi said. "She's a genius and a charismatic. I know it better than most. Look, I should pay attention to where my feet are, before I break the other arm. Then you *will* have to extract me. And won't I feel like an idiot then?"

"Dhar—"

She broke the sat. She felt funny about it for hours afterward, but at least when she crawled into her cocoon that rest period, adaptshell and all, she was so exhausted she slept.

She woke up sixteen hours and twelve minutes later, disoriented and sore in every joint. After ninety seconds she recollected herself enough to figure out where she was—in her shell, in her cocoon, fifty meters up in the Ishtarean canopy, struggling out of an exhaustion and painkiller haze—and when she was, with a quick check of the time.

She stowed and packed by rote, slithered down a strangler vine, stood in contemplation on the forest floor. Night was coming—the long night—and while she still had ample time to get back to base camp without calling for a pickup, every day now cut into her margin of safety.

She ran.

Rested, she almost had the resources to deal with it when Kraken spoke in her mind, so she gritted her teeth and said, "Yes, dear?"

"Hi," Kraken said. There was a pause, in which Dharthi sensed a roil of suppressed emotion. Thump. Thump. As long as her feet kept running, nothing could catch her. That sharpness in her chest was just tight breath from running, she was sure. "Zamin says she's worried about you."

Dharthi snorted. She had slept too much, but now that the kinks were starting to shake out of her body, she realized that the rest had done her good. "You know what Zamin wanted to talk to me about? You. How *wonderful* you are. How caring. How made of charm." Dharthi sighed. "How often do people take you aside to gush about how wonderful I am?"

"You might," Kraken said, "be surprised."

"It's *hard* being the partner of somebody so perfect. When did you ever *struggle* for anything? You have led a charmed life, Kraken, from birth to now."

"Did I?" Kraken said. "I've been lucky, I don't deny. But I've worked hard. And lived through things. You think I'm perfect because that's how you see me, in between bouts of hating everything I do."

"It's how everyone sees you. If status in the afterlife is determined by praises sung, yours is assured."

"I wish you could hear how they talk about you. People hold you in awe, love."

Thump. Thump. The rhythm of her feet soothed her, when nothing else could. She was even getting resigned to the ceaseless damp, which collected between her toes, between her buttocks, behind her ears. "They *love* you. They tolerated me. No one *ever* saw what you saw in me."

"I did," Kraken replied. "And quit acting as if I *were* somehow perfect. You've been quick enough to remind me on occasion of how I'm not. This thing, this need to prove yourself . . . it's a sophipathology, Dhar. I love you. But this is not a healthy pattern of thought. Ambition is great, but you go beyond ambition. Nothing you do is ever good enough. You deny your own accomplishments and inflate those of everyone around you. You grew up in Aphrodite, and there are only thirty thousand people on the whole damned planet. You *can't* be surprised that, brilliant as you are, some of us are just as smart and capable as you are."

Thump. Thump—

She was watching ahead even as she was arguing, though her attention wasn't on it. That automatic caution was all that kept her from running off the edge of the world.

Before her—below her—a great cliff dropped away. The trees in the valley soared up. But this was not a tangled jungle: it was a climax forest, a species of tree taller and more densely canopied than any Dharthi had seen. The light below those trees was thick and crepuscular, and though she could hear the rain drumming on their leaves, very little of it dripped through.

Between them, until the foliage cut off her line of sight, Dharthi could see the familiar, crescent-shaped roofs of aboriginal Cytherean structures, some of them half-consumed in the accretions from the forest of smoking stone towers that rose among the trees.

She stood on the cliff edge overlooking the thing she had come half a world by airship and a thousand kilometers on foot to find, and pebbles crumbled from beneath the toes of her adaptshell, and she raised a hand to her face as if Kraken were really speaking into a device in her ear canal instead of into the patterns of electricity in her brain. The cavernous ruin stretched farther than her eyes could see—even dark-adapted, once the shell made the transition for her. Even in this strange, open forest filled with colorful, flitting, flying things.

"Love?"

"Yes?" Kraken said, then went silent and waited.

"I'll call you back," Dharthi said. "I just discovered the Lost City of Ishtar."

Dharthi walked among the ruins. It was not all she'd hoped.

Well, it was *more* than she had hoped. She rappelled down, and as soon as her shell sank ankle deep in the leaf litter she was overcome by a hush of awe. She turned from the wet, lichen-heavy cliff, scuffed with the temporary marks of her feet, and craned back to stare up at the forest of geysers and fumaroles and trees that stretched west and south as far as she could see. The cliff behind her was basalt—another root of the volcano whose shield was lost in mists and trees. This . . . this was the clearest air she had ever seen.

The trees were planted in rows, as perfectly arranged as pillars in some enormous Faerie hall. The King of the Giants lived here, and Dharthi was Jack, except she had climbed down the beanstalk for a change.

The trunks were as big around as ten men with linked hands, tall enough that their foliage vanished in the clouds overhead. Trees on Earth, Dharthi knew, were limited in height by capillary action: how high could they lift water to their thirsty leaves?

Perhaps these Cytherean giants drank from the clouds as well as the soil.

"Oh," Dharthi said, and the spaces between the trees both hushed and elevated her voice, so it sounded clear and thin. "Wait until Zamin sees these."

Dharthi suddenly realized that if they were a new species, she would get to name them.

They were so immense, and dominated the light so completely, that very little grew under them. Some native fernmorphs, some mosses. Lichens shaggy on their enormous trunks and roots. Where one had fallen, a miniature Cytherean rain forest had sprung up in the admitted light, and here there was drumming, dripping rain, rain falling like strings of glass beads. It was a muddy little puddle of the real world in this otherwise alien quiet.

The trees stood like attentive gods, their faces so high above her she could not even hear the leaves rustle.

Dharthi forced herself to turn away from the trees, at last, and begin examining the structures. There were dozens of them—hundreds—sculpted out of the same translucent, mysterious, impervious material as all of the ruins in Aphrodite. But this was six, ten times the scale of any such ruin. Maybe vaster. She needed a team. She needed a mapping expedition. She needed a base camp much closer to this. She needed to give the site a name—

She needed to get back to work.

She remembered, then, to start documenting. The structures—she could not say, of course, which were habitations, which served other purposes—or even if the aboriginals had used the same sorts of divisions of usage that human beings did—were of a variety of sizes and heights. They were all designed as arcs or crescents, however—singly, in series, or in several cases as a sort of stepped spectacular with each lower, smaller level fitting inside the curve of a higher, larger one. Several had obvious access points, open to the air, and Dharthi reminded herself sternly that going inside unprepared was not just a bad idea because of risk to herself, but because she might disturb the evidence.

She clenched her good hand and stayed outside.

Her shell had been recording, of course—now she began to narrate, and to satlink the files home. No fanfare, just an upload. Data and more data—and the soothing knowledge that while she was hogging her allocated bandwidth to send, nobody could call her to ask questions, or congratulate, or—

Nobody except Kraken, with whom she was entangled for life.

"Hey," her partner said in her head. "You found it."

"I found it," Dharthi said, pausing the narration but not the load. There was plenty of visual, olfactory, auditory, and kinesthetic data being sent even without her voice.

"How does it feel to be vindicated?"

She could hear the throb of Kraken's pride in her mental voice. She tried not to let it make her feel patronized. Kraken did not mean to sound parental, proprietary. That was Dharthi's own baggage.

"Vindicated?" She looked back over her shoulder. The valley was quiet and dark. A fumarole vented with a rushing hiss and a curve of wind brought the scent of sulfur to sting her eyes.

"Famous?"

"*Famous?*"

"Hell, Terran-famous. The homeworld is going to hear about this in oh, about five minutes, given light lag—unless somebody who's got an entangled partner back there shares sooner. You've just made the biggest Cytherean archaeological discovery in the past hundred days, love. And probably the next hundred. You are *not* going to have much of a challenge getting allocations now."

"I—"

"You worked hard for it."

"It feels like . . ." Dharthi picked at the bridge of her nose with a thumbnail. The skin was peeling off in flakes: too much time in her shell was wreaking havoc with the natural oil balance of her skin. "It feels like I should be figuring out the next thing."

"The next thing," Kraken said. "How about coming home to me? Have you proven yourself to yourself yet?"

Dharthi shrugged. She felt like a petulant child. She knew she was acting like one. "How about to you?"

"*I* never doubted you. You had nothing to prove to me. The self-sufficiency thing is your pathology, love, not mine. I love you as you are, not because I think I can make you perfect. I just wish you could see your strengths as well as you see your flaws— one second, bit of a squall up ahead—I'm back."

"Are you on an airship?" *Was she coming here?*

"Just an airjeep."

Relief *and* a stab of disappointment. You wouldn't get from Aphrodite to Ishtar in an AJ.

Well, Dharthi thought. *Looks like I might be walking home.*

And when she got there? Well, she wasn't quite ready to ask Kraken for help yet.

She would stay, she decided, two more sleeps. That would still give her time to get back to base camp before nightfall, and it wasn't as if her arm could get any *more* messed up between now and then. She was turning in a slow circle, contemplating where to sling her cocoon—the branches were really too high to be convenient—when the unmistakable low hum of an aircar broke the rustling silence of the enormous trees.

It dropped through the canopy, polished-copper belly reflecting a lensed fish-eye of forest, and settled down ten meters from Dharthi. Smiling, frowning, biting her lip, she went to meet it. The upper half was black hydrophobic polymer: she'd gotten a lift in one just like it at Ishtar base camp before she set out.

The hatch opened. In the cramped space within, Kraken sat behind the control board. She half rose, crouched under the low roof, came to the hatch, held out her right hand, reaching down to Dharthi. Dharthi looked at Kraken's hand, and Kraken sheepishly switched it for the other one. The left one, which Dharthi could take without strain.

"So I was going to take you to get your arm looked at," Kraken said.

"You spent your allocations—"

Kraken shrugged. "Gonna send me away?"

"This time," she said, ". . . no."

Kraken wiggled her fingers.

Dharthi took her hand, stepped up into the GEV, realized how exhausted she was as she settled back in a chair and suddenly could not lift her head without the assistance of her shell. She wondered if she should have hugged Kraken. She realized that she was sad that Kraken hadn't tried to hug her. But, well. The shell was sort of in the way.

Resuming her chair, Kraken fixed her eyes on the forward screen. "Hey. You did it."

"Hey. I did." She wished she felt it. Maybe she was too tired.

Maybe Kraken was right, and Dharthi should see about working on that.

Her eyes dragged shut. So heavy. The soft motion of the aircar lulled her. Its soundproofing had degraded, but even the noise wouldn't be enough to keep her awake. Was this what safe felt like? "Something else."

"I'm listening."

"If you don't mind, I was thinking of naming a tree after you."

"That's good," Kraken said. "I was thinking of naming a kid after you."

Dharthi grinned without opening her eyes. "We should use my Y chromosome. Color blindness on the X."

"Ehn. Ys are half-atrophied already. We'll just use two Xs," Kraken said decisively. "Maybe we'll get a tetrachromat."

JOE R. LANSDALE

Prolific Texas writer Joe R. Lansdale has won the Edgar Award, the British Fantasy Award, the American Horror Award, the American Mystery Award, the International Crime Writers' Award, and six Bram Stoker Awards. Although perhaps best known for horror/thrillers such as *The Nightrunners, Bubba Ho-Tep, The Bottoms, The God of the Razor,* and *The Drive-In,* he also writes the popular *Hap Collins and Leonard Pine* mystery series—*Savage Season, Mucho Mojo, The Two-Bear Mambo, Bad Chili, Rumble Tumble, Captains Outrageous, Devil Red,* and *Hyenas*—as well as Western novels such as *Texas Night Riders* and *Blood Dance,* and totally unclassifiable cross-genre novels such as *Zeppelins West, The Magic Wagon,* and *Flaming London.* His other novels include *Dead in the West, The Big Blow, Sunset and Sawdust, Act of Love, Freezer Burn, Waltz of Shadows, The Drive-In 2: Not Just One of Them Sequels, Leather Maiden, Deranged by Choice,* and *Edge of Dark Water.* He has also contributed novels to series such as *Batman* and *Tarzan.* His many short stories have been collected in *By Bizarre Hands, Tight Little Stitches in a Dead Man's Back, The Shadows, Kith and Kin, The Long Ones, Stories by Mama Lansdale's Youngest Boy, Bestsellers Guaranteed, On the Far Side of the Cadillac Desert with Dead Folks, Electric Gumbo, Writer of the Purple Rage, Fist Full of Stories, Steppin' Out, Summer '68, Bumper Crop, The Good, the Bad, and the Indifferent, Selected Stories by Joe R. Lansdale, For a Few Stories More, Mad Dog Summer and Other Stories, The King and Other Stories, Deadman's Road,* an omnibus, *Flaming Zeppelins: The Adventures of Ned the Seal, Shadows West* (with John L. Lansdale), *Trapped in the Saturday Matinee,* and *High Cotton: the Collected Stories of Joe R. Lansdale.* As editor, he has produced the anthologies *The*

Best of the West, *Retro Pulp Tales*, *Son of Retro Pulp Tales*, *Razored Saddles* (with Pat LoBrutto), *Dark at Heart: All New Tales of Dark Suspense* (with wife Karen Lansdale), *The Horror Hall of Fame: The Stoker Winners*, the Robert E. Howard tribute anthology, *Cross Plains Universe* (with Scott A. Cupp), *Crucified Dreams,* and *The Urban Fantasy Anthology* (edited with Peter S. Beagle). An anthology in tribute to Lansdale's work is *Lords of the Razor.* His most recent books are a new Hap and Leonard novel, *Dead Aim; The Thicket; The Ape Man's Brother;* and a big retrospective collection, *Bleeding Shadows.* He lives with his family in Nacogdoches, Texas.

Here he sweeps us along with a man who is wrenched out of his proper place and time and thrown headlong into another world, one that proves even *more* dangerous than going down with the sinking *Titantic* . . .

The Wizard of the Trees

JOE R. LANSDALE

I AM HERE BECAUSE OF A TERRIBLE HEADACHE. I KNOW you will want more of an explanation than that, but I can't give it to you. I can only say I was almost killed when the great ship *Titanic* went down. There was an explosion, a boiler blowing, perhaps. I can't say. When the ship dove down and broke in half, I felt as if I broke in half with it.

An object hit me in the head underwater. I remember there was something down there with me. Not anyone on the ship, not a corpse, but something. I remember its face, if you can call it that: full of teeth and eyes, big and luminous, lit up by a light from below, then I was gasping water into my lungs, and this thing was pulling me toward a glowing pool of whirling illumination. It dragged me into warmth and into light, and my last sight of the thing was a flipping of its fishlike tail; and then my head exploded.

Or so it seemed.

When I awoke, I was lying in a warm, muddy mire, almost floating, almost sinking. I grabbed at some roots jutting out from the shoreline and pulled myself out of it. I lay there with my headache for a while, warming myself in the sunlight, then the headache began to pass. I rolled over on my belly and looked at the pool of mud. It was a big pool. In fact, pool is incorrect. It was like a great lake of mud. I have no idea how I managed to be there, and that is the simple truth of it. I still don't know. It felt like a dream.

With some difficulty I had managed a bunk in steerage on the *Titanic*, heading back home to my country, the United States of America. I had played out my string in England, thought I might go back and journey out West where I had punched cows and shot buffalo for the railroad. I had even killed a couple of men in self-defense, and dime novels had been written about me, the Black Rider of the Plains. But that was mostly lies. The only thing they got right was the color of my skin. I'm half-black, half-Cherokee. In the dime novels I was described as mostly white, which is a serious lie. One look at me will tell you different.

I was a roughrider with Buffalo Bill's Wild West Show, and when it arrived in England to perform, they went back and I had stayed on. I liked it for a while, but as they say, there's no place like home. Not that I had really had one, but we're speaking generally here.

I struggled to my feet and looked around. Besides the lake of mud, there were trees. And I do mean trees. They rose up tall and mighty all around the lake, and there didn't seem anything to do but to go among them. The mud I wouldn't go back into. I couldn't figure what had happened to me, what had grabbed me and pulled me into that glowing whirlpool, but the idea of its laying a grip on me again was far less than inviting. It had hauled me here, wherever here was, and had retreated, left me to my own devices.

The mud I had ended up in was shallow, but I knew the rest of the lake wasn't. I knew this because as I looked out over the vast mire, I saw a great beast moving in it; a lizard, I guess you'd call it. At least that was my first thought, then I remembered the bones they had found out in Montana some years back and how they were called dinosaurs. I had read a little about it, and that's what I thought when I saw this thing in the mud, rising up gray and green of skin, lurching up and dipping down, dripping mud that plopped bright in the sunlight. Down it went, out of sight, and up again, and when it came up a third time it had a beast in its mouth; a kind of giant slick, purple-skinned seal, its blood oozing like strawberry jam from between the monster's teeth.

It may seem as if I'm nonchalant about all this, but the truth is I'm telling this well after the fact and have had time to accept it. But let me jump ahead a bit.

The world I am on is Venus, and now it is my world.

My arrival was not the only mystery. I am a man of forty-five, and in good shape, and I like to think of sound mind. But good as I felt at that age, I felt even better here on this warm, damp, tree-covered world. I would soon discover there was an even greater mystery I could not uncover. But I will come to that even if I will not arrive at a true explanation.

I pulled off my clothes, which were caked with mud, and shook them out. I had lost both my shoes when the ship went down; they had been sucked off me by the ocean's waters with the same enthusiasm as a kid sucking a peppermint stick. I stood naked with my clothes under my arm, my body covered in mud, my hair matted with it. I must have looked pretty foolish, but there I was with my muddy clothes and nowhere to go.

I glanced back at the muddy lake, saw the great lizard and his lunch were gone. The muddy lake, out in the center, appeared to boil. My guess was it was hot in the middle, warm at the edges. My host, the thing that had brought me here, had fortunately chosen one of the warm areas for me to surface.

I picked a wide path between the trees and took to the trail. It was shadowy on the path. I supposed it had been made by animals, and from the prints, some of them very large. Had I gone too far off the path I could easily have waded into darkness.

There was little to no brush beneath the trees because there wasn't enough sunlight to feed them. Unusual birds and indefinable critters flittered and leaped about in the trees and raced across my trail. I walked on for some time with no plans, no shoes, my clothes tucked neatly under my arm like a pet dog.

Now, if you think I was baffled, you are quite correct. For a while I tried to figure out what had nabbed me under the waters and taken me through the whirling light and left me almost out of the mud, then disappeared. No answers presented themselves, and I let it go and set my thoughts to survival. I can do that. I have a practical streak. One of the most practical things was I was still alive, wherever I was. I had survived in the wilderness before. Had gone up in the Rocky Mountains in the dead of winter with nothing but a rifle, a knife, and a small bag of possible. I had survived, come down in the spring with beaver and fox furs to sell.

I figured I could do that, I could make it here as well, though later on I will confess to an occasional doubt. I had had some close calls before, including a run-in with Wyatt Earp that almost turned ugly, a run-in with Johnny Ringo that left him dead under a tree, and a few things not worth mentioning, but this world made all of those adventures look mild.

Wandering in among those trees, my belly began to gnaw, and I figured I'd best find something I could eat, so I began looking about. Up in the trees near where I stood there were great balls of purple fruit and birds about my size, multicolored and feathered, with beaks like daggers. They were pecking at those fruits. I figured if they could eat them, so could I.

My next order of business was to shinny up one of those trees and lay hold of my next meal. I put my clothes under it, the trunk of which was as big around as a locomotive, grabbed a low-hanging limb, and scuttled up to where I could see a hanging fruit about the size of a buffalo's head. It proved an easy climb because the limbs were so broad and so plentiful.

The birds above me noticed my arrival but ignored me. I crawled out on the limb bearing my chosen meal, got hold of it, and yanked it loose, nearly sending myself off the limb in the process. It would have been a good and hard fall, but I liked to think all that soft earth down there, padded with loam, leaves, and rot, would have given me a soft landing.

I got my back against the tree trunk, took hold of the fruit, and tried to bite into it. It was as hard as leather. I looked about. There was a small broken limb jutting out above me. I stood on my perch, lifted the fruit, and slammed it into where the limb was broke off. It stuck there, like a fat tick with a knife through it. Juice started gushing out of the fruit. I lifted my face below it and let the nectar flood into my mouth and splash over me. It was somewhat sour and tangy in taste, but I was convinced that if it didn't poison me, I wouldn't die of hunger. I tugged on the fruit until it ripped apart. Inside it was pithy and good to eat. I scooped it out with my hands and filled up on it.

I had just finished my repast when above me I heard a noise, and when I looked up, what I saw was to me the most amazing sight yet in this wild new world.

Silver.

A bird.

But no, it was a kind of flying sled. I heard it before I saw it, a hum like a giant bee, and when I looked up the sunlight glinted off it, blinding me for a moment. When I looked back, the sled tore through the trees, spun about, and came to light with a smack in the fork of a massive limb. It was at an angle. I could see there were seats on the sled, and there were people in the seats, and there was a kind of shield of glass at the front of the craft. The occupants were all black of hair and yellow of skin, but my amazement at this was nothing compared to what amazed me next.

Another craft, similar in nature, came shining into view. It glided to a stop, gentle and swift, like a gas-filled balloon. It floated in the air next to the limb where the other had come to a stop. It was directed by a man sitting in an open seat who was like those in the other machine, a man with yellow skin and black hair. Another man, similar in appearance, sat behind him, his biggest distinction a large blue-green half-moon jewel on a chain hung around his neck. This fellow leaped to his feet, revealing himself nude other than for the sword harness and the medallion, drew a thin sword strapped across his back, dropped down on the other craft, and started hacking at the driver, who barely staggered to his feet in time to defend himself. The warrior's swords clanged together. The other two occupants of the wrecked craft had climbed out of the wells of their seats with drawn swords and were about to come to their comrades' aid when something even more fantastic occurred.

Flapping down from the sky were a half dozen winged men, carrying swords and battle-axes. Except for the harness that would serve to hold their weapons, and a small, hard, leather-looking pouch, they, like the others, were without clothes. Their eyes were somewhat to the side of their heads, there were beaklike growths jutting from their faces, and their skin was milk-white, and instead of hair were feathers. The colors of the feathers were varied. Their targets were the yellow men in the shiny machine on the tremendous tree limb.

It became clear then that the man with the necklace, though obviously not of the winged breed, was no doubt on their side. He skillfully dueled with the driver of the limb-beached craft, parried deftly, then with a shout ran his sword through his opponent's chest. The mortally wounded warrior dropped his weapon and fell backward off his foe's sword, collapsed across the fore of his vessel.

The two warriors in league with the dead man were fighting valiantly, but the numbers against them were overwhelming. The man with the medallion, or amulet, stood on the fore of the craft, straddling the carcass of his kill, and it was then that I got a clear view of his face. It has been said, and normally I believe it, that you can't judge someone by his appearance. But I tell you that I have never seen anyone with such an evil countenance as this man. It wasn't that his features were all that unusual, but there was an air about him that projected pure villainy. It was as if there was another person inside of him, one black of heart and devious of mind, and it seemed that spectral person was trying to pressure itself to the surface. I have never before or since had that feeling about anyone, not even Comanche and Apache warriors who had tried to kill me during my service with the Buffalo Soldiers.

It was then that one of the two defenders, having driven back a winged warrior he had been dueling with, pulled with his free hand a pistol. It was a crude-looking thing, reminiscent of an old flintlock. He raised the pistol in the direction of his adversary and fired. The pistol's bark was like the cough of a tubercular man. The winged man spouted blood, dropped his sword, brought both hands to his face, then relaxed and fell, diving headfirst like a dart. As the winged man dove between the limbs near me, crashed through some leaves, and plummeted to the ground, the sword he dropped stuck conveniently in the limb before me. I took hold of it thinking that now I had a weapon for self-defense, and that it was a good time to depart. I told myself that this fight, whatever it was about, was not my fight. They were so busy with one another, I had not even been seen. So, of course, casting aside common sense, I decided I had to get into the thick of it.

It might well have been the fact that the men in the craft were outnumbered, but I must admit that one glance at the man with the jeweled medallion and I knew where my sentiments lay. I know how that sounds, but I assure you, had you seen his face, you would have felt exactly the same way.

Why I thought one more sword might make a difference, considering the horde of winged men assisting the evil-faced man was enormous, I can't explain to you. But with the thin, light sword in my teeth, I began to climb upward to aid them.

This is when I realized certain things, certain abilities that I had sensed upon arrival, but were now proving to be true. I felt strong, agile, not only as I might have felt twenty years earlier but in a manner I had never experienced. I moved easily, squirrel-like is what I thought, and in no time I reached the craft caught in the fork of the limb.

The winged men were fluttering about the two survivors like flies on spilled molasses. The man with the necklace had paused to watch, no longer feeling the need to engage. He observed as his birds flapped and cawed and swung their weapons at his own kind. It was then that he saw me, rising up over the lip of the limb, finding my feet.

I removed the sword from my teeth and sprang forward with a stabbing motion, piercing the heart of one of the winged attackers. It fluttered, twisted, and fell.

The yellow-skinned couple glanced at me but accepted my help without question or protest for obvious reasons. I must have been a sight. Naked, having left my clothes at the base of the great tree. My skin and hair matted with mud. I looked like a wild man. And it was in that moment I noticed something I should have noticed right off, but the positioning and the leaves and smaller limbs of the tree had blocked my complete view. One of the yellow skins was a woman. She was lean and long and her hair was in a rough cut, as if someone had just gathered it up in a wad and chopped it off with a knife at her shoulders. She was not nude as her opponents were. She wore, as did her companion, a sort of black skirt, and a light covering of black leather breast armor. She had a delicate, but unquestionably feminine shape. When I saw her face I almost forgot what I was doing. Her bright green, almond-shaped eyes sucked me into them. I was so nearly lost in them that a winged man with an axe nearly took my head off. I ducked the axe swing, lunged forward, stretching my leg way out, thrusting with my sword, sticking him in the gut. When I pulled my sword back, his guts spilled out along with a gush of blood. As he fell out of view, more of the things came down from the sky and buzzed around us, beating their wings. They were plenty, but it was soon obvious our skills with weapons were superior to theirs. They used the swords and axes crudely. They handled them with less skill than a child with a mop and a broom.

My partners—such as they were—were well versed in the use of the blade, as was I, having learned swordsmanship from an older man while I was among the Buffalo Soldiers. My teacher was a black man, like me, and had once lived in France. There he had been trained well in the use of the steel, and I in turn had learned this skill from him. So it was not surprising that in short order we had killed most of our attackers and sent the others soaring away in fear. The necklace-wearing man, who had been observing, now joined in, attempting to take me out of the fray, and I engaged him. He was good with the sword, quick. But I was quicker and more skilled, blessed with whatever strange abilities this world gave me. He caused me a moment's trouble, but it only took me a few parries to grasp his method, which was not too unlike my own. A high-and-low attack, a way of using the eyes to mislead the opponent. I was gradually getting the better of him when his driver coasted his machine next to the limb. My opponent gave out with a wild cry, came at me with a surge of renewed energy, driving me back slightly, then he wheeled, leaped onto his machine, and slid quickly into his seat, smooth as a woman slipping sleek fingers into a calfskin glove. The sled with the two yellow men in it darted away.

I turned, lowered my bloodstained blade, and looked at those whose side I had joined. The woman spoke, and her words, though simple, hit me like a train.

She said, "Thank you."

It was another side effect of my arrival here. I was not only stronger and more agile, I could understand a language I had never heard before. As soon as the words left her mouth they translated in my head. It was so immediate it was as if their language were my native tongue.

"You're welcome," I said. This seemed a trite thing to say, me standing there on a limb holding a sword, mud-covered and naked, with my business hanging out, but I was even more astonished to have my words understood by her without any true awareness that I was speaking my own language.

"Who are you?" the woman asked.

"Jack Davis," I said. "Formerly of the United States Buffalo Soldiers."

"The United States?" she asked.

"It's a bit hard to explain."

"You are covered in mud," the man said, sheathing his sword.

"You are correct," I said. I decided to keep it simple. "I fell into a mud lake."

The man grinned. "That must have took some doing."

"I consider myself a man of special talents," I said.

The young woman turned her head in a curious fashion, glanced down at me. "Is your skin black, or is it painted?"

I realized what part of me she was studying. Under all that mud had I been Irish and not part Negro, my blush would have been as bright as the sinking sun. Before long it would become obvious to me that on this world nudity was not something shameful or indecent in their minds. Clothes for them were ornaments, or were designed to protect them from the weather, but they were not bothered by the sight of the flesh.

"Correct," I said. "I am black. Very much so."

"We have heard of black men," she said. "But we have never seen them."

"There are others like me?" I said.

"We have heard that this is so," said the woman. "In the far south, though I suspect they are less muddy."

"Again," said the man, "we thank you. We were very much outnumbered and your sword was appreciated."

"You seemed to be doing well without me, but I was glad to help," I said.

"You flatter us," he said.

"I am Devel, and this is my sister, Jerrel."

I nodded at them. By this time Devel had turned to the sled and to the dead man lying on its front, bleeding. He bent down and touched his face. "Bandel is dead by Tordo's hand, the traitor."

"I'm sorry," I said.

"He was a warrior, and there is nothing else to say," said Jerrel, but she and Devel, despite their matter-of-fact tone, were obviously hurt and moved. That's why what happened next was so surprising.

Devel dragged the corpse to the edge of the sled, then the limb, and without ceremony, flipped it over the side. "To the soil again," he said.

This seemed more than unusual and disrespectful, but I was later to learn this is their custom. When one of their number dies, and since they live in high cities and populate the trees, this is a common method. If they die on the ground, they are left where they fell. This treatment was considered an honor.

I processed this slowly but kept my composure. My survival might depend on it. I said, "May I ask who these men were and why they were trying to kill you?"

Jerrel glanced at Devel, said, "He chose to help us without question. He is bonded to us in blood."

"True," Devel said, but I could tell he wasn't convinced.

Jerrel, however, decided to speak. "They are the Varnin. And we are warriors of Sheldan. Prince and princess, actually. We are going to their country, in pursuit of the talisman."

"You're warring over a trinket?" I said.

"It is far more than a trinket," she said. "And since there are only us two, it is hardly a war."

"I would call in reinforcements."

She nodded. "If there were time, but there is not."

She did not elaborate. We left it at that for the time being, and set about releasing the silver craft from the limbs where it had lodged. This seemed like a precarious job to me, but I helped them do it. The craft proved light as air. When it came loose of the limbs it didn't fall, but began to hum and float. Devel climbed into the front-seat position, where the dead man had been, touched a silver rod, and the machine hummed louder than before.

Jerrel climbed into one of the seats behind him, said, "Come with us."

Devel glanced at her.

"We can't leave him," she said. "He looks to be lost."

"You have no idea," I said.

"And he helped us when we needed it," she said. "He risked his life."

"We have our mission," he said.

"We will find a safe place for him," she said. "We still have a long distance to go. We can not just abandon him."

This discussion had gone on as if I were not standing there.

I said, "I would appreciate your taking me somewhere other than this tree."

Devel nodded, but I could tell he wasn't entirely convinced.

I stepped into the machine, took a seat. Devel looked back at me. I could tell this was a development he was not fond of, in spite of the fact I had taken their side in the fight.

But he said nothing. He turned forward, touched the rod. The machine growled softly, glided away through a cluster of leaves and limbs. I ducked so as not to be struck by them. When I looked up, the machine had risen high in the sky, above the tree line, up into the sunny blue. I was astonished. It was such a delicate and agile craft, so far ahead of what we had achieved back home. This made me consider that, interestingly enough, their understanding of firearms was far behind ours. There was a part of me that felt that it would be nice if it stayed that way. It seemed humans and bird-men were quite capable of doing enough damage with swords and axes. As for the pistol Devel had fired, he had discarded it as if it had been nothing more than a worn-out handkerchief.

I glanced over the side, saw below all manner of creatures. There were huge, leather-winged monsters flying beneath us and in the clear areas between the trees. On the ground in the rare open spaces I could see monstrous lizards of assorted colors. The beasts looked up at the sound of our humming machine, their mouths falling open as if in surprise, revealing great rows of massive teeth. We passed over hot, muddy lakes boiling and churning with heat. Huge snakes slithered through the mud and onto the land and into the trees. It was beautiful and frightening. In a short time I had survived the sinking of a great ocean liner, an uncommon arrival in a hot mud lake, climbed a tree to eat, found a fight against a yellow man with a strange talisman who was assisted by winged creatures, and had taken sides in the fight. Now, here I was, lost and confused, flying above massive trees in a featherlight craft at tremendous speed, my body feeling more amazing than ever, as if someone had split open my skin and stuck a twenty-year-old inside me. It made my head spin.

"Exactly where are you going?" I had to raise my voice to be heard above the wind.

"Perhaps it is best we do not speak of it," Devel said. "You aided us, but our mission is personal. You know what you know about the talisman and need know no more."

"Understood, but where are you taking me?"

"I am uncertain," Devel said.

"Very well," I said, not wishing to be put out of the craft and left to my own devices. I needed to try to stay with them as long as I could to learn more about this world. Here was better than wandering the forest below; how much better off remained to be seen. As an old sergeant told me around a wad of chewing tobacco once, "If you ain't dead, you're living, and that's a good thing." It was one of the few bits of advice he had given me I had taken to heart, as he was always jealous of my education, which he called white man's talk. I had been blessed with a Cherokee mother who had learned reading and writing in white man's schools and had become a teacher. She always said education didn't belong to anyone other than the one who was willing to take it. She also said education was more than words and marks on paper. She taught me the customs of the Cherokee, taught me tracking, about living in the wild. All the things I might need to survive.

That said, I preferred the comfort of the flying sled to the rawness of the wild world below. This way I had time to consider and plan, though I must admit my considerations and planning were not accomplishing a lot. It was more as if wheels were spinning inside my head but wouldn't gain traction.

Besides, let me be entirely honest. The woman was why I

wanted to remain. I was smitten. Those green eyes were like cool pools and I wanted to dive right into them. I wanted to believe there had been some kind of connection on her part, but considering my current appearance the only person or thing that might love me was a hog that had mistaken me for a puddle to wallow in.

I can't say how long we flew, but I feel certain it was hours. I know that exhaustion claimed me after a while, the cool wind blowing against me, me snug in my seat. I might have felt better and stronger, but I had swum in the cold ocean, pulled myself from a hot mud pit, climbed a great tree, and fought a great fight, so I was tired. I drifted asleep for a while.

When I awoke the sun had dipped low in the sky, and so had we. We were coasting down between large gaps in the great trees. We came to trees so huge they would have dwarfed the redwoods of home. There was even one with shadowy gaps in it the size of small caves.

That's when I saw that nearly all the trees had large gaps in them, from head to foot. It was part of their natural construct. As the sun finally set, we flew into one of those tight wooden caverns, Devel parked his airship, and we stepped out.

The night was dark as in the inside of a hole. No moon was visible. What stars there were made a thin light. But then, as I stood there looking out of the gap, soaking in the night, an amazing thing happened. It was as if there was suddenly dust in the air, and the dust glowed. I was confused for a moment, then some of the dust landed on me. It wasn't dust at all, but little bugs that were as silver as the flying sled, shinier. The entire night was filled with them. They gave a glow to everything, bright as the missing moonlight.

I should pause here and jump ahead with something I later learned. There was no moonlight because there was no moon. This world was without one. Of all the things I had trouble getting used to, that was the one that most pained me. No bright coin of light coasting along in the night sky. In place of it were glowing insects, lovely in their own way, but they could not replace in my mind the moon that circled Earth.

Jerrel pulled a length of dark cloth from inside a container in the craft, fastened it to the top and bottom of our cavern. It stuck to where she put it without button or brace or tack or spike. The cloth was the same color as the tree we were in. I realized immediately, that at night, and perhaps in day at a decent distance, it would appear to be a solid part of the tree. We were concealed.

There were cloaks inside the craft's container, red and thick. Jerrel gave Devel one, me one, took one for herself. She turned on a small lamp inside the craft. The source of its power I assumed was some kind of storage battery. It lit up the interior of our cavern quite comfortably.

Jerrel broke out some foodstuffs, and though I couldn't identify what she gave me, except for a container of water, I lit into that chow like it was my last meal. For all I knew it was. It wasn't good, but it wasn't bad, either.

Before long, Devel lay down and pulled his cloak over him and fell asleep. I was near that point myself, but I could tell Jerrel wanted to talk, that she was interested in me. She began with a few simple questions, most of which I couldn't answer. I told her about the great ocean liner and what had happened to me, how I thought I might be in a dream. She assured me she was real and not a dream. When she laughed a little, the way she laughed, sweet and musical, it assured me my ears were hearing a real voice and that my eyes were seeing a strange and rare beauty.

Jerrel tried her best to explain to me where I was. She called the world she knew Zunsun. She took a slate from the craft with a marker, drew a crude drawing of the sun, then placed her planet two places from it. I knew enough basic astronomy to know she was talking about the planet we called Venus.

I learned there was only one language on Zunsun, and everyone spoke it, with varying degrees of accent according to region. I told her about the moon I missed, and she laughed, saying such a thing seemed odd to her, and it was impossible for her to grasp what it was I so sorely missed.

After a time, she opened the back of the sled and took out a large container of water. She also found a cloth and gave that to me to clean up with. I was nervous wiping myself down in front of her, but as she seemed disinterested, I went about it. Running water through my hair and fingers, wiping myself as clean as possible with what was provided. When I was nearly finished, I caught her eye appraising me. She was more interested than I had first thought.

I don't know why, but Jerrel took me into her confidence. Had Devel been awake, I don't know she would have. But I could tell she trusted me. It was an immediate bond. I have heard of and read of such things, but never believed them until then. Love at first sight was always a romantic writer's foolishness to me, but now I saw the idea in an entirely new light, even if it was the light from a battery.

"Tordo has taken our half of the talisman," she said. "The other half is in the city of the bird-men. Once it was whole, and its powers gave the bird-men a great advantage against us. Our people warred constantly against them. We had no real land to call our own. We moved among the trees, for we couldn't defend ourselves well in a direct fight against the bird-men, not with them having both halves of the talisman and aided by wings."

"Where does it come from?" I said. "What does it do?"

"I can only speak of legend. The halves have been separated a long time. One half was with our people, the other with theirs. It is said that in the far past the two tribes, weary of war, divided the talisman. This was not something the bird-men had to do, as they were winning the conflict, and we would not have lasted.

But their warrior-king, Darat, felt we could live together. Against the advice of his council, he gave our people one half of the talisman and kept the other. Divided, it is powerless. United, it was a dangerous tool of war. No one remembers how it was made or of what it was made, or even what powers it possesses. When Darat died the tradition of peace carried on for many years with new rulers, but then the recent king of the bird-men, Canrad, was of a different mind. After many generations he wanted the lost power back."

"And one of your people, Tordo, betrayed you?" I said.

Jerrel nodded. "He was a priest. It was his job to protect our half of the talisman. It was kept in a house of worship."

"You worship half of a talisman?"

"Not the talisman. The peace it gives us. Peace from the bird-men, anyway. There are others who war against us, but they are less powerful. The bird-men could be a true threat. It surprises me that Canrad has taken this approach. The peace between us had worked for so long.

"What we are trying to do is stop Tordo before he delivers our half of the talisman. My father, King Ran, sent us. We did not want to alarm our people. We thought to overtake the thief swiftly, as we got news of his treachery immediately, Tordo's and that of the lesser priest, the one who was with him in the flier. But it turned out Tordo was prepared for our pursuit. His actions hadn't been of the moment, but were long prepared. He had the winged men waiting. An assistance given him by King Canrad. Tordo knows how my father thinks, knew he would try to catch him with as little alarm as possible by using a small force. He knew this because Tordo is my father's brother, our uncle."

"Betrayed by family," I said. "There isn't much worse."

"We could go back and raise an army, but it would be too late. Two days and he will be in the city of the Varnin, and they will have both pieces of the talisman, and all of its power."

"Seems to me, that being the case, you should have flown all night."

Jerrel grimaced. "You may be telling the truth about being from another world."

"You doubt me?" I asked.

She smiled, and it was brighter than the light from the battery. I melted like butter on a hot skillet.

"Let me show you why we do not fly at night. Why no one in his right mind does."

She took hold of the cloth she had placed over the entrance to the tree cave, tugged it loose at one edge, said, "Come look."

I looked, and what I saw astonished me. The sky was bright with the glowing insects, thicker than before. Their light showed me the sky was also full of great batlike creatures, swooping this way and that. They were the size of Conestoga wagons, but moved more lightly than the flying sled. They were snapping and devouring the shiny bugs in large bites, gulping thousands at a time.

"Fly at night, they will make sure you do not fly for long. We call them Night Wings. They rule the sky from solid dark until near first light, then they go away, far beyond the trees and into the mountains where they dwell."

"This means your uncle has to stop for the night as well," I said.

"Exactly," she said. "When the Night Wings depart in the early morning, we will start out again, hope to catch up with them. They don't have a tremendous lead, but it's lead enough if they are able to arrive at the city of the Varnin and my uncle delivers the talisman."

"Were you and your uncle ever close?"

"Close?" she said. "No. He was not close to my father. He felt he should have his place of rule. My guess is he hopes to do just that under the agreement of Canrad of Varnin. He would rather rule with a cloud over his head than not rule at all."

"I would like to assist you. I have a good sword arm. I can help you stop your uncle. I pledge my allegiance to you."

Jerrel grinned when I said that.

"I accept," she said. "But Devel must accept as well."

"That sounds good to me," I said.

"For now, let us rest."

We took our cloaks, stretched out on the floor of our wooden cave. I tried to sleep, and thought I would have no trouble, exhausted as I was. But I merely dozed, then I would awake thinking I was fighting the waters of the Great Atlantic, only to find I was indeed on Venus, sleeping in a tree, and sleeping not far away was the most beautiful and enticing woman I had ever known.

I was up when Jerrel and Devel rose.

It was partially dark, but some light was creeping through the cloth over the gap in the tree. Jerrel pulled it loose, let the beginnings of early morning seep in.

Jerrel and Devel moved to an area of our cave away from me and whispered. As they did, Devel would glance at me from time to time. His face was a mixture of emotions, none of them appeared to be amused.

After a moment Devel came to me, said, "Jerrel trusts you. I feel I must. Her judgment is generally sound."

"I assure you," I said, "I am trustworthy."

"Words are easy, but you will have your chance to prove your loyalty," he said. "Don't let us down."

"Did I let you down in the fight?"

"No. But what we face from here on out will be much worse. It will try all of us."

"Then put me to the test," I said.

We flew away from the tree and into the morning sky. As we went, the sun grew large and the sky grew bright. The glowing bugs were long gone to wherever they go—some in the gullets of the Night Fliers—and the hungry bat things were gone as well. We sailed on into the bright light and before long it was less bright and the clouds above were dark and plump with rain. Finally, the rain came, and it came hard and fast and began to flood the seats on the craft.

Devel guided our flying sled down and under the lower limbs of the trees. We dodged in between them swiftly, and close to limbs that for a moment looked like inevitable crash sites. But he avoided them, flicked us through clusters of leaves, then down under a series of trees that were smaller in height than the others, yet wide and numerous of branch with leaves so thick the rain could hardly get through. It was as if a great umbrella had been thrown over us. As we went, the sky darkened more and the rain hammered the trees and shook the leaves; random drops seeped through. Then came the lightning, sizzling across the sky with great gongs of thunder. There was a great crack and a flash, a hum of electricity, and a monstrous limb fell from one of the trees.

The lightning, as if seeking us out for dodging the rain, flicked down through a gap in the larger trees and hit one of the smaller ones just before we glided under it. A spot on the limb burst into a great ball of flame and there was an explosion of wood. It struck the front of the craft, hit so hard it was as if a great hand had taken hold of the front of the flying machine and flung it to the ground.

Fortunately we were not flying high at the time, but it was still a vicious drop. Had it not been for the centuries' buildup of loam from leaves and needles and rotting fruit to cushion our fall, we would have burst apart like a tossed china cup.

We smacked the ground hard enough to rattle our teeth. The machine skidded through the loam like a plow breaking a field. It went along like that for a great distance beneath the trees, then hit something solid that caused us to veer hard left and wreck against the trunk of one of the smaller trees.

It was such an impact that for a long moment I was dazed. When I gathered my thoughts and put them into some reasonable shape of understanding, I examined my surroundings. I was in the middle seat of the flying sled, Devel ahead of me, Jerrel behind. But she wasn't. She was missing. I struggled out of my seat, got up close to Devel. He wasn't moving. He couldn't. He was dead. A short limb jutting out from the tree had been driven securely through his chest, bursting his heart. His body was painted in blood.

I fell off the crumpled craft, landed on the ground, and started to crawl. When I got enough strength back to manage my feet under me, I searched around for Jerrel, screamed her name.

"Here," she said. I turned, saw her rising up from behind a pile of leaves and branches. She was scratched up, but from where I stood she looked well enough, all things considered.

When I got to her she surprised me by taking me into her arms, clutching me to her.

"Devel?" she asked.

I gently freed myself from her embrace, shook my head. She made a squeaking noise and fell to her knees. I squatted beside her, held her as she shook and cried. As if to mock us, the sky grew light and the rain stopped. The world took on a pleasant, emerald glow.

I was still astonished to find that at death all that was done in way of ceremony was that the dead were placed on the ground. I assumed that in the humid air of Venus, aided by insects and internal decay, bodies would soon lose their flesh and find their way into the soil. But it was still disconcerting to see Devel pulled from the machine by Jerrel, stretched out on the soil to be left. Jerrel wept over him, violently, then she was through. She left him, as she said, to Become One With The All. I convinced her to stretch his cloak over him though she thought it was a waste of material. I know how this makes her sound, but I assure you, this was custom. I guess it was a little bit similar to some American Indian tribes leaving the corpses of the dead on platforms to be consumed by time and elements.

We traveled forward. The sky had completely cleared and the storm had moved on. We could hear it in the distance, roaring at the trees and the sky. I don't know how long we walked, but finally we came to a clearing in the wilderness, and in the clearing were mounds of giant bones. Some were fresh enough that stinking flesh clung to them, others had almost disappeared into the ground itself. Teeth gleamed in the sunlight. In the distance the dark rain clouds moved as if stalking something, lightning flashed and thunder rolled and the wind sighed.

"It's a kind of graveyard for the great beasts," Jerrel said, looking around.

It was indeed. It went on for what I estimate to be ten or fifteen miles long, a half mile wide.

We had brought some supplies from the crippled flying sled with us, and we found the shade of some very large and well-aged bones, sat down in the shade the bones made, ignored the smell from still-rotting flesh, and ate our lunch. It was an odd place for a meal, but our stamina had played out. We sat and Jerrel talked about Devel. It was minor stuff, really. Childhood memories, some of it funny, some of it poignant, some of it just odd, but all of it loving. She talked for quite a while.

When our strength was renewed, we continued. I guess we had walked about a mile among the bones when we found her uncle's airship. It was blackened and twisted and smacked down among a rib cage that looked like the frame of a large ship. The man I had seen before, the one who had been driving the craft, was still in it, though some creature had been at him—had actually sucked the flesh from his head and face. But it was him. I could tell that, and if I had any doubts Jerrel dismantled them. She drew her sword and cut off his fleshless head and kicked it into a pile of the bones.

"Traitor," she said. I saw then not only the beautiful woman I had fallen in love with but the warrior, and it frightened me a little.

"The question," I said, "is where is your uncle? Wait. Look there."

A little farther up, among the bones, were the wrecked bodies of several bird-men, blackened and twisted and scorched by fire.

"The lightning hit them same as us," I said. "Maybe your uncle was killed."

But we didn't locate his body. Perhaps a beast had found him, but it was also possible that he was journeying on foot to the kingdom of the Varnin.

"This means we might catch up with him," I said.

Before long I spied his tracks in the soft soil, pointed them out. Jerrel could find Varnin without tracking her uncle, but it was him and the talisman we wanted, so the tracks were encouraging.

It was near night when we finally passed the lengthy stacks of bones. We edged toward the forest. The trees, low down and high up, were full of ravaging beasts, but the open land worried me most. Anyone or anything could easily spot us there.

Edging along the trees, moving swiftly and carefully as possible, we were taken aback by the sudden appearance of half a dozen beasts with men mounted on them. My fear had been realized. They spotted us.

The beasts they were riding looked remarkably like horses, if horses could have horns and were shorter and wider with red-

and-white stripes. They were guided in a way similar to horses as well, bits and bridles, long, thin reins. The riders were seated in high-set saddles, and as they came closer it became apparent they were not human at all.

Humans have flesh, but these things had something else. Their skin was yellow like Jerrel's skin, but it was coarse and gave one the impression of alligator hide. They had flaring scales around their necks. Their features were generally human-like, but their noses were flat as a coin, little more than two small holes. Their foreheads slanted and the tops of their heads peaked. Their mouths were wide and packed with stained teeth and their round eyes were red and full of fiery licks of light. They were carrying long lances tipped with bright tips of metal. Short swords with bone handles bounced in scabbards at their hips. Closer yet, I saw there were little glowing parasites flowing over their skin like minnows in a creek.

Jerrel said, "Galminions. They are eaters of human flesh. Robbers. They run in packs. And they smell."

They came ever closer. Jerrel was right. They did smell, like something dead left under a house.

"Ah," said the foremost rider, reining his mount directly in front of us. The others sat in a row behind him, smiling their filthy teeth. "Travelers. And such a good day for it."

"It is," Jerrel said. "We thought a stroll would be nice."

The one who had spoken laughed. The laugh sounded like ice cracking. He had a peculiar way of turning his head from side to side, as if one eye were bad. When the sunlight shifted I saw that was exactly the problem. He was blind in that eye; no red flecks there. It was white as the first drifts of snow in the Rockies.

"How is your stroll?" said Dead Eye.

"It's been warm, and it's quite the hike," Jerrel said, "but it has been amusing. It has been so good to speak to you. We must be on our way. We wish you good day."

"Do you now?" said Dead Eye. He turned in his saddle and looked back at his companions. "They wish us good day."

The companions laughed that similar laugh, the one that sounded like ice cracking, then made leathery shifts in their saddles.

"It's good to see we're all in a cheery mood," Jerrel said.

When Dead Eye turned back to us, he said, "I am cheery because we are going to kill you and eat you and take your swords. But mainly we're going to kill you and eat you. Maybe we'll start eating you while you're alive. Of course we will. That's how we like it. The screams are loud and the blood is hot."

"You will dance on the tip of my sword," I said. "That is what you will do."

"And what are you exactly?" said Dead Eye.

"A black man."

"I can see that. Were you burned?"

"By the fires of hell. Perhaps you would like a taste of hell itself."

"What is hell?"

I had wasted my wit. "Never mind," I said. "Let us pass, or—"

"I will dance on the tip of your sword," Dead Eye said.

"Exactly," I said.

"What about the rest of us," he said. "Shall they dance as well?"

"I suppose that between our two swords there will be dancing partners for all of you."

This really got a laugh.

"He is not joking," said Jerrel.

"We will be the judge of that," Dead Eye said. "For we are not jokesters either."

"Oh, I don't know," I said. "You look pretty funny to me."

My comment was like the starter shot.

They came as one in a wild charge. Jerrel and I worked as one. We seemed to understand the other's next move. We dodged into the trees, and the Galminions followed. The trees made it difficult for them to maneuver their beasts, but we moved easily. I sprang high in the air and came down on the rider nearest me with a slash of my sword, severing his head, spurting warm blood from his body like the gush from a fountain.

Jerrel lunged from behind a tree, and avoiding the ducking horned head of one of the mounts, stuck it in the chest. With a bleating sound it stumbled and fell, rolled about kicking its legs, tumbling over the fallen rider, crushing him with a snap of bone and a crackle of bumpy skin.

That was when Dead Eye swung off his steed and came for me, driving his lance directly at my chest. I moved to the side, parried his lance with my sword. The tip of his weapon stuck deep in a tree, and the impact caused him to lose his footing. When he fell, it was never to rise again. I bounded to him and drove my sword deep in his throat. He squirmed like a bug stuck through by a pin. His white eye widened. He half spun on my sword, spat a geyser of blood, shook and lay still.

The others fled like deer.

"Are you all right?" she asked.

"I am, and believe it or not," I said, "fortune has smiled on us."

For Jerrel riding one of the beasts was uncomfortable and she rode awkwardly. For me it was like being back in the cavalry. I felt in control. The creatures handled very similar to horses though they seemed smarter. That said, they had a gait similar to mules, making for a less smooth ride.

"You call this fortune?" Jerrel said.

"If your uncle is on foot, yes," I said.

As we rode on, in front of us the clearing went away and a mountain range rose before us. It was at first a bump, then a hump, and finally we could see it for what it was. The mountain was covered in dark clouds and flashes of lightning, all of it seen to the sound of rumbling thunder. The patches of forest that climbed up the mountain were blacker than the trees that gave the Black Hills of the Dakotas their name.

The day moved along, the sun shifted, and so did the shadows. They fell out of the forests and grew longer, thicker, cooler, and darker. A few of the shiny bugs came out. We shifted into the woods, found a spot where old wood had fallen, and made a kind of hut of trees and limbs. We dismounted and led our animals inside through a gap. I found some deadwood and pulled it in front of the opening. I chopped a lean but strong limb off a tree with my sword and used it to stretch from one side of our haven to the other. On one side of it I placed our mounts, the limb serving as a kind of corral. After removing their saddles and bridles, I used bits of rope from the bag of supplies we had brought from the wreck of the sled to hobble them, a trick Jerrel had never seen before.

Finally we stretched out on our side of the barrier with our cloaks as our beds. We lay there and talked, and you would have thought we had known each other forever. In time the Night Wings were out. They flew down low and we could hear their wings sweeping past where we were holed up. Many of the bugs outside slipped in between the gaps of fallen wood and made our little room, such as it was, glow with shimmering light.

Jerrel and I came together at some point, and anything beyond that is not for a gentleman to tell. I will say this, and excuse the dime-novel feel to it. My soul soared like a hawk.

Next morning we were up early, just after the Night Wings and the glowing bugs abandoned the sky. We saddled up and rode on out. From time to time I got down off my critter and checked the ground, found signs of our quarry's tracks, remounted, and we continued. By the middle of the day we had reached the mountain and were climbing up, riding a narrow trail between the great dark trees.

The weather had shifted. The dark clouds, the lightning and thunder had flown. As we rode from time to time I saw strange beasts watching us from the shadows of the forest, but we were not bothered and continued on.

Late in the day I got down and looked at our man's tracks, and they were fresh. Our mounts were giving us the final edge on his head start.

"He is not far ahead," I said, swinging back into the saddle.

"Good. Then I will kill him."

"Maybe you could just arrest him."

"Arrest him?"

"Take him prisoner."

"No. I will kill him and take back the talisman."

I figured she would too.

The trail widened and so did our view. Up there in the mountains, nowhere near its peak, but right in front of us at the far end of the wide trail, we could see the city of the bird-men. The great trees there had grown, or been groomed, to twist together in a monstrous wad of leaves and limbs, and mixed into them was a rock fortress that must have taken thousands of bird-men and a good many years to build. It was like a castle and a nest blended together with the natural formations of the mountain; in places it was rambling, in others tight as a drum.

I said, "Before we come any closer, we had best get off this trail and sneak up on our man. If we can jump him before he enters the city, then that's the best way, and if he is inside already, well, it's going to be difficult, to put it mildly."

Jerrel nodded, and just as we rode off the trail and into the dark forest, a horde of bird-men came down from the sky and into the thicket with a screech and a flash of swords.

Surprised, we whirled on our mounts and struck out at

them. It was like swatting at yellow jackets. I managed to stick one of the creatures and cause him to fall dead, but as he fell his body struck me and knocked me off my mount. I hustled to my feet just as Jerrell ducked a sword swing, but was hit in the head by the passing hilt of the sword. She fell off her beast and onto her back and didn't move.

I went savage.

I remember very little about what happened after that, but I was swinging my sword with both skill and insane fury. Bird-men lost wings and limbs and faces and skulls. My sword stabbed and slashed and shattered. I was wet and hot with the blood of my enemies.

To protect themselves they flapped their wings, lifted up higher, and dove, but they were never quick enough and were hindered by the thickness of the trees and my speed was beyond measure. I leaped and dodged, parried and thrust. I raged among the flapping demons like a lion among sheep.

Finally it was as if all the bird-men in the world appeared. The sky darkened above me and the darkness fell over me, and down they came in a fluttering wave of screeches and sword slashes and axe swings.

I was a crazed dervish. I spun and slung my blade like the Reaper's scythe, and once again they began to pile up, but then I was struck in the head from the side, and as I tumbled to the ground, I thought it was the end of me.

I couldn't have been down but for a moment when I felt a blade at my throat and heard a voice say, "No. Bring him."

Jerrel and I were lifted up and carried. My sword was gone. I was bleeding. I saw walking before the pack of bird-men, Tordo, Jerrel's traitorous uncle.

We were hoisted out of the forest and onto the trail, carried up toward the amazing twists of forest and stone. As we neared I saw small clouds of smoke rising from stone chimneys, and in loops of groomed limbs I saw large nests made of vines and sticks and all manner of refuse. The nests were wide open, but they were built under the great limbs and leaves of trees that served as a roof. Beyond them there was an enormous tree, the biggest I had seen on my world or this one, and there was a gap in it that served as an opening into the city proper. A great drawbridge had been dropped, and it stretched out over a gap between trees and mountain, and the gap was wide and deep beyond comprehension. Over the drawbridge we were carried, and into the great fortress of wood and stone.

My thought was that Jerrel was already dead and I was next, and let me tell you true as the direction north, I didn't care if I died. With Jerrel lost, I wished to die.

As it turned out, I didn't die. And neither did Jerrel. I didn't realize she was alive until we found ourselves in the bowels of the fortress in a prison that was deep inside the cave of a tree; a series of metal bars served as our doorway. Looking through the bars I could see a long corridor that was also the inside of a tree, and there were two guards nearby, one with a lance, one with an axe, both with expressions that would make a child cry.

In our cell they dropped us down on some limbs and leaves that served as beds. There was a peculiar odor. The only thing I can equate it with is the smell of a henhouse on a hot, damp afternoon.

I knelt over Jerrel, lifted her head gently. "My love," I said.

"My head hurts," she said. The sound of her voice elated me.

"I guess so. You took quite a lick."

She sat up slowly. "Are you okay?"

"I got a bump myself, behind my ear."

She gingerly touched it with the tips of her fingers. "Ow," she said.

"My sentiments exactly. What I don't understand is why they didn't kill us."

"I think, in my case, my uncle wants me to see the ceremony."

"What ceremony?"

"The linking of the two halves of the talisman. The acquisition of the greatest power on our planet. He wants me to see what he has achieved before he puts me to death. Wants me to know the deed is done, and I have failed to prevent it, then we die."

"If you ain't dead, you're living, and that's a good thing," I said.

It took her a moment to take that in. It was as if whatever power allowed my words to be translated to her language had lost a beat. After a moment she laughed her musical laugh. "I think I understand."

"We won't give up until we're beyond considering on the matter one way or the other," I said.

"I love you, Jack," she said.

"And I you." We allowed ourselves a kiss. Yet, in spite of my bravado, in spite of the repeating of my old sergeant's words, I feared it might be our last.

"Love is a wonderful steed," said a voice, "ride it as long as you can."

We looked up, and there above us, sitting on a ridge of stone was a bird-man, his feet dangling. He looked youngish, if I can claim any ability of judging the age of a man who looks a lot like a giant chicken crossed with the body of a man. A very weak-looking chicken. He appeared near starved to death. His head hung weak. His ribs showed. His legs were skinny as sticks, but there was still something youthful about him.

"Who are you?" I asked. It wasn't a brilliant question, but it was all I had.

"Gar-don," he said, and dropped off the ledge, his wings taking hold with a fanning of air. He settled down near us, his legs weak and shaky. He sat down on the floor, his head sagged, he sighed. "I am a prisoner, same as you."

"Gar-don," Jerrel said. "The former king's son. His heir."

"That was how it was supposed to be, but no longer. I was usurped."

"Canrad," said Jerrel.

"Yes," Gar-don said, "now he is king. And I am here, awaiting the moment when he is able to acquire the rest of the talisman, and from what I overheard, that moment has arrived."

"Yes," Jerrel said. "For all of us. I am Jerrel, Princess of Sheldan."

Gar-don lifted his head, took a deep breath, said, "I know of you. I am sorry for your fate, and his."

"Jack," I said. "I am called Jack."

"I shall go out as a prince," Gar-don said. "I will not beg. My horror is not my death but what the two halves of the talisman can do. Canrad will possess immense power."

"What does this power do?" I asked.

"We only have legend to explain it to us. It gives him the power over spirits and demons from the old trees."

"The old trees?" I said.

"Giant trees that contain spirits of power," Jerrel said. "Those kinds of trees no longer exist. They ceased to exist before I was born, before my father was born, his grandfather and so on. The spirits are contained in the two halves of the talisman."

"Canrad will be able to control the people then," Gar-don said. "They, like my father, and myself, were perfectly happy with our peace treaty. Only an insane being wants war. The people only follow Canrad because they fear him. All uprisings have been destroyed, or the participants have gone into hiding. After today, they might as well never have existed, for he will control anyone and everyone with his new powers. He will not be able to be defeated."

"But you don't actually know how he will do that?" I asked.

"I have only heard of the legend," Gar-don said. "The power of the spirits, the demons of the trees. Exactly what they are capable of, I do not know. Our people have always feared the talisman, and knowing now that it will be united, no one will resist him. It would be useless."

There was a clatter of sound in the hallway. Gar-don stood weakly, and said, "It seems we are about to find out the exactness of the talisman's power."

They came for us, unlocking our cell, entering quickly. To be sure of our compliance there was a horde of them with long spikes and strong nets and an angry attitude. I managed to hit one with my fist, knocking him to the floor in a swirl of dust and feathers. Jerrel kicked another. Gar-don tried to fight, but he was as weak as a dove. They netted the three of us, bagged us, kicked us awhile, then hauled us away like trapped vermin being taken to a lake to be drowned.

We were brought to a large throne room, that like the overall stronghold was made of stone and was combined with the natural strength of trees and limbs and leaves. Enormous branches jutted out of the walls high above our heads, and perched on them like a murder of ravens were bird-men and bird-women—the first females I had seen of that race. An occasional feather drifted down from above, coasted in the light.

Above that perch on which the bird-people were seated was a tight canopy of leaves, so thick and layered it would have taken an army of strong warriors many days to hack their way through it; actually, I'm not even sure they could do it in years.

They brought us in and held us close to the floor in our nets. We could see through the gaps in the netting. Besides the bird-people on the limbs above, the throne room was packed with others, some of them warriors, many of them nobles, and some citizens. We were the spectacle, and all of the bird-people had been summoned to witness whatever ceremony was at hand. I assumed it would not be a parade in our honor.

On a dais was a throne and on the throne was a large winged man who looked as if an ancient human being, fat of body, thin of legs, with a head like a warped melon, had been mated to a condor and a buzzard, all of him swathed over with warts and scars and age. A golden cloak draped his shoulders, and except for half the talisman on a chain around his neck, he wore nothing else. His eyes were dark and the color of old, dried pinesap. This, of course, was King Canrad.

Tordo stood near the throne, one hand on its back support. There were guards on either side of King Canrad and Tordo. The room was full of warriors as well.

Canrad nodded at Tordo. Tordo stepped to the center of the dais, removed his half of the talisman from his neck, and lifted it up with both hands. Sunlight coming through an open gap behind the king glittered across the talisman like sunlight on a trout's back.

"What say you?" said the king.

The crowed cheered. It sounded like the sort of cheers we Buffalo Soldiers used to give the lieutenant when he rode by on horseback. A white man who led us like we couldn't lead ourselves, as if our color tainted our intelligence. It was a cheer, but it came from the mouth, not the soul.

The king said, "The old order is here. Gar-don, son of the former king, who was not worthy and shall not be named is also here. He will see how a true king shows his power."

"It is you who is not worthy," Gar-don called out from his netted position on the floor.

"Strike him," said the king. One of the warriors stepped forward and brought the staff of his spear sharply across Gar-don's back. Gar-don grunted.

"We also have among us the daughter of King Ran of the Sheldan," said the king. "A rather inferior race in my opinion. Add a black man-thing that I can not define, nor can anyone else, and we have three enemies of the throne. The gods will welcome their deaths. They will be the first to die by the power of the talisman. I will call up all the demons of the trees, and they will render these worthless creatures into wet rags."

"I know your law," Jerrel said, pushing herself to her knees under the net. "I ask my right to challenge you, or your second. If I win, our lives will be spared."

"I am too old to be challenged," said the king. "I have no intention of sullying myself with a duel. Nor will I sully one of my men. Why should I? You have the right by our law to make a challenge, and I, as king, have the right to refuse. I refuse. Be silent."

King Canrad leaned forward on his throne. I could almost hear his bones creak. His wings trembled slightly. He looked like a gargoyle rocking on its ledge. He said to Tordo, "Bring me the power."

Tordo hesitated, then moved toward him. King Canrad held out his hand. "Give it to me."

Tordo held his half of the talisman forward with his left hand, and as the King reached to take it, Tordo sprang forward, snatched at the talisman around the king's neck, yanked it loose of its chain.

Links of chain clattered on the floor as Tordo slammed the two pieces of the talisman together with a loud *click*. He lifted it above his head with a smile. He yelled out a series of words, an incantation. I understood the words, but not their jumbled purpose.

And then the spell was finished, and . . .

. . . Well, nothing. It was as quiet in the throne room as a mouse in house slippers. From somewhere in the crowd there was a cough, as if someone had a mouthful of feathers, which considering who was in the room, could have actually been the case.

Tordo's gleeful expression died slowly. He said a word that didn't translate, but I had an idea what it meant. He turned slowly and looked over his shoulder. He had gone from a potential wizard of the trees to a fool with two connected pieces of jewelry.

The guards hustled up from the bottom of the dais, their spears raised, ready to stick Tordo.

"No," said the king. "Give me the talisman first."

One of the warriors tugged it from Tordo's hands, removed his sword as well, gave the talisman to the king. The king held it in his hands. He looked at it the way a fisherman might look at his catch, realizing it had appeared much larger underwater. "It is useless. It is a lie." He lifted his eyes to Tordo. "I will make your death a long one."

While they were so engaged, and all eyes were on them, I lifted an edge of the net, crawled out from under it and seized one of the bird-men. I drew his sword from its sheath and shoved him back. I sprang toward the dais. A warrior stepped in front of me, but I jabbed quickly and the sharp blade went through his eye and down he went.

With my newfound abilities renewed, I leaped easily to the dais and put my sword to the king's throat.

The guards on either side of the throne started toward me.

I said to the king, "Give the order to free the lady and Gardon, or I will run this through your throat."

The king's body shook. "Free them," he said.

The net was lifted. The warriors around them parted. I noticed there was a rearranging of soldiers, some shifted out of one group and into another. It was a good sign. They were showing their division.

I said, "Those who wish the king well, fear the point of my sword. Those who wish him ill, perhaps you would enjoy my sword thrust. We shall see which is more popular."

There was a slight murmur.

By this time Jerrel and Gar-don had joined me on the dais. They stood near me and the king. Jerrel picked up the pike of the guard I had killed. Tordo hadn't moved; he feared to move.

Gar-don said, "I am your king. I am the son of the true king, who was the son of a king, and the king before that. Today the talisman failed Canrad and Tordo. The spirits within it do not wish their will to succeed. They do not wish their powers used for something so pointless as killing and destruction and war. It is peace they want. It is peace they have allowed. And I suggest we obey their will and continue on that path, lest they turn on us and destroy us all."

Someone said, "Gar-don, our king."

A moment later this was repeated, then someone else said the same, and voices rose up from the crowd and filled the room, and the voices came not from the mouths of the frightened but from the souls of true believers.

There were a few who for a moment seemed unwilling to make the change to Gar-don, but they were vastly outnumbered, and those who tried to defend Canrad were quickly dispatched in a wave of bloody anger. If there was a lesson to be learned from Gar-don's remarks about the talisman, they hadn't actually learned it, which meant the bird-people were as human as the wingless. They were not ready to accept that the talisman was nothing more than an ancient myth.

Gar-don took the talisman, held it up as Tordo had done. He was still weak and struggled to hold it aloft. But his spirit was strong. He spoke so loudly his words could be heard at the back of the room and up into the leafy canopy.

"The power of the talisman will remain unused. Half of it will go back with Princess Jerrel, back to her city and her king, where it will continue to remain powerless, and our peace will continue."

"What of him," said a bird-woman, stepping forward to point a long finger at Tordo.

Gar-don turned his head to Tordo, studied him. He was about to speak when Jerrel beat him to it. "Gar-don, King of the Varnin," she said, "I ask you to sanction my right to combat with Tordo. He has stolen from my family. He has insulted my family. And I desire to insult him with the edge of my blade."

"And if you lose?" said Gar-don.

"I won't," Jerrel said. "But if I do, let him go. Banish him."

"Don't do this," I said. "Let me take your place."

"I am as good a warrior as any other, my love."

"Very well," said Gar-don. "But before that . . ."

He turned to the former King Canrad.

"I banish you. As of now, you will rise and you will go away, and you will never come back."

The old man rose, and in that moment, seeing how weak he was, I almost felt sorry for him. Then a blade came out from under his cloak and he stabbed at Gar-don. I caught Canrad's arm just in time, twisted. It snapped easily. He screeched and dropped the dagger. I let him go.

Gar-don leaned forward and looked into Canrad's eyes. "I see emptiness."

Gar-don weakly picked up the dagger Canrad had dropped. He seemed strong all of a sudden. "It will not matter what I do, Canrad, you are dead already." With that, he jammed the blade into the former king's chest. The old man collapsed in a cloaked wad, and immediately a pool of blood flowed around him.

"Give Tordo a sword," Gar-don said, turning back to the situation at hand. "Death is your loss, Tordo. Banishment is your victory."

Jerrel dropped the pike and was given a sword.

* * *

Tordo was given a sword. All of the disappointment of the moment, every foul thing he was, bubbled up and spewed out of him. He attacked with a yell. He bounced forward on the balls of his feet, attempting to stick Jerrel. Jerrel glided back as if walking on air.

Everyone on the dais moved wide of their blades as they battled back and forth, the throne sometimes coming between them. Once Jerrel slipped in Canrad's blood, and in spite of this being a private duel, I almost leaped to her aid, but Gar-don touched me on the arm.

"It is not done," he said.

Tordo put one boot on Canrad's lifeless neck and used it as a kind of support to lift him up and give him more of a downward thrust. But Jerrel slipped the lunge.

Tordo sprang off Canrad's lifeless neck and made a beautiful thrust for her face. I let out a gasp of air. It was right on target.

At the last moment Jerrel dropped under his thrust, which lifted the hair on her head slightly, and drove her weapon up and into his belly. He held his position, as if waiting for his form to be admired, then made a noise like an old dog with a chicken bone in its throat and fell flat on his face. Blood poured out of him and flowed into the puddle of gore that had fanned out from beneath Canrad.

Jerrel studied the corpse of Tordo for a moment. She took a deep breath, said, "I have drawn my kin's own blood, but I have avenged Tordo's treachery and honored my father."

Gar-don stepped forward and surveyed the crowd. He lifted his chin slightly. The response to this was another cheer from the multitude, and this one was more than from the throat. It was from deep within the soul.

There were great celebrations, and we were part of it. It was pleasant and necessary to the new agreement between kingdoms, but I was glad when it ended and we were given back the mounts we had taken from the Galminions, sent on our way with supplies, fanfare, and of course Jerrel's half of the talisman.

As we rode along the wide trail in the morning light, winding down from the great lair of the bird-people, I said, "Do you think Gar-don's people believed what he said about the talisman?"

"Perhaps they did," Jerrel said. "Perhaps some did. Perhaps none did. The only thing that matters is there was no great power when the two pieces were united. It's just a legend."

"Designed to prevent war between your people and theirs," I said. "That seems like a legend worth believing. The halves of a great power divided so neither has a unique and overwhelming power over the other."

"Devel would be amused," she said.

We experienced a few adventures on our way to Jerrel's kingdom, but they were minor, mostly involving brigands we dispatched with little effort, a few encounters with wild beasts. When we arrived in the land of Sheldan and Jerrel explained all that had happened to her father, I was afforded much curiosity, mostly due to the color of my skin.

I was thanked. I was rewarded with a fine sword and scabbard. I was given a prominent place at King Ran's table, and it was there that Jerrel told him that we were to marry.

It was the first I had heard of it, but I was delighted with the idea.

That was some time ago. I am sitting now at a writing desk in a great room in this Sheldan castle made of clay and stone. It is dark except for a small candle. I am writing with a feather pen on yellow parchment. My wife, the beautiful warrior Jerrel, sleeps not far away in our great round bed.

Tonight, before I rose to write, I dreamed, as I have the last three nights. In the dream I was being pulled down a long bright tunnel, and finally into the cold, dark waters of the Atlantic, washing about in the icy waves like a cork. The great light of a ship moved my way, and in the shadows of that light were the bobbing heads of dying swimmers and the bouncing of the *Titanic*'s human-stuffed rafts. The screams of the desperate, the cries of the dying filled the air.

I have no idea what the dream means, or if it means anything, but each night that I experience it, it seems a little clearer. Tonight there was another part to it. I glimpsed the thing that brought me here, pulled me down and through that lit tunnel to Venus. I fear it wishes to take me back.

I finish this with no plans of its being read, and without complete understanding as to why I feel compelled to have written it. But written it is.

Now I will put my pen and parchment away, blow out the candle, lie gently down beside my love, hoping I will never be forced to leave her side, and that she and this world will be mine forever.

MIKE RESNICK

Mike Resnick is one of the bestselling authors in science fiction, and one of the most prolific. His many novels include *Kirinyaga, Santiago, The Dark Lady, Stalking the Unicorn, Birthright: The Book of Man, Paradise, Ivory, Soothsayer, Oracle, Lucifer Jones, Purgatory, Inferno, A Miracle of Rare Design, The Widowmaker, The Soul Eater, A Hunger in the Soul, The Return of Santiago, Starship: Mercenary, Starship: Rebel,* and *Stalking the Vampire.* His collections include *Will the Last Person to Leave the Planet Please Shut Off the Sun?, An Alien Land, A Safari of the Mind, Hunting the Snark and Other Short Novels,* and *The Other Teddy Roosevelts.* As editor, he's produced *Inside the Funhouse: 17 SF Stories About SF, Whatdunits, More Whatdunits, Shaggy B.E.M. Stories, New Voices in Science Fiction, This Is My Funniest,* a long string of anthologies coedited with Martin H. Greenberg—*Alternate Presidents, Alternate Kennedys, Alternate Warriors, Aladdin: Master of the Lamp, Dinosaur Fantastic, By Any Other Fame, Alternate Outlaws,* and *Sherlock Holmes in Orbit,* among others—as well as two anthologies coedited with Gardner Dozois, and *Stars: Original Stories Based on the Songs of Janis Ian,* edited with Janis Ian. He won the Hugo Award in 1989 for "Kirinyaga." He won another Hugo Award in 1991 for another story in the *Kirinyaga* series, "The Manamouki," and another Hugo and Nebula in 1995 for his novella "Seven Views of Olduvai Gorge." His most recent books are a number of new collections, *The Incarceration of Captain Nebula and Other Lost Futures, Win Some, Lose Some: The Hugo-Award Winning (and Nominated) Short Science Fiction and Fantasy of Mike Resnick,* and *Masters of the Galaxy,* and two new novels, *The Doctor and the Rough Rider* and *The Doctor and the Dinosaurs.* He lives with his wife, Carol, in Cincinnati, Ohio.

Here a soldier of fortune sets off into the hostile Venusian jungle in company with a very unusual partner, in search of the most fabulous treasure on the planet—and finds much more than he bargained for.

The Godstone of Venus

MIKE RESNICK

"DOES IT *EVER* STOP RAINING?" ASKED SCORPIO, looking out the window as the rain splashed into the ocean.

"They say it did once, for almost a whole week, about thirty years ago," replied the bartender, carrying a pair of purple concoctions over to Scorpio, handing one to him and drinking the other himself as he walked back to the bar.

Marcus Aurelius Scorpio was seated at a wooden table next to a large window. The tavern sat atop a huge rocky promontory, with a vast ocean surrounding three sides of it, and a crushed-rock path leading down to a dense jungle behind it.

"That was a rhetorical question," replied Scorpio.

"Yeah, you don't look drunk enough for it to be a serious one—yet," replied the bartender. "Where's your partner?"

Scorpio shrugged. "Beats me. He'll be by later."

"How'd you ever hook up with something like him?" asked the bartender. "Or is he an it?"

"Not unless one of his ladyfriends got mad at him since this morning," replied Scorpio.

"You know, Venus has got a lot of races, some of 'em bright, some of 'em barely able to scratch without instructions, but your partner is the strangest of 'em all, or my name ain't Lucius Aloisius McAnany."

"When you get right down to it, your name *isn't* Lucius

anymore. Most of the locals can't pronounce it, so it's Luke."

"But when I pay my taxes it's Lucius."

Scorpio looked amused. "When did you ever pay taxes?"

"Well, *if* I did," said McAnany, "it'd be as Lucius."

"I think I'll go back to listening to the rain hit the windows," said Scorpio. "It makes more sense."

McAnany was about to reply when he was drowned out by the hooting of a huge golden fish that stuck its head out of the tank that rested on a shelf behind the bar.

"All right, all right!" he muttered, pouring the remainder of his drink into the tank. The fish swam right through the spreading purple liquid, hooted happily, and turned a trio of back somersaults.

"Look at that," said McAnany disgustedly. "A goddamned alcoholic fish." He pointed to a bright orange creature that hung upside down on the ceiling. "And what passes for a bat on this idiot world, and eats nothing but cigar butts. Damned lucky for him none of the Venusian races ever get lung cancer. Probably just their bartenders." He paused, then slammed a fist down on the bar. "What the hell are a couple of Earthmen like us doing on this godforsaken world anyway?"

"Drinking purple stuff."

"Damn it, you know what I mean!" growled McAnany. "I could have been a bartender back in Klamath Falls. I mean, hell, we had enough goddamned water there. No, I had to come to the Planet of Opportunity to make my millions." He spat on the bare wooden floor. "Opportunity, my ass!"

"So go home," said Scorpio.

"And do what? I'm sixty-three years old, and I've been bartending here for more than thirty years. I'm too old to retrain."

"So go home and tend bar there."

"To tell the truth, I'm afraid to," admitted McAnany. "Thirty years is a long time. Who the hell knows what it's like there now?"

Scorpio made no reply, and McAnany glared at him. "Anyone ever tell you that sympathy's not your long and strong suit?"

"From time to time."

"Didn't have any effect on you then, either, I'll bet."

Scorpio looked over McAnany's shoulder at the door, which was just opening. A couple walked in, drenched despite all their protections against the weather.

"Hell of a day!" muttered the burly man, removing his outer garments and tossing them carelessly on the end of the bar, revealing a pockmarked, mustached face with a thick head of wavy gray hair. He then helped the woman out of her protective gear, and Scorpio saw that she was a curvaceous, expensively clad woman—or at least female—with light blue skin and matching hair.

"Pretty much the same as all the other days around here," replied McAnany.

"*That's* a depressing thought," said the woman. "What have you got to drink?"

"You name it, and I've either got it or I'll fake it."

The woman looked at Scorpio. "I'll have what that man is drinking."

"Me, too," said the man. He turned to the bartender. "I'm supposed to meet someone here."

"Must be him," said McAnany, gesturing to Scorpio. "Ain't no one else been here all day."

The man approached Scorpio. "Are you the one they call The Scorpion?"

"At your service," replied Scorpio. "You must be Rand Quintaro."

Quintaro nodded and extended his hand, then sat down and gestured the woman to sit next to him, which she did. "You could have chosen a more convenient place," he said.

"This is my office when I'm on Venus," replied Scorpio.

"I understand you have a partner," continued Quintaro. "Where is he?"

"He'll be along."

"We'll wait."

"That's up to you," said Scorpio. "Could be a couple of days."

"He's on a job?" asked Quintaro.

"It's confidential. I can't discuss it."

The man nodded his head knowingly. McAnany emitted a sarcastic snort, then brought the blue-skinned woman her drink.

"It's strong!" she breathed after taking a sip.

"I can dilute it," offered McAnany.

"No," she said, never taking her eyes off Scorpio. "I like strong."

"You got a name, lady?"

"It's Sapphire," she replied.

"Sapphire what?" asked McAnany.

"Just Sapphire."

"Pleased to meet you, Just Sapphire," said Scorpio. He turned back to Quintaro. "You sure you don't want to talk a little business now?"

Quintaro sighed, and his mustache quivered. "All right. There's no sense wasting any more time. It took me two months just to decide you and your partner were the men for the job."

"He's not exactly a man," noted Scorpio.

"Anyway, you come highly recommended."

"I'd ask by who, but you'd probably tell me, and I'd have to lecture you about the company you keep," said Scorpio with just the trace of a smile.

McAnany looked at a small screen that was hidden behind the bar. "He's coming!" he announced.

"Your partner?" asked Quintaro.

Scorpio nodded. "I guess he accomplished his mission faster than anticipated."

Shut up, said a familiar voice inside his head.

A moment later the door opened, and a strange-looking creature entered. He was a dark blue quadruped, perhaps the size of a mastiff. He had four nostrils, two in front, one on each cheek, eyes that seemed to glow even though they were totally shielded from the dim lights, and a tail that ended in such a sharp point that it could very well be used as a weapon. He was covered by a dull curly down, and when he opened his mouth he displayed a double row of coal-black fangs.

"This is Merlin," announced Scorpio. "He doesn't talk, but he understands everything you say."

Quintaro studied Merlin for a moment. "I've never seen anything like him," he said. "What world is he from?"

"This one."

"Really?"

"Why would I lie to you?" said Scorpio. "Not every planet produces just one sentient race."

Quintaro stared at Merlin for another moment, then shrugged and turned back to Scorpio. "He won't be offended if I speak directly to you? I'd feel . . . awkward . . . speaking to him."

I just may bite his foot off.

Practice a little anger management, thought Scorpio. *I got the repair estimate on the ship while you were off hunting for ladyfriends, and we need a quick seventy-three thousand* mojuri *or we're stuck on this ball of dirt—well, ball of jungle and water.*

Seventy-three thousand mojuri? *That's outrageous!*

Probably, agreed Scorpio. *How much is that in real money?*

Twenty thousand credits.

That's *why you're not biting his foot off.*

Yet.

Scorpio turned to Quintaro. "All right—we're all ears. What exactly are you here about?"

"I want to hire your services," said Quintaro.

"Which particular services?"

"Whatever's required. I'll be honest. I expect to run into some danger in the pursuit of my goal, and I'm told you're the deadliest man on Venus, now that Cemetery Smith has moved to Titan."

"Suppose you tell me what goal you're in pursuit of?" said Scorpio.

Quintaro leaned forward. "Have you ever heard of the Godstone of Venus?"

Scorpio shook his head. "What is it—some kind of gem, or a carving, or what?"

"I don't know," answered Quintaro.

Scorpio frowned. "Then what do you want it for?"

"It's supposed to imbue its possessor with certain mystical powers."

"You've been reading too many bad adventure stories, Mr. Quintaro," said Scorpio.

"It exists!" insisted Quintaro. "Even if it's just a stone with no mystical powers, it's worth a king's ransom. Men and Venusians have been searching for it for eons." Suddenly a sly smile crossed his face. "But I've got something they didn't have."

"Let me guess," said Scorpio in bored tones. "An ancient treasure map?"

"Even better," said Quintaro, pointing at Sapphire. "I've got *her*!"

Scorpio turned to look at Sapphire, who hadn't said a word since commenting on her drink. "What do you think you know?" he asked.

"It was my race that created the Godstone," she said, "and my race that hid it."

"What makes you think you can find it no matter who created and hid it?" demanded Scorpio.

"My race is not like yours," she said. "We are born with a racial memory, back to the very first member of our species that crawled up out of the sea, breathed air, and developed limbs."

"If every member of your race knows where it is, what makes you think one of them hasn't found it already?"

"I would know if they had," said Sapphire.

"Anyway," said Quintaro, "it's not necessary that *you* believe in the stone. Just believe in the money." He paused. "You just have to lead us to where she knows it is, and I'll offer you thirty thousand credits for the job, in any currency that's accepted in the system—half now and half when we find it . . . or when we reach the location and it's not there."

"Thirty thousand buys us for one month maximum," replied Scorpio.

"It's a deal."

We don't want any part of this, said Merlin wordlessly.

Why not?

He doesn't have the slightest idea what he's after. She put him up to this, and that description, vague as it was, of a godstone was planted in his mind by her. I was born on Venus, and I've never heard of it. As for him, he plans to kill us and take back the down payment when we reach our destination.

Then read her mind and see if the damned thing really exists.

I can't.

Scorpio frowned. *You never came across a sentient being of any race where you couldn't read their minds, or at least their emotions.*

This one's different came Merlin's answer. *She looks human, but she's not—not human, and not a mutation as far as I can tell.*

Is she Venusian?

I don't know.

What do you know about her?

Nothing—and that scares me.

I've never seen you afraid of anything before. Now you're scaring me.

"Well, Scorpion?" said Quintaro.

We need the money, thought Scorpio. *And we'll be on our guard. What the hell—the breeding season's ending.*

I take that as an agreement.

Yeah, thought Merlin. *This really isn't much of a world once the females are out of heat.*

I'm sure they share that conviction.

"All right, Mr. Quintaro," said Scorpio. "You've got yourself a deal."

"I assume you paused because you were consulting with your partner?"

Assuage his fears, thought Merlin.

"Yeah." Scorpio blinked his eyes rapidly and shook his head. "Whenever he's reading my mind," he lied, "I feel a kind of buzzing inside my head and I go blank for a moment."

Quintaro, convinced that his plans and motives remained unknown, relaxed noticeably.

"We'll start in the morning," he announced. "I've got the transportation we'll need."

"Where are you staying?" asked Scorpio.

"We thought we'd spend the night here."

Scorpio turned to McAnany. "Got a spare room?"

"Got five of 'em," answered the bartender.

"Well, now you have four," said Scorpio. He turned back to Quintaro. "Where's your vehicle?"

"Down the trail a bit," he answered, gesturing toward the door.

"It had better be a VZ Model 3 or 4," said Scorpio. "Anything else will sink right into this mud if it's carrying the four of us plus our gear."

"It's a VZ4," confirmed Quintaro.

"Okay," said Scorpio. "All that's left is your down payment."

Quintaro reached into a pocket, pulled out a wad of thousand-credit notes, peeled off fifteen of them, and pushed them across the table to Scorpio.

Scorpio pocketed the money and turned to Sapphire. "You don't say much, do you?"

"Not much," she agreed.

"How did you two meet?"

"It was the strangest damned thing," said Quintaro. "I was actually getting set to take my leave of this world—I hear they've discovered a couple of truly phenomenal diamond pipes on Ganymede, and since I'm a jeweler by trade, I was thinking of going there—"

He's lying. He's a gambler, and he's got a criminal record as long as your arm.

"—when I ran into this lovely lady as I was checking out of my hotel by the Amber City spaceport. We got to talking, found we had a lot in common, and eventually she mentioned the godstone. Well, hell, everyone on Venus has heard about it . . ."

"Not me," said Scorpio.

Not him, either—until she planted his interest in his head.

"Well, you're a transient," said Quintaro. "People talk about you all over the system. I've heard about your exploits on Mars and half a dozen moons. They say you can't go back to Earth, but I figure that's either just romantic bullshit or else at least you had a good reason for whatever you did."

"You don't have to sell, Mr. Quintaro," said Scorpio. "I've already accepted your offer."

"Anyway, it's perfectly understandable that someone who spends so little time here—or anywhere—wouldn't know about the godstone."

"Interesting name: godstone," said Scorpio.

"I find it very evocative. Even if it was worthless, I'd spend this much money just to say I was the guy who found it."

"Well, I hope we can make you feel you've gotten your money's worth," said Scorpio. "We'll be leaving at daybreak, which comes pretty early around here. You might want to grab some sleep."

"Good idea," said Quintaro. He got to his feet. "Come, my dear."

Sapphire stood up with an alien grace, linked her arm in his, and walked to the door.

"Where *is* our room?" Quintaro asked McAnany.

"Down the corridor, last room on the right," answered the bartender. "Door's unlocked. You're just staying one night. I'll lock it from here once you're inside the room, and just open it tomorrow when you're leaving."

"Thanks," said Quintaro. He handed a bill to McAnany. "This ought to cover it."

"That'll buy you three rooms," answered McAnany, "each with a woman in it." Suddenly he looked embarrassed. "Sorry, Miss Sapphire, ma'am . . . Just a figure of speech."

She'd shown no annoyance when he uttered the remark, and she showed no reaction when he apologized. A moment later the couple walked out of the bar and down the corridor, and though they were still arm in arm Scorpio got the feeling that she was leading him. He got up and placed his empty glass on the bar.

"You ever heard of this godstone?" he asked.

McAnany shook his head. "Nope. He makes it sound like you and me are the only ones who haven't."

"Yeah," said Scorpio. "Well, don't believe everything you hear." He looked over at Merlin. "You all through making a new generation? We've got work to do if we're heading out in the morning."

My race has sexual seasons, just like many mammals on your home world. Live with it. At least I'm not chasing a new female on every world we visit like some partners I could mention.

Only because it wouldn't do you the least bit of good, thought Scorpio. *Now, what kind of equipment are we going to need for this foolishness?*

It's only foolish if you consider Quintaro. He thinks he's looking for a valuable gem, and he intends to kill us when he finds it.

It's probably just what he hopes it is—something worth a few million on the black market—or even the open market if the government doesn't claim it as a planetary treasure.

Don't think about it or him. She is the wild card.

She's one of the better-looking cards in the deck.

That's all you can say—or think—after what I've told you?

What do you want me to say?

Idiot.

Scorpio reached behind the bar, grabbed a bottle, and filled his glass.

"You look annoyed," noted McAnany.

"There are two blue creatures in this place," answered Scorpio. "Quintaro went off with the gorgeous one, and I'm stuck with the ugly one who doesn't trust anyone, including his partner."

"If he's worried about you running off with the money that guy gave you, I can stick it in the safe until you get back," offered McAnany.

"Bad trade," muttered Scorpio.

"Trade? What trade?"

"You get fifteen thousand credits, and I get a deserted, beat-up tavern when I get back."

"You think I'd do that to you?" said McAnany in hurt tones.

"Even Merlin thinks so, and he hates to agree with me." Scorpio picked up his bottle and began walking to the door. "Unlock my room for me. I got a feeling this is the last night I'm going to be sleeping in a bed for a month."

Scorpio dragged himself out of bed at sunrise, staggered to the bathroom, and rinsed his face off. He wasn't thrilled with the smell or taste of Venus's water, but he remembered all the worlds where water was almost impossible to come by. He considered shaving, decided not to, stuck a trio of fresh outfits into a cloth bag, slung it over his shoulder, strapped on a holster and a modified laser pistol, donned his boots, and walked out into the corridor, almost tripping over Merlin.

Good morning, said the Venusian silently.

I think what I hate most about you is that you never have to sleep, Scorpio replied grumpily.

Right. It's only saved your life three or four times.

Okay, I'll find something else to hate about you. Where are our clients—up or still snoring?

They were eating what passes for breakfast in the bar about an hour ago. They're outside now.

"Why?" said Scorpio aloud. "It's been pouring for the past month. I can't imagine it stopped in the last six hours."

They've got all kinds of protective gear. Also, I think they're probably sitting in the vehicle.

"A car or a boat?"

A little of each, I think.

"And there's room for all four of us and our gear?" said Scorpio. "This guy's not a piker."

Whatever that is.

"Okay, well, we might as well get this show on the road," said Scorpio, walking down the crushed-rock path with Merlin falling into step behind him. He descended until the ground leveled out, and came to the Venusian version of a safari car, an amphibious vehicle that could negotiate oceans, rivers, streams, muddy jungles, just about every kind of unfriendly landscape the planet could provide.

Scorpio briefly looked up from force of habit, but there was no sun to be seen, nor had there been in many millennia, just incredibly thick cloud cover. He then paused to wipe the rain from his face.

"Good morning, Scorpion," said Quintaro from where he and Sapphire sat in the back of the vehicle. "I assume you're doing the driving. That is, unless your partner can . . ."

"I'll drive," answered Scorpio, tossing his bag into the very back. "Nice vehicle."

"Actually, it belongs to a friend."

And the friend has issued an arrest warrant against him for stealing it.

You're surprised? thought Scorpio. He opened a door for Merlin, waited for his partner to find a comfortable position in a vehicle that was never meant for his species.

"Where's the control?" he asked.

"This is the latest model," answered Quintaro. "Put your thumb on the pad there . . . yes, that's right . . . and now, as long as you keep your thumb there it'll follow your orders, whether on land or water. That green button on the side of it will morph it into a boat or whatever else we need."

Scorpio mentally ordered the vehicle to move forward slowly, down the crushed-stone path leading away from the tavern, and it was soon skimming over the muddy jungle trail.

"Got the hang of it?" asked Quintaro.

"Yeah," answered Scorpio. "I've never driven anything as expensive as one of these VZ4's, but I've piloted ships that responded to mental commands."

"This is a goddamned vehicle, not a ship," said Quintaro irritably. "Just remember that." It was the first time his smooth façade had slipped, and Scorpio wondered why.

He's scared to death.

Why?

We're not going for a friendly ride in the park. Most people who go more than a few miles into this jungle don't come out. That goes for my race, too.

Shit! We didn't charge him enough.

I told you not to take it.

They'd gone a mile into the jungle when Scorpio saw something moving off to his left . . . something *large*. He stopped the vehicle and stared.

"What is it?" asked Quintaro nervously.

"I don't know. Merlin, has Venus got something black and shaggy about the height of Tritonian *lymix*, only half again as long?"

It's a herbivore.

Even herbivores can kill you when they're that big. We'll give him a wide berth.

"Well, what does he say?"

"He says yes," lied Scorpio, partially to see the man's reaction, but mostly to see if Sapphire would contradict him. He checked her reaction in a small dashboard screen, and saw that she was smiling in amusement.

"Well, as long as we're going to be cooped up in this thing for a while, perhaps Sapphire will enlighten my partner and me about the history of the godstone."

Why bother? thought Merlin. *If she's lying, and she probably will be, I won't be able to tell.*

There's got to be a little truth to it. Maybe, like a famous detective of literature, we can construct the comprehensive whole from some of the disparate parts.

Oh, well, we've got nothing better to do.

"Miss Sapphire, ma'am?" said Scorpion.

"It is the greatest treasure on all of Venus," she replied emotionlessly, as if by rote. "The man who finds it will become wealthy beyond all imagining."

"What's it made of?"

"I'm no meteorologist."

"Neither am I," said Scorpio. "But if I was spending all this money, and possibly risking my life, I'd sure as hell know what I *think* it's made of."

"Rare stones," she replied. "Rarer than diamonds, than rubies, than emeralds. Stones that exist nowhere else in the universe."

Possible? asked Scorpio.

I'm no gemologist. It seems unlikely, except . . .

Except?

Except why has she taken over Quintaro's mind, and why is she risking her life by coming along?

"Are there any holographs of it?" asked Scorpio.

"Not to my knowledge," replied Sapphire.

"Does it show up in any history books?"

"Of course. That's how I know it exists."

"Which ones?"

"I can't remember."

I don't have to read her mind to know she's lying, thought Scorpio.

I still can't read it. All I get is a feeling of danger.

Let me know when it feels imminent.

You'll know, replied Merlin with absolute certainty.

They were three days out from the tavern. The rain had diminished but not stopped, and Scorpio was inclined to think of his surroundings as a rainjungle, which in his mind was one step more impenetrable and uncomfortable than a rain forest. Finally they came to a river that didn't have endless trees poking out of it, and he moved the vehicle onto it, where it floated smoothly and began picking up speed.

Overhead were a variety of avians—mostly bright red and yellow, a few blue, one large one that seemed to prey on the others a rich green, all of them seemingly impervious to the constant rain. There were myriads of water flowers of every imaginable shape and color, each reaching high and opening up its petals to the life-giving rain.

There were a few large beasts in the water. Most ignored them, and the vehicle, now a vessel, easily avoided the others. Scorpio found that he was actually relaxing and enjoying the trip when Sapphire leaned forward.

"Slow down," she said.

"We're not going that fast," he replied.

"Nevertheless," she said. "We're going to leave the river and go back on land very soon now."

Scorpio looked ahead. The trackless jungle bordering the river looked exactly the same as it had for the past fifty miles.

"Are you sure?" he said, frowning.

"Absolutely."

"I can't believe this area's ever been mapped," he continued. "What makes you think—?"

"Just do it!" she snapped.

Out of the corner of his eye, he could see her elbow Quintaro.

"Just do what I'm paying you to do and stop bitching," he said.

"Yes, sir, right away, sir," said Scorpio.

Subservience doesn't become you, noted Merlin.

If you've got a quicker way to make the twenty grand we need to repair the ship, I'll punch him out. Otherwise, we play the game.

"Here," said Sapphire in another half mile.

Scorpio ordered the boat onto a sandy beach, paused until it had morphed back into a vehicle, and began driving it along a narrow animal trail, all the while wondering how Sapphire could know that this particular trail was the one she wanted, even if she'd had some treasure map and committed it to memory. The tides rose; they fell; and what was a trail today might have been an ocean bottom or an empty plain in antiquity, when the map would have been created, if indeed there was a map and a godstone at all.

They proceeded along the trail for three hours. Then, as the sun was starting to set, spreading a soft golden hue through the thick cloud layer, Scorpio brought the vehicle to a sudden stop.

"What is it?" demanded Quintaro, but Scorpio and Merlin, who had a better view of the trail, were out of the car and racing ahead on foot. They reached the object of their attention in seconds and knelt next to a blood-covered, thick-bearded man dressed in tattered rags.

Scorpio was about to pull him off the trail when he realized that there probably wouldn't be another vehicle along for years, maybe decades, so he decided against moving the wounded man. Instead, he made a very crude pillow out of a stand of weeds and used it to prop up the man's head, then opened what was left of the man's shirt and began examining his body for wounds.

"Something with claws has ripped him up pretty badly," he reported, as Quintaro ran up to them. "I've never seen paws on a herbivore, so it's almost certainly a predator, and that means the claws were probably carrying half a dozen diseases picked up from victims."

He's very groggy, and perhaps a bit delusional, said Merlin silently. *But something's very strange here. I mean, other than his being here at all.*

What is?

He was ripped to shreds by a predator, but pull what's left of his shirt off his left shoulder.

Scorpio did so. "Son of a bitch!" he muttered, as the shoulder displayed a fresh laser burn, clearly just a few hours old.

"Let me suggest that whatever ripped him up did so as he was escaping from whoever burned his shoulder," said Scorpio.

"Makes sense," said Quintaro. He frowned. "But who else would be in this godforsaken wilderness?"

"Who indeed?" said Sapphire, joining them. Scorpio couldn't get over the notion that she sounded amused though her expression gave nothing away.

Scorpio examined the man's body to see where to staunch the bleeding and realized that there were just too many flesh wounds to close them all, or even half of them, before he bled to death.

Merlin, go to my bag and find the strongest stimulant I've got in the med kit.

Why waste it? He's as good as dead.

Let's see if we can wake him up long enough for him to tell us who the hell did this to him. I don't know about you, but I'd like to know what areas to avoid.

Merlin took off without sending another thought and was back a moment later with the entire kit.

Why the whole thing?

I don't know one stimulant from another.

Scorpio opened the kit, pulled out the one he wanted, pulled out a lozenge, and pressed it against the inside of the man's upper lip, holding it in place for the count of ten. By eight, the man had opened his pain-filled eyes.

"What . . . where?" he mumbled.

"You're among friends," said Scorpio. "Do you remember what happened to you?"

"Some kind of monster ran right through camp . . . killed about half of us . . . I got in the way when one of my team took a shot at it . . . I don't remember anything after that . . ."

"What are you—your group—doing out here in the middle of nowhere?" asked Scorpio.

You're not going to believe it, thought Merlin.

"Looking for . . ." The man's voice trailed off. Scorpio thought he had perhaps twenty seconds of life left, but then he looked past Scorpio's shoulder and tensed. "I'm sorry, Miss Sapphire, ma'am," he said. "I did my best. I hope you find it."

All the tension went out of his body then, his eyes rolled back into his head, and Scorpio knew that he was dead.

He laid the man's body back, stood up, and turned to

Sapphire. "What the hell was *that* all about?" he demanded.

"I don't know," she replied.

"He *knew* you, even knew your name and what you're searching for."

"He didn't mention the godstone," replied Sapphire. "He might have seen me around Amber City, might have heard my name."

"Bullshit!" snapped Scorpio.

"You're not thinking of quitting?" demanded Quintaro.

"I've got to discuss it with my partner," said Scorpio. "We've been lied to, and I don't know how or why."

"We'll go stand by that tree while you talk," said Quintaro, taking Sapphire's arm and starting off through the mud.

"Don't bother," said Scorpio. "You can't hear us wherever you are."

Well? thought Scorpio.

He wasn't delusional, replied Merlin. *He knew her, knew her name, knew she's after the godstone. What makes no sense is that, as I say, he wasn't delusional or delirious.*

This whole thing doesn't make any sense, thought Scorpio.

That's what's disturbing.

So do we quit or not?

It's up to you.

Scorpio considered his options. *I say we stay.*

The money means that much to you? I mean, we can make it elsewhere. We always manage.

Right now the money's got nothing to do with it. This is a hell of a mystery, and I don't plan to spend the rest of my life wondering about it.

Merlin shrugged, a gesture that sent ripples down both of his sides. *Okay.*

Scorpio turned to Sapphire. "We'll continue—for now."

If he expected to see anything—gratitude, arrogance, any change of expression at all—he was disappointed.

"Then let's get back to the vehicle and get started before it gets bogged down in the mud," said Quintaro. "If there's another group hunting for the stone, we don't want to lose any time."

Acting or telling the truth? asked Scorpio.

I keep telling you—he's the dupe, she's the brain. He hasn't got enough sense to act, except when it comes to lying about paying us.

"All right," said Scorpio. "Let's climb back in."

"What about *him?*" asked Quintaro, indicating the dead man.

"There won't be a bone left by morning," answered Scorpio. "And if we bury him in this muck, they'll just dig him up five minutes after we're gone."

They reached the vehicle and were soon heading deeper into the jungle, with Sapphire directing Scorpio to make minor course corrections every few miles.

When it was too dark to go any farther, Scorpio tried to decide—as he did every night—whether they'd be safer on land or on the nearby river.

You ask every night, and my answer's always the same: There's stuff that can cause you problems either way, replied Merlin when Scorpio queried him.

Scorpio considered his options and decided to remain on the land. If something was going to sneak up and attack, it didn't make much difference whether it hid in the thick jungle or beneath the surface of the water, but *he* would feel better defending himself on dry—well, soggy—land.

He tried to find a place where at least they couldn't be attacked from above, but there was no escaping the huge, towering trees that gave shelter to arboreal predators. Finally he found an area that looked minimally flatter and more protected from the rain, and announced that they were spending the night there.

"Can't you find something with less bugs, at least?" complained Quintaro.

"Shut up," said Sapphire, coldly and emotionlessly, and

Quintaro immediately fell silent.

The four of them sat in total silence for half an hour. Scorpio was about to drift off to sleep when something nudged his arm. He thought it was Merlin, but when he opened his eyes he found that it was Sapphire.

"Yeah?" he said.

She placed a finger to her lips. "Softly. There's movement out there. Intelligent movement."

He stared at her. "You sure it's not the group our dead friend belonged to—the one with a blue woman named Sapphire?"

She stared at him for a long moment, no emotion crossing her face. Finally she said, "There are seven distinct sentient races on Venus."

"That we know about," he answered, staring at her meaningfully.

"The movement out there is directed by intellect," she continued. "They are not human, and they have never heard of the godstone."

"Then I say live and let live," said Scorpio.

"Do not be a fool," she said. "I would not awaken and warn you if there was no danger. They are creatures that are endemic to the jungle, and they prey on strangers."

"They must be starving," said Scorpio, unimpressed. "Nobody wanders through here without a purpose. That can't afford them much sustenance."

"They plan to eat you, you and Quintaro—but only after they rob us first."

"But not you?"

She stared at him for a long moment. "I was mistaken," she said.

"About what?"

"You *are* a fool."

She got up and walked back to where she had been sitting.

Merlin, were you listening?

Well, observing, anyway.

Are these critters really out there, and are they intelligent?

They're out there. They're sentient; I would question "intelligent."

They plan to attack?

That's a given.

How did she know?

We'll worry about that later. Tell Quintaro not to fire his weapon when the fighting starts. He might hit me in the dark.

You need some help?

If I do, I'll let you know.

Scorpio looked around and saw that Merlin had already departed in what he assumed was the direction of what he now thought of as the enemy. He decided that they needed a term for them—not for their race, of which he was still ignorant—but for their occupation, because given his surroundings "highwayman" seemed ridiculous. There wasn't a highway within a thousand miles, and except for himself and Quintaro, there weren't any men within miles.

He considered giving Sapphire a reassuring smile, decided she didn't need one, and sat perfectly still, trying to pick up any unusual sounds through the driving rain. Nothing happened for almost ten minutes. Then the calm was shattered by a hideous scream. A minute later came another. The area two miles to the east was briefly illuminated by weapons fire, then another scream came to his ears.

Three dead, two running away as fast as they can.

Good! thought Scorpio. *What race were they?*

Tabolla. They just crossed over the barrier to sentience about two millennia ago. They're the most primitive of our sentient races.

Okay. Bring back their weapons if they're any better than ours—

They aren't.

And I'll see you in a few minutes.

I'll be back in the morning. I haven't eaten in two days.

Did you have to say that? thought Scorpio disgustedly.

Well, you did ask.

Scorpio shut his eyes for a moment, trying to rid himself of the mental image of Merlin eating his enemies—the fact that they were raw didn't help—and then reopened them and found himself staring at Sapphire, who stared back, unblinking.

"It's over," he said. "But you know that, don't you?"

She offered no answer, and her expression never changed.

"Who the hell *are* you?" he continued after a moment.

Still no answer.

"Or perhaps I should ask: *what* are you?"

"Leave her alone," said Quintaro.

"To quote your blue friend, shut up," said Scorpio.

Quintaro's face darkened, and he seemed about to get to his feet, when Sapphire laid a hand lightly on his arm.

"He's right," she said coldly. "Shut up."

The anger didn't vanish, but he didn't say another word.

They sat silently, facing each other. Scorpio paid no attention to Quintaro but stared directly at Sapphire. His only observation by the time he fell asleep twenty minutes later was that she never blinked.

Merlin had rejoined them by the time Scorpio awoke. Quintaro was sprawled in a water-resistant one-man tent, snoring, and Sapphire was sitting motionless, her back against a tree trunk, protected from the rain by the overhanging branches, exactly as she'd been when he'd fallen asleep. His first thought was that she had somehow died during the night, but when he got to his feet, she did the same.

"Wake your friend and we'll be on our way," said Scorpio.

She stepped on the splayed fingers of Quintaro's left hand.

"Damn!" he yelled, getting to his knees and shaking the

hand vigorously. Then he saw who had been responsible for it, and all anger vanished.

"Five minutes to take care of your morning ablutions," announced Scorpio. "We'll eat in the vehicle."

Why do I detect added tension? asked Merlin. *I thought I was the one taking all the risks last night.*

You ever see her eat, or sneak off to relieve herself?

No. But I already told you she wasn't human.

I could fill a book with things she isn't, replied Scorpio. *What the hell is she?*

I have no idea.

Was she in any danger last night? Can she even feel pain?

There's an easy way to find out.

Oh?

You'll see.

Quintaro returned a couple of minutes later, Scorpio walked off for a few minutes and returned, and the four of them began approaching the vehicle, which was about ten yards away. As they did so, Merlin "accidentally" bumped against Sapphire, and her upper arm made contact with the branch of a thorn-covered bush.

"Merlin apologizes," said Scorpio quickly.

"Not a problem," she replied.

"You're bleeding," he noted, indicating a pair of dark spots that suddenly appeared at the point of contact.

She looked at her arm, said "Oh," and continued walking to the vehicle.

Hypothesis, thought Merlin. *If you cut her, she bleeds. She just doesn't feel it or care about it.*

They reached the vehicle, climbed into it, and began moving. Scorpio tried to think of the direction as "inland," but he was so thoroughly lost and so completely surrounded by jungle except for a handful of narrow, winding trails that the whole planet seemed inland from where he was.

"Any idea how much farther we have to go?" he asked Quintaro, on the assumption that there was no sense asking Sapphire.

"Beats me," he said. He jerked a thumb toward Sapphire. "She's my map."

"Has she deigned to tell you what we do when we get there?"

"Pick it up and go home," answered Quintaro.

"I mean, is it above the ground? Is it in plain sight? Is it guarded, and if so, by who or by what?"

"I don't know," said Quintaro. "I just know it'll put us on easy street for life."

Is he holding back anything, or maybe out-and-out lying? asked Scorpio.

Nope. View him as one hundred percent dupe.

Why did she choose him, I wonder?

Half the reason's in your pocket.

After an uneventful three hours, the rain finally became no more than a light drizzle. Scorpio stopped, just to rest his eyes for a few minutes. Quintaro got out to stretch his legs, as did Merlin, who found the vehicle especially unsuited to a member of his race.

"How's your arm?" Scorpio asked Sapphire, who had remained seated.

"It's fine," she replied. "But you knew that."

"We could talk about all the things I don't know instead," offered Scorpio. "Quantum mechanics, ancient Mercurian pottery, godstones . . ."

"You know what you need to know," said Sapphire.

"I hope you don't think I want the damned thing for myself," said Scorpio. "If I did, I wouldn't be driving *you* to it."

"That is not a satisfactory answer, Mr. Scorpio."

"Oh?"

"Mr. Quintaro and I are in your power. He is a fool, as well you know."

"And you are . . . ?"

"A weak, helpless woman," she answered.

"That may be a record," said Scorpio, smiling at her. "Three lies in a four-word sentence."

She did not return his smile, but she took no offense, and indeed didn't react at all.

"So what does a godstone *do*?" continued Scorpio.

She stared at him and did not answer.

"You said it was worth more than diamonds. Forgive my ignorance, but what *is* worth more than diamonds?"

Silence.

"How long have you been looking for it?"

No answer.

"A year? Three years?" A pause. "Ten thousand years?"

No reaction, and no answer.

"Sooner or later, we really have to have a little talk," said Scorpio. "A two-sided talk. I'm sure you think my partner and I are expendable, just as I know you think Quintaro is. Leaving aside whether Merlin and I can take care of ourselves, if there *is* a godstone, whatever the hell that means, is *Venus* expendable?"

"Venus is my home," she said in cold, flat, emotionless tones.

"So you *can* answer when you want to."

She stared at him and offered no reply.

"What makes you want to?" he asked. "For example, how about an identical blue woman named Sapphire who is leading an expedition that's looking for something called—you'll never believe this—a godstone? You think that might be an interesting topic of conversation?"

"Try not to be as big a fool as Quintaro."

"You sure know how to hurt a guy," said Scorpio.

"Yes, I do," replied Sapphire. "You would do well to remember that."

"It's never far from my mind," he assured her. "One last question."

"Good."

"For *this* conversation," he qualified. He stared at her. "Did you pick us, or did Quintaro?" He held up a hand. "Before you say it was him, I know who approached us and made the offer. But was it his idea or yours?"

"He has no ideas," said Sapphire.

"All right," said Scorpio. "Then let me ask you: why us?"

"He told you why. You are said to be the most lethal man on the planet, and even I do not know who or what will be guarding the godstone."

He stared at her for a long moment. "Okay," he said at last. "We'll talk again later."

She neither confirmed nor contradicted him but merely stared at him. Or *through* him, he decided.

He climbed out of the vehicle, walked around for a few moments to get a little life back into his legs, then joined Merlin, who was staring at some large golden fish in a stream.

"You're hungry after everything—or every*one*—that you ate last night?" he asked with a smile.

No, I just like their colors, and the patterns they make when the light hits them through the water.

Our blue-skinned passenger thinks we're going to run into some trouble when we finally reach the godstone.

I know. I see the conversation in your mind.

What do you think? asked Scorpio. *We're just pawns in whatever game she's playing. We could steal the vehicle right now, strand them here, and go back to McAnany's tavern. Quintaro probably won't last a day, but somehow I think it would only prove a minor inconvenience to her.*

I think we don't want to be looking over our shoulders for the rest of our lives.

"Okay," said Scorpio aloud. "It was just a suggestion. Let's get back to the vehicle."

He called to Quintaro, and a few moments later the vehicle was making its way along the muddy trail.

They came to the first fork they'd encountered in almost two days, and Sapphire directed Scorpio to keep to the left. He did so, and soon the road began winding downhill. By nightfall, they were running alongside a major river, perhaps two miles across. The rain returned with a vengeance, and they spent the night inside the vehicle, doing their best to ignore the thunder and the discomfort.

At dawn, they began again, but within a mile the trail had totally washed away, and Sapphire directed Scorpio to take the amphibious vehicle into the river, which paralleled the trail for quite a few miles, and simply keep to the water until the trail was passable again.

"I *hate* all this water!" complained Quintaro.

"Be glad you have it," replied Scorpio, plunging the vehicle into the river as it morphed into a boat.

"Be glad of *this*?"

"Comes from the clouds," said Scorpio. "No clouds, no rain—but also no clouds and this is a desert world too hot for anything to live on it."

"They live on Mercury, don't they?" said Quintaro irritably.

"Not on the sunward side, they don't," replied Scorpio. "They stick to the terminator zone and the dark side."

"You've been there, I presume?" said Quintaro dubiously.

"A couple of times," Scorpio confirmed. "Not my favorite place."

"Scorpion!" said Sapphire suddenly. "Hard left!"

Scorpio instantly did as she ordered and saw a huge creature, about the size of a humpback whale, far more reptilian than fish or mammal, suddenly surface where they had been, pluck three low-flying avians out of the sky in its gaping jaws, then vanish beneath the water again.

"I've seen stuff like that in the ocean!" remarked Quintaro. "But inland, in a river?"

"This isn't like Earth," explained Scorpio. "It's *all* freshwater, and every creature that lives in the one can swim in the other."

"God, I hate this world!" snapped Quintaro.

"Then what are you doing here?"

Quintaro made a face. "Looking for action. I'd been hearing about *baxitla*—that's the Venusian card game—for years, so I thought I might as well give it a try." A smug smile. "Did okay, too. You cost me less than one night's winnings. And I met *her*"—he jerked a thumb in Sapphire's direction—"and once we get our hands on the godstone, I plan to open my own casino in Marsport."

Just what Marsport needs, thought Scorpio. *An eighty-fourth casino—or is it the eighty-fifth?*

It's all academic, answered Merlin. *However this ends up, you don't think he's going make any money, do you?*

Scorpio gave the creature five minutes to get sufficiently downstream, then guided the VZ4 back to the center of the river.

They proceeded for another seven miles, then he decided that the trail was safe enough to handle the vehicle, so he ordered the wheels to emerge, withdrew the rudder into the interior, and was soon traversing the jungle road once more.

"How's this thing fixed for fuel?" asked Quintaro. "I haven't noticed you refreshing the pile or whatever the hell it runs on since we started."

"It's got a series of atomic batteries," answered Scorpio. "We started with a dozen, and we've drained two of them and are on our third." He paused, then added with a smile, "It's your vehicle. I figure you'd have asked the salesman."

"Took it right out of the showroom," answered Quintaro smoothly. Then: "Will we have enough to get back?"

"Depends on where we're going," said Scorpio. "Ask your ladyfriend."

Which ended the conversation.

* * *

The rain increased as night fell, the trees weren't clustered enough or carrying enough foliage to provide sufficient shelter, and they slept in the vehicle once more. Merlin was gone when Scorpio awoke, but that wasn't unusual. The Venusian was out hunting for a meal, and he'd be back when he'd killed and eaten it.

"Does it ever cool off?" muttered Quintaro as he climbed out of the vehicle and went off toward a cluster of trees.

"Sure," said Scorpio. "As soon as the rain stops."

Quintaro glared at him, then disappeared behind the trees.

"We're alone again," noted Scorpio. "Care to continue our conversation?"

No answer.

"May I take your silence as an affirmative?"

"Does that pass for wit on Earth?" she asked coldly.

"Haven't you been there?"

She stared at him without speaking.

"I hope to hell this damned stone exists, and it's everything you think it is."

"It exists," she said with absolute certainty.

"With a name like 'godstone' it must be part of some religion," he continued.

She remained silent.

"You might tell me a little something about it, including where you think it is. I'd hate to have the other Dragon Lady get there first."

She gave him a contemptuous glare, then got out of the vehicle, walked to the far side of the clearing, and raised her unblinking face to the sky, oblivious of the rain cascading down.

"Come on back!" he said, half shouting to be heard over the rain. "I won't ask any more questions." *This morning,* he added mentally.

She stood motionless for a full minute. He sat where he was, watching her, thinking that under other circumstances he could admire a figure like that all day, especially the way the water made her outfit cling to it, but all he could do was wonder what was going on inside that head.

Finally, she returned to the vehicle just as Quintaro reappeared. Then it was simply a matter of waiting for Merlin.

When he hadn't shown up for another half hour, Scorpio got out of the vehicle. He couldn't search for tracks—they were washing away almost as fast as they were made, and besides, Merlin's had probably been made hours ago, but he felt he had to do *something*, even if just get wet. He heard chattering in the branches above him, looked up, and saw a family of monkeylike bipeds huddled against the rain. They didn't have tails like the monkeys of Earth did, but growing out of each wrist was not only a hand but a long, thin tentacle that functioned like a tail, wrapping around limbs to secure the owner's position.

After another few minutes a thought reached him.

Stop standing in the rain, you idiot, and get the med kit ready. I'll be there in another minute.

Scorpio rushed around to the back of the vehicle, opened it up, and got the kit. As he did so, Merlin broke through the foliage and came into view, limping painfully across the small clearing.

"What the hell happened to you?" said Scorpio. "You need help getting into the vehicle?"

No, I can make it, thought Merlin, and proved it by jumping up into it, emitting a pained grunt. *I can't reach my wounds. Rub some antiseptic and painkiller on them.*

Scorpio applied the proper medications. "I take it breakfast fought back?" he said as he rubbed them in.

No. There's another safari out here.

A safari?

I don't know what else you'd call it.

They can't be on foot?

No, they're in a pair of vehicles. There are only four of them left—well, three now. One of the men took a shot at me—probably thought I was dinner. He did me some damage, as you can see. When he knew I was hit, he left the vehicle and came after me.

You killed him, of course, thought Scorpio.

Of course.

I wonder what the devil they're hunting for this far from what passes for civilization?

I thought you'd never ask, replied Merlin. *They're after the godstone—and they've got a blue-skinned lady guiding them.*

Oh, shit! Scorpio paused for a moment. *Is this the same group as the guy we found a couple of days ago?*

Probably.

Probably?

He died before I could find out.

How far are they from us?

Maybe four miles west. Five at the outside.

Okay, try to get some rest.

Scorpio closed and latched the back, then walked around and climbed onto his seat.

"Is he all right?" asked Quintaro without much interest.

"He's a hard one to kill," answered Scorpio. He turned to face Sapphire. "Mind if I ask you a question or two?"

"Yes," she answered.

"Live with it," he said. "My first question: have you got a sister?"

She didn't answer, but he thought he could see the muscles in her face suddenly become tense.

"Okay," he said. "I've got another one, and this time I'm going to insist on an answer."

"Leave her alone!" snapped Quintaro.

"Be quiet," said Scorpio. "This doesn't concern you." He turned back to Sapphire. "Are we in a race?"

"No," she said.

"You're sure?"

She merely stared at him.

You might as well proceed, thought Merlin. *You can't turn back, not now that you've as much as told her we're within walking distance of her double's safari.*

You really think she can stop us or do us harm if we do turn back?

I'm incapacitated, and you're in no more danger going forward than going back to the tavern against her wishes.

Shit! I hate it when you make sense.

Scorpio put the vehicle in gear and began proceeding once again along the muddy trail.

They traveled for two more hours, and suddenly Scorpio could see another river—or an equally broad branch of the river he was paralleling—sweeping toward them from his right. He brought the vehicle to a halt and turned once again to Sapphire.

"All right," he said. "Either I'm going to have to cross the river at some point in the next couple of miles, or I'm going to turn to the right, but even then we're going to be confronted by another river. So which way do you want me to go?"

"Straight," she said.

"You're sure?"

She merely stared at him. He shrugged and began moving forward again. The forest began thinning out, and suddenly he came to a valley that was almost devoid of trees, and again he stopped.

"What now?" demanded Quintaro.

"That ground looks awfully soft," replied Scorpio. "I know this is a VZ4, but I don't know if even *it* has enough muscle to get us out of there if we bog down."

"It's not there," said Sapphire.

"What's not there?" asked Scorpio, surprised that she'd offered an unsolicited comment.

"What I want," she replied. "Go around it."

"Okay."

"To the right," she added.

"You sure?" he said. "If Merlin's correct, that's the direction your kid sister's coming from."

"Shut up," she said, and turned to look out over the landscape.

Scorpio followed her instructions, found a long-unused path—he hesitated to call it even a trail—and began carefully moving along it.

How are you doing back there? he asked.

I'll live, answered Merlin. *Or if I don't, it won't be the wounds that kill me. We're getting close.*

We're getting close to the guys that tried to kill you. I don't know that we're getting close to the godstone.

I still can't read her mind, but she's getting so excited the whole vehicle reeks of it.

It does?

Well, it does if you're a Venusian.

Scorpio kept to the path. In about a mile it widened, and suddenly the rain completely stopped. One minute it was pouring as it had been doing for months, and one minute it was like a dry summer day on Earth.

"What happened to the rain?" asked Quintaro. "It's like there's an invisible wall, and nothing's falling on this side of it."

"I don't know," replied Scorpio. He glanced at Sapphire. "One of us doesn't seem surprised."

She offered no reply, as he had known she wouldn't, and he continued moving forward. The path, which was once again a trail, remained thoroughly muddy.

That's damned strange, he thought.

What is?

The rain's stopped. Yet the trail's as muddy as if it has been pouring for weeks, right up to a minute ago.

I have no answer.

I'll settle for a guess. I don't feel good about this.

Scorpio waited for a comment from anyone, even Quintaro. When none was forthcoming, he sent the vehicle forward. He proceeded for three hundred yards, then four, then five—and then he heard it, like the loudest kind of thunder, but it was coming from ahead and below, not above.

"What the hell is that?" demanded Quintaro nervously.

"A waterfall," said Scorpio. "Like it or not, this is the end of the line."

"Not quite," said Sapphire. "Keep going."

"Those falls can't be a mile away," protested Scorpio. "Just where the hell do you want me to go?"

"I'll tell you when to stop," she said.

What do you think?

You might as well, answered Merlin. *One way or another we're going to her destination. Why walk?*

Scorpio began moving the vehicle very slowly. He'd gone another quarter mile when two slightly older, less elegant, mud-covered vehicles came into sight off to his right.

Quintaro pulled a pulse gun out of his pocket and started to take aim when Sapphire brought the edge of her hand down on his wrist, so hard that Scorpio could hear the bone crack even over Quintaro's scream of pain.

"You goddamned bitch!" he bellowed. "I'm trying to protect our fucking interest!"

"You don't even know what our interest is," she replied, her voice thick with contempt.

"I know what *mine* is," he snarled, "and no one's going to double-cross me!"

He turned and took a swing at her with his uninjured hand. Scorpio didn't see what happened next, but an instant later Quintaro collapsed, unconscious, on the floor of the vehicle.

Suddenly, Sapphire reached forward and handed Scorpio a wad of bills. "Here is what he owed you," she said. "You know, of course, that he had no intention of ever paying it."

"I know," said Scorpio, pocketing the cash.

"He is of no further use to us," she continued. "Stop the vehicle."

Scorpio came to a stop, and she opened a door and shoved Quintaro's body out into the mud.

"Is he dead or alive?" asked Scorpio.

"One or the other," said Sapphire. "Now proceed."

"To *where*?"

"Do you see that tall skeleton of a dead tree ahead of us?"

"Hard to miss. First dead tree I've seen since we started."

"That is our destination."

"We've come all this way for a barren tree?" said Scorpio.

"Do not appear a bigger fool than I think you to be," replied Sapphire.

"Are we trying to beat the other party to it?"

"It makes no difference, for they are the same."

Scorpio frowned. *Does that make any sense to you?*

None.

Scorpio drove to within fifty feet on the tree and came to a stop. He and Sapphire got out immediately, and he walked around the back, unlatched it, and helped Merlin to the ground. The Venusian was still unsteady on his feet, but he walked by his partner's side, trying his best to ignore his pain.

The two other vehicles had stopped also, and Scorpio observed them closely, waiting to see just how much this other blue-skinned woman resembled Sapphire—but when she emerged from the second vehicle, he stared, blinked, rubbed his eyes, and stared again.

They could be twins! he thought.

Or somehow even closer, answered Merlin.

"There will be protections, of course," said Sapphire.

The woman Scorpio now thought of as The Other Sapphire uttered a terse command, and two men who had been driving the vehicles walked cautiously toward the tree, weapons in hand. When they got within five feet of it there was a sound of static and both men collapsed, one screaming, one unconscious or dead.

"Now it is our turn," said Sapphire.

"I'm not going to walk right up to it," answered Scorpio. "I just saw what happens to men who do that."

"Nevertheless."

"It might help if you tell me what I'm looking for."

"You already know," she said.

"Is the tree the godstone?"

"Of course not."

"Then what is it, where is it, and what does it look like?"

"The stone is irregularly shaped, perhaps a foot in width. Do you see that hole at the base of the tree?"

"Yeah. Looks like some animal has burrowed in."

"Eons ago, one probably did. But now that is where the godstone is. You will approach on hands and knees, hopefully below the tree's ability to see or detect you, and bring it back."

"That's suicidal," said Scorpio.

"Perhaps not."

"I'll prove it to you," he said. He reached into the vehicle, pulled out Quintaro's pulse gun from where it had fallen, bent over, and hurled it sidearm at the hole. It was never more than eighteen inches above the ground—and it burst into flame when it was within three feet of the tree. Scorpio straightened up. "Like I said, suicide."

"It must be retrieved," she said, and for the first time he detected a trace—more than a trace—of emotion in her voice.

"Oh, Merlin and I can get it for you," said Scorpio. "I'm just trying to come up with a price."

"You've been paid."

"I've been paid for taking you here. Risking our lives to retrieve a protected treasure wasn't part of the bargain."

"You will get it *now!*" she demanded, her face suddenly a mask of fury.

"I'm thinking," he said. "I'd ask for this vehicle, which would certainly bring a healthy price once we clean it up, but we both know it's stolen property. And something tells me that you're not going to share the godstone with me, no matter what you promise. You're really not in a very good bargaining position, Blue Lady."

"I can kill you right now," she said. "You know that, don't you?"

"I'm a little harder to kill than you think," said Scorpio. "But even if you can, you'd better be sure you know how to get the stone without me."

She glared hatefully at him but said nothing.

"Okay," he said after a moment's consideration. "There's got to be a black-market dealer who's not too fussy and has a market for a VZ4. I'll take the vehicle once we're done here. Do we have an agreement?"

She nodded.

"All right." He pulled out his laser pistol and aimed a beam right at the tree trunk, about ten feet above the ground.

"What are you doing?" demanded Sapphire.

"It'll take a lot more than this to melt a stone," said Scorpio. As the trunk began smoldering, then burst into flame, he trained his beam on a low-hanging branch. "Damned good thing it's not raining here. No way I could set it on fire if it were." He turned to Sapphire. "Somebody on your side has a hell of a lot of powers but very little brain."

In seconds, the branch was aflame, and Scorpio trained his weapon on another branch. As he did so he leaned down, picked up a heavy stick, and hurled it at the opening. Nothing happened, except that the stick bounced off the trunk.

"Okay, Merlin," he said. "In and out quick. I don't know when this damned tree might collapse."

The Venusian limped ahead, reached the tree, inserted his head and neck into the opening, and emerged a moment later with an irregularly shaped crystal in his mouth.

"The stone!" breathed Sapphire.

And suddenly Scorpio became aware of the other blue woman racing forward, an ecstatic expression on her face, the mirror image of Sapphire's. At first he thought she was intending to stop at Sapphire's side. Then he realized that she was heading straight *at* Sapphire, probably to give her a hug of shared triumph. But finally he saw that she wasn't slowing down, and that Sapphire had turned to face her and was making no effort to avoid the collision—except that there wasn't a collision at all. He couldn't tell which of them absorbed the other, or if both had somehow formed halves of a totally new body, but suddenly there was just one female—he hesitated to think of her as a woman—standing before him.

She took the stone from Merlin and held it up. Scorpio noticed that there was an irregularly shaped hole in it, maybe two inches across, very near the center.

Sapphire began uttering a chant, not quite singing it but more than merely reciting it.

You recognize the language? asked Scorpio.

I know every tongue in current use on Venus, but I've never heard this one before.

Suddenly, the stone became brighter, then brighter still, and finally blindingly bright. Scorpio had to close his eyes, and though he was standing right next to it, he couldn't feel any additional heat.

Then a powerful masculine voice broke the silence.

"At last!" it bellowed. "At last I live again!"

Scorpio opened one eye, expecting to be blinded again. Instead he saw a huge blue man, twelve feet tall, burly and heavily muscled, sporting a thick beard, and clad in a glittering robe that seemed to be a softer, pliable version of the stone.

"A thousand times a thousand years I have waited for the day I always knew would come!"

He reached out and enclosed Sapphire's extended hand in his powerful fingers. As he made physical contact with her, as their hands touched, both of them became as bright as the stone had been a moment ago, and they began growing until they soon were taller than the tallest of the surrounding trees. He spoke once more, his voice as loud as a thunderclap: "I am complete again!"

Scorpio tried to watch them, but again his eyes could not stand the brightness, and he had to close them. He kept them closed for almost a minute, then he suddenly sensed that the brightness had dissipated.

He opened his eyes, as did Merlin, and found that they were alone, that there was no trace of either Sapphire or the being—he couldn't help thinking of it as a god—that had been imprisoned in the stone.

He suddenly remembered the stone, leaned down, and picked it up.

The hole is gone, observed Merlin.

I know, answered Scorpio silently. *He's complete again.*

Scorpio carried the stone to his vehicle and placed it on a cushioned seat.

Pity to leave the other two vehicles behind, but hot or not, the VZ4 is worth more than both of them put together. Let's head back to McAnany's tavern, and get those repairs made to the ship.

And the stone?

I think we'll keep it as a souvenir, replied Scorpio. *After all, how many bona fide gods and goddesses do we plan to meet in the future?* He helped Merlin into the vehicle, climbed in himself, and began heading back the way they'd come. *Now let's get the hell off of Venus as quick as we can.* He increased the speed.

Why so fast? asked Merlin.

I'm not a practitioner of any religion, and I like it that way.

What's that got to do with anything?

Scorpio shrugged. "Maybe nothing," he said aloud. "But we've just turned a god loose on the world, and I don't think he plans on going back into retirement anytime soon."

IAN McDONALD

British author Ian McDonald is an ambitious and daring writer with a wide range and an impressive amount of talent. His first story was published in 1982, and since then he has appeared with some frequency in *Interzone, Asimov's Science Fiction,* and elsewhere. In 1989 he won the *Locus* "Best First Novel" Award for his novel *Desolation Road.* He won the Philip K. Dick Award in 1991 for *King of Morning, Queen of Day.* His other books include *Out on Blue Six* and *Hearts, Hands and Voices, Terminal Café, Sacrifice of Fools, Evolution's Shore, Kirinya, Ares Express, Brasyl,* as well as three collections of his short fiction, *Empire Dreams, Speaking in Tongues,* and *Cyberabad Days.* His novel, *River of Gods,* was a finalist for both the Hugo Award and the Arthur C. Clarke Award in 2005, and a novella drawn from it, "The Little Goddess," was a finalist for the Hugo and the Nebula. He won a Hugo Award in 2007 for his novelette "The Djinn's Wife," won the Theodore Sturgeon Award for his story "Tendeleo's Story," and in 2011 won the John W. Campbell Memorial Award for his novel *The Dervish House.* His most recent books are the starting volume of a YA series, *Planesrunner,* another new novel, *Be My Enemy,* and a big retrospective collection, *The Best of Ian McDonald.* His latest novel is *Empress of the Sun.* Born in Manchester, England, in 1960, McDonald has spent most of his life in Northern Ireland, and now lives and works in Belfast.

In the eloquent and evocative story that follows, we trace a trail of flowers across the planet Venus toward a troubled and uncertain destiny.

Botanica Veneris: Thirteen Papercuts by Ida Countess Rathangan

IAN McDONALD

INTRODUCTION BY MAUREEN N. GELLARD
MY MOTHER HAD FIRM INSTRUCTIONS THAT, IN CASE of a house fire, two things required saving: the family photograph album and the Granville-Hydes. I grew up beneath five original floral papercuts, utterly heedless of their history or their value. It was only in maturity that I came to appreciate, like so many on this and other worlds, my great-aunt's unique art.

Collectors avidly seek original Granville-Hydes on those rare occasions when they turn up at auction. Originals sell for tens of thousands of pounds (this would have amused Ida); two years ago, an exhibition at the Victoria and Albert Museum was sold out months in advance. Dozens of anthologies of prints are still in print: the *Botanica Veneris*, in particular, is in fifteen editions in twenty-three languages, some of them non-Terrene.

The last thing the world needs, it would seem, is another *Botanica Veneris*. Yet the mystery of her final (and only) visit to Venus still intrigues half a century since her disappearance. When the collected diaries, sketchbooks, and field notes came to me after fifty years in the possession of the Dukes of Yoo, I realized that I had a precious opportunity to tell the true story of my great-aunt's expedition—and of a forgotten chapter in my family's history. The books were in very poor condition, mildewed and blighted in Venus's humid, hot climate. Large parts were illegible or simply missing. The narrative was frustratingly incomplete. I have resisted the urge to fill in those blank spaces. It would have been easy to dramatize, fictionalize, even sensationalize. Instead I have let Ida Granville-Hyde speak. Hers is a strong, characterful, attractive voice, of a different class, age, and sensibility from ours, but it is authentic, and it is a true voice.

The papercuts, of course, speak for themselves.

Plate I: *V strutio ambulans:* the Ducrot's Peripatetic Wort, known locally as Daytime Walker (Thent) or Wanderflower (Thekh).
Cut paper, ink and card.

Such a show!

At lunch, Het Oi-Kranh mentioned that a space-crosser—the *Quest for the Harvest of the Stars,* a Marsman—was due to splash down in the lagoon. I said I should like to see that—apparently I slept through it when I arrived on this world. It meant forgoing the sorbet course, but one does not come to the Inner Worlds for sorbet! Het Oi-Kranh put his spider-car at our disposal. Within moments, the Princess Latufui and I were swaying in the richly upholstered bubble beneath the six strong mechanical legs. Upward it carried us, up the vertiginous lanes and winding staircases, over the walls and balcony gardens, along the buttresses and roof walks and up the ancient iron ladderways of Ledekh-Olkoi. The islands of the archipelago are small, their populations vast, and the only way for them to build is upward. Ledekh-Olkoi resembles Mont St. Michel vastly enlarged and coarsened. Streets have been bridged and built over into a web of tunnels quite impenetrable to non-Ledekhers. The Hets simply clamber over the homes and lives of the inferior classes in their nimble spider-cars.

We came to the belvedere atop the Starostry, the ancient pharos of Ledekh-Olkoi that once guided mariners past the reefs and atolls of the Tol Archipelago. There we clung—my companion, the Princess Latufui, was queasy—vertigo, she claimed, though it might have been the proximity of lunch—the whole of Ledekh-Olkoi beneath us in myriad levels and layers, like the folded petals of a rose.

"Should we need glasses?" my companion asked.

No need! For at the instant, the perpetual layer of grey cloud parted and a bolt of light, like a glowing lance, stabbed down from the sky. I glimpsed a dark object fall though the air, then a titanic gout of water go up like a dozen Niagaras. The sky danced with brief rainbows, my companion wrung her hands in delight—she misses the sun terribly—then the clouds closed again. Rings of waves rippled away from the hull of the space-crosser, which floated like a great whale low in the water, though this world boasts marine fauna even more prodigious than Terrene whales.

My companion clapped her hands and cried aloud in wonder.

Indeed, a very fine sight!

Already the tugs were heading out from the protecting arms of Ocean Dock to bring the ship in to berth.

But this was not the finest Ledekh-Olkoi had to offer. The custom in the archipelago is to sleep on divan-balconies, for respite from the foul exudations from the inner layers of the city. I had retired for my afternoon reviver—by my watch, though by Venusian Great Day it was still midmorning and would continue to be so for another two weeks. A movement by the leg of my divan. What's this? My heart surged. *V strutio ambulans:* the Ambulatory Wort, blindly, blithely climbing my divan!

Through my glass, I observed its motion. The fat, succulent leaves hold reserves of water, which fuel the coiling and uncoiling of the three ambulae—surely modified roots—by hydraulic pressure. A simple mechanism, yet human minds see movement and attribute personality and motive. This was not pure hydraulics attracted to light and liquid, this was a plucky little wort on an epic journey of peril and adventure. Over two hours, I sketched the plant as it climbed my divan, crossed to the balustrade, and continued its journey up the side of Ledekh-Olkoi. I suppose at any time millions of such flowers are in constant migration across the archipelago, yet a single Ambulatory Wort was miracle enough for me.

Reviver be damned! I went to my space trunk and unrolled my scissors from their soft chamois wallet. Snip snap! When a cut demands to be made, my fingers literally itch for the blades!

When he learned of my intent, Gen Lahl-Khet implored me not to go down to Ledekh Port, but if I insisted (I insisted: oh I insisted!), at least take a bodyguard or go armed. I surprised him greatly by asking the name of the best armorer his city could supply. Best Shot at the Clarecourt November shoot, ten years on the trot! Ledbekh-Teltai is the most famous gunsmith in the archipelago. It is illegal to import weaponry from off-planet—an impost, I suspect, resulting from the immense popularity of hunting Ishtari janthars. The pistol they have made me is built to my hand and strength: small, as requested; powerful, as required; and so worked with spiral-and-circle Archipelagan intaglio that it is a piece of jewelry.

Ledekh Port was indeed a loathsome bruise of alleys and tunnels, lit by shifts of grey, watery light through high skylights. Such reeks and stenches! Still, no one ever died of a bad smell. An Earthwoman alone in an inappropriate place was a novelty, but from the nonhumanoid Venusians, I drew little more than a look. In my latter years, I have been graced with a physical *presence* and a destroying stare. The Thekh, descended from Central Asian nomads abducted en masse in the eleventh century from their bracing steppe, now believe themselves the original humanity, and so consider Terrenes beneath them, and they expected no better of a subhuman Earthwoman.

I did turn heads in the bar. I was the only female—humanoid, that is. From Carfax's *Bestiary of the Inner Worlds*, I understand that among the semiaquatic Krid, the male is a small, ineffectual symbiotic parasite lodging in the mantle of the female. The barman, a four-armed Thent, guided me to the snug where I was to meet my contact. The bar overlooked the Ocean Harbor. I watched dockworkers scurry over the vast body of the space-crosser, in and out of hatches that had opened in the skin of the ship. I did not like to see those hatches; they ruined its perfection, the precise, intact curve of its skin.

"Lady Granville-Hyde?"

What an oily man, so well lubricated that I did not hear his approach.

"Stafford Grimes, at your service."

He offered to buy me a drink, but I drew the line at that unseemliness. That did not stop him ordering one for himself and sipping it—and several successors—noisily during the course of my questions. Years of Venusian light had turned his skin to wrinkled brown leather: drinker's eyes looked out from heavily hooded lids—years of squinting into the ultraviolet. His neck and hands were mottled white with pockmarks where melanomas had been frozen out. Sunburn, melancholy, and alcoholism: the classic recipe for honorary consuls systemwide, not just on Venus.

"Thank you for agreeing to meet me. So, you met him."

"I will never forget him. Pearls of Aphrodite. Size of your head, Lady Ida. There's a fortune waiting for the man . . ."

"Or woman," I chided, and surreptitiously activated the recording ring beneath my glove.

Plate 2: *V flor scopulum*: the Ocean Mist Flower. The name is a misnomer: the Ocean Mist Flower is not a flower, but a coral animalcule of the aerial reefs of the Tellus Ocean. The seeming petals are absorption surfaces drawing moisture from the frequent ocean fogs of those latitudes. Pistils and stamen bear sticky palps, which function in the same fashion as Terrene spiderwebs, trapping prey. Venus boasts an entire ecosystem of marine insects unknown on Earth.

This cut is the most three-dimensional of Lady Ida's Botanica Veneris. Reproductions only hint at the sculptural quality of the original. The "petals" have been curled at the edges over the blunt side of a pair of scissors. Each of the 208 palps has been sprung so that they stand proud from the black paper background.

Onion paper, hard-painted card.

THE HONORARY CONSUL'S TALE

PEARLS OF APHRODITE. TRULY, THE PEARLS BEYOND price. The pearls of Starosts and Aztars. But the cloud reefs are perilous, Lady Ida. Snap a man's body clean in half, those bivalves. Crush his head like a Vulpeculan melon. Snare a hand or an ankle and drown him. Aphrodite's Pearls are blood pearls. A fortune awaits anyone, my dear, who can culture them. A charming man, Arthur Hyde—that brogue of his made anything sound like the blessing of heaven itself. Charm the avios from the trees—but natural, unaffected. It was no surprise to learn he was of aristocratic stock. Quality: you can't hide it. In those days,

I owned a company—fishing trips across the archipelago. The legend of the Ourogoonta, the Island that is a Fish, was a potent draw. Imagine hooking one of those! Of course, they never did. No, I'd take them out, show them the cloud reefs, the Krid hives, the wing-fish migration, the air-jellies; get them pissed on the boat, take their photographs next to some thawed-out javelin-fish they hadn't caught. Simple, easy, honest money. Why wasn't it enough for me? I had done the trick enough times myself, drink one for the punter's two, yet I fell for it that evening in the Windward Tavern, drinking hot, spiced kashash and the night wind whistling up in the spires of the dead Krid nest-haven like the caged souls of drowned sailors. Drinking for days down the Great Twilight, his one for my two. Charming, so charming, until I had pledged my boat on his plan. He would buy a planktoneer—an old bucket of a sea skimmer with nary a straight plate or a true rivet in her. He would seed her with spores and send her north on the great circulatory current, like a maritime cloud reef. Five years that current takes to circulate the globe before it returns to the arctic waters that birthed it. Five years is also the time it takes the Clam of Aphrodite to mature—what we call pearls are no such thing. Sperm, Lady Ida. Compressed sperm. In waters, it dissolves and disperses. Each Great Dawn the Tellus Ocean is white with it. In the air, it remains compact—the most prized of all jewels. Enough of fluids. By the time the reef ship reached the deep north, the clams would be mature and the cold water would kill them. It would be a simple task to strip the hulk with high-pressure hoses, harvest the pearls, and bank the fortune.

Five years makes a man fidgety for his investment. Arthur sent us weekly reports from the Sea Wardens and the Krid argosies. Month on month, year on year, I began to suspect that the truth had wandered far from those chart coordinates. I was not alone. I formed a consortium with my fellow investors and chartered a 'rigible.

And there at Map 60 North, 175 East, we found the ship—or what was left of it, so overgrown was it with Clams of Aphrodite. Our investment had been lined and lashed by four Krid cantoons: as we arrived, they were in the process of stripping it with halberds and grappling hooks. Already the decks and superstructure were green with clam meat and purple with Krid blood. Arthur stood in the stern frantically waving a Cross of St. Patrick flag, gesturing for us to get out, get away.

Krid pirates were plundering our investment! Worse, Arthur was their prisoner. We were an unarmed aerial gadabout, so we turned tail and headed for the nearest Sea Warden castle to call for aid.

Charmer. Bloody buggering charmer. I know he's your flesh and blood, but . . . I should have thought! If he'd been captured by Krid pirates, they wouldn't have let him wave a bloody flag to warn us.

When we arrived with a constabulary cruiser, all we found was the capsized hulk of the planktoneer and a flock of avios gorging on clam offal. Duped! Pirates my arse—excuse me. Those four cantoons were laden to the gunwales with contract workers. He never had any intention of splitting the profits with us.

The last we heard of him, he had converted the lot into Bank of Ishtar bearer bonds—better than gold—at Yez Tok and headed in-country. That was twelve years ago.

Your brother cost me my business, Lady Granville-Hyde. It was a good business; I could have sold it, made a little pile. Bought a place on Ledekh Syant—maybe even made it back to Earth to see out my days to a decent calendar. Instead . . . Ach, what's the use. Please believe me when I say that I bear your family no ill will—only your brother. If you do succeed in finding him—and if I haven't, I very much doubt you will—remind him of that, and that he still owes me.

Plate 3: *V lilium aphrodite:* the Archipelago sea lily. Walk-the-Water in Thekh: there is no comprehensible translation from Krid. A ubiquitous and fecund diurnal plant, it grows so aggressively in the Venerian Great Day that by Great Evening bays and harbors are clogged with blossoms and passage must be cleared by special bloom-breaker ships.

Painted paper, watermarked Venerian tissue, inks, and scissor-scrolled card.

So dear, so admirable a companion, the Princess Latufui. She knew I had been stinting with the truth in my excuse of shopping for paper, when I went to see the honorary consul down in Ledekh Port. Especially when I returned without any paper. I busied myself in the days before our sailing to Ishtaria on two cuts—the Sea Lily and the Ocean Mist Flower—even if it is not a flower, according to my Carfax's *Bestiary of the Inner Worlds*. She was not fooled by my industry and I felt soiled and venal. All Tongan women have dignity, but the princess possesses such innate nobility that the thought of lying to her offends nature itself. The moral order of the universe is upset. How can I tell her that my entire visit to this world is a tissue of fabrications?

Weather again fair, with the invariable light winds and interminable grey sky. I am of Ireland, supposedly we thrive on permanent overcast, but even I find myself pining for a glimpse of sun. Poor Latufui: she grows wan for want of light. Her skin is waxy, her hair lustreless. We have a long time to wait for a glimpse of sun: Carfax states that the sky clears partially at the dawn and sunset of Venus's Great Day. I hope to be off this world by then.

Our ship, the *Seventeen Notable Navigators,* is a well-built, swift Krid *jaicoona*—among the Krid the females are the seafarers, but they equal the males of my world in the richness and fecundity of their taxonomy of ships. A *jaicoona*, it seems, is a fast catamaran steam packet, built for the archipelago trade. I have no sea legs, but the *Seventeen Notable Navigators* was the only option that would get us to Ishtaria in reasonable time. Princess Latufui tells me it is a fine and sturdy craft though built to alien dimensions: she has banged her head most painfully several times. Captain Highly-Able-at-Forecasting, recognizing a sister seafarer, engages the princess in lengthy conversations of an island-hopping, archipelagan nature, which remind Latufui greatly of her home islands. The other humans aboard are a lofty Thekh, and Hugo von Trachtenberg, a German in very high regard of himself, of that feckless type who think themselves gentleman adventurers but are little more than grandiose fraudsters. Nevertheless, he speaks Krid (as truly as any Terrene can) and acts as translator between princess and captain. It is a Venerian truth universally recognized that two unaccompanied women travelers must be in need of a male protector. The dreary hours Herr von Trachtenberg fills with his notion of gay chitchat! And in the evenings, the interminable games of Barrington. Von Trachtenberg claims to have gambled the game professionally in the cloud casinos: I let him win enough for the sensation to go to his head, then take him game after game. Ten times champion of the County Kildare mixed bridge championships is more than enough to beat his hide at Barrington. Still he does not get the message—yes, I am a wealthy widow, but I have no interest in jejune Prussians. Thus I retire to my cabin to begin my studies for the *crescite dolium* cut.

Has this world a more splendid sight than the harbor of Yez Tok? It is a city most perpendicular, of pillars and towers, masts and spires. The tall funnels of the ships, bright with the heraldry of the Krid maritime families, blend with god-poles and lighthouse and customs towers and cranes of the harbor, which in turn yield to the tower houses and campaniles of the Bourse, the whole rising to merge with the trees of the Ishtarian Littoral Forest—pierced here and there by the comical roofs of the estancias of the Thent *zavars* and the gilded figures of the star gods on their minarets. That forest also rises, a cloth of green, to break into the rocky palisades of the Exx Palisades. And there—oh how thrilling!—glimpsed through mountain passes unimaginably high, a glittering glimpse of the snows of the altiplano. Snow. Cold. Bliss!

It is only now, after reams of purple prose, that I realize what I was trying to say of Yez Tok: simply, it is city as botany—stems and trunks, boles and bracts, root and branch!

And out there, in the city-that-is-a-forest, is the man who will guide me farther in my brother's footsteps: Mr. Daniel Okiring.

Plate 4: *V crescite dolium:* the Gourd of Plenty. A ubiquitous climbing plant of the Ishtari littoral, the Gourd of Plenty is so well adapted to urban environments that it would be considered a weed, but for the gourds, which contains a nectar prized as a delicacy among the coastal Thents. It is toxic to both Krid and humans.

The papercut bears a note on the true scale, written in gold ink.

THE HUNTER'S TALE

HAVE YOU SEEN A JANTHAR? REALLY SEEN A JANTHAR? Bloody magnificent, in the same way that a hurricane or an exploding volcano is magnificent. Magnificent and appalling.

The films can never capture the sense of scale. Imagine a house, with fangs. And tusks. And spines. A house that can hit forty miles per hour. The films can never get the sheer sense of mass and speed—or the elegance and grace—that something so huge can be so nimble, so agile! And what the films can never, ever capture is the smell. They smell of curry. Vindaloo curry. Venerian body chemistry. But that's why you never, ever eat curry on *asjan*. Out in the Stalva, the grass is tall enough to hide even a janthar. The smell is the only warning you get. You catch a whiff of vindaloo, you run.

You always run. When you hunt janthar, there will always be a moment when it turns, and the janthar hunts you. You run. If you're lucky, you'll draw it on to the gun line. If not . . . The 'thones of the Stalva have been hunting them this way for centuries. Coming-of-age thing. Like my own Maasai people. They give you a spear and point you in the general direction of a lion. Yes, I've killed a lion. I've also killed janthar—and run from even more.

The 'thones have a word for it: the *pnem*. The fool who runs.

That's how I met your brother. He applied to be a pnem for Okiring *Asjans*. Claimed experience over at Hunderewe with Costa's hunting company. I didn't need to call Costa to know he was a bullshitter. But I liked the fellow—he had charm and didn't take himself too seriously. I knew he'd never last five minutes as a *pnem*. Took him on as a camp steward. They like the personal service, the hunting types. If you can afford to fly yourself and your friends on a jolly to Venus, you expect to have someone to wipe your arse for you. Charm works on these bastards. He'd wheedle his way into their affections and get them drinking. They'd invite him and before you knew it he was getting their life-stories—and a lot more beside—out of them. He was a careful cove too—he'd always stay one drink behind them and be up early and sharp-eyed as a hawk the next morning.

Bring them their bed tea. Fluff up their pillows. Always came back with the fattest tip. I knew what he was doing, but he did it so well—I'd taken him on, hadn't I? So, an aristocrat. Why am I not surprised? Within three trips, I'd made him Maître de la Chasse. Heard he'd made and lost one fortune already . . . is that true? A jewel thief? Why am I not surprised by that either?

The Thirtieth Earl of Mar fancied himself as a sporting type. Booked a three-month Grand *Asjan;* he and five friends, shooting their way up the Great Littoral to the Stalva. Wives, husbands, lovers, personal servants, twenty Thent *asjanis* and a caravan of forty *graapa* to carry their bags and baggage. They had one *graap* just for the champagne—they'd shipped every last drop of it from Earth. Made so much noise we cleared the forest for ten miles around. Bloody brutes—we'd set up hides at water holes so they could blast away from point-blank range. That's not hunting. Every day they'd send a dozen bearers back with hides and trophies. I'm surprised there was anything left, the amount of metal they pumped into those poor beasts. The stench of rot . . . God! The sky was black with carrion avios.

Your brother excelled himself: suave, in control, charming, witty, the soul of attention. Oh, most attentive. Especially to the Lady Mar . . . She was no kack-hand with the guns, but I think she tired of the boys-club antics of the gents. Or maybe it was just the sheer relentless slaughter. Either way, she increasingly remained in camp. Where your brother attended to her. Aristocrats—they sniff each other out.

So Arthur poled the Lady Mar while we blasted our bloody, brutal, bestial way up onto the High Stalva. Nothing would do the thirtieth earl but to go after janthar. Three out of five *asjanis* never even come across a janthar. Ten percent of hunters who go for janthar don't come back. Only ten percent! He liked those odds.

Twenty-five sleeps we were up there, while Great Day turned to Great Evening. I wasn't staying for night on the Stalva. It's not

just a different season, it's a different world. Things come out of
sleep, out of dens, out of the ground. No, not for all the fortune
of the earls of Mar would I spend night on the Stalva.

By then, we had abandoned the main camp. We carried bare
rations, sleeping out beside our mounts with one ear tuned to
the radio. Then the call came: Janthar sign! An *asjani* had seen a
fresh path through a speargrass meadow five miles to the north
of us. In a moment, we were mounted and tearing through the
High Stalva. The earl rode like a madman, whipping his *graap* to
reckless speed. Damn fool: of all the Stalva's many grasslands,
the tall pike-grass meadows were the most dangerous. A janthar
could be right next to you and you wouldn't see it. And the pike
grass disorients, reflects sounds, turns you around. There was
no advising the Earl of Mar and his chums, though. His wife
hung back—she claimed her mount had picked up a little
lameness. Why did I not say something when Arthur went back
to accompany the Lady Mar! But my concern was how to get
everyone out of the pike grass alive.

Then the earl stabbed his shock goad into the flank of his
graap, and before I could do anything he was off. My radio
crackled—form a gun line! The mad fool was going to run the
janthar himself. Aristocrats! Your pardon, ma'am. Moments
later, his *graap* came crashing back through the pike grass to
find its herd mates. My only hope was to form a gun line and
hope—and pray—that he would lead the janthar right into our
cross fire. It takes a lot of ordnance to stop a janthar. And in this
kind of tall-grass terrain, where you can hardly see your hand in
front of your face, I had to set the firing positions just right so
the idiots wouldn't blow each other to bits.

I got them into some semblance of position. I held the
center—the *lakoo.* Your brother and the Lady Mar I ordered to take
jeft and *garoon*—the last two positions of the left wing of the gun
line. Finally, I got them all to radio silence. The 'thones teach you

how to be still, and how to listen, and how to know what is safe and what is death. Silence, then a sustained crashing. My spotter called me, but I did not need her to tell me: that was the sound of death. I could only hope that the earl remembered to run in a straight line, and not to trip over anything, and that the gun line would fire in time . . . a hundred hopes. A hundred ways to die.

Most terrifying sound in the world, a janthar in full pursuit! It sounds like it's coming from everywhere at once. I yelled to the gun line; steady there, steady. Hold your fire! Then I smelled it. Clear, sharp: unmistakable. Curry. I put up the cry: Vindaloo! Vindaloo! And there was the mad earl, breaking out of the cane. Madman! What was he thinking! He was in the wrong place, headed in the wrong direction. The only ones who could cover him were Arthur and Lady Mar. And there, behind him: the janthar. Bigger than any I had ever seen. The Mother of All Janthar. The Queen of the High Stalva. I froze. We all froze. We might as well try to kill a mountain. I yelled to Arthur and Lady Mar. Shoot! Shoot now! Nothing. Shoot for the love of all the stars! Nothing. Shoot! Why didn't they shoot?

The 'thones found the Thirtieth Earl of Mar spread over a hundred yards.

They hadn't shot because they weren't there. They were at it like dogs—your brother and the Lady Mar, back where they had left the party. They hadn't even heard the janthar.

Strange woman, the Lady Mar. Her face barely moved when she learned of her husband's terrible death. Like it was no surprise to her. Of course, she became immensely rich when the will went through. There was no question of your brother's ever working for me again. Shame. I liked him. But I can't help thinking that he was as much used as user in that sordid little affair. Did the Lady of Mar murder her husband? Too much left to chance. Yet it was a very convenient accident. And I can't help but think that the thirtieth earl knew what his lady was up to;

and a surfeit of cuckoldry drove him to prove he was a man.

The janthar haunted the highlands for years. Became a legend. Every aristo idiot on the Inner Worlds who fancied himself a Great Terrene Hunter went after it. None of them ever got it though it claimed five more lives. The Human-Slayer of the Selva. In the end it stumbled into a 'thone clutch trap and died on a pungi stake, eaten away by gangrene. So we all pass. No final run, no gun line, no trophies.

Your brother—as I said, I liked him though I never trusted him. He left when the scandal broke—went up-country, over the Stalva into the Palisade country. I heard a rumor he'd joined a mercenary *javrost* unit, fighting up on the altiplano.

Botany, is it? Safer business than Big Game.

Plate 5: *V trifex aculeatum:* Stannage's Bird-Eating Trifid. Native of the Great Littoral Forest of Ishtaria. Carnivorous in its habits; it lures smaller, nectar-feeding avios with its sweet exudate, then stings them to death with its whiplike style and sticky, poisoned stigma.
Cutpaper, inks, folded tissue.

The princess is brushing her hair. This she does every night, whether in Tonga, or Ireland, on Earth, or aboard a space-crosser, or on Venus. The ritual is invariable. She kneels, unpins, and uncoils her tight bun and lets her hair fall to its natural length, which is to the waist. Then she takes two silver-backed brushes, and, with great and vigorous strokes, brushes her hair from the crown of her head to the tips. One hundred strokes, which she counts in a Tongan rhyme that I very much love to hear.

When she is done, she cleans the brushes, returns them to the baize-lined case, then takes a bottle of coconut oil and works it through her hair. The air is suffused with the sweet smell of coconut. It reminds me so much of the whin flowers of home, in the spring. She works patiently and painstakingly, and when she has finished, she rolls her hair back into its bun and pins it. A simple, dedicated, repetitive task, but it moves me almost to tears.

Her beautiful hair! How dearly I love my friend Latufui!

We are sleeping at a *hohvandha*, a Thent roadside inn, on the Grand North Road in Canton Hoa in the Great Littoral Forest. Tree branches scratch at my window shutters. The heat, the humidity, the animal noise are all overpowering. We are far from the cooling breezes of the Vestal Sea. I wilt, though Latufui relishes the warmth. The arboreal creatures of this forest are deeper-voiced than in Ireland; bellings and honkings and deep booms. How I wish we could spend the night here—Great Night—for my Carfax tells me that the Ishtarian Littoral Forest contains this world's greatest concentration of luminous creatures—fungi, plants, animals, and those peculiarly Venerian phyla in between. It is almost as bright as day. I have made some daytime studies of the Star Flower—no Venerian Botanica can be complete without it—but for it to succeed, I must hope that there is a supply of luminous paint at Loogaza, where we embark for the crossing of the Stalva.

My dear Latufui has finished now and closed away her brushes in their green baize-lined box. So faithful and true a friend! We met in Nuku'alofa on the Tongan leg of my Botanica of the South Pacific. The king, her father, had issued the invitation—he was a keen collector—and at the reception I was introduced to his very large family, including Latufui, and was immediately charmed by her sense, dignity, and vivacity. She invited me to tea the following day—a very grand affair—where she confessed that as a minor princess, her only hope of fulfilment was in marrying well—an institution in which she had no interest. I replied that I had visited the South Pacific as a time apart from Lord Rathangan—it had been clear for some years that he had no interest in me (nor I in him). We were two noble ladies of compatible needs and temperaments, and there and then we became firmest friends and inseparable companions. When Patrick shot himself and Rathangan passed into my possession, it was only natural that the princess move in with me.

I cannot conceive of life without Latufui; yet I am deeply ashamed that I have not been totally honest in my motivations for this Venerian expedition. Why can I not trust? Oh secrets! Oh simulations!

> *V   stellafloris   noctecandentis:*   the   Venerian Starflower. Its name is the same in Thent, Thekh, and Krid. Now a popular Terrestrial garden plant, where it is known as glow berry, though the name is a misnomer. Its appearance is a bunch of night-luminous white berries, though the berries are in fact globular bracts, with the bioluminous flower at the center. Selective strains of this flower traditionally provide illumination in Venerian settlements during the Great Night.
>
> Paper, luminous paint (not reproduced). The original papercut is mildly radioactive.

By high train to Camahoo.

We have our own carriage. It is of aged gothar wood, still fragrant and spicy. The hammocks do not suit me at all. Indeed, the whole train has a rocking, swaying lollop that makes me seasick. In the caravanserai at Loogaza, the contraption looked both ridiculous and impractical. But here, in the high grass, its ingenuity reveals itself. The twenty-foot-high wheels carry us high above the grass, though I am in fear of grass fires—the steam tractor at the head of the train does throw off the most ferocious pother of soot and embers.

I am quite content to remain in my carriage and work on my Stalva-grass study—I think this may be most sculptural. The swaying makes for many a slip with the scissor, but I think I have caught the feathery, almost downy nature of the flower heads. Of a maritime people, the princess is at home in this rolling ocean of grass and spends much of her time on the observation balcony, watching the patterns the wind draws across the grasslands.

It was there that she fell into conversation with the Honorable Cormac de Buitlear, a fellow Irishman. Inevitably, he ingratiated himself and within minutes was taking tea in our carriage. The Inner Worlds are infested with young men claiming to be the junior sons of minor Irish gentry, but a few minutes' gentle questioning revealed not only that he was indeed the Honorable Cormac—of the Bagenalstown De Buitlears—but a relative, close enough to know of my husband's demise, and the scandal of the Blue Empress.

Our conversation went like this.

HIMSELF: The Grangegorman Hydes. My father used to knock around with your elder brother—what was he called?

MYSELF: Richard.

HIMSELF: The younger brother—wasn't he a bit of a black sheep? I remember there was this tremendous scandal. Some jewel—a sapphire as big as a thrush's egg. Yes—that was the expression they used in the papers. A thrush's egg. What was it called?

MYSELF: The Blue Empress.

HIMSELF: Yes! That was it. Your grandfather was

presented it by some Martian princess. Services rendered.

MYSELF: He helped her escape across the Tharsis steppe in the revolution of 'II, then organized the White Brigades to help her regain the Jasper Throne.

HIMSELF: Your brother, not the old boy. You woke up one morning to find the stone gone and him vanished. Stolen.

I could see that Princess Latufui found the Honorable Cormac's bluntness distressing, but if one claims the privileges of a noble family, one must also claim the shames.

MYSELF: It was never proved that Arthur stole the Blue Empress.

HIMSELF: No, no. But you know how tongues wag in the country. And his disappearance was, you must admit, *timely*. How long ago was that now? God, I must have been a wee gossoon.

MYSELF: Fifteen years.

HIMSELF: Fifteen years! And not a word? Do you know if he's even alive?

MYSELF: We believe he fled to the Inner Worlds. Every few years we hear of a sighting, but most of them are so contrary, we dismiss them. He made his choice. As for the Blue Empress: broken up and sold long ago, I don't doubt.

HIMSELF: And here I find you on a jaunt across one of the Inner Worlds.

MYSELF: I am creating a new album of papercuts. The Botanica Veneris.

HIMSELF: Of course. If I might make so bold, Lady Rathangan: the Blue Empress: do you believe Arthur took it?

And I made him no verbal answer but gave the smallest shake of my head.

Princess Latufui had been restless all this evening—the time before sleep, that is: Great Evening was still many Terrene days off. Can we ever truly adapt to the monstrous Venerian calendar? Arthur has been on this world for fifteen years—has he drifted not just to another world, but another clock, another calendar? I worked on my Stalva-grass cut—I find that curving the leaf-bearing nodes gives the necessary three-dimensionality—but my heart was not in it. Latufui sipped at tea and fumbled at stitching and pushed newspapers around until eventually she threw open the cabin door in frustration and demanded that I join her on the balcony.

The rolling travel of the high train made me grip the rail for dear life, but the high plain was as sharp and fresh as if starched, and there, a long line on the horizon beyond the belching smokestack and pumping pistons of the tractor, were the Palisades of Exx: a grey wall from one horizon to the other. Clouds hid the peaks, like a curtain lowered from the sky.

Dark against the grey mountains, I saw the spires of the observatories of Camahoo. This was the Thent homeland; and I was apprehensive, for among those towers and minarets is a *hoondahvi*, a Thent opium den, owned by the person who might be able to tell me the next part of my brother's story—a story increasingly disturbing and dark. A person who is not human.

"Ida, dear friend. There is a thing I must ask you."

"Anything, dear Latufui."

"I must tell you, it is not a thing that can be asked softly."

My heart turned over in my chest. I knew what Latufui would ask.

"Ida: have you come to this world to look for your brother?"

She did me the courtesy of a direct question. No preamble, no preliminary sifting through her doubts and evidences. I owed it a direct answer.

"Yes," I said. "I have come to find Arthur."

"I thought so."

"For how long?"

"Since Ledekh-Olkoi. Ah, I cannot say the words right. When you went to get papers and gum and returned empty-handed."

"I went to see a Mr. Stafford Grimes. I had information that he had met my brother soon after his arrival on this world. He directed me to Mr. Okiring, a retired *asjan*-hunter in Yez Tok."

"And Cama-oo? Is this another link in the chain?"

"It is. But the Botanica is no sham. I have an obligation to my backers—you know the state of my finances as well as I, Latufui. The late Count Rathangan was a profligate man. He ran the estate into the ground."

"I could wish you had trusted me. All those weeks of planning and organizing. The maps, the itineraries, the tickets, the transplanetary calls to agents and factors. I was so excited! A journey to another world! But for you, there was always something else. None of that was the whole truth. None of it was honest."

"Oh, my dear Latufui . . ." But how could I say that I had not told her because I feared what Arthur might have become. Fears that seemed to be borne out by every ruined life that had touched his. What would I find? Did anything remain of the wild, carefree boy I remembered chasing old Bunty the dog across the summer lawns of Grangegorman? Would I recognize him? Worse, would he listen to me? "There is a wrong to right. An old debt to be canceled. It's a family thing."

"I live in your house but not in your family," Princess Latufui said. Her words were barbed with truth. They tore me. "We would not do that in Tonga. Your ways are different. And I thought I was more than a companion."

"Oh, my dear Latufui." I took her hands in mine. "My dear dear Latufui. Your are far far more to me than a companion. You are my life. But you of all people should understand my family. We are on another world, but we are not so far from Rathangan, I think. I am seeking Arthur, and I do not know what I will find, but I promise you, what he says to me, I will tell to you. Everything."

Now she laid her hands over mine, and there we stood, cupping hands on the balcony rail, watching the needle spires of Camahoo rise from the grass spears of the Stalva.

> *V vallumque foenum:* Stalva Pike Grass. Another non-Terrene that is finding favor in Terrestrial ornamental gardens. Earth never receives sufficient sunlight for it to attain its full Stalva height. *Yetten* in the Stalva Thent dialect.
>
> Card, onionskin paper, corrugated paper, paint. This papercut is unique in that it unfolds into three parts. The original, in the Chester Beatty Library in Dublin, is always displayed unfolded.

THE MERCENARY'S TALE

IN THE NAME OF THE LEADER OF THE STARRY SKIES and the Ever-Circling Spiritual Family, welcome to my *hoondahvi*. May *apsas* speak; may *gavanda* sing, may the *thoo* impart their secrets!

I understand completely that you have not come to drink. But the greeting is standard. We pride ourself on being the most traditional *hoondahvi* in Exxaa Canton.

Is the music annoying? No? Most Terrenes find it aggravating. It's an essential part of the *hoondahvi* experience, I am afraid.

Your brother, yes. How could I forget him? I owe him my life.

He fought like a man who hated fighting. Up on the altiplano, when we smashed open the potteries and set the Porcelain Towns afire up and down the Valley of the Kilns, there were those who blazed with love and joy at the slaughter and those whose faces were so dark it was as if their souls were clogged with soot. Your brother was one of those. Human expressions are hard for us to read—your faces are wood, like masks. But I saw his face and knew that he loathed what he did. That was what made him the best of *javrosts*. I am an old career soldier; I have seen many many come to our band. The ones in love with violence: unless they can take discipline, we turn them away. But when a mercenary hates what he does for his silver, there must be a greater darkness driving him. There is a thing they hate more than the violence they do.

Are you sure the music is tolerable? Our harmonies and chord patterns apparently create unpleasant electrical resonance in the human brain. Like small seizures. We find it most reassuring. Like the rhythm of the kittening womb.

Your brother came to us in the dawn of Great Day 6817. He could ride a *graap*, bivouac, cook, and was handy with both bolt and blade. We never ask questions of our *javrosts*—in time they answer them all themselves—but rumors blow on the wind like *thagoon* down. He was a minor aristocrat, he was a gambler; he was a thief, he was a murderer; he was a seducer, he was a traitor. Nothing to disqualify him. Sufficient to recommend him.

In Old Days the Duke of Yoo disputed mightily with her neighbor the Duke of Hetteten over who rightly ruled the altiplano and its profitable potteries. From time immemorial, it had been a place beyond: independently minded and stubborn of spirit, with little respect for gods or dukes. Wars were fought down generations, laying waste to fames and fortunes, and when in the end, the House of Yoo prevailed, the peoples of the plateau had forgotten they ever had lords and mistresses and debts of fealty. It is a law of earth and stars alike that people should be well governed, obedient, and quiet in their ways, so the Duke of Yoo embarked on a campaign of civil discipline. Her house corps had been decimated in the Porcelain Wars, so House Yoo hired mercenaries. Among them, my former unit, Gellet's *Javrosts*.

They speak of us still, up on the plateau. We are the monsters of their Great Nights, the haunters of their children's dreams. We are legend. We are Gellet's *Javrosts*. We are the new demons.

For one Great Day and Great Night, we ran free. We torched the topless star shrines of Javapanda and watched them burn like chimneys. We smashed the funerary jars and trampled the bones of the illustrious dead of Toohren. We overturned the houses of the holy, burned elders and kits in their homes. We lassoed rebels and dragged them behind our *graapa*, round and round the village, until all that remained was a bloody rope. We forced whole communities from their homes, driving them across the altiplano until the snow heaped their bodies. And Arthur was at my side. We were not friends—there is too much history on this world for human and Thent ever to be that. He was my *badoon*. You do not have a concept for it, let alone a word. A passionate colleague. A brother who is not related. A fellow devotee . . .

We killed and we killed and we killed. And in our wake came the Duke of Yoo's soldiers—restoring order, rebuilding towns, offering defense against the murderous renegades. It was all strategy. The Duke of Yoo knew the plateauneers would never love her, but she could be their savior. Therefore, a campaign of final outrages was planned. Such vileness! We were ordered to Glehenta, a pottery town at the head of Valley of the Kilns. There we would enter the *glotoonas*—the birthing creches—and slaughter every infant down to the last kit. We rode, Arthur at my side, and though human emotions are strange and distant to me, I knew them well enough to read the storm in his heart.

Night snow was falling as we entered Glehenta, lit by ten thousand starflowers. The people locked their doors and cowered from us. Through the heart of town we rode; past the great conical kilns, to the *glotoonas*. Matres flung themselves before our *graapa*—we rode them down. Arthur's face was darker than the Great Midnight. He broke formation and rode up to Gellet himself. I went to him. I saw words between your brother and our commander. I did not hear them. Then Arthur drew his blasket and in a single shot blew the entire top of Gellet's body to ash. In the fracas, I shot down three of our troop; then we were racing through the glowing streets, our hooves clattering on the porcelain cobbles, the erstwhile Gellet's *Javrosts* behind us.

And so we saved them. For the Duke of Yoo had arranged it so that her Ducal Guard would fall upon us even as we attacked, annihilate us, and achieve two notable victories: presenting themselves as the saviors of Glehenta and destroying any evidence of their scheme. Your brother and I sprung the trap. But we did not know until leagues and months later, far from the altiplano. At the foot of the Ten Thousand Stairs, we parted—we thought it safer. We never saw each other again though I heard he had gone back up the stairs, to the Pelerines. And if you do find him, please don't tell him what became of me. This is a shameful place.

And I am ashamed that I have told you such dark and bloody truths about your brother. But at the end, he was honorable. He was right. That he saved the guilty—an unintended consequence. Our lives are made up of such.

Certainly, we can continue outside on the *hoondahvi* porch. I did warn you that the music was irritating to human sensibilities.

V *lucerna vesperum:* Schaefferia: the Evening Candle. A solitary tree of the foothills of the Exx Palisades of Ishtaria, the Schaefferia is noted for its many upright, luminous blossoms, which flower in

Venerian Great Evening and Great Dawn.

Only the blossoms are reproduced. Card, folded and cut tissue, luminous paint (not reproduced). The original is also slightly radioactive.

A cog railway runs from Camahoo Terminus to the Convent of the Starry Pelerines. The Starsview Special takes pilgrims to see the stars and planets. Our carriage is small, luxurious, intricate, and ingenious in that typically Thent fashion, and terribly tedious. The track has been constructed in a helix inside Awk Mountain, so our journey consists of interminable, noisy spells inside the tunnel, punctuated by brief, blinding moments of clarity as we emerge onto the open face of the mountain. Not for the vertiginous!

Thus, hour upon hour, we spiral our way up Mount Awk.

Princess Latufui and I play endless games of Moon Whist, but our minds are not in it. My forebodings have darkened after my conversation with the Thent *hoondahvi* owner in Camahoo. The princess is troubled by my anxiety. Finally, she can bear it no more.

"Tell me about the Blue Empress. Tell me everything."

I grew up with two injunctions in case of fire: save the dogs and the Blue Empress. For almost all my life, the jewel was a ghost stone—present but unseen, haunting Grangegorman and the lives it held. I have a memory from earliest childhood of seeing the stone—never touching it—but I do not trust the memory. Imaginings too easily become memories, memories imaginings.

We are not free in so many things, we of the landed class. Richard would inherit, Arthur would make a way in the worlds, and I would marry as well as I could—land to land. The Barony of Rathangan was considered one of the most desirable in

Kildare, despite Patrick's seeming determination to drag it to the bankruptcy court. A match was made, and he was charming and bold; a fine sportsman and a very handsome man. It was an equal match: snide comments from both halves of the county. The Blue Empress was part of my treasure—on the strict understanding that it remain in the custody of my lawyers. Patrick argued—and it was there that I first got an inkling of his true character—and the wedding was off the wedding was on the wedding was off the wedding was on again and the banns posted. A viewing was arranged, for his people to itemize and value the Hyde treasure. For the first time in long memory, the Blue Empress was taken from its safe and displayed to human view. Blue as the wide Atlantic it was, and as boundless and clear. You could lose yourself forever in the light inside that gem. And yes, it was the size of a thrush's egg.

And then the moment that all the stories agree on: the lights failed. Not so unusual at Grangegorman—the same grandfather who brought back the Blue Empress installed the hydro plant—and when they came back on again; the sapphire was gone: baize and case and everything.

We called upon the honor of all present, ladies and gentlemen alike. The lights would be put out for five minutes, and when they were switched back on, the Blue Empress would be back in the Hyde treasury. It was not. Our people demanded we call the police, Patrick's people, mindful of their client's attraction to scandal, were less insistent. We would make a further appeal to honor: if the Blue Empress was not back by morning, then we would call the guards.

Not only was the Blue Empress still missing, so was Arthur.

We called the Garda Siochana. The last we heard was that Arthur had left for the Inner Worlds.

The wedding went ahead. It would have been a greater scandal to call it off. We were two families alike in notoriety.

Patrick could not let it go: he went to his grave believing that Arthur and I had conspired to keep the Blue Empress out of his hands. I have no doubt that Patrick would have found a way of forcing me to sign over possession of the gem to him and would have sold it. Wastrel.

As for the Blue Empress: I feel I am very near to Arthur now. One cannot run forever. We will meet, and the truth will be told.

Then light flooded our carriage as the train emerged from the tunnel onto the final ramp and there, before us, its spires and domes dusted with snow blown from the high peaks, was the Convent of the Starry Pelerines.

> *V aquilonis vitis visionum:* the Northern Littoral, or Ghost Vine. A common climber of the forests of the southern slopes of the Ishtari altiplano, domesticated and widely grown in Thent garden terraces. Its white, trumpet-shaped flowers are attractive, but the plant is revered for its berries. When crushed, the infused liquor known as *pula* creates powerful auditory hallucinations in Venerian physiology and forms the basis of the Thent mystical *hoondahvi* cult. In Terrenes, it produces a strong euphoria and a sense of omnipotence.
>
> Alkaloid-infused paper. Ida Granville-Hyde used Thent Ghost-Vine liquor to tint and infuse the paper in this cut. It is reported to be still mildly hallucinogenic.

THE PILGRIM'S TALE

YOU'LL COME OUT ONTO THE BELVEDERE? IT'S SUPPOSED to be off-limits to Terrenes—technically blasphemy—sacred space and all that—but the pelerines turn a blind eye. Do excuse the cough . . . ghastly, isn't it? Sounds like a bag of bloody loose change. I don't suppose the cold air does much for my dear old alveoli, but at this stage it's all a matter of damn.

That's Gloaming Peak there. You won't see it until the cloud clears. Every Great Evening, every Great Dawn, for a few Earth-days at a time, the cloud breaks. It goes up, oh so much farther than you could ever imagine. You look up, and up, and up—and beyond it, you see the stars. That's why the pelerines came here. Such a sensible religion. The stars are gods. One star, one god. Simple. No faith, no heaven, no punishment, no sin. Just look up and wonder. The Blue Pearl: that's what they call our Earth. I wonder if that's why they care for us. Because we're descended from divinity? If only they knew! They really are very kind.

Excuse me. Bloody marvelous stuff, this Thent brew. I'm in no pain at all. I find it quite reassuring that I shall slip from this too too rancid flesh swaddled in a blanket of beatific thoughts and analgesic glow. They're very kind, the pelerines. Very kind.

Now, look to your right. There. Do you see? That staircase, cut into the rock, winding up up up. The Ten Thousand Stairs. That's the old way to the altiplano. Everything went up and down those steps: people, animals, goods, palanquins and stick-stick men, traders and pilgrims and armies. Your brother. I watched him go, from this very belvedere. Three years ago, or was it five? You never really get used to the Great Day. Time blurs.

We were tremendous friends, the way that addicts are. You wouldn't have come this far without realizing some truths about your brother. Our degradation unites us. Dear thing. How we'd set the world to rights, over flask after flask of this stuff! He realized the truth of this place early on. It's the way to the stars. God's waiting room. And we, this choir of shambling wrecks, wander through it, dazzled by our glimpses of the stars. But he was a dear friend, a dear dear friend. Dear Arthur.

We're all darkened souls here, but he was haunted. Things

done and things left undone, like the prayer book says. My father was a vicar—can't you tell? Arthur never spoke completely about his time with the *javrosts*. He hinted—I think he wanted to tell me, very much, but was afraid of giving me his nightmares. That old saw about a problem shared being a problem halved? Damnable lie. A problem shared is a problem doubled. But I would find him up here all times of the Great Day and Night, watching the staircase and the caravans and stick convoys going up and down. Altiplano porcelain, he'd say. Finest in all the worlds. So fine you can read the Bible through it. Every cup, every plate, every vase and bowl, was portered down those stairs on the shoulders of a stickman. You know he served up on the altiplano, in the Duke of Yoo's Pacification. I wasn't here then, but Aggers was, and he said you could see the smoke going up—endless plumes of smoke, so thick the sky didn't clear and the pelerines went for a whole Great Day without seeing the stars. All Arthur would say about it was, that'll make some fine china. That's what made porcelain from the Valley of the Kilns so fine: bones—the bones of the dead, ground up into powder. He would never drink from a Valley cup—he said it was drinking from a skull.

Here's another thing about addicts—you never get rid of it. All you do is replace one addiction with another. The best you can hope for is that it's a better addiction. Some become god addicts, some throw themselves into worthy deeds, or self-improvement, or fine thoughts, or helping others, God help us all. Me, my lovely little vice is sloth—I really am an idle little bugger. It's so easy, letting the seasons slip away; slothful days and indolent nights, coughing my life up one chunk at a time. For Arthur, it was the visions. Arthur saw wonders and horrors, angels and demons, hopes and fears. True visions—the things that drive men to glory or death. Visionary visions. It lay up on the altiplano, beyond the twists and turns of the Ten Thousand Steps. I could never comprehend what it was, but it drove him.

Devoured him. Ate his sleep, ate his appetite, ate his body and his soul and his sanity.

It was worse in the Great Night . . . Everything's worse in the Great Night. The snow would come swirling down the staircase and he saw things in it—faces—heard voices. The faces and voices of the people who had died, up there on the altiplano. He had to follow them, go up, into the Valley of the Kilns, where he would ask the people to forgive him—or kill him.

And he went. I couldn't stop him—I didn't want to stop him. Can you understand that? I watched him from this very belvedere. The pelerines are not our warders, any of us is free to leave at any time though I've never seen anyone leave but Arthur. He left in the evening, with the lilac light catching Gloaming Peak. He never looked back. Not a glance to me. I watched him climb the steps to that bend there. That's where I lost sight of him. I never saw or heard of him again. But stories come down the stairs with the stickmen and they make their way even to this little aerie, stories of a seer—a visionary. I look and I imagine I see smoke rising, up there on the altiplano.

It's a pity you won't be here to see the clouds break around the Gloaming, or look at the stars.

> *V genetic nives:* Mother-of-snows (direct translation from Thent). Ground-civer hi-alpine of the Exx Palisades. The plant forms extensive carpets of thousands of minute white blossoms.
>
> The most intricate papercut in the *Botanica Veneris*. Each floret is three millimeters in diameter. Paper, ink, gouache.

A high-stepping spider-car took me up the Ten Thousand Steps, past caravans of stickmen, spines bent, shoulders warped beneath brutal loads of finest porcelain.

The twelve cuts of the *Botanica Veneris* I have given to the princess, along with descriptions and botanical notes. She would not let me leave, clung to me, wracked with great sobs of loss and fear. It was dangerous; a sullen land with Great Night coming. I could not convince her of my reason for heading up the stairs alone, for they did not convince even me. The one, true reason I could not tell her. Oh, I have been despicable to her! My dearest friend, my love. But worse even than that, false.

She stood watching my spider-car climb the steps until a curve in the staircase took me out of her sight. Must the currency of truth always be falsehood?

Now I think of her spreading her long hair out, and brushing it, firmly, directly, beautifully, and the pen falls from my fingers . . .

Egayhazy is a closed city; hunched, hiding, tight. Its streets are narrow, its buildings lean toward one another; their gables so festooned with starflower that it looks like a perpetual festival. Nothing could be further from the truth: Egayhazy is an angry city, aggressive and cowed: sullen. I keep my Ledbekh-Teltai in my bag. But the anger is not directed at me, though from the story I heard at the Camahoo *hoondahvi,* my fellow humans on this world have not graced our species. It is the anger of a country under occupation. On walls and doors, the proclamations of the Duke of Yoo are plastered layer upon layer: her pennant, emblazoned with the four white hands of House Yoo, flies from public buildings, the radio-station mast, tower tops, and the gallows. Her *Javrosts* patrol streets so narrow that their *graapa* can barely squeeze through them. At their passage, the citizens of Egayhazy flash jagged glares, mutter altiplano oaths. And there is another sigil: an eight-petaled flower; a blue so deep it seems almost to shine. I see it stenciled hastily on walls and doors and the occupation-force posters. I see it in little badges sewn to the quilted jackets of the Egayhazians; and in tiny glass jars in low-set windows. In the market of Yent, I witnessed *Javrosts* overturn and smash a vegetable stall that dared to offer a few posies of this blue bloom.

The staff at my hotel were suspicious when they saw me working up some sketches from memory of this blue flower of dissent. I explained my work and showed some photographs and asked, what was this flower? A common plant of the high altiplano, they said. It grows up under the breath of the high snow; small and tough and stubborn. It's most remarkable feature is that it blooms when no other flower does—in the dead of the Great Night. The Midnight Glory was one name though it had another, newer, which entered common use since the occupation: the Blue Empress.

I knew there and then that I had found Arthur.

A pall of sulfurous smoke hangs permanently over the Valley of Kilns, lit with hellish tints from the glow of the kilns below. A major ceramics center on a high, treeless plateau? How are the kilns fueled? Volcanic vents do the firing, but they turn this long defile in the flank of Mount Tooloowera into a little hell of clay, bones, smashed porcelain, sand, slag, and throat-searing sulfur. Glehenta is the last of the Porcelain Towns, wedged into the head of the valley, where the river Iddis still carries a memory of freshness and cleanliness. The pottery houses, like upturned vases, lean toward one another like companionable women.

And there is the house to which my questions guided me: as my informants described; not the greatest but perhaps the meanest; not the foremost but perhaps the most prominent, tucked away in an alley. From its roof flies a flag, and my breath caught: not the Four White Hands of Yoo—never that, but neither the Blue Empress. The smoggy wind tugged at the hand-and-dagger of the Hydes of Grangegorman.

Swift action: to hesitate would be to falter and fail, to turn and walk away, back down the Valley of the Kilns and the Ten Thousand Steps. I rattle the ceramic chimes. From inside, a huff and sigh. Then a voice: worn ragged, stretched and tired, but unmistakable.

"Come on in. I've been expecting you."

V crepitant movebitvolutans: Wescott's Wandering Star. A wind-mobile vine, native of the Ishtaria altiplano, that grows into a tight spherical web of vines which, in the Venerian Great Day, becomes detached from an atrophied root stock and rolls cross-country, carried on the wind. A central calyx contains woody nuts that produce a pleasant rattling sound as the Wandering Star is in motion.

Cut paper, painted, layed, and gummed. Perhaps the most intricate of the Venerian papercuts.

THE SEER'S STORY

TEA?

I have it sent up from Camahoo when the stickmen make the return trip. Proper tea. Irish breakfast. It's very hard to get the water hot enough at this altitude, but it's my little ritual. I should have asked you to bring some. I've known you were looking for me from the moment you set out from Loogaza. You think anyone can wander blithely into Glehenta?

Tea.

You look well. The years have been kind to you. I look like shit. Don't deny it. I know it. I have an excuse. I'm dying, you know. The liquor of the vine—it takes as much as it gives. And this world is hard on humans. The Great Days—you never completely adjust—and the climate: if it's not the thin air up here, it's the molds and fungi and spores down there. And the ultraviolet. It dries you out, withers you up. The town healer must have frozen twenty melanomas off me. No, I'm dying. Rotten inside. A leather bag of mush and bones. But you look very well, Ida. So, Patrick shot himself? Fifteen years too late, says I. He could have spared all of us . . . enough of that. But I'm glad you're happy. I'm glad you have someone who cares, to treat you the way you should be treated.

I am the Merciful One, the Seer, the Prophet of the Blue Pearl, the Earth Man, and I am dying.

I walked down that same street you walked down. I didn't ride, I walked, right through the center of town. I didn't know what to expect. Silence. A mob. Stones. Bullets. To walk right through and out the other side without a door opening to me. I almost did. At the very last house, the door opened and an old man came out and stood in front of me so that I could not pass. "I know you." He pointed at me. "You came the night of the *Javrosts*." I was certain then that I would die, and that seemed not so bad a thing to me. "You were the merciful one, the one who spared our young." And he went into the house and brought me a porcelain cup of water and I drank it down, and here I remain. The Merciful One.

They have decided that I am to lead them to glory, or, more likely, to death. It's justice, I suppose. I have visions you see— *pula* flashbacks. It works differently on Terrenes than Thents. Oh, they're hardheaded enough not to believe in divine ¡spiration or any of that rubbish. They need a figurehead—the repentant mercenary is a good role, and the odd bit of mumbo jumbo from the inside of my addled head doesn't go amiss.

Is your tea all right? It's very hard to get the water hot enough this high. Have I said that before? Ignore me—the flashbacks. Did I tell you I'm dying? But it's good to see you; oh how long is it?

And Richard? The children? And Grangegorman? And is Ireland . . . of course. What I would give for an eyeful of green, for a glimpse of summer sun, a blue sky.

So, I have been a con man and a lover, a soldier and an addict, and now I end my time as a revolutionary. It is surprisingly easy. The Group of Seven Altiplano Peoples' Liberation Army do the work: I release gnomic pronouncements that run like grass fire from here to Egayhazy. I did come up with the Blue Empress motif: the Midnight Glory: blooming in the dark, under the breath of the high snows. Apt. They're not the most poetic of people, these potters. We drove the Duke of Yoo from the Valley of the Kilns and the Ishtar Plain: she is resisted everywhere, but she will not relinquish her claim on the altiplano so lightly. You've been in Egayhazy—you've seen the forces she's moving up here. Armies are mustering, and my agents report 'rigibles coming through the passes in the Palisades. An assault will come. The Duke has an alliance with House Shorth—some agreement to divide the altiplano up between them. We're outnumbered. Outmaneuvered and outsupplied, and we have nowhere to run. They'll be at each other's throats within a Great Day, but that's a matter of damn for us. The Duke may spare the kilns—they're the source of wealth. Matter of damn to me. I'll not see it, one way or other. You should leave, Ida. *Pula* and local wars—never get sucked into them.

Ah. Unh. Another flashback. They're getting briefer, but more intense.

Ida, you are in danger. Leave before night—they'll attack in the night. I have to stay. The Merciful One, the Seer, the Prophet of the Blue Pearl, can't abandon his people. But it was good, so good of you to come. This is a terrible place. I should never have come here. The best traps are the slowest. In you walk, through all the places and all the lives and all the years, never thinking that you are already in the trap, then you go to turn around, and it has closed behind you. Ida, go as soon as you can . . . go right now. You should never have come. But . . . oh, how I hate the thought of dying up here on this terrible plain! To see Ireland again . . .

> *V volanti musco:* Altiplano Air-moss. The papercut shows part of a symbiotic lighter-than-air creature of the Ishtari altiplano. The plant part consists of curtains of extremely light hanging moss that gather water from the air and low clouds. The animal part is not reproduced.
> Shredded paper, gum.

He came to the door of his porcelain house, leaning heavily on a stick, a handkerchief pressed to mouth and nose against the volcanic fumes. I had tried to plead with him to leave, but whatever else he has become, he is a Hyde of Grangegorman, and stubborn as an old donkey. There is a wish for death in him; something old and strangling and relentless with the gentlest eyes.

"I have something for you," I said, and I gave him the box without ceremony.

His eyebrows rose when he opened it.

"Ah."

"I stole the Blue Empress."

"I know."

"I had to keep it out of Patrick's hands. He would have broken and wasted it, like he broke and wasted everything." Then my slow mind, so intent on saying this confession right, I had practiced on the space-crosser, and in every room and mode of conveyance on my journey across this world, flower to flower, story to story: my middle-aged mind tripped over Arthur's two words. "You knew?"

"All along."

"You never thought that maybe Richard, maybe Father, or Mammy, or one of the staff had taken it?"

"I had no doubt that it was you, for those very reasons you said. I chose to keep your secret, and I have."

"Arthur, Patrick is dead, Rathangan is mine. You can come home now."

"Ah, if it were so easy!"

"I have a great forgiveness to ask from you, Arthur."

"No need. I did it freely. And do you know what, I don't regret what I did. I was notorious—the Honorable Arthur Hyde, jewel thief and scoundrel. That has currency out in the worlds. It speaks reams that none of the people I used it on asked to see the jewel, or the fortune I presumably had earned from selling it. Not one. Everything I have done, I have done on reputation alone. It's an achievement. No, I won't go home, Ida. Don't ask me to. Don't raise that phantom before me. Fields of green and soft Kildare mornings. I'm valued here. The people are very kind. I'm accepted. I have virtues. I'm not the minor son of Irish gentry with no land and the arse hanging out of his pants. I am the Merciful One, the Prophet of the Blue Pearl."

"Arthur, I want you to have the jewel."

He recoiled as if I had offered him a scorpion.

"I will not have it. I will not touch it. It's an ill-favored thing. Unlucky. There are no sapphires on this world. You can never touch the Blue Pearl. Take it back to the place it came from."

For a moment, I wondered if he was suffering from another one of his hallucinating seizures. His eyes, his voice were firm.

"You should go, Ida. Leave me. This is my place now. People have tremendous ideas of family—loyalty and undying love and affection: tremendous expectations and ideals that drive them across worlds to confess and receive forgiveness. Families are whatever works. Thank you for coming. I'm sorry I wasn't what you wanted me to be. I forgive you—though as I said there is nothing to forgive. There. Does that make us a family now? The Duke of Yoo is coming, Ida. Be away from here before that. Go. The townspeople will help you."

And with a wave of his handkerchief, he turned and closed his door to me.

I wrote that last over a bowl of altiplano mate at the stickmen's caravanserai in Yelta, the last town in the Valley of the Kilns. I recalled every word, clearly and precisely. Then I had an idea; as clear and precise as my recall of that sad, unresolved conversation with Arthur. I turned to my valise of papers, took out my scissors and a sheet of the deepest indigo and carefully, from memory, began to cut. The stickmen watched curiously, then with wonder. The clean precision of the scissors, so fine and intricate, the difficulty and accuracy of the cut, absorbed me entirely. Doubts fell from me: why had I come to this world? Why had I ventured alone into this noisome valley? Why had Arthur's casual acceptance of what I had done, the act that shaped both his life and mine, so disappointed me? What had I expected from him? Snip went the scissors, fine curls of indigo paper fell from them onto the table. It had always been the scissors I turned to when the ways of men grew too much. It was a simple cut. I had the heart of it right away, no false starts, no new beginnings. Pure and simple. My onlookers hummed in appreciation. Then I folded the cut into my diary, gathered up my valises, and went out to the waiting spider-car. The eternal clouds seem lower today, like a storm front rolling in. Evening is coming.

* * *

I write quickly, briefly.

Those are no clouds. Those are the 'rigibles of the Duke of Yoo. The way is shut. Armies are camped across the altiplano. Thousands of soldiers and *javrosts*. I am trapped here. What am I to do? If I retreat to Glehenta, I will meet the same fate as Arthur and the Valley people—if they even allow me to do that. They might think that I was trying to carry a warning. I might be captured as a spy. I do not want to imagine how the Duke of Yoo treats spies. I do not imagine my Terrene identity will protect me. And the sister of the Seer, the Blue Empress! Do I hide in Yelta and hope that they will pass me by? But how could I live with myself knowing that I had abandoned Arthur?

There is no way forward, no way back, no way around.

I am an aristocrat. A minor one, but of stock. I understand the rules of class, and breeding. The Duke is vastly more powerful than I, but we are of a class. I can speak with her, gentry to gentry. We can communicate as equals.

I must persuade her to call off the attack.

Impossible! A middle-aged Irish widow, armed only with a pair of scissors. What can she do? Kill an army with gum and tissue? The death of a thousand papercuts?

Perhaps I could buy her off. A prize beyond prize: a jewel from the stars, from their goddess itself. Arthur said that sapphires are unknown on this world. A stone beyond compare.

I am writing as fast as I am thinking now.

I must go and face the Duke of Yoo, female to female. I am of Ireland, a citizen of no mean nation. We confront the powerful, we defeat empires. I will go to her and name myself and I shall offer her the Blue Empress. The true Blue Empress. Beyond that, I cannot say. But I must do it and do it now.

I cannot make the driver of my spider-car take me into the camp of the enemy. I have asked her to leave me and make her own way back to Yelta. I am writing this with a stub of pencil. I am alone on the high altiplano. Above the shield wall, the cloud layer is breaking up. Enormous shafts of dazzling light spread across the high plain. Two mounted figures have broken from the line and ride toward me. I am afraid—and yet I am calm. I take the Blue Empress from its box and grasp it tight in my gloved hand. Hard to write now. No more diary. They are here.

V. *Gloria medianocte:* the Midnight Glory, or Blue Empress.

Card, paper, ink.

ABOUT THE EDITORS

GEORGE R. R. MARTIN IS THE #1 *NEW YORK TIMES* bestselling author of many novels, including the acclaimed series A Song of Ice and Fire—*A Game of Thrones, A Clash of Kings, A Storm of Swords, A Feast for Crows,* and *A Dance with Dragons.* As a writer-producer, he has worked on *The Twilight Zone, Beauty and the Beast,* and various feature films and pilots that were never made. He lives with the lovely Parris in Santa Fe, New Mexico.

GARDNER DOZOIS HAS WON FIFTEEN HUGO AWARDS and thirty-two Locus Awards for his editing work, plus two Nebula Awards for his own writing. He was the editor of *Asimov's Science Fiction* for twenty years and is the author or editor of over a hundred books, including *The Year's Best Science Fiction.*

ABOUT THE TYPE

THIS BOOK WAS SET IN SCALA, A TYPEFACE DESIGNED by Martin Majoor in 1991. It was originally designed for a music company in the Netherlands and then was published by the international type house FSI FontShop. Its distinctive extended serifs add to the articulation of the letterforms to make it a very readable typeface.